⁓ CATO ⁓
SUPREME COURT
REVIEW

2 0 0 9 — 2 0 1 0

⌉CATO⌐
SUPREME COURT
REVIEW
2 0 0 9 — 2 0 1 0

ROGER PILON
Publisher

ILYA SHAPIRO
Editor in Chief

ROBERT A. LEVY
Associate Editor

TIMOTHY LYNCH
Associate Editor

Editorial Board

CENTER FOR CONSTITUTIONAL STUDIES
CATO
INSTITUTE
Washington, D.C.

THE CATO SUPREME COURT REVIEW (ISBN 978-1-935308-37-9) is published annually at the close of each Supreme Court term by the Cato Institute, 1000 Massachusetts Ave., N.W., Washington, D.C. 20001-5403.

CORRESPONDENCE. Correspondence regarding subscriptions, changes of address, procurement of back issues, advertising and marketing matters, and so forth, should be addressed to:

Publications Department
The Cato Institute
1000 Massachusetts Ave., N.W.
Washington, D.C. 20001

All other correspondence, including requests to quote or reproduce material, should be addressed to the editor.

CITATIONS: Citation to this volume of the Review should conform to the following style: 2009-2010 Cato Sup. Ct. Rev. (2010).

DISCLAIMER. The views expressed by the authors of the articles are their own and are not attributable to the editor, the editorial board, or the Cato Institute.

INTERNET ADDRESS. Articles from past editions are available to the general public, free of charge, at www.cato.org/pubs/scr.

ISBN 978-1-935308-37-9

Printed in the United States of America.

Cato Institute
1000 Massachusetts Ave., N.W.
Washington, D.C. 20001
www.cato.org

Contents

CONTENTS

FOREWORD

Can the Government Do That?

*Roger Pilon**

The Cato Institute's Center for Constitutional Studies is pleased to publish this ninth volume of the *Cato Supreme Court Review*, an annual critique of the Court's most important decisions from the term just ended, plus a look at the cases ahead—all from a classical Madisonian perspective, grounded in the nation's first principles, liberty and limited government. We release this volume each year at Cato's annual Constitution Day conference. And each year in this space I discuss briefly a theme that seemed to emerge from the Court's term or from the larger setting in which the term unfolded.

That larger setting for the Court's October 2009 Term was colored, above all else, by the sheer ambition of the Obama administration and its congressional agenda: The massive federal "bailout" schemes; the governmental intrusions into the banking, investment, and mortgage fields, concerning even executive pay and benefits; the auto industry takeovers, including the upending of traditional bankruptcy law; and of course ObamaCare, presently the subject of unprecedented suits by some 21 states, among others. That is but a sampling of recent events beyond the Court's doors that have brought to the fore that most basic of constitutional questions: Where does the federal government find its authority to do all of that?

More than once during her recently concluded Senate confirmation hearings was that question put before the Court's newest member, Justice Elena Kagan. And for good reason, what with mid-term elections just ahead and the growing Tea Party movement, sure to figure prominently in their outcome, taking as its leitmotif the restoration of limited constitutional government. But the Court, too,

* Roger Pilon is vice president for legal affairs at the Cato Institute, director of Cato's Center for Constitutional Studies, and publisher of the *Cato Supreme Court Review*.

began its term with that question—more precisely, ended its prior term with a special September session to hear additional oral argument on the question that had stopped it in June: Can the government ban books? Or ban guns in Chicago, to move to the term before us? Or ban law student groups in San Francisco from enjoying the same benefits that other groups enjoy if they're selective in choosing their members? Or incarcerate "sexually dangerous" inmates after they've completed their sentences? Or, to bring matters to the moment, can government order individuals to buy government prescribed health insurance policies from private vendors?

In each of those cases and many others before the Court this term or soon to come before it, the same basic question kept coming up: Can the government do that? That's the question, globally, behind the cover story of *The Economist* as we edit this volume, "Leviathan Inc: The state goes back into business." Yet in America the state is not supposed to be in the business of business. Our Constitution was written not simply to separate church and state but, far more broadly, to separate society and state. Government sets the rules and enforces them. It's not supposed to be a player in the game— the game of life. (As the Declaration put it, "That *to secure these Rights*, Governments are instituted among Men.") And the reason is simple: To the extent that government is in the game, decisions are made collectively, not individually. The vote one gets biennially, at best, is the palest reflection of the countless votes we get daily in our private capacities. In a word, our Constitution was written to secure individual, not collective, freedom.

And so we ask how the Court, the non-political branch, did this term in holding the political branches and the states within their constitutional bounds. The problem in answering that question, of course, is that those bounds, at least since the New Deal, have been largely ignored by the Court, the political branches, and the people themselves. But as noted above, there are signs today, owing in large part to the excesses of the Obama administration, that at least some of the people and some in the political class are coming to appreciate the vast gap between modern "constitutional law" and the Constitution itself. Thus, in asking whether the Court this term stood as "an impenetrable bulwark against every assumption of power in the Legislative or Executive," the role Madison envisioned for it, we have to temper the question and ask simply whether the

Court was moving in the right direction, back toward the Constitution; for the restoration of constitutional government is not the work of a day or of the Court alone.

This term, as usual, the record was mixed, but on balance the Roberts Court seemed to be moving in the right direction, however haltingly at times. Thus, in policing one of the government's proper functions, the Court limited the reach of a vague statute that afforded prosecutors unbridled power to charge individuals with depriving another of "the intangible right of honest services," albeit in a set of opinions that themselves were hardly models of precision. Similarly, concerning the fiduciary duty of investment advisors, the Court affirmed the limited power of courts to interfere with contractual agreements fairly reached. And in a challenge to the sweeping Sarbanes-Oxley Act, the Court modestly enhanced the political accountability of public officials by reaffirming the separation-of-powers and unitary-executive principles. But let's look more fully at a few of the Court's other decisions to try to discern where it may be going, beginning with that special case from the prior term, *Citizens United v. Federal Election Commission*.

When the Court announced its decision at last on January 21, the political reaction was immediate and intense, culminating, one could say, with the unseemly spectacle of President Obama berating captured justices on national TV during his State of the Union address—and misstating the case's holding at that. Yet the *Citizens United* majority, unable to speak for itself in that setting, had simply stood up for the rights of the rest of us to speak freely at election time in the only way most of us are able to speak, by joining with others of like mind and pooling our financial resources to try thereby to better be heard. That we should so speak through corporations or unions would be noteworthy only if doing so led to corruption or its appearance, the sole rationale for campaign finance restrictions the Court allowed in its seminal 1976 *Buckley v. Valeo* decision. Yet there was no evidence of corruption here, so the Court, to its credit, struck down the relevant provisions of the 2002 McCain-Feingold Act and reversed its own anomalous 1990 decision in *Austin v. Michigan Chamber of Commerce*. That the government had actually claimed during earlier oral argument that under *Austin* it could ban books expressly advocating the election or defeat of a candidate that were published or distributed by a corporation or union is a mark of how far we've strayed from our founding principles. In this case, then, the Court moved smartly to restore a lost liberty, telling the government in the process, you can't do that.

The disquieting aspect of the case, of course, was Justice John Paul Stevens's lengthy dissent for himself and three other justices. Obsessed, it seems, with the concept of corporate "personality"—the *persona ficta* that our law has long recognized because it enables all manner of market and legal efficiencies—the dissent was unable or unwilling to notice that there are real people with real interests standing behind the corporate entity, much like behind the union entity, and those people may have reasons to want to speak through *their* entity. But how could the dissent have thought otherwise, after decades of teachings about the modern business corporation as a creature of the state, imbued with only those rights the state gives it, rather than as a creature of contract? Here, the Court "pierced the corporate veil"—for the right reason—whereas the dissent saw only the surface, which it read in simple "powerful v. powerless" terms.

Nor did the dissent's analysis improve when it turned to procedural matters. Making much of the majority's having sustained a facial challenge that the parties had agreed to dismiss, the dissent would have entertained only an as-applied challenge. But this was a First Amendment case, where facial challenges are the rule owing to the chilling effect that successful as-applied challenges leave in their wake. Thus, the charge of judicial overreaching fails because the real defendant here was Congress, not the FEC, Congress's agent. It was Congress that had overstepped its constitutional bounds. The Court had allowed that in *Austin*. That mistake needed correcting.

Other mistakes the Court has made are more longstanding, but no less in need of correction—in fact, more in need, because they have long distorted our understanding of the Constitution. And none, perhaps, cries out more for correction than the Court's 1873 decision in the infamous *Slaughterhouse Cases*. Arising from "a fetid stew of corruption" in the city of New Orleans in the aftermath of the Civil War, the case has stood ever since for the Court's having eviscerated the Privileges or Immunities Clause from the recently ratified Fourteenth Amendment. As much scholarship has since shown, the debates in the 39th Congress and in the state ratifying conventions make it clear that the clause was meant to be the principal font of substantive rights under the amendment, not only for the newly freed slaves but for all American citizens. But the *Slaughterhouse* majority rendered the clause "a vain and idle enactment," as the four dissenters put it, bitterly, leaving the Court to decide cases thereafter under the amendment's less substantive Due Process Clause. From that has come the uneven history of "substantive due process"—including the Court's episodic, unsystematic "incorporation" of rights as constitutionally protected against infringement by the states.

In the century and a half that has ensued since the *Slaughterhouse* decision came down, a few halting efforts have been made to revive the Privileges or Immunities Clause and the jurisprudence it was intended to effect, but none was more promising than the one mounted this term in *McDonald v. Chicago*. Two years ago in *District of Columbia v. Heller*, a case effectively of first impression, the Court gave life and meaning at last to the individual right to keep and bear arms under the Second Amendment. But because *Heller* was decided only against the federal government, it remained to be determined whether the right was good against state governments as well under the Fourteenth Amendment's "incorporation" doctrine.

That was the immediate question before the Court in *McDonald*, given Chicago's draconian handgun ban. But because *Heller* had been a case of first impression, taking the Court to a searching discussion of the nation's first principles and early history, its further development in *McDonald* seemed a perfect opportunity to revisit the *Slaughterhouse Cases*. For not only was the Privileges or Immunities Clause meant above all, with newly freed slaves in mind, to protect the right of self-defense—the very right at issue in *McDonald*—but *Slaughterhouse*, like *Heller*, on which *McDonald* was building, was also a case of first impression; it concerned the very issue at stake in *McDonald*, the bearing of the newly settled law upon the states; and its focus, again as in *Heller*, was on a period when the American people had made fundamental changes in their constitutional order—on the founding, in *Heller*, and on the aftermath of the Civil War, in *Slaughterhouse*. In short, the stars were aligned for revisiting the egregious *Slaughterhouse* mistakes.

But it was not to be. True, in *McDonald* the Court got the immediate question right in holding that the Second Amendment was good against the states, leaving it to future courts to determine the precise contours of the right to keep and bear arms. Few thought it would be otherwise, however—that states, but not the federal government, could ignore Second Amendment rights. Yet that, in effect, is what the Court's four liberals argued in dissent as they essentially restated their *Heller* dissent—an approach not unlike the one they took to banning books in *Citizens United*.

But on the deeper constitutional question of whether the Court should bring the Privileges or Immunities Clause back to life, only Justice Clarence Thomas was prepared to be an originalist. Justice Antonin Scalia, whose trenchant historical analysis in *Heller* only two years before had breathed life into the uncertain Second Amendment, seized the opportunity at oral argument in *McDonald* to summarily dismiss the case for reviving the Privileges or Immunities Clause. It is near impossible to square Scalia's sound textualist approach to constitutional interpretation in general with his dismissal of the plain text before him in this case, especially since that text's rich historical pedigree renders it far more determinate than the substantive due process jurisprudence he invoked here, against which he has so often railed, finding it the source of endless judicial mischief. He's often right about that, which makes it all the more curious that he would dismiss a better tool that was readily at hand—and in the Constitution besides.

Nonetheless, it is worth noting that Thomas's originalist interpretation was not disputed by any other member of the Court. Rather, both the plurality and dissenting justices chose not to revisit the Privileges or Immunities question but instead to decide the case by applying the settled law of the Due Process Clause. Thus, the door is now open for reviving the Privileges or Immunities Clause in a future case, using Thomas's concurrence as a roadmap. We should remember that Justice John Marshall Harlan's dissent in *Plessy v. Ferguson* kept alive the hope of overturning that decision's separate-but-equal ruling, and that too was a long time coming.

Here also, then, the Court told the government what it could not do, even if its opinion was not properly grounded and it missed an all-too-rare opportunity to restore the Constitution the Framers of the Fourteenth Amendment had crafted after the bloodiest war in the nation's history. There were other important decisions this term, however, where the Court got it quite wrong. *Christian Legal Society v. Martinez* was one. The question at issue in that case was whether Hastings Law School, a public entity, could require CLS, a small student organization formed around Christian beliefs, to admit any Hastings student as a member or officer, failing which it would be ineligible for benefits such as funding, meeting space, school recognition, and the like that were otherwise available to student organizations. If CLS discriminated in its membership, that is, Hastings would discriminate in turn against CLS by denying the group the benefits it gave to some 60 other student groups organized around all manner of interests.

During the course of litigation below, however, Hastings' nondiscrimination policy, which singled out certain legally recognized grounds on which discrimination might be forbidden, became an "all-comers" policy, which swept far more broadly by forbidding student groups from discriminating on *any* ground. Thus, this theretofore unnoticed policy was content neutral. Unfortunately, Justice Ruth Bader Ginsburg, writing for the Court's majority, bought that argument, dismissing out of hand its implications—among other things, if a student group must admit anyone as a member or officer, it could easily lose its identity as the group it wants to be. In this case, not surprisingly, CLS required its members to subscribe to certain religious beliefs and practices, including abstention from premarital and homosexual sex.

The deeper problem here, however, is with the strained antidiscrimination law the Court has sanctioned over the years: Arising from the civil rights movement of the 1960s, it has compromised private freedom of association—perhaps understandably, given the context in which it arose. While rightly prohibiting public discrimination on a variety of grounds, this body of law has prohibited private discrimination as well, except for certain "intimate expressive associations." Thus, the Boy Scouts may discriminate against homosexuals and atheists who might wish to join or be scout leaders; the Jaycees may not. The Court has drawn a line rooted in value judgments—the Court's—not in the far clearer and far more justifiable distinction between private and public associations.

Clearly, CLS, a group formed around religious beliefs, is an intimate expressive association entitled to discriminate in its selection of members and officers. Accordingly, Hastings could not *directly* prohibit CLS from doing so. But neither may it reach that same result *indirectly* by conditioning the receipt of benefits available to other similarly situated groups on CLS's giving up its constitutional right to freedom of association. We have here the classic doctrine of unconstitutional conditions—sometimes difficult to apply, but not here—which Justice Ginsburg utterly ignored. Beguiled perhaps by the "content neutral" all-comers policy, perhaps also by her own prior experience in this area of the law, she not only found for Hastings but took the occasion to label Justice Samuel Alito's powerful dissent for himself and the Court's three other conservatives "desperate" and "warped"—unseemly comment coming from an institution noted for its comity.

Here, then, the Court failed to tell the government that it could not do what it did, that it could not put a private group to a choice between two of its entitlements: its right to freedom of association, and its right to access benefits otherwise available to similar organizations. And in the process it upheld a patently absurd policy, with Democrats able to join the Republican student group, Muslims able to join the Jewish student group, and conversely, *ad infinitum*. That result, inconsistent as it is with other recent decisions in this area, marks how far modern antidiscrimination policy and law are capable of straying not only from basic constitutional principles but from simple common sense.

Turning back to federal power, yet another decision this term that found the Court wrongly allowing the government to act was *United States v. Comstock*. Here the Court upheld Section 4248 of the Adam Walsh Child Protection Act of 2006, which authorizes the Department of Justice to civilly commit "sexually dangerous" persons *after* they've completed their federal sentences. The case was not about the serious due process questions that surround that power but simply about that most basic of constitutional questions: Where does Congress find its authority to enact such a statute? As a model for future Courts inclined to assist federal expansion, the implications are far-reaching.

Under their general police power, *states* can civilly commit dangerous people, of course, provided due process has been afforded. And the federal government can too—but only in federal territory. Otherwise, the bedrock principle of constitutional design is that Congress's powers are enumerated and hence limited, and a general police power of the kind at issue here is not among them. So where does the federal government find its authority?

Justice Stephen Breyer, writing for the Court with brief concurrences in the judgment by Justices Anthony Kennedy and Alito, found it in the Constitution's Necessary and Proper Clause, in Congress's power "to make all Laws which shall be necessary and proper for carrying into Execution" its other powers. But which of Congress's 17 other enumerated powers does Section 4248 "carry into execution"? And is Section 4248 necessary and proper for executing that power?

Unfortunately, the Court focused mainly on the second question, arguing that Congress has "broad authority" to enact laws to further its enumerated powers. And the five-factor test Breyer offered asked not whether Section 4248 was necessary and proper for executing an *enumerated* power but for "a jumble of *unenumerated* 'authorities,'" as Justice Thomas put it in a searching dissent for himself and Justice Scalia. In fact, the closest the Court ever got to that core first question was to say, in Thomas's clearer words, "that the civil detention of a 'sexually dangerous person' under §4248 carries into execution the enumerated power that justified that person's arrest or conviction in the first place."

And what exactly is that enumerated power? Well it turns out that three of the five respondents who brought this case were in federal custody for possession of child pornography, a federal crime under the 1977 Protection of Children Against Sexual Exploitation Act. (The other two were charged with crimes committed in federal territory, so the federal government was home free there.) But since Congress has no enumerated power to criminalize such possession, we're still short of the Constitution. To complete the chain of argument, therefore, we have to turn to the ground for that 1977 Act. And it is, no surprise, that boundless congressional power, under modern readings, to regulate interstate commerce. So criminalizing the possession of child pornography, the argument runs, is a necessary and proper means for carrying into execution the regulation of interstate commerce. Thus, the federal power to civilly commit sexually dangerous people after they've completed their sentence is derived ultimately from Congress's power to regulate interstate commerce. If that seems a stretch, it is, especially if we consider the history of the matter.

What that history shows is that the commerce power was granted mainly to enable Congress to ensure the free flow of goods and services among the states, given that states under the Articles of Confederation had imposed various protectionist impediments to interstate commerce. One of the main reasons for drafting a new constitution, in fact, was to address that problem, which the Framers thought they had done by giving Congress the power to regulate, or "make regular," interstate commerce. Chief Justice John Marshall said as much in 1824 in the first great Commerce Clause case, *Gibbons v. Ogden*. And in his concurrence, Justice William Johnson stated the matter explicitly: "If there was any one object riding over every other in the adoption of the constitution, it was to keep the commercial intercourse among the States free from all invidious and partial restraints."

But abandon that functional understanding of the commerce power and it's only a matter of time before Congress uses the power not to ensure a free national market but to regulate and even criminalize all manner of activities having nothing to do with unimpeded interstate commerce—many of those regulations serving, ironically, to impede a free market. Thus does the Commerce Clause, in conjunction with the Necessary and Proper Clause, become in effect a general police power of a kind that was reserved to the states—and with that, a Constitution of *limited* government evolves into its opposite.

Speaking for the government at oral argument, then-Solicitor General Kagan granted that Congress would have no power to civilly commit sexually dangerous people who were outside of federal detention, but she was hard-pressed to explain why mere detention, after completion of sentence, justified commitment. Her core contention was that the commitment power "is necessary and proper to the responsible exercise of the Federal power to operate a criminal justice system." But she added that "these are the people who are most likely to violate Federal laws based on the Commerce Clause in the future"—presumably by possessing child pornography *in the future*. That sounds like a straightforward general police power rationale.

Citing *New York v. United States*, Justice Breyer concluded that "the Framers would not have believed that the *Federal* Government, rather than the States, would assume such responsibilities. Yet the powers conferred upon the Federal Government by the Constitution were phrased in language broad enough to allow for the expansion of the Federal Government's role" (original emphasis). Language has its limits, to be sure, which is why judgment is needed as well, and that was sorely lacking in this decision. As Justice Thomas noted, sexual abuse is despicable, but "the Constitution does not vest in Congress the authority to protect society from every bad act that might befall it." In the matter at hand, states have all the power they need to protect us from sexually dangerous people.

Conservatives have long lamented the expansion of the commerce power in ways that have undermined its original purpose. But the modern reading that so often limits economic liberty, championed by liberals, has no principled bounds. Today it serves as a font, through the Necessary and Proper Clause, for civilly committing people we might want to see committed anyway, but only through proper authority. Tomorrow it could be expanded in ways we would not want to see. The Austrian-English philosopher Ludwig Wittgenstein wrote that when language goes on holiday, philosophical problems begin. So too do constitutional problems.

And nowhere do those problems loom more clearly before the nation today than in the many legal challenges to ObamaCare that are currently in our courts, because no legislation Congress has ever passed has more clearly raised that most fundamental of constitutional questions: Are there any limits on what Congress may do? The main focus of the suits, of course, is on the so-called individual mandate, which forces individuals to buy federally prescribed health insurance or pay a "penalty" (or tax—one of the crucial constitutional questions). Enacted pursuant to the Commerce Clause, that mandate takes the commerce power into uncharted territory, as many have noted. Indeed, the furthest reaches of the power—as sanctioned by the Court in *Wickard v. Filburn* and, even more, in *Gonzales v. Raich*—were confined to *prohibiting* action, not requiring it. And so we are left with the question: Under our Constitution, written to secure liberty through limited government, can the government do that?

We will have answers from the courts soon enough, and from the Supreme Court in time. But in the end it is the people, through the political process and all that it entails, who will give the ultimate answer. And on that score, there is mounting evidence that the people are awakening to the widening gap between the Constitution and what has been made of it—and that is good.

Introduction

*Ilya Shapiro**

This is the ninth volume of the *Cato Supreme Court Review*, the nation's first in-depth critique of the Supreme Court term just ended. We release this journal every year in conjunction with our annual Constitution Day symposium, about two and a half months after the previous term concludes and two weeks before the next one begins. We are proud of the speed with which we publish this tome—authors of articles about the last-decided cases have no more than a month to provide us full drafts—and of its accessibility, at least insofar as the Court's opinions allow for that. This is not a typical law review, after all, whose prolix submissions use more space for obscure footnotes than for article text. Instead, this is a book of articles about law intended for everyone from lawyers and judges to educated laymen and interested citizens.

And we are happy to confess our biases: We approach our subject matter from a classical Madisonian perspective, with a focus on individual liberty, property rights, and federalism, and a vision of a government of delegated, enumerated, and thus limited powers. We also try to maintain a strict separation of politics (or policy) and law; just because something is good policy doesn't mean it's legal, and vice versa. Similarly, certain decisions must necessarily be left to the political process: We aim to be governed by laws, not lawyers, so just as a good lawyer will present all plausibly legal options to his client, a good public official will recognize that the ultimate buck stops with him.

Having said that, let's take a quick survey of the term that was. October Term 2009 produced fewer divisions but more headlines than the previous term. Of the 86 cases with decisions on the merits—

---

* Senior Fellow in Constitutional Studies, Cato Institute and Editor-in-Chief, *Cato Supreme Court Review*.

72 after argument, 11 summary reversals, two decided before argument, and one certified question—16 went 5–4 (19 percent, down from 30 percent last year but close to OT07's 17 percent) and 40 had no dissenters (47 percent, up from 33 percent last year and continuing a general Roberts Court trend).[1] More interestingly, the total number of dissenting votes was notably low, with an average decision producing only 1.33 justices in dissent, down from an average of 1.70 over the preceding 10 years. Still, this apparent judicial "era of good feelings"—is the Chief Justice finally succeeding in his quest for less divisiveness?—was overshadowed by stark splits in big cases such as *Citizens United v. FEC* (campaign finance), *McDonald v. Chicago* (right to keep and bear arms), *Christian Legal Society v. Martinez* (freedom of association), and *Free Enterprise Fund v. PCAOB* (separation of powers).

Chief Justice John Roberts tied Justice Anthony Kennedy for the title of "winning justice," voting with the majority in 91 percent of cases (though Kennedy joined the majority in 12 of the 5–4 decisions, beating Roberts's 10 such votes). Justice John Paul Stevens was again most likely to dissent (26 percent of all cases and 48 percent of cases with dissenters), but less so than last year, when the senior associate justice dissented in over half of all cases that had dissents. Justices Antonin Scalia and Clarence Thomas were the justices most likely to agree—ousting last year's most-collegial duo of the Chief Justice and Justice Samuel Alito and voting the same way, at least in judgment, in 79 of the 86 merits cases (92 percent, followed by "rookie" Justice Sonia Sotomayor's 90 percent agreement with each of Justices Ruth Bader Ginsburg and Stephen Breyer). Justices Stevens and Thomas again found themselves on opposite sides of a judicial outcome most often, voting together in only 51 cases (60 percent).

Looking beyond the statistics, this was of course the last term for Justice Stevens. The long-time leader of the Court's "liberal" wing—

---

[1] All statistics taken from SCOTUSblog, Super Stack Pack OT09 Available, July 7, 2010, available at http://www.scotusblog.com/blog/2010/07/07/super-stat-pack-ot09-available/. Note that SCOTUSblog classifies *Citizens United v. FEC* as an OT08 case (meaning one from the previous term) because it was argued and reargued before the official start of October Term 2009. I disagree with this classification—not least because the *Cato Supreme Court Review* article examining the case appears in this volume, not last year's—but will accept it here in order to use the invaluable statistical analysis that SCOTUSblog provides.

and therefore the assigning justice for the majority opinions and lead dissents in all those "conventional" 5–4 splits—Stevens did not retire quietly to that Florida condo. While he only wrote for the Court six times this term, he had two of its most memorable dissents—the stem-winders in *Citizens United* and *McDonald* that will go down among his most memorable writings. With Stevens's departure, perhaps we will finally stop hearing the media's lament about how the "moderate Republican" stood in place while the Court shifted right around him.[2]

Replacing Justice Stevens is Justice Elena Kagan, who had a cup of coffee as the "tenth justice"—the honorific given the solicitor general—before being nominated to be the ninth. While her confirmation was never in any serious doubt, Kagan faced strong criticism from legal analysts and senators on a variety of issues—most importantly on her refusal to "grade" past Court decisions or identify any specific limits to government power.[3] The 37 votes against Kagan were the most ever for a successful Democratic nominee, which statistic is emblematic of a turbulent political environment in which the Constitution and the basic question of where government derives its power figure prominently. Only time will tell what kind of justice Kagan will be now that she is, seemingly for the first time in her ambitious life, unconstrained to speak her mind.

Turning to the *Review*, the volume begins, as always, with the text of the previous year's B. Kenneth Simon Lecture in Constitutional Thought, which in 2009 was delivered by Professor Michael McConnell of Stanford University Law School. Although some characterize the Ninth Amendment as an "inkblot," McConnell—formerly of the Tenth Circuit Court of Appeals—analyzes "The Ninth Amendment in Light of Text and History," demonstrating how this vital 21-word

---

[2] For a fascinating article taking issue with this narrative—which Stevens himself has done much to propagate—see Justin Driver, The Stevens Myth, The New Republic, April 7, 2010, at 19.

[3] This editor was one of the critics. See, e.g., Ilya Shapiro, Kagan's Confirmation Could Be High-Water Mark for Big Government, Cato@Liberty, August 5, 2010, http://www.cato-at-liberty.org/kagans-confirmation-could-be-high-water-mark-for-big-government/; Sallie James and Ilya Shapiro, Elena Kagan Balances Your Diet, The Daily Caller, July 2, 2010, http://dailycaller.com/2010/07/02/elena-kagan-balances-your-diet/; Ilya Shapiro, Kagan Failed the Kagan Standard, Reuters, July 2, 2010, http://blogs.reuters.com/great-debate/2010/07/02/kagan-failed-the-kagan-standard/.

provision is designed to "helps us understand the constitutional structure of powers granted and rights reserved, the relation of the Bill of Rights to the original Constitution of 1787, and the role of natural rights in American constitutionalism." As a basic rule, McConnell declares that "natural rights control in the absence of sufficiently explicit positive law to the contrary." He parses historical evidence regarding pre- and post-constitutional natural law jurisprudence to explain the need to return to the Blackstonian equitable interpretation of unenumerated rights claims.

We move then to the 2009 term, with four articles on an impressive array of First Amendment cases. The biggest of these is the most controversial case of the past couple of years, *Citizens United v. FEC*. This decision—liberalizing the rules surrounding independent expenditures and express advocacy by corporations and unions—caused President Obama to upbraid the Court at his State of the Union address (while misstating the Court's holding) and led Congress to launch an effort to chill political speech in the name of "leveling the playing field." Longtime campaign finance lawyers James Bopp Jr. and Richard E. Coleson tackle this fascinating ruling, describing the litigation strategy leading up to a rare two-argument Court appearance and outlining the case's implications. They conclude that, despite the overall liberalization, "the way *Citizens United* was decided has caused some damage to citizens' speech, association, and self-government rights with regard to imposed disclosure."

Nadine Strossen, New York Law School professor and former president of the ACLU, takes on the case of *United States v. Stevens*, which at base deals with the rationale behind content-based speech restrictions. In *Stevens*, the Supreme Court struck down a federal statute that criminalized the commercial creation, sale, or possession of certain depictions of treatment of animals. The law was intended to "dry up" the production of so-called crush videos—don't ask, just read Strossen's piece—but in effect extended to all sorts of speech and activity. Strossen's analysis takes you through the Court's history of designating unprotected categories of speech, beginning with *Chaplinsky v. New Hampshire* (fighting words) and ending with *New York v. Ferber* (child pornography). Strossen notes that *Stevens* is part of a line of cases in which the Court has reversed this trend and, instead, "contract[ed] government power to enforce content-based regulations of expression, even when such regulations receive overwhelming [public] support." This trend started with *Texas v. Johnson*, the 1989 case striking down restrictions on flag burning, and continues here. It includes cases that uphold the burning of crosses, the advertising of tobacco products to minors, and the possession of images that only appear to depict minors. Strossen's article succinctly presents the importance of *Stevens*, in that the case "generated analysis and holdings that should significantly reinforce the general ban on content-based regulations of expression" by reining in *Chaplinsky* and *Ferber*'s "precedential force for further content-based restrictions."

Professor Richard Epstein—one of my mentors at the University of Chicago Law School—follows with an assessment of the state of Free Exercise and Establishment Clause jurisprudence after the "bitterly contested" case of *Christian Legal Society v. Martinez*, a decision that reflects, he says, "not the Court's finest hour." The Christian Legal Society applied for the privileges normally afforded to all registered student organizations at a public California law school and was turned down because it required members to subscribe to certain beliefs and practices concerning pre-marital sex and homosexuality, and that violated the school's anti-discrimination policy. In a 5–4 decision, the Court upheld the law school's decision on the ground that excluding CLS "encourages tolerance, cooperation, and learning among students." Epstein argues that public institutions cannot directly regulate the membership of private expressive associations like CLS; but neither can they do that indirectly by imposing unconstitutional conditions before benefits otherwise available will be granted. And he sees two other issues here. First, the law school's "all-comers" position was never a formal policy and was only adapted in light of the litigation—so whatever the case's outcome, "the causes of toleration and cooperation will not be served." Second, there is a question of how much the privileges/rights distinction will be reborn after *CLS* with regard to gay marriage. Epstein's guess is that the "doctrine of unconstitutional conditions that lay in ruins after *CLS* will rise again."

The final First Amendment case is *Doe v. Reed*. Here the Court addressed the question of whether disclosing the identities of petition signers violated the signers' rights to freedom of association, holding that states can require the public identification of those who seek issues placed on the electoral ballot. Steve Simpson, a senior attorney with the Institute for Justice, writes about the potential effects *Doe* will have on campaign finance rules. He notes how *Doe* works in conjunction with *Citizens United*, which, as noted above, struck down restrictions on corporate speech but didn't address how burdensome laws requiring disclosure of those who fund independent advocacy can be. While *Doe* came out at a time of "great controversy" surrounding campaign finance laws, Simpson believes that the case is "more important for what it did not say than for what it did." Disclosure requirements are allowed because the Court sees them as only *burdening* speech, not *preventing* it. Simpson suggests that readers should "recognize, as Justice Thomas did [in dissent], that if we take First Amendment rights seriously, *all* speakers must be protected from what amounts to state-sponsored harassment and intimidation."

Next we move to *McDonald v. Chicago*, the sort of case that was expected to reach the Court soon after *D.C. v. Heller*, in 2008, recognized that the Second Amendment guaranteed an individual right. In "The Tell-Tale Privileges or Immunities Clause," Alan Gura (who argued both *Heller* and *McDonald*), Josh Blackman, and I discuss the Court's reluctance—except for a significant concurrence by Justice Thomas—to use the Fourteenth Amendment's Privileges or Immunities Clause, rather than the Due Process Clause, as the textual vehicle for applying the right to keep and bear arms to the states. Despite the fact that the Court granted a cert petition specifically presenting the question of how exactly to "incorporate" the Second Amendment, the Court—and in particular Justice Antonin Scalia—seemed unwilling to seriously entertain the Privileges or Immunities issue. We argue that Justice Thomas—the necessary fifth vote for extending the right to the states—correctly found that the Privileges or Immunities Clause provides a method for extending rights "that is more faithful to the Fourteenth Amendment's text and history." There is extensive evidence, moreover, that the clause was understood to apply both enumerated and unenumerated rights. Justice Thomas's concurrence thus opens the door to future litigation regarding constitutional rights, such as the right to earn an honest living, that have long been disparaged.

In a trio of cases this term the Court rolled back one of the worst sources of federal overcriminalization and due process violations, the "honest services fraud" statute. The defendant in the leading case, Jeffrey Skilling, was the CEO of Enron. Like everyone else, however, he deserved a clear explanation of what the law prohibits; some of the worst abuses of tyrannical governments have occurred via vague criminal laws that can be stretched to encompass nearly any act or omission. Here, the honest services fraud statute failed to adequately describe just what conduct was prohibited. Thus, except for "core" prohibitions on bribery and kickbacks, the Court found it to be void for vagueness. As Harvey Silverglate and Monica Shah explain, the Court did not go nearly far enough in clarifying the void for vagueness doctrine and curbing federal abuses of the criminal law. Not only does vagueness infect the undisturbed "core" of the statute, but federal prosecutors are still free to "go after state and local politicians—whether under 'honest services' or extortion or other such statutes—for engaging in practices that are *not* criminalized under state and municipal law." Even post-*Skilling*, the problem remains: "As long as federal prosecutors and courts attempt to superimpose federal standards on local political culture, there is going to be a problem . . . that traps even the well-intentioned state or local politician."

Continuing the theme of expanding government power—and increasing challenges to it (for example, the ObamaCare lawsuits)—the Supreme Court in *United States v. Comstock* made it a little more difficult to limit the scope of federal authority. As George Mason law professor and Cato adjunct scholar Ilya Somin recounts in "Taking Stock of *Comstock*: The Necessary and Proper Clause and the Limits of Federal Power," the clause was never intended to be a free-standing expansion of federal power. It was instead intended to be tied to— to "carr[y] into execution"—one of Congress's enumerated powers as listed in Article I, Section 8 of the Constitution. Somin argues that the Court seems to have forgotten this vital source for *limiting* federal power in *Comstock*, where the issue was the power granted to the Bureau of Prisons to detain "sexually dangerous" federal prisoners after they have served their full sentences. The Court upheld the law as being "necessary and proper" to implement Congress's power to operate a penal system and to act as custodian of its prisoners. Somin illustrates how this reasoning threatens to stretch the enumeration of powers to the breaking point in that there is no independent enumerated power for the federal government to operate a penal system or act as custodian of its prisoners. Instead, the Court creates a chain of connected powers that gives Congress the power ultimately "to enact any law that might be connected to an ancillary power that is in turn somehow connected to an enumerated power, even if the challenged law does not actually do anything to enforce any enumerated power."

We next examine the constitutionality of a vital part of the Sarbanes-Oxley Act, which has cost the economy an estimated $1.4 trillion and caused many businesses to scratch their heads at the myriad rules and regulations now imposed on them. At the administrative center of Sarbanes-Oxley is the Public Company Accounting Oversight Board—and the PCAOB (pronounced "peek-a-boo") was in turn at the center of *Free Enterprise Fund v. PCAOB*. Hans Bader, a senior attorney at the Competitive Enterprise Institute and one of the lawyers on the case, explains the infirmities of the Court's half-a-loaf decision, which nevertheless struck down the PCAOB's two layers of protection from executive oversight as violating the separation of powers. The Court refused to sustain an Appointments Clause challenge, however, even though it is the Securities and Exchange Commission as a whole that appoints PCAOB members rather than—as the Constitution demands—either the president or a "head of department" (here, the SEC chairman). Bader is critical both of the denial of the Appointments Clause claim and the Court's preservation of Sarbanes-Oxley despite its constitutional infirmities and lack of severability clause. He explains how this sort of "judicial minimalism" demonstrates at least that the Roberts Court is not a "pro-business" entity as many have claimed. Instead, the Court seemed to bend over backwards to protect the anti-business Sarbanes-Oxley Act by "engaging in a radical judicial surgery that retroactively changed the relationship between the SEC and the PCAOB."

Further, as Congress enacts another round of financial regulations, University of Illinois law professor Larry E. Ribstein says that the case of *Jones v. Harris Associates* should serve as "a warning against the dangers of federal regulation of firms' structure and governance." Faced with a circuit split and two prominent intra-circuit views about the nature of mutual funds, a unanimous Court rejected Seventh Circuit Court of Appeals Judge Frank Easterbrook's rule for evaluating the appropriateness of compensation of investment advisers under the Investment Company Act (without siding with dissenting Seventh Circuit Judge Richard Posner either). Ribstein argues that while the ruling in *Jones* is not ideal, "the Court cannot do much more" without rewriting the law. As Justice Samuel Alito commented at the end of his opinion, "this really is a matter for Congress, not the courts."

Professor Michael Risch, newly of Villanova Law School, then reviews *Biksi v. Kappos*, which was supposed to be the patent case of the century but ultimately tread warily in this contentious area (to the relief of many practitioners). When the Federal Circuit Court of Appeals rejected a patent application based solely on the nature of the "invention" at issue—a method for hedging risk in commodities trading—the U.S. Patent and Trademark Office sought to force the Supreme Court to consider the "patentable subject matter" question. Although several Supreme Court decisions have made clear that abstract ideas, natural phenomena, and products of nature are not patentable subject matter, "it seems that no one can figure out what constitutes abstract ideas, natural phenomena, or products of nature." When the Court unanimously voted to deny the patent application here because the "concept of hedging is no more than an abstract idea," most considered the opinion a non-event. Risch, however, regards *Bilski* as "remarkably important." He provides analysis of the legal decision and reflects on "*Bilski*'s effect on business research and development," cautiously offering good news for those businesses and individuals seeking patents on software and business methods.

In our final article about the 2009–10 term, Judd Stone and Joshua Wright survey competing interpretations of the Court's intriguing antitrust decision, *American Needle v. NFL*. In this case, a clothing manufacturer alleged that the exclusive license the NFL granted to Reebok to manufacture team-branded headwear was an illegal conspiracy to restrain trade. For months, antitrust observers and football fans alike awaited the Supreme Court's decision—inspiring an article even from the quarterback of the defending champion New Orleans Saints. Yet the implications of the decision, which effectively narrowed the scope of "intra-enterprise immunity" to firms with a complete "unity of interests," are unclear. While some depict the decision as a departure from the last several decades of antitrust law, Stone and Wright explain why this interpretation is meritless and discuss the practical impact of the Court's holding.

They argue that the Court's antitrust jurisprudence has broadly embraced rules that are both relatively easy to administer and conscious of the error costs of deterring pro-competitive conduct. Intra-enterprise immunity potentially provided such a "filter" that enabled judges to dismiss a non-trivial subset of meritless claims prior to costly discovery. Rather than marking a drastic change in antitrust jurisprudence, *American Needle* should be viewed as the Supreme Court's replacement of an unreliable screening mechanism with a more cost-effective alternative.

Our volume concludes with a look ahead to October Term 2010—and what we can expect from Justice Kagan—by appellate specialist and longtime Cato contributor Erik S. Jaffe. While we have yet to see as many blockbuster constitutional cases as we did last term, we do look forward to: two big free speech challenges, one over a statute prohibiting the sale of violent video games to minors, another the offensive protesting of a fallen soldier's funeral; an Establishment Clause lawsuit against Arizona's tax credit for private tuition funds (an alternative to educational voucher programs); federal preemption cases involving safety standards for seatbelts, an Arizona statute regarding the hiring of illegal aliens, and the forbidding of class-arbitration waivers as unconscionable components of arbitration agreements; important ERISA and copyright cases; a case examining privacy concerns attending the federal government's background checks for contractors; and a criminal-procedure dispute regarding access to DNA testing that may support a claim of innocence. With some interesting cases still seeking Supreme Court review, it should be a good and varied year.

* * *

This is the third volume of the *Cato Supreme Court Review* that I have edited—and so I have reached the median tenure for someone in my position. (So far, so good!) While the learning curve keeps flattening, the amount of work has increased in parallel with the constitutional issues raised by various government actions. There are thus many people to thank for their contributions to this endeavor. I first need to thank our authors, without whom there obviously would not be anything to edit or read. My gratitude also goes to my colleagues at Cato's Center for Constitutional Studies, Bob Levy, Tim Lynch, and David Rittgers, who continue to provide valuable counsel in areas of law with which I'm less familiar. Wally Olson has also recently joined our group, and I look forward to exploring civil justice issues with him. A big thanks to research assistant Jonathan Blanks for making the trains run on time and keeping me honest, as well as to legal associates Trevor Burrus, Nicholas Mosvick, Evan Turgeon, and Caitlyn Walsh, and legal interns Jennifer Fry and Jonathan Wood, for doing the more thankless (except here) tasks. Neither the *Review* nor our Constitution Day symposium would be the successes they are without them. Finally, thanks to Roger Pilon, the ageless founder of this now well-established journal—and of Cato's legal policy shop—who gave me the first job that I've managed to stay in for more than two years (a lifetime in Washington).

I reiterate our hope that this collection of essays will deepen and promote the Madisonian first principles of our Constitution, giving renewed voice to the Framers' fervent wish that we have a government of laws and not of men. In so doing, we hope also to do justice to a rich legal tradition in which judges, politicians, and ordinary citizens alike understood that the Constitution reflects and protects the natural rights of life, liberty, and property, and serves as a bulwark against the abuse of power. In this uncertain time of individual mandates, endless "stimulus," financial "reform," and general government overreach, it is more important than ever to remember our proud roots in the Enlightenment tradition.

We hope you enjoy this ninth volume of the *Cato Supreme Court Review*.

The Ninth Amendment in Light of Text and History

*Michael W. McConnell**

The Ninth Amendment may seem a strange subject for a lecture at a conference on the recent decisions of the Supreme Court. After all, the Court has never squarely based a holding on the Ninth Amendment and has scarcely even discussed its meaning. Some scholars regard the amendment as an "inkblot"[1] or as nothing more than a warning not to read the enumeration of powers too liberally or the enumerated rights too narrowly.[2] It plays virtually no role in modern constitutional litigation. And yet the Ninth Amendment is the subject of two recent books[3] and many articles, and rightly so: the amendment, properly understood in light of its text and history, helps us understand the constitutional structure of powers granted and rights reserved, the relation of the Bill of Rights to the original

* Richard and Frances Mallery Professor and director of the Constitutional Law Center, Stanford Law School; senior fellow, Hoover Institution; formerly Circuit Judge, U.S. Court of Appeals for the Tenth Circuit. Portions of this lecture were originally delivered as the Hayek Lecture at New York University School of Law and will be published in the *New York University Journal of Law and Liberty* under the title "Natural Rights and the Ninth Amendment: How Does Lockean Legal Theory Assist in Interpretation?" The author wishes to thank Sam Bray, Kurt Lash, and Randy Barnett for useful comments and suggestions.

[1] Nomination of Robert H. Bork to Be Associate Justice of the Supreme Court of the United States: Hearings Before the S. Comm. on the Judiciary, 100th Cong. 248-49 (1987) (statement of Judge Robert H. Bork) (comparing the Ninth Amendment to an indecipherable "ink blot"); see also Robert H. Bork, The Tempting of America: The Political Seduction of the Law 166 (1990).

[2] See, e.g., Thomas B. McAfee, The Original Meaning of the Ninth Amendment, 90 Colum. L. Rev. 1215 (1990).

[3] Daniel A. Farber, Retained by the People: The "Silent" Ninth Amendment and the Constitutional Rights Americans Don't Know They Have (2007); Kurt T. Lash, The Forgotten History of the Ninth Amendment (2009); see also Randy E. Barnett, Restoring the Lost Constitution: The Presumption of Liberty (2004).

Constitution of 1787, and the role of natural rights in American constitutionalism.

I. Text

The Ninth Amendment is only 21 words long: "The enumeration in the Constitution, of certain rights, shall not be construed to deny or disparage others retained by the people." What are these rights? What is their legal status? What is their relation to the enumerated rights of the Bill of Rights? We know that we must not regard the enumeration as "denying" or "disparaging" these other rights, but what does that mean? Does it mean that these other rights are now judicially enforceable constitutional rights, just like the rights of freedom of speech and due process, and the right to confront witnesses?

Let us begin with the text. The Ninth Amendment refers to two different sets of rights. First are "certain rights" that are the subject of "enumeration in the Constitution." These are the rights (some positive, some natural) that are spelled out in the Bill of Rights, as well as in the few rights-reserving provisions of the original Constitution, such as Article I, Sections 9 and 10 (the prohibitions on bills of attainder, ex post facto laws, and state laws impairing the obligation of contracts), plus Article III's guarantee of jury trials in criminal cases. Because these are express constitutional rights, they have the status in our law as judicially-enforceable "trumps": even if violation of these rights would be an otherwise appropriate means of effectuating an enumerated power, the government may not infringe or abridge them.[4] As James Madison explained to the First Congress, if protections for these rights

> are incorporated into the Constitution, independent tribunals of justice will consider themselves in a peculiar manner the guardians of those rights; they will be an impenetrable bulwark against every assumption of power in the Legislative or Executive; *they will be naturally led to resist every encroachment upon rights expressly stipulated for in the Constitution by the declaration of rights.*[5]

[4] I borrow the terminology of "trumps" from Ronald Dworkin, Taking Rights Seriously, at xi (1977).

[5] 1 Annals of Cong. 457 (Joseph Gales & William Seaton eds., 1834) (statement of Rep. Madison) (emphasis added).

Significantly, as positive law, Madison insisted that these rights were judicially enforceable, and by the logic of constitutionalism, superior to enacted law, whether federal or state.

The second set of rights to which the Ninth Amendment refers are the "other" rights that are "retained by the people." This is the language of Lockean social compact theory.[6] At the time of the social compact—which for late-18th-century America meant the time of constitution-making—the people make an authoritative decision regarding which powers to delegate to the government and which rights to retain. As the delegates to the Constitutional Convention explained in the letter transmitting the proposed Constitution to Congress for submission to the ratifying conventions:

> Individuals entering into society, must give up a share of liberty to preserve the rest. The magnitude of the sacrifice must depend as well on situation and circumstances, as on the object to be obtained. It is at all times difficult to draw with precision the line between those rights which must be surrendered, and those which may be reserved . . . .[7]

The essence of the Lockean social compact is that we relinquish certain of our natural rights and we receive, in return, more effectual protection for certain of our rights, plus the enjoyment of positive rights, that is, rights created by the action of political society.[8] As articulated by the New York Anti-Federalist writing as Brutus:

> The common good, therefore, is the end of civil government, and common consent, the foundation on which it is established. To effect this end, it was necessary that a certain portion of natural liberty should be surrendered, in order, that what remained should be preserved: how great a proportion of natural freedom is necessary to be yielded by individuals, when they submit to government, I shall now enquire. So much, however, must be given up, as will be sufficient to enable those, to whom the administration of the government is committed, to establish laws for the promoting the

---

[6] See generally John Locke, The Second Treatise of Government, in Two Treatises of Government §§ 95–140 (1690) (constructing a social compact theory of government).

[7] Letter to Congress (Sept. 17, 1787), in 2 The Records of the Federal Convention of 1787, at 666 (Max Farrand ed., 1911).

[8] Locke, *supra* note 6, at §§ 122–131.

> happiness of the community, and to carry those laws into
> effect. But it is not necessary, for this purpose, that individu-
> als should relinquish all their natural rights. Some are of
> such a nature that they cannot be surrendered. Of this kind
> are the rights of conscience, the right of enjoying and defend-
> ing life, etc. Others are not necessary to be resigned, in order
> to attain the end for which government is instituted, these
> therefore ought not be given up. To surrender them, would
> counteract the very end of government, to wit, the common
> good. From these observations it appears, that in forming a
> government on its true principles, the foundation should be
> laid in the manner I before stated, by expressly reserving to
> the people such of their essential natural rights, as are not
> necessary to be parted with.[9]

Madison offered a similar account of social compact theory on
the floor of the House in the First Congress. He explained that a bill
of rights would "specify" two types of rights: those "which are
retained when particular powers are given up to be exercised by
the Legislature," and "positive rights," like trial by jury, which
"cannot be considered as a natural right, but a right resulting from
a social compact."[10]

Brutus and Madison thus employed the common language of
Lockean rights theory. Certain natural rights are "surrendered" or
"relinquished," while others are "retained" or "reserved." In interpreting the rights language of the Constitution, it is important to
understand the meanings then attached to these words, and to bear
in mind the differences between those meanings and modern usage.

The key words here, as used by Brutus, Madison, and the transmit-
tal letter, are *natural* rights, *positive* rights, *retained* rights (also called
reserved rights), and *relinquished* rights. "Natural rights" are rights
human beings possess in the state of nature—principally ownership
of one's own body and the product of one's labors, and the right to
use violence against others to punish violations of the law of nature.[11]
Importantly, these natural rights do not necessarily survive into
civil society; some are "retained" and others are "surrendered" in

---

[9] Brutus, On the Lack of a Bill of Rights, in The Complete Federalist and Anti-Federalist Papers 749, 750 (2009).

[10] 1 Annals of Cong., *supra* note 5, at 454.

[11] Locke, *supra* note 6, at §§ 26–28.

exchange for greater security in those that are retained.[12] They are not the same as modern "human rights," which governments everywhere and always must respect. "Positive rights" are rights not enjoyed in the state of nature.[13] Madison gives the example of trial by jury; no one has the right to a jury trial in the state of nature. "Retained rights" comprise only a subset of natural rights. No positive rights—no rights that are the product of civil society—are included. As the Federal Farmer explained, many important rights, such as the right to trial by jury, to the writ of habeas corpus, to the assistance of counsel, and to confront witnesses, are not "reserved" natural rights but "stipulated rights" that "individuals acquire by compact."[14] And in this compact some natural rights—such as freedom from taxation or military conscription—are relinquished.

Thus, the "other rights" to which the Ninth Amendment refers, which are "retained" by the people, comprise the set of natural rights that have not been surrendered or relinquished under the social compact in order to promote the good, prosperity, and safety of society. This set does not include positive rights, which are not "retained" but rather are created by the social compact—such as the enforcement of contracts. Nor does it include those rights "expressly stipulated for in the Constitution by the declaration of rights."[15] Examples of unenumerated natural rights that might be "retained by the people" include the right to control the upbringing of one's children, the right to travel, the right to engage in nonprocreative sex, the right to read, the right to control one's own medical care, the right to choose one's own friends and associates, the right to pursue a job or profession, the right of self-defense, and many others.[16] During the Bill of Rights debates, reference was jokingly made to the right to wear a hat, and to go to bed when one pleases.[17]

---

[12] *Id*. at §§ 128–31.

[13] *Id*. at §§ 136–39.

[14] Federal Farmer No. 16 (Jan. 20, 1788), reprinted in Empire and Nation 157, 158 (Forrest McDonald ed., 1962).

[15] 1 Annals of Cong., *supra* note 5, at 457.

[16] I make no argument as to whether any of these natural rights would be constitutionally protected under a proper interpretation of the Constitution, but only mention them as examples of rights enjoyed in the state of nature that might arguably have been retained by the people.

[17] 1 Annals of Cong., *supra* note 5, at 759–60 (statement of Rep. Sedgwick). Professor Kurt Lash argues that, in addition to its application to individual natural rights, the Ninth Amendment protected the people's collective political right to enact policies

II. Legal Status of Natural Rights Before and After the Bill of Rights

What is the legal status of retained natural rights? The Ninth Amendment seems to say that retained natural rights have precisely the same status they had before adoption of the Bill of Rights or the rights-protecting provisions of the original Constitution. They are neither "denied or disparaged," nor are they elevated to the status of expressly enumerated rights. As Professor Randy Barnett has written, "The purpose of the Ninth Amendment was to ensure that all individual natural rights had the same stature and force after some of them were enumerated as they had before."[18]

In order to understand what force these unenumerated retained rights have under the law, we must therefore examine how natural rights were invoked before the Constitution. Some scholars, among them Professor Barnett, argue that unenumerated natural rights are now constitutional rights, with the same status as rights spelled out by the First through Eighth Amendments. Other scholars regard the Ninth Amendment as a protection for federalism, for certain collective rights of a republican nature, or as a unenforceable truism or inkblot.[19] My reading of the historical materials suggests a middle ground: that unenumerated natural rights are protected through some combination of political self-control on the part of the political branches (reinforced by the separation of powers) and equitable interpretation by the courts, which entails the narrow construction of statutes so as to avoid violations of natural rights. In other words, *natural rights control in the absence of sufficiently explicit positive law to the contrary.* This can be understood as a clear statement rule for abrogating unenumerated natural rights.

The historical evidence indicates that natural rights in the pre-constitutional world did *not* have the status we now ascribe to constitutional rights—meaning supreme over positive law. With the possible exception of *Dr. Bonham's Case*,[20] a hotly contested and frequently

at the state and local level. See Kurt T. Lash, A Textual-Historical Theory of the Ninth Amendment, 60 Stan. L. Rev. 895 (2008). This article will focus only on individual rights.

[18] Randy E. Barnett, The Ninth Amendment: It Means What It Says, 85 Tex. L. Rev. 1, 2 (2006).

[19] For a summary of five leading views on the meaning of the Ninth Amendment, see *id.* at 10–21.

[20] 8 Co. Rep. 107a, 113b (1610); see Theodore F.T. Plunknett, Bonham's Case and Judicial Review, 40 Harv. L. Rev. 30 (1926).

misinterpreted decision by the great Chief Justice of the Court of Common Pleas, Sir Edward Coke, there appear to be no examples in English jurisprudence of courts upholding natural rights claims in the teeth of contrary statutes passed by sovereign authorities.[21] John Locke himself presupposed that "the body of the people" is the only available judge of "whether the prince or legislative act contrary to their trust," and that if the government should "decline that way of determination," the people's only recourse is rebellion: the "appeal . . . to heaven."[22] As Blackstone explained in his *Commentaries on the Laws of England,* Parliament had "no superior on earth," and if Parliament made its intent clear, "there is no court that has power to defeat the intent of the legislature."[23] With minor departures, this became established doctrine in American colonial and state courts as well.[24]

A striking example of pre-constitutional natural law jurisprudence was Lord Mansfield's 1772 decision in *Somersett's Case,* involving the legality of slavery within the Kingdom of England. Mansfield operated on the premise that "[t]he state of slavery is of such a nature, that it is incapable of being introduced on any reasons, moral or political, but only by positive law . . . . It is so odious, that nothing can be suffered to support it, but positive law."[25] Finding no positive law to support slavery within England, Mansfield required Somersett's captors to set him free. This famous decision, well known to the American colonists, illustrates how natural law could be enforced in court, but it also made plain that natural law cannot trump explicit positive law, however odious. Despite its odiousness, under the logic of the *Somersett* decision, slavery remained legal and enforceable in parts of the empire where there were slave codes or other authoritative pronouncements establishing slavery.

A particularly clear illustration of the relation of natural rights to positive law may be found in the famed Virginia Bill for Establishing

---

[21] See Philip Hamburger, Law and Judicial Duty 237–54 (2008).

[22] Locke, *supra* note 6, at § 242.

[23] William Blackstone, 1 Commentaries *90–91.

[24] For this proposition, I rely on the definitive research of Professor Philip Hamburger. See Hamburger, *supra* note 21, at 274–80.

[25] R. v. Knowles, ex parte Somersett, 20 State Tr 1 (1772), reprinted in The Eighteenth-Century Constitution 1688–1815, at 387–88 (E. Neville Williams ed., 1960).

Religious Freedom, authored by Thomas Jefferson and championed by Madison. It concludes with the following observation:

> And though we well know that this assembly elected by the people for the ordinary purposes of legislation only, have no power to restrain the acts of succeeding assemblies, constituted with powers equal to our own, and that therefore to declare this act to be irrevocable would be of no effect in law; yet we are free to declare, and do declare, that the rights hereby asserted are of the natural rights of mankind, and that if any act shall be hereafter passed to repeal the present, or to narrow its operation, such act will be an infringement of natural right.[26]

This concluding observation makes clear that the founding generation, despite its regard for "the natural rights of mankind," believed that in the absence of express constitutional protections, legislatures had the power (if not the right) to infringe those natural rights. If the rights affirmed by the Virginia Bill, which Madison regarded as not only "natural" but "unalienable,"[27] could in fact be revoked, repealed, or narrowed by future legislatures, this demonstrates that (at least prior to express constitutionalization) "natural" and "unalienable" rights enjoyed a status inferior to legislation.

That natural law did not trump positive law as a legal matter in court did not mean that it was wholly without effect. To begin with, legal theorists regarded natural law as morally binding on Parliament itself. It may have been true that courts were not free to hold acts of Parliament "unconstitutional" or "void," but Parliament remained subject to the unwritten constitution of the realm, and was under an obligation, albeit not judicially enforceable, to control itself.[28] Even after the ratification of a written constitution, Americans expected that Congress and the president, and ultimately an alert and engaged citizenry, would be the principal bulwarks against

---

[26] A Bill for Establishing Religious Freedom § III (1786), reprinted in Jefferson and Madison on Separation of Church and State 50 (Lenni Brenner ed., 2004).

[27] James Madison, Memorial and Remonstrance against Religious Assessments (1785), reprinted in Jefferson and Madison, *supra* note 26, at 68.

[28] See Hamburger, *supra* note 21, at 252–54.

violations.[29] This was, indeed, the principal reason the Federal Farmer gave for supporting enactment of a Bill of Rights: "If a nation means its systems, religious or political, shall have duration, it ought to recognize the leading principles of them in the front page of every family book."[30] Rights should be declared so "that the people might not forget these rights, and gradually become prepared for arbitrary government."[31] Recall the stern warning the enactors of the Virginia Bill for Establishing Religious Freedom gave to future legislators who might contemplate repeal.

But natural rights were not merely political principles. They also had purchase in court, albeit not as constitutional rights—that is, not as superior to positive law. It was understood that courts had the power to engage in equitable interpretation, under which statutes were interpreted narrowly so as to avoid violating the law of nature.[32] As Blackstone explained:

> [I]f the parliament will positively enact a thing to be done which is unreasonable, I know of no power in the ordinary forms of the constitution, that is vested with authority to control it. . . . But where some collateral matter arises out of the general words, and happens to be unreasonable; there the judges are in decency to conclude that this consequence was not foreseen by the parliament, and therefore they are at liberty to expound the statute by equity, and only *quoad hoc* disregard it. . . . [T]here is no court that has power to defeat the intent of the legislature, when couched in such

[29] See The Federalist No. 33, at 199 (Hamilton) (Clinton Rossiter, ed. 1961[1788]) ("If the federal government should overpass the just bounds of its authority and make a tyrannical use of its powers, the people, whose creature it is, must appeal to the standard they have formed, and take such measures to redress the injury done to the Constitution as the exigency may suggest and prudence justify."). For an interpretation stressing popular enforcement of constitutional principles, see Larry D. Kramer, The People Themselves: Popular Constitutionalism and Judicial Review (2004).

[30] Federal Farmer No. 16 (Jan. 20, 1788), reprinted in 1 Classics of American Political and Constitutional Thought: Origins through Civil War 568 (Scott J. Hammond et. al. eds., 2007).

[31] Federal Farmer No. 16, *supra* note 14, at 153.

[32] See generally Hamburger, *supra* note 21, at 344–57, 622–30; J.H. Baker, The Law's Two Bodies: Some Evidential Problems in English Legal History 28, 28 n.96 (2001); S.E. Thorne, Dr. Bonham's Case, Essays in English Legal History 275 (1985).

21

evidence and express words, as leave no doubt whether it
was the intent of the legislature or no.[33]

In part, this equitable interpretation was predicated on the charitable
assumption that the legislature likely did not intend, by the use of
broad language not explicitly addressed to the point at issue, to
violate the law of nature. As one American judge stated in a 1784
decision that closely followed and quoted from the above Blackstone
passage: "When the judicial make these distinctions, they do not
controul the Legislature; they endeavour to give their intention its
proper effect."[34] Equitable interpretation was interpretation according to the animating purpose or spirit of a law, rather than its letter.[35]

This equitable approach to the enforcement of constitutional rights
changed with adoption of the Constitution. By declaring the docu-
ment part of the "supreme Law of the Land,"[36] the sovereign people
made the Constitution positive law, superior to any act of the legislature. By authorizing the federal courts to hear cases "arising under"
the Constitution,[37] the people made clear that the positive law of the
Constitution would be judicially cognizable. And by enumerating
certain rights through the Bill of Rights, the people made those rights
as much a part of the positive law of the land as any power of
Congress. They did not, however, constitutionalize those natural
rights that remained unenumerated.

The Framers thus drew upon natural rights when they created
a written constitution, but they recognized a distinction between
constitutional law, which is a species of judicially enforceable positive law, and natural law or natural justice. As George Mason
explained at the Constitutional Convention: "[Judges] could declare
an unconstitutional law void. But with regard to every law however
unjust oppressive or pernicious, which did not come plainly under

---

[33] Blackstone, *supra* note 23, at *90.

[34] Rutgers v. Waddington (N.Y. City Mayor's Ct. 1784), quoted in Hamburger, *supra*
note 21, at 351.

[35] See Hamburger, *supra* note 21, at 344–57; Brutus, No. 15, in 2 The Complete Anti-
Federalist 437–41 (Herbert Storing ed., 1981).

[36] U.S. Const. art. VI, cl. 2.

[37] U.S. Const. art. III, § 2, cl. 1.

this description, they would be under the necessity as Judges to give it a free course."[38]

With this background, the Ninth Amendment can best be understood as ensuring that rights arising from natural law or natural justice are not abrogated on account of the *expressio unius* effect of incomplete enumeration. But it did not elevate those rights to the status of constitutional positive law, superior to ordinary legislation.

III. How Does This Work?

We are left with this construction of the Ninth Amendment: Courts should give presumptive protection to natural rights (but not make up new positive rights), but natural rights are subject to congressional override through explicit and specific legislation. In other words, the rights retained by the people are indeed individual natural rights, but those rights enjoy precisely the same status, and are protected in the same way, as before the Bill of Rights was added to the Constitution. They are not relinquished, denied, or disparaged. Nor do natural rights become "constitutional rights." They are simply what all retained rights were before the enactment of the Bill of Rights: a guide to equitable interpretation and a rationale for narrow construction of statutes that might be thought to infringe them, but not superior to explicit positive law. This understanding of the relation of unenumerated natural rights to positive law closely resembles the relation between common law and legislation: the common law governs in the absence of contrary legislation, and sometimes even guides or limits the interpretation of ambiguous or overbroad statutes, but does not prevail in the teeth of specific statutory overrides.

This mode of interpretation offers a middle way between the two usual poles of unenumerated rights jurisprudence. One pole maintains that if a claimed right cannot be found in the Constitution, even applying a liberal construction to its terms, it is entitled to no protection at all. That is the jurisprudence of *Bowers v. Hardwick*.[39] The other pole maintains that there are unwritten natural rights

---

[38] Records of the Federal Convention, *supra* note 7, at 78. This was not an argument on Mason's part for judicial restraint, but rather an argument to augment judicial authority with regard to unjust or pernicious laws, by creation of a council of revision.

[39] 478 U.S. 186 (1986) (upholding constitutionality of state law criminalizing sodomy).

whose content must inevitably be determined, finally and without possibility of legislative override, by judges. These rights then receive full constitutional protection even when the representatives of the people have reached the contrary conclusion. That is the jurisprudence of *Roe v. Wade*[40] and *Lochner v. New York*.[41] If I am correct about the meaning of the Ninth Amendment, neither of these approaches is entirely correct. Rather, an assertion of natural right (generally founded on common law or other long-standing practice) will be judicially enforceable unless there is specific and explicit positive law to the contrary. This allows the representatives of the people, rather than members of the judiciary, to make the ultimate determination of when natural rights should yield to the peace, safety, and happiness of society.

For example, suppose that a federal statute defined the crime of murder without reference to traditional common-law justifications such as self-defense. The Ninth Amendment would come into play because a defendant could show that the right of self-defense is a natural right, and that the relevant statute was silent on the subject. The court would conclude that the natural right to self-defense would continue to prevail, because there was no specific indication of an intention of the legislature to abrogate the right.[42] This mode of analysis differs from finding that there is a "constitutional right of self-defense," because such a right would be judicially defined and impervious to legislation. Under an equitable understanding of the Ninth Amendment, if Congress were to pass a statute explicitly defining or narrowing the traditional common law defense—for example, by denying the right to inflict injury on another in defense of one's property—the statute would prevail.

---

[40] 410 U.S. 113 (1973) (holding that a woman's right to terminate her pregnancy by means of abortion prevails over state statute protecting unborn child, at least prior to viability).

[41] 198 U.S. 45 (1905) (holding that a worker's "liberty of contract" prevails over a state law limiting the number of hours bakers could contract to work).

[42] It should go without saying that this is not how the Supreme Court has actually approached the question. See United States v. Oakland Cannabis Buyers' Coop., 532 U.S. 483, 490 (2001) (calling it "an open question whether federal courts ever have authority to recognize a necessity defense not provided by statute"); cf. United States v. Patton, 451 F.3d 615, 637 (10th Cir. 2006) (assuming the existence of a common-law defense of necessity).

This may sound unfamiliar but it should not. In fact, without alluding to the Ninth Amendment or to pre-constitutional natural rights jurisprudence, the Supreme Court frequently employs the adjudicative method I have outlined here. For example, in *Zadvydas v. Davis*,[43] the Court was faced with a statute providing that aliens subject to a final order of removal may be held in custody for 90 days, but that they "may be detained beyond the removal period" if the attorney general determines they pose a risk to the community.[44] Can this detention be indefinite? The United States argued that it could. The Court summarized the government's argument as follows:

> The Government argues that the statute means what it literally says. It sets no "limit on the length of time beyond the removal period that an alien who falls within one of the Section 1231(a)(6) categories may be detained." Hence, "whether to continue to detain such an alien and, if so, in what circumstances and for how long" is up to the Attorney General, not up to the courts.[45]

A lower court granted habeas relief to Zadvydas on due process grounds, but the applicability of due process to aliens subject to removal is at least questionable, and the boundaries of the due process right are hard to define. The Supreme Court took a different tack, concluding, without reaching the constitutional question:

> We have found nothing in the history of these statutes that clearly demonstrates a congressional intent to authorize indefinite, perhaps permanent, detention. Consequently, interpreting the statute to avoid a serious constitutional threat, we conclude that, once removal is no longer reasonably foreseeable, continued detention is no longer authorized by statute. See 1 E. Coke, Institutes *70b ("*Cessante ratione legis cessat ipse lex*") (the rationale of a legal rule no longer being applicable, that rule itself no longer applies).[46]

---

[43] 533 U.S. 678 (2001).

[44] *Id*. at 689.

[45] *Id*. (quoting Br. for Pet'rs 22).

[46] *Id*. at 699.

This reasoning bears close resemblance to a proper Ninth Amendment analysis. Under the Ninth Amendment, the habeas petitioner would invoke the natural right to freedom from indefinite restraint, and the question would become whether the statute invoked by the executive specifically and explicitly abrogated that right. If the Court is correct that neither the text nor the history of the statute demonstrates such an intent, it would follow that Zadvydas was entitled to habeas relief.[47] However, this is not the same as saying that Zadvydas had a due process right to release; when Congress (or the executive, through delegated authority) subsequently amended the statute to be more specific, as it did, the subsequent enactment was enforceable.[48]

The Supreme Court followed a similar approach in *Hamdan v. Rumsfeld*.[49] There, the government argued that the congressional Authorization for Use of Military Force provided authorization for the military commission that was convened to try Hamdan.[50] Again, there were important issues under due process and international law, but the Court did not reach or resolve them. The Court stated: "we assume that the AUMF activated the President's war powers, and that those powers include the authority to convene military commissions in appropriate circumstances, [but] there is nothing in the text or legislative history of the AUMF even hinting that Congress intended to expand or alter the authorization set forth in Article 21 of the Uniform Code of Military Justice."[51] Thus, "[a]bsent a more specific congressional authorization, the task of this Court is . . . to decide whether Hamdan's military commission is so justified."[52] There was no mention of the Ninth Amendment, but the mode of

---

[47] I do not necessarily mean to endorse the result in *Zadvydas* in all respects. Zadvydas sought not just freedom from indefinite detention, which vindicates the natural right of liberty, but release *into the United States*. It is not clear to me that any alien has a natural right to that.

[48] See Hernandez-Carrera v. Carlson, 547 F.3d 1237, 1251–56 (10th Cir. 2008). The main difference between my suggested approach and that taken by the Court is that the Court's approach hinges on the existence of constitutional doubt; under my approach, natural rights could be protected even if not plausibly covered by an enumerated right.

[49] 548 U.S. 557 (2006).

[50] *Id*. at 594.

[51] *Id*.

[52] *Id*. at 595.

reasoning is familiar. A broad and indefinite statute like the AUMF is not a sufficient basis for overcoming deeply rooted natural and international law norms. Only when and if there were "a more specific congressional authorization" would the Court have to answer the ultimate constitutional question.

IV. Implications

I have offered this interpretation of the Ninth Amendment because it best comports with the text and history of the provision. But some may ask why it would make a difference and whether constitutional adjudication would be improved if it were adopted. I think it would. As a middle way between the no legal effect and the fully enforceable rights approaches, Blackstonian equitable interpretation achieves much of the purpose of the latter while mitigating its judicial imperialism.

The most controversial of Supreme Court decisions have involved the identification and enforcement of unenumerated rights. Some such decisions have so enraged parts of the citizenry as to call the legitimacy of the judicial power into question. If the Court were to take a middle-ground position of equitable interpretation grounded in the Ninth Amendment, its decisions might well gain democratic legitimacy. Most likely, if the Court's explication of natural rights is persuasive, Congress would follow the Court's lead. In some cases, politicians will be able to forge pragmatic compromises that are beyond the institutional competency of the courts. (That seems to have been what happened to the *Zadvydas* decision.) In other cases, the representatives of the people may squarely reject the Court's conclusion (as Congress rejected the Supreme Court's conclusions about partial-birth abortion and the meaning of free exercise of religion). These will be difficult cases, but I see no reason to presuppose that courts are wiser (or even necessarily more libertarian) than legislatures when it comes to controversial moral questions; they certainly are less representative.

Equitable interpretation in cases of unenumerated natural rights would permit further public deliberation. Instead of a judicial pronouncement purporting to place an issue outside democratic debate,[53] a judicial decision would govern by the force of its reason

---

[53] See Planned Parenthood of Se. Pa. v. Casey, 505 U.S. 833, 867 (1992).

27

and persuasiveness, with the possibility of a democratic override if the representatives of the people reject the court's arguments. Courts are not, after all, infallible. Some of the most grievous injuries to American constitutional principle have been inflicted by judicial error: think of *Dred Scott*, *Plessy v. Ferguson*, *Buck v. Bell*, or others too recent in memory to be uncontroversial examples. And it should be remembered that courts do not always err on the side of rights, or of vulnerable minorities. Perhaps judicial review would be improved if, when courts stray beyond the "rights expressly stipulated for in the Constitution," as Madison called them, their judgments were subject to further debate and revision by more representative institutions. Introduction of a democratic element might embolden courts to act when they should, and ameliorate the effects when they should not. In any event, a return to Blackstonian equitable interpretation of unenumerated rights claims would, in my judgment, make more sense of the text of the Ninth Amendment in light of its history.

Citizens United v. Federal Election Commission: "Precisely What WRTL Sought to Avoid"

*James Bopp Jr. & Richard E. Coleson**

In *Citizens United v. FEC*[1] the Supreme Court overturned both *Austin v. Michigan State Chamber of Commerce*,[2] which permitted the prohibition of corporate election-related speech, and the part of *McConnell v. FEC*[3] that facially upheld the ban on corporate "electioneering communications."[4] *Citizens United* declared that the regime the Federal Election Commission created in implementing the "appeal to vote" test in *FEC v. Wisconsin Right to Life (WRTL)*[5] was "precisely what *WRTL* sought to avoid."[6]

Incorporated citizen groups and unions may now independently and expressly advocate candidates' election or defeat like other groups. That is constitutionally correct. However, the Supreme Court's reasoning in *Citizens United* causes problems in campaign-finance law. In this article, we analyze how the case was decided, what it means, and the problems it leaves in its wake.

---

* Attorneys, Bopp, Coleson & Bostrom, Terre Haute, Indiana. James Bopp is also general counsel for the James Madison Center for Free Speech.

[1] 558 U.S. ___, 130 S. Ct. 876 (2010).

[2] 494 U.S. 652 (1990).

[3] 540 U.S. 93 (2003).

[4] Citizens United, 130 S. Ct. at 913. Electioneering communications are essentially targeted, broadcast ads naming federal candidates in 30- and 60-day periods before primaries and general elections, respectively. See 2 U.S.C. § 434(f)(3).

[5] 551 U.S. 449, 470 (2007) (controlling opinion by Roberts, C.J., joined by Alito, J.). The appeal-to-vote test distinguished protected issue advocacy from regulable electioneering communications. *Id.* at 451–52.

[6] Citizens United, 130 S. Ct. at 896.

We base our analysis on our role as counsel in *McConnell*, *WRTL*, and *Citizens United* and as petitioners for an FEC rule implementing *WRTL*. We served as Citizens United's counsel in the lower court and prepared its jurisdictional statement—the equivalent of a petition for certiorari in cases with statutory rights of appeal. After *Citizens United* was accepted we hosted its amici curiae conference (attended by the editor of this journal, among many others). When Citizens United retained Theodore Olson as lead counsel, we withdrew. We approached the case differently than Olson did. The approaches are contrasted below.

I. *Buckley*: Foundational Protection for Political Speech

To understand the background and significance of *Citizens United*, we begin with the foundational *Buckley v. Valeo* decision.[7] *Buckley* provided nine relevant principles:

1. "In a republic . . . the people are sovereign," and their "[d]iscussion of public issues and debate on the qualifications of candidates are integral to the operation of the system of government established by our Constitution."[8]

2. "The First Amendment affords the broadest protection to . . . political expression . . . 'to assure [the] unfettered interchange of ideas for the bringing about of political and social changes desired by the people,'" and "'debate on public issues should be uninhibited, robust, and wide-open.'"[9]

3. If a law restricts speech before an upcoming election, it must have clear constitutional authority and be narrowly tailored to a compelling governmental interest.[10]

4. Congress's authority to enact campaign-finance laws stems from its constitutional authority to regulate federal elections. This authority is inherently self-limiting because unless the regulated activity is *clearly* election-related, the regulation is not constitutionally

---

[7] 424 U.S. 1 (1976).

[8] *Id.* at 14.

[9] *Id.* (citations omitted).

[10] *Buckley* imposed "exacting scrutiny," *id.* at 16, 44, 64, which means "[t]he strict test," *id.* at 66. Its requirements are debated for contribution limits and disclosure, but expenditure limits are always subject to strict scrutiny.

authorized. A regulation may not be overbroad (*Buckley*-overbreadth[11]) by reaching beyond this constitutional authority. In *Buckley*'s most specific description of the problem to avoid, it allowed campaign-finance regulation to reach only First Amendment activity *"unambiguously related to the campaign* of a particular federal candidate."[12]

5. Regulation requires bright lines protecting issue advocacy because of a dissolving-distinction problem. As *Buckley* explained:

> [T]he distinction between *discussion of issues and candidates* and *advocacy of election or defeat of candidates* may often dissolve in practical application. Candidates, especially incumbents, are intimately tied to public issues involving legislative proposals and governmental actions. Not only do candidates campaign on the basis of their positions on various public issues, but campaigns themselves generate issues of public interest.[13]

6. A bright line distinguishing ordinary political speech from electioneering is the "express advocacy" test, which permits the government to regulate only those communications with explicit words expressly advocating for or against federal candidates' election, "such as 'vote for.'"[14] Such "magic words" communications are "unambiguously related to the campaign of a particular federal candidate."[15]

---

[11] *Buckley* overbreadth concerns whether regulated First Amendment activity is unambiguously campaign related. The substantial-overbreadth doctrine, by contrast, requires *facial* invalidation of statutes sweeping in *too much* protected speech, as set forth in *Broadrick v. Oklahoma*, 413 U.S. 601, 611–14 (1973).

[12] 424 U.S. at 80 (emphasis added). See James Bopp Jr. and Richard E. Coleson, Comments of the James Madison Center for Free Speech on Notice of Proposed Rulemaking 2007-16 (Electioneering Communications) at 4–9 (Sept. 29, 2007) (explaining *Buckley*'s analysis), available at http://www.fec.gov/pdf/nprm/electioneering_comm/2007/james_madison_center_for_free_speech_eccomment16.pdf. See also James Bopp Jr. & Josiah Neeley, How Not to Reform Judicial Elections: *Davis, White,* and the Future of Judicial Campaign Financing, 86 Denv. U. L. Rev. 195, 222–25 (2008).

[13] 424 U.S. at 42 (emphasis added).

[14] *Id.* at 43–44 & n.52. See James Bopp Jr. & Richard E. Coleson, The First Amendment Is Not a Loophole: Protecting Free Expression in the Election Campaign Context, 28 UWLA L. Rev. 1, 9, 11–15 (1997) (explaining long-standing express-advocacy-test speech protection).

[15] Buckley, 424 U.S. at 80.

7. The only cognizable interest justifying speech restriction is preventing quid pro quo corruption (political favors for campaign contributions) or the appearance thereof, and this interest justifies restricting only political contributions, not speech.[16]

8. Any equality (level-the-playing-field) justification for restricting speech is not cognizable.[17]

9. *Buckley* was not asked to address whether a federal prohibition on corporate "independent expenditures" (express advocacy) was constitutional, though it cited favorably a dissent (in another case) arguing that it was unconstitutional.[18]

Buckley's express-advocacy test and issue-advocacy protection were reaffirmed in *FEC v. Massachusetts Citizens for Life*[19] and widely recognized by lower federal courts in numerous cases that we brought.[20]

II. *Austin* and *McConnell*: A Shaky Superstructure

Given *Buckley*'s rejection of speech-equalizing justifications, *Austin* was anomalous in approving a ban on corporate express advocacy with a new corporate-form corruption rationale that the dissent identified as the rejected equality rationale.[21] But after *Austin*, corporations could still engage in issue advocacy that mentioned candidates because *Buckley* protected such speech.

That changed when the Bipartisan Campaign Reform Act (commonly known as McCain-Feingold) banned corporate electioneering communications.[22] The line was bright but not speech-protective in that it subsumed formerly protected issue advocacy. But *McConnell*,

---

[16] *Id.* at 26, 45.

[17] *Id.* at 48–49.

[18] *Id.* at 43 (citing United States v. Auto. Workers, 352 U.S. 567, 595–96, (1957) (Douglas, J., dissenting)).

[19] 479 U.S. 238 (1986).

[20] See, e.g., Faucher v. FEC, 928 F.2d 468, 470 (1st Cir. 1991); Virginia Society for Human Life v. FEC, 263 F.3d 379, 329 (4th Cir. 2001); North Carolina Right to Life v. Leake, 525 F.3d 274, 283 (4th Cir. 2008); Brownsburg Area Patrons Affecting Change v. Baldwin, 137 F.3d 503, 506 (7th Cir. 1998); Iowa Right to Life Committee v. Williams, 187 F.3d 963, 969 (8th Cir. 1999)); California Pro-Life Council v. Getman, 328 F.3d 1088, 1098 (9th Cir. 2003).

[21] Austin v. Mich. State Chamber of Commerce, 494 U.S 652, 704–705 (1990) (Kennedy, J., joined by O'Connor & Scalia, JJ., dissenting).

[22] Bipartisan Campaign Reform Act of 2002, Pub. L. No. 107-155, 116 Stat. 81 (2002).

which involved a challenge to much of McCain-Feingold, rejected the express-advocacy line as controlling and facially upheld the prohibition "to the extent that the issue ads broadcast during the 30- and 60-day periods preceding federal primary and general elections are the functional equivalent of express advocacy."[23] *McConnell* failed to provide any test for functional equivalence and recognized that the opinion's rationale might not apply to "genuine issue ads."[24] It simply relied on *Austin* to uphold the corporate electioneering-communication ban.[25]

McConnell's facial upholding of the ban on corporate electioneering communications set the stage for a case challenging the ban as applied to particular ads—a case about how to distinguish "genuine" from so-called sham issue ads and what "functional equivalent" meant. That case was *WRTL*.

III. *WRTL*: Issue-Advocacy Protection Reasserted

In July 2004, Wisconsin Right to Life, a nonprofit, ideological corporation, broadcast ads challenging filibusters of President George W. Bush's judicial nominees. The ads asked citizens to ask Senators Herb Kohl and Russ Feingold to oppose the filibusters. Since Senator Feingold was a candidate, WRTL had to stop the broadcasts before August 15 (30 days before Wisconsin's primary), at which point the ads became illegal electioneering communications. Broadcasting the ads remained criminal through the November election under the 60-day pre-general-election prohibition.

We challenged the prohibition as applied to WRTL's ads, noting that *McConnell* had left open the question of whether its rationale applied to "genuine issue ads" and asserting that WRTL's ads were genuine issue ads. The *WRTL* district court agreed with the FEC and intervening McCain-Feingold sponsors that *McConnell* precluded as-applied challenges, but the Supreme Court unanimously rejected

---

[23] McConnell v. FEC, 540 U.S. 93, 206 (2003). See James Bopp Jr. & Richard E. Coleson, The First Amendment Is Still Not a Loophole: Examining *McConnell*'s Exception to *Buckley*'s General Rule Protecting Issue Advocacy, 31 N. Ky. L. Rev. 289 (2004) (*McConnell* analysis).

[24] 540 U.S. at 206 n.88.

[25] *Id*. at 204–205.

that contention.[26] The district court then ruled in our favor,[27] and the FEC appealed.

We advised the Supreme Court of the burdensome litigation to which WRTL was subjected in its effort to vindicate its First Amendment rights and that the necessity of as-applied challenges functioned like a prior restraint. We asked the Court to overrule *McConnell*'s facial upholding of the electioneering-communication prohibition unless it provided a workable test to reduce the need for litigation and make as-applied challenges an adequate remedy.

WRTL's controlling opinion (by Chief Justice John Roberts, joined by Justice Samuel Alito) mandated that such as-applied challenges be conducted quickly, simply, and with little or no discovery; it also protected issue advocacy with the "appeal to vote" test.[28] Justice Antonin Scalia, joined by Justices Anthony Kennedy and Clarence Thomas, argued that only the express-advocacy test protected speech and the new appeal-to-vote test would lead to chilled political speech.[29] Justice Alito said that if a chill on issue advocacy became evident there would certainly be a request to reconsider *McConnell* and *WRTL*.[30] So if the problems we identified in *WRTL* were not fixed, reconsideration was expected.

Key to understanding our approach to *Citizens United* is *how* the Court decided *WRTL*. The controlling *WRTL* opinion chose between basing the holding on the nature of the *money*, the *speaker*, or the *speech*. That choice would guide how we litigated *Citizens United*.

In *WRTL* we argued—regarding the nature of the *money*—that WRTL would be willing to pay for the ads from a fund to which only individuals could donate (reducing the corporate-form corruption concern).[31] This was set out last in the complaint as an alternative to our primary speech-based argument. Regarding the nature of the *speaker*, an amicus curiae argued that nonprofits did not fit *Austin*'s

[26] Wisc. Right to Life v. FEC, 546 U.S. 410 (2006) (per curiam).

[27] Wisc. Right to Life v. FEC, 466 F. Supp. 2d 195 (D.D.C. 2006).

[28] FEC v. Wisc. Right to Life, 551 U.S. 449, 469-70 (2007).

[29] *Id.* at 494-95 (Scalia, J., joined by Kennedy & Thomas, JJ., concurring).

[30] *Id.* at 582-83.

[31] See Brief of Appellee at 48, FEC v. Wisc. Right to Life, 551 U.S. 449 (2007) (Nos. 06–969 & 06–970) (hereinafter "WRTL Brief"). *WRTL* briefs and complaints are available at http://www.jamesmadisoncenter.org under "Wisconsin Right to Life's McCain-Feingold Challenge."

corporate-form corruption rationale.[32] Regarding the nature of the *speech*, we argued for a test based on the grassroots-lobbying nature of the ads.[33]

Our test was designed to distinguish "genuine" from "sham" issue ads, in keeping with the debate that ran through *McConnell*. A range of other tests to distinguish genuine from sham grassroots lobbying had been suggested by groups responding to a proposed FEC rule-making to allow genuine grassroots lobbying, which the FEC foolishly decided to forgo.[34] The *WRTL* district court had also established a test for distinguishing between genuine and sham grassroots lobbying.[35] We collected these tests in an appendix to an article that we published and cited in briefing to the Supreme Court.[36] In the same appendix we collected examples of genuine issue ads, including a grassroots-lobbying ad promoting a federal partial-birth abortion bill that was also targeted to Senators Feingold and Kohl. That "PBA Ad" had been recognized by the government's own expert in *McConnell* as a "genuine issue ad."[37] So we argued that when *McConnell* left open as-applied challenges as to "genuine issue ads" it had in mind just such an ad, which we used as a template for our proposed test.

Which of the three options did the *WRTL* Court choose? It based its holding on the nature of the *speech*. And it employed a test that protected all issue advocacy, not just the grassroots-lobbying

---

[32] The brief was prepared by then-Dean of Stanford Law School Kathleen M. Sullivan and the Stanford Constitutional Law Center. See Brief of Family Research Council, Free Market Foundation, and Home School Legal Defense Association as Amici Curiae in Support of Appellee at 17–18, FEC v. Wisc. Right to Life, 551 U.S. 449 (2007) (Nos. 06–969 & 06–970).

[33] WRTL Brief, *supra* note 31, at 55–57.

[34] The petition for rulemaking was filed by lawyers for OMB Watch (by Robert Bauer, President Obama's present counsel), Chamber of Commerce of the United States, AFL-CIO, National Education Association, and Alliance for Justice. The petition is available at http://www.fec.gov/pdf/nprm/lobbying/orig_petition.pdf.

[35] Wis. Right to Life v. FEC, 466 F. Supp. 2d 195, 207 (D.D.C. 2006).

[36] See James Bopp Jr. & Richard E. Coleson, Distinguishing "Genuine" from "Sham" in Grassroots Lobbying: Protecting the Right to Petition during Elections, 29 Campbell L. Rev. 353, 406–412 (2007), available at http://law.campbell.edu/lawreview/articles/29-3-353.pdf.

[37] McConnell v. FEC, 251 F. Supp. 2d 176, 312 (D.D.C. 2003) (Henderson, J.); *id.* at 905 (Leon, J.); *id.* at 748 (Kollar-Kotelly, J.).

subset.[38] It chose a test that was so broad and protective that corporations could engage in extensive issue advocacy naming candidates near elections. It was so broad that the *WRTL* dissent proclaimed *McConnell*'s facial upholding of the prohibition effectively overturned.[39] Consequently, after *WRTL*, there was little practical need to overturn *Austin* because, while corporations still could not expressly advocate for candidates, they could do most of the issue advocacy they had done before the electioneering-communication prohibition—the issue advocacy that *McConnell* said was preferred as more effective than express advocacy.[40] That choice and the language of the controlling opinion indicated that the *WRTL* Court was restoring *Buckley*'s strong protection for issue advocacy.[41] It also indicated that the Court was interested in broad, speech-based protections, not narrow protections based on the nature of the money or speaker. That choice would guide our approach to *Citizens United*.

WRTL's test showed how the Court intended to protect issue advocacy. The test declared that no ad could be, in *McConnell*'s language, "the functional equivalent of express advocacy" (subject to the corporate prohibition) unless it "is susceptible of no reasonable interpretation other than as an appeal to vote for or against a specific candidate."[42] Conversely, no ad may be prohibited that "may reasonably be interpreted as something other than as an appeal to vote for or against a specific candidate."[43]

This appeal-to-vote test was borrowed from prior campaign-finance jurisprudence. It is consistent with the *Buckley*-overbreadth principle on which the express-advocacy test was based, which principle required that regulated First Amendment activity be "unambiguously related to the campaign of a particular federal candidate." The test's focus on an actual "appeal" that can only be about voting parallels (in weaker form) the express-advocacy test's requirement

---

[38] WRTL, 551 U.S. at 470.

[39] *Id.* at 525.

[40] 540 U.S. at 193 & n.77.

[41] *WRTL* defined issue advocacy: "Issue advocacy conveys information and educates. An issue ad's impact on an election, if it exists at all, will come only after the voters hear the information and choose—uninvited by the ad—to factor it into their voting decisions." 551 U.S. at 470.

[42] *Id.*

[43] *Id.* at 476.

that there be "express words of *advocacy* of election or defeat, such as *'vote* for.'"[44] And most importantly, it is nearly identical to an express-advocacy test fashioned by the Ninth Circuit in *FEC v. Furgatch.*[45]

The *Furgatch* test was an attempt to craft a "non-magic-words" express-advocacy test. It is unconstitutional as an express-advocacy test because *Buckley* made clear that express advocacy requires "magic words"[46] and because *WRTL* explicitly held that its appeal-to-vote test—for "the functional equivalent of express advocacy"— would be unconstitutionally vague if applied to ads that did not already fit the electioneering-communication definition (i.e., targeted broadcast ads naming candidates shortly before elections).[47] But the *Furgatch* test was the basis of the backup electioneering-communication definition[48] and *WRTL's* appeal-to-vote test. *Furgatch's* language shows as much: An ad "must, when read as a whole, and with limited reference to external events, be *susceptible of no other reasonable interpretation but as an exhortation to vote for or against a specific candidate.*"[49] *WRTL* forbade all but the most general reliance on context,[50] but the rest of *WRTL's* test was nearly verbatim: "susceptible of no reasonable interpretation other than as an appeal to vote for or against a specific candidate."[51]

Furgatch's formula was significantly narrowed when the Ninth Circuit explained that "speech may only be termed 'advocacy' if it presents a *clear plea for action*, and . . . it must be clear what action is advocated[, *that is*,] . . . a *vote* for or against a candidate . . . ."[52]

---

[44] Buckley, 424 U.S. at 44 n.52 (emphasis added).

[45] 807 F.2d 857 (9th Cir. 1987).

[46] See *supra*, as was reiterated in *McConnell*, 540 U.S. at 126, 191, 216–217, *WRTL*, 551 U.S. at 513 (Souter, J., dissenting) and *Citizens United* 130 S. Ct. at 935 n.8 (Stevens, J., dissenting).

[47] 551 U.S. at 474 n.7.

[48] See 2 U.S.C. § 434(f)(3)(A)(ii) (2010) (functional if primary definition held unconstitutional) (applicable if communication "promotes[,] . . . supports[,] . . . attacks[,] or opposes a candidate . . . and . . . is suggestive of no plausible meaning other than an exhortation to vote for or against a specific candidate").

[49] 807 F.2d at 864 (emphasis added).

[50] 551 U.S. at 473–74.

[51] *Id.* at 470.

[52] 807 F.2d at 864 (emphasis added).

Furgatch applied this to an anti-Carter ad that proclaimed "DON'T LET HIM DO IT!" where the only way not to "let him do it" was to vote against him.[53] The Ninth Circuit decided that there was a "clear plea for action" and the action solicited was "a vote for or against a candidate," so the communication at issue failed the test.[54]

Since *WRTL* and its appeal-to-vote test sought to protect issue advocacy, surely the test must require a "clear plea for action" where the "appeal to vote" meant what it said, that is, there must be an actual "appeal" (an invitation or exhortation) "to vote"; mere indications of support for or opposition to candidates will not suffice. That analysis would also guide our approach in *Citizens United*.

The tensions within the *WRTL* majority and the probationary nature of the holding revealed that the FEC would need to exercise care in implementing the appeal-to-vote test. The majority clearly opposed any FEC rule chilling political speech.

IV. FEC Rule: How to Invite Reconsideration

The appeal-to-vote test might have worked, but the FEC seemed intent on ensuring that it did not. As *WRTL*'s successful counsel, we petitioned for a rule implementing the appeal-to-vote test.[55] We filed extensive comments on the FEC's proposals for a rulemaking, explaining what the FEC needed to do to comply with *WRTL*. When the FEC was going astray with the flawed final rule it was about to adopt, we filed two letters objecting to that rule. In our comments, we advised the FEC that in *WRTL* we had

> expressly asked the Supreme Court to overrule its facial upholding of the electioneering communication restrictions in *McConnell* unless the Court provided the relief of both (a) stating a generally-applicable test to reduce the need for

---

[53] *Id*. at 864–85.

[54] *Id*. The *Furgatch* test was also narrowed in *California Pro-Life Council v. Getman*, 328 F.3d 1088 (9th Cir. 2003) (which we litigated), which made clear that context was subordinate to the actual words used and that "a close reading of *Furgatch* indicates that we presumed express advocacy must contain some explicit *words* of advocacy (emphasis in original)."

[55] See James Madison Center for Free Speech, Petition for Rulemaking Protecting "Genuine Issue Ads" From the "Electioneering Communication" Prohibition & Repealing 11 C.F.R. § 100.22(b) (2007), http://www.fec.gov/pdf/nprm/electioneering_comm/2007/petition_center_for_free_speech.pdf (last visited June 11, 2010).

litigation and (b) making as-applied challenges an adequate remedy for protecting the First Amendment liberties of groups seeking to broadcast genuine issue ads by limiting the burdens of litigation.[56]

So, we said, the rule needed to remain protective and workable. We warned:

> [I]mplicit in the Chief Justice's opinion and explicit in Justice Alito's concurring opinion is the position that if the as-applied remedy remains inadequate to protect the First Amendment rights of groups seeking to broadcast genuine issue ads trapped by the electioneering communication restrictions, then *McConnell*'s facial upholding of the restrictions will need to be reconsidered.[57]

Ignoring our warnings, the FEC subverted the Court's simple, objective, protective test into a complex, subjective, unprotective rule. It reduced the Court's own test to a mere *part* of the FEC's "two-part, 11-factor balancing test," as *Citizens United* described it.[58] Any time a constitutional test is reduced to merely being *part* of an administrative agency's test, the latter test is clearly unconstitutional. Against our advice, the FEC made details of the *application* of the appeal-to-vote test to particular grassroots lobbying ads a part of its test. Ignoring *WRTL*'s declaration of liberty for issue advocacy, the FEC imposed maximum control over it. It made a rule so prolix and vague that *Citizens United* declared it akin to a prior restraint because it compelled speakers to seek FEC advisory opinions to know whether they could speak.[59] And *Citizens United* noted that many citizen groups could not afford the protracted litigation necessary to dispute the FEC's de facto licensing scheme (including the discovery that the FEC insisted on in *Citizens United* despite *WRTL*'s mandate of "minimal if any discovery, to allow parties to resolve

---

[56] James Bopp Jr. & Richard E. Coleson, Comments of the James Madison Center for Free Speech on Notice of Proposed Rulemaking 2007-16 (Electioneering Communications) 2 (2007), http://www.jamesmadisoncenter.org/Finance/MadisonCenter CommentsReWRTLII.pdf (last visited June 11, 2010). See also WRTL Brief, *supra* note 31, at i, 62, 65–70.

[57] Bopp & Coleson, *supra* note 56, at 3–4.

[58] 130 S. Ct. at 895.

[59] *Id*. at 895–96.

disputes quickly without chilling speech through the threat of burdensome litigation").[60] The FEC became the arbiter of what citizens could say and thus did "precisely what *WRTL* sought to avoid."[61] That is, it chilled political speech.

Of course, the Supreme Court's repudiation of the FEC's rule lay in the future when Citizens United sought our help. But it was clear after the rulemaking that the appeal-to-vote test required rehabilitation to avoid reconsideration. We would show the Court how its rule had become unworkable in application and offer a way to fix it in *Citizens United* based on the Court's own analysis in *WRTL*.

V. *Citizens United*: Different Approaches

In framing the case initially, we approached the case differently than Olson would later. Our approach was dictated by (1) Citizens United's goal and concern in bringing the suit, (2) how the Court decided *WRTL*, and (3) the need for a broad, speech-protective rule protecting issue advocacy from all regulation for all speakers.

What was Citizens United's original goal in bringing this suit? That may be seen from the original complaint, filed December 13, 2007, which only challenged the *reporting* (requiring disclosure of donors) and *disclaimer* requirements as applied to three ads that fit the electioneering-communication definition.[62] They were ads for *Hillary: The Movie* and then-Senator Hillary Clinton was a presidential candidate. We did not challenge the electioneering-communication prohibition because we considered the ads permitted under FEC rules and *WRTL*'s appeal-to-vote test. Citizens United stated its concern about retaliation:

> One of the chief concerns with the Reporting Requirement is the disclosure of donors who may then be subject to various forms of retaliation by political opponents. On information and belief, the Clinton White House had in its possession over 1,000 FBI files on political opponents.[63]

[60] *Id.*

[61] *Id.* at 896.

[62] Complaint at 1, Citizens United v. FEC, No. 1:07-CV-02240, 2008 WL 2788753 (D.D.C. Dec. 13, 2007).

[63] *Id.* at 8. See also Neil A. Lewis, White House Got More Files Than Disclosed, N.Y. Times, June 26, 1996, at 1.

Citizens United stated that disclosure "will, in Citizens United's belief based on long experience, substantially reduce the number of donors and amount of donations to Citizens United because many potential donors do not wish to be publicly so identified for a variety of legitimate reasons."[64]

Did Citizens United ever get this requested protection from disclosing donors? Not from *Citizens United*, perhaps for reasons of changed focus and altered strategy in the case.[65]

How does one pursue an as-applied challenge to the disclosure requirements facially upheld in *McConnell*? We had developed a constitutional analysis, based on *Buckley* and adopted by federal

---

[64] Compl., *supra* note 62, at 9.

[65] Citizens United subsequently filed an FEC advisory opinion request seeking an exemption for media and commercial activity, which would free it from disclosure requirements. See Op. Request Fed. Election Comm'n 2010–08 (Mar. 29, 2010), available at http://saos.nictusa.com/saos/searchao?SUBMIT = ao&AO = 3053. The FEC denied an earlier similar request. See Op. Fed. Election Comm'n 2004-30, at 8 (Sept. 10, 2004), available at http://ao.nictusa.com/ao/no/030012.html. On June 11, 2010, the FEC "conclude[d] that Citizens United's costs of producing and distributing its films, in addition to related marketing activities, are covered by the press exemption," making its movies and ads not subject to the disclosure requirements. Op. FEC 2010-08, available at http://saos.nictusa.com/saos/searchao?SUBMIT = continue& PAGE_NO = -1. This was based on the facts that (a) Citizens United had made 12 more documentaries since its first advisory-opinion request (comprising 25 percent of its budget), *id.* at 5, and (b) "Citizens United will not pay to air its documentaries on television; instead it will receive compensation from the broadcasters," *id.* at 7. That Citizens United planned to pay broadcasters to air its materials was a key factor in its denial of the press exemption earlier. FEC Op. 2004-30 at 7. Of course, in *Citizens United*, that Citizens United planned to pay to broadcast *Hillary* on video-on-demand was a central fact, 130 S. Ct. at 887, and the second advisory opinion request says that more video-on-demand broadcasting is in negotiation, but the request does not say that video-on-demand broadcast would *not* be paid for by Citizens United. See Citizens United Op. Request 2010-08 at 3, available at http://saos.nictusa.com/saos/searchao?SUBMIT = continue&PAGE_NO = -1. How far the FEC will go in extending the press exemption to other organizations, especially those with fewer such activities to their credit, remains to be seen, but the government's asserted interest in "disclosure" for nonprofit advocacy groups has been undermined by the FEC's decision that there will be no disclosure for this advocacy group but full disclosure for similar activity, such as an editorial, by another. And recent disclosure that traditional journalists have been operating as advocates will further enhance this underinclusiveness and undercut the government's disclosure interest. See Jonathon Strong, Documents Show Media Plotting to Kill Stories about Rev. Jeremiah Wright, The Daily Caller, July 20, 2010, http://dailycaller.com/2010/07/20/documents-show-media-plotting-to-kill-stories-about-rev-jeremiah-wright/print/.

courts, that provided a way. We noted in the fourth *Buckley* foundational principle above that *Buckley* required that campaign-finance regulations be closely tied to congressional authority to regulate federal elections. In that case, the Court said that campaign-finance regulation may only reach First Amendment activity that is "unambiguously related to the campaign of a particular federal candidate."[66] *Buckley* imposed this requirement precisely in the context of a *reporting* requirement to be sure that reporting did not reach communications that were "too remote," that is, not "unambiguously campaign related."[67]

The Fourth Circuit, in *North Carolina Right to Life, Inc. v. Leake*,[68] had expressly recognized this unambiguously-campaign-related requirement as *Buckley's* means of cabining Congress to its sole authority to regulate in this area:

> The *Buckley* Court . . . recognized the need to cabin legislative authority over elections in a manner that sufficiently safeguards vital First Amendment freedoms. It did so by demarcating a boundary between regulable election-related activity and constitutionally protected political speech: after *Buckley*, campaign finance laws may constitutionally regulate only those actions that are *"unambiguously related to the campaign of a particular . . . candidate."* . . . This is because only *unambiguously campaign related* communications have a sufficiently close relationship to the government's acknowledged interest in preventing corruption to be constitutionally regulable.[69]

Leake reiterated this *Buckley*-overbreadth principle:

> Pursuant to their power to regulate elections, legislatures may establish campaign finance laws, so long as those laws are addressed to communications that are *unambiguously campaign related*. The Supreme Court has identified two categories of communication as being *unambiguously campaign related*. First, "express advocacy," defined as a communication that uses specific election-related words. Second, "the functional equivalent of express advocacy," defined as an

[66] 424 U.S. at 80.

[67] *Id* at 80, 81.

[68] 525 F.3d 274 (4th Cir. 2008).

[69] *Id*. at 281 (emphasis added).

"electioneering communication" that "is susceptible of no reasonable interpretation other than as an appeal to vote for or against a specific candidate."[70]

The Fourth Circuit's recognition of *Buckley*-overbreadth analysis was not anomalous. Other federal courts had employed it to decide cases.[71] The primary sponsors of McCain-Feingold and the rest of the campaign "reform" lobby expressly endorsed the unambiguously-campaign-related requirement to support the electioneering-communication definition in *McConnell*.[72] They argued that the definition was constitutional under *Buckley* because it is not vague or overbroad, that is, an electioneering communication was "unambiguously related to the campaign of a particular federal candidate."[73] And they insisted that this was the analysis that Congress employed in enacting McCain-Feingold.[74] *McConnell* held that the electioneering communication definition was constitutional because it was neither vague nor overbroad, citing the very part of *Buckley* that the reform lobby cited, which stated the unambiguously-campaign-related requirement.[75] For everyone to use the requirement to facially *uphold* the electioneering communication but to deny us the use of the same requirement, especially after *WRTL* clearly used the same sort of analysis to *narrow* the scope of regulable electioneering communications, would be an intolerable bait-and-switch. Chief Justice Roberts had decried just such a bait-and-switch in *WRTL*.[76]

Because *Buckley* mandated the unambiguously-campaign-related requirement precisely in the *disclosure* context, and *Leake* expressly identified *WRTL*'s appeal-to-vote test as the implementation of the requirement in the *electioneering-communication* context, we hoped that the justices who decided *WRTL* would hold that Citizens United's ads were subject to neither prohibition nor disclosure because

---

[70] *Id*. at 282–83 (emphasis added).

[71] See, e.g., N.M. Youth Organized v. Herrera, ____ F.3d ____, 2010 WL 2598314 (10th Cir. June 30, 2010).

[72] Brief for Intervenor-Defendants Senator John McCain et al. at 57-62, McConnell v. FEC, 540 U.S. 93 (2003).

[73] *Id*. at 62 (quoting *Buckley*, 424 U.S. at 80).

[74] *Id*.

[75] 540 U.S. at 191 (quoting *Buckley*, 424 U.S. at 80).

[76] FEC v. Wis. Right to Life, Inc., 551 U.S. 449, 480 (2007).

they were not unambiguously campaign related under *WRTL*'s appeal-to-vote test.[77] Citizens United challenged the reporting, disclosure, and disclaimer requirements as applied to "(a) communications that may not be prohibited as electioneering communications under *WRTL* . . . and (b) Citizens United's Ads . . . because the activity is not 'unambiguously related to the campaign of a particular federal candidate'" and because the provisions "are unconstitutional under the First Amendment guarantees of free expression and association."[78]

On December 20, 2007, two important events occurred that affected the nature of the case. First, Citizens United was invited to broadcast *Hillary* on video-on-demand, making the movie itself an electioneering communication. It would thus be subject to reporting, disclosure, and disclaimer requirements and, if it contained an "appeal to vote" under *WRTL*'s test, it would be prohibited from airing. Second, the FEC filed its opposition to preliminary injunction, stating, "Although plaintiff's first two proposed ads appear to come within the *WRTL* exemption . . . [a third ad entitled] 'Questions' poses a closer question that the Commission has not had an adequate opportunity to address."[79]

The next day, we filed an amended complaint. It included a challenge to both the electioneering-communication prohibition and the reporting, disclosure, and disclaimer requirements as applied to the movie. It also included a *facial* challenge to the prohibition, "because it has not proven workable in application, as required by [*WRTL*]" and so was unconstitutional under the First Amendment.

---

[77] The controlling *WRTL* opinion had also been extraordinarily careful to distinguish protected "issue advocacy" or "political speech" from "electioneering" or "campaign speech." This indicated a determination to permit regulation of *campaign* speech ("unambiguously campaign related"), not ordinary political speech.

[78] A benefit of the unambiguously-campaign-related requirement is that it is employed before a court subjects the provision to the appropriate level of scrutiny. There is substantial confusion on the appropriate level of scrutiny for disclosure requirements. Compare McIntyre v. Ohio Elections Comm'n, 514 U.S. 334, 347 (1995) (strict scrutiny) with Citizens United, 130 S. Ct. at 914 (intermediate scrutiny). The intermediate scrutiny trap is thus avoided if the provision is deemed not to be unambiguously campaign related.

[79] Defendant's Memorandum in Opposition to Plaintiff's Motion for Consolidation at 8–9, Citizens United v. FEC, No. 1:07-CV-02240, 2008 WL 2788753 (D.D.C. Dec. 20, 2007).

This facial challenge was based on the fact that the FEC could not "tell by looking at an ad whether it meets the FEC's own [rule]." The FEC had reviewed the ad for seven days and still had not figured out whether it was prohibited. When the FEC conceded that the ad could not be prohibited, 17 days later, we dismissed the facial challenge. In our opinion, *WRTL*'s reluctance to overrule *McConnell*—though three justices in the *WRTL* majority argued for a return to the express-advocacy line—indicated a disinterest in a facial challenge, likely for reasons of judicial restraint and respecting precedent. Chief Justice Roberts and Justice Alito had invested in the appeal-to-vote test despite strong pressure from both sides on the Court, so if it could be made to work it should be allowed to do so. And there were sound arguments for how *WRTL*'s rule could be made workable, employing *Furgatch*'s "clear plea for action" that can only be about voting. But the FEC's rule and tardy confession that the ads passed the appeal-to-vote test demonstrated the unworkability of the appeal-to-vote test, placing the reconsideration of *McConnell* and even *Austin* squarely before the Court.[80] So we dismissed the facial challenge.

Our as-applied challenges remained, as to both the ads and the movie, as to both disclosure and prohibition. In press reports, the issue of whether the movie could be prohibited was becoming the central focus, with the disclosure issue being pushed to the background. To keep the vital disclosure issue from getting lost, we consistently placed it first in briefing. It was important to Citizens United and, as will be discussed, disclosure is causing serious intimidation problems that result in chilled speech.

Regarding the movie, we argued that it could not be regulated as an electioneering communication because it was not unambiguously related to the campaign of a federal candidate. After all, under *WRTL*'s appeal-to-vote test, the movie contained no clear plea for action. Mere criticism of Hillary Clinton was insufficient, absent an appeal involving voting. We made an additional argument that eventually would capture the attention of the Supreme Court and

---

[80] Reconsideration of a precedent is always appropriate if the Court is being asked to apply it. See James Bopp Jr., Richard E. Coleson & Barry A. Bostrom, Does the United States Supreme Court Have a Constitutional Duty to Expressly Reconsider and Overrule *Roe v. Wade?*, 1 Seton Hall Const. L.J. 55 (1990) (discussing principles governing whether judicial review is appropriate).

the press: full-length movies are like books—which may not be banned. We argued:

> *Hillary* also "may reasonably be interpreted as *something other* than as an appeal to vote," *WRTL II*, 127 S. Ct. at 2670 (emphasis added). A reasonable interpretation is that it is a full-length, documentary movie about Senator Clinton, and such a movie enjoys all the protection historically afforded to any book about a public figure. *Hillary* is the functional equivalent of a book, not of the 30- or 60-second ads that were the target of Congress in BCRA and at issue in *McConnell.* . . . If the difference in medium matters when it comes to First Amendment protection . . . , then the government could freely engage in high-tech "book burnings" without restriction.[81]

These were the arguments in our jurisdictional statement, upon which the Supreme Court accepted the appeal for full briefing and argument. With these arguments, we were confident of victory on the disclosure and prohibition provisions that applied to the ads and movie. The arguments sought incremental remedies; we did not explicitly ask the Court to overrule *McConnell*, but we provided it the opportunity to do so if it thought it appropriate. Our arguments were based on the sort of analysis employed in *WRTL* and showed the Court how to rule in our favor under its own appeal-to-vote test by improving the test to make it more workable and protective. Our arguments did not rely on the nature of the *speaker* or the nature of the *money* used (following *WRTL's* focus on the nature of the *speech*) both because of *WRTL's* focus and because the result would be a broad, speech-protective ruling—not a narrow one of limited applicability. We anticipated a rule distinguishing regulable "campaign speech" from unregulable "issue advocacy" or "political speech" that would protect all speakers and bring considerable clarity to campaign finance law. The need for a bright line was vital because the FEC was asserting that its interest in compelling disclosure extended "beyond speech about candidate elections and encompasse[d] activity that attempts to sway public opinions on issues[.]"[82]

---

[81] Plaintiff's Summary Judgment Motion at 39, Citizens United v. FEC, No. 1:07-CV-02240 (D.D.C. May 16, 2008).

[82] Defendant FEC's Motion for Summary Judgment at 22, Citizens United v. FEC, No. 1:07-CV-02240 (D.D.C. June 6, 2008).

When Olson took over representation of Citizens United at the merits stage, the emphasis and arguments changed. His opening brief addressed the movie first.[83] *Buckley*'s unambiguously-campaign-related requirement was only mentioned in passing.[84] The argument that the appeal-to-vote test required an actual "appeal" was made without any discussion of the analytical underpinnings of the requirement of "a clear plea for action."[85] Moreover, whether there was an appeal was said to "depend frequently on the context in which it arises,"[86] even though *WRTL* had expressly eschewed context for employing its test.

In addition, the brief made several arguments for narrower rulings that we had not proposed to the Court in our jurisdictional statement. These served to urge the Court to avoid overruling both *Austin* and *McConnell* and later became the focus of attacks on the Court's majority decision. The brief made a *statutory* argument that the electioneering-communication definition did not encompass video-on-demand, asserting that the movie therefore could not be prohibited.[87] We did not make this argument because it would have been of no practical benefit to Citizens United; they wanted to broadcast the movie on commercial television, not just on video-on-demand. Furthermore, such a narrow ground for relief would not have been of practical benefit to anyone else. Such a ruling would have prevented the Court from providing broad protection from the electioneering-communication prohibition, thereby failing to safeguard free expression in a meaningful way.

The brief also made money-based and speaker-based arguments, arguing that since most of the funds (99 percent) used for the movie were donated by individuals, the movie constituted speech from an organization like Massachusetts Citizens for Life, which the Court in *McConnell* had exempted from the electioneering-communication prohibition.[88] This exemption was first recognized in *Massachusetts*

---

[83] Brief for Appellant at 16, *Citizens*, 130 S. Ct. 876 (No. 08-205).

[84] *Id.* at 52. *Buckley*'s unambiguously-campaign-related quote was only mentioned in a parenthetical for a cite to *Leake* (which was only mentioned as to the public's informational interest in disclosure, which was not central to *Leake*'s analysis). *Id.*

[85] *Id.* at 36–37.

[86] *Id.* at 38.

[87] *Id.* at 26 n.2.

[88] *Id.* at 29–34.

Citizens for Life[89] (from the independent-expenditure prohibition) for ideological, non-stock, nonprofit corporations neither engaging in business activity nor accepting corporate or union contributions.[90] Citizens United, however, did not qualify for the *MCFL* exemption because it both engaged in business activities and received corporate donations, and thus did not seek the *MCFL* exemption in its complaint. The exemption is based on the nature of the *corporation*, and, if the Court had based its ruling on this ground, the decision would have only benefited corporations with a tiny bit of business income or business corporation contributions. Analytically, this would be a slight expansion of the *MCFL* exemption, but in order to claim it organizations would have to expose themselves to very intrusive investigations by the FEC regarding all their activities. Consequently, while this expanded version of the *MCFL* exemption has already been recognized by several circuits,[91] few organizations have sought it.

The brief then turned to a speech-based argument, asserting that the movie was not the functional equivalent of express advocacy because it was "not remotely an 'appeal to vote'"[92] but rather "similar to the numerous critical candidate biographies found in bookstores" and the government could prove no corruption interest in such movies.[93] This was the best and most appropriate argument, but, as noted above, it was made without the necessary analytical foundation from *Furgatch* and *Buckley*-overbreadth that an "appeal to vote" required a call to action.

Finally, the brief made an argument that took the form of an assertion: "*Austin* was wrongly decided and should be overruled."[94] The brief noted that *Austin*'s equality rationale was inconsistent with other precedent and briefly addressed flaws in *Austin*'s analysis, but

---

[89] FEC v. Mass. Citizens for Life, Inc., 479 U.S. 238, 263–64 (1986) [hereinafter *MCFL*].

[90] See 11 C.F.R. § 114.10(c) (2010) (FEC rule defining *MCFL*-corporations and disallowing even *de minimis* proscribed activity or contributions).

[91] See FEC v. NRA of Am., 254 F.3d 173, 192 (D.C. Cir. 2001); N.C. Right to Life, Inc. v. Bartlett, 168 F.3d 705, 714 (4th Cir. 1999); Minn. Citizens Concerned for Life v. FEC, 113 F.3d 129, 130 (8th Cir. 1997); FEC v. Survival Educ. Fund, Inc., 65 F.3d 285, 292 (2d Cir. 1995); Day v. Holahan, 34 F.3d 1356, 1364 (8th Cir. 1994).

[92] Brief for Appellant at 35, Citizens, 130 S. Ct. 876 (No. 08-205).

[93] *Id.* at 36.

[94] *Id.* at 30.

then drew the Court back to one of its narrow-ruling arguments: "But whatever the continuing vitality of *Austin*, its rationales clearly do not support a ban on speech that . . . is funded predominantly by individuals."[95]

Despite mentioning in his brief, that *Austin* should be overturned, at oral argument Olson essentially waived any facial challenge to the prohibition and any overruling of *Austin* and *McConnell* by, "conceding that [the prohibition] could be applied to General Motors . . . [and] stating that 'we accept the Court's decision in *Wisconsin Right to Life*.'"[96] The only way that GM could be subject to the prohibition was if *Austin* were *not* overruled; *WRTL*'s appeal-to-vote test was an effort to *prevent* overruling *Austin* and *McConnell*.

A decision in *Citizens United* was expected at the end of the Supreme Court's 2008–09 term. Instead, surprisingly, the Court ordered briefing and argument on this question: "For the proper disposition of this case, should the Court overrule either or both *Austin* . . . and the part of *McConnell*. . . which addresses the facial validity of [the electioneering-communication prohibition]?"

Our response, in an amici curiae brief for seven former FEC chairmen and one former FEC commissioner, was that

> "proper disposition" of this case d[id] not *require* overruling *Austin* . . . or . . . *McConnell* . . . because this case may be decided for Appellant on other grounds. The application of this Court's unambiguously-campaign-related ("UCR") principle would resolve the challenges to both the Prohibition and Disclosure Requirements.[97]

We rejected the notion that a precedent could only be overruled when it is *necessary* for the decision because it can and should be done when *appropriate*. We continued:

---

[95] *Id.* at 31. We made our arguments in an amicus curiae brief for the Center for Truth in Politics, which was directly affected by the outcome of the challenge to the disclosure requirements. But absent party reiteration, the Court does not typically employ dispositive analyses advanced only by amici.

[96] 130 S. Ct. at 932.

[97] Brief Amici Curiae of Seven Former Chairmen and One Former Commissioner of the Federal Election Commission Supporting Appellant on Supplemental Question at 2, Citizens United, 130 S. Ct. 876 (No. 08-205) (emphasis in original).

> However, it would be appropriate, and in fact desirable, for the Court to overrule these troublesome precedents because (1) both are properly implicated for reconsideration, (2) "Congress shall make no law . . . abridging the freedom of speech" has special force in protecting political speech, (3) *Austin* and *McConnell* have proven to be unworkable, having spawned many complex, multi-factor tests, and (4) the FEC and lower courts have made the appeal-to-vote test in [*WRTL*] unworkable. *Austin* and its progeny *should* be overruled.[98]

So our position was that wherever a precedent controls it is always inherently at issue and thus the Court may reconsider it without any analytical "necessity" and without being explicitly requested to do so.

Given the unworkability of *WRTL*'s test, *Austin* and *McConnell* could still be overruled. To that end, we explained the unworkability of the appeal-to-vote test. We explained the prolix and complex federal laws, regulations, and advisory opinions spawned by *Austin* and *McConnell* and how the federal courts and the FEC could not even agree on whether an ad in one of our cases was covered by *WRTL*'s appeal-to-vote test.[99] We also explained that the FEC had taken more than two months to respond to an advisory opinion request filed on behalf of the National Right to Life Committee that asked for approval for two ads under the FEC's own "*WRTL*" test, only ultimately to get approval for one (long after the election) and receive a notice that the FEC commissioners could not agree on the other. Clearly the appeal-to-vote test had proved unworkable unless the Court required a "clear plea for action" that entails voting, affirmed its unambiguously-campaign-related requirement, and made it clear that the FEC had gotten the rule wrong. But, we said, overruling the anomalous *Austin* decision would certainly be proper because the prohibition at issue originated in it, and *Austin should* be overruled because it was constitutionally flawed.

In contrast, Olson not only *expressly* requested that *Austin* be overruled, but argued that "a reexamination of *Austin*'s . . . rationale

---

[98] *Id* (emphasis in original).

[99] See The Real Truth About Obama v. FEC, No. 08-483, 2008 WL 4416282, at *7 (E.D. Va., Sept. 24, 2008) (order denying preliminary injunction). The FEC said the ad contained no appeal to vote, but the court decided that the ad was express advocacy.

[wa]s *essential* to the proper disposition of this case" and was "necessary."[100] The problem here was not the overruling of *Austin* but the erroneous assumption that overruling can only be done when "necessary" and "essential" to the ruling.

VI. *Citizens United*: Why and How *Austin* Was Overruled

Austin was clearly anomalous and deserved overruling, but two events particularly motivated the Court's decision to overrule it here.

First, the FEC had subverted *WRTL*'s appeal-to-vote test, which was intended to protect ordinary "political speech" (or "issue advocacy"). The FEC reduced *WRTL*'s "objective" test to a mere *part* of the FEC's "two-part, 11-factor balancing test."[101] The outcome of *Citizens United* may thus be largely explained by this subversion of *WRTL*'s rule. The Court's indignation was clear: "This is precisely what *WRTL* sought to avoid."[102] *WRTL* "refrained from holding the statute invalid," the Court said, "except as applied to the facts then before the Court, [and it] was a careful attempt to accept the essential elements of the Court's opinion in *McConnell*, while vindicating the First Amendment arguments made by the *WRTL* parties."[103] Having attempted a protective test focused on the nature of the *speech* at issue, only to see that test subverted, the Court found it "necessary" to decide *Citizens United* because the prohibition of that speech was based on the nature of the *speaker*. *Citizens United* overturned *Austin*'s holding that the corporate form poses a corruption risk. The FEC and the reform lobby had underestimated the tenuous probationary status of the electioneering-communication prohibition and had tried to limit the appeal-to-vote test instead of embracing it.

Second, at the first oral argument, the government asserted that the rationale of *Austin* would permit banning corporate-published books. The reaction on the bench was predictable, and the fact that the government apparently did not anticipate it shows how diluted free speech rights have become. At the second oral argument—the first for then-Solicitor General Elena Kagan—the government sought

---

[100] Supplemental Brief for Appellant at 15, 21, Citizens United, 130 S. Ct. 876 (No. 08-205) (emphasis added).

[101] Citizens United, 130 S. Ct. at 895.

[102] *Id.* at 896.

[103] *Id.* at 894.

to backtrack, asserting that although the statute would prohibit such books, the FEC had never done so. Chief Justice Roberts responded, "[W]e don't put our First Amendment rights in the hands of FEC bureaucrats . . . ."[104]

Given FEC subversion of the protective ruling in *WRTL* and the book-banning specter, the Court felt compelled to reexamine the foundation to this censorship regime and overturned *Austin* and *McConnell*. But the Court's analysis of why overturning was "necessary" has created problems in campaign-finance law requiring repair. Having entertained the suggestion of overruling *Austin*, the Court apparently felt constrained to find it "necessary" to overrule *Austin*. The notion that an absolute *necessity* was the only appropriate situation for reconsidering *Austin* should have been resisted, even at the risk of not having *Austin* overruled, because framing the issue in that fashion drove the analysis in the wrong direction on analytical points crucial for First Amendment protection.

In that analysis, the Court examined whether there were "narrower grounds" for deciding the case. *Citizens United* rejected Olson's arguments that "electioneering communication" does not include video-on-demand and that video-on-demand poses insufficient risks based on its nature—arguments the Court was able to reject without causing any analytical harm.[105] It likewise rejected Olson's invitation to decide the case based on the amount of business corporation contributions Citizens United received, which caused no analytical harm.[106] But the decision did cause analytical harm to free speech when the Court decided that the movie was the functional equivalent of express advocacy under the appeal-to-vote test,[107] as discussed next. The fact that this harm was done in service to proving it "necessary" to overrule *Austin* demonstrates the twin errors of expressly seeking *Austin*'s reversal in this case and the notion that overruling may happen only when there is no other way to decide a case—an approach that values institutional concerns over the Court's constitutional mandate. In any event, the strong backlash from the Court's dissenters, the executive and legislative

---

[104] Transcript of Oral Argument at 61, Citizens United, 130 S. Ct. 876 (No. 08-205).

[105] 130 S. Ct. at 888–91.

[106] *Id.* at 891–92.

[107] *Id.* at 889–90.

branches, and the general public—even though most critics misunderstand *Citizens United*'s holding—indicates that institutional concerns may not have been well served by the appeal to necessity, since it served little purpose and was unconvincing in its key application. A constitutional speech-based rationale for the decision would have been more consistent with *WRTL* and would have better protected free speech.

The harm caused by *Citizens United* in finding that it was "necessary" to reconsider *Austin* is immense. After *Buckley*, the primary protection for issue advocacy has been a bright, protective line based on the *nature* of the speech. The express-advocacy test long protected robust issue advocacy, in which corporations were as free to engage as everyone else. So long as speakers avoided expressly advocating the election or defeat of candidates, they were free to talk about candidates and issues as much as they desired without having to put disclaimers on their speech, file reports, or disclose donors because *Buckley* expressly excluded any reporting of "expenditures" for issue advocacy. Instead, *Buckley* limited such disclosures to expenditures for express advocacy—that is, for "spending that is unambiguously related to the campaign of a particular federal candidate."[108] This was the robust, wide-open debate on public issues that the First Amendment was designed to protect. No one had to hire a lawyer to decipher complex campaign-finance laws, as long as a simple, bright line was observed. No one had to hire staff to comply with burdensome recordkeeping and reporting requirements for issue advocacy. People of ordinary means could pool their resources for effective advocacy. Groups advocating their positions on issues such as abortion, gun control, the environment, immigration, health care, taxation, war, and so on could form as the need arose and speak their minds without the advance planning and significant funding necessary for both FEC compliance and effective advocacy. Issue advocacy was unburdened and unchilled.

McConnell's upholding of McCain-Feingold disrupted the liberty of issue advocacy. *WRTL* partially restored bright-line protection to it. And the logic of *WRTL*'s line should have extended to disclosure, just as the express-advocacy line had protected against disclosure as to issue advocacy. That was what we asked the Court to do in

[108] 424 U.S. at 80.

Citizens United, and that was what was shoved aside, inadequately argued, and ultimately rejected by the Court. So Citizens United and American citizens alike remain burdened and chilled in their issue advocacy. That corporations and unions may engage in express advocacy in addition to the issue advocacy they already could pursue after *WRTL* hardly compensates for this loss of liberty.

The way that the *Citizens United* Court decided that it was "necessary" to reach *Austin* was to fail to give plain meaning to the words "appeal to vote" in its appeal-to-vote test. There was no such "appeal" (such as *Furgatch*'s "DON'T LET HIM DO IT!") in the movie, so the Court could only point to many criticisms of Senator Clinton and statements such as, "Could [Senator Clinton] become the first female President?" and "Before America decides on our next president, voters should need no reminders of . . . what's at stake—the well being and prosperity of our nation." But criticism is essential to robust issue advocacy and does not by itself constitute an "appeal." One could fully support a senator's reelection yet fervently assail her positions on certain issues. Nonetheless, from such criticisms and statements the Court concluded that "there is no reasonable interpretation of *Hillary* other than as an appeal to vote against Senator Clinton."[109] That is an appalling departure from the protection afforded by the express-advocacy test and even the *Furgatch* version of that test. The appeal-to-vote test was fatally wounded instead of being strengthened, as it should have been. Consequently, the appeal-to-vote test slipped into the dustbin of history.

The Court also held that the disclosure requirements could not be limited to communications that were the functional equivalent of express advocacy (containing an "appeal to vote") but applied to all electioneering communications.[110] The Court was compelled to do this by the gutting of the "appeal to vote" test itself and the failure to argue a solid analytical basis for it—the unambiguously-campaign-related requirement. Without these bases, there was no sensible analytic line to be drawn, and the Court was left to apply "exacting scrutiny" without any evidence of real disclosure harm. So, ironically, a case originally brought to restrain disclosure—for

[109] Citizens United, 130 S. Ct. at 890.
[110] *Id.* at 915.

all the good the eventual Supreme Court decision did—has now become the proffered justification for a new round of disclosure requirements. It did not have to be this way.

VII. *Citizens United*: Its Meaning for Campaign-Finance Law Generally

Beside the obvious facts that corporations and unions may now spend independently to engage in express advocacy, what does *Citizens United* mean to campaign-finance law? In a coincidence with our *Buckley* analysis above, *Citizens United* made nine vital points controlling future legislation and litigation:

1. It powerfully reaffirmed the strong protection for, and necessity of, political speech as "an essential mechanism of democracy."[111] This extends to speech by associations choosing to incorporate. Concern over "factions" is addressed by "permitting them all to speak, . . . and by entrusting the people to judge what is true and what is false."[112]

2. It stressed the need to avoid chilling political speech by giving it "breathing space."[113] It proscribed complex rules: "The First Amendment does not permit laws that force speakers to retain a campaign finance attorney . . . or seek declaratory rulings before discussing the most salient political issues of our day. Prolix laws chill speech for the same reason that vague laws chill speech . . . ."[114] The decision prohibited subjective, "intricate case-by-case determinations" in favor of bright-line, "objective" tests.[115] It further decried restrictions that prevented organizing and speaking on short notice with little expense, deciding that such "onerous restrictions . . . function as the equivalent of prior restraint . . . ."[116]

3. It noted that the First Amendment is "[p]remised on mistrust of governmental power" and that the "FEC's business is to censor."[117] So government efforts to chill speech by, for example, turning the

---

[111] *Id.* at 898.
[112] *Id.* at 907.
[113] *Id.* at 892 (quoting WRTL, 551 U.S. at 469).
[114] *Id.* at 889.
[115] *Id.* at 889, 892, 895.
[116] *Id.* at 895–96.
[117] *Id.* at 896, 898.

Court's objective appeal-to-vote test into "a two-part, 11-factor balancing test,"[118] must be viewed with skepticism, not deference, and subjected to strict scrutiny.[119]

4. It pronounced the death (again) of the equality rationale, the true basis of the corporate-form corruption interest recognized in *Austin*.[120] This was facilitated by Solicitor General Kagan's abandonment of that rationale as a basis for defending *Austin* in *Citizens United*.[121] The equality rationale was rejected in *Buckley*, *Davis*, and now *Citizens United*, and should play no further role. Campaign-finance laws seeking to regulate corporations based on their corporate form will encounter strict scrutiny to ensure that this phoenix-like asserted interest does not rise again.

5. It held that the only cognizable anti-corruption interest is in preventing quid pro quo corruption.[122] This interest does not permit the restriction of independent expenditures, but it does permit restrictions on "large direct contributions."[123] The emphasis on *large* contributions cites *Buckley* and precludes low contribution limits.[124] There is no risk of corruption or its appearance with low contributions, and the Court held that this interest did not justify the corporate prohibition on independent expenditures. It said, "The fact that speakers may have influence over or access to elected officials does not mean that these officials are corrupt[.]"[125] Such a "generic favoritism or influence theory . . . is unbounded and susceptible to no limiting principle," it added, and "[t]he appearance of influence or access . . . will not cause the electorate to lose faith in our democracy."[126] The Court held that "there is only scant evidence that independent expenditures even ingratiate," but "[i]ngratiation and access, in any event, are not corruption."[127]

---

[118] *Id.* at 895.

[119] *Id.* at 898.

[120] *Id.* at 922–23.

[121] *Id.* at 923–24.

[122] *Id.* at 909–10.

[123] *Id.* 908–909.

[124] See Randall v. Sorrell, 548 U.S. 230, 262 (2006) (striking down contribution limits as too low).

[125] *Id.* at 910.

[126] *Id.*

[127] *Id.*

The Court distinguished *McConnell*'s upholding of the ban on so-called soft-money donations to political parties because soft money, not independent expenditures, was involved.[128] But because the soft-money ban was based on access and gratitude as corruption,[129] the *Citizens United* holding—that those are not corruptive influences—undercuts the soft-money ban. Nonetheless, the Supreme Court has summarily affirmed the D.C. Circuit in rejecting an as-applied challenge to the ban in *Republican National Committee v. FEC*.[130] The Court also discounted any interest in preventing the "circumvention" of contribution limits; an interest that has been used to justify limits on political party expenditures coordinated with party candidates (and is at issue in *Cao v. FEC*).[131] The Court said that "[p]olitical speech is so ingrained in our culture that speakers find ways to circumvent campaign finance laws," but that "informative voices should not have to circumvent onerous restrictions to exercise their First Amendment rights."[132] Political parties' voices are just as "informative" as corporations'.[133]

And since there is no longer any anti-corruption interest in restricting corporate speech, corporations must be free to contribute to political action committees (PACs) that only make independent expenditures (i.e., no political contributions). Lower courts have already held that noncorporate contributions to independent-expenditure PACs may not be limited since there is no quid pro quo corruption.[134] With *Austin*'s corporate-form corruption interest now gone, corporate contributions to such PACs must also be unlimited.[135]

---

[128] *Id.* at 910–11.

[129] McConnell, 540 U.S. at 125, 129, 145, 169.

[130] Republican Nat'l Comm. v. FEC, 130 S.Ct. 3544 (2010), aff'g 698 F.Supp. 2d 150 (D.D.C. 2010) (3-judge district court).

[131] Cao v. FEC, 2010 U.S. Dist. LEXIS 12846 (E.D. La. Jan. 27, 2010), appeal docketed, Nos. 10-30080 (5th Cir. Jan. 29, 2010) & 10-30146 (5th Cir. Feb. 22, 2010).

[132] Citizens United, 130 S. Ct. at 912.

[133] *Id.* WRTL also rejected a circumvention argument, declaring that "[e]nough is enough" and rejecting "a prophylaxis-upon-prophylaxis approach to regulating expression." 551 U.S. at 478–79.

[134] See SpeechNow.org v. FEC, 599 F.3d 686 (D.C. Cir. 2010); Long Beach Area Chamber of Commerce v. City of Long Beach, 603 F.3d 684 (9th Cir. 2010); EMILY's List v. FEC, 581 F.3d 1 (D.C. Cir. 2009); N.C. Right to Life v. Leake, 525 F.3d 274 (4th Cir. 2008). The FEC has now recognized that independent-expenditure PACs may receive unlimited contributions from both corporations and noncorporate entities. See FEC Ops. 2010-09 (Club for Growth) (unlimited contributions solely from individuals),

6. It overruled the portion of *McConnell* facially upholding the electioneering-communication prohibition.[136] As a result, the language about government being able to prohibit the "functional equivalent of express advocacy" is gone, just as *WRTL*'s appeal-to-vote test (stating what constitutes a "functional equivalent") is gone. Until now, the FEC and states have justified speech restrictions based on the notion that functional equivalence is a permissible test or that appeal-to-vote-test language applies beyond the electioneering-communication context. One immediate application of *Citizens United* is to the FEC's regulation at 11 C.F.R. § 100.22, which defines "expressly advocating" in two ways. The first essentially follows *Buckley*'s "express words of advocacy" definition, but the second employs a *Furgatch*-style definition that the FEC has justified as consistent with *WRTL*'s appeal-to-vote test. That justification is now gone, and the *Citizens United* dissent reaffirmed what the justices said in *WRTL* and *McConnell*—that the express-advocacy test requires so-called magic words, such as "vote for."[137] So *Citizens United* again makes clear that any "express advocacy" or "independent expenditure" definition not requiring magic words is unconstitutional. The FEC's definition is at issue in *The Real Truth About Obama v. FEC*,[138] in which the Supreme Court granted certiorari to vacate a Fourth Circuit opinion upholding the definition and remanded the case for consideration in light of *Citizens United*.

7. It made several important statements regarding PACs. For one, *Citizens United* applied strict scrutiny to the government's limitation of corporate speech to the PAC option.[139] The Court held that having a PAC option does not allow a corporation itself to speak, so the

---

2010-11 (Commonsense Ten) (unlimited contributions from individuals, PACs, corporations, and labor unions). And SpeechNow.org has filed a petition for certiorari (No. 09A1212) asking the Supreme Court to determine the issue it lost in *SpeechNow.org*, whether PAC-status disclosure must apply to such groups receiving such contributions to make only independent expenditures or if ordinary independent-expenditure disclosure satisfies any interest the government may have.

[135] See Thalheimer v. City of San Diego, No. 09-CV-2862-IEG, 2010 WL 596397, at *6-9 (S.D. Cal. Feb. 16, 2010) (preliminary injunction opinion) (enjoining ban on corporate contributions to independent-expenditure PACs).

[136] Citizens United, 130 S. Ct. at 913.

[137] *Id.* at 935 n.8.

[138] 130 S.Ct. 2371 (2010).

[139] Citizens United, 130 S. Ct. at 898.

corporate ban was in fact a speech ban.[140] And even if the PAC option did allow corporations to speak, PAC status imposes such "onerous" burdens that it is inadequate to satisfy corporations' right to political speech.[141] This holding as to the onerous, insufficient nature of PAC options was decided without mentioning the federal source-and-amount limitations on contributions to PACs. In other words, the *other* PAC burdens (registration, recordkeeping, periodic reporting of all receipts and disbursements, and mandatory organization before speaking) were sufficient to make PAC burdens onerous and inadequate means of speech. This means that cases such as *Alaska Right to Life Committee v. Miles*,[142] which relied on the absence of source-and-amount restrictions to hold that Alaska's PAC-style requirements were not particularly onerous and therefore constitutional, are no longer viable.

8. Its express endorsement of bright-line, protective, objective tests, its rejection of subjective, "intricate case-by-case determinations," and its pronouncement that PAC burdens are onerous all doom the FEC's current method of determining PAC status. Declining to make a bright-line rule, the FEC opted to make no rule, instead stating that determining an organization's "major purpose" (which *Buckley* said must be to nominate or elect candidates before PAC status may be imposed[143]) would be a case-by-case determination based on ambiguously defined, subjective criteria.[144] The FEC must now make an objective, easily determined rule or enforcement policy. For example, it may apply PAC status only to groups that spend more than 50 percent of their annual budget on regulable, election-related speech (and meet the statutory threshold of $1,000 in regulable expenditures or contributions per year). The FEC's PAC-status enforcement policy is at issue in *The Real Truth About Obama*, remanded for reconsideration in light of *Citizens United*.[145]

9. It held that facial invalidation was required because of "the primary importance of speech itself to the integrity of the election

---

[140] *Id.* at 897–98.

[141] *Id.*

[142] 441 F.3d 773 (9th Cir. 2006).

[143] 424 U.S. at 79.

[144] Political Committee Status, 72 Fed. Reg. 5595 (Feb. 7, 2007).

[145] 130 S.Ct. 2371.

process," and the necessity of protecting speakers from the substantial burdens required to clarify the law through multiple as-applied challenges.[146] This is an important recognition that courts must lighten the litigation burden of challenges to campaign-finance restrictions. With *WRTL* and *Citizens United*, it is clear that *McConnell* was the highwater mark of a rapidly receding "reform" flood. *Citizens United*, despite its faults, is a robust reassertion of the First Amendment and the rights of citizens to participate in the political speech essential to self-governance. Apparently, liberty is coming back into fashion.

These nine transferable analyses are positive developments for liberty, the First Amendment, citizen self-governance, and the Republic. For example, their application has already led to *Speechnow.org*, which cited *Citizens United* in an important ruling protecting citizens' rights to organize and engage in core political speech.[147]

VIII. *Citizens United*: Its Meaning for Disclosure

Still, it should be noted that the way *Citizens United* was decided has caused some damage to citizens' speech, association, and self-government rights with regard to imposed disclosure (including mandated disclaimers, reporting, and donor disclosure). Can this damage be limited? To evaluate this we must answer further questions:

What did Buckley *hold regarding disclosure?* Buckley expressly excluded genuine issue advocacy from the required reporting of "expenditures," defined as disbursements "'for the purpose of influencing' the nomination or election of candidates for federal office." *Buckley* noted that the definition had "potential for encompassing both issue discussion and advocacy of a political result."[148] To "ensure that the reach" of the disclosure statute was not "impermissibly broad," the Court construed "expenditure" to reach only express advocacy.[149] "This reading is directed precisely to that spending that is unambiguously related to the campaign of a particular

---

[146] Citizens United, 130 S. Ct. at 895.

[147] See *supra*, note 134.

[148] 424 U.S. at 79.

[149] *Id.* at 80.

federal candidate," the Court stated.[150] It continued, "As narrowed, [it] does not reach all partisan discussion for it only requires disclosure of those expenditures that expressly advocate a particular election result."[151] In short, issue advocacy was not subject to disclosure, only "spending that is unambiguously related to the campaign of a particular federal candidate."

What disclosure line did Citizens United *reject?* The *McConnell* Court had already rejected express advocacy as the disclosure line by holding that disclosure could also be required for electioneering communications.[152] While *WRTL* drew the *prohibition* line for electioneering communications at its appeal-to-vote test, *Citizens United* declined to draw the electioneering-communication *disclosure* line at the same place.[153] This means, at present, that any communication merely meeting the express-advocacy *definition* is subject to disclosure.

Can a new electioneering-communication disclosure line (other than the mere electioneering-communication definition) be drawn that is consistent with Citizens United *and* Buckley? In other words, could the federal courts narrow the disclosure requirement in a way that protects the *issue* advocacy protected by *Buckley*, in a manner similar to *WRTL*'s narrowing of the scope of the electioneering-communication prohibition to protect genuine issue ads, but without drawing the line at the appeal-to-vote test? Stated yet another way, is there room for a new disclosure line (faithful to *Buckley*'s issue-advocacy protection) between a disclosure line at the appeal-to-vote test (now rejected) and a disclosure line at the bare electioneering-communication definition?

This analysis begins by asking what sort of communications were actually at issue in the as-applied challenge to the electioneering-communication disclosure requirements in *Citizens United*. The Court only considered the disclosure requirement as applied to two types of communications, a movie and ads. The *Citizens United* Court held that the movie at issue "would be understood by most viewers as an extended criticism of Senator Clinton's character and her fitness

---

[150] *Id.*

[151] *Id.*

[152] 540 U.S. at 194–99.

[153] 130 S. Ct. at 915.

for the office of the Presidency."[154] It noted references to candidacy, the election, and voting, and it declared the movie "the functional equivalent of express advocacy" under *WRTL*'s appeal-to-vote test.[155]

What did Citizens United argue about the ads and what did the Court say about them? Citizens United did not claim that the ads contained issue advocacy, arguing instead that there should be no disclosure because the ads were about commercial activity.[156] To this the Court countered, "Even if the ads only pertain to a commercial transaction, the public has an interest in knowing who is speaking about a candidate shortly before an election."[157] Moreover, the Court twice described the ads as "pejorative."[158]

Are either of these relevant to the hunt for a new disclosure line lying below the appeal-to-vote test and the bare electioneering-communication definition? The movie is not analytically helpful because it was subject to disclosure *even if* the disclosure line were drawn at the appeal-to-vote test. But the ads were *not* deemed to contain an appeal to vote, so what the Court said and held concerning them *is* analytically relevant to a possible new line. What the Court actually held is this: As applied to pejorative ads about commercial transactions (with no allegation that they advocated any public issue), the electioneering-communication disclosure regime is constitutional, in part because the disclosure trigger is not the appeal-to-vote test.

But would the disclosure regime be constitutional as applied to a communication that was about a public issue, not about a commercial transaction, and not pejorative toward a candidate? What if it were a genuine issue ad of the sort at issue in *WRTL*? *WRTL* described WRTL's ads as follows:

> First, their content is consistent with that of a genuine issue ad: The ads focus on a legislative issue, take a position on the issue, exhort the public to adopt that position, and urge the public to contact public officials with respect to the matter. Second, their content lacks indicia of express advocacy: The ads do not mention an election, candidacy, political

---

[154] *Id.* at 890.

[155] *Id.*

[156] *Id.* at 915.

[157] *Id.*

[158] *Id.* at 887, 915.

party, or challenger; and they do not take a position on a candidate's character, qualifications, or fitness for office.[159]

To be consistent with *Buckley*, such a genuine issue ad would have to be protected from disclosure.[160] That would mean that government could not require disclosure as to issue-advocacy electioneering communications that do not contain an appeal to vote; do not mention elections, candidacies, or political parties; do not address character, qualifications, or fitness of candidates; and are not pejorative.

That would be a new disclosure line between the appeal-to-vote test and the bare electioneering-communication definition. Such an as-applied challenge was not addressed in *Citizens United*, and would have to be successful unless *Buckley's* holding as to permissible disclosure is to be entirely overturned. Only time will tell if such a challenge succeeds.

In any event, this analysis shows that *Buckley's* unambiguously-campaign-related requirement remains viable, but damaged by not being argued and embraced in *Citizens United*. There must, after all, be some line cabining what Congress and the FEC may regulate under their congressional authority to regulate elections. Congress has acknowledged by its definitions that it may only regulate "contributions" and "expenditures" made "for the purpose of influencing" federal election campaigns.[161] The FEC has acknowledged the same in various explanations and justifications of its rules.[162] But it is not enough to say that disclosure may be required for disbursements made "for the purpose of influencing" because that is precisely the language that *Buckley* found vague and overbroad, and narrowed using the unambiguously-campaign-related requirement to protect issue advocacy. That there must be such a constitutionally mandated line is imperative in light of the FEC's assertion that it is authorized to regulate "beyond speech about candidate elections" to reach

---

[159] 551 U.S. 449, 470 (2007).

[160] Even *McConnell* "assume[d] that the regulation of campaign speech might not apply to the regulation of genuine issue ads." 540 U.S. at 206 n.88.

[161] See 2 U.S.C. §§ 431(8)(A)(i) ("contribution" definition) and (9)(A)(i) ("expenditure" definition).

[162] See, e.g., Coordinated Communications, 71 Fed. Reg. 33190, 33197 (June 8, 2006) (to be codified at 11 C.F.R. pt. 109) (investigations as to expenditures for coordinated party communications must not be for "activity . . . unlikely to be for the purpose of influencing Federal elections").

"attempts to sway public opinion on issues."[163] That is *not* the line that the Supreme Court drew in *Citizens United* and cannot be the constitutional line if *Buckley* and the First Amendment remain viable.

The unambiguously-campaign-related line is necessary if there is to be adequate protection from unwarranted disclosure because the Court applies "exacting scrutiny" to disclosure requirements. That scrutiny, while high in *Buckley*, is often watered down in application. The unambiguously-campaign-related requirement mandates that as a threshold matter the regulated speech must be shown to be unambiguously campaign related before scrutiny is applied. That was what *Buckley* did. Applying this threshold requirement restricts the regulatory scope before the appropriate level of scrutiny is applied. It fixes the analysis as to disclosure so that lowered intermediate scrutiny does not simply sanction whatever disclosure the government wants to impose.

So why was *Citizens United* not more protective as to electioneering-communication disclosure? Justice Thomas's dissent outlined the problems that developed in California following the disclosure of persons donating in support of a ballot initiative (Proposition 8) prohibiting gay marriage. Similar problems arose surrounding the public release of petitions to put a similar referendum on the ballot in Washington State. The Court was familiar with such problems because it had issued a stay protecting against release of the petitions until it had a chance to consider the case.[164] The social costs of disclosing citizens' political activities have clearly risen since 1976, when *Buckley* was decided. The ability to post individuals' names, addresses, places of employment, and even maps to individuals' homes on the Internet has facilitated vandalism, harassment, and threats of physical harm and death. Despite this growing problem, *Citizens United* seemed unconcerned about providing a high level of protection.

---

[163] Defendant FEC's Motion for Summary Judgment at 22, Citizens United v. FEC, No. 1:07-CV-02240, 2008 WL 2788753 (D.D.C. June 6, 2008).

[164] Doe v. Reed, 561 U.S. ____, 130 S.Ct.2811 (2010) (signatories of referendum petitions generally do not have a constitutional right to keep their identities private but courts should consider in any given case whether a particular referendum presents sufficiently unique circumstances that anonymity is required). For a larger discussion of *Doe*, see, elsewhere in this volume, Steve Simpson, *Doe v. Reed* and the Future of Disclosure Requirements 2009-2010 Cato Sup. Ct. Rev. 139 (2010).

What are some possible explanations? For one, the push to reverse *Austin*, which the public would (and did) consider a huge step, may have created pressure to balance that decision with strong disclosure requirements. Also, the unambiguously-campaign-related requirement, which *Buckley* employed to protect issue advocacy, was not argued to the Court by a party.

When confronted with a challenge to the electioneering-communication disclosure regime in a case dealing with ads like those at issue in *WRTL*, where briefing focuses on *Buckley*'s protection from disclosure for issue ads, and where there is no counterpressure from a major overruling in a different aspect of the case, the Court should recognize the need to protect issue advocacy and remove government-facilitated intimidation from the political toolbox.

United States v. Stevens:
Restricting Two Major Rationales for Content-Based Speech Restrictions
Nadine Strossen*

Introduction

In *United States v. Stevens*,[1] the Court continued a trend—one that has largely united the justices in recent decades—of contracting government power to enforce content-based regulations of expression, even when those regulations receive overwhelming support from elected officials[2] and the general public, and even when the expression conveys ideas or depicts actions that most people consider offensive or wrongful.[3] Content-based speech regulations pose

* Professor Strossen thanks New York Law School students David Henek and Russell Smith for their invaluable assistance with research and footnotes. Additional appreciated contributions were made by NYLS students Lisabeth Jorgensen, Joseph Schneiderman, and Trevor Timm. Important consultation, training and administrative support were provided by two NYLS staff colleagues: Michael Roffer, associate librarian for reader services and professor of legal research; and Steven Cunningham, senior administrative assistant.

[1] 559 U.S. ____, 130 S. Ct. 1577 (2010).

[2] The statute that the Court struck down in Stevens, 18 U.S.C. § 48, was passed in the Senate by unanimous consent and in the House of Representatives by a vote of 372–42. H.R. 1887, 106th Cong. (1999). See Bill Summary & Status, 106th Congress (1999–2000), H.R. 1887, Major Congressional Actions, available at http://thomas.loc.gov/cgi-bin/bdquery/z?d106:HR01887:@@@R; Office of the Clerk, House of Representatives, Final Vote Results for Roll Call 514 ,(October 19, 1999), available at http://clerk.house.gov/evs/1999/roll514.xml.

[3] The Court has struck down restrictions on burning the U.S. flag, see United States v. Eichman, 496 U.S. 310 (1990); Texas v. Johnson, 491 U.S. 397 (1989); burning a Ku Klux Klan-style cross, see Virginia v. Black, 538 U.S. 343 (2003); R.A.V. v. City of St. Paul, 505 U.S. 377 (1992); photographs or films that appear to depict children engaging in sexual conduct (but do not in fact portray actual minors), see Ashcroft v. Free Speech Coal., 535 U.S. 234 (2002); and advertising for tobacco products that is aimed at minors, see Lorillard Tobacco Co. v. Reilly, 533 U.S. 525 (2001).

the greatest danger to the core value underlying the First Amendment: the right of individuals to make their own choices about what ideas to express, receive, and believe, free of governmental limitations or manipulation.[4] Nonetheless, the Court has not categorically pronounced all content-based speech regulations automatically unconstitutional,[5] thus leaving the door open for those who continue to seek to regulate certain forms of controversial expression.

Congress stepped through this door in 1999 by enacting 18 U.S.C. § 48, which criminalized the commercial creation, sale, or possession of certain depictions of treatment of animals that is illegal in some U.S. jurisdictions.[6] In *Stevens*, the Supreme Court shut the door on

---

[4] As the Court has explained, in contrast with content-neutral regulations of the "time, place, and manner" of expression—for example, noise control regulations in residential neighborhoods—regulations that target the content of expression "pose the inherent risk that the Government seeks not to advance a legitimate regulatory goal, but to suppress unpopular ideas or information or to manipulate the public debate through coercion rather than persuasion." Turner Broad. Sys. v. FCC, 512 U.S. 622, 641 (1994).

[5] Justice Anthony Kennedy has advocated this position concerning any expression that is not within one of the traditional categorical exclusions from the First Amendment that the Court has recognized, such as for obscenity or defamation. For all content-based regulations of protected expression, Justice Kennedy has maintained that strict scrutiny is inappropriate; in his view, such regulations should be per se unconstitutional. See Republican Party of Minn. v. White, 536 U.S. 765, 792–93 (2002) (Kennedy, J., concurring); Simon & Schuster, Inc. v. Members of N.Y. Crime Victims Bd. 502 U.S. 105, 124 (1991) (Kennedy, J., concurring).

[6] The statute's title, as well as its legislative history, is aimed at depictions of "animal cruelty," but it actually sweeps more broadly, encompassing images of animal treatment that is illegal for any reason, even if there is no cruelty (a term that does not appear in the key statutory language). The statute reads in full:

Section 48. Depiction of animal cruelty

(a) CREATION, SALE, OR POSSESSION. – Whoever knowingly creates, sells, or possesses a depiction of animal cruelty with the intention of placing that depiction in interstate or foreign commerce for commercial gain, shall be fined under this title or imprisoned not more than 5 years, or both.

(b) EXCEPTIONS. – Subsection (a) does not apply to any depiction that has serious religious, political, scientific, educational, journalistic, historical or artistic value.

(c) DEFINITIONS. – In this section –

(1) the term "depiction of animal cruelty" means any visual or auditory depiction, including any photograph, motion-picture film, video recording, electronic image, or sound recording of conduct in which a living animal is intentionally maimed, mutilated, tortured, wounded, or killed, if such conduct is illegal under Federal law or the law of the State in which the creation, sale, or possession takes place, regardless of whether the maiming, mutilation, torture, wounding,

Section 48, which it struck down on facial overbreadth grounds.[7] Moreover, the Court came close to shutting the door on two major supporting rationales that have consistently been advanced by advocates of not only Section 48 but also other content-based regulations. The Court did this by reinterpreting two of its past rulings that did countenance content-based regulations, upon which proponents of such regulations routinely rely (as did the government in *Stevens*): *Chaplinsky v. New Hampshire*[8] and *New York v. Ferber*.[9]

Chaplinsky laid out criteria for excluding certain content-based categories of expression from First Amendment protection.[10] *Ferber* upheld a statute criminalizing child pornography—images recording sexual conduct by children—principally on a "drying-up-the-market" rationale, thereby allowing the government to pursue the unusually important goal of preventing child sexual abuse by criminalizing the resulting images and reducing the economic incentive to engage in the abuse.[11] In *Stevens*, the Court significantly recast both *Chaplinsky* and *Ferber* in ways that substantially rein in their precedential force as foundations for further inroads into the cardinal rule against content regulations.

The government's primary argument in *Stevens* was that the Court may expand the set of content-based speech categories that it deems wholly excluded from First Amendment protection whenever it concludes, under *Chaplinsky*'s general balancing test, that the expression is "of such slight social value as a step to truth that any benefit that may be derived from [it] is clearly outweighed by the social interest in order and morality."[12] In addition, the government argued that *Ferber*'s drying-up-the-market rationale also justified Section 48.[13]

---

or killing took place in the State; and

       (2) the term "State" means each of the several States, the District of Columbia, the Commonwealth of Puerto Rico, the Virgin Islands, Guam, American Samoa, the Commonwealth of the Northern Mariana Islands, and any other commonwealth, territory, or possession of the United States. 18 U.S.C. § 48 (2006).

[7] 130 S. Ct. at 1588.

[8] 315 U.S. 568 (1942).

[9] 458 U.S. 747 (1982).

[10] Chaplinsky, 315 U.S. at 571–72.

[11] Ferber, 458 U.S. at 759–60.

[12] Stevens, 130 S. Ct. at 1585 (quoting Chaplinsky, 315 U.S at 571–72).

[13] Reply Brief for the United States at 5, United States v. Stevens, 130 S. Ct. 1577 (2010) (No. 08-769).

Although the Court itself has rarely, if ever, actually accepted either of these rationales for expanding the range of permitted content-based speech regulations—the "*Chaplinsky* rationale"[14] or the "*Ferber* rationale"[15]—both rationales are regularly cited by Congress and other lawmakers in enacting censorial laws. Lower court judges have also accepted them, as illustrated by the statute at issue in *Stevens*. Both rationales were stressed in Section 48's legislative history, in support of the conclusion that Section 48 was constitutional.[16] In the *Stevens* litigation, one or both rationales were accepted by the federal district court judge,[17] who rejected Stevens's First Amendment challenge to Section 48, as well as by three Third Circuit judges[18] and Justice Samuel Alito.[19] Indeed, the Supreme Court's *Stevens* opinion acknowledged that the government's arguments were grounded in language that the Court had set out in *Chaplinsky* and repeatedly reiterated, including in *Ferber*.[20] Therefore, the Court

---

[14] The Court has rarely, if ever, actually sanctioned a new categorical First Amendment exception beyond the longstanding, traditional exceptions such as the ones that *Chaplinsky* itself listed, e.g., obscenity, defamation, and "fighting words." Before the Supreme Court's decision in *Stevens*, conventional wisdom had viewed the Court's 1982 decision in *Ferber* as classifying child pornography as a new category of constitutionally unprotected expression. However, the Court's *Stevens* opinion, as explained below, recasts *Ferber* as one specific instance of a prior, longstanding categorical exception for expression that is "an integral part of conduct in violation of a valid criminal statute." Stevens, 130 S. Ct. at 1586 (quoting Giboney v. Empire Storage & Ice Co., 336 U.S. 490, 498 (1949)). See also Free Speech Coal., 535 U.S. 246 (declaring that virtual child pornography is not "an additional category of unprotected speech"); Texas v. Johnson, 491 U.S. 397, 418 (1989) (stating that there is no "separate juridical category" for expression involving the U.S. flag).

[15] See Free Speech Coal., 535 U.S. at 254 (rejecting the drying-up-the-market rationale as a sufficient justification for outlawing "virtual child pornography," which is produced without using actual children, and distinguishing *Ferber*); Bartnicki v. Vopper, 532 U.S. 514, 529–31 & n.13 (2001) (rejecting the drying-up-the-market rationale as a sufficient justification for punishing the publication of illegally intercepted mobile phone conversations, where the media publishers did not participate in the illegal interception, and distinguishing *Ferber*).

[16] H.R. Rep. No. 106–397, at 4–5 (1999) (Conf. Rep).

[17] See Stevens, 130 S. Ct. at 1583 (describing the district court's decision, which is unreported).

[18] See United States v. Stevens, 533 F.3d 218, 236–37 (3d Cir. 2008) (Cowen, J., dissenting).

[19] See Stevens, 130 S. Ct. at 1599–1602 (Alito, J., dissenting).

[20] *Id.* at 1585–86 (majority opinion).

seized on the opportunity that the *Stevens* case presented to check the most far-ranging, speech-suppressive implications of both *Chaplinsky* and *Ferber*.

Part I of this article provides an overall analysis of Section 48 and the *Stevens* litigation. Part II summarizes the importance of the general prohibition on content-based speech regulations, and the two major types of exceptions to that prohibition that the Court has condoned, as illustrated by *Chaplinsky* and *Ferber*. Parts III and IV explore the two most important general issues the *Stevens* case presented: the appropriate limits on these two major exceptions to the ban on content regulation. Part III notes a counterintuitive aspect of *Stevens*'s tightened criteria for recognizing a categorical exclusion from the First Amendment: by insisting that any such exclusion is not new but simply the explicit identification of historically unprotected speech—whose implicit exclusion is deeply rooted in history and tradition—the Court actually increases free speech protection. Typically, however—or at least stereotypically—anchoring the scope of constitutional rights, including freedom of speech, in history and tradition has had the opposite effect; it has restricted protection of these rights. Finally, Part V applies *Stevens*'s sharply limited criteria for permissible content-based regulations to two narrower potential alternatives to Section 48, which would target only the two specific types of depictions that were the primary concern of Section 48's proponents: "crush" and dogfighting videos. It concludes that the government might be able to submit evidence justifying restrictions on crush videos under *Stevens*'s tightened First Amendment standards but the evidence that was introduced in *Stevens* itself suggest that the government would have a hard time restricting dogfighting videos.[21]

I. Analysis of Section 48 and the *Stevens* Decision

The Supreme Court rejected the government's primary argument: that the depictions targeted by Section 48 should be added to the few content-based categories of expression that the Court has held

---

[21] The government and other proponents of Section 48 sometimes focused specifically on dogfighting videos, and sometimes on videos (or other depictions) of animal fighting more generally. The same First Amendment analysis would apply to any of these depictions, although the pertinent empirical evidence would of course vary.

to be completely outside the First Amendment.[22] Once the Court determined that Section 48 outlawed protected expression—that is, expression that *prima facie* falls within the First Amendment's protective ambit—the Court subjected Section 48 to facial over-breadth analysis and struck it down as substantially overbroad.[23]

In light of this holding, it is noteworthy that Section 48 outlawed a much wider range of depictions than those on which its legislative history focused. Throughout the legislative process, supporters of Section 48 stressed that they were seeking to suppress "crush videos," which "feature the intentional torture and killing of helpless animals."[24] These videos "typically show 'mice, hamsters, and other small animals' being crushed to death," but "some crush videos have been made showing 'cats, dogs, and even monkeys being tortured.'"[25] Crush videos often depict women slowly crushing animals to death "with their bare feet or while wearing high heeled shoes," sometimes while "talking to the animals in a kind of dominatrix patter" over "[t]he cries and squeals of the animals, obviously in great pain."[26] These videos "appeal to persons with a very specific sexual fetish."[27] Accordingly, both parties in the *Stevens* litigation acknowledged that crush videos could be prosecuted under existing obscenity statutes.[28] Crush videos might well satisfy the Court's three criteria for the traditional obscenity exception to the First Amendment: the material, "taken as a whole, appeal[s] to the prurient interest in sex, . . . portray[s] sexual conduct in a patently offensive way," and "does not have serious literary, artistic, political, or scientific value."[29] Although the actions depicted in crush videos are outlawed throughout the United States,[30] the statute's proponents

---

[22] Stevens, 130 S. Ct. at 1586.

[23] *Id.* at 1587–89.

[24] H.R. Rep. No. 106–397, at 2 (1999) (Conf. Rep.).

[25] Brief for the United States at 17, United States v. Stevens, 130 S. Ct. 1577 (2010) (No. 08-769).

[26] *Id.* at 17.

[27] *Id.* at 42.

[28] See *id.* at 42–43; See Brief for the Respondent at 50-51, United States v. Stevens, 130 S. Ct. 1577 (2010) (No. 08-769).

[29] Miller v. California, 413 U.S. 15, 24 (1973).

[30] Stevens, 130 S. Ct. at 1599.

maintained that it is difficult to prosecute the participants because the videos typically do not provide any clues to their identities.[31]

Despite the legislative history's focus specifically on crush videos, Section 48 was written much more broadly, to encompass any depictions of specified treatment of animals that is illegal "under Federal law or the law of the State in which the creation, sale, or possession takes place," even if the conduct was perfectly legal where it occurred.[32] Moreover, the specified types of treatment were not limited to those that involved cruelty, but also included any illegal "wounding" or "killing."[33] Accordingly, the statute criminalized depictions of hunting or fishing that was legal where it took place but violated the specific regulations where the resulting image was sold or possessed—for example, because it took place on a date that was not within that jurisdiction's pertinent hunting or fishing season, or because it used a weapon that was not permitted in that jurisdiction. Recognizing the constitutional problems that this sweeping statutory language posed, and consistent with the legislative history's specific concern about crush videos, President Bill Clinton, when he signed Section 48, announced that, "to ensure that the Act does not chill protected speech," the executive branch would interpret it as covering only depictions "of wanton cruelty to animals designed to appeal to a prurient interest in sex."[34]

Notwithstanding the Clinton administration's limiting interpretation of Section 48, after the end of that administration, Robert J. Stevens was indicted under Section 48 because of three videos he sold that included depictions of dogfighting and fights between dogs and other animals.[35] The government never contended that any of these depictions was "designed to appeal to a prurient interest in sex," and the depictions were obviously not the crush videos that had been of central concern to Congress. Stevens moved to dismiss the indictment on First Amendment grounds. The district court

---

[31] See *id.* at 1598 (Alito, J., dissenting) (citing H.R. Rep. No. 106–397, at 3 (1999) (Conf. Rep.)).

[32] 18 U.S.C. § 48 (c)(1), *supra* at n. 6.

[33] *Id.*

[34] See Statement by President William J. Clinton upon Signing H.R. 1887 (Dec. 9, 1999), reprinted in 1999 U.S.C.C.A.N. 324.

[35] Stevens, 130 S. Ct. at 1583.

denied the motion, holding that the targeted depictions were categorically unprotected by the First Amendment. The jury convicted Stevens and the district court sentenced him to 37 months' imprisonment followed by three years of supervised release.[36] The *en banc* Third Circuit declared the statute facially unconstitutional and vacated Stevens's conviction.[37]

The Supreme Court affirmed the Third Circuit's judgment, but on different grounds. Although both the Third Circuit and the Supreme Court rejected the government's argument that the targeted depictions should be categorically unprotected by the First Amendment,[38] from that point on their analyses diverged. The Third Circuit concluded that Section 48 could not survive the strict scrutiny to which it was subject as a content-based regulation of protected speech.[39] While the Third Circuit observed in a footnote that the statute "might also be unconstitutionally overbroad," it did not resolve this issue.[40] In contrast, the Supreme Court did not subject Section 48 to strict scrutiny, but rather struck it down as substantially overbroad because its "presumptively impermissible applications . . . far outnumber any permissible ones."[41] The government could not deny that, as written, Section 48 did literally apply to many depictions beyond the only two kinds that, the government maintained, it should be construed to outlaw: crush videos and depictions of animal fighting. The government sought to defend against the facial overbreadth challenge by urging the Court to construe the statute more narrowly than it was written in several respects.

For example, although Section 48 expressly targets "depiction[s] of animal cruelty," it criminalized depictions of any "wounding" or "killing" of an animal that was illegal for any reason, even reasons having nothing to do with protecting animals against cruelty. Therefore, as mentioned above, Section 48 outlawed depictions of generally lawful activities such as hunting, fishing, slaughtering livestock,

---

[36] *Id.* Thirteen judges participated in the decision; ten joined in the majority ruling, and three dissented. See Stevens, 533 F. 3d at 236 (Cowen, J., dissenting).

[37] Stevens, 533 F.3d at 220.

[38] *Id.*; Stevens, 130 S. Ct. at 1584.

[39] Stevens, 533 F.3d at 232–33.

[40] *Id.* at 235 n.16.

[41] Stevens, 130 S. Ct. at 1592.

and exterminating pests, if the particular activity depicted did not comply with regulations designed to promote various interests, such as human health and environmental concerns. In an effort to avert the resulting overbreadth, the government argued that the Court should read into the statutory language an additional requirement that there be "accompanying acts of cruelty."[42]

Another aspect of Section 48 that the government urged the Court to read more narrowly than written was its exception for "any depiction that has serious religious, political, scientific, educational, journalistic, historical, or artistic value." The government apparently recognized that this exception would not necessarily shelter the hunting depictions that, it maintained, the statute did not intend to target, because such depictions would not necessarily be found to have "*serious* value."[43] Therefore, the government asked the Court to interpret the "serious value" requirement as meaning "at least some minimal value" or value that is not "scant," even though at trial the government had endorsed the jury instructions on point, which required value that is "significant and of great import."[44] Likewise, the government asked the Court to read into Section 48 a requirement that the value of any targeted depiction must be "determined based on an assessment of the work as a whole,"[45] even though Section 48 refers to "any . . . depiction," including "any photograph" or "electronic image," and even though the government's own expert witnesses supported their arguments that Stevens's videos lacked sufficient value by focusing on brief segments.[46] In sum, as the Court concluded, the government was asking it not to construe the statute, but rather to rewrite it.[47]

---

[42] *Id.* at 1588.

[43] See Reply Brief for the United States, *supra* note 13, at 5–6 (emphasis added) (citing H.R. Rep. No. 397, at 24–5, 31 (1999) (Conf. Rep)).

[44] Stevens, 130 S. Ct. at 1590.

[45] Brief for the United States, *supra* note 25, at 26; Reply Brief for the United States, *supra* note 13, at 6.

[46] See Brief for the Respondent, *supra* note 28, at 8 (detailing how one of the government's expert witnesses concluded that one of the three targeted videotapes was valueless because, in his view, a single one-minute scene in an hour-long movie was too long).

[47] Stevens, 130 S. Ct. at 1592.

In addition to asking the Court to correct Congress's substantially overbroad drafting through a judicial rewriting, the government also asked the Court to rely on the executive branch to achieve the same result by exercising prosecutorial discretion to enforce the statute only in cases involving depictions of "'extreme' cruelty."[48] This "trust us" argument flies in the face of the most fundamental constitutional principles that secure First Amendment and other constitutional freedoms against infringements, rather than relegating them to the discretion of government officials.[49]

Moreover, this argument is especially unpersuasive in light of the *Stevens* litigation itself. Stevens was prosecuted for selling videos that contained some footage of pit bulls engaging in dogfights, at least some of which were apparently legal where and when they occurred,[50] as well as attacks against other animals. Stevens maintained that he had long opposed dogfighting and that these videos were designed to educate pit bull owners and trainers about the breed's special strengths and qualities that make it well-suited for non-dogfighting activities such as hunting, tracking, and weight pulling.[51] At trial, several expert witnesses attested to the serious value in each of these films. Notably, one such expert was the acting vice president of the American Canine Foundation, which works to end animal cruelty.[52] This expert testimony highlighted several valuable aspects of the films, including their educational value for law enforcement officials who regularly work with or encounter pit bulls.[53] In any event, even assuming for the sake of argument that these videos could fairly be considered to comply with the government's malleable proposed criterion of depicting "extreme cruelty," they are certainly excluded by the additional limiting construction that President Clinton announced when he signed Section 48, confining it to depictions that are "designed to appeal to a prurient interest in sex."[54]

---

[48] *Id.* at 1581.

[49] See, e.g., W. Va. Bd. of Educ. v. Barnette, 319 U.S. 624, 647 (1947).

[50] Stevens, 130 S. Ct. at 1583.

[51] See Brief for the Respondent, *supra* note 28, at 58–59.

[52] See American Canine Foundation home page, http://www.americancaninefoundation.com.

[53] See Brief for the Respondent, *supra* note 28, at 7.

[54] See Statement by President William J. Clinton upon Signing H.R. 1887, *supra* note 34.

The Supreme Court's sole dissenter, Justice Samuel Alito, criticized the majority for invalidating the statute on facial grounds, rather than confining its review to the statute as applied to the particular videotapes at issue.[55] Justice Alito then analyzed the statute as if it had actually outlawed only crush videos and videos of "brutal animal fights."[56] Accepting the government's proffered analogy to child pornography, Justice Alito concluded that both types of depictions should be excluded from First Amendment protection because the crimes they depict "cannot be effectively controlled without targeting the videos."[57]

II. The Importance of the General Prohibition on Content-Based Speech Regulations—and the Exceptions to That Prohibition

The Supreme Court has stressed that "above all else, the First Amendment means that government has no power to restrict expression because of its message, its ideas, its subject matter or its content."[58] In recent decades, the Court has consistently held that content-based restrictions on speech are presumptively unconstitutional.[59] Notwithstanding this cardinal general rule, the Court has held that content-based speech restrictions are permissible in two situations. First, the Court has recognized a series of content-based categorical exceptions to First Amendment coverage, categories of expression that it has deemed wholly outside the First Amendment's scope. Once expression is held to satisfy the defining criteria for any such categorical exclusion—for example, the tripartite definition of constitutionally unprotected "obscenity"[60]—the First Amendment analysis ends; government is free to regulate or even prohibit such categorically unprotected expression.[61] Second, the Court has held that even expression that is within the First Amendment's scope—

---

[55] Stevens, 130 S. Ct. at 1593 (Alito, J., dissenting).

[56] *Id.* at 1601.

[57] *Id.*

[58] Police Dep't of Chicago v. Mosley, 408 U.S. 92, 95–96 (1972).

[59] See Erwin Chemerinsky, Constitutional Law: Principles and Policies 932–33 (3d ed. 2006).

[60] Miller v. California, 413 U.S. 15, 24 (1973).

[61] See Chemerinsky, *supra* note 59, at 986. The Court has held, however, that even concerning categorically unprotected expression, regulations may not discriminate on the basis of viewpoint. R.A.V. v. City of St. Paul, 505 U.S. 377 (1992).

that is, it does not satisfy the criteria for any categorical exception—may still be subject to content-based regulation if the government can satisfy "strict judicial scrutiny" by showing that the regulation is "narrowly tailored" and necessary to advance a goal of "compelling" importance, such that no "less restrictive alternative" measure would suffice.[62]

In light of the fundamental First Amendment concerns underlying the general proscription on content-based regulations, it is important to constrain the two exceptional situations in which they are nonetheless tolerated. The Supreme Court's *Stevens* opinion constitutes a significant step toward reining in the first such exception: categorical content-based exclusions from First Amendment protection. Specifically, the Court reformulated the passage from *Chaplinsky* that had initially described the Court's approach to such exclusions. The *Stevens* litigation also provides support for reining in the second exception, for regulations that the government can demonstrate to satisfy strict scrutiny. In particular, the Third Circuit's opinion, which reviewed Section 48 under strict scrutiny, rejected the government's drying-up-the-market rationale that the Supreme Court had validated in *Ferber* in the child pornography context.[63] Moreover, although the Supreme Court did not engage in strict scrutiny analysis because of its substantial overbreadth holding, what it said about *Ferber* indicates that the Court will likely continue to construe that case narrowly—making it difficult to extend *Ferber*'s rationale beyond the "special case" of child sexual abuse and child pornography.[64]

---

[62] See Chemerinsky, *supra* note 59, at 986–87, 1005–06.

[63] See United States v. Stevens, 533 F.3d 218, 230–31 (3d Cir. 2008); see also Stevens, 130 S. Ct. 1577, 1583–84 (2010); but see Stevens, 533 F.3d at 245–46 (Cowen, J., dissenting) ("Congress could have thus reasonably concluded that targeting the distributors would be the most effective way of drying up the animal-cruelty depictions market"); Stevens, 130 S. Ct. at 1601–02 (Alito, J., dissenting) ("In short, because videos depicting live dogfights are essential to the success of the criminal dogfighting subculture, the commercial sale of such videos helps to fuel the market for, and thus to perpetuate the perpetration of, the criminal conduct depicted in them.").

[64] See Stevens, 130 S. Ct. at 1586 ("We made clear that *Ferber* presented a special case.").

III. Putting the Lid on Content-Based Categories of Unprotected Speech

A. Contrast between Key Passages in Chaplinsky *and* Stevens *Regarding Categorical First Amendment Exceptions*

The U.S. government's primary argument in *Stevens* was that the depictions Section 48 outlawed should be added to the few categories of expression that the Court has held to be excluded from First Amendment protection.[65] The rationale for this conclusion would have warranted wide-ranging suppression of any controversial or extreme expression. The government maintained that "[w]hether a given category of speech enjoys First Amendment protection depends upon a categorical balancing of the value of the speech against its societal costs."[66] The Court rejected this argument in unusually strong language as "startling and dangerous."[67] Nonetheless, the trial court had accepted this very argument, as did the three dissenting Third Circuit judges, and the Supreme Court recognized that it was derived from a widely quoted passage in *Chaplinsky*, which first explicated the Court's approach to categorically unprotected expression.[68]

In the *Stevens* litigation, the government had relied on the broadest language in *Chaplinsky*'s pertinent passage to support its request that the Court carve out from the First Amendment a new category of unprotected expression. In contrast, the *Stevens* Court treated that language as dicta and instead focused on narrower language in the *Chaplinsky* passage, which it integrated into an updated statement of the pertinent principles concerning categorically unprotected expression. That updated statement also drew on several of the

---

[65] See Brief for the United States, *supra* note 25, at 9–14.

[66] Stevens, 130 S. Ct. at 1585 (citing Brief for the United States, *supra* note 25, at 8).

[67] *Id.* The government also proffered other arguments, which the Court did not address, that were at least as deserving of this strong critique. For example, the government argued that "Section 48 furthers the substantial interest in preventing the erosion of public morality that attends" the depicted acts. Brief for the United States, *supra* note 25, at 34. Another example is the government's argument that the targeted depictions could be criminalized under an expanded concept of constitutionally unprotected obscenity, as material that is "depraved and loathsome to the senses." *Id.* at 37.

[68] Stevens, 130 S. Ct. at 1585.

Court's post-*Chaplinsky* rulings, which had sharply curtailed *Chaplinsky*'s speech-suppressive slant. The *Stevens* reformulation transforms *Chaplinsky*'s broad invitation to recognize unprotected categories of expression into strictly limited preconditions for doing so.

The pertinent, often quoted *Chaplinsky* passage reads:

> There are certain *well-defined and narrowly limited classes of speech, the prevention and punishment of which has never been thought to raise any Constitutional problem.* These include the lewd and obscene, the profane, the libelous, and the insulting or "fighting" words—those which by their very utterance inflict injury or tend to incite an immediate breach of the peace. It has been well observed that such utterances are no essential part of any exposition of ideas, and are of such slight social value as a step to truth that any benefit that may be derived from them is clearly outweighed by the social interest in order and morality.[69]

In contrast, *Stevens*'s corresponding passage draws very selectively from this *Chaplinsky* excerpt, quoting only the italicized language near its beginning, while also drawing on post-*Chaplinsky* decisions that are much more speech-protective:[70]

> "From 1791 to the present," . . . the First Amendment has "permitted restrictions upon the content of speech in a few limited areas," . . . These "historic and traditional categories long familiar to the bar," including obscenity, defamation, fraud, incitement, and speech integral to criminal conduct, are "*well-defined and narrowly limited classes of speech, the prevention and punishment of which have never been thought to raise any Constitutional problem.*"[71]

Although both the *Chaplinsky* and *Stevens* passages acknowledge that there are *some* content-based categorical exceptions to First

---

[69] 315 U.S. 568, 571–72 (1942) (emphasis added).

[70] This central passage in Stevens quotes the following post-*Chaplinsky* decisions that expanded free speech protection beyond what the Court had recognized when it decided *Chaplinsky*: R.A.V. v. St. Paul, 505 U.S. 377 (1992); Simon & Schuster, Inc. v. Members of N.Y. Crime Victims Bd., 502 U.S. 105 (1991) (Kennedy, J., concurring in judgment); Virginia Bd. of Pharmacy v. Virginia Citizens Consumer Council, Inc., 425 U.S. 748 (1976); Brandenburg v. Ohio, 395 U.S. 444 (1969) (per curiam).

[71] Stevens, 130 S. Ct. at 1584 (citations omitted and emphasis added).

Amendment protection, they reflect dramatically different perspectives on the appropriate criteria for identifying those exceptions.[72] The *Stevens* approach is essentially backward-looking, treating the finite exceptions that had been generally accepted since the First Amendment's adoption as a closed, fixed set of all such exceptions. In contrast, *Chaplinsky* invites the very argument that the government made in *Stevens*: that the Court may now and in the future continue the process of recognizing potentially unlimited new categories of unprotected expression, beyond those with a longstanding historical pedigree, so long as the Court deems the expression at issue to fail the open-ended, subjective balancing test that the last sentence of the *Chaplinsky* passage sets out.

Accordingly, in the *Stevens* litigation, the government argued that the targeted depictions of illegal treatment of animals should constitute categorically unprotected expression because they are "no essential part of any exposition of ideas" and "of such slight social value as a step to truth that any benefit that may be derived from them is clearly outweighed by the social interest in order and morality."[73] The *Stevens* opinion acknowledged, "[t]o be fair to the Government," that past decisions had quoted this language from *Chaplinsky* with apparent approval.[74]

The *Stevens* Court went on to impose an important limitation on the significance of this language, however, by stressing that it was only "descriptive," merely describing the "historically unprotected categories of speech."[75] The *Stevens* Court emphatically rejected any reading of this language as normative, declaring that it does "not set forth a test that may be applied as a general matter to permit

---

[72] Both *Chaplinsky* and *Stevens* list particular examples of categorically unprotected expression, and neither purports to provide a full roster. Nonetheless, it is interesting to contrast these (partial) lists. The only two categories that both cases cite are obscenity and defamation. The *Stevens* list omits several categories that *Chaplinsky* had specified as unprotected: "lewd" speech, "profane" speech, and "insulting or 'fighting' words." These omissions are consistent with post-*Chaplinsky* rulings that have effectively removed these categories from the unprotected list. Conversely, the *Stevens* listing of unprotected categories adds several others that the *Chaplinsky* roster had not included: fraud, incitement, and speech integral to criminal conduct. See Stevens, 130 S. Ct. at 1584.

[73] Brief for the United States, *supra* note 25, at 11–12.

[74] 130 S. Ct. at 1585.

[75] *Id.*

the Government to imprison any speaker so long as his speech is deemed valueless or unnecessary, or so long as an ad hoc calculus of costs and benefits tilts in a statute's favor."[76]

Stevens did not rule out the possibility that the Court could in the future recognize a category of "historically unprotected" expression that had "not yet been specifically identified or discussed as such in our case law."[77] The Court *did* foreclose, however, the possibility of carving out from First Amendment protection any expression that had been protected historically. The Court flatly rejected the government's contention "that categories of speech may be exempted from the First Amendment's protection without any long-settled tradition of subjecting that speech to regulation."[78] And Stevens's Supreme Court brief persuasively explained why this "historically unprotected" criterion is dictated by the First Amendment's text and purpose:

> [The] focus on history and tradition is critical because it ensures that the First Amendment's shield is withheld only from those narrow categories of speech for which the Constitution itself never intended protection, but not from those forms of speech that the legislative majority just prefers not to protect. Protection against legislative hostility or constantly shifting public sentiment is, after all, the whole purpose of the First Amendment.[79]

As indicated by the *Stevens* passage quoted above, the Court read two phrases in the corresponding *Chaplinsky* passage as setting out essential prerequisites for any newly stated recognition of another longstanding content-based First Amendment carve-out. First, the exception must be "historic and traditional," a test that the *Stevens* Court indicated it would construe narrowly. It signaled that any such exception must extend from 1791 to the present. Moreover, the sole sentence that the Court approvingly quoted from *Chaplinsky* stated that any such exception has "never been thought to raise any Constitutional problem."[80] If these requirements are enforced

[76] *Id.* at 1586.

[77] *Id.*

[78] *Id.* at 1585.

[79] Brief for the Respondent, *supra* note 28, at 15.

[80] Stevens, 130 S. Ct. at 1584 (quoting Chaplinsky, 315 U.S. at 571–72).

strictly, it is hard to imagine any future expansion of the list of unprotected speech categories beyond those the Court has previously recognized. At the very least, this criterion would bar recognition of any admittedly new categorical exceptions to the First Amendment that various advocates have proposed: for example, for "hate speech" that expresses discriminatory views on the basis of race, religion, gender, and other personal characteristics;[81] or "pornography" that is "demeaning" or "degrading" to women.[82]

The second phrase from *Chaplinsky* that the *Stevens* Court approvingly quotes as a prerequisite for recognizing any newly identified category of historically unprotected speech refers to such First Amendment exceptions as "well-defined and narrowly limited classes of speech."[83] This second prerequisite also serves as a significant check upon the Court's recognition of new categories of unprotected speech content. It requires that any alleged historical exception for certain expression would have to be demonstrated at a narrow level of specificity, rather than at a higher level of abstraction. For example, in *Stevens* the government could not rely on the longstanding obscenity exception, as it sought to do, by describing that exception at a relatively high level of abstraction; the government described the obscenity exception as encompassing expression that "offends the sensibilities of most citizens,"[84] and thus includes depictions of animal cruelty. In contrast, the *Stevens* decision noted the government's failure to produce any evidence about any historic lack of protection for the particular depictions that Section 48 sought to suppress.[85]

Stevens's refusal to recognize any novel additions to the traditional roster of unprotected categories of expression was ratified by the Court's subsequent decision in another free speech case during its 2009–10 term, *Holder v. Humanitarian Law Project*.[86] To be sure, the majority rejected the particular First Amendment claim in that case;

---

[81] See, e.g., Mari J. Matsuda, et al., Words that Wound (1993).

[82] See, e.g., Andrea Dworkin, Pornography: Men Possessing Women (1991); Andrea Dworkin & Catharine MacKinnon, Pornography and Civil Rights: A New Day for Women's Equality (1988).

[83] Stevens, 130 S. Ct. at 1584 (quoting Chaplinsky, 315 U.S. at 571–72).

[84] Brief for the United States, *supra* note 25, at 37.

[85] 130 S. Ct. at 1585.

[86] 559 U.S.____, 130 S. Ct. 2705 (2010).

the plaintiffs had challenged a federal statute that criminalized the "knowing" provision of "material support" to "foreign terrorist organizations" insofar as it barred them from providing training and engaging in advocacy in support of peaceful, humanitarian goals. Nonetheless, it is noteworthy that the Court did not accept the government's suggestion that the expression at issue should be treated as categorically unprotected.[87] Instead, the Court subjected the statute, as applied to plaintiffs' expression, to strict scrutiny.[88] Moreover, the dissenting justices expressly cited *Stevens* in stressing that plaintiffs' expression was not "deprive[d] . . . of First Amendment protection under any traditional 'categorical' exception to its protection."[89]

B. Stevens's *Recharacterization of* Ferber's *Child Pornography Exception, Limiting Its Potential as a Model for Future New Exceptions*

The Court's effort in *Stevens* to limit categories of unprotected expression to the finite set that it has historically recognized is underscored by *Stevens*'s novel characterization of the child pornography exception to First Amendment protection.[90] That exception, which the Court initially recognized in *Ferber*, is invariably described as the Court's most recent addition to the list of content-based categories of unprotected expression. For example, this description was used even by Stevens's own Supreme Court brief[91] and by the Third Circuit,[92] although they both read *Ferber* narrowly in other respects. The *Ferber* Court's own language was certainly consistent with this reading. For example, the Court said that it was "[r]ecognizing and classifying

---

[87] *Id.* at 2724 n.5 ("We do not consider any such argument because the Government does not develop it."). *Stevens* would require any "developed" argument in support of this point to demonstrate that the expression was within a "well-defined and narrowly limited class of speech, the prevention and punishment of which [has] never been thought to raise any Constitutional problem." Stevens, 130 S. Ct. at 1584. Accordingly, the fact that the Court did not view the government's argument on this point in *Holder* as sufficiently "develop[ed]" is consistent with *Stevens*'s strict specification of the necessary showings to do so.

[88] Humanitarian Law Project, 130 S. Ct. at 2724.

[89] *Id.* at 2733 (Breyer, J., dissenting).

[90] See Ferber, 458 U.S. 747, 763–64 (1982).

[91] Brief for the Respondent, *supra* note 28, at 15–16.

[92] 533 F.3d 218, 224 (3d Cir. 2008).

child pornography as a category of material outside the protection of the First Amendment."[93]

In contrast, the Supreme Court's *Stevens* opinion did not acknowledge that the Court had recognized child pornography as a new category of unprotected expression. To the contrary, the *Stevens* Court treated child pornography as a specific example of a long-standing more general category of unprotected expression, citing a case that had recognized this broader excluded category just five years after *Chaplinsky*. Specifically, *Stevens* assimilated child pornography to the traditionally unprotected category of "speech integral to criminal conduct," citing the 1947 case of *Giboney v. Empire Storage & Ice Co.*[94] The Court quoted language in *Ferber* itself, as well as its two major subsequent decisions concerning child pornography,[95] which stressed that "[t]he market for child pornography was 'intrinsically related' to the underlying abuse, and was therefore 'an integral part of the production of such materials, an activity illegal throughout the Nation.'"[96]

Given *Stevens*'s recasting of child pornography as a newly identified example of "a previously recognized, long-established category of unprotected speech,"[97] rather than a newly minted category, *Ferber* has only limited capacity to serve as a springboard for judicial recognition of additional categories of unprotected expression, which is how the U.S. government and other proponents of Section 48 had invoked it. In the wake of *Stevens*, *Ferber* cannot serve as precedent for creating a new category of unprotected expression, but rather

---

[93] Ferber, 458 U.S. at 763. See also *id.* at 764 (referring to child pornography as "a definable class of material . . . that . . . is . . . without the protection of the First Amendment.").

[94] Stevens, 130 S. Ct. at 1585 (citing Giboney, 336 U.S. 490, 498 (1949)). For a critique of *Giboney*, as well as *Ferber*, see Eugene Volokh, Speech as Conduct: Generally Applicable Laws, Illegal Courses of Conduct, "Situation-Altering Utterances," and the Uncharted Zones, 90 Cornell L. Rev. 1277, 1324–25 (2005).

[95] Ashcroft v. Free Speech Coal., 535 U.S. 234, 249–50 (2002); Osborne v. Ohio, 495 U.S. 103, 110 (1990).

[96] Stevens, 130 S. Ct. at 1586 (citing Giboney, 336 U.S. at 498). In the same vein, during the oral argument in *Stevens*, Justice Scalia twice referred to child pornography as a subspecies of the longstanding obscenity exception, thus also not acknowledging it as a distinct new category of unprotected expression. See Transcript of Oral Argument at 8–9, 21, Stevens, 130 S. Ct. 1577 (2010) (No. 08-769).

[97] Stevens, 130 S. Ct. at 1586.

only for identifying a new, specific subset of a traditional, historical exception. In particular, *Stevens* stressed that child pornography was "integrally related" to the underlying crime of child sexual abuse because of the drying-up-the-market rationale. Therefore, if this rationale could be extended to other expression, one could argue that such other expression should likewise fall within the longstanding categorical exception for speech that is "an integral part of [the criminal] conduct" it depicts.[98]

However, the Court has consistently resisted attempts to extend the drying-up-the-market rationale beyond the specific context of child pornography.[99] For example, in *Bartnicki v. Vopper*,[100] the Court held that the First Amendment barred any penalty on media for disclosing a cell phone conversation that another party had illegally intercepted in violation of wiretapping laws. The proponents of penalizing the media argued that it was difficult to enforce direct prohibitions on wiretapping and therefore that it was necessary and appropriate to "dry up the market" for the fruits of such illegal interceptions by penalizing the media for disclosing them. The Court emphatically rejected this argument, and indicated that *Ferber*'s drying-up-the-market rationale may well be confined to the "special case" of child pornography.[101] The drying-up-the-market rationale

---

[98] *Id.* In *Ferber* itself, the Court explained this general rationale as follows: "The advertising and selling of child pornography provide an economic motive for and are thus an integral part of the production of such materials, an activity illegal throughout the Nation." 458 U.S. at 761–62. The *Ferber* Court then quoted the very passage from *Giboney* that the Supreme Court quoted in *Stevens. Id.*

[99] See Amy Adler, Inverting the First Amendment, 149 U. Pa. L. Rev. 921, 936 (2001) (child pornography "is the only place in First Amendment law where the Supreme Court has accepted the idea that we can constitutionally criminalize the depiction of a crime.").

[100] 532 U.S. 514 (2001). See also Free Speech Coal., 535 U.S. at 254 (rejecting the drying-up-the-market rationale as a sufficient justification for outlawing "virtual child pornography," which is produced without using actual children); Stanley v. Georgia, 394 U.S. 557, 567–68 (1969) (rejecting the state's argument that its prohibition on possessing obscenity was a necessary complement to its prohibition on distributing obscenity).

[101] Stevens, 130 S. Ct. at 1586.

for punishing expression that depicts or results from illegal conduct also has been criticized by individual justices[102] and by scholars.[103]

C. Stevens's *Criteria for Identifying Categorical First Amendment Exceptions: Comparisons and Contrasts to Other Constitutional Law Contexts*

As discussed above, the two criteria that *Stevens* endorses for identifying any category of unprotected expression are that such category is (1) grounded in history and tradition and (2) "well-defined and narrowly limited." These two criteria also have been used by the Court in another important constitutional context: to identify rights that are sufficiently "fundamental" to be deemed implicitly protected under the Due Process Clauses of the Fifth and Fourteenth Amendments as a matter of "substantive due process."[104] Somewhat ironically, the justices who have most consistently stressed these prerequisites for recognizing a new substantive due process right are the justices who generally take the narrowest view of such rights—notably, on the current Court, Justices Antonin Scalia and Clarence Thomas.[105] In the substantive due process context,

---

[102] See Osborne v. Ohio, 495 U.S. 103, 145 n.19 (1990) (Brennan, J., dissenting) ("The notion that possession of pornography may be penalized in order to facilitate a prohibition on its production . . . is not unlike a proposal that newspaper subscribers be held criminally liable for receiving the newspaper if they are aware of the publisher's violations of child labor laws.").

[103] See Volokh, *supra* note 94, at 1324–26 (criticizing *Giboney, Ferber, Osborne* and the drying-up-the-market rationale, noting that "When the New York Times publishes illegally leaked documents, or transcripts of an illegally [intercepted] conversation, it would have a strong First Amendment defense . . . even though the prospect of such publication may provide a motive for the illegal leaks or illegal interception."). See also Adler, *supra* note 99, at 970–93 ("Child pornography law has validated a renegade vision of how speech works. It is a vision that we have rejected in every other First Amendment context. Child pornography law has collapsed the 'speech/action' distinction that occupies a central role in First Amendment law.").

[104] See Washington v. Glucksberg, 521 U.S. 702, 720–21(1997) (citations omitted):

> Our established method of substantive-due-process analysis has two primary features: First, we have regularly observed that the Due Process Clause specially protects those fundamental rights and liberties which are, objectively, 'deeply rooted in this Nation's history and tradition' . . . . Second, we have required . . . a 'careful description' of the asserted fundamental liberty interest.

[105] See, e.g., Lawrence v. Texas, 539 U.S. 558, 588 (2003) (Scalia, J., with whom Thomas, J., and Rehnquist, C.J., join, dissenting) ("*Washington v. Glucksberg* . . . held that only fundamental rights which are 'deeply rooted in this Nation's history and tradition'

strictly enforcing these prerequisites for recognizing an implicit right has the effect of limiting the protection for the constitutional right at issue. In stark contrast, in the First Amendment context, strictly enforcing these same prerequisites for recognizing a categorical exemption from the right has the opposite effect: to maximize protection for the constitutional right at issue.

Stevens's strict reliance on history and tradition constitutes an unusual twist on such sources of constitutional interpretation even in the specific context of identifying categorical exemptions from First Amendment protection. Typically, a judge who invokes history and tradition in this context does so in support of limiting First Amendment protection.[106] That is exactly the purpose for which the key *Chaplinsky* passage itself invoked history and tradition: *Chaplinsky*'s specific holding was to reject a First Amendment challenge to a conviction for expressing provocative religious and political opinions because of the historically enshrined "fighting words" exception to free speech.[107] Therefore, it is noteworthy that the *Stevens* Court turns that typical use of history and tradition on its head, and converts it into a criterion that forestalls limits on First Amendment protection.

This situation illustrates how overly simplistic it is to equate a particular approach to constitutional interpretation, such as originalism, with a particular ideology or result.[108] That oversimplified equation was likewise belied by another decision that the Court issued

---

qualify for anything other than rational basis scrutiny under the doctrine of 'substantive due process.'") (citations omitted).

[106] See, e.g., United States v. Williams, 128 S. Ct. 1830 (2008) ("offers to engage in illegal transactions"); Brandenburg, 395 U.S. 444, 447 (1969) (per curiam) (intentional incitement of imminent illegal conduct); New York Times v. Sullivan, 376 U.S. 254, 279–80 (1964) (defamation); Roth v. United States, 354 U.S. 476, 484–85 (1957) (obscenity).

[107] Chaplinsky, 315 U.S. at 569 (Chaplinsky, a member of the Jehovah's Witnesses, said the following to a city marshal: "You are a God damned racketeer" and "a damned Fascist and the whole government of Rochester are Fascists or agents of Fascists.").

[108] See generally Jeffrey Rosen, Conservatives v. Originalism, 19 Harv. J.L. & Pub. Pol'y 465 (1996) (arguing that certain justices who generally adhere to originalism nonetheless choose not to analyze three issues with that approach—race-conscious voting districts, gay rights, and minority set-asides—because the results conflict with their conservative political beliefs). Major constitutional law cases illustrate that the same general historical, originalist approach can well yield very different conclusions. See, e.g., McDonald v. City of Chicago, 130 S. Ct. 3020, 3036–42 (2010) (concluding

during its 2009–10 term, which also illustrates the Court's longstanding reliance on the history and tradition criterion it stressed in *Stevens* in yet another important constitutional law context. Specifically, *McDonald v. City of Chicago* invoked that established criterion for determining whether a right that is set out in the Bill of Rights (and hence directly constrains the federal government) should also be deemed to be "incorporated" into the Fourteenth Amendment—and thus also enforceable against state and local governments.[109] *McDonald* posed this question concerning the Second Amendment right that the Court had recognized in *District of Columbia v. Heller*,[110] the right to keep and bear arms in the home for the purpose of self-defense. In *McDonald*, the Court divided 5–4 along "conservative" and "liberal" lines,[111] with the justices who are generally considered more conservative concluding that the right at issue was enforceable against state and local governments,[112] and the justices considered more liberal reaching the opposite conclusion.[113] This alignment constitutes a reversal of the typical roles in incorporation debates.[114]

---

that the Constitution's Framers and ratifiers considered the individual right to bear arms "among those fundamental rights necessary to our system of ordered liberty"); see also *id*. at 3111–14 (Stevens, J., dissenting) (acknowledging that the individual right to bear arms is rooted in history and tradition, but concluding that the states' right to restrict gun ownership is a far "older and more deeply rooted tradition").

[109] 130 S. Ct. at 3036.

[110] 128 S.Ct. 2783 (2008).

[111] I put these words in quotation marks to flag how inaccurate and oversimplified they are. See, e.g., Jeffrey Rosen, So What's the 'Right' Pick?, N.Y.Times, July 3, 2005, at 41.

[112] Justice Thomas agreed with the conclusion, supported by four other justices, that "the Fourteenth Amendment makes the right to keep and bear arms set forth in the Second Amendment 'fully applicable to the States.'" McDonald, 130 S. Ct. at 3058–59 (Thomas, J., concurring in part and concurring in the judgment). Justice Thomas also concurred in some portions of the Court's analysis of the Fourteenth Amendment's Due Process Clause. However, Justice Thomas rested his conclusion on the Fourteenth Amendment's Privileges or Immunities Clause. *Id*. at 3059. The justices who squarely concluded that the right at issue should be incorporated via the Fourteenth Amendment's Due Process Clause were Justice Alito (who authored the mixed majority/plurality opinion), Chief Justice Roberts, and Justices Scalia and Kennedy.

[113] Justice Stevens filed a dissenting opinion, *id*. at 3088, and Justice Breyer filed a dissenting opinion in which Justices Ginsburg and Sotomayor joined, *id*. at 3120. Indicative of the role reversal, Justice Stevens urged the Court to reverse "some 1960's opinions," noting that "[t]he Court has not hesitated to cut back on perceived Warren Court excesses."). *Id*. at 3095 (Stevens, J., dissenting).

[114] See generally Chemerinsky, *supra* note 59, at 501 (noting that the debate about incorporation "determined the reach of the Bill of Rights and the extent to which

IV. Confining the Drying-Up-the-Market Rationale to the Child Pornography Context

As Part III explained, in *Stevens* the Supreme Court recast its *Ferber* decision as having been squarely grounded in the longstanding categorical First Amendment exclusion of expression that is "an integral part of conduct in violation of a valid criminal statute."[115] In the *Ferber* case, the particular "integral" relationship between the expressive material at issue—child pornography—and the underlying criminal conduct—sexual abuse of children—was the fact that the criminal conduct was carried out in order to generate the expressive material, thus leading to the "drying up the market" rationale. The *Ferber* opinion elaborated on that rationale as follows:

> [T]he distribution network for child pornography must be closed if the production of material which requires the sexual exploitation of children is to be effectively controlled. Indeed, there is no serious contention that the legislature was unjustified in believing that it is difficult, if not impossible, to halt the exploitation of children by pursuing only those who produce the photographs and movies. While the production of pornographic materials is a low-profile, clandestine industry, the need to market the resulting products requires a visible apparatus of distribution. The most expeditious if not the only practical method of law enforcement may be to dry up the market for this material by imposing severe criminal penalties on persons selling, advertising, or otherwise promoting the product.[116]

In *Ferber* the Court also cited three additional rationales in support of its conclusion that child pornography is beyond the First Amendment pale:[117]

---

individuals could turn to the federal courts for protection from state and local governments.").

[115] Stevens, 130 S. Ct. at 1586.

[116] Ferber, 458 U.S. at 759–60.

[117] The *Ferber* Court listed various "reasons" why government is "entitled to greater leeway in the regulation of pornographic depictions of children," 458 U.S. at 756, and it then discussed several reasons, numbering them "First" through "Fifth." *Id.* at 756–64. However, the Court's numbering is confusing because it does not strictly correspond to the distinct rationales that the Court proffers in support of its conclusion concerning child pornography, in several respects. Of most relevance, the Court's discussion of what it labels its "second" reason actually addresses two distinct rationales, one of which is the "drying up the market theory," *id.* at 759–60, which the Court also discussed under what it labeled its "third" reason, *id.* at 761–62. Moreover,

1. The goal that the statute was designed to serve, preventing the sexual abuse of children, is of exceptionally compelling importance.[118]
2. Child pornography constitutes a permanent record of the sexual abuse to which the child was subject, and the child suffers continuing harm from its circulation.[119]
3. The targeted expression has only "exceedingly modest, if not *de minimis*" value.[120]

In the *Stevens* litigation, as well as in other cases, advocates of content-based regulations of expression other than child pornography have relied on the rationales the Court set out in *Ferber* in two ways. First, they cite one or more of *Ferber's* rationales as supporting the recognition of additional categorical exclusions from the First Amendment. Second, as a fallback position, they cite one or more of these rationales as satisfying judicial strict scrutiny. Now that the Court's *Stevens* ruling has specified two quite narrow criteria for identifying content-based categorical exclusions from free speech protection, as Part III discussed, most of the *Ferber* rationales will henceforth save a content-based speech regulation only if these rationales satisfy strict scrutiny.[121] This is unlikely to occur.

In *Ferber* itself, the Court did not subject the challenged statute to strict scrutiny, given the Court's holding that child pornography, which the statute outlawed, was categorically unprotected expression. Therefore, even though the *Ferber* Court endorsed the rationales it articulated as generally supporting its conclusion that child pornography constitutes categorically unprotected expression, the Court might well find that not all these rationales are sufficiently

---

the Court designates as its "fifth" reason the general proposition that its past decisions have recognized certain content-based categorical exclusions from free speech protection, *id.* at 763–64, which of course provides no logical support for the specific proposition that child pornography should constitute such an exclusion.

[118] Ferber, 458 U.S. at 756–58.

[119] *Id.* at 759.

[120] *Id.* at 762.

[121] Additionally, as discussed above, *Ferber's* drying-up-the-market rationale could potentially support an argument that another category of expression should also be recognized, along with child pornography, as a specific instance of the general, historically recognized categorical exclusion for expression that is "integrally related" to illegal conduct. Accordingly, that particular *Ferber* rationale could potentially support a claim for a newly recognized categorical exclusion.

persuasive to withstand strict scrutiny when offered to support other censorial measures, including Section 48.

To be sure, the Court will always hold that protecting children's welfare—which closely corresponds to one of its *Ferber* rationales—is a goal of compelling importance. That said, the *Ferber* Court understandably accorded extraordinary importance to the more specific child protection goal it stressed, of protecting children from sexual abuse. Therefore, one could plausibly argue that any content-based regulation that was designed to promote any other goal—even any other goal concerning children's welfare—could be distinguished from *Ferber* on this basis. In *Ferber*, the Court described the specific objective of protecting children from sexual abuse as being "of surpassing importance,"[122] a phrase that adds a special emphasis, in contrast with the usual strict scrutiny parlance, which refers to a goal of "compelling" importance.[123]

The Third Circuit's opinion in *Stevens* stresses this unique aspect of *Ferber* and concludes that the *Ferber* Court was willing to accept the drying-up-the-market rationale as a sufficient justification for criminalizing depictions of criminal conduct only in that specific context,[124] given the particular heinousness of the crime.[125] Indeed, the Supreme Court itself has said that "the interests underlying child pornography prohibitions far exceed the interests justifying" an anti-obscenity law, even though obscenity is a more longstanding exception to First Amendment protection than child pornography.[126]

---

[122] 458 U.S. at 757.

[123] The *Ferber* Court also indicated that it might well be uniquely deferential to government power to regulate child pornography when it contrasted the traditional obscenity exception with its newly recognized child pornography exception; it said that "the States are entitled to greater leeway in the regulation of pornographic depictions of children." *Id.* at 756.

[124] See Stevens, 533 F.3d at 226 ("assum[es]," for the sake of argument only, that "*Ferber* may, in limited circumstances . . . be applied to other categories of speech").

[125] See *id.* at 228 (noting that in *Ferber*, "the Supreme Court went to great lengths to cabin its discussion of the depiction/act conflation because of the special role that children play in our society."). See also Osborne, 495 U.S. at 108 (Brennan, J., dissenting) (attributing what he views as the Court's deviation from First Amendment principles and precedents, in upholding a law criminalizing the mere possession of child pornography, to the fact that "the Court . . . is so disquieted by the possible exploitation of children in the production of . . . pornography.").

[126] Osborne, 495 U.S. at 108.

In the same vein, the Supreme Court has also distinguished child pornography from other expression, including even constitutionally unprotected obscenity, in terms of another rationale it stressed in *Ferber*: that the targeted expression has only "exceedingly modest, if not *de minimis* value."[127] By definition, obscenity lacks "serious . . . value."[128] Therefore, the Court's indication that child pornography has even less "value" than obscenity[129] signals that the Court has relegated child pornography to a singularly outcast status in this regard. Consequently, the Court is unlikely to conclude that any other expression, other than child pornography, has such minimal value.

In sum, building on the Third Circuit's analysis in *Stevens*, one could argue that the drying-up-the-market rationale for punishing expression in order to deter unlawful conduct should be confined *only* to the child pornography context because of two unique factors that the Supreme Court has repeatedly stressed: (1) the "surpassing importance" of protecting children from sexual abuse and (2) child pornography's especially *de minimis* value. Some commentators have read *Ferber* and the Court's other child pornography cases in this strictly limited fashion.[130]

---

[127] *Id.* (quoting Ferber, 458 U.S. at 759).

[128] Miller v. California, 413 U.S. 15, 22 (1973) (explaining that this is one of the three prerequisites for expression to be deemed "obscene" and hence excluded from the First Amendment).

[129] *Osborne* distinguished the Court's holding in Stanley v. Georgia, 394 U.S. 557 (1969), in which it had struck down a statute outlawing the private possession of obscene material; in contrast, *Osborne* itself rejected a First Amendment challenge to a statute outlawing the private possession of child pornography. In support of this distinction, *Osborne* stressed that "*Stanley* was a narrow holding, . . . and, since the decision in that case, the value of permitting child pornography has been characterized as 'exceedingly modest, if not *de minimis*.'" 495 U.S. at 108 (quoting *Ferber*).

[130] When the Court issued its *Ferber* decision, at least one commentary urged that its drying-up-the-market rationale, which was then a novel justification for a censorial measure, should be strictly limited to the child pornography context. See Child Pornography and Unprotected Speech, 96 Harv. L. Rev. 141, 148 (1982). This commentary recognized, however, that the *Ferber* opinion did not itself explicitly spell out such a limitation, thus making it a potential foundation for additional speech-suppressive measures. See *id.* at 150 ("[T]he *Ferber* opinion emerges as a sympathetic response to piteous exploitation. The decision represents the confluence of three concerns—sexually explicit speech, child welfare, and illegal conduct—and should be viewed as a narrow decision legitimized only because of that convergence. The Court's failure to articulate any such limitation, however, leaves each of the three lines of analysis precariously susceptible to extension in future First Amendment decisions."). See

Even if the government can show that a content-based speech regulation is designed to promote a sufficiently important purpose, it is always harder for the government to satisfy the second prong of the strict scrutiny test, which requires that the challenged measure is narrowly tailored and necessary to promote the government's goal, and that no alternative measure, less restrictive of expression, will suffice. In particular, in *Stevens* and other cases concerning different content-based speech regulations, proponents of such regulations have invoked *Ferber*'s central rationale and argued that the speech regulations are necessary to promote the government's goal of deterring certain conduct, due to the difficulties of directly prosecuting the conduct itself.

Under strict scrutiny, the government cannot justify suppressing speech that depicts criminal conduct merely by asserting that it is difficult to prosecute the underlying conduct, or that prosecuting the depictions would have some additional impact in deterring the criminal conduct above and beyond direct prosecutions of such conduct.[131] If such assertions could justify a speech-suppressive measure, then the government could outlaw almost any depictions of any crime.[132] Instead, though, the Supreme Court has rejected this drying-up-the-market rationale for targeting any expression other than child pornography. If this rationale were to survive strict scrutiny, which it did not have to do in the child pornography context, the government would have to demonstrate the following supporting facts:

---

also Geoffrey R. Stone, Dog-Fighting and the First Amendment, Huffington Post, April 25, 2010, http://www.huffingtonpost.com/geoffrey-r-stone/dog-fighting-and-the-first-amendment (describing as "a . . . basic principle of First Amendment doctrine" that "even though speech was produced by an unlawful act, the speech may not be restricted for that reason," and says that "child pornography is a unique exception to [this] principle" because "society has a uniquely 'compelling' interest in preventing" children from being "forced to engage in actual sexual conduct in order to produce the expression").

[131] In *Ferber*, the Court explained that it is difficult to enforce laws criminalizing the production of child pornography because "the production of pornographic materials is a low-profile, clandestine industry." 458 U.S. at 759–60. However, the same could be said of essentially all criminal activity.

[132] See Stevens, 533 F.3d at 230 ("Restriction of the depiction of almost any activity can work to dry up, or at least restrain, the activity's market.").

1. That laws criminalizing the underlying conduct are unusually difficult to enforce—that is, beyond the usual difficulties that routinely impede the enforcement of any criminal laws. Conversely, if these laws are as effective as criminal laws in general, enforcing them is a less restrictive alternative to suppressing the associated expression. Moreover, the government would have to show that it had exhausted alternative measures for increasing the effectiveness of the laws that criminalize the underlying conduct, including increasing the penalties for violating them and increasing the resources allocated to enforcing them.[133]

2. That the underlying criminal conduct is substantially motivated by the desire to create the depiction; in other words, if the depictions were criminalized, the underlying criminal conduct would substantially cease. Conversely, if the underlying criminal conduct would continue to a significant extent in any event, because there are other economic or non-economic incentives for engaging in it, then criminalizing the depictions would not sufficiently promote the goal of deterring the criminal conduct.

3. That the depictions do not materially aid in law enforcement efforts to suppress the underlying criminal conduct. Conversely, if the depictions did materially aid in prosecuting such conduct, outlawing them would be counterproductive. It might even fail rational basis review,[134] and it would certainly fail strict scrutiny.

Because the *Ferber* Court did not subject the challenged statute to strict scrutiny, it did not strictly scrutinize the drying-up-the-market rationale, even in the special context of child pornography. To the contrary, the Court applied only deferential, rational basis review. It did not demand actual empirical evidence that criminalizing child pornography was the only means by which to prevent the underlying child abuse, let alone that criminalization would be effective in preventing such abuse. Neither did the Court demand any evidence

---

[133] See Bartnicki v. Vopper, 532 U.S. 514, 529 (2001) (rejecting argument that expression that results from illegal conduct should be criminalized in order to deter the illegal conduct, noting that "[i]f the sanctions that presently attach to a violation of" the statute making the conduct illegal "do not provide sufficient deterrence, perhaps those sanctions should be made more severe.").

[134] See Chemerinsky, *supra* note 59, at 540 (explaining that under this standard, the Court will strike down a law if its challenger shows that it has no rational relationship to a legitimate government purpose).

of the ineffectiveness of the less restrictive alternative that is typically used to deter criminal conduct—namely, prosecuting those who engage in that conduct; in this context, that would mean prosecuting those who actually abuse children in producing child pornography. Instead, using classic rational basis review terminology, the *Ferber* Court asserted that the legislature was "justified in believing" that this usual approach for halting illegal conduct would not be sufficiently effective.[135] The Court similarly speculated that "[t]he most expeditious if not the only practical method of law enforcement *may* be to dry up the market for this material by imposing severe criminal penalties on persons selling, advertising, or otherwise promoting the product."[136]

Not only did the *Ferber* majority not cite any empirical evidence in support of these conclusions, but the empirical evidence it did cite actually supported a less restrictive alternative to criminalizing the expression at issue: enforcing obscenity statutes. Justice Stevens's separate opinion in *Ferber* stressed this point. Specifically, the very congressional committee reports that the majority cited had concluded that the problem of child sexual abuse for the purpose of producing child pornography could be adequately addressed by imposing stiff penalties for violating obscenity laws, because "virtually all" child pornography satisfies the standards for constitutionally unprotected obscenity.[137]

In sum, the drying-up-the-market rationale might not satisfy strict scrutiny even in the unique context of child pornography. That was one reason for Justice Stevens's conclusion that the Court should not have treated child pornography as categorically unprotected expression.[138] It is also one reason why the *Ferber* decision was strongly criticized by contemporary commentators.[139] In any event, regardless of whether or not the drying-up-the-market rationale could

---

[135] 458 U.S. at 759.

[136] *Id.* at 760 (emphasis added). See also Osborne, 495 U.S. at 109–10 (upholding a statute that criminalized the mere possession of child pornography under rational basis review, asserting that "[i]t is . . . surely reasonable for the State to conclude that it will decrease the production of child pornography if it penalizes those who possess and view the product, thereby decreasing demand.").

[137] Ferber, 458 U.S. at 779 n.4 (Stevens, J., concurring in the judgment) (citing S. Rep. No. 95-438, at 13 (1977)); see also H.R. Rep. No. 95-697, at 7–8 (1977).

[138] Ferber, 458 U.S. at 778 (Stevens, J., concurring in the judgment) ("A holding that respondent may be punished for selling these two films does not require us to conclude that other users of these very same films, or that other motion pictures

satisfy strict scrutiny in the "special case" of child pornography,[140] that rationale is less likely to satisfy strict scrutiny in any other context, as the Third Circuit explained in detail in its *Stevens* opinion.

The Third Circuit expressed its deep skepticism toward *Ferber's* "conflation of the underlying act with its depiction."[141] It cited NYU law professor Amy Adler's exhaustive analysis of child pornography jurisprudence for the proposition that it "is the only place in First Amendment law where the Supreme Court has accepted the idea that we can constitutionally criminalize the depiction of a crime."[142] The Third Circuit posited that in *Ferber* the Supreme Court was willing to "collapse[] the 'speech/action' distinction that occupies a central role in First Amendment law,"[143] because of the unique importance of protecting children from sexual abuse.[144] In contrast, even though the goal of preventing cruelty to animals is surely important, the Third Circuit concluded that neither this goal nor any other would justify criminalizing depictions in an effort to deter the underlying conduct, a type of measure that the Court has upheld only in the context of child pornography.

Strictly scrutinizing the drying-up-the-market rationale that the government invoked in support of Section 48, the Third Circuit concluded that it was not narrowly tailored to promote the government's asserted goal of preventing cruelty to animals.[145] To survive strict scrutiny, the Third Circuit clarified, the government would have to show that Section 48 "prevent[s] cruelty to animals that

---

containing similar scenes, are beyond the pale of constitutional protection."). Although the Court's judgment in *Ferber* was unanimous, the majority's opinion only received a bare five-vote majority. See *id.* at 774 (Blackmun, J., concurring in the result); *Id.* at 775 (Brennan, J., with whom Marshall, J., joins, concurring in the judgment); *Id.* at 777 (Stevens, J., concurring in the judgment).

[139] See Adler, *supra* note 99, at 982 (quoting Supreme Court, 1981 Term, Child Pornography and Unprotected Speech, 96 Harv. L. Rev. 141, 148, 150 (1982)); and Frederick Schauer, Codifying the First Amendment: *New York v. Ferber*, 1982 Sup. Ct. Rev. 285, 303–04).

[140] Stevens, 130 S. Ct. at 1586.

[141] 533 F.3d 218, 226 (3d Cir. 2008).

[142] Adler, *supra* note 99, at 984.

[143] *Id.* at 970.

[144] Stevens, 533 F.3d at 228.

[145] *Id.*

state and federal statutes *directly* regulating animal cruelty under-enforce."[146] As the Supreme Court has stressed, under strict scrutiny the appropriate inquiry is not whether the challenged measure advances the government's goal to some marginal extent, but rather whether it significantly advances the government's goal, above and beyond other, alternative measures that do not intrude on First Amendment freedoms.[147] This is only logical, as surely every government measure, including censorial ones, would have *some* impact in promoting the government's goal. If these measures had no impact whatsoever, they would be struck down as irrational or arbitrary because they would fail to pass even the highly deferential standard of rational basis review.

Specifically concerning the government's drying-up-the-market rationale for Section 48, the Third Circuit noted that the government had submitted no empirical evidence to substantiate that criminalizing depictions of the outlawed conduct was effective, let alone that it was necessary and the least restrictive alternative for significantly advancing the goal of deterring animal cruelty.[148] The Third Circuit acknowledged that the government made a "plausible" argument that the perpetrators of animal abuse depicted in crush videos "are very difficult to find and prosecute for those underlying acts . . . because the only person typically onscreen is the 'actress,' and only her legs or feet are typically shown."[149] Accordingly, if the government could substantiate that argument with evidence,[150] a statute that outlawed crush videos might potentially survive strict

---

[146] *Id* (emphasis added).

[147] See Edenfield v. Fane, 507 U.S. 761, 770–71 (1993) (explaining that under strict scrutiny, government must prove that the challenged speech regulation will alleviate the posited harm "to a material degree").

[148] Stevens, 533 F.3d at 230–31.

[149] *Id.* at 229, 234.

[150] See Reno v. ACLU, 521 U.S. 844, 885 (1997) ("The interest in . . . freedom of expression . . . outweighs any theoretical but unproven benefit of censorship."). See also U.S. v. Williams, 53 U.S. 285, 324–25 & n.3 (2008) (Souter, J., dissenting) (noting that "the Government does not get a free pass whenever it claims a worthy objective for curtailing speech" and rejecting government's claim that it is necessary to criminalize offers to sell and solicitations of virtual child pornography because of difficulty in prosecuting actual child pornography; citing extensive empirical evidence and concluding that the government "appears to be highly successful in convicting child pornographers").

scrutiny. Weighing against this conclusion, though, are the two *Ferber* rationales that are arguably unique to the child pornography context, as discussed above: the "surpassing importance" of protecting children from sexual abuse and the *de minimis* value of child pornography.[151] Accordingly, in any other factual context, the Court might well reject the drying-up-the-market rationale, insisting instead that government must pursue "[t]he normal method of deterring unlawful conduct," which "is to impose an appropriate punishment on the person who engages in it."[152]

The Third Circuit expressed even more skepticism about the government's drying-up-the-market rationale as a potential justification for outlawing dogfighting videos, in contrast to crush videos. Specifically, the Third Circuit questioned the government's potential ability to produce empirical evidence that would demonstrate even the effectiveness, let alone the necessity, of outlawing dogfighting videos as a means of deterring dogfighting, for several reasons. First, the Third Circuit cited evidence that most dogfights take place before live audiences, attracting substantial numbers of spectators who pay admission fees and generate gambling revenues. In short, the evidence indicates that producing videos is not the primary economic motive for the underlying animal cruelty.[153] Notably, the Humane Society of the United States, a supporter of Section 48, attested to these facts.[154] Second, in contrast to crush videos, animal-fighting videos apparently do not routinely obscure the identity of human participants, as indicated by the videos in the *Stevens* case itself. The Third Circuit pointed out that these videos made no attempt to conceal any of the faces of the people depicted, and they also provided the names and addresses of some participants, as well as the locations of the depicted activities.[155] A survey of the success rates of prosecutions under laws criminalizing dogfighting and other

---

[151] Ferber, 458 U.S. at 757, 759.

[152] Bartnicki v. Vopper, 532 U.S. 514, 529 (2001).

[153] Stevens, 533 F.3d at 230; accord People v. Bergen, 883 P.2d 532, 545 (Colo. Ct. App. 1994) ("[W]ithout the knowing presence of spectators, much of the 'sport' of the fights would be eliminated.").

[154] The Humane Society of the United States, Dogfighting Fact Sheet, available at http://www.hsus.org/hsus_field/animal_fighting_the_final_round/dogfighting_fact_sheet/.

[155] Stevens, 533 F.3d at 234.

kinds of animal fighting concluded that they enjoy a high success rate.[156] Likewise, the director of the Humane Society's campaign against animal fighting pegged the success rate of federal prosecutions of dogfighting at more than 98 percent.[157] The government did not submit any evidence to counter these statistics.

The foregoing points that the Third Circuit cited as weighing against a drying-up-the-market justification for criminalizing dogfighting videos are bolstered by yet another one: that, because dogfighting videos do provide identifying information about the depicted animal abuse, they can be valuable aids for law enforcement officials in prosecuting and deterring those underlying abuses. The aforementioned survey of prosecution success rates for animal fighting cases concluded that "[p]rosecutors seem more willing to go forward when there is videotape evidence, and juries seem more willing to convict in such cases."[158] Consequently, criminalizing these depictions, far from significantly advancing the government's goal of deterring the underlying conduct, could well undermine that important goal.

---

[156] Adam Ezra Schulman, Animal-cruelty videos & free speech: some observations from data, http://www.firstamendmentcenter.org/analysis.aspx?id = 21814 (July 7, 2009) (citing an overall success rate of 90 percent for prosecutions of all types of animal fighting).

[157] See Joe Biddle, Vick Raises Bar on Cruelty, The Tennessean, July 21, 2007. The overall success rate for criminal prosecution nationwide is not a compiled statistic but one can find local prosecution rates from city council and district attorney websites. For example, the New York County District Attorney's Office boasts a conviction rate of "close to 90 percent" since 1980. New York County District Attorney's Office: History, http://manhattanda.org/officeoverview/history.shtml (last visited July 29, 2010). This rate is consistent with information found for New York County on the Bureau of Justice Statistics website, http://bjs.ojp.usdoj.gov/dataonline/Search/Prosecutors/bydiscomp_table.cfm (last visited July 29, 2010). Local prosecution success rates can also be gleaned from data in the National Survey of Prosecutors, 2001. See Carol J. DeFrances, Prosecutors in State Courts, 2001, U.S. Dep't of Justice, Bureau of Justice Statistics, NJC 193441 (2002), available at http://bjs.ojp.usdoj.gov/content/pub/pdf/psc01.pdf. Comparing these separately compiled statistics (with no clear indication of the time periods they each cover) may well be like comparing apples and oranges, but at least they indicate that the government will not be able to demonstrate the necessity of criminalizing depictions of animal cruelty merely by asserting that prosecuting animal cruelty is unusually difficult.

[158] Schulman, *supra* note 156.

V. How Would More Narrowly Drafted Statutes, Focusing Only on Crush and/or Dogfighting Videos, Fare under *Stevens*'s First Amendment Analysis?

Because Section 48's legislative history focused specifically on crush videos, and because the government's defense of Section 48 focused only on crush videos plus dogfighting videos, it is worth considering how the *Stevens* ruling would bear on any new statute that criminalized only depictions of these two specific kinds of criminal activities. Indeed, in the wake of *Stevens*, legislation along these narrower contours has been introduced in Congress.[159] It should also be recalled that crush videos could well be successfully prosecuted without any new statute specifically on point, as constituting constitutionally unprotected obscenity.[160] This part of the article will focus on other potential bases for concluding that the First Amendment would permit criminalizing the production of either crush or dogfighting videos.

After *Stevens*, neither type of video could be categorically excluded from First Amendment protection as independent, stand-alone categories of unprotected speech. That is because of the *Stevens* Court's insistence that it will recognize as categories of unprotected speech only "well-defined and narrowly limited classes of speech," which "[f]rom 1791 to the present" have been understood to be excluded from the First Amendment.[161] As the Court stressed in *Stevens*, no such showing could be made concerning the broadly defined depictions of illegal treatment of animals that Section 48 criminalized,[162] and the same is true for these two particular subsets of such depictions.

Nonetheless, the Court could potentially treat either subset of depictions the way it treated child pornography in *Stevens*: as a specific example of another, more general, historically recognized category of unprotected expression—namely, expression that is an

---

[159] See Animal Torture Prevention Act of 2010, H.R. 5337, 111th Cong., (2d Sess., as introduced May 18, 2010) (amending 18 U.S.C. Section 48); H.R. 5092, 111th Cong., (2d Sess., as introduced Apr. 21, 2010) (amending 18 U.S.C. Section 48) (focusing exclusively on "animal crush videos").

[160] See, e.g., Brief for the United States, *supra* note 25, at 42–43; see also Brief for the Respondent, *supra* note 28, at 50–51.

[161] Stevens, 130 S. Ct. at 1584.

[162] *Id.* at 1586.

integral part of illegal conduct. *Stevens* stressed that child pornography could be subsumed within this general categorical exclusion because it was "integrally related" to the underlying child abuse involved in the production process. Accordingly, proponents of criminalizing crush or dogfighting videos would have to show that these videos are also "integrally related" to the depicted animal abuse. The most persuasive showing would be that the abuse takes place solely—or at least largely—for purposes of generating the videos. In these situations, drying up the market for the depictions would completely, or almost completely, end the underlying abuse. In other words, given the necessary and direct causal connection that would then exist between the conduct and the expression, suppressing the expression would have a directly proportionate suppressive impact on the conduct.[163] One bill that was introduced in Congress after the Supreme Court's *Stevens* decision incorporates this principle. It criminalizes depictions of "extreme animal cruelty" only if the cruel conduct "is committed for the primary purpose of creating the depiction."[164]

Proponents of criminalizing crush videos have maintained that the animal abuse they depict takes place only for purposes of producing and selling videos, and that there is no live audience for these "performances."[165] If the government could support this contention through empirical evidence,[166] that could be enough to encompass crush videos within the historic, traditional First Amendment exception for expression that is an integral aspect of criminal conduct.[167]

---

[163] Adler, *supra* note 99, at 987 (acknowledging, although highly critical of *Ferber*, that punishing the production of child pornography could be justified when it "serve[s] as an inducement to commit" the crime of child abuse, and is "not just the product of a crime of child abuse.").

[164] H.R. 5337, 111th Cong. (2010).

[165] See Brief of Amicus Curiae the Humane Society of the United States in Support of Petitioner at 9, United States v. Stevens, 130 S. Ct. 1577 (2010) (No. 08-769).

[166] See Bartnicki, 532 U.S. at 530–31 (rejecting a drying-up-the-market rationale for punishing expression that resulted from illegal conduct, and stressing that "there is no empirical evidence to support the assumption that the prohibition against" the expression would reduce the illegal conduct).

[167] But see Editorial, Disgusting but Not Illegal, N.Y. Times, Aug. 2, 2010, at A16. (reading *Stevens* as precluding any First Amendment exclusion for crush videos, and as rejecting both the child pornography analogy and the applicability of the obscenity exception to such videos).

In contrast, as discussed above, the evidence that was adduced in the *Stevens* litigation indicates that the parallel contention could probably not be sustained as to dogfighting videos, because dogfights are conducted for reasons other than producing and selling videos.

If either crush videos or dogfighting videos are not treated as falling within a longstanding categorical exception to free speech, then a law that criminalized either one could be upheld only if it satisfied strict scrutiny. Justice Alito's dissenting opinion in *Stevens* concludes that a statute that criminalized only crush videos and depictions of "brutal animal fights" would survive strict scrutiny because "the crimes depicted in these videos cannot be effectively controlled without targeting the videos."[168] For the reasons discussed above, the government could potentially demonstrate that the drying-up-the-market rationale is the least restrictive alternative for deterring the crimes that crush videos depict, but it could probably not do so concerning dogfighting videos. Moreover, as also explained above, the drying-up-the-market rationale might be strictly confined to the "special case" of child pornography,[169] so that deterring any criminal conduct other than sexual abuse of children would continue to depend on prosecuting that conduct, not on prosecuting any resulting expression.

Conclusion

Although the Supreme Court has championed as a First Amendment "bedrock"[170] the principle that government may not regulate expression based on its content, the Court has condoned two major exceptions to that principle: for certain categories of expression that are deemed wholly outside the First Amendment and for any content-based regulation that can survive strict scrutiny. The 1942 case of *Chaplinsky v. New Hampshire* contains broad language suggesting that the Court can relegate new categories of expression to unprotected status based on a subjective balancing test, assessing the costs and benefits of the expression. Before its ruling in *Stevens*, the Court had repeatedly cited that language with apparent approval. The

---

[168] Stevens, 130 S. Ct. at 1601 (Alito, J., dissenting).

[169] *Id.* at 1586.

[170] Texas v. Johnson, 491 U.S. 397, 414 (1989).

1982 case of *New York v. Ferber* suggests that expression may be outlawed when it depicts illegal conduct, even though fundamental First Amendment principles call for punishing the conduct, not the expression. In *Ferber*, though, the Court concluded that there was a sufficiently close nexus between child pornography and the child sexual abuse it portrayed to warrant punishing the expression as a means of deterring the conduct.

Ferber's drying-up-the-market rationale has been regularly cited by proponents of various content-based speech regulations, in support of both kinds of exceptions to the general rule against such regulations. Accordingly, in the *Stevens* litigation, proponents of the challenged ban on certain depictions of illegal treatment of animals relied on this rationale as supporting either a new categorical First Amendment exception or a conclusion that the ban satisfied strict scrutiny. In rejecting these arguments, the Supreme Court took the opportunity to reformulate the key passage in *Chaplinsky* and to recharacterize *Ferber* in ways that should strictly limit both decisions' precedential force for further content-based restrictions. Moreover, using a different approach to the issues than the Supreme Court did, the Third Circuit analyzed the weaknesses of *Ferber*'s drying-up-the-market rationale, making a persuasive case that it should be strictly confined to the specific context of child pornography.

In sum, the *Stevens* litigation generated analysis and holdings that should significantly reinforce the general ban on content-based regulations of expression. This is of course a positive development for defenders of free speech, and it also has positive ramifications for defenders of animal welfare. Culpability and law enforcement resources should not be deflected from those who actually abuse animals to those who merely distribute images of abuse, especially when the images can be employed as valuable aids for identifying and prosecuting the abusers and for mobilizing public support for such prosecutions.

Church and State at the Crossroads:
Christian Legal Society v. Martinez
*Richard A. Epstein**

Introduction

One of the recurrent battlegrounds in American constitutional law concerns the vexed relationship between church and state. At an abstract level, the discussion is often cast as a disagreement between those who wish to retain a strong wall of separation between the two and those who think that some accommodation between them better fits the national landscape. To be sure, this account is somewhat overdrawn. The strictest separationist recognizes that some public services must be supplied to private churches, and the most ardent accommodationist recognizes the need to place some limits on the level of interaction between church and state. The disagreements often come over just how all that is to be achieved. These crosscurrents recently came to a head in the bitterly contested decision of *Christian Legal Society v. Martinez*, issued on the last day of the October 2009 term.[1] The decision illustrates both the built-in tension between the Free Exercise and Establishment clauses and the important role that the doctrine of unconstitutional conditions may play in setting the ground rules for state interaction with religious organizations.

As with many great cases, the facts of *CLS* were stark in their simplicity. The Christian Legal Society applied for the privileges

* Laurence A. Tisch Professor of Law, New York University Law School; Peter and Kirsten Bedford Senior Fellow, Hoover Institution; The James Parker Hall Distinguished Service Professor of Law, University of Chicago. I co-authored an amicus curiae brief for the Cato Institute with Ilya Shapiro and Evan Turgeon. I would like to thank Todd Gaziano and Geoffrey Stone for their detailed comments on an earlier draft of this article.

[1] Christian Legal Soc'y Chapter of the Univ. of Cal., Hastings Coll. of the Law v. Martinez, 561 U.S. ____, 130 S. Ct. 2971 (2010) [hereinafter "CLS"].

that Hastings Law School, a public institution, normally affords to all "Registered Student Organizations," and was turned down because of its unwillingness to admit into its ranks those students who did not share its fundamental commitments, which included a rejection of homosexuality and a strong commitment to sex only within marriage.

CLS held that the Hastings Law School was within its rights to exclude CLS from most of the privileges that it routinely extended to RSOs. Justice Ruth Bader Ginsburg, writing for an uneasy five-member coalition, vindicated Hastings's position, at least for the moment, on the ground that its exclusion of CLS rested on a permissible "all-comers" policy that required all Hastings RSOs to admit all interested students to their ranks, regardless of any clash in belief or worldview. She insisted that its policy could be rationally defended on the ground that it "encourages tolerance, cooperation, and learning among students."[2] She also remanded the case to see if CLS could still pursue its claim that Hastings had used its all-comers policy as a pretext for impermissible viewpoint discrimination.[3] The preservation point will prove knotty on remand, but it will not be examined in any detail here, except to say that no one knows whether an exception to a theory is preserved when the theory itself was never argued.

Justice Ginsburg's majority decision was accompanied by two uneasy concurrences by Justices John Paul Stevens and Anthony Kennedy, who fretted about the possible implications of this decision. Ginsburg's decision also provoked a strong dissent from Justice Samuel Alito, who insisted that the record had already shown that the all-comers policy was, in fact, a sham used to conceal Hastings's animus toward CLS.[4] As so often happens in constitutional law, the level of scrutiny applied to government policies often determines the outcome of the case. Justice Ginsburg ended up where she did because she took a deferential view toward how Hastings ran its law school, on the ground that the case "merely" involved a benefit

---

[2] CLS, 130 S. Ct. at 2990.

[3] "Neither the district court nor the Ninth Circuit addressed an argument that Hastings selectively enforces its all-comers policy, and this Court is not the proper forum to air the issue in the first instance. On remand, the Ninth Circuit may consider CLS's pretext argument if, and to the extent, it is preserved." *Id.* at 2995.

[4] CLS, 130 S. Ct. at 3001.

that the school could, but need not, confer on CLS. Justice Alito ended up on the opposite side because he exercised far higher scrutiny of Hastings's policy. There is no ironclad resolution to the deference/ oversight controversy that works in all cases. But in the instant context, judicial deference had the unfortunate consequence of letting Hastings run roughshod over a weak and defenseless religious organization under its banner of toleration, cooperation, and learning. It was not the Court's finest hour.

To put the case in context, the Hastings chapter of CLS contains fewer than a dozen students whose distinctive religious views were, and are, out of step with the majority of the administration, faculty, and students at Hastings Law School. In early September 2004, CLS applied to become an RSO at Hastings, a California public institution of higher learning that has about 426 students per class. Hastings had long followed a policy that offered recognition and tangible support to all student organizations on a nondiscriminatory basis. These benefits included the use of the Hastings name and logo, the use of its bulletin boards and email systems, funding for activities and travel, and office space on the campus. After a prolonged internal review, however, Hastings refused to certify CLS as an RSO, thereby cutting it off from these benefits, which were routinely afforded to about 60 other RSOs with widely disparate views on legal, political, social, and moral issues.[5] At the time, Hastings based its refusal to register CLS on the ground that key provisions of CLS's charter conflicted with the school's nondiscrimination policy, which bars discrimination on grounds of sexual orientation. CLS requires its members and officers to abide by key tenets of the Christian faith and comport themselves to serve CLS's fundamental mission as

---

[5] Here was a brief rundown from Justice Alito:

> During the 2004–2005 school year, Hastings had more than 60 registered groups, including political groups (*e.g.*, the Hastings Democratic Caucus and the Hastings Republicans), religious groups (*e.g.*, the Hastings Jewish Law Students Association and the Hastings Association of Muslim Law Students), groups that promote social causes (*e.g.*, both pro-choice and pro-life groups), groups organized around racial or ethnic identity (*e.g.*, the Black Law Students Association, the Korean American Law Society, La Raza Law Students Association, and the Middle Eastern Law Students Association), and groups that focus on gender or sexuality (*e.g.*, the Clara Foltz Feminist Association and Students Raising Consciousness at Hastings).

Id. at 3001–02.

followers of Jesus Christ in the law. That commitment, in turn, requires its members and officers to abstain from extramarital sexual relations and bars from membership any person who engages in "unrepentant homosexual conduct."[6] CLS imposes these restrictions only on membership and governance; its meetings have always been open to all members of the Hastings community. By way of offsetting the effects of its decision to exclude CLS from RSO membership, Hastings was prepared to allow CLS to use its facilities for certain meetings, but refused to go any further. In essence, Hastings preferred a policy of discrimination to one of total exclusion. On September 23, 2004, CLS lawyers sent Hastings a letter demanding full recognition. After a tense exchange of letters between the two sides, this lawsuit followed.

At first look, it appears as though the issue raised in *CLS* was whether Hastings's nondiscrimination policy could trump CLS's claim of associational autonomy. It turns out, however, that the exact articulation of the Hastings policy as it applied to CLS was itself a major source of disagreement. Justice Ginsburg, speaking for the majority, held that the case was, by stipulation, to be examined on the assumption that the all-comers policy held sway. Justice Alito's dissent insisted that the nondiscrimination policy, as it related to sexual orientation, governed.

In order to analyze *CLS*, it is necessary to proceed as follows. I first examine which of these two policies controlled Hastings's rejection of CLS. After these procedural wrangles are sorted out, I next analyze the First Amendment claims for freedom of speech and the free exercise of religion under *both* the more focused anti-discrimination policy and the broader all-comers policy. That inquiry proceeds in two stages. Its first part asks how these policies would fare under the First Amendment if the government had *by direct regulation* imposed them on all groups in society. That novel approach, of course, did not happen here, as all the disputed regulations and policies applied only to students who were selected for admission into Hastings Law School. Accordingly, the second portion of that analysis invokes the doctrine of unconstitutional conditions to see

---

[6] *Id.* at 2974.

how that fact changes the overall analysis.[7] Under that doctrine, the government does not have a free hand when it decides to confer licenses, benefits, or privileges on various groups. To be sure, it must be allowed to attach some conditions on its various dispensations of power, given the budget constraints under which all such organizations necessarily labor. But while some conditions are acceptable, others are not. No state, for example, can allow a foreign corporation to do business within its boundaries on condition that it abandons all access to federal courts.[8] A state also may not condition private entry to a public highway on its willingness to waive its First Amendment right to freedom of speech or its Fourth Amendment right to be free from unreasonable searches and seizures.[9] Yet, by the same token, the state can condition private entry on the willingness of drivers to abide by the appropriate traffic rules and to litigate accidents on the highways in state court.[10]

The situation at Hastings is, of course, not exactly on all fours with the highway cases, given that the state must use the school for its own educational purposes. To capture the differences between the highway and the campus, the analysis must further consider the way in which the doctrine of unconstitutional conditions applies to what is commonly termed a "limited public forum," a category into which the Court explicitly placed Hastings.[11] These locations, as their name suggests, lie somewhere between the private and public poles. Finally, I explore some of the ramifications of *CLS* for other recent and ongoing controversies relating to religion, speech, and sex discrimination.

---

[7] For my systematic analysis of the doctrine, see Richard A. Epstein, Bargaining with the State 5 (1993) ("Stated in its canonical form, this doctrine holds that even if a state has absolute discretion to grant or deny any individual a privilege or benefit, it cannot grant the privilege subject to conditions that improperly coerce, pressure, or induce the waiver of that person's constitutional rights.").

[8] Terral v. Burke Constr. Co., 257 U.S. 529, 532 (1922) (noting that a state cannot require a foreign corporation to waive its access to federal courts in diversity cases as a condition for doing business within the state).

[9] See, e.g., Frost & Frost Trucking Co. v. R.R. Comm'n, 271 U.S. 583 (1926). This point is discussed at length in Epstein, *supra* note 7, at 162–70.

[10] Opinion of the Justices, 147 N.E. 681 (Mass. 1925).

[11] See, for the definition, Perry Educ. Ass'n v. Perry Local Educators' Ass'n, 460 U.S. 37, 44–45 (1983) (stating that a limited public forum lies somewhere between a government building dedicated to private purposes only and the public roads).

My conclusions are as follows: First, Justice Ginsburg was wrong to assume that the all-comers policy governed this case by stipulation. Second, she understated the level of protection that intimate private associations, of which CLS is one, receive from direct government regulation. Third, by ignoring the unconstitutional conditions doctrine, she allowed Hastings far too much discretion in how it treated its student organizations. More specifically, she drew all the wrong implications from her correct classification of Hastings as a limited public forum. That classification allows the state to make policy choices, governed by a rational basis standard of review, in running its organizations. But to the extent that its nonessential facilities—such as after-hours use of classrooms—are used by students, its power to exclude or discriminate remains as restricted as it is in any open public forum. Justice Ginsburg wrongly concluded that Hastings should, by its all-comers policy, treat all student groups as de facto common carriers. The correct analysis runs in precisely the opposite direction: Hastings itself functions as a limited common carrier that must admit into its ranks all groups regardless of their substantive positions. The net effect of these mistakes is to legitimate intolerance against small and isolated religious groups—an error that has had, and will continue to have, negative consequences on key issues dealing with the treatment of speech and religion under a wide range of anti-discrimination norms.

I. Finding the Relevant Hastings Policy

Many First Amendment challenges to government policies or rules often turn on a distinction between those policies that single out or target certain religious or speech practices for special sanction, and those that apply a general and neutral condition to those same practices. The rationale behind that distinction is clear enough.[12] Those policies that single out certain parties for their speech or religious activities carry within them greater peril to their interests in individual and institutional autonomy. The application of general policies poses less of a threat in that regard, at least in theory, because the only way that the state can attack the religious or speech activities

---

[12] See generally Geoffrey R. Stone, Content-Neutral Restrictions, 54 U. Chi. L. Rev. 46 (1987); Geoffrey R. Stone, Content Regulation and the First Amendment, 25 Wm. & Mary L. Rev. 189 (1983).

of one group is to impose similar limitations on all others. The group whose freedom of speech or religion may well be impaired thus has natural allies whose influence on the political process can easily counteract the political or legal isolation of the religious group in question. No one, in principle, could ever deny that a general nondiscrimination norm is an important form of protection for what are commonly called "discrete and insular minorities."[13]

It is, therefore, of some importance that the initial dispute in *CLS* depended on the articulation of the policy that applied to the case. The district court affirmed Hastings's decision to limit CLS's access to the law school's facilities under the nondiscrimination policy, which reads in full as follows:

> [Hastings] is committed to a policy against legally impermissible, arbitrary or unreasonable discriminatory practices. All groups, including administration, faculty, student governments, [Hastings]-owned student residence facilities and programs sponsored by [Hastings], are governed by this policy of nondiscrimination. [Hastings's] policy on nondiscrimination is to comply fully with applicable law.
>
> [Hastings] shall not discriminate unlawfully on the basis of race, color, religion, national origin, ancestry, disability, age, sex or sexual orientation. This nondiscrimination policy covers admission, access and treatment in Hastings-sponsored programs and activities.[14]

In the view of the district court, this policy counted as both "neutral" and "reasonable" because it "requires that student groups be open to all interested students, without discrimination on the basis of any protected status."[15] That argument did not deny that the policy applied to religious organizations. Rather, it held that this generalized prohibition was insulated from a First Amendment challenge that treated the policy as a burden on an "expressive association," that is, one devoted to the advance of certain personal and moral beliefs, in contradistinction to business or commercial ends. In effect, its position was that the general nondiscrimination policy

---

[13] See United States v. Carolene Prods. Co., 304 U.S. 144, 153 n.4 (1938).

[14] CLS, 130 S. Ct. at 2979.

[15] Christian Legal Soc'y v. Kane, 2006 U.S. Dist. LEXIS 27347 at *45 (N.D. Cal. 2006).

should be regarded as neutral and reasonable because it was not directed solely toward religious groups. Every student organization at Hastings had to meet these conditions in order to gain access to the listed facilities and treatment. At this point, it looks as if the question is whether, under the First Amendment, disparate *treatment* of religious groups is required or whether it suffices that the disparate *impact* of the rule hits religious groups far harder than anyone else.

On the record, moreover, there is little doubt that this nondiscrimination policy governed the negotiations between Hastings and CLS from September 2004 to May 2005, when all its applications to stage events and use facilities were either ignored or rejected by the Hastings administration.[16] The definition of neutrality during these tense discussions was that the anti-discrimination norm that applied to CLS was that which applied to all other organizations. Under that policy, Hastings admitted that its nondiscrimination policy "permits political, social, and cultural student organizations to select officers and members who are dedicated to a particular set of ideals or beliefs."[17]

Up to this point, there is no mention of a different general policy, the more inclusive all-comers rule. The first mention of this policy was in the deposition of Mary Kay Kane, then the Hastings dean, who stated: "It is my view that in order to be a registered student organization you have to allow all of our students to be members and full participants if they want to."[18] There was, of course, no all-comers policy on the books comparable to that of the nondiscrimination policy. None had been debated, discussed, or approved by the faculty.

The new all-comers policy was first advanced as an extemporized gloss on the official nondiscrimination policy, from which, as Justice Alito points out, it plainly differed. The nondiscrimination policy identifies, in the fashion of the Civil Rights Acts, an explicit set of grounds on which it is forbidden to discriminate. The all-comers policy requires all individuals to be admitted into all groups. Any

---

[16] See CLS, 130 S. Ct. at 3002 (noting that Hastings's director of student services, Judy Hansen Chapman, relied on that policy in correspondence with CLS).

[17] *Id.* at 3003.

[18] *Id.*

grounds for discrimination, not just those listed in the nondiscrimination policy, are off-limits. The effect of this policy is to treat all voluntary organizations under the Hastings umbrella as common carriers, required to take all traffic on equal terms.[19] Indeed, as drafted, the duty to serve is still broader than that because it does not make way even for the traditional "for cause" reasons that allow common carriers to refuse service: the unwillingness of customers to follow the rules of the organization, to pay dues, or to behave in an orderly manner. In addition, the nondiscrimination policy is capable of universal application within Hastings, which is why it covers both admissions and hiring, for all its actions can refuse to take into account certain student traits. But the all-comers policy plainly cannot be universal: even if it is possible (although unwise) to admit all registered students into all Hastings RSOs, it is just not possible to hire all applicants to the faculty or to admit all applicants into the student body under that kind of rule. The only context in which that rule can work at all is *after* the hiring or admissions process is over, so that the privileges are extended only to the limited group of individuals that have been chosen under an overtly exclusionary regime.

The all-comers policy is not mentioned once in the long district court opinion, which stressed only the generality of the nondiscrimination policy that it upheld. The all-comers policy makes its official debut in a cryptic Ninth Circuit decision affirming the result below, which in its entirety reads:

> The parties stipulate that Hastings imposes an open membership rule on all student groups—all groups must accept all comers as voting members even if those individuals disagree with the mission of the group. The conditions on recognition are therefore viewpoint neutral and reasonable.[20]

---

[19] For an early discussion of common carrier obligations, see H. W. Chaplin, Limitations upon the Right of Withdrawal from Public Employment, 16 Harv. L. Rev. 555, 556–57 (1903).

[20] 319 Fed. Appx. 645, 646 (9th Cir. 2009). The opinion cited Truth v. Kent Sch. Dist., 542 F.3d 634, 649–50 (9th Cir. 2008), which dealt only with the refusal to certify a high school Christian organization under the school's nondiscrimination policy. No all-comers policy was mentioned in that case.

The key stipulation that was mentioned in the Ninth Circuit opinion reads as follows:

> Hastings requires that registered student organizations allow *any* student to participate, become a member, or seek leadership positions in the organization, regardless of [her] status or beliefs. Thus, for example, the Hastings Democratic Caucus cannot bar students holding Republican political beliefs from becoming members or seeking leadership positions in the organization.[21]

Justice Ginsburg held that that stipulation necessarily insulated the underlying factual record from playing any role in the case.[22] Consistent with her aggressive policy of procedural preclusions, she did not discuss these principles, even though the Hastings officials that handled the matter acted under the written nondiscrimination policy. In her view, the word "any" (which she duly italicized) limited the scope of the litigation so that the written nondiscrimination policy no longer mattered. The greater scope of the reformulated rule could only strengthen the generality and neutrality of the rule, which in turn increases its ability to survive a constitutional attack relating either to speech or to free exercise.

The impressive weight that Justice Ginsburg attaches to the stipulation is questionable in light of the surrounding circumstances. The stipulation is written in the timeless present tense; the key verb is "requires." That stipulation did not, in so many words, say that Hastings "required"—past tense—all organizations to follow the all-comers policy at the time the critical decisions were made about CLS, before the all-comers policy had been formulated. Nor does the stipulation say that the actual decision in this case had been made pursuant to this all-comers policy, when clearly that was not possible. In addition, the statement does not take into account the wrinkle that this policy did not quite mean what it said. At the Supreme Court level, the implicit for-cause limitations available to common carriers to refuse service were built back into the record (saying that the policy "does not foreclose neutral and generally applicable membership requirements unrelated to 'status or

---

[21] CLS, 130 S. Ct. at 2982 (emphasis in original).
[22] *Id.* at 2982–84.

beliefs'"),[23] presumably to take into account the usual grounds that allow common carriers to refuse service. Finally, the stipulation clashes with the position that Hastings took in the answer to the complaint, by insisting that Hastings had no all-comers policy in place, but rather permitted "political, social, and cultural student organizations to select officers and members who are dedicated to a particular set of ideals or beliefs."[24] On issues of this importance, it seems most unwise to truncate the substantive examination by a stipulation that could be read more narrowly in ways that are more consistent with the record. Both versions of the policy raise real questions of principle, and it is to those issues that I now turn.

II. Government Regulation of Associational Freedom

One fundamental distinction that runs through all areas of constitutional law concerns the government's role as regulator on the one hand and manager on the other. Traditionally, most constitutional doctrine asks what restrictions the government-as-regulator can impose on the private conduct of individuals undertaken on their own property and with their own resources when engaged in certain forms of protected conduct—in this instance, involving a cross between speech and religion. The level of protection that these activities receive against government intrusion is normally quite high in these two contexts because the Supreme Court prizes the interests in question.

That basic attitude does not, of course, translate into an absolutist position, even in pure regulation cases. The laws against incitement to riot, fraud, defamation, industrial espionage, and conspiracy to kill people or fix prices remain in place, as does the law that prohibits human sacrifice and pollution in the name of religious liberty. This article is no place to examine each of these areas in detail, but it is important to note one key thread in the analysis. This emphasis on force, fraud, and monopoly lines up well with the standard classical liberal justifications for overriding private choice. As such, the model of limited government prevails, which puts the jurisprudence on the First Amendment in obvious tension with the judicial attitudes that are taken toward the protections of property and contract, for

[23] *Id.* at 2980 n.2.
[24] *Id.* at 3003.

which the Supreme Court offers far more limited protection from direct government regulation.

The point where the small-government approach to freedom of speech and religion receives perhaps its greatest pressure is with freedom of association. As an initial matter, associational freedom has received strong protection in a wide variety of contexts. The famous decision in *NAACP v. Alabama* allowed the NAACP to keep its membership records from the prying eyes of Alabama's attorney general.[25] In a similar fashion, it is clearly beyond argument that the free exercise of religion allows people not only to think and pray as they choose but also to associate through churches and other organizations in pursuit of their common ends. In recent times, one great counterweight to these associational freedoms has been the ever more popular anti-discrimination laws dealing with race, sex, age, disability, and, of course, sexual orientation. There is no question that common carriers were long subject to take-all-comers rules that prohibited them from engaging in certain forms of invidious discrimination in dealing with their customers. Yet, by the same token, the common-law rule always allowed those firms that did not have common carrier status, and the monopoly power that went along with it, to choose their trading partners free from these restraints.[26] The same is true of antitrust law, a central tenet of which is that one competitor ordinarily may refuse to deal with another for any reason at all.[27] The only exceptions are the few cases of "essential facilities" that give one competitor a monopoly position vis-à-vis the other.[28] The scope of the all-comers doctrine is, therefore, limited. Freedom of association and contract are the norm for market firms as well as private clubs and churches.

The modern anti-discrimination laws are in many ways patterned on the earlier rules applicable to common carriers. However, their application is not limited to common carriers, but extends to cover all sorts of public accommodations that exercise no hint or whisper

---

[25] NAACP v. Alabama ex rel. Patterson, 357 U.S. 449 (1958).

[26] See, e.g., Allnut v. Inglis, 104 Eng. Rep. 206 (K.B. 1810), which was carried over into American law in Munn v. Illinois, 94 U.S. 113 (1876); see also Duquesne Light Co. v. Barasch, 488 U.S. 299 (1989) (stating the modern synthesis).

[27] Verizon Commc'ns Inc. v. Law Offices of Curtis V. Trinko, LLP, 540 U.S. 398 (2004).

[28] See, e.g., Florida Fuels, Inc. v. Belcher Oil Co., 717 F. Supp. 1528 (S.D. Fla. 1989) (giving a narrow reading of the doctrine).

of monopoly power.[29] These rules necessarily interfere with the rights of freedom of association because they truncate the right *not* to associate, which Justice Ginsburg, in line with conventional theory, recognizes as part of the basic right.[30] In dealing with the clash between these associational rights and the general anti-discrimination law, Justice Ginsburg notes the level of "close scrutiny" that is applied to these regulations.[31] In dealing with these points, she cites two cases to which she gives but passing attention: *Roberts v. United States Jaycees*[32] and *Boy Scouts of America v. Dale*.[33] She then quickly sidesteps their implications by noting that both are cases where the states applied an anti-discrimination law "that *compelled* a group to include unwanted members, with no choice to opt out."[34]

For the moment, it is best to treat *Roberts* and *Dale* on their own terms to see how anti-discrimination laws in general fare against challenges based on freedom of association. Once that is done, we can turn to the distinction between compulsion and benefits that drives her opinion. In dealing with the regulation of private organizations, the Court has stuck with the three-part classification that it announced in *Roberts*: economic associations, expressive associations, and intimate associations. For economic activities, the modern synthesis recognizes, without question, the dominance of the antidiscrimination laws over any claim of freedom of association. That position is inconsistent with the classical liberal view, which treats the principle of freedom of association (subject to the limitations already noted) as paramount in all areas of life. Put otherwise, any anti-discrimination law that undermines the preservation of a competitive economic system falls outside the scope of the state's traditional police powers.[35]

For these purposes, however, this claim has been put to rest, but in ways that leave untouched the analysis of the two forms of

---

[29] See, e.g., the broad definition of a public accommodation in New Jersey's Law Against Discrimination, N.J. Stat. Ann. § 10:5–4 (2010).

[30] CLS, 130 S. Ct. at 2984–85.

[31] *Id*. at 2985.

[32] Roberts v. United States Jaycees, 468 U.S. 609 (1984).

[33] Boy Scouts of Am. v. Dale, 530 U.S. 640 (2000).

[34] CLS, 130 S. Ct. at 2975.

[35] See Richard A. Epstein, Forbidden Grounds: The Case against Employment Discrimination Laws 98–108 (1992).

117

associational freedoms outside the economic arena—globally expressive, and deeply intimate. *Roberts* gives the highest value to the intensely personal arrangements involved with CLS, matters that go to the core of individual identity. Justice Brennan's decision intimates quite clearly that the anti-discrimination law could *not* apply to those situations because "the Court has concluded that choices to enter into and maintain certain intimate human relationships must be secured against undue intrusion by the State because of the role of such relationships in safeguarding the individual freedom that is central to our constitutional scheme."[36] The question that matters is where to draw the line. Justice Brennan had no hesitation about putting family relationships on the intimate side of the line and those of large commercial enterprises on the other. But he also had little hesitation in allowing Minnesota's public accommodation law[37] to apply to the Jaycees, a broad-based service organization that does not exhibit the social cohesion and moral commitment to its mission that define groups like CLS.[38] Yet he said nothing about the large terrain that exists between the Jaycees and the family unit, leaving that issue for another day.

A classical liberal theory of freedom of association does not have to decide which type of associations matter or why. It is enough that all of these associations generate gains from cooperation for their members—gains that, outside the common carrier setting, are likely to be systematically larger than losses to excluded parties who are able to form or join other organizations on grounds of mutual consent. But the modern tripartite synthesis requires some theory to delineate between noncommercial operations like the Jaycees and intimate operations by the family, and to make that line clear enough to sort out the interim cases. Justice Brennan sought to supply this theory by noting that subjective values count for much more in intimate settings than in larger, all-purpose organizations lacking such focused beliefs.

The question of whether to draw the line was still unanswered. When it came up to the Supreme Court in *Dale*, the side of protected,

---

[36] Roberts, 468 U.S. at 617–18.

[37] Minn. Stat. §§ 363.01 et seq. (1982).

[38] Roberts, 468 U.S. at 621–23.

"intimate" organizations was drawn more broadly than Justice Brennan was likely to accept. The precise question in the case was this: do the Boy Scouts, who have certain definite moral principles that they impose on their broad membership, merit protection as an intimate, expressive organization that falls on the other side of the line from *Roberts*?[39] The line-drawing problem does not have an easy solution. The New Jersey Supreme Court had rejected the Boy Scouts' claim of intimate association because its "large size, nonselectivity, inclusive rather than exclusive purpose, and practice of inviting or allowing nonmembers to attend meetings, establish that the organization is not 'sufficiently personal or private to warrant constitutional protection' under the freedom of intimate association."[40] The New Jersey Supreme Court also held that "the reinstatement of *Dale* does not compel the Boy Scouts to express any message."[41]

The first claim is plausible; the second is wishful thinking. In the Establishment Clause area, the Supreme Court—especially its liberal members—has been quick to find that any involvement of the state in the activities of religious organizations counts as an endorsement of their views.[42] In this context, it is not just a matter of false appearances. It is an explicit requirement of forced membership by openly gay individuals in key positions within the Boy Scouts. Of course, that appearance conveys the message that the Boy Scouts approve of homosexual conduct, when they do not. What an organization says depends on the people to whom it chooses to say it. So a deeply divided Supreme Court, through Chief Justice William Rehnquist, took the Boy Scouts at their word and allowed them to resist the application of New Jersey's Law Against Discrimination, a result with which I agree.[43] The Court emphatically and repeatedly stated

[39] Dale, 530 U.S. at 649–50 (listing Boy Scout principles).

[40] Dale v. Boy Scouts of America, 734 A.2d 1196, 1221 (N.J. 1999) (quoted in Dale, 530 U.S. at 646).

[41] Dale, 734 A.2d at 1229 (quoted in Dale, 530 U.S. at 647).

[42] See, e.g., Grand Rapids Sch. Dist. v. Ball, 473 U.S. 373 (1985); Aguilar v. Felton, 473 U.S. 402 (1985).

[43] Richard A. Epstein, The Constitutional Perils of Moderation: The Case of the Boy Scouts, 74 So. Cal. L. Rev. 119 (2000). The case has been heavily commented on. See, e.g., Louis Michael Seidman, The *Dale* Problem: Property and Speech under the Regulatory State, 75 U. Chi. L. Rev. 1541 (2008) (noting how difficult it is to have strong speech rights with weak property rights); Andrew Koppelman, Signs of the Times: *Dale v. Boy Scouts of America* and the Changing Meaning of Nondiscrimination, 23 Cardozo L. Rev. 1819 (2002) (decrying expansive reach of *Dale*'s view of expressive

that the evaluation of the group's goals and purposes necessarily resided with the group itself, and it refused to reject that position, pointing to the internal divisions within the group's ranks that led, from time to time, to deviations in practice from its core principles.[44] More concretely, the Court treated the Boy Scouts' mission statement as unassailable proof of its core beliefs.[45] Nor was the Boy Scouts' right of intimate association lost because the Boy Scouts had declined to include any explicit references to its opposition to homosexual activity in its handbook.

Judged by this metric, *CLS* is a far easier case for freedom of association than was *Dale*. The CLS chapter at Hastings is small and cohesive. It has no ambiguity about its meaning or purposes. It is a charter member of the class of intimate associations that every justice who participated in the *Roberts* decision placed beyond the pale of the anti-discrimination laws. In the context of direct regulation, at least, CLS enjoys strong protection of its associational, speech, and religious interests as intimate expression associations.

The next question, then, is what kinds of restrictions might pass muster? The obvious case is any effort to single out religious beliefs for extra scrutiny. But I have no doubt that if the government imposed an all-comers statute on all organizations, it would be struck down. The only question is how. The enormity of the rule would leave every organization in the United States in an untenable position because it could not take refuge behind an admission-and-hiring system that independently limits the scope of that all-comers obligation. Businesses would have to hire without limit, or take people on a first-come, first-served basis. All sorts of voluntary associations would find themselves stuffed to the gills. The rate-making implementation of this mad proposal alone would be sufficient to doom it to perdition. Does any court want to decide the rates at which unwelcome applicants can join the organizations whose members don't want them? This system works with common carriers because of their monopoly position, their clear capacity restraints, their ability to set rates, and the simple fact that passengers are, generally,

---

associations; David E. Bernstein, Antidiscrimination Laws and the First Amendment, 66 Mo. L. Rev. 83 (2001) (noting how religious schools could use free speech guarantees to defeat employment discrimination laws).

[44] Dale, 530 U.S. at 648–49.

[45] *Id.* at 649.

pretty fungible. Queuing is tolerable for all sorts of common carriers, at least when price can shorten the queue to match capacity. No one hires employees or forms partnerships this way. Quite literally, this unheard-of rule could never pass in a legislature because it would produce no net winners.

But do this mental experiment: suppose that some adventurous legislature passed a universal all-comers statute for all firms. Manifestly, the courts would strike it down *in toto*, which in turn would allow all religious organizations to tuck themselves into the lee of all the business organizations that would lead the general charge against this rule. But what happens next with a rule that knocks out some selective grounds for refusing to associate, as is done with the civil rights laws? There is no question that this type of regime is far more sustainable because it negates only a few possible reasons for not hiring without creating a free-for-all. But the question of which grounds are appropriate for which organizations is troublesome. That said, no court in the land would say to a church or other religious organization, "You may keep out rich people or poor, but you cannot keep out those people who detest your faith and are determined to overthrow it." The organization is allowed to have its viewpoint determine its membership under the *Roberts* formulation. An organization can discriminate on the basis of status, on the basis of belief, on the basis of neither, or on the basis of both. But this is a case where the anti-discrimination norm comes out second best.

III. From Coercion Imposed to Benefit Denied

A. The Right/Privilege Distinction

We thus come up with the situation where a religious organization is protected against compelled membership that might be ordered under either the all-comers policy or the selective admission standard. The critical transitional question is what happens when we move from the government-as-regulator to the government-as-owner of certain forms of property? It is a fair reading of Justice Ginsburg's opinion in *CLS* that the sole ground that distinguishes *Dale* turns on the mode of state involvement. In a critical passage, she notes that Hastings does not impose any positive restrictions on what CLS can do off campus with its own resources, but only indicates that it has to accept reasonable conditions in order to be eligible for the benefits that Hastings metes out to the various registered student organizations. In essence, the denial of the privilege should not be regarded as compulsion, so that the special protection for intimate associations recognized in *Roberts* and *Dale* is simply beside the point under this mocked up version of the long-discredited right/privilege distinction. In *Commonwealth v. Davis*, then-Massachusetts Supreme Court Justice Oliver Wendell Holmes put the issue as follows:

> For the legislature absolutely or conditionally to forbid public speaking in a highway or public park is no more an infringement of the rights of a member of the public than for the owner of a private house to forbid it in his house. When no proprietary right interferes, the legislature may end the right of the public to enter upon the public place by putting an end to the dedication to public uses.[46]

When the case got to the U.S. Supreme Court, Justice Edward White gave it a slightly different version that put the distinction in terms of the greater/lesser power: "The right to absolutely exclude all right to use, necessarily includes the authority to determine under what circumstances such use may be availed of, as the greater power contains the lesser."[47] This version of the doctrine did not survive. Indeed, in 1939, that view was decisively repudiated in *Hague v. CIO*, which held that the government ownership of the streets did not preclude their use as a public forum.[48] That theme was endorsed in the academic literature as well. For example, whatever was left of the older right/privilege distinction was the object of a well-known 1968 attack by William Van Alstyne, who observed that "[i]f this view were uniformly applied, the devastating effect it would have on any constitutional claims within the public sector can be readily perceived."[49]

---

[46] Commonwealth v. Davis, 39 N.E. 113, 113 (1895).

[47] Davis v. Massachusetts, 167 U.S. 43, 48 (1897).

[48] Hague v. CIO, 307 U.S. 496, 515 (1939) ("Wherever the title of streets and parks may rest, they have immemorially been held in trust for the use of the public and, time out of mind, have been used for purposes of assembly, communicating thoughts between citizens, and discussing public questions. Such use of the streets and public places has, from ancient times, been a part of the privileges, immunities, rights, and liberties of citizens.").

[49] William Van Alstyne, The Demise of the Right-Privilege Distinction in Constitutional Law, 81 Harv. L. Rev. 1439, 1441 (1968).

Ironically, in *CLS*, Justice Ginsburg writes as if none of these developments had taken place when she holds that CLS has no constitutional claims against Hastings, a public institution, when it merely refuses to supply this packet of benefits to CLS. Thus, suppose in this case that Hastings Law School did not admit any students into its entering class who refused to accept all the tenets of the school's nondiscrimination policy, or to sign on to an oath to that effect. Does anyone think that this refusal to admit members of CLS into the law school would be acceptable?

B. Open Public Forums

So the next question asks how the unmentioned doctrine of unconstitutional conditions ties into the decision of Hastings to deny CLS most of the benefits routinely conferred on other RSOs. In order to answer that question, Justice Ginsburg quickly motored past *Roberts* to evaluate the CLS claim in connection with the doctrine of a limited public forum that lies, as noted earlier, midway between the public square and the use of Hastings facilities for its core missions of teaching and research. It is here that Justice Ginsburg's argument falls apart, whether we consider the case under the rubric of either the nondiscrimination policy or the all-comers approach.

To see why, start with actions on the public square. The state must be able to stop some speech in some cases, but it could not restrict access to public forums on either of the two policies in play in *CLS*. To do so on the strength of the nondiscrimination policy would count as a form of viewpoint discrimination that prefers groups with some positions over groups that hold other positions. Instead, these highway cases adopt an all-comers policy, which, in this instance, imposes a duty to take all comers subject to time, place, and manner that are neutral in both form and effect. One position that is manifestly precluded by this approach is the insistence that the users of the public forum adopt take-all-comers policies similar to those that Hastings imposed. Just imagine a similar requirement that all vehicles that use the public highways take all comers, even if they do not choose to act as a common carrier.

This issue made it to the Supreme Court in *Hurley v. Irish-American Gay, Lesbian and Bisexual Group*, which held that the South Boston Allied War Veterans Council did not have to admit into its St. Patrick's Day parade a gay, lesbian, and bisexual (GLIB) group that sought to march as a separate contingent under its own banner as part of the council's larger St. Patrick's Day celebration.[50] The Supreme Court held that the private organization's First Amendment associational and expressive rights trumped a Massachusetts statute that banned discrimination on account of sexual orientation.[51] This issue was somewhat clouded because the Court also held that the anti-discrimination law applied to the extent that it permitted individual members of GLIB to join the float so long as they did not march under their GLIB banner or profess their own views. Still, that concession to the anti-discrimination laws is of no relevance here because it applies only to nonexpressive activities. Indeed, CLS was prepared to go further than this exception required, by its willingness to let any nonmember attend its meetings and say whatever he or she liked. But the essential point remains: state ownership over the roads does not add to the power of Massachusetts to tell the Veterans Council how to select its members and project its own message. Needless to say, the usual time, place, and manner restrictions allow the state to control for nuisance-like behavior, just as it can with activities on private property.[52]

In an open public forum, therefore, the state cannot impose either a nondiscrimination policy or an all-comers policy on private associations for matters that pertain to speech and religion. The state has to act as the common carrier. It cannot force the veterans to project messages with which they disagree. Whatever the rule in pure economic relationships, the principle of freedom of association keeps the state from using its monopoly power over the highway to run roughshod over the Veterans Council. Indeed, it is possible that it could not impose its all-comers policy even in economic affairs. Thus, it is doubtful that even standards of minimal constitutional rationality are met by a rule that requires IBM or any other corporation to hire all job applicants because the company makes use of public roads from which it could, in principle, be excluded. In some instances, the generality of a rule protects it from constitutional invalidation, simply because everyone is made worse off. But in this

---

[50] Hurley v. Irish-American Gay, Lesbian and Bisexual Group, 515 U.S. 557 (1995).

[51] See Mass. Gen. Laws Ann. ch. 272, § 98 (1992).

[52] See, e.g. Ward v. Rock Against Racism, 491 U.S. 781 (1989) (allowing "narrowly tailored" regulations to deal with noise and other time, place, and manner issues).

case, its perverse consequences are manifest whether it applies to one company or a hundred.

It takes little ingenuity to see that these general considerations carry over to religion and speech. No one could be told that he is only allowed to enter the public highways if he will provide transportation to members of rival religious groups on the same terms and conditions that he supplies it to members of his own group. And it would not reduce the sting in the slightest if this requirement were at the same time imposed on bridge club members to the benefit of chess club members. The all-comers policy and the nondiscrimination policy, which do not work as forms of direct regulation, do not work when transformed into conditions for entry onto public roads.

C. Limited Public Forums

The next step in the argument is to determine whether the rules that apply to a open public forum like the roads could carry over to a limited public forum like Hastings Law School. Justice Ginsburg takes the position that it cannot, saying that "this case fits comfortably within the limited-public-forum category, for CLS, in seeking what is effectively a state subsidy, faces only indirect pressure to modify its membership policies; CLS may exclude any person for any reason if it forgoes the benefits of official recognition."[53] Clearly, there are obvious distinctions between open and limited public forums.

Unfortunately, Justice Ginsburg turns the analysis upside down when she seeks to account for that difference. Her key mistake is to argue that the limited nature of the public forum necessarily alters the calculus under both the nondiscrimination policy and the all-comers policy from how it comes out on the public highway. She is right that the change of place matters, but it still must be understood what those differences are. Initially, no one would care to deny that Hastings University need not follow the all-comers policy that it wishes to impose on CLS in deciding which applicants to admit. Nor does it have to take people in on a first-come, first-served basis until its class is filled. Nor is it required to sell places in its class to the highest bidder. The ability for Hastings to function as a

[53] CLS, 130 S. Ct. at 2986.

law school depends, of course, on its power to exclude—and on its power to admit. Even though it is a government agency, it has to receive a fair measure of management discretion to run its essential programs. Justice Stevens sounds the same theme when he writes, "It is critical, in evaluating CLS's challenge to the nondiscrimination policy, to keep in mind that an RSO program is a *limited* forum— the boundaries of which may be *delimited* by the proprietor."[54]

Once Justices Ginsburg and Stevens treat Hastings as a limited public forum, they have two tasks: First, they must identify situations in which Hastings can exercise its ordinary right to exclude like a private owner. Second, they must also identify the public forum aspects of its operations in which it functions like the proprietor of a public forum lacking that right to exclude, because otherwise a limited public forum just becomes a form of government-run private property. On the former point, Hastings clearly does not have complete power to hire faculty and admit students for whatever reason it sees fit. The Equal Protection Clause, for example, prevents the school from refusing to admit students into the law school on the grounds of race or sex. I have no doubt that it would also prevent Hastings from adopting a policy that excluded members of CLS because of their religious beliefs. The clear implication is that some neutral criteria of academic excellence, fitness to study law, and ability to pay tuition are part of that mix.

Justice Ginsburg makes a modest concession to Justice Alito when she concedes that Hastings would be on thin constitutional ice if

> the State of California tried to "demand that all Christian groups admit members who believe that Jesus was merely human." But the CLS chapter that brought this lawsuit does not want to be just a Christian group; it aspires to be a recognized student organization. The Hastings College of Law is not a legislature. And no state actor has demanded that anyone do anything outside the confines of a discrete, voluntary academic program.[55]

There is a certain irony in drawing a distinction between a legislature and a school, for that distinction could have been used in *United*

---

[54] *Id.* at 2997 (emphasis in original).

[55] *Id.* (internal citation omitted).

States v. Virginia to spare the Virginia Military Institute from an order to admit women, which Justice Ginsburg imposed.[56] The point, of course, is that institutions that manage complex programs need more discretion than legislatures, and that it is somewhat odd to require a school to admit women under the Equal Protection Clause, only to recognize that, once admitted, they must receive, in practice, separate treatment on a wide number of issues. Make no mistake about it, compared to *CLS*, the level of intrusion was far greater in *Virginia*, where Justice Ginsburg required (but did not find) an "exceedingly persuasive justification" for the exclusion of women from VMI.[57] CLS makes, at most, modest demands on Hastings for routine services. At VMI, an educational program had to be revamped from top to bottom. At Hastings, there is merely a need to create a new email portal.

The importance of getting the boundaries right is clear. Initially, CLS cannot demand that Hastings construct its academic program in line with its own beliefs. But in this case, none of its demands concern anything other than how the various facilities of Hastings should be allocated when they are not dedicated to the school's educational mission. This problem comes all the time in connection with high schools and universities where the rule is that religious groups cannot be excluded from the use of facilities outside the regular academic program so long as other groups within the institution are allowed to use the facilities.[58]

Here are some of the relevant precedents:

In *Rosenberger v. Rector and Visitors of the University of Virginia*, the University of Virginia was not obligated to fund any student publications.[59] But it could not refuse to cover the printing costs of an explicitly Christian publication if it were prepared to fund printing costs for other campus publications dealing with similar religious and social issues. To the extent that the university was not engaged in its distinctive academic mission, it had to treat all groups in the same fashion, without discrimination.

[56] United States v. Virginia, 518 U.S. 515 (1996).

[57] *Id.* at 524.

[58] DiLoreto v. Downey Unified Sch. Dist. Bd. of Educ., 196 F.3d 958, 965 (9th Cir. 1999) ("The government may limit expressive activity in nonpublic fora if the limitation is reasonable and not based on the speaker's viewpoint.").

[59] Rosenberger v. Rector & Visitors of the Univ. of Va., 515 U.S. 819 (1995).

Similarly, in *Widmar v. Vincent*, the Court overturned a decision of the University of Missouri at Kansas City to deny religious groups access to its facilities after hours when it held those same facilities open to nonreligious groups.[60] There seems to be no meaningful distinction between the cases. Interestingly enough, the Court rejected the view that this restriction was needed to promote a greater separation of church and state. As a common carrier, it had to be impartial with respect to the ends of its constituent organizations, and thus was under a duty not to "inhibit" the advancement of religion.[61] There is no reason to think that the adoption of any self-serving nondiscrimination policy would have altered the outcome.

Finally, in *Lamb's Chapel v. Center Moriches Union Free School District*, the same basic principles prevented the Central Moriches school district from refusing to let Lamb's Chapel use its facilities after hours to run a religiously oriented film series that stressed the importance of family values.[62] As a limited public forum, the district did not need to allow any group to use its facilities after hours. But once the district opened its doors to some outside organizations, it could not discriminate against others. Thus, the Court held, first, that the equal access policy to this limited public forum did not create an establishment of religion and, second, that the district's rules impermissibly authorized viewpoint discrimination that cut against Lamb's Chapel. The articulation of formal regulations here did not save the policy.

As these cases indicate, Hastings is properly treated as a limited public forum to which common carrier obligations *do* attach so long as it is *not* engaged in its essential academic mission. Put otherwise, the classrooms and the bulletin boards, when used after hours, function as a public square limited to all Hastings students. These internal public features of Hastings Law School are like the public roads in *Hurley* or the public classrooms in *Lamb's Chapel*. Thus, if other student groups could use, for a fixed fee, the Hastings auditorium to run a meeting on a Sunday afternoon, so too could CLS, even though outsiders to the Hastings community could be excluded. Hastings is the common carrier that has to take all comers, not CLS.

---

[60] Widmar v. Vincent, 454 U.S. 263 (1981) (cited in Rosenberger, 515 U.S. at 834–35).

[61] See, e.g., Lemon v. Kurtzman, 403 U.S. 602, 612–13 (1971).

[62] Lamb's Chapel v. Ctr. Moriches Union Free Sch. Dist., 508 U.S. 384 (1993).

It is not availing in this context, moreover, to change the example by stating that parity is restored if the auditorium is open only to those student groups that satisfy an all-comers policy, which CLS does not. At this point, the question should be whether there is any reasonable basis to exclude those groups that fail to sign the all-comers policy, which has only been used against common carriers and never against ordinary associational groups. Hastings bears at least some burden to explain why it adopts, in such a haphazard manner, a policy that is never used anywhere else. If it states that the reason is to prevent organizations like CLS from using facilities because they discriminate on grounds of sexual orientation, the all-comers policy becomes a pretext for a much more focused discriminatory activity that runs headlong into the conventional First Amendment prohibition against viewpoint discrimination in the distribution of university funds.[63] But if it denies that explanation, what other reason does it have for imposing this restriction, knowing that it has a disparate impact on isolated groups like CLS?

There is, of course, a tradition that indicates that neutral rules that limit speech are valid so long as they do so without regard to the beliefs of that organization. "Incidental"—I hate that word—burdens get little traction in First Amendment cases. In the best-known case of this sort, *United States v. O'Brien*, the Supreme Court held that the United States could punish people for burning draft cards to protest the Vietnam War. Its need to preserve the integrity of the Selective Service System was said to be "unrelated to the suppression of free expression."[64]

O'Brien is an unpersuasive decision for two reasons. First, the burning of the draft card was known by everyone to be symbolic speech of the sort that is strongly protected. Second, the purported state interest in administrative order can be easily satisfied in so many other ways. Burning the card does not remove the registrant from the system. The simple requirement that the protestor keep a copy of the original card should allow for ready identification of the individual if necessary. The powerful expressive element is overwhelmed by the obvious fixes to the administrative problems. The case rationale is flimsy and utterly unworthy of extension. When

---

[63] See, e.g., Rosenberger, 515 U.S. at 819.
[64] United States v. O'Brien, 391 U.S. 367, 377 (1968).

129

the decision came down it was subject to widespread criticism that remains valid today.[65]

Yet, let it be supposed that *O'Brien* is correct. The United States at least offered what the Court regarded as sufficient reasons for imposing criminal sanctions on draft card burners. By parity of reasoning, the United States should have to offer similar justifications to criminalize private religious organizations that meet and pray on private property, or even to impose on them duties not to discriminate, subject to civil sanctions. But it can do neither so long as *Roberts* and *Dale* remain the law. It is, therefore, one thing for the state to refuse to supply benefits to people who burn draft cards, given that their actions are criminal. It is quite another to refuse to supply benefits to CLS, given that its underlying actions receive the highest level of constitutional protection. There is quite simply no parallel between criminal and fully protected conduct. In other words, if the twin rationales of toleration and cooperation cannot justify imposing the nondiscrimination norm on private parties on their own premises, it does not justify imposing that norm when they enter a limited public forum. To do otherwise is to revive the discredited privilege/ right distinction.

There is a second confusion with Justice Ginsburg's argument, when taken on its own terms. Her stated justification for the all-comers policy and the nondiscrimination policy is the desire to advance toleration and cooperation that students will need in some larger environment.[66] But she fundamentally misconstrues the social meaning of both terms. The term "toleration" in religious affairs has a precise meaning: individuals "tolerate" the right of other people to practice a religion with which they profoundly disagree. The historical account here always stressed the position that mutual noninterference is the only way in which people of different faiths can get along. My dictionary puts the point as follows: "Toleration: The recognition of the rights of the individual to his own opinions and customs, as in matters pertaining to religious worship, when they do not interfere with the rights of others or with decency and order."[67]

---

[65] See, e.g. Dean Alfange Jr., Free Speech and Symbolic Conduct: The Draft-Card Burning Case, 1968 Sup. Ct. Rev. 1.

[66] See CLS, 130 S. Ct. at 2990.

[67] Funk & Wagnalls New Int'l Dictionary of the English Language 1320 (1996).

That definition, stressing negative liberties, is consistent with the historical record. In speaking about toleration, John Locke wrote: "It is not the diversity of opinions (which cannot be avoided), but the refusal of toleration to those that are of different opinions (which might have been granted), that has produced all the bustles and wars that have been in the Christian world upon account of religion."[68] Locke's letter was written in 1689, the same year as the passage of the Act of Toleration, whose title was "An Act for Exempting their Majestyes Protestant Subjects dissenting from the Church of England from the Penalties of certaine Lawes."[69] In this instance, toleration was needed to allow Protestants (but not others) to deviate from the Book of Common Prayer, whose dangers of excessive orthodoxy and centralization were neatly summed up by Justice Hugo Black as follows:

> Powerful groups representing some of the varying religious views of the people struggled among themselves to impress their particular views upon the Government and obtain amendments of the Book [of Common Prayer] more suitable to their respective notions of how religious services should be conducted in order that the official religious establishment would advance their particular religious beliefs.[70]

The doctrine of unconstitutional conditions is one safeguard against that risk.

Read in context, therefore, the lesson of toleration at Hastings Law School is best achieved by letting CLS go about its own business. The opponents of CLS need to learn, if they do not already know, that they will not wilt by being present in the same building in which CLS conducts its meetings. Toleration requires adopting a live-and-let-live attitude about those with whom you disagree. It does not require any religious group to suffer a forced surrender of essential group characteristics, by admitting non-believers into its ranks. This purported justification for the rule gets matters exactly backward.

---

[68] Letter from John Locke, A Letter Concerning Toleration (1689), available at http://www.constitution.org/jl/tolerati.htm.

[69] 1 Will. & Mar. c. 18 (1689).

[70] Engel v. Vitale, 370 U.S. 421, 426–27 (1962).

Justice Ginsburg does no better when she defends the Hastings policy for fostering cooperation. Cooperation, for its part, requires only that a group be prepared to work with other groups on common issues. It does not require that any group sacrifice its core identity or admit members of other groups, whose principles it does not accept, into its own ranks. That is, these twin virtues presuppose that organizations are allowed to maintain their separate identities, and then explains how different groups and individuals should think about and interact with others. Forced association in important extracurricular activities done in a limited public forum turns toleration into feigned agreement, and turns cooperation into forced association. Toleration outside the confines of Hastings has never had the connotation that Justice Ginsburg gives it in *CLS*. Her Orwellian abuse of language does not supply the needed justification for Hastings's all-comers policy.

Justice Ginsburg and Justice Stevens also relied on *Employment Division v. Smith* to support the proposition that a neutral rule of general application could not be resisted on free exercise grounds.[71] In their view, *Smith* explained why Hastings could not be required to grant the exemption from the all-comers policy to CLS even if it were allowed to do so.[72] But *Smith* does not so hold. The key holding from Justice Antonin Scalia reads: "We have never held that an individual's religious beliefs excuse him from compliance with an otherwise valid law prohibiting conduct that the State is free to regulate."[73] That last clause is critical because the state is *not* free to regulate the activities of religious groups on private property insofar as they relate to religious beliefs and practices. That observation is consistent with *Smith*'s holding, which allowed for the direct enforcement of a criminal law that forbade all individuals to smoke peyote, against a member of the Native American Church who smoked peyote for ritual purposes. The disparate impact of the law on religious activities was an "incidental" burden that could not defeat the general rule. It therefore followed that if the criminal law were valid, Oregon could deny Smith unemployment benefits for engaging in what was criminal action.

---

[71] Employment Div., Dep't of Human Res. v. Smith, 494 U.S. 872 (1990).

[72] CLS, 130 S. Ct. at 2993, 2997 n.2.

[73] Smith, 494 U.S. at 878–79.

The narrow objection to the use of *Smith* is the same as the objection to the application of *O'Brien*. The doctrine of unconstitutional conditions may not protect people who engage in criminal activity in seeking government benefits. But it does protect those, like CLS, whose conduct has constitutional immunity from suit. If the state cannot punish private meetings of CLS, it cannot withhold benefits from them. The cases are distinguishable.

The second argument goes to the weakness of *Smith* on its own terms. *Smith* has been widely attacked for its rigid approach. Justice Scalia's insistence on neutrality made little sense when a modest accommodation, limited to allowing the use of peyote in these sacramental activities, posed no threat of systematic drug abuse, which is why the statute was never, in practice, criminally enforced. *Smith* also raised enormous hackles from liberals and conservatives alike who could not understand why the Free Exercise and Establishment Clauses should be reduced to a weak form of equal protection pabulum. That sorry episode provoked congressional efforts to undo the statute, first in the form of the Religious Freedom Restoration Act[74]—which was promptly struck down[75]—and then in the Religious Land Use and Institutionalized Persons Act,[76] which has thus far escaped constitutional challenge.

Smith is no decision worthy of emulation and expansion. The brutal truth is that this neutrality rule does a very bad job of reconciling the relevant interests in free exercise cases. The disparate treatment test is manifestly underinclusive of First Amendment concerns in areas that call not for judicial deference, but for strict scrutiny of state actors. There are no intolerable demands on judicial competence, for the application of a disparate impact case in these settings yields a simple and straightforward result. There is no excuse for using the disparate impact test to prop up an all-comers policy that has nothing to condemn outside the area of common carriers.

The case for the all-comers rule is, moreover, not salvaged by the observation from both Justice Ginsburg and Justice Stevens that Hastings is not required to offer a subsidy to groups like CLS. No

---

[74] 42 U.S.C. § 2000bb (2006).

[75] City of Boerne v. Flores, 521 U.S. 507 (1997).

[76] Religious Land Use and Institutionalized Persons Act of 2000, 42 U.S.C. § 2000cc et seq. (2006).

subsidy is said to be a far cry from the use of coercion. But to call the payments and benefits supplied to CLS a "subsidy" ignores the larger context in which Hastings makes these payments. Justice Ginsburg puts the situation this way: "RSOs are eligible to seek financial assistance from the Law School, which subsidizes their events using funds from a mandatory student-activity fee imposed on all students."[77]

This simple sentence explains what is wrong with her argument. This supposed subsidy is not manna from heaven, courtesy of an anonymous Hastings alumnus who is antagonistic to CLS. It is collected by taxes on all students, including members of CLS. To make this an economic subsidy requires proof that it is paid by others to CLS. But viewed in context, the subsidies run the other way. CLS members must put money into a pot from which they are not allowed to withdraw cash. They are systematic net losers from a policy that requires them to subsidize all other groups. Only if we turn a blind eye to the source of the money does the subsidy argument make sense. That is not what First Amendment law is about. In the end, the usual rules for a limited public forum apply: if the state cannot sanction the activity when done privately, it cannot refuse to extend benefits to persons who engage in those activities in a limited public forum.

Conclusion: Where Do We Go from Here?

The *CLS* case is a peculiar amalgam that in some instances follows old precedent, in other instances repudiates precedent, and in other instances goes beyond precedent. The question is, what lies in the future?

At this juncture, the case has two separate strands. The first is case-specific: on remand, can CLS make out that the all-comers policy was an effort to target CLS? The record on this point seems to be clear: There has at no time been a formal all-comers policy. The Hastings administration routinely gave CLS the runaround on dates and places. The policy was adopted by the dean during litigation, but never systematically implemented. The clear inference was

---

[77] CLS, 130 S. Ct. at 2979.

that it was an effort to throw a viewpoint-neutral façade on a viewpoint-biased policy. Unless the notion of pretext is given a narrowness that it has nowhere else in the law, the case should come out in favor of CLS. But, of course, anything is possible, including a hostile decision coupled with a new application in which the policies will be monitored for consistency across other organizations. Whatever the outcome in the case, the causes of toleration and cooperation will not be served.

Second, *CLS* also has real implications for larger social issues, including the constitutional status of gay marriage in connection with Equal Protection Clause challenges. As matters now stand, the Supreme Court in *Lawrence v. Texas* held that the state could not criminalize homosexual sodomy as a form of "deviate sexual intercourse."[78] The majority of the Court did not decide *Lawrence* on equal protection grounds, however; that is, on the ground that the Texas law covered not only homosexual sodomy but also heterosexual sodomy. Instead, it found in an application of substantive due process that all persons had a constitutional liberty interest in sexual relations free from state interference to engage in a "transcendent" personal experience. The opinion thus has serious libertarian overtones because it defines a broad sphere of sexual autonomy into which the state cannot enter. But the next question on the agenda is that if homosexual sodomy cannot be criminalized, why do the liberty interests of gay couples not allow them to marry on the same terms and conditions of heterosexual couples? The Supreme Court has thus far ducked this question—in part because of the furor that it would create however the Court rules—but it will not be able to do so for long.

So let us assume that *Lawrence* states the law of the land. If so, it is hard to think of a solid doctrinal justification that explains why these arrangements cannot be blessed by the state. Once the first step is taken in *Lawrence* on criminalization, it is difficult not to take the second step on same-sex marriage. After all, the state has a monopoly on the ability to issue licenses and should not be able to use that to benefit one group of persons at the expense of others. Churches and other organizations should not, on this view, be forced to accept gay couples in their ranks, or for that matter straight

---

[78] Lawrence v. Texas, 539 U.S. 558 (2003).

couples, if they so choose. The doctrine of unconstitutional conditions rightly applies, carrying *Lawrence* to the next step.

Or does it, after *CLS*? At this point, the grand question is whether the right/privilege distinction in *CLS* will have some renaissance. That rebirth is surely not evidenced in the two recent decisions in Massachusetts, *Gill v. Office of Personnel Management*[79] and *Massachusetts v. HHS*,[80] in which Judge Joseph Tauro struck down key provisions of the Defense of Marriage Act, which had, for the purposes of federal benefit programs, defined marriage as a union between one man and one woman.[81] His two decisions blew by, at breakneck speed, the right/privilege distinction with the categorical judgment that all rationales in favor of the traditional definition of marriage lacked even the most minimal level of rationality[82] to fend off any sort of an equal protection challenge under either the Fourteenth Amendment or the Fifth Amendment, which has long read equal protection into due process.[83] Not to be outdone, Judge Vaughn Walker, in *Perry v. Schwarzenegger*, recently struck down California's gay-marriage ban (Proposition 8) on the grounds that its definition of marriage as between one man and one woman could not be

---

[79] Gill v. Office of Pers. Mgmt., 2010 U.S. Dist. LEXIS 67874 (D. Mass. 2010).

[80] Massachusetts v. United States Dep't of Health and Human Serv., 698 F. Supp. 2d 234 (D. Mass. 2010). For sheer intellectual chutzpah, this Tenth Amendment argument takes the cake. First, it is held that the Equal Protection Clause requires that the states admit same-sex married couples. Clearly, Congress could enforce that command if it were valid under Section 5 of the Fourteenth Amendment. Nonetheless, these rights are reserved to the states, none of which, after *Gill*, may choose to keep to the traditional definitions of marriage.

[81] Defense of Marriage Act, § 1 U.S.C. § 7 (2006) reads:

In determining the meaning of any Act of Congress, or of any ruling, regulation, or interpretation of the various administrative bureaus and agencies of the United States, the word "marriage" means only a legal union between one man and one woman as husband and wife, and the word "spouse" refers only to a person of the opposite sex who is a husband or a wife.

[82] "This court need not address these arguments [for heightened scrutiny based on abridgment of fundamental rights and suspect classes], however, because DOMA fails to pass constitutional muster even under the highly deferential rational basis test. As set forth in detail below, this court is convinced that 'there exists no fairly conceivable set of facts that could ground a rational relationship' between DOMA and a legitimate government objective. DOMA, therefore, violates core constitutional principles of equal protection." Gill, 699 F. Supp. 2d 374 at 387 (internal citation omitted). The categories, at this point, are completely malleable.

[83] See, e.g., Bolling v. Sharpe, 347 U.S. 497, 499 (1954).

defended on any rational grounds.[84] It is worth noting that neither the U.S. government nor Governor Schwarzenegger chose to defend their respective laws on the merits.

The question is whether that juggernaut will be stopped in the Supreme Court, given that it appears that there are at least five firm votes in favor of the legalization of gay marriage: four liberal justices—Ginsburg, Breyer, Sotomayor, and Kagan—plus Kennedy. Doctrine is, of course, a transient thing at the Supreme Court level, but it appears that the only line that could possibly hold back that outcome is *CLS*. Under *CLS*, the state does not have to "subsidize" gay marriage through its recognition, even though it need not criminalize it. Of course, no one knows how this will play out as the attacks on DOMA and Proposition 8 march onward through the legal system. But the betting here is that *CLS* will provide little resistance against an attack on traditional morals legislation that, when read against the early background of the Fourteenth Amendment, was squarely within the state power.

Still, doctrine is, as previously mentioned, a malleable thing, even a bird of passage. No one doubts that the move toward the constitutionalization of gay marriage is hopeless under any originalist reading of the Fourteenth Amendment. But in the end my prediction is that constitutional politics will conquer what is left of constitutional law. The doctrine of unconstitutional conditions that lay in ruins after *CLS* will rise again.

---

[84] Perry v. Schwarzenegger, 2010 U.S. Dist. LEXIS 78817 (N.D. Cal. 2010).

Doe v. Reed and the Future of Disclosure Requirements

*Steve Simpson**

Introduction

In *Doe v. Reed*, the Supreme Court waded into the contentious politics of gay marriage to decide whether government-mandated disclosure of petition signatures in a referendum violates the First Amendment.[1] The issue arose in the context of a Washington State referendum to repeal a recently enacted gay marriage law. Under Washington's version of the Freedom of Information Act, petition signatures must not only be disclosed to state officials for verification, they may also be publicly disclosed, along with the signers' addresses, to anyone who requests them. Fearing threats and harassment of the type that occurred during the debate over California's Proposition 8, the proponents of the Washington referendum and a group of petition signers sought to block public disclosure of the petitions, arguing that disclosure would violate the First Amendment.

The Supreme Court answered the question narrowly. Construing the plaintiffs' challenge as a facial attack—a challenge to petition-signature disclosure as such, regardless of the subject of the referendum or the precise burdens plaintiffs face—the Court ruled against them and held that states have the authority to require the disclosure of the identities of those who sign petitions to have issues placed on the ballot.

On its face, *Doe* is unexceptional. The Supreme Court has long recognized that states have the authority to regulate the process of

---

* Steve Simpson is a senior attorney with the Institute for Justice. He would like to thank Joseph Gay, one of IJ's constitutional fellows, for his tremendous help with this article.

[1] Doe v. Reed, 561 U.S. ____, 130 S. Ct. 2811 (2010).

elections.[2] Every state that allows laws to be passed by initiative or referendum requires proponents to circulate petitions and obtain the requisite number of signatures before the issue may be placed on the ballot.[3] The Court's decision in *Doe* can thus be seen as a recognition that states must have some discretion to determine how to validate signatures in order to maintain the integrity of their elections. And, mindful that disclosure implicates First Amendment rights, the Court sent the case back to the district court to allow the plaintiffs to try to prove, in a subsequent as-applied challenge, that disclosure would violate their First Amendment rights by chilling their speech and their ability to associate for political purposes.[4]

But as is so often the case with Supreme Court decisions, there is much more to this story than meets the eye. Not only is *Doe* at the heart of a heated cultural battle over gay marriage, it is the latest skirmish in a broader war over the future of campaign finance and election laws. That conflict reached a crescendo with the recent and highly controversial decision in *Citizens United v. FEC*, in which the Court struck down the ban on corporate funding of independent electioneering ads. Although the Court upheld disclosure laws in principle, it left many questions about disclosure unanswered. For example, how burdensome may disclosure laws be? In *Citizens United*, the Court upheld relatively straightforward disclosure laws for those who engage in independent advocacy.[5] It struck down as unduly burdensome, however, a requirement that corporations run independent political ads only through separate political action committees or "PACs."[6] Many of the PAC regulations serve the purpose of disclosure, so there is obviously some limit to the burden that government may impose in the name of disclosure.[7]

---

[2] See, e.g., Buckley v. Am. Constitutional Law Found., Inc., 525 U.S. 182, 191–92 (1999) ("States allowing ballot initiatives have considerable leeway to protect the integrity and reliability of the initiative process."); Timmons v. Twin Cities Area New Party, 520 U.S. 351, 358 (1997) ("States may, and inevitably must, enact reasonable regulations of parties, elections and ballots.").

[3] See Initiative & Referendum Institute, What Are Ballot Propositions, Initiatives, and Referendums?, available at http://www.iandrinstitute.org/Quick%20Fact%20-%20What%20is%20I&R.htm (last visited August 12, 2010).

[4] Doe, 130 S. Ct. at 2821.

[5] Citizens United v. FEC, 558 U.S. ____, 130 S. Ct. 876, 914–16 (2010).

[6] *Id.* at 897.

[7] Compare 2 U.S.C. § 434(f) (2006) (upheld by Citizens United, 130 S. Ct. at 914-16) and § 434(c) (disclosure requirements substantially similar to section 434(f) that apply

Another unanswered question about disclosure is what purposes may the laws serve and in what contexts are they constitutionally permissible. In *Citizens United*, the Court held that disclosure laws inform the public about who is speaking and help citizens make informed choices in the political marketplace.[8] But the Court has only clearly endorsed disclosure of funding sources in the candidate context.[9] It remains to be seen whether the same analysis will apply to laws requiring the disclosure of funds spent to support or oppose ballot initiatives and referendums, where the Court has made clear that there is no possibility of corruption, the primary interest that justifies campaign finance laws in the candidate context.[10]

These questions are especially important as Congress and the states grapple with the implications of *Citizens United*. President Obama and many other voices on the left harshly criticized the decision,[11] and congressional Democrats swiftly moved to counter its effects with new legislation. Dubbed the "DISCLOSE Act," the proposed legislation seemed designed more to impede corporate efforts to speak during elections than to provide the public with information about those efforts.[12] Indeed, the bill largely exempted unions,[13] provided a special carve-out for the NRA and similar

---

to independent expenditures by persons "other than political committees") with §§ 432, 433, 434(a) (detailed administrative, organizational, and continuous reporting requirements applicable only to PACs).

[8] Citizens United, 130 S. Ct. at 914–15.

[9] See, e.g., Buckley v. Valeo, 424 U.S. 1, 66–67 (1976) (describing one of the goals of the informational interest as "alert[ing] the voter to the interests to which a *candidate* is most likely to be responsive and thus facilitat[ing] predictions of future performance *in office*" (emphases added)).

[10] See, e.g., Citizens Against Rent Control v. City of Berkeley, 454 U.S. 290, 296–98 (1981); First Nat'l Bank of Boston v. Bellotti, 435 U.S. 765, 790–91 (1978).

[11] See, e.g., Robert Barnes, Alito Dissents on Obama Critique of Court Decision, Wash. Post., Jan. 28, 2010, at A6 (noting Obama's criticism of *Citizens United* during his State of the Union address, and the accompanying Democratic applause).

[12] DISCLOSE Act, H.R. 5175, 111th Cong. § 101 (2010); see also Shareholder Protection Act of 2010, H.R. 4790, 111th Cong. (2010) (requiring corporations to seek shareholder preapproval for expenditures for political speech).

[13] H.R. 5175 § 101 (banning corporations that have contracts with the government of $7 million or more from engaging in express advocacy or electioneering communications, but not applying similar restrictions to unions that bargain with the government for salaries and benefits). The companion bill in the Senate is S. 3628 (2010).

groups,[14] prevented companies that had accepted Troubled Asset Relief Program funds from spending money on independent ads,[15] and imposed harsher disclosure obligations on corporations than had preexisted *Citizens United*.[16] Senator Chuck Schumer, one of the bill's cosponsors, helped erase any doubts of the bill's purpose when he pointed out to supporters that the act's "deterrent effect should not be underestimated."[17] President Obama echoed Schumer's sentiment when he said that DISCLOSE would help "reduc[e] corporate and even foreign influence over our elections."[18] Although DISCLOSE failed to pass, supporters have vowed to introduce it again,[19] and at least 11 states have enacted legislation designed to deal with the implications of *Citizens United*.[20]

Thus, *Doe* comes at a time of great controversy over campaign-finance laws and the growing realization among reformers that disclosure is one area in which the courts may take a more deferential approach. Unfortunately, the Court's decision in *Doe* sheds little

---

[14] *Id.* § 211(c) (exempting currently established groups with 500,000 dues-paying members and at least one member in each state).

[15] *Id.* § 101.

[16] *Id.* §§ 201-02 (broadening the definitions of express advocacy and electioneering communication subject to reporting requirements and bans); *Id.* § 211(a), (b) (broadening donor disclosure requirements for organizations speaking about candidates); *Id.* § 214 (imposing multiple new disclaimer requirements on broadcast ads). See generally Center for Competitive Politics, Policy Briefing: "DISCLOSE Act": H.R. 5175 and S. 3628 (July 22, 2010), available at http://www.campaignfreedom.org/docLib/20100527_DISCLOSEpolicybriefing.pdf.

[17] See Jess Bravin & Brody Mullins, New Rules Proposed on Campaign Donors, Wall St. J., Feb. 12, 2010 (quoting Senator Schumer (D-NY)). Representative Hank Johnson (D-GA) made this point even more blatantly when he told fellow House Democrats that if they vote against DISCLOSE "we will see more Republicans getting elected." Real Clear Politics Video, Dem Congressman: We Must Have Campaign Finance Disclosure to Stop Republicans from Getting Elected (June 24, 2010), available at http://www.realclearpolitics.com/video/2010/06/24/dem_congressman_we_must_have_campaign_finance_disclosure_to_stop_republicans_from_getting_elected.html.

[18] Remarks by the President on the DISCLOSE Act (July 26, 2010) (transcript available at http://www.whitehouse.gov/the-press-office/remarks-president-disclose-act).

[19] Dan Eggen, Bill on Political Ad Disclosures Falls Short in Senate, Wash. Post, July 28, 2010, at A3 ("Schumer vowed to try again.").

[20] Nat'l Conference of State Legislatures, Life after *Citizens United*, http://www.ncsl.org/default.aspx?tabid=19607 (last visited August 12, 2010) (listing 11 states with updated laws as of August 10, 2010).

light on what will happen in future cases. Indeed, the decision is perhaps more important for what it did not say than for what it did. The Court scrupulously avoided going beyond the narrow question of whether public disclosure of all petition signatures in a referendum was per se invalid under the First Amendment. The decision says nothing about the constitutionality of laws that require disclosure of those who contribute money to support or oppose ballot initiatives. Twenty-four states and many local jurisdictions have such laws on the books.[21] The laws have been challenged, but the Supreme Court has not yet taken up the issue. However, in light of ballot issue controversies such as California's Proposition 8—in which both sides of the gay marriage issue sought to intimidate opponents[22]—it seems likely that a case will reach the Court some day soon.

Although the Court's decision in *Doe* itself tells us little about what the future may hold, four justices wrote separately to express their views about the majority decision and the as-applied challenge on remand. Examining those opinions may shed light on how the Court will rule in a future case.

Part I of this article describes the factual background of the case. Part II discusses the Chief Justice's majority opinion. Part III examines the concurring and dissenting opinions with an eye toward understanding what the Court is likely to rule in the as-applied challenge, should it return to the Court, and in any future challenges to other ballot issue disclosure laws.

I. Background

Like California's Proposition 8, the Washington referendum at issue in *Doe* sought to revoke recent recognition of gay marriage rights. In May 2009, Washington's legislature passed a law treating

---

[21] See Initiative & Referendum Institute, *supra* note 3.

[22] See Citizens United, 130 S. Ct. at 916 (citing Brief for Inst. for Justice as Amicus Curiae in Support of Appellant on Supplemental Question at 13, 17–19) (noting that "donors to certain causes," including those supporting proposition 8, "were blacklisted, threatened, or otherwise targeted for retaliation," and calling this a "cause for concern"); Lisa Leff, Proposition 8 Backers Target Businesses, Associated Press, Oct. 23, 2008 (describing how businesses listed as donors on website of anti-Proposition 8 group received letters from pro-Proposition 8 group asking for money and threatening boycotts over their support of gay marriage).

same-sex domestic partnerships essentially the same as opposite-sex marriages.[23] Almost immediately after passage, however, a group known as Protect Marriage Washington began working on a referendum to repeal the law.[24]

Washington, like most states that allow legislative action through initiative and referendum, requires proponents to qualify their issue for the ballot by submitting petitions signed by a certain number of registered voters. Under Washington law, proponents must gather enough signatures to equal four percent of the votes cast in the preceding gubernatorial election. Petitions must also include the addresses of the signers.[25]

Washington law also requires the state's secretary of state to verify petition signatures. The secretary's office takes a statistical sample of the submitted signatures and compares them against the signatures on the voter registration cards, removing non-matching signatures, signatures with no valid voter registration, and any duplicate signatures.[26] If the sample does not verify that a sufficient number of valid signatures were submitted within an acceptable margin of error, the entire list of petition signatures must be verified.[27] This process allows petition-signature information to be disclosed only to the secretary of state and to a court in any subsequent suit challenging the validity of signatures, but it does not permit full public disclosure of signatures.[28]

In July 2009, Protect Marriage Washington submitted petition signatures to the secretary of state.[29] The number of signatures was close to the minimum number necessary to place the referendum on the ballot, requiring examination of the entire list.[30] After checking

---

[23] Doe, 130 S. Ct. at 2816 (citing S. Bill 5688, 61st Leg., Reg. Sess. (Wash. 2009)).

[24] Id.

[25] Id. (citing Wash. Const. art. II, § 1(b)).

[26] Wash. Rev. Code § 29A.72.230 (2010); Wash. Admin. Code §§ 434-379-010, -020 (2010).

[27] Wash. Admin. Code § 434-379-010 (2010).

[28] Wash. Rev. Code § 29A.72.230.

[29] Doe, 130 S. Ct. at 2816.

[30] Sam Reed, Washington Secretary of State, Certification of Referendum 71 (Sept. 2, 2009), available at http://wei.secstate.wa.gov/osos/en/initiativesReferenda/Documents/R-71%20Certification.pdf.

each signature, the secretary certified that a sufficient number were valid and placed the measure on the November 2009 ballot.[31]

In the meantime, several groups had announced their intention to invoke Washington's Public Records Act to obtain the names and addresses of petition signers and to publicly disclose the information in an online, searchable database.[32] Passed in 1972, the PRA is a fairly typical state freedom-of-information-type act in that it makes any records deemed "public records" available for release to the general public.[33] Originally, petition signatures were not considered "public records" and thus were not subject to disclosure under the PRA.[34] However, in 1998 the secretary of state reversed that interpretation and made petition signatures subject to public disclosure.[35] To make a request, one simply asks the secretary of state for specific and identifiable records, which may be received as physical photocopies or as digital copies.[36]

In July and August 2009, six organizations and individuals made PRA requests for the petition signatures from the gay marriage repeal referendum.[37] The organizations included the Associated Press, the Washington Coalition for Open Government, and two groups called WhoSigned.org and KnowThyNeighbor.org.[38] WhoSigned.org, working with KnowThyNeighbor.org, promised to put the names and addresses in an online, searchable database with the avowed purpose of allowing gay marriage supporters "to use its

---

[31] *Id.*

[32] See Washington Secretary of State, Referendum 71 Litigation in Federal Court, http://wei.secstate.wa.gov/osos/en/initiativesReferenda/Pages/R-71Information.aspx (last visited August 12, 2010).

[33] Doe, 130 S. Ct. at 2815; *Id.* at 2826 (Alito, J., concurring).

[34] See *id.* at 2826 (Alito, J., concurring) (discussing secretary of state's position, between 1973 and 1998, that petition signatures were not public records subject to disclosure); Wash. Rev. Code § 29A.72.230 (2010) (permitting observers of the signature verification process but prohibiting the recording of names and addresses).

[35] Brian Zylstra, The Disclosure History of Petition Sheets, Washington Secretary of State Blogs: From Our Corner (Sept. 17, 2009), http://blogs.sos.wa.gov/FromOurCorner/index.php/2009/09/the-disclosure-history-of-petition-sheets; Doe, 130 S. Ct. at 2826 (Alito, J., concurring).

[36] Washington Secretary of State, Public Records, http://www.sos.wa.gov/publicrecords/ (last visited July 29, 2010).

[37] See Washington Secretary of State, *supra* note 32.

[38] See *Id.*

online tools to find the names of people they know" and to engage in "uncomfortable" conversations.[39] Announcing the release of similar signatures in Arkansas, KnowThyNeighbor.org said it "expect[ed] that many petition signers will be confronted about their actions as their names are discovered on the website by family members, friends, coworkers, customers, and acquaintances."[40]

In July 2009, Protect Marriage Washington and some of the individuals who had signed the petition sued the secretary of state in federal court challenging the release of the names and addresses of the petition signers as a violation of the First Amendment.[41] The complaint asserted two counts, one broad and one narrow. The first count attacked the application of the PRA to ballot issues and referendums at all. In essence, it claimed that the post-1998 interpretation of the PRA, under which petition signatures were considered "public records," was unconstitutional. The second count claimed that applying the PRA to the referendum at issue was unconstitutional.[42] Along with their complaint, the plaintiffs filed a motion to enjoin the release of the signatures pending the resolution of the case.

The plaintiffs relied on a line of Supreme Court cases beginning with *NAACP v. Alabama*, in which the Court blocked efforts by the State of Alabama to obtain NAACP membership lists as a violation of the right of association under the First Amendment.[43] The theory of the plaintiffs' case in *Doe* was simple: the groups seeking disclosure had openly admitted that their purpose was to intimidate individuals who wished to sign the petitions. This result would necessarily chill plaintiffs' speech and thus violate their First Amendment rights.[44]

---

[39] KnowThyNeighbor.org Blog, Press Release, KnowThyNeighbor.org Partners with WhoSigned.org in Washington State (June 1, 2009), http://knowthyneighbor.blogs.com/home/2009/06/knowthyneighbororg-partners-with-whosignedorg-in-washington-state.html.

[40] KnowThyNeighbor.org Blog, Press Release, Names of Anti-Gay Petition Signers Posted Online (Apr. 28, 2009), http://knowthyneighbor.blogs.com/home/2009/04/press-release-names-of-arkansas-antigay-petition-signers-posted-online.html.

[41] Doe v. Reed, 661 F. Supp. 2d 1194, 1195–96 (W.D. Wash. 2009).

[42] *Id.* at 1196.

[43] NAACP v. Alabama ex rel. Patterson, 357 U.S. 449, 460–66 (1958).

[44] See Pls.' Mem. in Support of Mot. for TRO and Prelim. Inj. at 26–28, Doe v. Reed, 661 F.Supp.2d 1194 (W.D. Wash. 2009) (No. C09-5456BHS).

The district court accepted this argument, applying the highest level of, or "strict," scrutiny and holding that the release of names and addresses of petition sponsors under the PRA in general unjustifiably burdens political speech.[45] The Court thus issued an injunction based on the plaintiffs' broader claim that the application of the PRA to any referendum petitions violated the First Amendment without reaching their narrower claim that the application of the PRA in this instance was unconstitutional. As a result, only the broader claim was at issue in the resulting appeals.[46]

The U.S. Court of Appeals for the Ninth Circuit reversed. Construing the PRA as a "regulation that has an incidental effect on expressive conduct," it applied a lesser form of First Amendment scrutiny, under which the government has more leeway to regulate. It found the burden on First Amendment rights to be sufficiently justified by the state's interest in preventing fraud or mistake in the petition process and providing voters with information about who signed the petitions.[47] With release of the petition signatures imminent, the plaintiffs sought a stay of the Ninth Circuit's order from Justice Anthony Kennedy, sitting as circuit justice for the Ninth Circuit. The stay was granted[48] and remained in effect after the Supreme Court accepted the case for review in January 2010.[49]

In November 2009, Washington voters rejected the referendum, affirming the legislature's extension of marriage rights to gay couples.[50] The lawsuit, however, continued.

II. The Majority Opinion in *Doe*

The Court's decision in *Doe* is a good illustration of the fact that the outcome of a constitutional case often depends as much on how the Court characterizes the law and the right at issue as it does on what arguments are made about those subjects. The Supreme Court

[45] See Doe, 661 F. Supp. 2d at 1203–05.

[46] *Id.* at 1205.

[47] Doe v. Reed, 586 F.3d 671, 678–80 (9th Cir. 2009). The panel stayed the injunction without opinion, noting only that the lower court had applied "an incorrect legal standard." The opinion issued several days after the Supreme Court stayed the panel's judgment. See Petitioners' Brief at 11, Doe v. Reed, 130 S. Ct. 2811 (2010).

[48] Doe v. Reed, 130 S. Ct. 486 (2009).

[49] Doe v. Reed, 130 S. Ct. 1133 (2010).

[50] Doe, 130 S. Ct. at 2816.

has long recognized that the states must have the authority to regulate the process of elections to ensure their fairness and to prevent fraud. At the same time, it has also recognized that election regulations will often implicate First Amendment rights such as freedom of speech and association.[51] The difficulty in these cases is deciding how to reconcile these competing interests.[52]

The facts of *Doe* provided what seemed to be a relatively easy answer to this dilemma, for the law at issue in *Doe* was not a typical regulation of the election *process*, it was a generally applicable public records statute. As Justice Clarence Thomas pointed out in his dissent, the plaintiffs "do not argue that the Constitution allows them to support a referendum measure without disclosing their names *to the State*."[53] Instead, they challenged the designation of signature information as a "public record" under the PRA, which made the information subject to disclosure to anyone who asked for it.

The Court could have decided *Doe* simply by recognizing this distinction. Indeed, that is precisely the approach Justice Thomas would have taken. As he saw it, although the state has the constitutional authority to verify signatures, it does not follow that the state may make signatures and addresses available to everyone. Doing so, according to Justice Thomas, imposes a severe burden on First Amendment rights to speech and political association and is entirely unnecessary, because the state can easily verify signatures without such disclosure.[54] Accordingly, Justice Thomas would have applied strict scrutiny to the application of the PRA to signature information and invalidated this practice as vastly broader than necessary to achieve the state's legitimate interest in regulating the election process.[55]

---

[51] See, e.g., Timmons v. Twin Cities Area New Party, 520 U.S. 351, 357–58 (1997); Anderson v. Celebrezze, 460 U.S. 780, 786–87 (1983); Storer v. Brown, 415 U.S. 724, 738 (1974).

[52] See, e.g., Timmons, 520 U.S. at 358–59 (The Court must weigh the "character and magnitude" of burdens of state election law on associational rights against the need for "reasonable regulations of parties, elections, and ballots to reduce election- and campaign-related disorder.").

[53] Doe, 130 S. Ct. at 2837 (Thomas, J., dissenting) (emphasis in original).

[54] See *id.* at 2837, 2839–41.

[55] *Id.* at 2839–44.

On the other end of the spectrum, Justice Antonin Scalia, who concurred in the judgment, would have held that signing a petition receives no First Amendment protection at all.[56] In his view, signing a petition to place a referendum on the ballot is a legislative act rather than an exercise of First Amendment rights.[57] In keeping with his dissent in *McIntyre v. Ohio Elections Commission*,[58] Justice Scalia expressed skepticism that the First Amendment protects a right of anonymity at all.[59] Even if a right to anonymous speech exists, however, there can be no right to anonymously participate in lawmaking, in Justice Scalia's view. "[H]arsh criticism, short of unlawful action, is a price our people have traditionally been willing to pay for self-governance. Requiring people to stand up in public for their political acts fosters civic courage, without which democracy is doomed."[60]

Chief Justice John Roberts's majority opinion[61] took a position between these poles. The majority recognized, along with Justice Thomas, that signing a petition constitutes protected speech under the First Amendment, because the individual is expressing a view that either the law should be repealed or the matter should at least be put to a vote.[62] Nevertheless, the majority was willing to grant far more leeway to the state than Justice Thomas would have granted it. The majority characterized the PRA in this context not as a general public records provision that was redundant of preexisting and more specific election process laws but as a necessary part of those laws.[63] As the Court stated, "[w]e allow States significant flexibility in implementing their own voting systems."[64] Moreover, as a disclosure

---

[56] See *id.* at 2832 (Scalia, J., concurring in the judgment) ("I doubt whether signing a petition that has the effect of suspending a law fits within 'the freedom of speech' at all.").

[57] *Id.* (contrasting a "general right to 'speak' anonymously about a referendum" with the "disclosure . . . of those who took this legislative action").

[58] McIntyre v. Ohio Elections Comm'n, 514 U.S. 334, 371–78 (1995) (Scalia, J., dissenting) (arguing on originalist grounds against a First Amendment right to anonymous speech).

[59] Doe, 130 S. Ct. at 2832–33 (Scalia, J., concurring in the judgment).

[60] *Id.* at 2837.

[61] Joined by Justices Kennedy, Ginsburg, Breyer, Alito, and Sotomayor.

[62] Doe, 130 S. Ct. at 2817.

[63] See *id.* at 2818–19.

[64] *Id.* at 2818.

provision, the PRA "do[es] not prevent anyone from speaking."[65] The Court thus applied what it has termed "exacting scrutiny," rather than the strict scrutiny Justice Thomas would have applied. Under this standard there must be a "substantial relation between the disclosure requirement and a sufficiently important governmental interest" and "the strength of the governmental interest must reflect the seriousness of the actual burden on First Amendment rights."[66]

The case thus came down to two questions. First, is the state's interest in requiring disclosure of all the petition signatures and addresses sufficiently important? Second, does the state's interest outweigh the burden on the plaintiffs' First Amendment rights?

The state asserted two interests to justify its application of the PRA to signature information: "preserving the integrity of the electoral process" and "providing information to the electorate." If there is a standard interest states offer to justify their election laws, preserving the integrity of elections is it.[67] The phrase is a catchall that covers laws designed to prevent fraud or mistake and to promote transparency and accountability of the election process.[68] The Supreme Court has often found this interest sufficient to justify reasonably tailored election laws.

The informational interest is more controversial, however. It boils down to the idea that the government should try to educate voters about issues by requiring those who support or oppose initiatives and referendums to disclose information about themselves.[69] In *Doe*, that meant disclosing the identities and addresses of those who signed petitions to place the referendum on the ballot. The state and the other respondents argued that this information would provide

---

[65] *Id.* (quoting Citizens United, 130 S. Ct. at 914).

[66] Doe, 130 S. Ct. at 2818 (internal quotations and citations omitted). Although the Court referred to "exacting scrutiny," it has used that term in the past to refer interchangeably to intermediate and strict scrutiny. Compare Citizens United, 130 S. Ct. at 914, and Doe, 130 S. Ct. at 2818, with McIntyre, 514 U.S. at 347 (1995) (stating that exacting scrutiny requires an overriding state interest and narrow tailoring).

[67] See, e.g., Buckley v. Am. Constitutional Law Found. 525 U.S. 182, 191–92 (1999); Anderson v. Celebrezze, 460 U.S. at 788 n.9 (collecting cases).

[68] Doe, 130 S. Ct. at 2819.

[69] See, e.g., Cal. Pro-Life Council, Inc. v. Getman, 328 F.3d 1088, 1104–06 (9th Cir. 2003); Richey v. Tyson, 120 F. Supp. 2d 1298, 1314 (S.D. Ala. 2000) (citing Buckley, 424 U.S. at 66–67).

voters with "insight into whether support for holding a vote comes predominantly from particular interest groups, political or religious organizations, or other group[s] of citizens."[70]

The informational interest has most often been offered as the justification for state laws that require people who finance efforts to speak out for or against ballot initiatives or referendums to disclose their identities.[71] The idea is that requiring this sort of disclosure provides voters with what amounts to a sort of endorsement, albeit an unwilling one, from those who fund speech for or against initiatives and referendums.[72] The theory seems to be that if voters will not educate themselves about the issues, perhaps they will educate themselves about what other people think about the issues. Why spend time trying to figure out the issues, after all, when you can consult the secretary of state's website and learn what your neighbor thinks about them?

The reality is debatable, not least because voters seldom consult disclosure information and the media rarely report any of it.[73] It seems that voters either can already figure out what interests line up on each side of an issue or simply do not care. Still, debate rages on in the academy about the utility of using contributor and other information as "cues" to help better educate voters.[74]

---

[70] Doe, 130 S. Ct. at 2824 (Alito, J., concurring) (quoting Brief of Resp't Wash. Families Standing Together at 58 and citing Brief of Resp't Reed at 46–48).

[71] See, e.g., Cal. Pro-Life v. Getman, 328 F.3d at 1092; Richey v. Tyson, 120 F. Supp. 2d at 1302.

[72] See, e.g., Michael S. Kang, Democratizing Direct Democracy: Restoring Voter Competence through Heuristic Cues and "Disclosure Plus," 50 UCLA L. Rev. 1141, 1164 (2003) (arguing that disclosure should be widely broadcast to "inform [voters] who supports which side of a ballot question and help them to understand in a quick, familiar manner what the ballot question is really about"); Elizabeth Garrett, Commentaries on Bruce Ackerman and Ian Ayres's Voting with Dollars: A New Paradigm for Campaign Finance Reform: Voting with Cues, 37 U. Rich. L. Rev. 1011, 1035 (2003) ("A focus on these notorious groups is important for any assessment of disclosure statutes because these groups are the most likely to strongly resist publicity. . . . Thus, mandatory disclosure of campaign spending may be the only way to provide voters with credible signals based on notorious-group-support.").

[73] See Dick M. Carpenter, Institute for Justice, Disclosure Costs: Unintended Consequences of Campaign Finance Reform 11–13 (2007), available at http://www.ij.org/publications/other/disclosurecosts.html; Dick M. Carpenter, Mandatory Disclosure for Ballot-Initiative Campaigns, 13 Indep. Rev. 567, 579 (2009), available at http://www.independent.org/pdf/tir/tir_13_04_6_carpenter.pdf.

[74] See, e.g., James H. Kuklinski & Paul J. Quirk, Reconsidering the Rational Public: Cognition, Heuristics, and Mass Opinion in Elements of Reason 153, 155–63 (Arthur

What is far less debatable are the implications of the informational interest. Justice Samuel Alito described them effectively in his concurrence:

> The implications of accepting such an argument are breath-taking. Were we to accept respondents' asserted informational interest, the State would be free to require petition signers to disclose all kinds of demographic information, including the signer's race, religion, political affiliation, sexual orientation, ethnic background, and interest-group memberships. Requiring such disclosures, however, runs headfirst into a half century of our case law, which firmly establishes that individuals have a right to privacy of belief and association.[75]

Perhaps to avoid these breathtaking implications, the majority in *Doe* avoided the informational interest altogether simply by deciding that the far less controversial and more constitutionally sound interest in preserving the integrity of elections—that is, preventing fraud and mistake—would suffice. The Court's analysis of this interest is questionable, and, indeed, Justice Thomas did question it in dissent by pointing out that the state could easily ensure the validity of petition signatures by simply cross-referencing that information—which it keeps in digitized form—with voter registration information and then checking for duplicate signatures.[76] The state's desire to backstop its own efforts at signature verification through on-demand public disclosure was therefore, in Justice Thomas's view, a "blunderbuss approach" that went far beyond anything the state needed to do to prevent fraud.[77]

Nevertheless, as the majority noted, the Court has often given states wide latitude to implement their own election laws. The secretary of state's own verification procedures might not catch every invalid signature, the Court noted, and disclosure helps prevent

---

Lupia et al. eds., 2000) (discussing the academic literature supporting the cognitive heuristics theory, and its shortcomings).

[75] Doe, 130 S. Ct. at 2824 (Alito, J., concurring).

[76] See *id.* at 2840–41 (Thomas, J., dissenting). Justice Alito also expressed strong doubts about the strength of the state's interest in the integrity of the petition-gathering process and the availability of alternative mechanisms. See *id.* at 2825–27 (Alito, J., concurring).

[77] *Id.* at 2840 (Thomas, J., dissenting).

some types of fraud that are difficult to detect.[78] These points may not have addressed all of Justice Thomas's arguments, but the majority was applying only intermediate scrutiny, under which being wrong is not necessarily the same thing as being unconstitutional.[79]

The Court thus turned to the final question to decide whether the state's interest outweighed the burden on the plaintiffs' rights. Here, the plaintiffs faced difficulty based on the nature of the claim on which they had prevailed in the lower courts. They had claimed both that applying the PRA to any initiative and referendum petitions violated the First Amendment and that applying it to the petitions at issue in their case violated the First Amendment by chilling their rights to speech and association. The district court ruled for the plaintiffs only on the former claim, however, which resulted in only that claim coming before the Supreme Court. Thus, the majority felt constrained to treat the plaintiffs' claim as a facial challenge, meaning that they had to show that public disclosure would not only chill their speech in this instance, but that it would chill the speech of petition signers in a typical referendum or ballot issue election.[80]

Most initiatives and referendums are not controversial, noted the Court. Although the plaintiffs could show a potential for harassment and intimidation in a referendums concerning gay marriage, "typical referendum petitions 'concern tax policy, revenue, budget, or other state law issues.'"[81] According to the Court, the plaintiffs had little to offer in response to the state's claim that disclosure of a typical petition involved only modest burdens on the right of association.[82] It thus felt compelled to reject their broad challenge and to remand back to the district court to allow the plaintiffs the opportunity to demonstrate that the PRA violates the First Amendment as applied to them.

Here, again, however, Justice Thomas's dissent seemed a ready response to the majority's approach. The PRA is not part of the typical set of election regulations that Washington has long used to

---

[78] *Id.* at 2820 (Roberts, C.J.) (majority opinion).

[79] *Id.* at 2820 n.2.

[80] *Id.* at 2821.

[81] *Id.* (quoting Br. for Resp't Wash. Families Standing Together at 36).

[82] *Id.*

validate signatures. It is a generally applicable freedom-of-information statute that was interpreted to apply to petition signatures only in 1998, several decades after enactment.[83] One might just as easily argue that state income tax returns should be subject to the PRA, but one hopes that such a "blunderbuss" approach to rooting out tax fraud would be met with somewhat more skepticism than the majority expressed for the state's argument in *Doe*. It is not clear why that should be so, however. As Justice Thomas pointed out, signing a petition is an exercise of both freedom of speech and freedom of association—rights the Court has long held may be regulated only narrowly and only where the government demonstrates a compelling interest. As the Court has said, "the tie goes to the speaker, not the censor."[84]

Alas, when it comes to election process laws, the tie apparently goes to the state.

III. What Does the Future Hold?

The Court's decision in *Doe* raises two immediate questions: what comes next for the plaintiffs—who return to the district court to litigate their as-applied challenge—and what are the implications of the decision for future challenges to disclosure laws? The first question appears easier to answer, at least from the Supreme Court's perspective, because five justices wrote or joined concurrences that seemed clearly to take the position that the plaintiffs should lose their as-applied challenge. However, one of them was Justice John Paul Stevens, who has since been replaced by former Solicitor General Elena Kagan (whose views on the subject of disclosure are unknown).

The second question—the implications for future challenges to disclosure laws—is more difficult, at least outside of the strict context of disclosure laws that apply to petition signatures. Within that context, the answer is relatively straightforward. The states have substantial discretion to choose the means of implementing their election process regulations, meaning that challenges to the public disclosure of petition signatures are subject to intermediate (or

---

[83] *Id.* at 2826 (Alito, J., concurring).
[84] FEC v. Wis. Right to Life, Inc., 551 U.S. 449, 474 (2007).

"exacting") rather than strict scrutiny. Unless challengers can demonstrate that public disclosure substantially burdens the rights of all who wish to sign a petition, they are stuck with as-applied challenges. While one can certainly take issue with the majority's approach, as Justice Thomas did, the outcome of the decision is not terribly surprising. As stated above, the Court has long given the states discretion to implement their election process laws, and in the candidate context, as-applied challenges that require case-specific harm are the rule for disclosure laws.[85]

Outside the narrow context of laws that regulate the process of elections, however, it is very difficult to detect any implications of *Doe* at all. Indeed, about the only inference one can draw from *Doe* is that the majority and the various concurring justices *wanted* to avoid any implications for other types of disclosure laws. They could have broadly embraced disclosure in the initiative and referendum context—for example, by extolling the virtues of disclosure as a means of educating voters about issues—but they did not. And the only concurring justice to discuss an issue that would apply to disclosure laws more broadly was Justice Alito, who rejected the so-called informational interest as fundamentally illegitimate and at odds with the First Amendment. The informational interest is the primary grounds on which states have defended laws requiring the disclosure of those who spend money for speech supporting or opposing ballot issues and referendums.[86] Yet not one justice took issue with Justice Alito's position or attempted to defend the informational interest. All stayed focused on the question of whether the disclosure of petition signatures violated the First Amendment, not whether other types of disclosure laws might.

A. The As-Applied Challenge

The majority decision in *Doe* offered little insight into the remaining as-applied challenge other than to state, quoting *Buckley v. Valeo*, that to prevail, the plaintiffs must show "'a reasonable probability that the compelled disclosure [of personal information] will subject

---

[85] See, e.g., Brown v. Socialist Workers '74 Campaign Comm., 459 U.S. 87, 88 (1982) (holding that disclosure requirements were unconstitutional as applied to Socialist Workers Party based on evidence that supporters would be subject to reasonable probability of threats, harassment, or reprisals).

[86] See, e.g., Cal. Pro-Life, 328 F.3d at 1101; Richey, 120 F. Supp. 2d at 1312–15.

them to threats, harassment, or reprisals.'"[87] However, five justices—Stevens, Scalia, Ruth Bader Ginsburg, Stephen Breyer, and Sonia Sotomayor—indicated in separate concurrences that they did not believe the plaintiffs could prevail. Justices Sotomayor and Stevens wrote the principal concurrences arguing that the plaintiffs are unlikely to prevail in their as-applied challenge. Justices Ginsburg and Stevens joined in Justice Sotomayor's concurrence and Justice Breyer joined in Justice Stevens's concurrence. Justice Scalia wrote separately, expressing his view, which no other justice joined, that the First Amendment does not protect the right to anonymously sign a referendum petition at all.

Both Justice Sotomayor and Justice Stevens began by noting the narrow context in which the case arose. For Justice Sotomayor, the case fell "squarely within the realm of permissible election-related regulations" as opposed to more general laws that implicate the "communicative aspect of petitioning."[88] Likewise, in Justice Stevens's view, *Doe* merely involves the disclosure of information already in the state's possession, which the state requires to prevent petition fraud.[89] Thus, both justices emphasized, as did the majority, that states have broad latitude to legislate for the purpose of ensuring the integrity of their elections.[90] As a result, according to these justices, the plaintiffs will bear a heavy burden in their as-applied challenge.[91]

For Justice Sotomayor, plaintiffs would be able to prevail in an as-applied challenge only in "the rare circumstance in which disclosure poses a reasonable probability of serious and widespread harassment that the State is unwilling or unable to control."[92] Justice Stevens similarly viewed plaintiffs' success on the as-applied challenge as "unlikely."[93] Despite the evidence of harassment for petition signers, including harassing and threatening e-mails, veiled threats, and

---

[87] Doe, 130 S. Ct. at 2820 (quoting Buckley, 424 U.S. 1, at 74 (alterations in original)).

[88] *Id.* at 2828 (Sotomayor, J., concurring).

[89] *Id.* at 2829–30 (Stevens, J., concurring).

[90] *Id.* at 2828 (Sotomayor, J., concurring); *id.* at 2829–31 (Stevens, J., concurring).

[91] *Id.* at 2829 (Sotomayor, J., concurring); *id.* at 2831 (Stevens, J., concurring).

[92] *Id.* at 2829 (Sotomayor, J., concurring).

[93] *Id.* at 2831 (Stevens, J., concurring).

the prospect of boycotts,[94] Justice Stevens saw the burden on First Amendment rights as "speculative as well as indirect."[95] Like Justice Sotomayor, he believed that only a threat that "cannot be mitigated by law enforcement measures" would suffice to justify preventing disclosure of petition signatures.[96]

In striking contrast to Justices Stevens and Sotomayor, Justice Alito argued in his solo concurrence that the plaintiffs have "a strong argument that the PRA violates the First Amendment" as applied to them.[97] Justice Alito recognized the central paradox with using as-applied remedies to address a chilling effect—by the time the remedy is available, the chilling effect has already occurred, thus rendering the remedy too little, too late. As Justice Alito put it, an "as-applied remedy becomes practically worthless if speakers cannot obtain the exemption quickly and well in advance of speaking."[98] Accordingly, Justice Alito stressed that the standard for as-applied challenges from *Buckley*—which required plaintiffs to show only a *"reasonable probability"* that disclosure will lead to threats, harassment, or reprisals—was meant to be a realistic standard that plaintiffs could actually meet.[99] In his view, the evidence plaintiffs had produced along with the evidence of threats and harassment from Proposition 8 in California was easily enough to justify blocking disclosure in this case. "Indeed, if the evidence relating to Proposition 8 is not sufficient to obtain an as-applied exemption in this case, one may wonder whether that vehicle provides any meaningful protection for the First Amendment rights of persons who circulate and sign referendum and initiative petitions."[100]

One may indeed wonder about the utility of as-applied challenges in cases like *Doe* when Justices Sotomayor and Stevens are setting the standards. To wit, it is not at all clear that the standard they advocate—under which plaintiffs must show a reasonable probability of serious and widespread harassment that the state is unwilling

---

[94] Br. of Pet'rs., *supra* note 47, at 10–11.

[95] Doe, 130 S. Ct. at 2831 (Stevens, J., concurring).

[96] *Id.*

[97] *Id.* at 2823 (Alito, J., concurring).

[98] *Id.* at 2822.

[99] *Id.* at 2822–23 (quoting Buckley, 424 U.S. at 74) (emphasis in original).

[100] *Id.* at 2823–24.

or unable to control—is an as-applied standard at all. An as-applied challenge is supposed to focus on harm to the plaintiffs themselves, yet the Sotomayor-Stevens standard requires harm that is *widespread*. A standard is not as-applied simply because one uses the phrase "as-applied," especially if the class of individuals whose rights must have been violated amounts to everyone. It is not clear how large a group of people must have suffered harassment for it to become "serious and widespread," but judging by the views of Justices Sotomayor and Stevens, it is clearly a much larger group than was at issue here. With the added condition that the state must be unable or unwilling to control the harassment, the Sotomayor-Stevens standard starts to sound suspiciously like a facial, rather than an as-applied standard.

One may also wonder why Justice Alito did not simply sign on to Justice Thomas's dissent. It seems unlikely that an as-applied standard will ever suffice in a situation like *Doe*, for those who are truly concerned about harassment are far more likely to avoid exercising First Amendment rights than to bring a lawsuit to enjoin a disclosure law. Indeed, this is a large part of the reason that chilling-effect rulings tend to be facial—because the existence of the law and the possibility of sanctions or some other injury to First Amendment rights are enough to prevent their exercise in the first place.[101] Justice Thomas appears to be the only member of the Court who recognized this point.

Unfortunately for the plaintiffs in *Doe*, the merits or demerits of these points are secondary to the fact that, unless Justice Kagan takes a different approach from Justice Stevens, they likely will not be able to find the votes to prevail.

B. Future Disclosure Challenges

It may come as small consolation to the plaintiffs in *Doe*, but one silver lining of the case for those who oppose disclosure laws is that the case provides little support for anything other than the disclosure of petition signatures. The majority upheld this disclosure on the

---

[101] See, e.g., NAACP v. Button, 371 U.S. 415, 433 (1963) ("These freedoms are delicate and vulnerable, as well as supremely precious in our society. The threat of sanctions may deter their exercise almost as potently as the actual application of sanctions. Because First Amendment freedoms need breathing space to survive, government may regulate in the area only with narrow specificity." (internal citations omitted)).

same grounds that it has often upheld election process regulations. Even the concurring justices who obviously supported disclosure focused narrowly on laws that, in Justice Sotomayor's words, fall "squarely within the realm of permissible election-related regulations."[102] Justice Stevens was even more adamant about the narrow context of the case: "This is not a hard case. It is not about a restriction on voting or on speech and does not involve a classic disclosure requirement."[103] The law at issue "is not 'a regulation of pure speech. . . . It does not prohibit expression, nor does it require that any person signing a petition disclose or say anything at all."[104] "The PRA does not necessarily make it more difficult to circulate or obtain signatures on a petition . . . or to communicate one's views more generally."[105] And although signing a petition is an expressive act, according to Justice Stevens, it "does not involve any 'interactive communication' . . . and 'is not principally' a method of 'individual expression of political sentiment.'"[106]

Every one of these points on which Justice Stevens distinguished *Doe* would arguably apply to a "classic disclosure requirement," such as a law requiring those who speak out for or against ballot issues or referendums to disclose anyone who contributes to their efforts. Typical disclosure laws of this sort do indeed require speakers to disclose information as a condition of speaking, and, indeed, even require associational speakers to register with the government prior to speaking.[107] These laws can be burdensome, thus making it more difficult for speakers to get out their messages, and the types of speech that trigger such laws—typically anything that costs money, such as print or broadcast ads or even flyers, post cards, or yard signs—are unquestionably methods by which individuals express political sentiments.[108] Indeed, even Justice Scalia, who

[102] Doe, 130 S. Ct. at 2828 (Sotomayor, J., concurring).

[103] *Id.* at 2829 (Stevens, J., concurring).

[104] *Id.*

[105] *Id.* at 2830.

[106] *Id.*

[107] Jeffrey Milyo, Institute for Justice, Campaign Finance Red Tape: Strangling Free Speech & Political Debate 2 (2007), available at http://www.ij.org/images/pdf_folder/other_pubs/CampaignFinanceRedTape.pdf.

[108] *Id.* at 8–10, 14–18 (in experiment based on typical disclosure laws, finding that participants on average completed only 41 percent of the required tasks correctly, and describing participants' frustration while trying to complete the forms and their belief that this would deter political activity).

opposes the idea that the First Amendment protects a right of anonymity, recognized a distinction between disclosure laws that apply to "legislative action," like the one in *Doe*, and those that apply "to political speech" during an election.[109]

Finally, any states defending future challenges to contributor disclosure laws will have to grapple with Justice Alito's point that the so-called informational interest logically leads to mandatory disclosure of all sorts of other demographic information, such as race, sex, financial status, religion, and much more. Knowing whether those who support a ballot issue are predominantly black or rich or Republican or Muslim tells us far more about their interest-group affiliation than knowing their identities, addresses, and employers. If educating voters about interest groups in elections is the goal, then this sort of information would logically be subject to disclosure as well. Yet, as Justice Alito pointed out, the "State's informational interest paints such a chilling picture of the role of government in our lives that at oral argument the Washington attorney general balked when confronted with the logical implications of accepting such an argument."[110] Anyone supporting contributor disclosure laws in the future will have to do more than balk.

Conclusion

Doe is in many ways a frustrating case because the Court decided much less than many on both sides of the campaign-finance divide were expecting and perhaps hoping for. That frustration is perhaps more the fault of the spectators than the Court, but the expectations were understandable in light of the Court's greater protections for First Amendment freedoms and greater skepticism for laws that burden speech in recent cases, most notably, *Citizens United*.

Unfortunately, the Court's approach to disclosure laws has always been somewhat of a compromise position between the two extremes of campaign-finance law, one being that the government should have the same amount of discretion to regulate speech as it does other things like the right to property and to contract and the other being that the opening words of the First Amendment—"Congress shall make no law"—mean what they say. Thus, as the Court put

---

[109] Doe, 130 S. Ct. at 2833 n.3 (Scalia, J., concurring in the judgment).
[110] *Id*. at 2824–25 (Alito, J., concurring) (internal citations omitted).

it in *Doe*, "'disclosure requirements may burden the ability to speak, but they ... do not prevent anyone from speaking.'"[111]

However, few restrictions on speech actually "prevent anyone from speaking." Most impose burdens of varying degrees. One can argue that disclosure laws are typically the less burdensome alternative, but that is highly debatable. In *Citizens United*, for instance, the Court declined to require corporations to speak through PACs, many of whose restrictions are designed to facilitate full disclosure.[112] And if one takes the rights to anonymous speech and association that the Court protected in cases like *McIntyre* and *NAACP v. Alabama* seriously, it is hard to understand how requiring the disclosure of a speaker's identity as a condition of speaking is constitutionally acceptable. The Court recognized in *Buckley* that a cap on the amount one wishes to spend on speech amounts to a ban on speech for everyone who wishes to spend more than the cap.[113] By the same token, mandatory disclosure should amount to a violation of the rights of anyone who does not wish to disclose their identity when they speak. Stating up front that disclosure is "less burdensome" or does not "prevent anyone from speaking" simply assumes, at the outset, that disclosure does not violate First Amendment rights. This approach treats anonymous speech and association as second-class rights under the First Amendment, which is not only contrary to cases like *McIntyre* and *NAACP v. Alabama*, it is also inconsistent with a long national tradition of speaking and associating anonymously.[114] It also finds no support in the text of the First Amendment, which does not bar government merely from banning speech outright; it prevents laws that "abridge" the freedom of speech.

Justice Thomas's approach to disclosure is thus the far better one, especially in cases like *Doe*. There is much to say for simplicity in First Amendment cases, and Justice Thomas's dissenting opinion in

---

[111] *Id.* at 2818 (majority opinion) (quoting Citizens United, 130 S. Ct. at 914).

[112] See Citizens United, 130 S. Ct. at 897–98.

[113] See Buckley, 424 U.S. at 19 n.18 ("Being free to engage in unlimited political expression subject to a ceiling on expenditures is like being free to drive an automobile as far and as often as one desires on a single tank of gasoline.").

[114] See, e.g., McIntyre, 514 U.S. at 341–43 (discussing the tradition of anonymous speech in the founding era and since, in the realms of literature and politics); *id.* at 360–70 (detailed discussion of historical basis for the right to speak anonymously about politics).

Doe was as elegantly simple as it was based in common sense. The plaintiffs were not challenging election process laws as such, so the Court could have ruled for them and kept its election process precedents intact. In light of modern technology, the state's argument that it needed the public's help to verify signatures is almost laughable.[115] Indeed, public disclosure under the PRA is not automatic; someone must make a request for signatures. What happens if no one requests signature information in a given referendum election? Must the state conclude that that election lacked integrity and throw out the results? *Doe* involved individuals and groups who made clear that they wished to use disclosure laws for exactly the reasons that the Supreme Court has prevented disclosure in the past—to intimidate those who wish to take a political position and express certain views.[116] Despise those views if you wish, but recognize, as Justice Thomas did, that if we take First Amendment rights seriously, *all* speakers must be protected from what amounts to state-sponsored harassment and intimidation.

Despite the Court's less-than-principled approach to First Amendment rights in *Doe*, those who favor greater protections for speech during elections can at least take heart in this: Although the Court did not give them the principled protections for privacy of association that they wanted, it did not foreclose the possibility that those protections will come in a case in which the states have fewer grounds for regulating than in *Doe*. Optimists can say that they live to fight another day; pessimists can wait for the other shoe to drop. But both will have to wait for the next disclosure case before claiming vindication.

---

[115] See Doe, 130 S. Ct. at 2840–42 (Thomas, J., dissenting) (referring to public disclosure as a "blunderbuss approach" to furthering interest in reliability of petition-gathering process); see also *id.* at 2827 (Alito, J., concurring) (questioning strength of state's interest in detecting fraud and mistakes, in light of other, less burdensome alternatives).

[116] See, e.g., NAACP v. Alabama ex rel. Patterson, 357 U.S. 449, 460–66 (1958) (holding that compelled disclosure of membership violated speech and associational rights, based on evidence that past disclosure led to "economic reprisal, loss of employment, threat of physical coercion, and other manifestations of public hostility").

The Tell-Tale Privileges or Immunities Clause

Alan Gura,* Ilya Shapiro,** and Josh Blackman***

Help is on the way! That's the Supreme Court's most readily obvious message for those Americans living in the handful of states that don't respect the right to keep and bear arms. It should not have been a surprise. Two years ago, in striking down the District of Columbia's handgun and functional firearms bans, the high court provided a none-too-subtle message to recalcitrant politicians unwilling to obey national civil rights standards. Ancient cases refusing to apply the right to arms against the states, said the Court, had also failed to apply the First Amendment and were based on obsolete thinking.[1] This term, in *McDonald v. City of Chicago*,[2] *Heller*'s wink-and-nudge became a shove, finally dragging anti-gun politicians into the late-19th century.

* Member, Gura & Possessky, PLLC; Counsel for Petitioners in *McDonald v. City of Chicago* and for Respondents in *District of Columbia v. Heller*; J.D., Georgetown University Law Center; B.A., Cornell University.

** Senior Fellow in Constitutional Studies, Cato Institute, and Editor-in-Chief, *Cato Supreme Court Review*; J.D., University of Chicago Law School; M.Sc., London School of Economics; A.B., Princeton University; signatory to Cato's amicus brief in *McDonald*.

*** Teaching Fellow, Pennsylvania State University Dickinson School of Law; Law Clerk to the Hon. Kim R. Gibson, U.S. District Court for the Western District of Pennsylvania; President, Harlan Institute; J.D., George Mason University School of Law; B.S., Pennsylvania State University. The authors would like to thank Bob Levy for his helpful comments and suggestions. This article—and especially its expedited publication—would not have been possible without the assistance of Trevor Burrus. We dedicate this article to John Bingham.

[1] District of Columbia v. Heller, 128 S. Ct. 2783, 2813 n.23 (2008) ("With respect to *Cruikshank*'s continuing validity on incorporation, a question not presented by this case, we note that *Cruikshank* also said that the First Amendment did not apply against the States and did not engage in the sort of Fourteenth Amendment inquiry required by our later cases. Our later decisions in Presser v. Illinois, 116 U. S. 252, 265 (1886) and Miller v. Texas, 153 U.S. 535, 538 (1894), reaffirmed that the Second Amendment applies only to the Federal Government.") (referencing United States v. Cruikshank, 92 U.S. 542 (1876)).

[2] McDonald v. City of Chicago, 561 U.S. ____; 130 S. Ct. 3020 (2010).

But at exactly what part of the late-19th century have they arrived? The heady days of the Fourteenth Amendment's first five years, when it was understood that states were actually bound to respect Americans' basic rights?[3] Or the century's last three years, with the Fourteenth Amendment's central guarantee of freedom having been parodied into a dead letter, the Supreme Court picking and choosing which rights are worth securing, and to what extent?[4] It is the answer to that question, more than the result applying the right to arms, that promises to make *McDonald* an enduring landmark of American liberty for years to come.

I. The Second Amendment Returns to the Supreme Court

A. *Heller* Begets *McDonald*

In its landmark 2008 opinion, *District of Columbia v. Heller*, the Supreme Court found that the Second Amendment protects an individual right to keep and bear arms unconnected to service in a militia.[5] The Court accordingly struck down D.C. laws banning the keeping of handguns, and the keeping of all functional firearms within the home. The *Heller* decision was "everything a Second Amendment supporter could realistically have hoped for,"[6] but for one inherent limitation. The case having arisen as a challenge to the law of the federal capital, the Court could not reach the question of whether, and to what extent, the right to keep and bear arms applies to the states and their units of local government. Justice Antonin Scalia's opinion for the Court did, however, observe that its 19th-century precedent declining to apply the Second Amendment right against the states "also said that the First Amendment did not apply

---

[3] See, e.g., Live-Stock Dealers' & Butchers' Ass'n v. Crescent City Live-Stock Landing & Slaughter-House Co., 15 F. Cas. 649 (C.C.D. La. 1870); United States v. Hall, 26 F. Cas. 79, 81–82 (C.C. S.D. Ala. 1871).

[4] See, e.g., Chicago, Burlington & Quincy R.R. Co. v. Chicago, 166 U.S. 226 (1897). See also Cruikshank, 92 U.S. 542, and Presser, 116 U.S. 252 (declining to incorporate the First and Second Amendments, respectively against the states).

[5] Heller, 128 S. Ct. at 2821–22. For a thorough and insightful look at the story behind *District of Columbia v. Heller*, see Clark Neily, District of Columbia v. Heller: The Second Amendment Is Back, Baby!, 2007–2008 Cato Sup. Ct. Rev. 127 (2008).

[6] Neily, *supra* note 5, at 147.

against the states and did not engage in the sort of Fourteenth Amendment inquiry required by our later cases."[7]

Ancient precedent from a dark time in American history, precedent that deprived people of basic rights, was still technically on the books. But much had happened since the days when the Supreme Court turned a blind eye to the rise of Jim Crow, and was congratulated by the Civil War's losers for having "dared to withstand the popular will as expressed in the letter of [the Fourteenth] amendment."[8] The Court had spent the past century repairing its Reconstruction-era damage, selectively applying additional rights as against the states. Would the Second Amendment follow the same path, marking merely the latest step in the long piecemeal "incorporation" process?

Within minutes of the Supreme Court's decision in *Heller*, petitioners in *McDonald v. City of Chicago* brought suit challenging the city's handgun ban and several overly burdensome features of its gun registration system.[9] The following day, the National Rifle Association filed suits challenging the Chicago ordinances, as well as ordinances in the suburb of Oak Park.

Chicago residents face one of the highest murder rates in the United States, and rates of violent crime far exceeding the average for comparably sized cities.[10] Yet since 1982, Chicago's firearm laws effectively banned the possession of handguns by almost all city residents.[11] Despite enactment of the handgun ban, the murder rate in Chicago had increased.[12] Several of the petitioners had been the

---

[7] Heller, 128 S. Ct. at 2783 n.23.

[8] Christopher G. Tiedeman, The Unwritten Constitution of the United States: A Philosophical Inquiry into the Fundamentals of American Constitutional Law 102–03 (1890).

[9] The plaintiffs (later petitioners) were Otis McDonald, Adam Orlov, Colleen Lawson, David Lawson, the Illinois State Rifle Association, and the Second Amendment Foundation. Contrary to the facts recited by Justice Alito, McDonald, 130 S. Ct. at 3027 n.4, the Illinois State Rifle Association and the Second Amendment Foundation were indeed petitioners in this case.

[10] McDonald, 130 S. Ct. at 3026.

[11] The ordinance provided that "[n]o person shall . . . possess . . . any firearm unless such person is the holder of a valid registration certificate for such firearm." Chicago, Ill., Municipal Code § 8-20-040(a) (2009), Chicago, Ill., Municipal Code § 8-20-050(c) barred the registration of handguns.

[12] McDonald, 130 S. Ct. at 3026.

targets of violence. Otis McDonald, a retiree from a rough neighborhood in Chicago, had been threatened by drug dealers, and the Lawsons had been targeted by burglars in their home.

B. Lower Court Opinions

The district court, considering all three cases, rejected the plaintiffs' arguments, noting that the Seventh Circuit Court of Appeals had "squarely upheld the constitutionality of a ban on handguns a quarter century ago."[13] *Heller* had refrained from "opin[ing] on the subject of incorporation" of the Second Amendment,[14] and the district court judge in *McDonald* noted that he had a "duty to follow established precedent in the Court of Appeals . . . even though the logic of more recent caselaw may point in a different direction."[15]

The Seventh Circuit affirmed, deciding against Second Amendment incorporation because of three prior cases.[16] Although the court noted that the rationales of the restrictive 19th-century precedents were "defunct," it did not consider whether the Due Process Clause of the Fourteenth Amendment incorporated the Second Amendment, and declined to predict how the right to keep and bear arms would fare under the Court's modern "selective incorporation" jurisprudence.[17]

In so holding, the Seventh Circuit pointed to *Heller*'s discussion of Reconstruction-era precedents but carefully avoided quoting the Supreme Court's caveat that those decisions "did not engage in the sort of Fourteenth Amendment inquiry required by our later cases." Only by tip-toeing around this rather obvious admonition to conduct an incorporation analysis could the court of appeals claim fidelity to the Supreme Court's precedents. In this manner, the Seventh Circuit agreed with the 19th-century Supreme Court regarding application of the Second Amendment to the states—but the court was

[13] NRA, Inc. v. Vill. of Oak Park, 617 F.Supp.2d 752, 753 (N.D.Ill. 2008) (citing Quilici v. Vill. of Morton Grove, 695 F.2d 261 (7th Cir. 1982)).

[14] Oak Park, 617 F.Supp.2d at 754.

[15] *Id.* at 753.

[16] NRA, Inc. v. City of Chicago, 567 F.3d 856, 857 (2009) (citing United States v. Cruikshank, 92 U.S. 542 (1876); Presser v. Illinois, 116 U.S. 252 (1886); Miller v. Texas, 153 U.S. 535 (1894)).

[17] NRA, 567 F.3d at 857–58.

unfaithful to the century of case law that followed, culminating with *Heller*'s instruction to perform a modern due process analysis.

The Seventh Circuit asserted that precedent having direct application must be followed even if it "rest[s] on reasons rejected in some other line of decisions."[18] But the Supreme Court's Reconstruction-era decisions hadn't applied the due process incorporation doctrine at all. Indeed, that doctrine would not be invoked by the Supreme Court in securing individual rights for decades following the ratification of the Fourteenth Amendment.[19] The earlier cases thus had no direct application to this question. "[C]ases cannot be read as foreclosing an argument that they never dealt with."[20] "[W]hen a lower court perceives a pronounced new doctrinal trend in Supreme Court decisions, it is its duty, cautiously to be sure, to follow not to resist it."[21] As the Seventh Circuit itself once acknowledged, "[a] court need not blindly follow decisions that have been undercut by subsequent cases . . . ."[22]

Or, as that same court recognized nearly 30 years ago,

> sometimes later decisions, though not explicitly overruling or even mentioning an earlier decision, indicate that the Court very probably will not decide the issue the same way the next time. In such a case, to continue to follow the earlier case blindly until it is formally overruled is to apply the dead, not the living, law.[23]

Time and again, courts have rejected a result under one theory, only to adopt the same result under another. For example, the Supreme Court rejected a challenge to the mandatory federal sentencing

[18] Rodriguez de Quijas v. Shearson/Am. Express, Inc., 490 U.S. 477, 484 (1989).

[19] See, e.g., Josh Blackman & Ilya Shapiro, Keeping Pandora's Box Sealed: Privileges or Immunities, *The Constitution in 2020*, and Properly Extending the Right to Keep and Bear Arms to the States, 8 Geo. J.L. & Pub. Pol'y 1, 57–59 (2010) ("Indeed, the concept of [selective due process] 'incorporation' was anachronistically inserted into our Constitutional jurisprudence decades after the ratification of the Fourteenth Amendment.").

[20] Waters v. Churchill, 511 U.S. 661, 678 (1994) (plurality opinion) (citation omitted).

[21] Perkins v. Endicott Johnson Corp., 128 F.2d 208, 218 (2d Cir. 1942), aff'd, 317 U.S. 501 (1943) (footnotes omitted).

[22] United States v. Burke, 781 F.2d 1234, 1239 n.2 (7th Cir. 1985) (citations omitted).

[23] Norris v. United States, 687 F.2d 899, 904 (7th Cir. 1982).

guidelines under separation of powers and non-delegation theories,[24] but that did not stop the Seventh Circuit from sustaining a similar challenge under the Sixth Amendment right to a jury trial—and the Supreme Court affirmed.[25]

This has been the history of due process incorporation. Virtually all rights selectively incorporated under the Due Process Clause had at one point been denied incorporation or application against the states under other theories.[26] And the lower federal courts had a leading role in incorporating some of these rights, without awaiting a green light from the Supreme Court.[27]

Instead, the Seventh Circuit followed a non-binding line of cases, ignored *Heller*'s directive to apply later cases, and excluded the Second Amendment from the broad application given other rights. By contrast, the Ninth Circuit—in a case that may yet come before the Supreme Court—recognized *Heller*'s pro-incorporation signal and found that the Second Amendment secured fundamental rights incorporated through the Due Process Clause.[28] Presaging the framework that Justice Samuel Alito would use in *McDonald*, the Ninth Circuit applied *Washington v. Glucksberg* and determined that because the right to keep and bear arms is a fundamental right, "meaning, 'necessary to an Anglo-American regime of ordered liberty'" and "deeply rooted in this Nation's history and tradition," the Fourteenth Amendment incorporates the Second Amendment.[29]

---

[24] Mistretta v. United States, 488 U.S. 361 (1989).

[25] Booker v. United States, 375 F.3d 508 (7th Cir. 2004), aff'd, 543 U.S. 220 (2005).

[26] Compare, e.g., United States v. Cruikshank, 92 U.S. 542 (1876) (First Amendment not directly applicable to the states) with Gitlow v. New York, 268 U.S. 652 (1925) (First Amendment incorporated), and Fox v. Ohio, 46 U.S. (5 How.) 410 (1847) (Fifth Amendment's Double Jeopardy Clause not directly applicable to the states) with Benton v. Maryland, 395 U.S. 784 (1969) (Double Jeopardy Clause incorporated).

[27] See, e.g., United States ex rel. Hetenyi v. Wilkins, 348 F.2d 844 (2d Cir. 1965) (incorporating Fifth Amendment Double Jeopardy Clause); United States ex rel. Bennett v. Rundle, 419 F.2d 599 (3d Cir. 1969) (en banc) (incorporating Sixth Amendment public trial right).

[28] Nordyke v. King, 563 F.3d 439, 457 n.16 (9th Cir. 2009) ("Because, as *Heller* itself points out, 128 S. Ct. at 2813 n.23, *Cruikshank* and *Presser* did not discuss selective incorporation through the Due Process Clause, there is no Supreme Court precedent directly on point that bars us from heeding *Heller*'s suggestions.").

[29] *Id.* at 449 (citing Duncan v. Louisiana, 391 U.S. 145, 150 n.14 (1968)).

C. Seeking Supreme Court Review

McDonald took a curious path to the Supreme Court. The Seventh Circuit had consolidated the NRA and McDonald appeals but the Supreme Court granted only McDonald's petition; the NRA's petition would be held pending the outcome in *McDonald*, which would necessarily control the NRA case.

As petitioners, McDonald and company got the first crack at framing the "question presented," which controls the scope of the briefing on the merits. They posed the following question: "Whether the Second Amendment right to keep and bear arms is incorporated as against the States by the Fourteenth Amendment's *Privileges or Immunities or Due Process Clauses*."[30] That meant, not only would "incorporation" via the Fourteenth Amendment be at issue, but the *manner* of incorporation would be as well.

Stated another way, had the Seventh Circuit incorporated the Second Amendment through the Due Process Clause—as did the Ninth Circuit in *Nordyke*—the validity of that analysis would have likely been the primary question on review. But the Seventh Circuit rejected incorporation altogether, so the *McDonald* petitioners had a blank slate on which to make their case. And logically, the full weight of constitutional text, structure, and history called for application of the Privileges and Immunities Clause. In accepting McDonald's formulation of the question, the Supreme Court agreed to decide both whether and how to incorporate.

Recall that *Heller* had just decided the basic Second Amendment issue on originalist grounds: "We are guided by the principle that the Constitution was written to be understood by the voters; its words and phrases were used in their normal and ordinary as distinguished from technical meaning."[31] Even the *Heller* dissenters adopted a version of originalism, but focused more on legislative intent.[32] Following either approach, *McDonald* should have relied on

---

[30] Petition for Writ of Certiorari, McDonald, 130 S. Ct. 3020 (No. 08-1521) (emphasis added).

[31] Heller, 128 S. Ct. at 2788 (citations and internal quotation marks omitted).

[32] *Id.* at 2822 (Stevens, J., dissenting). See also Josh Blackman, Originalism for Dummies, Pragmatic Unoriginalism, and Passive Liberty, available at http://ssrn.com/abstract= 1318387 ("Rather than ascertaining the original public meaning, [Justice Stevens] focuses almost exclusively on the drafting history, and improperly attempts to guess the intentions of our framers.").

the Privileges or Immunities Clause—which was understood and intended to bind the states to national civil rights standards—to extend the Second Amendment to the states.

To be sure, there may have been a technical conception of "substantive" due process among some 19th-century legal scholars.[33] But there was no evidence—none—that the ratifiers of the Fourteenth Amendment understood the Due Process Clause to transmit substantive rights (beyond the bare minimum needed to prevent "due process of law" from becoming a kangaroo court). Nor was there any evidence that the clause's authors believed it contained such powers.

Thus, the original understanding of the Fourteenth Amendment plainly favored applying Privileges or Immunities, not "substantive" due process. That should have mattered to the Court and, therefore, to the litigants. Justice Antonin Scalia recently put it this way:

> Twenty years ago, when I joined the Supreme Court, I was the only originalist among its numbers. By and large, counsel did not know I was an originalist—and indeed, probably did not know what an originalist was. In their briefs and oral arguments on constitutional issues they generally discussed only the most recent Supreme Court cases and policy considerations; not a word about what the text was thought to mean when the people adopted it. If any light was to be shed on the latter question, it would be through research by me and my law clerks. Today, the secret is out that I am an originalist, and there is even a second one sitting with me, Justice Clarence Thomas. *Rarely, nowadays, does counsel fritter away two out of nine votes by failing to address what Justice Thomas and I consider dispositive. Originalism is in the game, even if it does not always prevail.*[34]

And quite apart from the originalist sympathies of some justices, there was the practical aspect of litigating before a Supreme Court on which sit intractable opponents of substantive due process—

---

[33] See Timothy Sandefur, Privileges, Immunities, and Substantive Due Process, 5 N.Y.U. J. L. & Liberty 115 (2009); Frederick Mark Gedicks, An Originalist Defense of Substantive Due Process: Magna Carta, Higher-Law Constitutionalism, and the Fifth Amendment, 58 Emory L.J. 585 (2009).

[34] Justice Antonin Scalia, Foreword, 31 Harv. J. L. & Pub. Pol'y 871, 871 (2008) (emphasis added).

including, most notably, *Heller*'s author. In the last major civil rights case reaching the Court from Chicago, Justice Scalia famously derided substantive due process as an "atrocity" and an act of "judicial usurpation."[35] It would have been folly to assume that this Court had on it five votes for substantive due process incorporation.

Indeed, ultimately, as we all now know, there were not five votes.

Whatever its merits or ultimate level of acceptance among the justices, substantive due process incorporation had one unique feature: it was familiar. The Court had been down this well-worn path many times before. The Seventh Circuit avoided incorporating the Second Amendment on due process grounds only by avoiding the question. For the Supreme Court, the question of whether to incorporate the Second Amendment on due process grounds would merely be a test of the justices' commitment to existing incorporation principles. Either they believed in it, or they didn't; they would either apply the familiar standards to the Second Amendment or alter those familiar standards to make an anti-gun exception. Either way, it would be a poor use of litigation resources to beat the drum on a theory where every justice's vote, whatever it might be, was a foregone conclusion.

Or was it? Maybe those justices unwilling to carry originalism to its logical result—defining the right to bear arms as one of the privileges or immunities of citizenship—would nonetheless utilize originalist grounds in an exercise of substantive due process noseholding. That is, some faint-hearted originalist justices generally hostile to substantive due process might vote for due process incorporation if they could be convinced that the outcome was historically correct. There is strong evidence that this occurred among the *McDonald* plurality.[36]

Accordingly, the failure to make a strong originalist case could have seriously jeopardized the outcome. Justices unrepentantly hostile to substantive due process might not have forged their own

---

[35] City of Chicago v. Morales, 527 U.S. 41, 85 (1999) (Scalia, J., dissenting). See also Stop the Beach Renourishment v. Fla. Dep't. of Envtl. Prot., 130 S. Ct. 2592, 2607–08 (2010) (Scalia, J., plurality opinion) (attacking as vague and undefined Justice Anthony Kennedy's use of substantive due process to protect against judicial takings).

[36] McDonald, 130 S. Ct. at 3033 n.9 (Alito, J., plurality opinion) (referencing Privileges or Immunities sources); *id.* at 3050–51 (Scalia, J., concurring).

originalist path unless meaningfully asked to do so by the petitioners. In *Gonzales v. Carhart,* for example, the Supreme Court upheld the federal partial-birth abortion ban against a substantive due process challenge.[37] Justices Scalia and Clarence Thomas, predictably, were not enthusiastic about the doctors' due process abortion-rights claim. But this pair was also skeptical of congressional power to regulate abortion under the Commerce Clause—Justice Thomas having endorsed the idea that "health laws of every description" were "not surrendered to a general government."[38] *Carhart* proved to be a 5–4 decision, in which Justice Thomas, joined by Justice Scalia (two of the five), "note[d] that whether the Act constitutes a permissible exercise of Congress' power under the Commerce Clause is not before the Court. The parties did not raise or brief that issue; it is outside the question presented; and the lower courts did not address it."[39] Had the abortion-rights lawyers raised an originalist Commerce Clause challenge—arguing that Congress lacked the power to enact this law—they might well have prevailed 6–3.[40]

In the end none of the Court's more "liberal" justices voted in McDonald's favor, but the case's reception among self-described progressives and others normally unenthusiastic about gun rights was quite positive. At the petition stage, liberal academic luminaries including Yale's Jack Balkin and UCLA's Adam Winkler joined a brief by the Constitutional Accountability Center endorsing the originalist arguments for incorporation via the Privileges or Immunities Clause.[41] On the eve of argument, even the *New York Times* editorial page—no friend of the Second Amendment—opined that McDonald should prevail on that same basis.[42]

Chicago's attorneys understood at least some if not all of this dynamic. The city's lawyers had reason to believe they might prevail

---

[37] 550 U.S. 124 (2007).

[38] United States v. Lopez, 514 U.S. 549, 594 (1995) (Thomas, J., concurring) (quoting Gibbons v. Ogden, 22 U.S. (9 Wheat.) 1, 203 (1824)).

[39] Carhart, 550 U.S. at 169 (Thomas, J., concurring) (citation omitted).

[40] See David S. Cohen, The Paradox of *McDonald v. City of Chicago,* Geo. Wash. L. Rev. Arguendo (forthcoming), available at http://papers.ssrn.com/sol3/papers.cfm?abstract_id= 1653524.

[41] See Brief of Constitutional Law Professors as Amici Curiae in Support of Petitioners, McDonald, 130 S. Ct. 3020 (2010) (No. 08-1521).

[42] Editorial, The Second Amendment's Reach, N.Y. Times, March 1, 2010, at A22.

on the substantive due process question, but wished to avoid arguing their case on originalist grounds.[43] And so, in opposition to McDonald's petition for certiorari, Chicago offered, "If the Court believes the time is right to address whether the Second Amendment restrains state and local governments under the Due Process Clause, the petitions should be granted to address this issue only [but t]his Court should decline to address whether the Second Amendment is incorporated under the Privileges or Immunities Clause."[44]

McDonald petitioners replied that there was no way to divorce the historical record of the Fourteenth Amendment's ratification from the case. Arguing that the Supreme Court had erred in its basic approach to the Fourteenth Amendment, *McDonald* petitioners' reply brief on petition for certiorari contained section headings entitled, "The Privileges or Immunities Clause Cannot Be Avoided" and "Overruling *Slaughterhouse* Remains Imperative."[45]

The Supreme Court accepted the *McDonald* case, only the *McDonald* case and—over Chicago's objections—accepted McDonald's framing of the question. Anyone surprised by the subsequent emphasis on originalist (that is, Privileges or Immunities Clause) arguments was not paying attention to the petition process.[46]

---

[43] On the merits, Chicago indeed offered argument as to why it believed the Due Process Clause does not incorporate the Second Amendment. But as to the originalist Privileges or Immunities argument, Chicago offered only that the Privileges or Immunities Clause is indeterminate or duplicative of other guarantees, and should not be revisited.

[44] Brief for Respondents in Opposition to Petition for Writ of Certiorari at 6, NRA of Am., Inc. v. City of Chicago & Oak Park, 567 F.3d 856 (7th Cir. 2009), rev'd sub nom. McDonald v. City of Chicago, 130 S. Ct. 3020 (2010).

[45] Reply Brief on Petition for Writ of Certiorari at 7, 10, McDonald, 130 S. Ct. 3020 (No. 08-1521). *Slaughterhouse*, of course, is the set of 1873 cases that all but erased the Privileges or Immunities Clause from the Constitution. Slaughterhouse Cases, 83 U.S. (16 Wall.) 36 (1873).

[46] McDonald's counsel repeatedly and emphatically explained to certain conservative lawyers (1) the concerns—validated by the case's outcome—about the potential lack of five votes for substantive due process incorporation; (2) the utility—also demonstrated by the result—of an originalist argument in swaying votes even for due process incorporation; and (3) the benefits—realized—of attracting support to the case from non-traditional allies. Regrettably, political hostility to restoring the Fourteenth Amendment's original meaning and irrational fears about the consequences of doing so could not always be overcome. For further commentary, see, e.g., Ilya Shapiro, *Heller* Counsel Argues for an Originalist Revolution, Cato-at-Liberty, http://www.cato-at-liberty.org/2009/11/17/heller-counsel-argues-for-an-originalist-revolution/ (Nov. 17, 2009, 8:54 EST).

II. Split Decision

The Supreme Court reversed the Seventh Circuit and held in a 4–1–4 split that the Constitution guarantees the right to keep and bear arms for all individuals regardless of where in the country they live. How the Court got there is a little more complicated.

Justice Alito, writing for the plurality on behalf of Chief Justice John Roberts, Justice Scalia, and Justice Anthony Kennedy, held that the Second Amendment was incorporated through the Fourteenth Amendment's Due Process Clause. Justice Scalia concurred and also wrote separately to dispute much of Justice John Paul Stevens's dissent (much as he had in the term's other big case, *Citizens United*[47]). Justice Thomas did not join in most of Justice Alito's opinion, but he concurred in the judgment, thereby providing the all-important fifth vote for incorporation. While Thomas agreed that the right to keep and bear arms should be applied to the states, and agreed that the right is "fundamental," he found that this fundamental right was properly extended to the states by the Privileges or Immunities Clause. Justice Stevens dissented. No one else joined his opinion. Stevens found that the Second Amendment should not be incorporated and, even if it were, it need not provide as much protection to people of the states as it provides to people in federal enclaves. Justice Stephen Breyer also dissented, joined by Justices Ruth Bader Ginsburg and Sonia Sotomayor. Breyer argued that (1) *Heller* was wrongly decided; (2) the Second Amendment should not be incorporated; and (3) *McDonald* would result in more crime and violence.

A. Justice Alito's Plurality Opinion

The bulk of Justice Alito's opinion focused on the history of the right to keep and bear arms from revolutionary times to Reconstruction and attempted to apply that history—and what it says about the nature of the right—to incorporation doctrine. Justice Alito observed that the Court had never embraced the "total incorporation" theory advanced by Justice Hugo Black, who argued that "[Section] 1 of the Fourteenth Amendment totally incorporated all of the provisions of the Bill of Rights,"[48] but Alito took "no position with respect

---

[47] Citizens United v. FEC, 558 U.S. ____, 130 S. Ct. 876, 925 (2010) (Scalia, J., concurring).
[48] McDonald, 130 S. Ct. at 3033 (citing Adamson v. California, 332 U.S. 46, 71–72 (1947) (Black, J., dissenting); Duncan v. Louisiana, 391 U.S. 145, 166 (1968) (Black, J., concurring)).

to t[he] academic debate" over this theory.[49] He continued to sketch the evolution of the Court's disjointed due process jurisprudence and noted that the Warren Court—the Court under Chief Justice Earl Warren in the 1950s and '60s—initiated "what has been called a process of 'selective incorporation'" wherein the Court held that the "Due Process Clause fully incorporates particular rights contained in the first eight Amendments."[50] These opinions "inquired whether a particular Bill of Rights guarantee is fundamental to our scheme of ordered liberty and system of justice."[51] Alito proceeded to list all the rights that had been incorporated under the Due Process Clause and the rights that had not been incorporated—most importantly, the Second Amendment.[52]

In order to reconcile the hodgepodge incorporation jurisprudence of the Supreme Court during the early-20th century, Justice Alito compiled "[f]ive features of the approaches taken."[53] First, "the Court viewed the due process question as entirely separate from the question whether a right was a privilege or immunity of national citizenship."[54] Second, the Court explained that the only rights protected against state infringement were those rights "of such a nature that they are included in the conception of due process of law,"[55] and that their protection was not due solely to their "enumerat[ion] in the first eight Amendments."[56] Alito listed several different formulations relied on by the Court to "describ[e] the boundaries of [rights protected by] due process," including the "famous[]" *Palko v. Connecticut* version, which protected rights that are "the very essence of a scheme of ordered liberty" and essential to "a fair and enlightened system of justice."[57]

Third, citing the standard from *Duncan v. Louisiana*, Justice Alito remarked that "during this era the Court 'can be seen as having

---

[49] McDonald, 130 S. Ct., at 3033 n.10.

[50] *Id.* at 3034 (citations omitted).

[51] Duncan, 391 U.S. at 149 n.14.

[52] McDonald, 130 S. Ct. at 3034–35 n.12.

[53] *Id.* at 3031.

[54] *Id.* (citing Twining v. New Jersey, 211 U.S. 78, 99 (1908)).

[55] *Id.*

[56] *Id.*

[57] *Id.* at 3032 (citing Palko v. Connecticut, 302 U.S. 319, 325 (1937)).

asked, when inquiring into whether some particular procedural safe-guard was required of a State, if a civilized system could be imagined that would not accord the particular protection.'"[58] By accepting this broader rationale of due process, the Court was able to reconcile the precedent of *Chicago, Burlington & Quincy Railroad*, which held that states cannot violate the Takings Clause of the Fifth Amend-ment, even though the provision was never explicitly "incorpo-rated."[59] Fourth, the Court found that some rights had "failed to meet the test for inclusion"; the rights of freedom of speech and press, assistance of counsel in capital cases, freedom of assembly, and free exercise "qualified," while others, such as to grand jury indictment, "did not" qualify.[60]

Fifth, even for rights in the Bill of Rights that "f[ell] within the conception of due process, the protection or remedies afforded against state infringement sometimes differed from the protection or remedies" provided against federal infringement.[61] However, the two examples Justice Alito gave of rights applying differently to the state and federal governments—the right of appointed counsel[62] and the exclusionary rule[63]—were subsequently overruled by Warren Court precedents.[64] The only extant precedent that supports this "watered-down" version of rights, *Apodaca v. Oregon*[65]—which held

---

[58] *Id.* (citing Duncan, 391 U.S. at 149, n.14).

[59] Chicago, Burlington & Quincy R.R. Co. v. Chicago, 166 U.S. 226 (1897) (opinion by Harlan, J.) (due process prohibits states from taking private property for public use without just compensation).

[60] McDonald, 130 S. Ct. at 3032 (citations omitted).

[61] *Id.*

[62] Betts v. Brady, 316 U.S. 455, 462 (1942) (holding that the Due Process Clause required appointment of counsel in state criminal proceedings only where "want of counsel in [the] particular case . . . result[ed] in a conviction lacking in . . . fundamental fairness"), overruled by Gideon v. Wainright, 372 U.S. 335 (1963).

[63] Wolf v. Colorado, 338 U.S. 25, 27–28 (1949) (holding that while the Fourth Amend-ment is "implicit in the concept of ordered liberty" and "enforceable against the States through the Due Process Clause," the exclusionary rule does not apply to the states), overruled by Mapp v. Ohio, 367 U.S. 643 (1961).

[64] Malloy v. Hogan, 378 U.S. 1, 10 (holding that the Bill of Rights provisions incorpo-rated "are all to be enforced against the States under the Fourteenth Amendment according to the same standards that protect those personal rights against federal encroachment").

[65] 406 U.S. 404 (1972).

that the "Due Process Clause does not require unanimous jury verdicts in state criminal trials"—was "the result of an unusual division among the Justices" and does not endorse the "two-track approach to incorporation."[66] Alito noted that it is "far too late to exhume what Justice Brennan . . . derided as 'the notion that the Fourteenth Amendment applies to the States only a watered-down, subjective version of the individual guarantees of the Bill of Rights.'"[67]

After considering this century-long train of precedents, Justice Alito concluded that the Court "must decide whether the right to keep and bear arms is fundamental to our scheme of ordered liberty or as we have said in a related context, whether this right is 'deeply rooted in this Nation's history and tradition.'"[68]

According to the plurality, the Court's "decision in *Heller* points unmistakably to the answer": yes.[69] Repeating *Heller's* holding, Justice Alito recounted that "individual self-defense is 'the central component' of the Second Amendment" and "citizens must be permitted 'to use [handguns] for the core lawful purpose of self-defense.' "[70] He then recited that the right described in *Heller* is "deeply rooted in this Nation's history and traditions"[71]

The plurality's treatment of the Privileges or Immunities Clause, meanwhile, was uncharacteristically curt. First, the plurality acknowledged that "many legal scholars dispute the correctness of the narrow *Slaughterhouse* interpretation."[72] Second, the Court noted that petitioners wanted the Court to overrule *Slaughterhouse* and "hold that the right to keep and bear arms is one of the 'privileges or immunities of citizens of the United States.'"[73] Third, the Court remarked that while the petitioners contend that the "Privileges or

---

[66] McDonald, 130 S. Ct. at 3035 n.14.

[67] *Id.* at 3047 (citing Malloy, 378 U.S. at 10–11) (internal quotation marks omitted).

[68] *Id.* at 3036 (citing Duncan, 391 U.S. at 149, and Wash. v. Glucksberg, 521 U.S. 702, 721) (internal citations and quotation marks omitted).

[69] McDonald, 130 S. Ct. at 3036.

[70] *Id.* (citing Heller, 128 S. Ct. at 2081–82, 2818).

[71] Glucksberg, 521 U.S. at 720.

[72] McDonald, 130 S. Ct. at 3029. This is an understatement akin to noting that "many" astrophysicists believe the Earth is essentially round and revolves around the Sun— but nevertheless an important first step in overcoming the *Slaughterhouse* Court's medieval view, as it were, of the Privileges or Immunities Clause.

[73] *Id.* at 3030 (quoting U.S. Const. amend. XIV § 1, cl. 2).

Immunities Clause protects all of the rights set out in the Bill of Rights, as well as some others"—that is, unenumerated rights—"petitioners are unable to identify the Clause's full scope."[74] Similarly, scholars who think *Slaughterhouse* was wrong are also unable to arrive at a "consensus on th[e] question" about the scope of unenumerated rights.[75] Without any substantive discussion, the plurality thus saw no need to reconsider *Slaughterhouse*—not that it would have had to demarcate there and then the full panoply of protected unenumerated rights to decide whether this particular (enumerated) right was covered by a properly interpreted Privileges or Immunities Clause. The Court merely noted that "for decades, the question of the rights"—both enumerated, and unenumerated—"protected by the Fourteenth Amendment against state infringement has been analyzed under the Due Process Clause of that Amendment and not under the Privileges or Immunities Clause."[76] Accordingly, the plurality "decline[d] to disturb the *Slaughterhouse* holding."[77] That's all, folks.

This short treatment is indeed remarkable. Regardless of the unknowable politics behind the adoption of petitioners' question presented, the Court did take that question. To exert merely 172 words on such a profound topic, barely acknowledging the proverbial elephant in the room in light of Justice Thomas's lengthy, historic concurrence seems odd.

Furthermore, that nobody can agree on the Privileges or Immunities Clause's full scope is hardly a reason to ignore it. The Fourteenth Amendment's authors refused to define its full scope, too. Introducing the amendment on the Senate floor, Michigan's Jacob Howard declared,

> To these privileges and immunities, whatever they may be— for they are not and cannot be fully defined in their entire extent and precise nature—to these should be added the personal rights guarantied and secured by the first eight

[74] *Id.*

[75] *Id.* Of course, to continue the metaphor from note 72, *supra*, astrophysicists adopting the Copernican view rather than the Ptolemaic still disagree among themselves regarding, for example, whether Pluto is a planet.

[76] *Id.*

[77] *Id.* at 3031.

amendments of the Constitution; such as the freedom of speech, . . . and the right to keep and to bear arms . . . .[78]

If the amendment's framers were not bothered by the inability to fully delineate the clause's scope, why should the Supreme Court be? Justice Robert Jackson had already replied to the *McDonald* plurality's concern nearly 70 years ago:

> [T]he difficulty of the task does not excuse us from giving these general and abstract words whatever of specific content and concreteness they will bear as we mark out their application, case by case. That is the method of the common law, and it has been the method of this Court with other no less general statements in our fundamental law.[79]

The argument would have quickly devolved into a circus had petitioners attempted to do what the Fourteenth Amendment's framers believed impossible and sought to offer a complete litany of rights included and excluded from the Privileges or Immunities Clause. The petitioners themselves had never considered, never mind agreed on, the full scope of the liberty protected by the amendment. Indeed, whether a particular right is or is not within the amendment is always a serious question warranting careful examination and deliberation; no Supreme Court case considering an unenumerated right has ever been a casual exercise.

Moreover, the fact that the Supreme Court happily announces new rules, including on occasion heretofore unknown rights, while never taking such opportunity to *fully* describe the scope of the relevant constitutional text, renders the sudden insistence on learning the Privileges or Immunities Clause's full catalog incongruent with the Court's approach to constitutional interpretation. "[The] Court has not been timorous about giving concrete meaning to such obscure and vagrant phrases as 'due process,' 'general welfare,' 'equal protection,' or even 'commerce among the several States.'"[80]

---

[78] Cong. Globe, 39th Cong., 1st Sess. 2765 (1866).

[79] Edwards v. California, 314 U.S. 160, 183 (1941) (Jackson, J., concurring).

[80] *Id.* at 183 (Jackson, J., concurring). As the Fifth and Fourteenth Amendment Due Process Clauses illustrate, not all rights must be specifically described. Cf. U.S. Const. amend. IX.

Refusing to interpret the relevant constitutional text in reaching as groundbreaking a decision as the application of the right to bear arms against the states takes a jarring leap of logic. As Professor Mark Tushnet observed in *Heller*'s wake:

> The debates over the Fourteenth Amendment's adoption are replete with comments that one of the Amendment's benefits would be to ensure that the South's freedmen would be able to protect themselves from marauding whites by guaranteeing their own right to arm themselves. The only embarrassment is a doctrinal one: *all these references described the right to keep and bear arms as one of the privileges of the citizenship that the Fourteenth Amendment guaranteed*, and contemporary incorporation doctrine rests not on the privileges or immunities clause of the Fourteenth Amendment, but rather on its due process clause.[81]

Indeed, the Privileges or Immunities Clause leaves quite a lump brushed under the constitutional carpet. Witness this remarkable passage from Justice Alito's plurality:

> Senator Jacob Howard, who spoke on behalf of the Joint Committee on Reconstruction and sponsored the Amendment in the Senate, stated that the Amendment protected all of "the personal rights guarantied and secured by the first eight amendments of the Constitution."[82]

No. Senator Howard did not state that "the Amendment" protected these rights. As shown in the fuller quote of the same speech above, the subject of Howard's speech was *the Privileges or Immunities Clause*. But Justice Alito continues:

> After ratification of the Amendment, Bingham maintained the view that the rights guaranteed by *§ 1 of the Fourteenth Amendment* "are chiefly defined in the first eight amendments to the Constitution of the United States." [83]

[81] Mark Tushnet, The Future of the Second Amendment, 1 Alb. Gov't L. Rev. 354, 355 n.4 (2008) (emphasis added).

[82] McDonald, 130 S. Ct. at 3033 n.9 (citing Cong. Globe, 39th Cong., 1st Sess., 2765 (1866)).

[83] *Id.* (quoting Cong. Globe, 42d Cong., 1st Sess., App. 84 (1871)) (emphasis added).

No. Representative Bingham, author of Section 1, did *not* maintain the view that "the rights guaranteed by § 1 of the Fourteenth Amendment" are so chiefly defined. Here is what Bingham stated on that particular page of the *Congressional Globe*:

> [P]ermit me to say that the *privileges or immunities of citizens of the United States*, as contradistinguished from citizens of a State, are chiefly defined in the first eight amendments to the Constitution of the United States.[84]

The nation's leading Fourteenth Amendment scholars stand in good company, likewise suffering the same gloss on their words. Justice Alito describes their brief as collecting authorities in stating that "[n]ot a single senator or representative disputed [the incorporationist] understanding' of the *Fourteenth Amendment*."[85] Well, not quite. The entire point of the law professors' brief was "to bring to the foreground of this case a remarkable scholarly consensus and well-documented history that shows that the Privileges or Immunities Clause of the Fourteenth Amendment was intended to protect substantive, fundamental rights, including the individual right to keep and bear arms at issue in this case."[86] And so, here is the sentence of the professors' brief immediately preceding that quoted by Justice Alito:

> [T]he most influential and knowledgeable members of the Reconstruction Congress went on record with their express belief that Section One of the Fourteenth Amendment—and, in most instances, the Privileges or Immunities Clause specifically—protected against state infringement of fundamental rights, including the liberties secured by the first eight articles of the Bill of Rights.[87]

The professors' brief explains, "Republicans in Congress affirmed two central points: the Privileges or Immunities Clause would safeguard the substantive liberties set out in the Bill of Rights, and that,

---

[84] Cong. Globe, 42d Cong., 1st Sess., App. 84 (1871).

[85] McDonald, 130 S. Ct. at 3033 n.9 (quoting Brief of Constitutional Law Professors as Amici Curiae, *supra* note 41, at 20) (emphasis added).

[86] Brief of Constitutional Law Professors as Amici Curiae, *supra* note 41, at 1.

[87] *Id.* at 20.

in line with *Corfield*, the Clause would give broad protection to substantive liberty, safeguarding all the fundamental rights of citizenship."[88]

And some people wonder why the Privileges or Immunities Clause was argued by petitioners. A better question, left unanswered, is why the plurality obfuscated the text it claimed to be interpreting. The *Slaughterhouse* majority might have (temporarily) gotten away with killing the Privileges or Immunities Clause, but Justice Alito's plurality suggests that like Poe's tell-tale heart, the Fourteenth Amendment's central guarantee of liberty is beating loudly under the floorboards.

B. *Justice Scalia's Quixotic Concurrence*

Justice Scalia's concurring opinion is perhaps most noteworthy for what he did not say—and what he attempted to sweep under the rug in a mere 55 words and a citation:

> Despite my misgivings about Substantive Due Process as an original matter, I have acquiesced in the Court's incorporation of certain guarantees in the Bill of Rights "because it is both long established and narrowly limited." *Albright v. Oliver*, 510 U.S. 266, 275 (1994) (SCALIA, J., concurring). This case does not require me to reconsider that view, since straightforward application of settled doctrine suffices to decide it.[89]

Justice Scalia's acquiescence in a theory he has recently termed "babble," "usurpation," and even an "atrocity," as part of his veritable holy war on behalf of originalism is startling enough. We now learn that Justice Scalia only has "misgivings" about substantive due process as an original matter and it is suddenly acceptable to "acquiesce" in the theory because it is "long established"? Imagine a hypothetical Supreme Court in the year 2073, with *Roe v. Wade* on the docket for reconsideration, and Justice Scalia, perhaps by virtue of the recent health care reform law, still advocating originalism from the bench. Would he acquiesce in *Roe* on its 100th birthday—coincidentally the 200th birthday of *Slaughterhouse*—because it

---

[88] *Id.* at 1.
[89] McDonald, 130 S. Ct. at 3050 (Scalia, J., concurring).

would by then be as long established as substantive due process is today?

After a 2008 speech in which Justice Scalia suggested that "maybe the original meaning of the Constitution is back,"[90] he was asked, "What rule or rules do you apply when deciding to set aside a precedent when reviewing a case that you feel was wrongly decided?"[91] Justice Scalia's response partly predicted his vote in favor of substantive due process incorporation, but it made his avoidance of *McDonald*'s originalist issues all the more perplexing.

"I believe in *stare decisis*," he said. "[T]he vast majority of that [wrongly decided] stuff is water under the bridge and I wouldn't go back and revise it. . . . I am a textualist, I am an originalist, I am not a nut."[92] But, he added: "There are some opinions that I do not accept. I think the most important criteria for me are, probably in ascending order, number one, how wrong was it? I mean there are some of them that are blatantly and maliciously wrong."[93]

This is an apt description of *Slaughterhouse*. Just five years after the 39th Congress labored to pass the Fourteenth Amendment, *Slaughterhouse* eviscerated the intent and purpose of the central part of that amendment, the Privileges or Immunities Clause. As the preponderance of modern scholarship shows, this interpretation was at least "blatantly" wrong, if not indeed "malicious," as were the decision's original propounders.[94] In *McDonald*, as we discuss below, Justice Thomas reviewed this scholarship and concluded that the

---

[90] Hon. Antonin Scalia, United States Supreme Court, Address to Federalist Society National Lawyers Convention at 9:40 (Nov. 22, 2008), video available at http://www.fed-soc.org/publications/pubid.1193/pub_detail.asp.

[91] *Id*. at 36:00.

[92] *Id*. at 36:32.

[93] *Id*. at 36:50.

[94] See generally Michael Kent Curtis, No State Shall Abridge: The Fourteenth Amendment and the Bill of Rights (1990); Akhil Reed Amar, The Bill of Rights: Creation and Reconstruction 161–70 (1995); Brief of the Constitutional Law Professors as Amici Curiae Supporting Petitioners at 3, McDonald, 130 S. Ct. 3020 (No. 08-1521) ("[*Slaughterhouse*] read the Privileges or Immunities Clause so narrowly as to render it practically meaningless—completely ignoring the contrary text, history and purpose of the Fourteenth Amendment."); see generally Brief for the Institute for Justice and the Cato Institute as Amici Curiae Supporting Petitioners, McDonald, 130 S. Ct. 3020 (No. 08-1521).

Slaughterhouse Cases had been wrongly decided and should be over-ruled.[95] In *his* opinion, however, Justice Scalia ignored Justice Thomas's able recounting of the errors of *Slaughterhouse*. But Scalia has another consideration when choosing *stare decisis* over originalism: the second point in his speech was, "how well has it been accepted?"[96] As an example, Scalia offers the incorporation doctrine, which he thinks is "probably wrong, but I wouldn't go back."[97]

That was clearly a harbinger of his "acquiescence" in *McDonald* to the "usurpative atrocity" of substantive due process. It does not, however, explain his silence regarding the Privileges or Immunities Clause. *Slaughterhouse* may be on the books, but "[v]irtually no serious modern scholar—left, right, and center—thinks that it is a plausible reading of the [Fourteenth] Amendment."[98] Indeed, one notable scholar described *Slaughterhouse* as "probably the worst holding, in its effect on human rights, ever uttered by the Supreme Court."[99]

The *Slaughterhouse* decision is so poorly accepted that Chicago's lawyers in *McDonald* would not explicitly defend its rationale. Yet Justice Scalia casually dismissed criticism of *Slaughterhouse* as mere academic concerns.[100] Apparently, he has forgotten his own advice in *Payne v. Tennessee*: "[W]hat would enshrine power as the governing principle of this Court is the notion that an important constitutional decision with plainly inadequate rational support *must* be left in place for the sole reason that it once attracted five votes."[101] And

---

[95] McDonald, 130 S. Ct. at 3058–88 (Thomas, J., concurring).

[96] Hon. Antonin Scalia, Address to the Federalist Society, *supra* note 90, at 37:16.

[97] *Id.* at 37:35.

[98] Akhil Amar, Substance and Method in the Year 2000, 28 Pepp. L. Rev. 601, 631 n.178 (2001).

[99] Charles Black Jr., A New Birth of Freedom: Human Rights, Named and Unnamed 55 (1997).

[100] Transcript of Oral Argument at 7–8, McDonald, 130 S. Ct. 3020 ("JUSTICE SCALIA: [W]hy are you asking us to overrule 150, 140 years of prior law, when—when you can reach your result under substantive due I mean, you know, unless you're *bucking for a—a place on some law school faculty* . . . JUSTICE SCALIA: Well, I mean, what you argue is the *darling of the professoriate*, for sure, but it's also contrary to 140 years of our jurisprudence. Why do you want to undertake that burden instead of just arguing substantive due process? Which, as much as I think it's wrong, I have—even I have acquiesced in it.") (emphasis added).

[101] Payne v. Tennessee, 501 U.S. 808, 834 (1991) (Scalia, J., concurring) (emphasis in original).

this admonition in *Planned Parenthood v. Casey*: "But in their [the plurality] exhaustive discussion of all the factors that go into the determination of when *stare decisis* should be observed and when disregarded, they never mention 'how wrong was the decision on its face?'"[102] Chief Justice John Roberts recently made a similar point about the virtues and limitations of *stare decisis* in *Citizens United v. FEC*: "When considering whether to reexamine a prior erroneous holding, we must balance the importance of having constitutional questions *decided* against the importance of having them *decided right*."[103]

Scalia's third "and probably . . . most important" question in weighing *stare decisis* is whether "that prior decision allow[s] me to behave like a judge"—that is, does the decision provide an adequate basis for judicial decisionmaking.[104] At oral argument, Scalia asked petitioners' counsel whether he was troubled that the Privileges or Immunities Clause would allow judges to enforce unenumerated rights. Counsel answered that the Court has already enforced some unenumerated rights, suggesting that reinvigorating the Privileges or Immunities Clause would not threaten the Court's established practices.[105] Scalia was not comforted.

More critically, of course, the enforcement of unenumerated rights would not have troubled the Framers. To the contrary, the Framers would have been disappointed in a timid judiciary that bends to the will of the political branches and shies from the trust placed in it by Article III to safeguard the Constitution.[106] The Framers of the original Constitution and the Bill of Rights explicitly endorsed—in the Ninth Amendment—the idea that some rights could not be enumerated. The Fourteenth Amendment's framers similarly codified language they understood to encompass a range of rights that could not be fully cataloged.[107]

---

[102] Planned Parenthood of Se. Pa. v. Casey, 505 U.S. 833, 982–83 (1992) (Scalia, J., dissenting).

[103] Citizens United, 130 S. Ct. at 920 (Roberts, C.J., concurring) (emphasis in original).

[104] Hon. Antonin Scalia, Address to the Federalist Society, *supra* note 90 at 37:53.

[105] Transcript of Oral Argument at 7–8, McDonald, 130 S. Ct. 3020.

[106] See, e.g., Alan Gura, *Heller* and the Triumph of Originalist Judicial Engagement: A Response to Judge Harvie Wilkinson 56 UCLA L. Rev. 1129, 1136–42 (2009).

[107] See Senator Jacob Howard's speech during ratification debates, Cong. Globe, 39th Cong., 1st Sess. 2765 (1866) (arguing that the Privileges or Immunities Clause of the Fourteenth Amendment gives protections to substantive liberty and fundamental rights enjoyed by "citizens of all free Governments": "protection by the government,

This is where Justice Scalia steps off the originalist bus.[108] Regardless of how "blatantly and maliciously wrong" a precedent might be, or how poorly accepted it is, Justice Scalia seems unwilling to bury its pernicious doctrine—perhaps because that process would call on him to engage in an historical exploration of which rights are to be enforced, rather than merely how rights are to be enforced.

Moreover, *McDonald* did not supply the only occasion during the 2009–10 term that Justice Scalia dealt with the scope and meaning of substantive due process. In *Stop the Beach Renourishment v. Florida Department of Environmental Protection*, Justice Scalia wrote for a plurality that chided Justice Kennedy's use of substantive due process to protect against judicial takings.[109] While holding that the Florida Supreme Court did not commit a judicial taking when it ruled that beachfront property owners did not have the right for their property to contact the waterline, Scalia rightly chose the Takings Clause as the proper clause under which takings—judicial or otherwise— should be reviewed. He also gave an accurate critique of substantive due process as a "wonderfully malleable" concept to which the "firm commitment to apply it would be a firm commitment to nothing in particular."[110] Instead, Scalia argues, textual provisions should be followed if germane textual provisions are available.[111] Indeed they should, and the same reasoning applies to Justice Scalia's dismissal of the germane textual provision—the Privileges or Immunities Clause—at issue in *McDonald*.[112]

---

the enjoyment of life and liberty, with the right to acquire and possess property of every kind, and to pursue and obtain happiness and safety, subject nevertheless to such restraints as the Government may justly prescribe for the general good of the whole") (quoting Corfield v. Coryell, 6 F. Cas. 546, 551 (C.C.E.D. Pa. 1823)).

[108] See Ilya Shapiro & Josh Blackman, Is Justice Scalia Abandoning Originalism?, Wash. Exam'r, March 8, 2010.

[109] Stop the Beach Renourishment v. Fla. Dep't of Envtl. Prot., 560 U.S. ____, 130 S. Ct. 2592, 2606–08 (2010) (Scalia, J., plurality opinion).

[110] *Id.* at 2608.

[111] *Id.* at 2606 ("Where a particular Amendment 'provides an explicit textual source of constitutional protection' against a particular sort of government behavior, 'that Amendment, not the more generalized notion of "substantive due process," must be the guide for analyzing these claims.'" (citations omitted)).

[112] For more on this contrast in Justice Scalia's reasoning see Ilya Shapiro & Trevor Burrus, Judicial Takings and Scalia's Shifting Sands, 35 Vt. L. Rev. ____ (forthcoming 2011), available at http://papers.ssrn.com/sol3/papers.cfm?abstract_id = 1652293.

The remainder of Justice Scalia's opinion addresses the philosophy advanced by Justice Stevens's dissent—"a broad condemnation of the theory of interpretation which underlies the Court's opinion, a theory that makes the traditions of our people paramount."[113] Scalia criticizes Stevens for excluding the right to keep and bear arms from incorporation, despite its being as "deeply rooted in this Nation's history and tradition as a right can be," while including other rights lacking historical grounding, simply because he "deeply believes it should be out."[114] Scalia also disparages Stevens's "subjective" conception of the Due Process Clause, which gives the court a "prerogative" and "duty" to update the Constitution "so that it encompasses new freedoms the Framers were too narrow-minded to imagine."[115]

Justice Scalia thus revisits the debate between the "living Constitution" approach to jurisprudence and originalism. He concludes that the issue "is not whether the historically focused method is a perfect means of restraining aristocratic judicial Constitution-writing; but whether it is the best means available in an imperfect world."[116] In other words, originalism is the least worst option because it is "much less subjective, and intrudes much less upon the democratic process."[117]

But ultimately, Justice Scalia's familiar observations ring hollow, coming as they do as a lengthy postscript to his declaration preferring application of substantive due process—a doctrine requiring him to apply those rights, and only those rights that *he* believes are fundamental—while scorning an originalist approach based on historical analysis of how the Fourteenth Amendment's framers understood the text they ratified. Justice Scalia could have demonstrated fidelity to the judicial method he would use to attack Justice Stevens by joining Justice Thomas's concurrence.

C. *Justice Thomas's Pivotal Concurrence*

"I believe this case presents an opportunity to re-examine, and begin the process of restoring, the meaning of the Fourteenth

---

[113] McDonald, 130 S. Ct. at 3050 (Scalia, J., concurring).

[114] *Id.* at 3051 (quoting Glucksberg, 521 U.S. at 721).

[115] *Id.* at 3051.

[116] *Id.* at 3057–58.

[117] *Id.* at 3058.

Amendment agreed upon by those who ratified it."[118] With these words, Justice Thomas broke with the plurality, turned to face the stark reality of the Fourteenth Amendment's central text, and launched an analysis that promises to fundamentally restore the proper relationship between Americans and their state governments.

Justice Thomas "agree[d] with the Court that the Fourteenth Amendment makes the right to keep and bear arms" applicable to the states, but "wr[ote] separately because I believe there is a more straightforward path to this conclusion, one that is more *faithful to the Fourteenth Amendment's text and history.*"[119] Though Thomas concurred with the result reached by the plurality, he argued that the right to keep and bear arms cannot be enforceable against the states through a clause that "speaks only to 'process.'"[120] Rather, "the right to keep and bear arms is a privilege of American citizenship that applies to the States through the Fourteenth Amendment's Privileges or Immunities Clause."[121]

Justice Thomas's opinion explores the right to keep and bear arms through the prism of the expansive notions of freedom, liberty, and equality vindicated by the Reconstruction amendments, "which were adopted to repair the Nation from the damage slavery had caused."[122] The Privileges or Immunities Clause, which provides that "[n]o State shall make or enforce any law which shall abridge the privileges or immunities of citizens of the United States," appears to secure to the persons just made U.S. citizens (freed slaves) a certain collection of rights—"privileges or immunities" in the parlance of the time—attributable to that status. This broad notion of freedom recognized certain fundamental freedoms that inhered in the newly ratified definition of citizenship.

Thomas noted that the Supreme Court's "marginalization" of the Privileges or Immunities Clause in the *Slaughterhouse Cases*, and the "circular" reasoning of *United States v. Cruikshank* constituted the "Court's last word" for over a century, and "in the intervening years" the Court held that the clause protected "only a handful of

---

[118] McDonald, 130 S. Ct. at 3063 (Thomas, J., concurring).

[119] *Id.* at 3058–59 (emphasis added).

[120] *Id.* at 3059.

[121] *Id.*

[122] *Id.* at 3060.

rights ... that are not readily described as essential to liberty.[123] Following these flawed precedents, "litigants seeking federal protection of fundamental rights turned to" the Due Process Clause—a "most curious place"—in order to find "an alternative fount of such rights."[124] Over time, the Court "conclude[d] that certain Bill of Rights guarantees," both substantive and procedural rights, "were sufficiently *fundamental* to fall within § 1's guarantee of 'due process'"—though the Court "has long struggled to define" the term "fundamental."[125] Justice Thomas criticized the disparate standard the Court has used to recognize "fundamental" rights, spanning from the *Glucksberg* "deeply rooted" test to the "less measurable range of criteria" of *Lawrence v. Texas* that recognized the nebulous protection of "liberty of the person both in its spatial and in its more transcendent dimensions."[126]

Taking an intrinsically originalist perspective, Thomas noted that neither the plurality nor the dissents even bother "argu[ing] the meaning they attribute to the Due Process Clause was consistent with public understanding at the time of its ratification."[127] Refusing to "accept a theory of constitutional interpretation that rests on such tenuous footing," Thomas opined that the "original meaning of the ... [Privileges or Immunities Clause] offers a superior alternative, and that a return to that meaning would allow this Court to enforce the rights the Fourteenth Amendment is designed to protect with greater clarity and predictability than the substantive due process framework has so far managed."[128]

Acknowledging the "importance of *stare decisis*," Justice Thomas noted that while significant number of cases have "been built upon the substantive due process framework," *stare decisis* is not "an

---

[123] McDonald, 130 S. Ct. at 3060–61 (Thomas, J., concurring) ("In other words, the reason the Framers codified the right to bear arms in the Second Amendment—its nature as an inalienable right that pre-existed the Constitution's adoption—was the very reason citizens could not enforce it against States through the Fourteenth."). See also Saenz v. Roe , 526 U. S. 489, 503 (1999).

[124] McDonald, 130 S. Ct. at 3061 (Thomas, J., concurring).

[125] *Id*. (emphasis added).

[126] *Id*. at 3062 (quoting Lawrence v. Texas, 539 U.S. 558, 562 (2003)).

[127] *Id*. at 3062.

[128] *Id*.

inexorable command."[129] Neither *McDonald* generally nor the originalist arguments propounded by petitioners' counsel called for reconsidering the entire Fourteenth Amendment. Rather, the "question in this case is only whether, and to what extent, a particular clause in the Constitution protects the particular right at issue here."[130]

Starting with the presumption that no clause in the Constitution could be "intended to be without effect,"[131] Thomas begins by inquiring what "'ordinary citizens' at the time of ratification would have understood" the Privileges or Immunities Clause to mean.[132] Gleaning from contemporary historical sources, Thomas makes three observations about the Privileges or Immunities Clause. First, the term "privileges or immunities" was a term of art, synonymous with "right[s]," "libert[ies]," or "freedom[s]," or in the words of William Blackstone, the "inalienable rights of individuals."[133] Second, "both the States and the Federal Government had long recognized the *inalienable rights* of their citizens."[134] Third, the "public's understanding of [the clause] was informed by its understanding of the [Privileges *and* Immunities Clause in Article IV]," as "famously" articulated by Justice Bushrod Washington in *Corfield v. Coryell*.[135]

Relying on an impressive array of historical sources, including popular and widely disseminated speeches by amendment sponsors Representative John Bingham[136] and Senator Jacob Howard,[137] as well

---

[129] *Id.* at 3063.

[130] *Id.*

[131] *Id.* (citing Marbury v. Madison, 5 U.S. (1 Cranch) 137, 174 (1803) (Marshall, C.J.)).

[132] McDonald, 130 S. Ct. at 3063 (Thomas, J., concurring) (citing Heller, 128 S. Ct. at 2788).

[133] *Id.* at 3064 (citing 1 William Blackstone, Commentaries *129).

[134] *Id.* at 3068 (emphasis added).

[135] *Id.* at 3066–67 (citing Corfield v. Coryell, 6 F. Cas. 546, 551–52 (C.C.E.D. Pa. 1825) (finding that the Privileges and Immunities Clause protects those rights "which are, in their nature, fundamental; which belong, of right, to the citizens of all free governments").

[136] *Id.* at 3072 ("Bingham emphasized that §1 was designed to arm the Congress of the United States, by the consent of the people of the United States, with the power to enforce the bill of rights as it stands in the Constitution today. It 'hath that extent—no more.') (quoting Cong. Globe, 39th Cong., 1st Sess. 2542–43 (1866)).

[137] See Senator Jacob Howard's speech introducing the new draft on the floor of the Senate, Cong. Globe, 39th Cong., 1st Sess. 2765 (1866) (explaining that the Constitution recognized "a mass of privileges, immunities, and rights, some of them secured by

as the Civil Rights Act of 1866[138] and the Freedmen's Bureau Act,[139] Thomas concluded that the "right to keep and bear arms was understood to be a privilege of American citizenship guaranteed by the Privileges or Immunities Clause."[140] The Privileges or Immunities Clause is not a mere anti-discrimination principle, but "establishes a minimum baseline of federal rights, and the constitutional right to keep and bear arms plainly was among them."[141]

Justice Thomas conceded that while his understanding is "contrary to this Court's precedents," "*stare decisis* is only an 'adjunct' of our duty as judges to decide by our best lights what the Constitution means," and so considered whether "*stare decisis* requires retention of those precedents."[142] He also cabined his analysis to the right to keep and bear arms—and expressly declined to evaluate the larger scope of the Privileges or Immunities Clause. Further, "the right to keep and bear arms was essential to the preservation of liberty" and the Framers and the ratifying-era public "deemed this right necessary to include in the minimum baseline of federal rights that the Privileges or Immunities Clause established in the wake of the War over slavery."[143]

As to *Slaughterhouse*, Thomas criticized the case for "interpreting the rights of state and federal citizenship as mutually exclusive." The *Slaughterhouse* majority had limited federal rights to a "handful" of rights that excluded rights of state citizenship.[144] But those latter,

---

the second section of the fourth article of the Constitution, . . . some by the first eight amendments of the Constitution," and that "there is no power given in the Constitution to enforce and to carry out any of these guarantees" against the states).

[138] McDonald, 130 S. Ct. at 3084 (Thomas, J., concurring) ("Both proponents and opponents of this Act described it as providing the 'privileges' of citizenship to freedmen, and defined those privileges to include constitutional rights, such as the right to keep and bear arms.").

[139] *Id.* at 3084 (The Freedmen's Bureau Act "entitled all citizens to the 'full and equal benefit of all laws and proceedings concerning personal liberty' and 'personal security.' The Act stated expressly that the rights of personal liberty and security protected by the Act 'includ[ed] the constitutional right to bear arms.'") (citing Act of July 16, 1866, ch. 200, §14, 14 Stat. 176).

[140] McDonald, 130 S. Ct. at 3076–77 (Thomas, J., concurring).

[141] *Id.* at 3083.

[142] *Id.* at 3084.

[143] *Id.* at 3063 (citing Planned Parenthood of Se. Pa. v. Casey, 505 U.S. 833, 963 (1992) (Rehnquist, C.J., concurring in judgment in part and dissenting in part)).

[144] *Id.* at 3084–85.

broader rights "'embraced nearly every civil right for the establishment and protection of which organized government is instituted'— that is, all those rights listed in *Corfield*."[145]

The artificial distinction between federal and state rights "led the Court in future cases to conclude that constitutionally enumerated rights were excluded from the Privileges or Immunities Clause's scope"—an understanding Justice Thomas "reject[ed]."[146] The Privileges or Immunities Clause was not meant to "protect every conceivable civil right from state abridgement," but "the privileges and immunities of state and federal citizenship overlap."[147] Thomas also found that *"Cruikshank* is not a precedent entitled to any respect" because it relied on the discredited *Slaughterhouse*.[148]

But does the Privileges or Immunities Clause protect certain rights beyond those enumerated in the Constitution—that is, unenumerated rights like the right of the *Slaughterhouse* butchers to "exercise their trade"?[149] Justice Thomas noted that the four dissenting justices in *Slaughterhouse*—whose view he generally supports—would have held the clause to protect the right to earn an honest living.[150] Of course the right to earn a living was not at issue in *McDonald*, but Justice Thomas was aware that his opinion would have broader application.[151]

"The mere fact that the Clause does not expressly list the rights it protects does not render it incapable of principled judicial application."[152] Fears about the "risks of granting judges broad discretion to recognize individual constitutional rights in the absence of textual or historical guideposts" apply equally whether those rights are recognized under the substantive due process doctrine or the Privileges or Immunities Clause.[153] Moreover, by employing an originalist

[145] *Id.* at 3084 (citing Slaughterhouse, 83 U.S. (16 Wall.) at 76).

[146] *Id.* at 3085.

[147] *Id.*

[148] *Id.* at 3086.

[149] Slaughterhouse, 83 U.S. (16 Wall.) at 60.

[150] McDonald, 130 S. Ct. at 3086 (Thomas, J., concurring).

[151] *Id.* at 3077 n.15 (Thomas, J., concurring) ("I address the coverage of the Privileges or Immunities Clause only as it applies to the Second Amendment right presented here, but I do so with the understanding that my conclusion may have implications for the broader argument.").

[152] *Id.* at 3086.

[153] *Id.* at 3089–90, 3096, 3099.

framework that seeks to learn "what the ratifying era understood the Privileges or Immunities Clause to mean," the interpretation of unenumerated rights "should be no more 'hazardous' than interpreting" other ambiguous clauses, such as the Necessary and Proper Clause.[154]

D. *Justice Stevens's Valedictory Dissent*

Justice Stevens, in one of his last public acts as a member of the Court, found that the Second Amendment did not protect a fundamental right, that even if it were fundamental it should not be incorporated, and that even if it were incorporated, it need not be protected equally at the state and federal levels. Stevens, who described incorporation as a "misnomer,"[155] adopted the second Justice John Marshall Harlan's view that "the Court's usual approach has been to ground the prohibitions against state action squarely on due process, without intermediate reliance on any of the first eight Amendments."[156] Relying on Justice Harlan's dissent in *Duncan*, Stevens argued it was "circular" to incorporate only rights "deeply rooted in our history" because "state actors have already been according the most extensive protection" to those same rights.[157]

Justice Stevens also remarked that *Glucksberg* "promises an objectivity it cannot deliver and masks the value judgments that pervade any analysis of what customs, defined in what manner, are sufficiently 'rooted'" in our history and traditions.[158] Stevens thus equates

---

[154] *Id*. at 3086.

[155] Compare *id*. at 3092 (Stevens, J., dissenting) ("It follows that the term 'incorporation,' like the term 'unenumerated rights,' is something of a misnomer. Whether an asserted substantive due process interest is explicitly named in one of the first eight Amendments to the Constitution or is not mentioned, the underlying inquiry is the same: We must ask whether the interest is 'comprised within the term liberty.'") (internal citations omitted) with Blackman & Shapiro, Pandora's Box, *supra* note 19, at 8 ("Indeed, 'incorporation' is a misnomer, a constitutional malapropism. The concept of 'incorporation' was anachronistically inserted into our constitutional jurisprudence decades after the ratification of the Fourteenth Amendment. Historical accounts of the ratification debates reveal that the Privileges or Immunities Clause was meant to protect both more and less than the Bill of Rights—but in any event not the eight particular amendments as such.").

[156] McDonald, 130 S. Ct. at 3092 (Stevens, J., dissenting) (citing Malloy v. Hogan, 378 U. S. 1, 24 (1964) (Harlan, J., dissenting)).

[157] *Id*. at 3098 (citing Duncan v. Louisiana, 391 U.S. 145, 183 (1968) (Harlan, J., dissenting) (critiquing "circular[ity]" of historicized test for incorporation).

[158] *Id*. at 3098–99.

the *Glucksberg* inquiry as "countenanc[ing] the most revolting past injustices in the name of continuity," such as "slavery" and the "subjugation of women and other rank forms of discrimination."[159]

In a somewhat confusing closing, Justice Stevens noted that the *Glucksberg* test is "judicial abdication in the guise of judicial modesty."[160] But it would seem that the justices abdicating their judicial role are those willing to delegate the interpretation of the Constitution to the City of Chicago and eschew federal judicial enforcement of the right to bear arms. The faux judicial modesty belongs to Stevens, and not the Court.

E.   *Justice Breyer's Multi-Factor Balancing Dissent*

Justice Breyer's dissenting opinion makes several points: First, like Stevens, Breyer briefly reopened the *Heller* debate by outlining his contrary version of the text and history of the right to keep and bear arms. Unlike Stevens's competing originalism, however, Breyer prefers his own (ahistorical) theory of "active liberty" to interpret the Constitution. Second, again somewhat like Stevens, Breyer would hold that the Second Amendment right to "private self defense" is not "fundamental" and should not be incorporated. That is, even "taking *Heller* as a given"—something none of the dissenters apparently do, even though Justice Sotomayor accepted during her confirmation hearing just last year that *Heller* was "settled law"[161]— Justice Breyer contended that the majority "fails" to show that the right to keep and bear arms is "fundamental to the American scheme of justice."[162] Third, Breyer seeks to distinguish the right to keep and bear arms from "other forms of substantive liberty" because the Second Amendment "often puts others' lives at risk," and "does

---

[159] *Id.* at 3099. Cf. Planned Parenthood of Se. Pa. v. Casey, 505 U.S. 833, 843 (1992) (plurality opinion) ("Liberty finds no refuge in a jurisprudence of doubt.").

[160] McDonald, 130 S. Ct. at 3099 (Stevens, J., dissecting).

[161] David B. Kopel, Sotomayor Targets Guns Now: Justice's Dissent Contradicts Confirmation Testimony, Wash. Times, June 29, 2010, at B1. Elena Kagan also commented that *Heller* was "settled law" during her confirmation hearing. See Elena Kagan, Confirmation Hearing Day 2 (June 29, 2010), available at http://www.c-spanvideo.org/program/294264-2; David Ingram, On Day 2, Kagan Tries to Appease Republicans, Nat'l. L. J., June 30, 2010, available at http://www.law.com/jsp/article.jsp?id= 1202463143586. Only time will tell whether she follows Justice Sotomayor's change of heart.

[162] McDonald, 130 S. Ct. at 3123 (Breyer, J., dissenting) (citing Duncan, 391 U.S. at 149).

not warrant federal constitutional regulation."[163] Finally, in an uncharacteristic paean to judicial minimalism, Breyer faults the majority for "transferring ultimate regulatory authority over the private uses of firearms from democratically elected legislatures to courts or from the States to the Federal Government."[164]

Continuing his disapproval of originalism, Justice Breyer remarked that "in the incorporation context, as elsewhere, history often is unclear about the answers"—even though Justice Stevens's *Heller* dissent relies almost exclusively on history—and "the historical status of a right is [not] the only relevant consideration."[165] Yet Breyer's preferred approach for determining whether a right is "fundamental" meanders even from established incorporation jurisprudence. Breyer seeks to consider a laundry list of factors, including "the nature of the right; any contemporary disagreement about whether the right is fundamental; the extent to which incorporation will further other, perhaps more basic, constitutional aims; and the extent to which incorporation will advance or hinder the Constitution's structural aims, including its division of powers among different governmental institutions (and the people as well)."[166] Questions of whether incorporation "further[s] the Constitution's effort to ensure that the government treats each individual with equal respect" and is consistent "with the Constitution's efforts to create governmental institutions well suited to the carrying out of its constitutional promises" are at the core of Breyer's approach to incorporation, one that seems inspired by "redemptive constitutionalism" that now constitutes the leading edge of progressive legal thought.[167]

In any event, Justice Breyer's critique of originalism makes two crucial errors: First, like Justice Stevens in *Heller*, Breyer conflates "original intent originalism"—which looks to constitutional framers' intent and "motivations"—with "original public meaning originalism"—the so-called New Originalism, which seeks to understand

[163] *Id.* at 3120.

[164] *Id.*

[165] *Id.* at 3123.

[166] *Id.* These aims largely mirror the considerations discussed in Jack Balkin & Reva Siegel, The Constitution in 2020 (2009), to discern when a right should be protected. See Blackman & Shapiro, Pandora's Box, *supra* note 19, at 31–41 (discussing and criticizing this view).

[167] See generally Balkin & Siegel, The Constitution in 2020, *supra* note 166; Stephen J. Breyer, Active Liberty: Interpreting Our Democratic Constitution (2005).

the semantic context of terms and how they were understood by the public at the time of ratification.[168] While the former has been seriously discredited, largely by scholars on the left, the latter has gained general acceptance. Second, Breyer considers originalism at the wrong time.[169] While it was appropriate in *Heller* to consider the meaning of the right to keep and bear arms at the time of the Second Amendment's ratification, the correct timeframe for analyzing the Fourteenth Amendment's substantive protections is the Reconstruction era. Breyer mistakenly grounds his analysis in 1791 rather than 1868—when the self-defense interest was perhaps the strongest it has been in American history—concluding that "the Framers did not write the Second Amendment in order to protect a private right of armed self-defense."[170]

III. *McDonald*'s Aftermath: Opening the Door to Liberty

The most common question about the state of the legal world after *McDonald*—no doubt what some readers of this article are looking for—relates to the future of "gun rights." That is, what does this "application of the Second Amendment to the states" mean in practice and what kinds of lawsuits will be successful? Each of us, for example, is regularly asked by friends, colleagues, and public interlocutors to explain the scope of this individual right to keep and bear arms.[171] One of us (Gura) is counsel in various lawsuits challenging "may issue" gun-carry permit systems (which require individuals to justify their need or show "good cause" to exercise

---

[168] See generally Antonin Scalia, A Matter of Interpretation, 16–18, 29–30, 37–41, 133–36, 140–42, 145–48 (1997); Randy Barnett, Restoring the Lost Constitution: The Presumption of Liberty (2005).

[169] See Blackman & Shapiro, Pandora's Box, *supra* note 19, at 51 ("Originalism demands that the interpreter select the proper temporal location in which to seek the text's original public meaning.").

[170] McDonald, 130 S. Ct. at 3136 (Breyer, J., dissenting).

[171] See, e.g., Ilya Shapiro, Guest Appearance on The Colbert Report, July 8, 2010 (replying "no personal rocket launchers" when asked by the host to name one acceptable firearm regulation), available at http://www.colbertnation.com/the-colbert-report-videos/340923/july-08-2010/automatics-for-the-people–ilya-shapiro–jackie-hilly.

their Second Amendment right),[172] a gun-range ban,[173] handgun-rostering schemes that turn legislators into gun designers,[174] and laws restricting access to arms during times of emergency.[175] Opinions citing *McDonald* in cases involving various municipal restrictions are already emerging from the lower courts[176] and the Ninth Circuit has specifically requested *McDonald*-related supplemental briefing in the continuing *Nordyke* saga.[177]

But all this Second Amendment litigation is almost beside *McDonald*'s point. Yes, the right at issue here—the one triggering, as it were, the fascinating seminar on incorporation doctrine—was one involving guns. But nowhere in *McDonald* will you find a discussion of the constitutionality of licensing or registration requirements, concealed-carry regimes, firearm- or ammunition-purchasing limits, automatic-rifle or "assault-weapon" prohibitions, or any of the myriad other issues at the heart of the legal and political battles over the future of gun regulations. Much like *Heller*—which decided "only" that the Second Amendment protected an individual right not connected to militia service—*McDonald* "merely" said that this right, whatever its scope, offered protection against all levels of government, not just the federal. In neither case did the Court even attempt to sketch the line between constitutional and unconstitutional gun laws. And that demurral is neither surprising nor disappointing; the Court simply didn't have to reach those issues to evaluate the claims made in the respective lawsuits.

---

[172] Kachalsky v. Cacase, No. 10-CV-5413 (S.D.N.Y. filed July 15, 2010); Woollard v. Sheridan, No 10-CV-2068 (D. Md. filed July 28, 2010); Sykes v. McGinness, No. 09-1235 (E.D. Cal. filed May 7, 2009).

[173] Ezell v. City of Chicago, No. 10-CV-5135 (N.D. Ill. filed Aug. 16, 2010).

[174] Pena v. Cid, No. 09-CV-1185 (E.D. Cal. filed Apr. 30, 2009).

[175] Bateman v. Perdue, No. 10-CV-265 (E.D.N.C. filed July 6, 2010).

[176] See, e.g., United States v. Marzzarella, No. 09-3185, 2010 U.S. App. LEXIS 15655 (3d Cir. July 29, 2010), available at http://www.ca3.uscourts.gov/opinarch/093185p.pdf (using intermediate scrutiny to uphold prohibition on serial-number removal as an incidental burden on Second Amendment rights); United States v. Skoien, No. 08-3770, 2010 U.S. App. LEXIS 14262 (7th Cir. July 13, 2010) (en banc), available at http://www.ca7.uscourts.gov/tmp/0H0O79JV.pdf (upholding a prohibition on gun possession by those previously convicted of a domestic violence misdemeanor).

[177] Nordyke v. King, 07-15763 (9th Cir. July 19, 2010) (order for parties to file supplemental briefs in light of *McDonald*).

What makes *McDonald* interesting and significant, therefore, is not what it said about the right to keep and bear arms or the "incorporation" of that right against the states, but what it said about rights generally. What rights do we have and how did we come to have them? Which constitutional provisions protect these rights? If we accept that the Constitution protects rights that are not explicitly enumerated therein—as we must if we are to give effect to the Ninth Amendment[178]—then what is the scope of these unenumerated rights? Most immediately, which state laws are now in jeopardy for violating the Fourteenth Amendment's substantive protections? These are the questions that are *McDonald*'s progeny.

Most of these questions were provoked not by the plurality opinion, however, or even by the debate between the plurality and the dissents. And they do not flow from the simple fact that the Court incorporated the Second Amendment. Instead, it was Justice Thomas's lone concurrence that, by reanimating the Privileges or Immunities Clause and starting a jurisprudential discourse on that clause's meaning, resurrected the old idea that we possess certain "unalienable rights." In stirring passages detailing the state oppressions rampant before and after the Civil War, Thomas showed the reasons for, first, the Civil Rights Act of 1866 and, soon after, the Fourteenth Amendment. Freed slaves needed guns to defend themselves against pervasive threats to life and liberty, to be sure—which is partly why extending the right to keep and bear arms is vitally important—but they also needed the freedom to secure employment in a variety of professions, to keep the fruits of their labors, to engage in economic transactions, and a host of other rights that in the parlance of the day were called privileges or immunities. These sorts of rights do not appear explicitly in the text of the Fourteenth Amendment, but in reviewing explanatory documents like the speeches of the amendment's framers and ratifiers, and sources such as *Corfield v. Coryell*, one finds that those unenumerated rights were very much understood to be constitutionally protected.

It is thus that Justice Thomas's forceful and scholarly opinion will influence litigation that has nothing to do with guns or the Second

---

[178] See, elsewhere in this volume, Michael W. McConnell, The Ninth Amendment in Light of Text and History, 2009–2010 Cato Sup. Ct. Rev. 13 (2010).

Amendment but with unenumerated rights—and especially the eco-nomic liberties that *Slaughterhouse* disparaged and that were sub-verted by the infamous *Carolene Products* footnote four.[179] Every complaint challenging the host of capricious laws impeding the fundamental right to earn an honest living—such as arbitrary licens-ing restrictions (typically sought by the very industry the law is supposed to be regulating) and other irrational barriers to entry—will now cite Thomas's *McDonald* concurrence. His opinion will also strengthen future challenges to the pervasive regulatory state that has exploded in recent years. When you think about it—and quite apart from the over-arching question of where the government gets the expansive power it asserts—legislation such as TARP and Oba-maCare offends a host of unenumerated rights as well.

Significantly, even though Justice Alito did not adopt Justice Thomas's approach, he took great pains in his plurality opinion not to reject or criticize it (as did, for that matter, Justices Stevens and Breyer in their dissents). *McDonald* as a whole thus represents a crucial first step down the path to constitutional liberty and opens the door to reviving a powerful constitutional provision. Thomas's clarion call for a liberty-focused originalism provides a foundation on which to build.

In the annals of Supreme Court history, solo or minority opinions that introduce novel ideas often start a trickle of discussions. These arguments swirl and strengthen, and over time flow into a sea change in constitutional law. Look no further than the first Justice John Marshall Harlan's opinion in *Plessy v. Ferguson*, which argued that separate is not equal. Harlan's lone dissent culminated in *Brown v. Board of Education*. Or consider Justice Owen Roberts's opinion for

---

[179] United States v. Carolene Products Co., 304 U.S. 144, 153 n.4 (1938) (subjecting to higher scrutiny legislative actions relating to "specific prohibitions of the Constitution, such as those of the first ten amendments," as well as those affecting "discrete and insular minorities"). Ironically, Chicago's handgun ban implicated just such a specific constitutional prohibition—the Second Amendment. Both dissenting opinions some-how missed this in arguing that gun-control regulations do not demand of judges a searching inquiry. See, e.g., McDonald, 130 S. Ct. at 3116 (Stevens, J., dissenting) ("[T]his is not a case, then, that involves a 'special condition' that 'may call for a correspondingly more searching judicial inquiry.'") (citing Carolene Products, 304 U.S. at 153, n.4.); *id.* at 3125 (Breyer, J., dissenting) ("We are aware of no argument that gun-control regulations target or are passed with the purpose of targeting 'discrete and insular minorities.'") (citing Carolene Products, 304 U.S. at 153, n.4).

himself and Justice Hugo Black in *Hague v. CIO*, which has become canonical within First Amendment law for its bold declaration of freedom in the public square.[180] Or the landmark case of *Griswold v. Connecticut*, in which only Justice Byron White squarely held that a state ban on the sale of contraceptives deprived married couples of substantive liberty under the Fourteenth Amendment's Due Process Clause.[181] Or to Justice Robert Jackson's concurrence in the *Steel Seizure Case* that now provides the framework by which the president's foreign policy powers are measured.[182] Indeed, law students in 25 or 50 years might look back at Justice Thomas's role in *McDonald* as most akin to that which Justice Lewis Powell played in *Regents of the University of California v. Bakke*, the unfortunate case allowing race to play a factor in university admissions.[183] There was no majority in *Bakke*, either, but Justice Powell's solo concurrence has come to be known as the controlling law of that case—think what you will of its (decidedly non-originalist) reasoning—and was essentially adopted by the Supreme Court a quarter-century later.[184]

In one respect, Thomas's position in *McDonald* is even more noteworthy than Harlan's was in *Plessy*, because Thomas represented the decisive fifth vote for a majority judgment rather than a dissent (or a superfluous concurring vote that might be disregarded as an outlier). In one opinion Justice Thomas has shown the way for the Privileges or Immunities Clause—long-hidden under the constitutional floorboards—to protect our most basic freedoms.

---

[180] Hague v. Comm. for Industrial Org., 309 U.S. 496, 515–16 (1939) (Roberts, J.).

[181] 381 U.S. 479, 502–07 (1964) (White, J., concurring).

[182] See, e.g., Medellin v.Texas, 552 U.S. 491, 524 (2008) (citing Youngstown Steel & Tube Co. v. Sawyer, 343 U.S. 579, 635 (1953) (Jackson, J., concurring)).

[183] 438 U.S. 265, 317–19 (1978) (Powell, J., concurring) (arguing that a policy that focused on diversity and only considered race a "plus," rather than a quota, could withstand strict scrutiny).

[184] Grutter v. Bollinger, 539 U.S. 306, 325 (2003) ("[T]oday we endorse Justice Powell's view [in *Bakke*] that student body diversity is a compelling state interest that can justify the use of race in university admissions.").

The Degradation of the "Void for Vagueness" Doctrine: Reversing Convictions While Saving the Unfathomable "Honest Services Fraud" Statute

Harvey A. Silverglate* and Monica R. Shah**

The "void for vagueness" doctrine is, in theory, rather simple to comprehend: in order to justify the deprivation of its citizens' liberty, government must give sufficiently clear notice of what its laws demand or prohibit. This fundamental aspect of due process of law, applied to federal legislation through the Constitution's Fifth Amendment and to the states via the Fourteenth, has long been a backstop against capricious enforcement of American laws. Its significance is perhaps best appreciated when compared to a legal system with no such safeguard. Soviet-era KGB secret police, confident that their elastic criminal statutes could be stretched to target all perceived enemies of the regime, were known to boast: "Show me the man and I'll find you the crime."

Notwithstanding its centrality to liberty and justice, the void for vagueness doctrine has fallen of late into a kind of desuetude in the arena of federal criminal legislation and prosecution. It remains alive in theory, but not terribly supportive of liberty in practice. This situation is particularly problematic because federal criminal law,

* Harvey A. Silverglate, of counsel to Boston's Zalkind, Rodriguez, Lunt & Duncan, LLP, practices criminal defense and civil liberties law. He is an adjunct scholar at the Cato Institute and contributed a chapter to In the Name of Justice: Leading Experts Reexamine the Classic Article "The Aims of the Criminal Law" (Timothy Lynch ed., 2009). Mr. Silverglate is the author, most recently, of Three Felonies a Day: How the Feds Target the Innocent (2009). Mr. Silverglate extends profuse thanks to his research assistant Kyle Smeallie for invaluable assistance in the preparation of this article.

** Monica R. Shah, an associate at Zalkind, Rodriguez, Lunt & Duncan, LLP, practices criminal defense, employment discrimination, and civil rights law.

unlike its state counterparts is entirely a creature of statute rather than of common law.[1] Hence, traditional common-law doctrines of willfulness and criminal intent, which cabin the application of state criminal statutes, do not apply on the federal side. Nor is federal statutory interpretation assisted very much by the hundreds of years of Anglo-Saxon common-law court opinions passed down from England and from the pre-colonial American courts. For a criminal statute to apply only to those who intentionally violate the law, Congress must specify the degree to which knowledge of the law and intent to violate it will factor into a potential prosecution.[2] Furthermore, much state law involves areas of human conduct where ordinary citizens, because of long tradition, have a good sense of the line between lawful conduct and crime. Murder and theft, for example, are not foreign concepts to most of us. Yet few citizens can be expected to have an intuitive grasp of what is entailed in "mail or wire fraud," or in rendering "material assistance" to terrorist groups, or the myriad other areas covered by the rapidly growing body of federal criminal statutes and regulations.[3] Therefore, the vagueness doctrine, one would think, has an even more vital role to play in federal criminal law than it does in the state criminal justice system. Yet the opposite often appears to be the truth.

Several cases decided in the past term highlight the inadequate amount of thought, as well as lack of practical common sense, that seems to characterize the Supreme Court's modern jurisprudence with regard to the due process aspects of the vagueness doctrine. The resolution of these cases is so unsatisfactory as to call for a reexamination of the role of due process vagueness analysis in all

---

[1] United States v. Hudson & Goodwin, 11 U.S. (7 Cranch) 32 (1812).

[2] According to a recent study, of the 446 nonviolent, non-drug-related criminal laws presented in the 109th Congress, more than half lacked a requirement that a defendant act with criminal intent. See Brian W. Walsh and Tiffany Joslyn, Without Intent: How Congress Is Eroding the Criminal Intent Requirement in Federal Law, the Heritage Found. and the Nat'l Ass'n for Criminal Def. Lawyers, May 2010, at 13, available at http://www.nacdl.org/withoutintent.

[3] A study by the Federalist Society reported that, by the year 2007, the U.S. Code (listing all statutes in force enacted by Congress) contained more than 4,450 criminal offenses, up from 3,000 in 1980. See John S. Baker Jr., Measuring the Explosive Growth of Federal Crime Legislation, Federalist Society for Law and Public Policy Studies White Paper, May 2004, updated June 16, 2008, available at http://www.heritage.org/Research/LegalIssues/lm26.cfm.

the high court's jurisprudence as it affects the validity of federal criminal statutes. Unless and until the vagueness doctrine becomes a viable tool for requiring that a citizen's obligations be clear before he can be punished for criminal transgressions, judges are going to be punishing citizens utterly innocent of evil intent, thus undermining the moral supports of the law.

An analysis of the Supreme Court's reasoning in this term's vagueness cases suggests that the time has come for the high court to begin to weed the garden of federal statutes that fail to inform the average citizen, or indeed even highly skilled lawyers, of what the law requires or prohibits.[4]

I. Introduction

In *Skilling v. United States*,[5] and the related cases *Black* and *Weyhrauch*,[6] the Supreme Court claimed to pare down 18 U.S.C. § 1346—

---

[4] The authors of this article are both practicing criminal defense attorneys, one of whom was involved in and has written about a Massachusetts federal wiretapping prosecution, *United States v. Bradford Councilman*, that, in many ways, typifies the lens through which life-tenured judges view the problem of statutory vagueness. That case involved the interpretation of the somewhat esoteric federal wiretapping statute and its application—or not—to an Internet service provider who routinely made copies of emails passing through its computer system. The district judge at first denied, then changed his mind based on a Ninth Circuit precedent, and finally allowed the defendant's motion to dismiss. United States v. Councilman, 245 F.Supp.2d 319 (D. Mass. 2003). A First Circuit panel affirmed the district court, United States v. Councilman, 373 F.3d 197 (1st Cir. 2004), but the en banc court, in a split decision, reversed the panel United States v. Councilman, 418 F.3d 67 (1st Cir. 2005) (en banc). What was remarkable about the en banc majority's decision was not so much that judges disagreed with one another, but rather that after the tortured history of the *Councilman* litigation and of the contrary statutory interpretation arrived at by another circuit as well as by the district judge and a majority of the panel that agreed with the district judge, the majority of the en banc First Circuit claimed that the rule of lenity toward the defendant did not apply. The case, the court reasoned, demonstrated simply a "garden-variety, textual ambiguity" rather than the kind of "grievous ambiguity in a penal statute" that would normally trigger a court's giving a defendant the benefit of the doubt. One dissenting judge, obviously exasperated at the notion that a citizen should be expected to understand, at his peril, the meaning of a statute that had eluded three of the eight judges (including the district judge) who opined in this very case, not to mention a split with another circuit, suggested that if the issue was indeed "garden-variety," then "this is a garden in need of a weed killer." United States v. Councilman, 418 F.3d 67, 90 (1st Cir. 2005) (en banc) (Torruella, J., dissenting). For an extended discussion, see Harvey A. Silverglate, Three Felonies a Day: How the Feds Target the Innocent 257–64 (2009).

[5] Skilling v. United States, 561 U.S. ____, 130 S. Ct. 2896 (2010).

the 28-word broadly defined and amorphous "honest services" fraud statute—to the point of clarity. For nearly a quarter century, federal prosecutors have exploited the statute's vagueness by pursuing state and local politicians and corporate executives for essentially what U.S. Attorneys deem to be morally or ethically questionable conduct. These overzealous prosecutions wreaked havoc on the federal courts, which had devised sometimes-conflicting views of the statute to save it from invalidation, all the while handing down honest services fraud convictions and decades-long sentences.[7]

Perhaps more importantly, the federal criminalization of certain business and political practices that enjoyed approval—or at least tacit acceptance—in the state and local culture left citizens without adequate guidance as to what was and was not a federal crime. When squarely faced with the honest services statute this term, the Court, without any textual basis or legislative history to guide it, reached back to decades-old case law, predating the statute itself, to conclude that the "core" of the statute involved cases of bribery or kickbacks and, therefore, if limited to only those cases, the statute passed constitutional muster.

The majority's mind-bending decision to effectively rewrite the honest services statute has been almost uniformly characterized by the media, legal scholars, and even seasoned white-collar criminal defense attorneys as a setback to the federal government's attempt to "clean up" state and local government and corporate America.[8]

---

[6] Black v. United States, 561 U.S. ____ , 130 S. Ct. 2963 (2010); Weyhrauch v. United States, 561 U.S. ____, 130 S. Ct. 2971 (2010) (per curiam).

[7] See Brief of Amicus Curiae Albert W. Alschuler in Support of Neither Party at 2–3, Weyhrauch v. United States, 130 S. Ct. 2971 (2010) (No. 08-1196) ("The Courts of Appeals have offered three views of the significance of state law in federal prosecutions for honest-services mail fraud: (1) A violation of state law is necessary to establish a federal violation; (2) although a violation of state law can establish the central element of honest-services fraud (breach of fiduciary duty or misuse of office), the Government may also establish this element without proving any state law violation; and (3) state law violations are immaterial, as the term 'honest services' must have a uniform national meaning.").

[8] See, e.g., Adam Liptak, Justices Limit Use of "Honest Services" Law against Fraud, N.Y. Times, June 24, 2010, available at http://www.nytimes.com/2010/06/25/us/25scotus.html ("The Supreme Court ... significantly narrowed the scope of a law often used by federal prosecutors in corruption cases[.]"); Lyle Denniston, "Honest Services" Law Pared Down: Three Cases, Three Rulings; Opinions Recapped, Scotusblog.com (June 24, 2010, 15:46 EST), http://www.scotusblog.com/2010/06/honest-services-law-pared-down ("Three separate rulings, threatening (though not quite

As we will demonstrate below, the decision is hardly a blow to the federal government's increasing encroachment on local political practices and culture, which should be the sole province of state and local governments. While the Court may have provided some modicum of clarity to a small subset of politicians and businessmen whose conduct cannot possibly be shoehorned into the definitions of briberies or kickbacks, the vagueness problem is far deeper and more pervasive than the Court's opinion suggests. The underlying reason why these federal prosecutions are so problematic is that there are no clear, uniform national standards of ethics in local politics or corporate governance (nor should there be, many would argue). Yet the Department of Justice nonetheless attempts to dictate local political culture or corporate behavior via federal criminal prosecutions. Whether federal authorities attack local political arrangements or corporate conduct as the "deprivation of honest services," or by deeming them "extortion," "bribery," or "kickbacks," is irrelevant. In the end, these prosecutions are based on vague notions of criminality that are governed by the political motivations of whichever party or clique controls the Department of Justice or by the public outrage of the day.

Consider the Enron scandal, for example. There is one school of thought holding that Enron's executives Kenneth Lay, Jeffrey Skilling, and others, engaged in "criminal greed" of the highest order, causing substantial financial losses to savvy investors, aging retirees, and their own employees. This theory is based on an assertion that these corporate executives concealed from investors the truth about Enron's financial picture. However, the notion that they actually concealed the facts from investors was somewhat controversial from the start, since some financial analysts very early blew the whistle on the company's true financial state, and others saw the true picture by simply paying sufficient attention to the details "hidden in plain

---

nullifying) convictions or prosecutions in three different criminal corruption cases, put an exclamation point on the defeat for government prosecutors in their efforts to salvage wide discretion in employing the so-called 'honest services fraud' law[.]'"); Elizabeth MacDonald, *Skilling* Ruling Could Affect Rite Aid, Adelphia, Qwest, AOL Cases, Emac's Stock Watch (June 24, 2010, 14:59 EST), http://emac.blogs.foxbusiness.com/2010/06/24/skilling-ruling-could-affect-rite-aid-adelphia-quest-aol-cases (quoting MaryJeanette Dee, a white-collar criminal defense attorney and a partner at Richards Kibbe & Orbe as stating, "Many pending prosecutions and appeals will be affected").

sight" in the company's financial reports.[9] Whether the defendants engaged in criminal conduct, therefore, was highly questionable to some market professionals, as well as to some federal prosecutors.[10] Now, nearly a decade after the Department of Justice invested untold time and resources into the investigation of the scandal and the prosecution of major and minor players, the Court's decision may nullify the convictions of Skilling and others. Coupled with the fact that the Court had already unanimously vacated the conviction of Arthur Andersen LLP, Enron's longtime auditor, for its role in the scandal,[11] the *Skilling* decision suggests that federal prosecutors abused their wide discretion to pursue criminal prosecutions. These prosecutions should never have been initiated in the first place.

Instead of reining in this wasteful manipulation of the criminal justice system, the Supreme Court, in addressing the honest services fraud statute, left just enough wiggle room to allow federal prosecutions to continue anew their mission of dictating, via the abusive use of *in terrorem* prosecutions, the ethical code of conduct in local politics and the corporate boardroom.

II. Background of the Three Cases

A. Jeffrey Skilling

Jeffrey Skilling presided over one of the most catastrophic collapses in the history of American business. In 2001, Houston-based Enron Corporation, then the seventh-largest company in America and one of the leading energy companies in the world,[12] was accused of accounting irregularities that vastly overstated the company's earnings.[13] Skilling, a longtime executive of the company, became its CEO in February 2001 and then abruptly resigned in August

---

[9] See, e.g., Malcolm Gladwell, Open Secrets: Enron, Intelligence, and the Perils of Too Much Information, The New Yorker, January 8, 2007, available at http://www.newyorker.com/reporting/2007/01/08/070108fa_fact_gladwell.

[10] Alexei Barrionuevo & Kurt Eichenwald, The Enron Case That Almost Wasn't, N.Y. Times, June 4, 2006, available at http://www.nytimes.com/2006/06/04/business/yourmoney/04enron.html.

[11] Arthur Andersen LLP v. United States, 544 U.S. 696, 706 (2005).

[12] Skilling, 130 S. Ct. at 2907.

[13] See Timeline: The Fall of Enron, Houston Chronicle, http://www.chron.com/news/specials/enron/timeline.html (last visited Aug. 25, 2010).

2001.[14] Within months, Enron's share price plummeted from a peak of $90 to virtually zero, and it filed for Chapter 11 bankruptcy.[15] Skilling, along with Enron's founder and chairman, Kenneth Lay, came to represent corporate excess, greed, and cronyism during the boom years of the late 1990s and early 2000s.

In response to the public outrage that ensued, the federal government initiated an investigation of Enron and ultimately prosecuted dozens of former Enron executives, as well as Arthur Andersen LLP, Enron's auditor and, at the time, one of the five largest accounting firms in the country.[16] On July 7, 2004, after working its way up Enron's corporate ladder, the government sought and received grand jury indictments for Enron's leadership, namely, Lay and Skilling, as well as Richard Causey, the company's former chief accounting officer.[17] The indictment alleged that each participated in a "wide-ranging scheme to deceive the investing public, including Enron's shareholders . . . about the true performance of Enron's businesses" by manipulating its financial results and making false and misleading public statements about its financial performance. Among numerous other counts, the indictment charged each defendant with conspiracy to commit securities and wire fraud based on the theory that they had "depriv[ed] Enron and its shareholders of the intangible right to [their] honest services."[18]

The government's theory of the case against Skilling at trial was straightforward and devastating. Prosecutors argued that Skilling violated his fiduciary duties to Enron's shareholders and duties to its employees by taking improper measures to prop up the company's share price, describing these duties as those of "honesty, candor, and fairness."[19] In its closing argument, the government claimed:

> This is a simple case, ladies and gentlemen. Because it's so simple, I'm probably going to end before my allotted time.

---

[14] *Id.*

[15] *Id.*

[16] Skilling, 130 S. Ct. at 2907; Silverglate, Three Felonies, *supra* note 4, at 131.

[17] Skilling, 130 S. Ct. at 2907.

[18] *Id.* at 2908 (quoting indictment).

[19] Brief for Petitioner at 3 & n.2, Skilling v. United States, 130 S. Ct. 2896 (2010) (No. 08-1394) (quoting Fifth Circuit record).

> It's black-and-white. Truth and lies. The shareholders, ladies
> and gentlemen, . . . buy a share of stock, and for that they're
> not entitled to much but they're entitled to the truth. They're
> entitled for the officers and employees of the company to
> put their interests ahead of their own. They're entitled to be
> told what the financial condition of the company is. They
> are entitled to honesty, ladies and gentlemen.[20]

Simple enough. But there was a problem with the application of
this theory: the case against Enron and its executives was not so
cut-and-dried. In fact, prosecutors privately expressed concerns
about the problems in the case against Skilling, suggesting, for example, that the case exhibited "fundamental weaknesses" because he
took "steps seemingly inconsistent with criminal intent," there were
"no 'smoking gun' documents," and the case rested on the testimony
of cooperating witnesses who had "marginal credibility."[21] Indeed,
the criminality of the defendants' conduct was not apparent, in
large part, because Enron's accounting practices, though "legally
questionable" and "extraordinarily risky," were openly disclosed
in its financial reports and other public statements and approved
by the company's auditor.[22]

Despite these misgivings, the government successfully characterized Skilling's conduct as criminal in nature by relying on the honest
services fraud theory, and the jury convicted Skilling of 19 counts.[23]
The district court judge found that Skilling had "repeatedly lied to
investors, including Enron's own employees, about various aspects
of Enron's business" and, as a result, sentenced him to 24 years in
prison, 3 years of supervised release, and $45 million in restitution.[24]
For the 52-year-old Skilling, it was effectively a term of life
imprisonment.

Skilling appealed to the Fifth Circuit Court of Appeals raising,
among other issues, a challenge to his conviction on the honest

---

[20] Gladwell, Open Secrets, *supra* note 9.

[21] Brief for Petitioner, *supra* note 19, at 2 (quoting John C. Hueston, Behind the Scenes
of the Enron Trial: Creating the Decisive Moments, 44 Am. Crim. L. Rev. 197, 197–98,
201 (2007)).

[22] Gladwell, Open Secrets, *supra* note 9; Silverglate, Three Felonies, *supra* note 4, at 127.

[23] Skilling, 130 S. Ct. at 2911.

[24] Gladwell, Open Secrets, *supra* note 9; Skilling, 130 S. Ct. at 2911.

services fraud conspiracy charge. The court of appeals rejected Skilling's claim that his conduct did not constitute conspiracy to commit honest services fraud, specifically finding that Skilling met all the elements of the crime, including: "(1) a material breach of a fiduciary duty imposed under state law, including duties defined by the employer-employee relationship, (2) that results in a detriment to the employer," specifically one caused "by an employee, contrary to his duty of honesty, to withhold material information, i.e., information that he had reason to believe would lead a reasonable employer to change its conduct."[25]

B. Conrad Black

In 2005, federal authorities in Chicago focused their attention on Lord Conrad Black, then the CEO and controlling shareholder of the media company Hollinger International, Inc., which owned and operated several large newspapers, including the *Chicago Sun-Times*, and a number of small community newspapers.[26] Black, along with three former executives of the firm, were charged with multiple counts of mail and wire fraud for devising and participating in corporate compensation schemes arising from non-competition agreements designed "to defraud International and International's public shareholders of money, property and their intangible right of honest services, to defraud the Canadian tax authorities of tax revenue, and to obtain money and property from these victims by means of materially false and fraudulent pretenses, representations, promises and omissions, in connection with the U.S. Community Newspaper Asset Sales."[27]

At trial, the government argued that Black and his colleagues "stole money from Hollinger by fraudulently paying themselves bogus and unapproved non-competition payments" and "that, in making the payments to themselves and failing to disclose them, [they] deprived Hollinger of their honest services as managers of the company."[28] In the government's view, that non-competition

---

[25] United States v. Skilling, 554 F.3d 529, 547 (5th Cir. 2009).

[26] Black v. United States, 130 S. Ct. 2963, 2966–67 (2010).

[27] First Superseding Indictment at 9, United States v. Black, No. 05 CR 727 (N.D. Ill. Nov. 17, 2005).

[28] Brief for the United States at 10, Black v. United States, 130 S. Ct. 2963 (2010) (No. 08-876).

agreement was worth little or nothing. But to Black, the nature of the agreement presented significant advantages under Canadian tax law,[29] and, to the willing buyers, removing an international media mogul from potential future business competition had its obvious upside as well. Thus, what was essentially a matter of business judgment governed by local law found the federal government second-guessing the parties to the sale by superimposing its own business judgments.

Following a four-month trial, the jury found the defendants, including Black, guilty of three of the mail fraud counts and also found Black guilty of obstruction of justice for removing file boxes from his office that were under protective order, but acquitted the defendants of nine other counts.[30] At the sentencing hearing, District Court Judge Amy St. Eve concluded, "Mr. Black, you have violated your duty to Hollinger International and its shareholders," and sentenced him to six and a half years in prison and a fine of $125,000.[31]

On appeal, the Seventh Circuit, in a surprisingly short and dismissive opinion written by Judge Richard Posner, affirmed defendants' convictions.[32] Characterizing some of defendants' challenges as "ridiculous," the court held there was sufficient evidence of "conventional fraud" demonstrating "a theft of money or other property from Hollinger by misrepresentations and misleading omissions amounting to fraud, in violation of 18 U.S.C. § 1341."[33] Posner also concluded that the conduct of Black and his colleagues satisfied the elements of honest services fraud under § 1341, holding that "[they] had a duty of candor in the conflict-of-interest situation in which they found themselves. Instead of coming clean they caused their corporation to make false filings with the Securities and Exchange Commission, and they did so for their private gain."[34] The court of

---

[29] *Id.* at 9.

[30] *Id.*

[31] Mary Vallis & Theresa Tedesco, Conrad Black Sentenced to More than Six Years in Jail, Nat'l Post, Dec. 13, 2007, p. 1, available at http://www.nationalpost.com/news/canada/Conrad + Black + gets + years + prison/156762/story.html.

[32] See United States v. Black, 530 F.3d 596 (7th Cir. 2008).

[33] *Id.* at 599, 600.

[34] *Id.* at 602.

appeals also rejected Black's challenge to his obstruction of justice conviction.[35]

C. Bruce Weyhrauch

In 2006, federal authorities in Alaska raided the offices of a number of state legislators in connection with the government's investigation of financial ties between VECO Corporation, an oil field services company, and several Alaska legislators. One of the politicians subjected to the raid was Bruce Weyhrauch, a licensed attorney and member of the Alaska House of Representatives representing Juneau since 2002.[36] Following the raid and subsequent investigation, the federal government indicted a dozen individuals, including Weyhrauch, U.S. Senator Ted Stevens, and VECO CEO Bill Allen.[37] The indictment against Weyhrauch alleged that he, former House Speaker Pete Kott, and VECO employees devised and participated in a scheme "to defraud and deprive the State of Alaska of the honest services of Kott and [Weyhrauch] performed free of deceit, self-dealing, bias, and concealment."[38] The specific charges against Weyhrauch are predicated on his failure to disclose to his constituents that he allegedly attempted to gain future legal work from VECO upon his retirement from the legislature in return for voting on a tax measure favored by the company. However, the government ran into an obstacle in the case—there was no state law or local rule compelling disclosure under such circumstances.[39]

Absent any state law or local ordinance to support its conflict-of-interest theory, the government attempted to introduce at trial evidence of Alaska ethics practices, the ethics training provided to Weyhrauch as a legislator, and Weyhrauch's own position on the legislature's ethics committee.[40] The district court granted Weyhrauch's motion *in limine* to exclude the evidence, finding that no Alaska statute or rule required Weyhrauch to publicly disclose his

---

[35] *Id.* at 603–05.

[36] Brief for Petitioner at 7, Weyhrauch v. United States, 130 S. Ct. 2971 (2010) (No. 08-1196).

[37] *Id.* at 10.

[38] *Id.*

[39] Weyhrauch v. United States, 548 F.3d 1237, 1240 (9th Cir. 2008).

[40] *Id.* at 1239–40.

negotiations with VECO before he took official action on the legislation at issue.[41]

The government filed an interlocutory appeal challenging the district court's ruling, which the Ninth Circuit Court of Appeals reversed on the grounds that a defendant may be convicted of honest services fraud without "proof that the conduct at issue also violated applicable state law."[42] The court of appeals further held that the government could proceed in its case against Weyhrauch, as the alleged conflict of interest and/or quid pro quo arrangement "falls comfortably within the two categories long recognized as the core of honest services fraud."[43]

III. The Supreme Court Invents a New Federal Crime

Federal law criminalizes use of the mails or wire communications to advance any "scheme or artifice to defraud, or for obtaining money or property by means of false or fraudulent pretenses, representations, or promises."[44] More than two decades ago, in *McNally v. United States*, the Supreme Court rejected the theory that this language proscribed public and private corruption that deprived individuals of their so-called intangible right to the honest and impartial services of their political representatives and fiduciaries.[45] Specifically, the Court declined to "construe the statute in a manner that leaves its outer boundaries ambiguous and involves the Federal Government in setting standards of disclosure and good government for local and state officials" and called on Congress "to speak more clearly than it has" should it "desire[] to go further."[46] Responding swiftly, Congress enacted a 28-word statute that purported to clear up the ambiguity in the law, stating, "For the purposes of this chapter, the term 'scheme or artifice to defraud' includes a scheme or artifice to deprive another of the intangible right of honest services."[47]

---

[41] *Id.*

[42] *Id.* at 1239.

[43] *Id.* at 1247.

[44] See 18 U.S.C. §§ 1341, 1343 (2006).

[45] 483 U.S. 350, 356 (1987).

[46] *Id.* at 360.

[47] 18 U.S.C. §1346 (2006).

There can be no doubt that, in the wake of *McNally*, Congress replaced an ambiguously interpreted law with a patently vague statute. Indeed, it offered no definition or guidance regarding the term "honest services." Since its enactment, federal prosecutors have exercised the wide discretion afforded by the statute to root out political corruption and corporate fraud. In an attempt to limit the scope of these prosecutions, federal courts have come up with various contradictory interpretations of the statute to save it from invalidation.[48] In his blistering dissent from the Supreme Court's denial of certiorari in an honest services case in the Court's previous term, Justice Antonin Scalia wrote, "Without some coherent limiting principle to define what 'the intangible right of honest services' is, whence it derives, and how it is violated, this expansive phrase invites abuse by headline-grabbing prosecutors in pursuit of local officials, state legislators, and corporate CEOs who engage in any manner of unappealing or ethically questionable conduct."[49]

When it finally faced this issue in the *Skilling*, *Black*, and *Weyhrauch* cases this term, the Court suggested that it had, indeed, found that coherent limiting principle. Justice Ruth Bader Ginsburg, writing for a 6–3 majority, including Chief Justice John Roberts and Justices John Paul Stevens, Stephen Breyer, Samuel Alito, and Sonia Sotomayor, rejected Skilling's argument that the honest services statute is impermissibly and fatally vague. Instead, the Court explained that "§ 1346 should be construed rather than invalidated."[50] Without any textual authority or legislative history to guide its interpretation of the statute's language, the Court instead took an inventive but dubious two-step approach to save the statute from invalidation—ostensibly in accord with the majority's stated aim of judicial modesty, shying away from invalidation of a statute on constitutional grounds. First, the majority attempted "to ascertain the meaning of the phrase 'intangible right of honest services.'"[51] To that end, the Court stated,

---

[48] Skilling, 130 S. Ct. at 2928 n.37 ("Courts have disagreed about whether § 1346 prosecutions must be based on a violation of state law ...; whether a defendant must contemplate that the victim suffer economic harm ...; and whether the defendant must act in pursuit of private gain ...." (internal citations omitted)).

[49] Sorich v. United States, 555 U.S. ____, 129 S. Ct. 1308, 1310 (2009) (Scalia, J., dissenting from denial of certiorari).

[50] Skilling, 130 S. Ct. at 2928.

[51] *Id.*

with little explanation, that the "intangible right of honest services" refers to "the honest-services doctrine recognized in the Court of Appeals' decisions before *McNally*."[52] While the majority acknowledged "there was considerable disarray over the statute's application" in pre-*McNally* case law, it nonetheless concluded that, in cases of bribery and kickbacks, there was no such confusion.[53]

In light of this apparent clarity, the Court proceeded to the second step of its analysis by "par[ing] that body of precedent down to its core," which the majority concluded consisted of "fraudulent schemes to deprive another of honest services through bribes or kickbacks supplied by a third party who had not been deceived."[54] In order to avoid constitutional invalidation, the Court therefore held that "§ 1346 criminalizes *only* the bribe-and-kickback core of the pre-*McNally* case law."[55] The Court excluded from its formulation the more amorphous outer boundaries of the statute, namely, undisclosed self-dealing by a public official or private employee—the very theories of guilt under which Skilling and Black were convicted and for which Weyhrauch was indicted.[56] In light of this holding, the Court remanded the *Skilling* case to the Fifth Circuit to determine whether the flawed jury instruction on the honest services fraud charge was harmless error.[57] The Court also remanded the *Black* case for harmless error review and recognized that his obstruction of justice charge may have been tainted by the flawed instruction on the honest services charge, and remanded the *Weyhrauch* case to reconsider whether the prosecution against him should go forward.[58]

The concurrence, authored by Justice Scalia and joined by Justices Anthony Kennedy and Clarence Thomas, tears into the majority's seemingly deferential, modest, and elegant holding. Justice Scalia observed that, by transforming the statute from "a prohibition of 'honest services fraud' into a prohibition of 'bribery and kickbacks,'"

---

[52] *Id.*

[53] *Id.* at 2929.

[54] *Id.* at 2928.

[55] *Id.* at 2896–97 (emphasis in original).

[56] *Id.* at 2931.

[57] *Id.* at 2934. It should be noted that the Court rejected Skilling's other argument that his jury pool was tainted and, therefore, constitutionally unfair, because he was tried in a charged atmosphere in Houston, where Enron was based. *Id.* at 2912–25.

[58] Black, 130 S. Ct. at 2970; Weyhrauch, 130 S. Ct. 2971.

the Court "wield[s] a power we long ago abjured: the power to define new federal crimes."[59] Specifically, Justice Scalia recognized that the majority's attempt to narrow the statute was based on several fallacies. First, contrary to the Court's suggestion, Justice Scalia observed that prior to (and following) *McNally*, the lower courts were hopelessly confused and recognized that honest services fraud could range from

> any action that is contrary to public policy or otherwise immoral, to only the disloyalty of a public official or employee to his principal, to only the secret use of a perpetrator's position of trust in order to harm whomever he is beholden to. The duty probably did not have to be rooted in state law, but maybe it did. It might have been more demanding in the case of public officials, but perhaps not.[60]

According to Justice Scalia and the other concurring justices, the majority's assumption that Congress adopted a clear body of precedent when it enacted the "intangible right" theory of honest services "is a step out of the frying pan into the fire."[61]

The concurrence also took issue with the Court's assumption that Congress intended the statute to encompass only bribes and kickbacks. Simply because the Court can now distill a paradigmatic or pure application of the honest services doctrine, with the benefit of hindsight, does not mean that Congress, when it enacted the statute in 1988, intended it to be so limited. "That," according to Justice Scalia and his concurring colleagues, "is a dish the Court has cooked up all on its own."[62] Moreover, as Justice Scalia explained in his concurrence, limiting the statute to briberies and kickbacks does not eliminate the vagueness of the statute because

> it does not solve the most fundamental indeterminacy: the character of the "fiduciary capacity" to which the bribery and kickback restriction applies. Does it apply only to public officials? Or in addition to private individuals who contract

---

[59] Skilling, 130 S. Ct. at 2935 (Scalia, J., concurring in part) (citing United States v. Hudson & Goodwin 11 U.S. (7 Cranch) 32 (1812)).

[60] *Id.* at 2938.

[61] *Id.*

[62] *Id.* at 2939.

> with the public? Or to everyone, including the corporate
> officer here? The pre-*McNally* case law does not provide an
> answer. Thus, even with the bribery and kickback limitation
> the statute does not answer the question "What is the crite-
> rion of guilt?"[63]

The Court summarily rejected the inherent indeterminacy of the
meaning of "fiduciary duty" as "rare in bribe and kickback cases"
and "beyond dispute."[64] However, it failed to provide answers to
the questions raised by the concurrence, leaving it for the lower
courts to grapple with. In fact, although it cited as examples federal
statutes and case law defining bribes and kickbacks, the Court failed
to even define with specificity whether state or federal law applies
to determine the elements of those crimes. In a footnote, the Court
recognized that Congress "would have to employ standards of sufficient definiteness and specificity to overcome due process concerns"
in order to criminalize undisclosed self-dealing by a public official
or private employee.[65] Yet it did not employ the same standard of
specificity and definiteness with respect to the pared-down statute
that remains.

According to the concurrence, in order to reach its conclusion to
save a patently vague statute, the Court engaged in an exercise of
judicial "invention" by rewriting the statute.[66] This, in the opinion
of Justice Scalia and the other concurring justices, was not an act of
"judicial humility," as claimed by the majority, but instead was an
act of judicial legislating. The concurrence would have invalidated
the convictions of Skilling and Black as unconstitutionally vague as
applied to them.

However, even the concurrence overlooked a more serious problem in the majority opinion. By rewriting the statute in a manner
thought by the majority to narrow the statute's judicially prescribed
ambit—according to congressional intent, so the majority posited—
the majority actually included within the federal statute's prohibition a wide variety of acts that would be *lawful* under *state* and *local*
statutes and ordinances, not because such statutes and ordinances

---

[63] *Id*. at 2938–39.

[64] *Id*. at 2931 n.42.

[65] *Id*. at 2933 n.45.

[66] *Id*. at 2939 (Scalia, J., concurring in part).

inadvertently omitted them from their ambit, and not because state and local prosecutors corruptly or incompetently looked the other way, but because the practices at issue might have been consistent with state and local political culture and practice. In short, the major defect of the vague federal honest services statute might well have been that it criminalized activities that were intentionally lawful under state and municipal law. But surely the legality of certain practices under state and local laws should be considered by the federal courts when they are called on to decide whether a *vague* federal prohibition should be deemed to outlaw accepted state and local practices. Of course, the newly minted definition of "honest services" also encompasses practices that have long been *criminalized* by state and local law, and while in such instances there is *no conflict* between federal and state laws, one does have to ask why the redundant federal statute is even necessary.

IV. Discussion

A. The Court Redefines the Vagueness Doctrine

A statute is unconstitutionally vague when it fails "to provide a person of ordinary intelligence fair notice of what is prohibited, or if it is so standardless that it authorizes or encourages seriously discriminatory enforcement."[67] In an earlier era, the Supreme Court readily recognized the risk of vague statutes:

> It would certainly be dangerous if the legislature could set a net large enough to catch all possible offenders, and leave it to the courts to step inside and say who could be rightfully detained, and who should be set at large. This would, to some extent, substitute the judicial for the legislative department of the government.[68]

---

[67] United States v. Williams, 553 U.S. 285, 304 (2008); see also U.S. Const. amend. V ("No person shall . . . be deprived of life, liberty, or property, without due process of law[.]"); Kolender v. Lawson, 461 U.S. 352, 357 (1983) ("[A] penal statute [must] define the criminal offense with sufficient definiteness that ordinary people can understand what conduct is prohibited and in a manner that does not encourage arbitrary and discriminatory enforcement."); Grayned v. City of Rockford, 408 U.S. 104, 108 (1972) ("[L]aws [must] give the person of ordinary intelligence a reasonable opportunity to know what is prohibited, so that he may act accordingly.").

[68] United States v. Reese, 92 U.S. 214, 221 (1875).

The vagueness doctrine is particularly applicable to criminal laws, which are to be strictly construed.[69] This principle, as Chief Justice John Marshall recognized long ago, "is founded on the tenderness of the law for the rights of individuals; and on the plain principle that the power of punishment is vested in the legislative, not in the judicial department."[70]

The honest services statute, and the Court's strained effort to save it from constitutional invalidation, reflect an unmooring of federal criminal laws from these fundamental principles. Even more disconcertingly, however, these principles have been distorted in a misguided attempt to protect the widespread use of federal criminal prosecutions in various areas, from national security to public corruption and white-collar fraud.

The plain language of the 28-word honest services statute provided no clue as to its meaning, and there was no substantive legislative history to guide the Court. The Court's inquiry should have ended there. With respect to vagueness and the rule of lenity, the Court has recognized that "[w]hen interpreting a criminal statute, we do not play the part of mind reader"[71] and that "[o]nce the meaning of an enactment is discerned and its constitutionality determined, the judicial process comes to an end."[72] Instead of relying on this principle, rooted in the vagueness doctrine and the rule of lenity, the *Skilling* majority relied on the canon of constitutional avoidance "to construe, rather than condemn Congress' enactments," reaching back to decades-old case law to divine congressional intent in enacting the honest services statute.[73] As Justice Scalia's concurrence made clear, the majority's ultimate interpretation—that the honest services statute is limited to its bribery and kickback "core"—is inconsistent with the legislature's intent, which was to restore pre-*McNally* case law supporting the intangible rights theory of fraud. As even the majority admitted, the lower courts prior to *McNally* imposed the theory on a range of conduct beyond simply bribes and kickbacks. There is no support, either in case law,

---

[69] United States v. Enmons, 410 U.S. 396, 411 (1973).

[70] United States v. Wiltberger, 18 U.S. (5 Wheat.) 76, 95 (1820).

[71] United States v. Santos, 553 U.S. 507, ____, 128 S. Ct. 2020, 2026 (2008).

[72] Tennessee Valley Auth. v. Hill, 437 U.S. 153, 194–95 (1978) (Burger, C.J.).

[73] Skilling, 130 S. Ct. at 2930–31.

legislative history, or the text of the statute itself, for the majority's suggestion that Congress intended to limit the statute to bribes and kickbacks.

Moreover, to reach this conclusion, the majority engaged in a form of common law-making by examining the underlying fact patterns of pre-*McNally* cases and attempting to identify a common standard most consistent with the results reached by these courts. For better or worse, the Court long ago relinquished its ability to create a federal common law. Only three decades after the Revolutionary War, a Pennsylvania federal court dismissed a bribery case because Congress had not enacted a bribery statute. The court ruled that federalism and the limited jurisdiction of federal courts precluded the existence of federal common-law crimes. The Supreme Court agreed, and, in *United States v. Hudson & Goodwin*, went on to announce that federal crimes were entirely creatures of congressional statute rather than judge-made common law.[74] "[W]hen assessing the reach of a federal criminal statute," the Court later held, "we must pay close heed to language, legislative history, and purpose in order to strictly determine the scope of the conduct the enactment forbids."[75] Thus, when the *Skilling* Court attempted to engage in common-law interpretation by analyzing pre-*McNally* case law rather than accepting the vague text of the statute, it failed to heed this longstanding principle set forth in *Hudson & Goodwin*. Furthermore, the *Hudson & Goodwin* decision clearly established that Congress, in writing statutes and the federal courts in interpreting them, do not have the full benefit of the common law's wisdom and experience.[76] The *Skilling* majority compounds the highly destructive effects of this decision not only by failing to pay close heed to the text and legislative history of the statute but also by relying on case law that predated the statute and was itself unhinged from the common law. Indeed, the federal courts' various contradictory decisions on the honest services statute reflect their detachment from the common law's emphasis on the requirements of clarity and "fair notice."

---

[74] 11 U.S. (7 Cranch) 32, 34 (1812).

[75] Dowling v. United States, 473 U.S. 207, 213 (1985) (citing Liparota v. United States, 471 U.S. 419, 424 (1985)).

[76] See Harvey Silverglate, Federal Criminal Law: Punishing Benign Intentions, in In the Name of Justice: Leading Experts Reexamine the Classic Article "The Aims of the Criminal Law" 67–68 (Timothy Lynch ed., 2009).

Professor Henry Hart recognized in his seminal essay, "The Aims of the Criminal Law," that such a detachment is a risk when society has transformed its criminal laws from merely prohibiting *malum in se* acts—that is, acts in which the blameworthiness is self-evident because the behavior in question is "intrinsically antisocial"—to also outlawing *malum prohibitum* acts—behaviors, such as the kind at issue in the honest services case, that are not intuitively evil but are barred by the legislature to "secure some ultimate social advantage."[77] In order for an offender to be considered "blameworthy" of the latter acts, Hart reasoned, he must be given fair notice that the conduct in question is prohibited and he must have willfully ignored this warning.[78] "[K]nowing or reckless disregard of the legal obligation affords an independent basis of blameworthiness justifying the actor's condemnation as a criminal, even when his conduct was not intrinsically antisocial."[79] As the law shifts from the *malum in se* to the *malum prohibitum* framework, as the federal criminal scheme clearly has, Hart recognized that "it necessarily shifts its ground from a demand that every responsible member of the community understand and respect the community's moral values to a demand that everyone know and understand what is written in the statute books."[80] If those statute books become too confusing and impractical, wrote Hart, they also become useless and unjust.[81] In this way, Hart pinpointed a necessary level of moral authority imbued in the criminal law. After all, to punish individuals for committing acts they had no reasonable way of knowing constituted crimes would be the moral equivalent of punishing an infant or a person with severely diminished mental capacity—something that the Western legal tradition has long avoided in order to preserve the moral underpinnings of the criminal law.[82]

As the *Skilling* decision demonstrates, the principles in Hart's monumentally important essay have been evaded by a steady erosion of this fundamental moral requirement in the law—punishing

---

[77] *Id.* at 65–66.

[78] *Id.*

[79] *Id.* at 66.

[80] *Id.*

[81] *Id.*

[82] *Id.*

only conduct committed in knowing violation of the criminal law —in the enforcement and interpretation of federal criminal statutes. Federal prosecutors find it easier to pursue criminal prosecutions at their whim when they are enforcing statutes with no apparent definitions of what constitutes the prohibited conduct—a luxury not available to prosecutors enforcing most state laws. Such statutes become a kind of roving commission, enabling federal prosecutors, within their respective districts, to single out political figures, businesspeople, political activists, and others whose practices are found unpopular, irksome, or otherwise offensive. As set forth below, that the Supreme Court chose to "pare down" rather than strike down a vague statute more than two decades after its enactment is not a solution to the fair notice problem in public and private corruption cases, nor does it give any comfort to the defendants who were long ago convicted of the vague portion of the crime and have served their sentences.

B. Vague Laws Permit the Continued Federalization of State Criminal Law

Academic discussions and judicial decisions concerning vagueness problems inherent in federal honest services and other public corruption prosecutions of state and local officials barely scratch the surface of the fundamental concern. In particular, solutions such as that adopted by the Supreme Court majority in *Skilling*—to limit the scope and meaning of the honest services statute to bribery and kickback schemes—are hardly solutions at all, since the vagueness problem afflicts federal definitions of bribery and kickback schemes themselves. This problem is particularly egregious when federal prosecutors go after state and local politicians, whether under honest services or extortion or other such statutes, for engaging in practices that are *not* criminalized under state and municipal law. Thus the majority's apparent resolution does not, as a practical matter, represent a move toward clarification of federal corruption laws.

Lawyers whose clients face indictments in this arena—and, of course, their public official clients—have a bird's-eye view of the abuse of the honest services and related formulations that inject both life and reality into problems of statutory vagueness and due process. The very undertaking by federal officials to control local political culture rather than restrict their oversight to practices that clearly interfere with interstate commerce or other core federal constitutionally designated interests virtually invites abuse. Add to this the litany of laws prosecutors can employ, and vagueness becomes a central problem. Put another way, as long as federal prosecutors and courts attempt to superimpose federal standards on local political culture, there is going to be a problem—perhaps best described as vagueness, but also demonstrating simply a clash of cultures—that traps even the well-intentioned state or local politician.

The situation is a quite practical one, hardly academic and theoretical, for the trial lawyer and his or her public official client. To understand how the statute unfairly traps even the innocent and well-meaning state or local public official, it is necessary to examine in some detail how these public officials, and the honest services and related corruption statutes, function "on the ground."[83]

Throughout the 1980s, state and federal investigators launched several probes into allegations of corruption among local political bodies in Hialeah, Florida, a heavily Cuban-American city just outside Miami. The *Miami Herald* published a series of articles in 1985 claiming that members of the Hialeah Zoning Board and City Council were "selling" their votes to developers in exchange for receiving lots or shares in the projects. As bad as that sounds, it's important to put these allegations in context. Florida laws governing local political office-holders are similar to those in most states. Local politicians are allowed, if not encouraged, to maintain private careers and businesses to support themselves and their families. Salaries paid to such political figures typically are modest, necessitating that anyone other than those with inherited or previously earned wealth maintain an income-generating occupation while in public office.

In the 1980s, members of the Hialeah Zoning Board were unsalaried volunteers, while city councilors were paid a mere $2,600 per year, and the mayor's salary hovered around $50,000. Since such officials are paid so little in their elected positions, it might well be seen as a perk of office that one is allowed to parlay one's importance and prestige into increased business success. At the very least, state and local laws and political culture tolerate local officials' engaging

---

[83] The following discussion relies heavily on the longer rendition of the Raul Martinez case in Chapter 1 of Harvey Silverglate's book, Three Felonies a Day: How the Feds Target the Innocent. See *supra* note 4.

in private business dealings that almost certainly benefit from their holding municipal office, as long as they do not engage in official acts, such as voting on municipal bodies on matters that directly affect their own financial interests. In an area where real estate development was exploding and where local city councils and zoning boards maintained dockets crowded with petitions for enactment of or relief from laws, some degree of fusion between civic and professional work among local officials was almost certainly inevitable and, indeed, even intended.

What is crucial to bear in mind here is that states and municipalities do prescribe limits to these relationships, often in fairly straightforward terms. Typically, state and municipal conflict-of-interest laws prohibit public officials from playing both ends of a project or business venture. There are also statutes prohibiting bribery and extortion. It is not as if these states and municipalities are lawless no-man's-lands screaming for the feds to march into town to redefine what is acceptable political culture.

Indeed, the state of Florida did not neglect Hialeah, nor its highly popular mayor, Raul Martinez. Elected to the Hialeah City Council in 1977 and to the mayor's office four years later, the highly popular Cuban-American, like many successful professionals in that fast-growing part of the state, dabbled in real estate development in addition to his career in public office. But to some in the local news media, Martinez's careers were too close, and their coverage led to state authorities' launching an investigation into whether he had parlayed his public office into improper personal gain. Finding neither bribery nor extortion to pin on the mayor, however, state investigators closed their inquiry in 1989.

Still, the federal investigation continued, and, after the death of long-time Democratic Congressman Claude Pepper, federal prosecutors ramped it up. The U.S. Attorney at the time was Dexter Lehtinen, whose wife expressed interest in replacing Pepper when he had fallen ill.[84] But it was widely thought that the up-and-coming Martinez was being groomed for Pepper's seat. Sure enough, when the corruption investigation made its way into the press, Martinez

---

[84] Alfonso Chardy, Sources: Lehtinen Rushed Probe after Pepper Fell Ill, The Miami Herald, Feb. 17, 1991.

dropped out of the congressional race. Ileana Ros-Lehtinen, the U.S. Attorney's wife, sought and won Pepper's seat after his death.

This political setback quickly became the least of Martinez's problems. On April 3, 1990, he was charged in a complex, 64-page indictment alleging, at its center, a "racketeering conspiracy" and the crime of extortion under the federal Hobbs Act. This indictment did not rely on supposedly vague formulations such as honest services fraud. Instead, it focused on the kinds of federal offenses held by the Supreme Court majority in *Skilling* to resolve any vagueness concerns. But in reality, the prosecution of Martinez evidenced the same infirmities as did the *Skilling* and other honest services cases.

The indictment alleged that real estate developers cut Martinez in on deals by selling him parcels of property at below-market prices, which prosecutors considered to be an extortionate arrangement. A typical deal for which Martinez was indicted was the Marivi Gardens project, purchased and developed by one Silvio Cardoso, a Hialeah City Council member and friend of the mayor. Cardoso believed that if Martinez were a partner in the project, it would attract buyers for the completed units.[85] Martinez indicated his interest, and Cardoso signed the purchase contract for the undeveloped property in January 1983. Martinez told Cardoso that he wanted to purchase one of the lots, but Cardoso replied that he intended to give, not sell, the lot to his valued business associate and political ally.

To the feds, this mutually beneficial arrangement was the stuff of extortion. Yet Cardoso testified that he and Martinez never discussed anything that Cardoso expected Martinez to do. And, it must be recalled, Cardoso by this time was an immunized cooperating witness for the government, under pressure to help the prosecution. Nonetheless, he never said that Martinez had ever threatened him in any way. Nor did Martinez threaten to veto Cardoso's zoning applications, even though a veto was within his power. Cardoso testified that his motive was more generalized: "I felt it would be to my benefit politically, and economically in the future."

As a result, Cardoso transferred the gift lot to Martinez, who duly declared it as income on his 1984 tax return. Three years later, Martinez sold the lot for $45,000. As Cardoso had anticipated, when

---

[85] Transcript of Record at 40, United States v. Martinez, 14 F.3d 543 (11th Cir. 1994) (Nos. 91-5619 & 92-4668) (testimony of Silvio Cardoso).

he ran for election to the city council in 1983, Martinez not only contributed to his campaign and helped get others to do so, he also escorted the candidate around Hialeah's campaign trail. Martinez even advised on the preparation of campaign literature. Cardoso was right: a business and friendship relationship with a popular and successful public official was not bad for business or political life.

Another government witness, Renan Delgado, testified similarly in connection with another real estate deal, Steve's Estates. Delgado sold property to Martinez on favorable terms, explaining that Martinez provided useful advice and assistance in his business. At trial, Delgado elaborated on the nature of his relationship with Martinez, and the rather obvious (and perfectly legal) business advantages: "If you're in business in a city, in any city, you want to be friend[s] with your people that run the city." Delgado explained that while he would have wanted to receive more of the money on the deal and give Martinez a less favorable price for the lots the mayor purchased, his decision to accept less money was "voluntary."

At this point, it helps to step back and take a look at the law federal prosecutors used to go after Martinez. The Hobbs Act was enacted in 1951 during a period of public outcry over organized crime, essentially to deter extortionate threats by both private thugs and public officials seeking payoffs. The situation of public officials is, of course, different from that of gangsters. The latter could threaten citizens with all manner and kinds of violence to extract payments or property. Corrupt public officials have a different tool to induce citizens to fork over money: the power inherent in political office by which officials can enrich or ruin private parties seeking government approval, assistance, or forbearance on a project. Public-sector extortion is in another way very different from extortion involving the neighborhood leg breaker. In our political system, citizens who run for public office often have to raise significant sums of money to finance their campaigns. Campaign contributors sometimes donate out of a sense of civic virtue. Often their motive has something to do with official or unofficial legislative or executive support, or simply "greasing the wheels" for a project.

Under federal law, bribery of state officials (typically payments initiated by the citizen) is not a distinct federal crime, although it might be punishable under circumstances in which the citizen uses the mails or other tools of interstate commerce to carry out a violation of state law. Only extortion engaged in by the official violates the Hobbs Act.[86]

Theoretically, this law is meant to prevent and punish the disruption to interstate commerce, over which the Constitution gives the federal government much control, when local officials impede economic and commercial activity by blocking projects unless paid off. A major purpose of such regulation of interstate commerce has been to remove untoward burdens on the free flow of commerce. A state cannot, for example, selectively impose a tax on products made in and exported from another state, as this would disadvantage and hence slow the flow of goods from one state to another. And so, in theory, it seems reasonable for the federal government to forbid state and local officials from superimposing a "corruption tax" on economic activity.

The trouble commenced because the Supreme Court interpreted the Hobbs Act in a way that eliminated any meaningful distinction between extortion and bribery. It regards payment to a state or local official as inherently a product of the official's position and power. This interpretation becomes a serious problem for local officials who choose to continue their businesses and professions while holding public office, as we shall see in the Martinez case. Indeed, the prosecution of Raul Martinez by Dexter Lehtinen's office demonstrates the ways in which the lack of clarity inherent in the Hobbs Act can be a prescription not so much for keeping interstate commerce free of debilitating corruption but rather for arbitrary federal intervention into local political systems and, not so incidentally, perhaps evening political scores and affecting electoral outcomes.

---

[86] The Hobbs Act reads, in relevant part:

> (a) Whoever in any way or degree obstructs, delays, or affects commerce or the movement of any article or commodity in commerce, by robbery or extortion or attempts or conspires so to do, or commits or threatens physical violence to any person or property in furtherance of a plan or purpose to do anything in violation of this section shall be fined under this title or imprisoned not more than twenty years, or both.
> (b) As used in this section—
> (2) The term "extortion" means the obtaining of property from another, with his consent, induced by wrongful use of actual or threatened force, violence, or fear, or under color of official right.

18 U.S.C. § 1951 (2006).

At bottom, the prosecution's case at the trial was all over the place: The mayor had used, or taken advantage of, or merely benefited from his official position in order to coerce, or accept, financial tribute from those whom he had the power to hurt or to refrain from helping. A delicate dance was played out, the feds alleged, between a fawning, sycophantic, and generous citizen-businessman, and a powerful local pol who remained in private business during his term in elective office and did not wall himself off from projects requiring government approvals.

Interestingly enough, Martinez's *defense* sounded very much like the government's *prosecution* theory. Businessmen gave Martinez good deals to encourage an alliance with them and their enterprises, because they believed that their association with Martinez would be of enormous benefit to them. To the U.S. Attorney's office, this was an extortionate (threatening) use of Martinez's official power. To the defense, it was a natural result of the combination of Martinez's golden career prospects, his official position and myriad contacts, and the realities and normal expectations of local politics involving, in particular, public officials who earn only token compensation.[87]

If there are to be legal limitations to this cozy and quite logical symbiotic arrangement, it would have to be imposed by clear conflict-of-interest or other laws limiting the business activities of public officials. It would also have to be accompanied, presumably, by increasing their salaries, without which there would be a clear risk that the middle class would absent itself from running for local elective office. Were public officials not allowed to earn a living while serving in public positions that pay very little, government would become the fiefdom of the wealthy (or, of course, the thoroughly corrupt). Martinez's business activities were conducted in the open, with money passing by check, not cash, and with properties passing by legal title held in the name of the mayor, not of a straw man. And still, he was indicted for extortion.

---

[87] The defense pointed out to the jury that in Hialeah, as in most of Florida at the time, local political officials were expected to maintain outside employment and business interests. It's worth keeping in mind, too, that in addition to traditionally low salaries for these offices, there is the matter of campaign expenses. Cardoso testified that in 1983 he spent some $100,000 on his own campaign and won a position that paid only $17,000 per year.

As Martinez's first trial concluded, it appeared that the scales were tipping toward the prosecution. Just before trial, Judge James Kehoe instructed the jurors about the law that would govern their deliberations. The prosecutors argued to the judge that the Hobbs Act did not require them to demonstrate a so-called specific quid pro quo, that is, something of value given by the public official to the businessman in exchange for something of value from the businessman. To convict Martinez, they had to prove only that the mayor engaged in merely "passive acceptance" of the benefits that his business dealings could bring him, "so long as the defendant knew or believed that the benefits he was receiving [were] motivated by a hope of influence." Betraying their complete ignorance of— or perhaps contempt for—the workings of local politics and the economic realities facing middle class candidates, the prosecutors added that "if a politician wants to make money in business transactions, then he can stay out of politics."[88]

Judge Kehoe bought the prosecution's argument and explained to the jury that the "passive acceptance of a benefit" by a public official constituted extortion "if the official [knew] he had been offered the payment in exchange for the exercise of his official power" or—and here is the rub that likely got Martinez convicted— "that such payment [was] motivated by hope of influence." As for the question of whether Martinez was "entitled" to the property given to him, that is a somewhat slippery concept. While Cardoso did not "owe" Martinez participation in the deal, the developer did perceive a business benefit to himself by involving the popular politician.

Given the testimony and the jury instructions, it was no surprise that the jury, while acquitting on several of the projects, convicted Martinez of extortion relating to four of the deals. On July 22, 1991, Judge Kehoe sentenced Martinez to a 10-year prison term. Martinez, now a convicted felon, nonetheless won reelection while awaiting appeal; and in 1994 the Court of Appeals for the Eleventh Circuit reversed Martinez's conviction, ruling that Judge Kehoe had erred in his instructions to the jury by blurring the line between extortionate threats and other non-threatening arrangements by which a citizen

---

[88] Brief for the Appellant at 51 United States v. Martinez, 14 F.3d543 (11th Cir. 1994) (Nos. 91-5619 & 92-4668).

might do business with a politician.[89] After a second trial resulted in a deadlocked jury and the prosecutors' bizarre decision to pursue a third trial ended in acquittals on some counts and deadlock on others, the government finally gave up.

The use of the extortion formulation in the *Martinez* case demonstrates with clarity and some drama the real-world consequences of federal prosecutors using even a statute *not* widely viewed as vague—and now deemed by the Supreme Court to constitute the heart of the deprivation of "honest services"—to pursue state and local public officials who, while operating fully in accord with state and local laws and political culture, can suddenly find their careers derailed and their lives trashed because it did not occur to them that following state and local rules would not necessarily protect them from a federal prosecution under federal statutes that give little useful—and certainly no protective—guidance.

C. The Skilling Decision Does Not Make a Dent in the Inevitable Federalization of Criminal Law

As demonstrated by federal prosecutors' use of the Hobbs Act to prosecute Hialeah Mayor Raul Martinez, the Supreme Court's "paring down" of the honest services statute still leaves federal prosecutors with an arsenal of legal weapons aimed at criminalizing acts of public and private corruption. These federal statutes will likely be utilized by prosecutors in much the same way they have exploited the vaguely construed intangible rights fraud theory for so many years. However, the impact of the *Skilling* case is that federal statutes now merely criminalize what is already prohibited under state law in all 50 states, namely, acts of bribery and extortion. This fact raises the question of why federal intervention is necessary in those areas, like public corruption and corporate fraud, where state and local policymakers have already spoken and no discernable federal constitutional interests appear to exist.

---

[89] The Eleventh Circuit also found that jurors had improperly considered outside materials, which contributed to its decision to reverse the lower court's verdict and grant Martinez a new trial. See United States v. Martinez, 14 F.3d 543, 550–51 (11th Cir. 1994). Unfortunately, the court of appeals, relying on Supreme Court opinions in the cases McCormick v. United States, 500 U.S. 257 (1991) and United States v. Evans, 504 U.S. 255 (1992), was little clearer on the definition of extortion than was Judge Kehoe. See Martinez, 14 F.3d at 552–53.

As set forth above, the *Skilling* decision did not invalidate the statute, but instead simply bars from federal prosecution a narrow category of honest services fraud cases, specifically those involving nondisclosure of conflicts of interest or self-dealing. While the Court limited the honest services doctrine to cases of bribery or kickbacks, by the Court's own admission such cases constitute the "lion's share" of prosecutions under § 1346.[90] Thus, although some § 1346 charges will be thrown out, many will be unaffected because they, in fact, involve bribery and kickbacks. For example, an ongoing federal corruption probe in Cleveland, in which more than two dozen public officials and business leaders have been charged, will be largely unaffected by the *Skilling* decision because the defendants have been charged in various bribery and kickback schemes.[91] In another case, involving corruption charges against New Orleans technology chief Greg Meffert, the prosecution simply added the phrase "bribery/kickbacks" to 24 honest services counts in the indictment to save the charges from dismissal.[92] And, in yet another case, Univision Services Inc., a wholly owned subsidiary of Univision Communications Inc., recently pled guilty to one count of conspiracy to commit mail fraud and paid a fine of $1 million in relation to "a nationwide scheme in which Univision Music Group executives, employees and agents made illegal cash payments to radio station programmers and managers in exchange for increased radio broadcast time for Univision Music Group recordings" absent "on-air acknowledgments or payment of broadcast fees to the radio stations, as required by law."[93]

---

[90] Skilling v. United States, 130 S. Ct. 2896, 2931 n.44.

[91] Supreme Court "Honest Services" Ruling Unlikely to Affect County Corruption Case, Cleveland Plain Dealer, (June 24, 2010, 02:55 EST), http://blog.cleveland.com/metro/2010/06/supreme_court_honest_services.html.

[92] Cindy Chan, Supreme Court's "Honest Services" Ruling Could Affect Local Public Corruption Cases, Times Picayune, July 11, 2010, available at http://www.nola.com/crime/index.ssf/2010/07/supreme_courts_honest_services.html.

[93] Mail Fraud Prosecutions Continue Despite *Skilling* Decision—Univision Services, Inc. to Pay One Million, White Collar Crime Prof Blog (July 27, 2010, 01:16 EST), http://lawprofessors.typepad.com/whitecollarcrime_blog/2010/07/mail-fraud-prosecutions-continue-despite-skilling-decision-univision-services-inc-to-pay-one-million.html (quoting Press Release, Dept. of Justice, Subsidiary of Univision Communications Inc. Pleads Guilty to Conspiracy to Commit Mail Fraud and Agrees to Pay $1 Million to Resolve Related Criminal and Administrative Cases (July 26, 2010), http://www.justice.gov/opa/pr/2010/July/10-crm-855.html)).

Moreover, in anticipation of the Court's decision in the honest services cases, prosecutors had avoided charging under the statute in many cases, or simply rearraigned defendants on charges safe from constitutional review. For example, the Hobbs Act, as already discussed, prohibits actual or attempted extortion affecting interstate commerce.[94] To establish extortion in public corruption cases the government's burden is no different from that in a bribery case.[95] In addition, as the *Skilling* majority pointed out, bribery of a federal official is also a crime,[96] as is theft or bribery of any program receiving federal funds[97] and accepting or providing kickbacks in relation to contracts with the federal government.[98] Moreover, prosecutors have the vague federal conspiracy statute at their disposal,[99] and can also fashion the allegations in the indictment as a racketeering enterprise, subjecting the defendants to the draconian penalties of the federal Racketeer Influenced and Corrupt Organizations Act.[100] On top of these charges, federal prosecutors can also rely on charges of obstruction of justice or making false statements.[101]

The case of Rod Blagojevich, the former governor of Illinois, is instructive as to the malleability of federal criminal law and the proclivity of federal prosecutors to ignore the guidance provided by state law. Blagojevich is notorious for allegedly attempting to sell the Senate seat vacated by then-President-Elect Barack Obama following his election in November 2008. In the early morning hours of December 9, 2008, federal authorities showed up on Blagojevich's front porch and arrested him for honest services fraud, racketeering, and extortion charges arising from his conduct and alleged attempts

---

[94] 18 U.S.C. § 1951(a) (2006).

[95] United States v. Evans, 504 U.S. 255, 260 (1992) (recognizing that at common law, "[e]xtortion by the public official was the rough equivalent of what we would now describe as 'taking a bribe.'").

[96] 18 U.S.C. § 201 (2006).

[97] *Id.* § 666.

[98] 41 U.S.C. § 53 (2006).

[99] 18 U.S.C. § 371 (2006).

[100] *Id.* § 1962(c).

[101] See, e.g., *id.* § 1510 (obstruction of criminal investigations); *id.* § 1511 (obstruction of state or local law enforcement); *id.* § 1512 (witness tampering); *id.* § 1001 (false statement statute).

to aggressively raise campaign funds from donors.[102] Illinois U.S. Attorney Patrick Fitzgerald framed the case, from the start, as a Department of Justice mission to clean up state and local politics. At the December 9, 2008, press conference, held immediately following the arrest, Fitzgerald announced that the governor had engaged in a "political-corruption crime spree," attempting to "get as much money from contractors, shaking them down, pay-to-play before the end of the year," when a new state ethics law would take effect.[103]

The nature of this accelerating "political-corruption crime spree" was attested to at trial by a key government witness, John Wyma, a lobbyist and one of Blagojevich's closest associates who turned on him to cooperate with the federal government. Wyma testified that he became increasingly "uncomfortable" with the governor's aggressive campaign fundraising tactics in late 2008 in light of Illinois' looming Ethics in Government Act, which was scheduled to take effect on January 1, 2009, and would have limited campaign contributions from individuals doing business with the state.[104] In effect, the government's own witness seemed to concede, or at least assume, that this aspect of Blagojevich's conduct was in accordance with *state law as it stood at the time.* This was precisely the point that Fitzgerald breathlessly touted at the December 2008 press conference, supposedly to show Blagojevich's criminality. At that press conference, not one reporter felt compelled to ask why this made the governor a crook, when it appeared that he and his cohorts were racing to do their fund raising under then-existing state law. Such timing is the sign of someone who actually takes pains to follow state law, is it not? Is it not common and perfectly lawful for a citizen to arrange his tax affairs, for example, to take advantage of existing law before a change in the law takes effect? Yet this political fundraising was featured in a federal prosecution as evidence of honest

---

[102] David Mendell, Letter from Chicago: What About Me?, The New Yorker, July 26, 2010, at 40–45.

[103] Mendell, *id.* at 45.

[104] Bill McMorris, Prosecution Rests in Blagojevich Trial as Defense Gets Extra Week, Washington Examiner, July 14, 2010, available at http://www.washingtonexaminer.com/opinion/columns/special-editorial-reports/Prosecution-Rests-in-Blagojevich-Trial-as-Defense-Gets-Extra-Week-98414739.html.

services fraud.[105] It is hard to imagine a more vivid example of the failure of federal anti-fraud laws in general and the honest services doctrine in particular to give some deference to political figures who try to conform their conduct to the requirements of state law. And, of course, if federal law is to eschew such deference, at least it should do so in clear terms.[106]

D. The Ideological Underpinnings of the Court's Vagueness Decisions

As we have attempted to demonstrate in this article—particularly in our discussion of the true depths of the vagueness problem as demonstrated by federal prosecutors' use of the Hobbs Act in prosecuting Hialeah mayor Raul Martinez—judges do not seem to have an adequate appreciation of the actual ways in which vague statutes allow the Department of Justice to proceed in the most confounding prosecutions against public officials. The same problem is seen in use of vague statutes against private citizens, including businesspeople, political activists, and others who provide targets of choice for prosecutors wishing to score points with future employers, the news media, or the general public.

A dramatic recent example is seen in the justices' various opinions in *Holder v. Humanitarian Law Project*, decided just three days before *Skilling* and the other honest services opinions were released.[107] In *Holder*, a group of plaintiffs sought a pre-enforcement judicial decree that particular national security laws were either unconstitutionally vague and hence in violation of the Due Process Clause of the Fifth Amendment, or otherwise in derogation of the First Amendment's free speech and freedom of association provisions.

---

[105] A fuller explanation of this aspect of the Blagojevich prosecution is found in Harvey Silverglate, How the 'Independent' Fourth Estate Has Failed in Its Critical Duty, Volokh Conspiracy (Dec. 17, 2009, 02:56 EST), http://volokh.com/2009/12/17/how-the-fourth-estate-has-failed.

[106] Although the press at Fitzgerald's news conference did not question as much of the government's evidence and legal theory as the prosecutor there disclosed, it later appeared that some members of the jury, upon hearing the evidence and, in particular, portions of the wiretap and eavesdrop tapes, were not convinced that Blagojevich was a felon rather than simply a politician trying to raise campaign funds and gain political power and leverage. The jury in varying combinations deadlocked on all of the counts, with the lone exception of a guilty verdict on a single count of lying to an FBI agent during a pre-indictment interview. Monica Davey & Susan Saulny, Blagojevich, Guilty on 1 of 24 Counts, Faces Retrial, N.Y. Times, Aug. 18, 2010, at A1.

[107] 561 U.S. ＿＿, 130 S. Ct. 2705 (2010).

Particularly at issue were provisions of the statute that prohibited four types of "material support" activities provided to any group designated by the secretary of state as a "foreign terrorist organization": "training," "expert advice or assistance," "service," and "personnel." (Between the filing of the lawsuit in 1998 and the case's final resolution by the Supreme Court a dozen years later, the statute was amended a number of times. The history of the statute's various formulations is set forth in the Court's opinion.)

The plaintiffs consisted of two American citizens and six domestic organizations, including the Humanitarian Law Project, described by the high court as "a human rights organization with consultative status to the United Nations."[108] The plaintiffs did not challenge all possible applications of the statute. Rather, they complained of their inability to determine how and whether the statute would or could be applied to certain of their intended activities, with regard to a number of organizations that engaged in both terrorist activities and non-terrorist political and humanitarian actions. The particular activities in which the organizational plaintiffs wished to participate but which they feared might be deemed in violation of some provisions of the statute included:

> (1)"train[ing] members of the PKK [Kurdistan Workers' Party] on how to use humanitarian and international law to peacefully resolve disputes"; (2) "engag[ing] in political advocacy on behalf of Kurds who live in Turkey"; (3) teach[ing] PKK members how to petition various representative bodies such as the United Nations for relief." Individual plaintiffs sought a declaration and clarification as to whether the statute would criminalize (1) "train[ing] members of [the] LTTE [Liberation Tigers of Tamil Eelam] to present claims for tsunami-related aid to mediators and international bodies; (2) "offer[ing] their legal expertise in negotiating peace agreements between the LTTE and the Sri Lankan government"; and (3) "engage[ing] in political advocacy on behalf of Tamils who live in Sri Lanka."[109]

The district court entered an injunction against the government's applying to the plaintiffs' activities the prohibitions on "personnel"

---

[108] *Id.* at 2713.
[109] *Id.* at 2716.

and "training support,"[110] which was affirmed by the Ninth Circuit.[111] The Supreme Court reversed in a 6–3 decision, with Chief Justice Roberts and Justices Stevens, Scalia, Kennedy, Thomas, and Alito in the majority.

The approach of the Supreme Court majority to the vagueness question is indicative of the difficulties encountered by ordinary— or even extraordinary—citizens in dealing with a statute where the terms are in the eyes of many seen as vague and inadequately informative for the provision of useful guidance. The majority wrote:

> Most of the activities in which plaintiffs seek to engage readily fall within the scope of the terms "training" and "expert advice or assistance." Plaintiffs want to "train members of [the] PKK on how to use humanitarian and international law to peacefully resolve disputes," and "teach PKK members how to petition various representative bodies such as the United Nations for relief." 552 F.3d at 921, n. 1. A person of ordinary intelligence would understand that instruction on resolving disputes through international law falls within the statute's definition of "training" because it imparts a "specific skill," not "general knowledge." . . . Plaintiffs' activities also fall comfortably within the scope of "expert advice or assistance": A reasonable person would recognize that teaching the PKK how to petition for humanitarian relief before the United Nations involves advice derived from, as the statute puts it, "specialized knowledge."[112]

All six justices in the *Holder* majority voted three days later to reverse and remand Skilling's conviction under a narrowing of the honest services statute that would encompass only allegations involving bribes and kickbacks, with three of them (Justices Scalia, Thomas, and Kennedy) expressing the view that the honest services statute should be invalidated altogether rather than rewritten by the Court. In dissent in *Holder*, Justice Breyer wrote, for himself and Justices Ginsburg and Sotomayor, that while "I do not think this statute is unconstitutionally vague," nonetheless the statute violates

---

[110] Humanitarian Law Project v. Reno, No. CV-98-1971 ABC (BQRx), 2001 U.S. Dist. LEXIS 16729, at *12 (C.D. Cal. Oct. 2, 2001).

[111] Humanitarian Law Project v. U.S. Dep't of Justice, 352 F.3d 382 (9th Cir. 2003).

[112] Holder, 130 S. Ct. at 2720.

First Amendment rights of speech and association.[113] "[T]he government has not made the strong showing," wrote Justice Breyer, "necessary to justify under the First Amendment the criminal prosecution of those who engage in these activities."[114] Justice Breyer also questioned the rational relationship between the ends of protecting national security and the means by which the statute's criminal prohibitions were formulated.

Thus, none of the justices were prepared to declare any portion of the statute to be unconstitutionally vague—not even the dissenters who recognized that, with regard to some people operating in good faith, the statute would criminalize language reasonably deemed by a citizen to be an exercise in free speech. A citizen is to understand that he or she can be criminally prosecuted for activities—in the words of the Breyer dissent—that "involve the communication and advocacy of political ideas and lawful means of achieving political ends," including "using international law to resolve disputes peacefully or petitioning the United Nations."[115] Were it not for the fact that this judicial explanation of the meaning and scope of the "material support" statute was made possible because pre-enforcement review happened to be available in this procedural context, one could readily envision the prosecution of perfectly well-meaning individuals and organizations for seeking to promote adherence to the rule of law and peaceful resolution of conflicts.

How is it that justices who understood (albeit to an incomplete extent) why the honest services statute was void or at least required a severe limiting interpretation would nonetheless find no Fifth Amendment due process vagueness infirmity in a statute that appears to transmogrify political advocacy into rendering "material assistance" to terrorism? In comparing the various opinions in the two cases, one gets the sense that the high court really does not understand the fundamental flaws that characterize vague statutes. There is insufficient appreciation of the challenge facing citizens who wish to conform their activities to the requirements of the criminal law, but who get woefully insufficient guidance from either the statutory text or even the judicial gloss on that language. (In

---

[113] *Id.* at 2731 (Breyer, J., dissenting).

[114] *Id.* at 2732.

[115] *Id.*

Holder, of course, the citizens had the benefit of being allowed to seek a pre-enforcement interpretation of the scope and meaning of the statute. Normally, given the rarity of federal court interpretations of statutes in the absence of an actual "case or controversy," the citizen has to proceed at his or her own peril.) The world becomes a terribly dangerous place for citizens active in the political arena, as well as for citizens engaged in the world of commerce, or those who choose public life and politics.

V. Conclusion

It is, surely, time for the high court to revisit the manner in which the void for vagueness doctrine has been allowed to degrade in the area of federal criminal law and enforcement. The lack of guidance afforded by federal criminal statutes should not be the basis for an intellectual game susceptible to different outcomes that depend on the political disposition of either the citizen or the government (or, for that matter, the judge). The inability of average intelligent citizens to understand modern federal criminal statutes is a growing problem that interferes not only with Fifth Amendment due process rights but even First Amendment speech and associational rights. Congress, effectively relieved of the discipline that should be imposed by the Due Process Clause, writes statutes that it pretends citizens will understand. Courts uphold, against vagueness attacks, statutes the scope and meaning of which divide scholars and judges. It seems, even to the citizen seeking to avoid cynicism, like a page out of *Alice in Wonderland*. The time has come to restore Fifth Amendment due process to one of its core meanings: if a criminal statute does not give the average citizen a clear notion of what conduct is intended to be outlawed, that statute should not serve as a basis for turning the citizen into a criminal.

Taking Stock of *Comstock*: The Necessary and Proper Clause and the Limits of Federal Power

*Ilya Somin**

Introduction

Constitutional limits on federal government power are once again a major focus of political debate. Those who argue that the federal government has nearly unlimited authority often cite the Necessary and Proper Clause to justify their view. That clause gives Congress the power to "make all Laws which shall be necessary and proper for carrying into Execution the foregoing Powers, and all other Powers vested by this Constitution in the Government of the United States, or in any Department or Officer thereof."[1] The Supreme Court's recent decision in *United States v. Comstock* is a step in the direction of interpreting the clause as a virtual blank check for Congress to regulate almost any activity it wants.[2] Justice Stephen Breyer's opinion for the Court, however, is vague on several key points. Moreover, it is difficult to say whether the coalition of justices that made up the *Comstock* majority will hold together in future cases. The ultimate impact of *Comstock* therefore remains to be seen.

Unlike much earlier litigation on the rights of potential "sexual predators," *Comstock* did not consider the defendants' individual rights under the Bill of Rights or the Due Process Clause of the Fourteenth Amendment. Rather, the case turned solely on the question of whether the Necessary and Proper Clause gives Congress the power to detain "sexually dangerous" former federal prisoners

* Associate Professor of Law, George Mason University School of Law. For helpful suggestions and comments, I would like to thank Randy Barnett, Roger Pilon, Ilya Shapiro, and Corey Young. I would also like to thank Desiree Mowry for her work as a research assistant for this article.

[1] U.S. Const. art. I, § 8, cl. 18.

[2] 561 U.S. ___, 130 S. Ct. 1949 (2010).

even after they have finished serving their sentences. In 1997, the Court had previously ruled that the Due Process Clause does not forbid the indefinite civil detention of mentally ill individuals who are considered likely to commit "predatory acts of sexual violence" in the future.[3] Thus, the *Comstock* defendants could not argue that their continued confinement violated an individual constitutional right. They could only claim that structural limits on federal government power precluded the federal government from detaining them even if a state government potentially could do so.

Part I of this article discusses Section 4248 of the Adam Walsh Act, the provision the Court upheld in *Comstock*. It also summarizes the Court's majority opinion, the two concurring opinions, and the dissent by Justice Clarence Thomas. Part II criticizes the Court's reasoning. The majority's extremely broad interpretation of the Necessary and Proper Clause may render much of the careful enumeration of congressional power in Article I of the Constitution superfluous. In addition, it tries to link the statute to a nebulous congressional authority to act as a "custodian" for federal prisoners that is itself not enumerated anywhere in the Constitution.

Part III considers the implications of *Comstock* for the future. The decision could strengthen the government's case in the ongoing litigation over the massive health care bill passed by Congress in March 2010. Lawsuits by 21 states, the National Federation of Independent Business, and various others have challenged the statute in court, arguing that key elements exceed Congress's powers under the Constitution.[4] *Comstock*'s broad interpretation of the Necessary and Proper Clause could be used to buttress the government's constitutional justifications for the new health care law's "individual mandate." Indeed, the government has already cited *Comstock* in its briefs urging dismissal of the state lawsuits.[5] Still, the mandate might run

---

[3] Kansas v. Hendricks, 521 U.S. 346, 352 (1997).

[4] Among the other lawsuits against the individual mandate is one undertaken by the conservative Thomas More Legal Center on behalf of itself and several individuals who refuse to obey the mandate. See Associated Press, 13 Attorneys General Sue Over Health Care Overhaul, Mar. 23, 2010, available at http://politics.usnews.com/news/articles/2010/03/23/13-attorneys-general-sue-over-healthcare-overhaul.html.

[5] See, e.g., Defendant's Motion to Dismiss at 47–48, Florida v. Department of Health and Human Services, No. 3:10-cv-91-RV/EMT (N.D. Fla. filed June 16, 2010), available at http://op.bna.com/hl.nsf/id/sfak-86hslb/$File/dojbrieflacase.pdf; Defendant's Motion to Dismiss at 34–35, Virginia ex. rel Cuccinelli v. Sebelius, No. 3:10-cv-00188-

afoul of the vague five-factor test that was a key element of *Comstock*. The ultimate impact of the decision on the health care litigation and other future cases may depend on how that test is interpreted and applied.

I. The Adam Walsh Act and the *Comstock* Decision

The litigation that culminated in the *Comstock* decision involved Section 4248 of the Adam Walsh Act, which gives the federal Bureau of Prisons the power to detain "sexually dangerous" federal prisoners even after they have served out their entire sentences.[6] The act marked a major expansion in the federal government's involvement in efforts to combat sexual predators.[7]

In late 2006, the federal government sought to use Section 4248 to confine Graydon Earl Comstock and four other soon-to-be-released federal inmates after their sentences ended.[8] The five defendants claimed that Section 4248 is unconstitutional because it exceeds the scope of Congress's authority under the Constitution. The U.S. Court of Appeals for the Fourth Circuit endorsed their argument.[9] It concluded that the provision went beyond Congress's authority under both the Commerce Clause (which gives Congress the authority to regulate interstate commerce) and the Necessary and Proper Clause.[10] It reached that decision despite the Supreme Court's

---

HEH, (E.D. Va. filed May 24, 2010), available at http://www.scribd.com/doc/ 31923230/Commonwealth-of-Virginia-v-Sibelius-Memorandum-In-Support-Of-Motion-To-Dismiss. It may be noteworthy, however, that both of these government briefs rely on *Comstock* to only a very limited degree.

[6] 18 U.S.C. § 4248(a) (2006). The Bureau's determination of "sexual dangerousness" must be confirmed by a court. See *id*. at § 4248(c).

[7] For detailed discussion of the Adam Walsh Act, see Corey Rayburn Yung, The Emerging Criminal War on Sex Offenders, Harv. C.R.-C.L. L. Rev. (forthcoming), available at http://papers.ssrn.com/sol3/papers.cfm?abstract_id=1456042.

[8] Comstock, 130 S. Ct. at 1955.

[9] United States v. Comstock, 551 F.3d 274 (4th Cir. 2009), rev'd, 130 S. Ct. 1949 (2010). The Fourth Circuit upheld a previous district court ruling to the same effect. See United States v. Comstock, 507 F. Supp. 2d 522 (E.D. N.C. 2009), aff'd, 551 F.3d 374, rev'd, 130 S. Ct. 1949 (2010).

[10] Comstock, 551 F.3d at 277–84.

extremely broad interpretation of the commerce power in the 2005 case of *Gonzales v. Raich*.[11]

In a 7–2 decision, with Justice Breyer writing for the majority, the Supreme Court reversed the Fourth Circuit and upheld Section 4248, relying exclusively on the Necessary and Proper Clause. The Court did not address the question of whether the provision might also be upheld under any of Congress's other powers, probably because then-Solicitor General Elena Kagan chose to focus her arguments exclusively on the Necessary and Proper Clause and did not press the Commerce Clause argument that federal prosecutors had raised in the lower courts.[12]

Justices Anthony Kennedy and Samuel Alito wrote concurring opinions where they agreed with the Court's bottom-line conclusion that Section 4248 was constitutional, but argued that the majority interpreted Congress's powers under the Necessary and Proper Clause too broadly. Interestingly, Chief Justice John Roberts joined the majority opinion in full, rather than signing onto either of the concurrences or writing separately. He was the only one of the five most conservative justices to embrace the majority's reasoning.[13]

A. The Majority Opinion

The main argument the majority relied on in upholding Section 4248 was that it was "necessary and proper" to the implementation of Congress's power to operate a penal system and act "as the custodian" of its prisoners.[14] The Court advanced several variations on this argument. First, it analogized the detention of "sexually dangerous" individuals after their sentences have ended to Congress's power to provide mental health and other services for federal prisoners during their incarceration.[15] It noted the possible precedent provided by numerous earlier statutes that provided for the hospitalization and care of mentally ill prisoners.[16] The Court described

---

[11] 545 U.S. 1 (2005). I have analyzed *Raich* in Ilya Somin, *Gonzales v. Raich*: Federalism as a Casualty of the War on Drugs, 15 Cornell J. L. & Pub. Pol'y 507 (2006) (symposium on the war on drugs).

[12] See Brief for Petitioners, United States v. Comstock, 130 S. Ct. 1949 (2010) (No. 08-1224), 2009 WL 2896312.

[13] I discuss the implications of Chief Justice Roberts's position *infra* § III.A.4.

[14] Comstock, 130 S. Ct. at 1958–64.

[15] *Id.* at 1958.

[16] *Id.* at 1958–61.

Section 4248 as merely "a modest addition to a set of federal prison-related mental-health statutes that have existed for many decades."[17] However, as the opinion itself noted, those earlier federal statutes provided for civil commitment of "dangerous" mentally ill prisoners only in cases that began during their term of incarceration, though the civil commitment could potentially continue afterward.[18] The Court also emphasized the extent to which Section 4248 "accommodat[es]" state interests by allowing state governments the option to detain the "sexually dangerous" persons themselves.[19] Section 4248 requires that the federal government consult with the state government in the area, and allow the state to assume custody of the former prisoner in question if state officials so choose.[20]

More generally, the Court concluded that the Necessary and Proper Clause authorizes any exercise of congressional power that "constitutes a means that is rationally related to the implementation of a constitutionally enumerated power."[21] In other areas of constitutional law, this "rational basis" test is usually applied in a way that is extremely deferential to the government.[22] Perhaps to reinforce this point, the *Comstock* opinion cites highly deferential Commerce Clause and Spending Clause decisions as relevant examples of the application of rational basis scrutiny.[23]

The majority lists five factors that determined their decision in this case:

> We take these five considerations *together*. They include: (1) the breadth of the Necessary and Proper Clause, (2) the long history of federal involvement in this arena, (3) the sound reasons for the statute's enactment in light of the Government's custodial interest in safeguarding the public from dangers posed by those in federal custody, (4) the statute's accommodation of state interests, and (5) the statute's narrow scope. *Taken together*, these considerations lead us to conclude

---

[17] *Id.* at 1958.

[18] *Id.* at 1958–60.

[19] *Id.* at 1961–62.

[20] 18 U.S.C. § 4248(d) (2006).

[21] Comstock, 130 S. Ct. at 1956.

[22] For discussion, see Somin, *supra* note 11, at 518–19.

[23] See Comstock, 130 S. Ct. at 1956–57 (citing Sabri v. United States, 541 U.S. 600, 605 (2004) and Gonzales v. Raich, 545 U.S. 1, 22 (2005)).

> that the statute is a "necessary and proper" means of exercis-
> ing the federal authority that permits Congress to create
> federal criminal laws, to punish their violation, to imprison
> violators, to provide appropriately for those imprisoned, and
> to maintain the security of those who are not imprisoned but
> who may be affected by the federal imprisonment of others.[24]

It is noteworthy that the majority emphasized that these "five considerations" determined the outcome when "[t]aken together."[25] This immediately raises the question of what happens in a case where one or more of the five cuts the other way. Does the government still win if, say, only three of the five considerations support its position? If not, the five-part test significantly undercuts the pro-government implications of the Court's use of the rational basis test. As discussed below, it also raises the possibility that *Comstock* could hurt the government's position in the present health care litigation, or at least not help it.[26] Unfortunately, the *Comstock* Court says very little about how the five-part test should be applied to future cases. As Justice Clarence Thomas asks in his dissent:

> Must each of the five considerations exist before the Court
> sustains future federal legislation as proper exercises of Con-
> gress' Necessary and Proper Clause authority? What if the
> facts of a given case support a finding of only four considera-
> tions? Or three? And if three or four will suffice, *which* three
> or four are imperative? At a minimum, . . . [the] five-consid-
> eration approach warrants an explanation as to . . . which
> of the five considerations will bear the most weight in future
> cases, assuming some number less than five suffices. (Or, if
> not, why all five are required.) The Court provides no
> answers to these questions.[27]

A final noteworthy element of the majority decision is the absence of any discussion of the meaning of the word "proper" in the Necessary and Proper Clause. While the Court explained in some detail why Section 4248 may be considered "necessary,"[28] it did not even

---

[24] *Id.* at 1965 (emphasis added).

[25] *Id.*

[26] See *infra* § III.A.1.

[27] Comstock, 130 S. Ct. at 1975 (Thomas, J., dissenting) (emphasis in original).

[28] Comstock, 130 S. Ct. at 1956–61.

consider the possibility that it might be "improper." This is notable because the fate of the state challenge to the newly enacted health care bill may depend in large part on how future decisions define "proper."[29]

B. *Justice Kennedy's and Justice Alito's Concurring Opinions*

Justice Kennedy's concurring opinion agrees with the majority's view that Section 4248 is constitutional under the Necessary and Proper Clause. Kennedy wrote separately, however, in order to express disagreement with some of the majority's arguments and "to caution that the Constitution does require the invalidation of congressional attempts to extend federal powers in some instances."[30] Kennedy's views are potentially significant because he is most often the Court's swing voter on important ideologically charged issues.

Kennedy argued against the use of the "rational basis" test adopted by the majority:

> The terms "rationally related" and "rational basis" must be employed with care, particularly if either is to be used as a stand-alone test. The phrase "rational basis" most often is employed to describe the standard for determining whether legislation that does not proscribe fundamental liberties nonetheless violates the Due Process Clause. Referring to this due process inquiry, and in what must be one of the most deferential formulations of the standard for reviewing legislation in all the Court's precedents, the Court has said: "But the law need not be in every respect logically consistent with its aims to be constitutional. It is enough that there is an evil at hand for correction, and that it might be thought that the particular legislative measure was a rational way to correct it . . . ." This formulation was in a case presenting a due process challenge and a challenge to a State's exercise of its own powers, powers not confined by the principles that control the limited nature of our National Government. The phrase, then, should not be extended uncritically to the issue before us.[31]

---

[29] See *infra* § III.A.3.

[30] Comstock, 130 S. Ct. at 1966 (Kennedy, J., concurring).

[31] *Id*. at 1966.

Justice Kennedy emphasized that Section 4248 should be upheld primarily because "this is a discrete and narrow exercise of authority over a small class of persons already subject to the federal power," which "involves little intrusion upon the ordinary processes and powers of the States."[32] He criticized the majority for asserting an excessively broad scope of federal power and "ignor[ing] important limitations [on congressional power] stemming from federalism principles."[33]

Justice Alito's concurring opinion also emphasized the narrow scope of Section 4248 and took the majority to task for "the breadth of [its] language."[34] He contended that "[t]he Necessary and Proper Clause does not give Congress *carte blanche*. Although the term 'necessary' does not mean 'absolutely necessary' or indispensable, the term requires an 'appropriate' link between a power conferred by the Constitution and the law enacted by Congress . . . . And it is an obligation of this Court to enforce compliance with that limitation."[35]

Nevertheless, Justice Alito argued that Section 4248 can be upheld as a necessary and proper adjunct to Congress's authority to operate a federal prison system because "[j]ust as it is necessary and proper for Congress to provide for the apprehension of escaped federal prisoners, it is necessary and proper for Congress to provide for the civil commitment of dangerous federal prisoners who would otherwise escape civil commitment as a result of federal imprisonment."[36] He cited evidence indicating that "in a disturbing number of cases, no State was willing to assume the financial burden of providing for the civil commitment of federal prisoners who, if left at large after the completion of their sentences, would present a danger to any communities in which they chose to live or visit."[37] States may be unwilling to detain these released federal prisoners because "having been held for years in a federal prison, [they] often had few ties to any State; it was a matter of speculation where they would choose to go upon release; and accordingly no State was

---

[32] *Id.* at 1968.

[33] *Id.*

[34] *Id.* at 1969 (Alito, J., concurring).

[35] *Id.* at 1970 (quoting M'Culloch v. Maryland, 17 U.S. (4 Wheat.) 316, 415 (1819)).

[36] *Id.* at 1970.

[37] *Id.*

enthusiastic about volunteering to shoulder the burden of civil commitment."[38]

C. *Justice Thomas's Dissent*

Justice Clarence Thomas wrote a forceful dissent, most of which was joined by Justice Antonin Scalia. Thomas's dissent emphasized that the Necessary and Proper Clause does not give Congress unconstrained authority to address whatever problems it sees fit. Rather, "Congress may act under that Clause only when its legislation 'carr[ies] into Execution' one of the Federal Government's enumerated powers."[39] Thomas argued that Section 4248 does not do so because it does not accomplish any "legitimate end" that implements one of Congress's other enumerated powers.[40] He concluded that "[n]o enumerated power in Article I, § 8 [of the Constitution], expressly delegates to Congress the power to enact a civil-commitment regime for sexually dangerous persons, nor does any other provision in the Constitution vest Congress or the other branches of the Federal Government with such a power. Accordingly, § 4248 can be a valid exercise of congressional authority only if it is 'necessary and proper for carrying into Execution' one or more of those federal powers actually enumerated in the Constitution."[41] Thomas argued that Section 4248 fails this test because "[t]he Government identifies no specific enumerated power or powers as a constitutional predicate for § 4248, and none are readily discernable."[42]

Thomas rejected the majority's argument that Section 4248 can be justified as an extension of Congress's power to operate a prison system and control its inmates because "[t]he Necessary and Proper Clause does not provide Congress with authority to enact any law simply because it furthers *other laws* Congress has enacted in the exercise of its incidental authority."[43] Rather, it can enact the additional law only insofar as that law facilitates the use of the previous law in implementing Congress's other enumerated powers. Even if the initial imprisonment of a given offender was necessary for the

---

[38] *Id.*

[39] *Id.* at 1974 (Thomas, J., dissenting) (quoting U.S. Const. art I, § 8, cl. 18).

[40] *Id.* at 1972–75.

[41] *Id.* at 1973 (quoting U.S. Const. art I, § 8, cl. 18).

[42] *Id.*

[43] *Id.* at 1976 (emphasis in original).

implementation of some other congressional power, it does not follow that civil confinement of the inmate after his sentence expires also facilitates that same purpose.

It is significant that Justice Thomas's opinion was joined by Justice Scalia, who endorsed all but one subsection of his colleague's dissent.[44] This may indicate a retreat by Scalia from the extremely broad interpretation of the Necessary and Proper Clause that he advanced in his concurring opinion in *Gonzales v. Raich*.[45]

II. Critique of the Court's Decision

In this part, I analyze several flaws in the Court's decision and the reasoning justifying it. As Justice Thomas's dissent showed, the majority failed to connect Section 4248 of the Adam Walsh Act to the implementation of any of Congress's enumerated powers. Justice Alito's more subtle argument for a connection between Section 4248 and enumerated powers also fails. And the Court's approach to the Necessary and Proper Clause is further flawed because it potentially renders many of Congress's enumerated powers redundant. Finally, the decision cannot be defended on the basis of precedent, including Chief Justice John Marshall's landmark decision in *M'Culloch v. Maryland*.[46]

A. Is There an Enumerated Power in the House?

The Necessary and Proper Clause does not give Congress a blank check to adopt any laws that might advance some useful purpose. Rather, it grants only the power to enact "Laws which shall be necessary and proper for carrying into Execution the foregoing Powers [listed in Article I], and all other Powers vested by this Constitution in the Government of the United States, or in any Department or Officer thereof."[47] This means that Section 4248 can be upheld only if it somehow "carrie[s] into Execution" some other power granted to the federal government elsewhere in the Constitution.

---

[44] The relevant section did not include most of Thomas's discussion of "legitimate" as opposed to impermissible ends, which forms the heart of his argument.

[45] Raich, 545 U.S. at 34–42 (Scalia, J., concurring). I criticized Scalia's *Raich* opinion in Somin, *supra* note 11, at 529–33.

[46] 17 U.S. (4 Wheat.) 316 (1819).

[47] U.S. Const. art. I, § 8, cl. 18.

Unfortunately, neither the majority opinion in *Comstock* nor the federal government in its brief shows any such connection.

The majority tries to justify Section 4248 by reference to the federal government's supposed power to act as a "custodian" for federal prisoners and protect the population against the danger posed by mentally ill federal inmates.[48] However, there is no independent congressional power to create "custodians" for federal prisoners. As the majority opinion points out, "[n]either Congress' power to criminalize conduct, nor its power to imprison individuals who engage in that conduct, nor its power to enact laws governing prisons and prisoners, is explicitly mentioned in the Constitution."[49]

Rather, this authority exists only insofar as it "executes" whatever enumerated federal power is implemented by the incarceration of the inmates in question. Even if we assume that Graydon Comstock and the other former inmates involved in the case were originally imprisoned for violating laws that Congress had the power to enact under its enumerated powers, confining these individuals after they have served their sentences does nothing to facilitate enforcement of those laws. By definition, those former prisoners have already been fully punished for their violations of federal law. Their continued confinement has no connection to their previous violations of federal law. Instead, it is justified solely on the ground that they are "sexually dangerous" persons who might commit unspecified crimes in the future.

The power to incarcerate "sexually dangerous" inmates who have completed their sentences does nothing to assist in the enforcement of federal laws that are actually authorized by any of Congress's enumerated powers. Not only does their confinement do nothing to implement any enumerated power, it may actually make it more difficult for the federal government to do so. The confinement and care of the "sexually dangerous" former inmates tie up federal penal system resources that could instead be used to facilitate the incarceration of inmates who have violated federal laws that actually implement one of Congress's enumerated powers. For these reasons, the majority's claim that "the same enumerated power that justifies the

---

[48] See *supra* § I.A..

[49] Comstock, 130 S. Ct. at 1958.

creation of a federal criminal statute . . . justifies civil commitment under § 4248 as well," is misguided.[50]

The government's brief relies on Congress's power to establish and operate a federal penal system.[51] This argument is vulnerable to the same textual objection as the majority's very similar "custodian" theory. Congress's power to operate a penal system is not an independent grant of constitutional authority. Rather, it exists only insofar as it enforces one of Congress's other enumerated powers by punishing offenders who violated laws enacted to implement those authorities.

To put the point in a more general way, let us assume that A is one of Congress's enumerated powers under the Constitution. Let us also assume that B is at least sometimes a permissible "necessary and proper" means to the implementation of A. Finally, let us posit that C is a power that is somehow connected to B. It does not follow from this that Congress has the authority to enact laws that do C any time there is some connection between C and B. Indeed, it *does not* have that power in cases where C's connection to B does nothing to facilitate A. Since B itself is permissible only insofar as it facilitates A, C is permissible only insofar as its connection to B assists the latter in a way that helps implement A. In this case, A is the power to implement Congress's enumerated powers, B is the authority to establish a federal penal system, and C is the supposed authority to confine "sexually dangerous" federal inmates after they have completed their sentences.

The majority tries to escape this conundrum by analogizing Section 4248 to previous statutes that enabled federal penal authorities to regulate and treat mentally ill inmates during the period of their incarceration.[52] These statutes are much more closely connected, however, to the enforcement of whatever laws the inmates in question violated in the first place. If mentally ill inmates can't be controlled in ways that prevent them from becoming a threat to guards or fellow prisoners, the operation of federal prisons becomes much more difficult or—in extreme cases—even impossible. This

---

[50] *Id.* at 1964.

[51] Brief for Petitioners at 22–48, United States v. Comstock, 130 S. Ct. 1949 (2010) (No. 08-1224), 2009 WL 2896312.

[52] Comstock, 130 S. Ct. at 1958–61.

in turn would make it hard to punish violators of federal laws by incarceration.[53] By contrast, Section 4248 does nothing to facilitate the punishment of inmates who violate federal law. Instead, it requires confinement of former prisoners who have *already* received their full punishment. If released from the federal penal system, they also pose little if any threat to its continued operation with respect to other inmates. Indeed, their release might actually make such operation easier by freeing up federal resources.

Justice Alito advances a more subtle argument connecting Section 4248 to enumerated federal power. As he puts it, it is "necessary and proper for Congress to protect the public from dangers created by the federal criminal justice and prison systems," in the same way that "it is necessary and proper for Congress to provide for the apprehension of escaped federal prisoners."[54] In this case, the relevant "danger created by the federal . . . prison system" is the risk created by "dangerous federal prisoners who would otherwise escape civil commitment as a result of federal imprisonment."[55]

The main flaw in Justice Alito's reasoning is that the supposed risks posed by "sexually dangerous" former federal inmates are not in fact "created" by the federal prison system. Unless incarceration by the federal government turned formerly nonviolent prisoners into "sexually dangerous" ones, they would have posed just as great a risk of becoming sexual predators had they never been incarcerated by the federal government in the first place. As Justice Thomas explains in his dissent: "A federal criminal defendant's 'sexually dangerous' propensities are not 'created by' the fact of his incarceration or his relationship with the federal prison system. The fact that the Federal Government has the authority to imprison a person for the purpose of punishing him for a federal crime—sex-related or otherwise—does not provide the Government with the additional power to exercise indefinite civil control over that person."[56]

Justice Alito's analogy to preventing prisoners from escaping is also off the mark. Forestalling escapes is essential to ensuring that

---

[53] Obviously, this assumes that the laws in question are themselves permissible exercises of congressional power. But none of the former inmates in the *Comstock* litigation challenged the validity of the statutes under which they were originally convicted.

[54] Comstock, 130 S. Ct. at 1970 (Alito, J., concurring).

[55] *Id.*

[56] *Id.* at 1979 (Thomas, J., dissenting).

prisoners are fully punished for violating federal laws that enforce Congress's enumerated powers. There is no such connection to the enforcement of enumerated powers when former inmates are civilly confined after they have already served their sentences.

Justice Alito does make a reasonable policy point when he notes that states might hesitate to confine potentially dangerous former federal inmates if it is not clear what state the ex-prisoners would otherwise settle in.[57] Rather than undertaking the expense of paying for their confinement, self-interested states might leave such individuals free in the hope that they will move somewhere else. This concern, however, may be overstated. After all, many former federal inmates probably do have significant connections to some particular state or region. In addition, it is not clear that either state or federal authorities can do a good job of predicting whether a particular former inmate is likely to become a dangerous sexual predator.[58] Federal officials might misclassify nonviolent prisoners as "sexually dangerous," just as state officials often do.[59] There are also serious moral objections to imprisoning people merely because we believe that they might commit a crime in the future.[60] Preventing the confinement of persons on the grounds that they might commit future crimes may therefore not be such a bad thing.

Even if Section 4248 does help solve a genuine problem, it does not necessarily follow that it is constitutional. The Necessary and Proper Clause gives Congress the authority to address only such problems as can be attacked using Congress's enumerated powers. Justice Thomas's dissent correctly reminds us that "[t]he Constitution does not vest in Congress the authority to protect society from every bad act that might befall it."[61]

---

[57] *Id.* at 1970 (Alito, J., concurring).

[58] See Yung, *supra* note 7, at 49–50 (noting evidence showing that authorities often misclassify innocent people who pose no danger, as sexual offenders).

[59] *Id.*

[60] See, e.g., Thomas Szasz, Psychiatry and the Control of Dangerousness: On the Apotropaic Function of the Term "Mental Illness," 29 J. Med. Ethics 227 (2003). See also the literature cited in Stephen J. Morse, Preventive Confinement of Dangerous Offenders, 32 J.L. Med. & Ethics 56 (2004).

[61] *Id.* at 1974 (Thomas, J., dissenting).

B. *Rendering the Rest of Congress's Powers Redundant?*

An additional problem with the Court's reasoning in *Comstock* is that it may render the vast majority of Congress's other enumerated powers redundant. As discussed above, the majority decided that Section 4248 is permissible because it helps the federal government act as a "custodian" of federal prisoners, which improves the operation of the federal prison system, which in turn is needed to enforce federal laws that implement Congress's enumerated powers.[62] At the same time, the Court fails to explain how Section 4248 improves the operation of the federal prison system in such a way as to actually assist in the enforcement of laws that implement enumerated powers.

If the Court's reasoning is valid, then the Necessary and Proper Clause gives Congress the power to enact any law that might be connected to an ancillary power that is in turn somehow connected to an enumerated power, even if the challenged law does not actually do anything to enforce any enumerated power. Moreover, even the required connection between the first ancillary power and the enumerated power is subject only to a weak "rational basis" test that imposes little if any constraint.[63]

This approach to the Necessary and Proper Clause makes most of Congress's enumerated powers under Article I completely superfluous. For example, Article I of the Constitution gives Congress the power to coin money and establish a system of weights and measures.[64] But under *Comstock*'s interpretation of the Necessary and Proper Clause, Congress already has these powers. After all, coining money and setting weights and measures can sometimes help implement Congress's power to regulate interstate commerce.[65] For example, a common set of weights and measures might make it easier for merchants to purchase and ship goods across state lines. And under *Comstock*'s reasoning, this is enough to give Congress the power to set weights and measures or coin money even in situations where doing so does *not* facilitate the regulation of interstate commerce.

---

[62] See *supra* § I.A.

[63] See *id*.

[64] U.S. Const. art. I. § 8. cl. 5.

[65] *Id*. at cl. 3.

Similarly, Congress is given the specifically enumerated power to establish post offices and post roads.[66] This power too becomes superfluous under *Comstock*. After all, post offices and post roads sometimes facilitate interstate commerce, and under *Comstock*, this gives Congress the power to establish and operate them even in situations where they don't, as when a post office is used for noncommercial mail. Similar reasoning renders superfluous even some of Congress's most important powers, such as the power to raise and support armed forces.[67] After all, the establishment of an army and navy could help protect interstate commerce against a variety of threats, and the armed forces can sometimes be used to enforce commercial regulations.[68] Under *Comstock*, this is potentially sufficient to authorize Congress to raise and support even those military forces that don't actually do anything to protect interstate commerce or enforce commercial regulations.

In sum, under the majority's reasoning in *Comstock*, Congress would have almost as much authority as it currently has even if the Constitution gave Congress only two enumerated powers: the power to regulate interstate commerce and the Necessary and Proper Clause itself. The rest of the enumerated powers in Article I become surplus verbiage.

There is an important caveat to this criticism of *Comstock*: the potential impact of the five-part test elaborated in the last part of the Court's opinion.[69] The more strictly this test is applied, the less likely it is that *Comstock* will render various other Article I powers redundant. For example, it could be that the majority's otherwise ultra-deferential approach to assertions of congressional power applies only in cases where the challenged statute addresses a field with a "long history of federal involvement" and has "a narrow scope" (factors two and five in the five-part test).[70] If so, then most of Congress's other enumerated powers would not be superfluous, since *Comstock*'s reasoning would apply only to relatively small-scale measures. However, the majority does not make clear how the

---

[66] *Id*. at cl. 7.

[67] *Id*. at cl. 12–13.

[68] For example, when the Coast Guard is used to combat the smuggling of illegal drugs.

[69] See discussion in *supra* § I.A.

[70] Comstock, 130 S. Ct. at 1965.

five factors should be weighed in cases where they do not all cut the same way.[71]

C. Arguments from Precedent

The majority's rationale for its decision relies heavily on three types of precedents: Chief Justice John Marshall's famous 1819 opinion in *M'Culloch v. Maryland*,[72] various federal statutes predating the Adam Walsh Act, and the Supreme Court's 1956 decision in *Greenwood v. United States*.[73] None of them provides much support for the Court's decision.

1. M'Culloch v. Maryland

Much ink has been spilled over *M'Culloch* since the case was decided in 1819, upholding the constitutionality of the Bank of the United States.[74] It is not possible to consider that debate in detail here. Instead, I confine myself to making the narrower point that nothing in that precedent required the Court to uphold Section 4248 in *Comstock*, or significantly strengthened the argument for doing so.

The *Comstock* majority cites *M'Culloch* for the proposition that "the Necessary and Proper Clause makes clear that the Constitution's grants of specific federal legislative authority are accompanied by broad power to enact laws that are 'convenient, or useful' or 'conducive' to the authority's 'beneficial exercise.'"[75] It is indeed true that *M'Culloch* gives Congress considerable discretion in selecting the means by which its enumerated powers are to be implemented. For example, Chief Justice Marshall famously wrote that the means in question need not be "absolutely necessary" to the implementation of an enumerated power, but need only be "useful" or "convenient" to that end.[76] At the same time, however, *M'Culloch* also noted several important limitations on the scope of the power granted by the Necessary and Proper Clause. Consider Marshall's most famous formulation of the clause's meaning:

---

[71] See *supra* § I.A.

[72] 17 U.S. (4 Wheat.) 316 (1819).

[73] 350 U.S. 366 (1956).

[74] For a recent discussion of the longstanding debate over *M'Culloch*, see Mark Robert Killenbeck, M'Culloch v. Maryland: Defining a Nation (2006).

[75] Comstock, 130 S. Ct. at 1956 (quoting M'Culloch, 17 U.S. (4 Wheat.) at 413, 418).

[76] M'Culloch, 17 U.S. (4 Wheat.) at 413–15.

> Let the end be legitimate, let it be within the scope of the constitution, and all means which are appropriate, which are plainly adapted to that end, which are not prohibited, but consist with the letter and spirit of the constitution, are constitutional.[77]

This passage suggests at least four constraints on the range of statutes authorized by the Necessary and Proper Clause: (1) the "end" pursued must be "legitimate" and "within the scope of the constitution," (2) the means must be "appropriate" and "plainly adapted to that end," (3) the means must "not [be] prohibited" elsewhere in the Constitution, and finally (4) they must be "consist[ent] with the letter and spirit of the Constitution."

At least two of these constraints are implicated in *Comstock*: the first and the fourth. For an end to be "legitimate" and "within the scope of the Constitution," it must presumably implement one of Congress's enumerated powers. As Marshall put it, "[t]he judiciary . . . must see that what has been done is not a mere evasive pretext, under which the national legislature travels out of the prescribed bounds of its authority."[78] Yet, as discussed above, Section 4248 does not satisfy this requirement. At most, it is connected to an ancillary power—the operation of a federal penal system—that is itself sometimes useful for implementing enumerated powers; but it is connected in a way that does not help promote that implementation.

Section 4248 also may not be "consist[ent] with the letter and spirit of the Constitution." As just argued, the Court's reasoning upholding it might render most of Congress's enumerated powers redundant. If so, that goes against both the letter of the Constitution and its spirit. It consigns much of the "letter" to uselessness by making it superfluous, and also undercuts the "spirit" at least insofar as that spirit includes the principle that "[t]his government is acknowledged by all, to be one of enumerated powers."[79]

---

[77] *Id.* at 421.

[78] *Id.* at 389; see also *id.* at 423 ("[S]hould congress, under the pretext of executing its powers, pass laws for the accomplishment of objects not entrusted to the government; it would become the painful duty of this tribunal, should a case requiring such a decision come before it, to say, that such an act was not the law of the land.").

[79] M'Culloch, 17 U.S. (4 Wheat.) at 405.

Finally, Section 4248 could also run afoul of Marshall's third requirement: that the means chosen by Congress must be "appropriate" and "plainly adapted to that end."[80] It is difficult to tell if it does, however, because neither the majority nor the government provides any argument connecting Section 4248 to an actual enumerated power. Thus, it is hard to tell what the relevant "end" is.

I do not mean to suggest that *M'Culloch* definitively required the Court to strike down Section 4248. Chief Justice Marshall's language was sufficiently vague that it could potentially be interpreted in a wide range of ways. It is clear, however, that the language of *M'Culloch* at least did not require *Comstock* to come out the way it did. Indeed, an interpretation of *M'Culloch* broad enough to uphold Section 4248 would render Marshall's limiting language almost meaningless. If a "legitimate end" includes just about any purpose that legislators might wish to pursue, it is not clear why Marshall bothered to list it as a supposed limiting factor in the first place.

2. *Statutory Precedents*

The Court relies in part on statutory precedents to buttress its case, citing various earlier federal statutes that provided for the care and management of mentally ill federal prison inmates.[81] The use of nonjudicial precedents in constitutional law is far from unknown. Courts and others have often relied on legislative and executive branch practice as evidence of constitutional meaning.[82]

Some of statutory precedents the Court cites are inapt because they involve regulation of the treatment of mentally ill inmates who have not yet completed their sentences. As discussed above, these regulations are readily distinguishable from Section 4248 because they help enforce Congress's power to punish violators of laws that enforce its enumerated powers.

However, the Court is on much stronger ground in citing statutes that permit the civil confinement of mentally ill federal prison

---

[80] *Id.* at 421.

[81] Comstock, 130 S. Ct. at 1958–60.

[82] See, e.g., Philip Bobbit, Constitutional Fate ch. 2 (1982) (describing longstanding use of appeals to tradition and history); Steven G. Calabresi & Christopher Yoo, The Unitary Executive (2008) (describing resort to executive branch practice to explicate the structure and scope of executive power).

inmates to continue even after their sentences have ended.[83] For example, there is a longstanding federal statute that, in its current form, permits the civil confinement of mentally ill inmates whose "release would create a substantial risk of bodily injury to another person or serious damage to the property of another."[84] While this statute and others like it refer to confinement that begins before the inmate completes his sentence, it can continue afterward.[85]

These statutes are relevantly similar to Section 4248 insofar as they permit confinement of mentally ill inmates even after they have completed their sentences, on the grounds that their release might pose a threat to others. As in the case of Section 4248, they do not have any clear connection to the enforcement of Congress's enumerated powers. That similarity, however, leaves them vulnerable to the same constitutional objections that have been leveled at Section 4248. Given the very strong textual case against Section 4248 described above, it is reasonable to conclude that these earlier statutes are also unconstitutional. As the Court admits, "even a longstanding history of related federal action does not demonstrate a statute's constitutionality."[86]

Less relevant are the Court's citations to various non-penal federal statutes that have been upheld under the Necessary and Proper Clause. For example, the majority refers to 19th century precedent holding that the clause gives Congress the power to provide pensions for former military servicemen and their dependents.[87] This policy, however, clearly helps implement Congress's enumerated power to raise and support armies.[88] The provision of pensions creates incentives for citizens to join the armed forces, which in turn enables Congress to raise a larger and more capable army than would otherwise be possible.

3. Greenwood v. United States

The *Comstock* majority also relied substantially on the 1956 case of *Greenwood v. United States*,[89] a precedent that was much cited in

---

[83] *Id.* at 1959–60.

[84] 18 U.S.C. § 4246(d) (2006).

[85] Comstock, 130 S. Ct. at 1959–60.

[86] *Id.* at 1958.

[87] *Id.* at 1964 (citing United States v. Hall, 98 U.S. 343 (1878)).

[88] U.S. Const. art. I. § 8, cl. 12.

[89] 350 U.S. 366 (1956). For the *Comstock* opinion's discussion of *Greenwood*, see Comstock, 130 S. Ct. at 1963–64.

the government's brief.[90] This case is arguably closer to *Comstock* than any previous Supreme Court decision. However, there are crucial distinctions between the two that undercut the parallel drawn by the Court and the government.

Greenwood upheld Congress's power to authorize detention of a suspect accused of violating federal law who was ruled incompetent to stand trial.[91] It did not create any freestanding congressional power to regulate anything that is in some way connected to the operation of a federal penal system. Rather, *Greenwood* merely addressed "the narrow constitutional issue" raised by Congress's authorization of federal authority to detain persons accused of federal crimes who are incompetent to stand trial, but could potentially be tried in the future.[92] According to the *Greenwood* Court, "[t]he power that put [the defendant] into such custody—the power to prosecute for federal offenses—is not exhausted" because the incompetent defendant might still be tried later if his psychiatric condition changes or psychiatrists change their diagnosis of the case.[93]

In *Greenwood*, the civil commitment at issue was simply an application of "the power to prosecute for federal offenses," which in turn rests on whatever Article I power is implemented by the initial criminalization of the offense in question.[94] As Justice Thomas noted in his dissent, "that statute's 'end' reasonably could be interpreted as preserving the Government's power to enforce a criminal law against the accused."[95]

By contrast, Section 4248 authorizes continued detention of former federal prisoners for reasons unconnected with the federal crimes with which they had previously been charged. Thomas correctly emphasizes that it "authorizes federal detention of a person even *after* the Government loses the authority to prosecute him for a federal crime."[96] In order to prove that Section 4248 is constitutional,

---

[90] Brief for Petitioners at 33–37, United States v. Comstock, 130 S. Ct. 1949 (2010) (No. 08-1224), 2009 WL 2896312.

[91] Greenwood, 350 U.S. at 374–80.

[92] *Id.* at 375.

[93] *Id.*

[94] *Id. Greenwood* did not claim that the underlying substantive criminal law under which he was charged exceeded the scope of congressional power.

[95] Comstock, 130 S. Ct. at 1978 (Thomas, J., dissenting).

[96] *Id.* (emphasis in original).

the government should have been required to show that it independently carries into execution one of Congress's enumerated Article I powers. It cannot rely on whatever authority might justify the substantive criminal law under which the "sexually dangerous" persons were previously convicted. As the Fourth Circuit decision in *Comstock* pointed out, "[t]he fact of previously lawful federal custody simply does not, in itself, provide Congress with any authority to regulate future conduct that occurs outside of the prison walls. For example, although the Government may regulate assaults occurring in federal prisons, the Government cannot criminalize all assaults committed by *former* federal prisoners."[97]

III. Implications for Future Cases

The *Comstock* case itself addressed the constitutionality of a relatively minor statute. Its long-term significance resides in its potential impact on future cases. In the near future, the most important of these is likely to be the litigation over the constitutionality of the Obama administration's health care plan, enacted by Congress in March 2010. *Comstock* could eventually also influence litigation over other issues.

A. Comstock *and ObamaCare*

Soon after the enactment of the new health care law, its constitutionality was challenged in court in two major lawsuits by 21 state governments, the National Federation of Independent Business, and others.[98] The most vulnerable provision in the new bill is the so-called individual mandate, under which most U.S. citizens and legal residents will be required to either purchase health insurance that meets federally mandated standards or to pay a fine of up to $695 per year, which by 2016 will rise to a maximum of $750 per year.[99]

[97] United States v. Comstock, 551 F.3d 274, 281 (4th Cir. 2009), rev'd, 130 S. Ct. 1949 (2010) (emphasis in original).

[98] See cases cited in note 5.

[99] Patient Protection and Affordable Care Act, Pub.L. No. 111-148, 124 Stat. 119, § 1501 (2010). Some American Indians, people with religious exemptions, and the very poor are exempt from the mandate. *Id.*

The government has already cited *Comstock* in arguing that the "individual mandate" created by the plan is constitutional.[100] Some academic and media commentary also suggests that *Comstock* will be an important precedent supporting the government's position in the health care cases.[101]

Defenders of the constitutionality of the individual mandate have mostly justified it as an exercise of Congress's power to regulate interstate commerce or its power to tax.[102] However, both the government in its briefs and some scholars have also cited the Necessary and Proper Clause as an alternative justification for the mandate.[103] Cornell law professor Michael Dorf argues that *Comstock* embraces the proposition that "federal power extend[s] to areas that are not independently regulable, so long as regulation in those areas is reasonably related to regulation that is within the scope of congressional power."[104] This rule, he contends, easily encompasses the individual mandate:

---

[100] Defendant's Motion to Dismiss at 47–48, Florida v. Department of Health and Human Services, No. 3:10-cv-91-RV/EMT (N.D. Fla. filed June 16, 2010), available at http://op.bna.com/hl.nsf/id/sfak-86hslb/$File/dojbrieflacase.pdf; Defendant's Motion to Dismiss at 34–35, Virginia v. Sebelius, No. 3:10-cv-00188-HEH (E.D. Va. filed May 24, 2010), available at http://www.scribd.com/doc/31923230/Commonwealth-of-Virginia-v-Sibelius-Memorandum-In-Support-Of-Motion-To-Dismiss.

[101] See, e.g., Michael Dorf, The Supreme Court's Decision about Sexually Dangerous Federal Prisoners: Could It Hold the Key to the Constitutionality of the Individual Mandate to Buy Health Insurance?, Findlaw, May 19, 2010, available at http://writ.news.findlaw.com/dorf/20100519.html; Abdon M. Pallasch, New Ruling Suggests High Court May Uphold Health Care Law, Chi. Sun-Times, July 12, 2010.

[102] See, e.g., Erwin Chemerinsky, Health Care Reform Is Constitutional, Politico, Oct. 23, 2009, available at http://www.politico.com/news/stories/1009/28620.html; Ruth Marcus, An "Illegal" Mandate? No, Wash. Post, Nov. 27, 2009; Robert A. Schapiro, Federalism Is No Bar to Health Care Reform, Atlanta Journal-Constitution, Nov. 2, 2009; David B. Rivkin Jr., Lee A. Casey & Jack M. Balkin, A Healthy Debate: The Constitutionality of an Individual Mandate, 158 U. Pa. L. Rev. PennUMBRA 93, 102 (2009), available at http://www.pennumbra.com/debates/pdfs/HealthyDebate.pdf. I have criticized these types of arguments in Ilya Somin, The Individual Health Insurance Mandate and the Constitutional Text, Engage, March 2010, at 49. For a good recent critique of several of them, see Ilya Shapiro, State Suits against Health Reform Are Well Grounded in Law—and Pose Serious Challenges, 29 Health Aff. 1229 (2010).

[103] See briefs cited in note 100; Dorf, *supra* note 101.

[104] Dorf, *supra* note 101.

> Applying that principle to the individual mandate to pur-
> chase health insurance is straightforward. The federal law
> forbids health insurers from refusing or dropping coverage
> based on pre-existing conditions. That prohibition is
> undoubtedly a regulation of "economic activity" [authorized
> by Congress' power under the Commerce Clause]. But the
> prohibition by itself would create an incentive for uninsured
> healthy people to game the system: They could take their
> chances without health insurance unless and until they got
> sick; at that point, they could buy health insurance without
> fear of being turned down for a pre-existing condition; and
> as a result, the system would not function, because a pool
> composed exclusively of sick people would not produce suf-
> ficient premiums to cover the cost of their medical treatment.
> Thus, Congress had a reasonable basis for including the indi-
> vidual mandate in the health care legislation as a means of
> effectuating the prohibition on refusing or dropping cover-
> age for pre-existing conditions.[105]

Dorf's analysis might turn out to be correct. It is certainly possible that the Supreme Court will ultimately uphold the individual mandate based on the Necessary and Proper Clause. The Court's four most liberal justices (including the newly confirmed Elena Kagan) are highly unlikely to strike down the mandate on any basis. If even one of the five more conservative justices endorses the Necessary and Proper Clause rationale for the mandate, a decision upholding it becomes almost inevitable.

1. The Five-Part Test

Dorf and the government fail to consider, however, the possible effect of the five-factor test developed by the *Comstock* majority. To recall, the five "considerations" were "(1) the breadth of the Neces-sary and Proper Clause, (2) the long history of federal involvement in this arena, (3) the sound reasons for the statute's enactment in light of the Government's custodial interest in safeguarding the public from dangers posed by those in federal custody, (4) the stat-ute's accommodation of state interests, and (5) the statute's nar-row scope."[106]

---

[105] *Id.*
[106] Comstock, 130 S. Ct. at 1965.

Unlike Section 4248 of the Adam Walsh Act, the individual mandate is potentially vulnerable on at least three of these five criteria. Since it forces millions of people to buy a product they may not want, it is certainly not "narrow in scope." It also does not "accommodate state interests" to the extent that the Court claims the *Comstock* legislation does. The majority concluded that Section 4248 accommodated state interests because it gives states the option of confining the "sexually dangerous" former prisoners themselves.[107] Indeed, the Court even suggested that Section 4248 gives states the option of assuming custody of the former prisoners and then releasing them.[108] Under the majority's interpretation of Section 4248, the federal government can only confine "sexually dangerous" former federal inmates if the state government consents to it. If it prefers, the state can instead assume custody of the person in question and immediately set him free.

By contrast, the individual mandate applies throughout the country, even in areas where the state government opposes it and would prefer a different system of health insurance regulation. Moreover, states are not given any right to avoid the mandate or exempt any of their citizens from it. At the very least, this is a much lesser degree of "accommodation" of state interests than the Court found with respect to Section 4248.

The individual mandate may also lack a comparable "long history of federal involvement." Although the federal government has often regulated health care, it has never previously forced private individuals to purchase health insurance or other health care products against their will. Congress has never enacted and the Court has never upheld a statute requiring private individuals to purchase a product merely because they happen to be citizens or permanent residents of the United States.[109] Whether the health insurance mandate is supported by a "long history of federal involvement" depends on the relevant frame of reference. If it is health care policy as a whole, then the requisite history is there. If it is regulations

---

[107] *Id.* at 1962–63.

[108] *Id.* at 1963.

[109] This point is effectively documented in Randy E. Barnett, Nathaniel Stewart & Todd Gaziano, Why the Personal Mandate to Ban Health Insurance Is Unprecedented and Unconstitutional, Heritage Foundation, Dec. 9, 2009, at 6–8, available at http://www.heritage.org/Research/LegalIssues/lm0049es.cfm.

forcing individuals to purchase products (health-related or otherwise), then it is not.

Finally, it is difficult to say whether a court would find "sound reasons for the statute's enactment in light of the Government's ... interest." Whether the government's reasoning on this point is "sound" is likely to be judged differently by people with diverging ideologies and political allegiances. Pro-market economists have proposed ways to cover preexisting conditions that do not require either an individual mandate or forcing insurers to accept customers they prefer to reject.[110] In an effort to avoid assessing the details of policy issues, courts could potentially interpret this prong of the test in a way that is highly deferential to the legislature. But the *Comstock* opinion does not make clear whether such deference is required.

2. The Proper Meaning of "Proper"

An additional reason why *Comstock*'s significance for the health care litigation is difficult to assess is that the Supreme Court did not consider the meaning of the key term "proper" in the Necessary and Proper Clause. The Court has never clearly defined the meaning of "proper" but there is a strong textual and historical argument that "proper" legislation cannot upset the overall structure of the Constitution or infringe on reserved state prerogatives.[111] It is arguable that a law is not "proper" if upholding it requires an interpretation of the Necessary and Proper Clause so broad that it renders many of Congress's other enumerated powers redundant.[112] The individual mandate can certainly be attacked as potentially "improper," and the state plaintiffs may well raise this point as the litigation proceeds. As Professor Randy Barnett pointed out in an

---

[110] See, e.g., John H. Cochrane, Health Status Insurance: How Markets Can Provide Health Security, Cato Institute Policy Analysis no. 633, Feb. 18, 2009; John H. Cochrane, What to Do about Preexisting Conditions, Wall St. J., Aug. 14, 2009, available at http://online.wsj.com/article/NA_WSJ_PUB: SB10001424052970203609204574316172512242220.html.

[111] See Randy E. Barnett, The Original Meaning of the Necessary and Proper Clause, 6 U. Pa. J. Const. L. 183, 215–20 (2003) (discussing the relevant evidence); Gary Lawson & Patricia Granger, The "Proper" Scope of Federal Power: A Jurisdictional Interpretation of the Sweeping Clause, 43 Duke L.J. 267, 297 (1993) (arguing that the evidence shows that "proper" means that laws "must be consistent with principles of separation of powers, principles of federalism, and individual rights").

[112] See discussion in *infra* § II.B.

early comment on *Comstock*, "[t]he problem with the mandate is whether it is a 'proper' means to achieve a constitutional end."[113] *Comstock* provides little or no guidance in addressing that issue.

3. The Recent Virginia Decision Denying the Federal Government's Motion to Dismiss

As this article went to press, federal district court Judge Henry Hudson had just issued a ruling denying the federal government's motion to dismiss the Virginia lawsuit against the individual mandate.[114] Hudson's opinion only briefly mentions *Comstock*, and does not discuss either the rational basis framework or the Court's five-part test.[115] Hudson did rule, however, that the Virginia's case was strong enough to reject the government's motion to dismiss the suit on the ground that Virginia's argument "lacks legal vitality and therefore fails to state a cause of action."[116] Moreover, he emphasized that the individual mandate "literally [sic] forges new ground" and that "[n]either the U.S. Supreme Court nor any circuit court of appeals has squarely addressed this issue."[117] At the very least, therefore, Judge Hudson seems to have concluded that *Comstock* does not clearly resolve the mandate case in the government's favor.

This ruling is not, of course, a final decision on the case. It merely denies the federal government's motion to dismiss Virginia's suit. Moreover, any decision the trial court makes will surely be appealed to the Fourth Circuit Court of Appeals and ultimately to the Supreme Court. Appellate judges may or may not interpret *Comstock* differently from Judge Hudson.

In sum, the fate of the Necessary and Proper Clause rationale for the health insurance mandate remains unclear after *Comstock*. Much will depend on how the Court interprets *Comstock*'s five-factor test and how this test relates to the deferential "rational basis" review outlined elsewhere in the Court's opinion.[118]

---

[113] Posting of Randy E. Barnett to Volokh Conspiracy Preliminary Thoughts on *Comstock*, June 17, 2010, available at http://volokh.com/2010/05/17/preliminary-thoughts-on-comstock/.

[114] Virginia ex rel. Cuccinnelli v. Sebelius, (E.D. Va. Aug. 2, 2010), 2010 WL 2991385.

[115] *Id.* at *11–12.

[116] *Id.* at *2.

[117] *Id.* at *10, 16.

[118] See *supra* § I.A.

4. The Pivotal Role of Chief Justice Roberts

A crucial question in the application of *Comstock* to the health insurance mandate will be the position taken by Chief Justice John Roberts. Only five justices endorsed the majority opinion in *Comstock*, and he was one of them. Justices Thomas and Scalia dissented, while Justices Alito and Kennedy concurred in the decision on narrow grounds that would not apply to the health care mandate. Roberts's vote was therefore pivotal.

The four most liberal justices are likely to conclude that the health care mandate is constitutional under *Comstock*'s interpretation of the Necessary and Proper Clause. However, it is not clear whether the more conservative Chief Justice will go along with this view. One possible reason for the vagueness and imprecision of the five-factor test is that it represents a lowest-common-denominator compromise between the four liberals and the Chief Justice. It is possible that he differs with the rest of the *Comstock* majority in his interpretation of vague phrases such as "narrow scope," "accommodation of state interests," and "long history of federal involvement."

Section 4248 was a relatively narrow statute that few if any justices objected to on ideological grounds. By contrast, the individual mandate is a far broader law that may well split the Court along classic right-left lines. This is not to suggest that either liberal or conservative justices will simply vote their ideological preferences. However, ideology does sometimes influence judicial decisionmaking on closely contested, politically divisive cases.[119]

It is possible that both *Comstock* and the Necessary and Proper Clause will turn out to be irrelevant to the ultimate outcome of the health care litigation. The Supreme Court might well uphold the individual mandate based on the Commerce Clause or the Tax Clause. However, the government's arguments on both of these clauses have important shortcomings. The Commerce Clause argument is weakened by the reality that even cases such as *Raich* that give Congress almost unlimited power to regulate "economic activity" still do not cover a regulation that forces people to purchase a product even if they haven't engaged in any "activity" at all.[120] The

---

[119] For a recent survey of the evidence, see Eileen Braman, Law, Politics, and Perception: How Policy Preferences Influence Legal Reasoning (2009).

[120] This point is emphasized in Barnett et al. *supra* note 113.

Tax Clause argument has a variety of logical flaws, including the fact that it is difficult to show that a financial penalty for failing to comply with a regulatory mandate counts as a tax.[121] In September 2009, President Barack Obama himself made the commonsense point that "for us to say that you've got to take a responsibility to get health insurance is absolutely not a tax increase."[122] And even if the mandate is a tax, it may not be a constitutionally permissible one.[123] If the Commerce Clause and tax arguments fail, the Necessary and Proper Clause rationale could take center stage.

B. *Potential Impact on Other Cases*

Comstock's influence is unlikely to be confined to the health care litigation. It could potentially affect other cases as well. One area where *Comstock*'s impact is mostly likely to be felt is in the field of constitutional challenges to various federal criminal statutes. Over the last several decades, federal criminal law has expanded to cover a bewildering array of conduct, to the point where the average American adult may commit as many as three federal felonies per day.[124] Many of these statutes have at best weak connections to enumerated federal powers. Thus, *Comstock*'s relatively broad interpretation of the Necessary and Proper Clause could potentially be used to defend them against constitutional challenges.

In the short run, *Comstock*'s impact may be limited by the fact that the Court has also adopted an extraordinarily broad interpretation of the Commerce Clause in *Gonzales v. Raich*. However, *Raich*'s more extreme language could potentially be pared back by the Supreme Court, especially if the Court ends up invalidating the individual mandate.

That said, the vagueness of the Court's reasoning makes it extremely difficult to make any forecast about the ultimate effect of

---

[121] See Somin, *supra* note 102, at 50.

[122] *Id.*

[123] See Steven Willis & Nakku Chung, Of Constitutional Decapitation and Health Care, Tax Notes, 128 Tax Notes No. 2, 169 (2010) (arguing that if the mandate is a tax, it is an unconstitutional capitation tax that has not been properly apportioned among the states, as required by the Constitution).

[124] Harvey Silverglate, Three Felonies a Day (2009); see also Alex Kozinski & Misha Tseytlin, You're (Probably) a Federal Criminal, in In the Name of Justice 43, 44–48 (Timothy Lynch, ed. 2009) (pointing out that most American adults have probably violated a federal criminal statute at some point in their lives).

Comstock. Much depends on how lower courts and the Supreme Court itself will choose to interpret *Comstock*'s five-factor test. A relatively restrictive interpretation might end up significantly constraining the use of the Necessary and Proper Clause as a rationale for expansive assertions of federal power. It could, for example, confine heavy judicial deference to cases where the challenged statute is "narrow," "accommodates" state interests, and is backed by a "long history of federal involvement."[125] On the other hand, a lax application of the test could turn *Comstock* into a virtual blank check for Congress.

Conclusion

United States v. Comstock is a severely flawed decision. One of its most important shortcomings is the uncertainty surrounding the application of the five-factor test used to rationalize the Court's ruling. As a result, it is difficult to predict the effect of this precedent on other cases. The one certain result is that there will be more Necessary and Proper Clause litigation in our future as courts struggle to define the limits of federal power.

---

[125] *Comstock*, 130 S. Ct. at 1965.

Free Enterprise Fund v. PCAOB: Narrow Separation-of-Powers Ruling Illustrates That the Supreme Court Is Not "Pro-Business"

*Hans Bader**

Introduction

Chief Justice John Roberts has often been depicted as an advocate of narrow rulings and a judicial philosophy of minimalism.[1] In his opinion for the Court in *Free Enterprise Fund v. Public Company Accounting Oversight Board*,[2] he took this philosophy to an extreme, refusing to invalidate much of the Sarbanes-Oxley Act despite the fact that its central provisions violated the Constitution's separation of powers. Enacted in 2002, Sarbanes-Oxley has cost the economy $1.4 trillion,[3] making it the biggest expansion of regulation of business since the New Deal.[4] The Supreme Court's decision to leave

---

* Senior attorney at the Competitive Enterprise Institute; J.D., Harvard Law School; of counsel to the petitioners in the case that is the subject of this article.

[1] See, e.g., Tara Leigh Grove, The Structural Case for Vertical Maximalism, 95 Cornell L. Rev. 1, 7 (2009); Jeffrey Rosen, John Roberts, Centrist? Partial Solution, The New Republic, Dec. 11, 2006, at 8; Robert Barnes, Roberts Court Moves Right, but with a Measured Step, Wash. Post, Apr. 20, 2007, at A3.

[2] 561 U.S. ____, 130 S. Ct. 3138 (2010).

[3] Henry Butler & Larry Ribstein, The Sarbanes-Oxley Debacle 5 (2006). See also Cesar Conda, A Detour Past Congress, Weekly Standard, Jan. 22, 2007, at 13 (trillion-dollar estimate by economist Ivy Zhang); Editorial, Sarbanes-Oxley on Trial, Wall St. J., Dec. 4, 2009, at A24 (similar estimate in study by the American Enterprise Institute and Brookings Institution).

[4] When President Bush signed it into law, he called it "the most far-reaching reforms of American business practices since the time of Franklin Delano Roosevelt." Elisabeth Bumiller, Bush Signs Bill Aimed at Fraud in Corporations, N.Y. Times, July 31, 2002, at A1. Sarbanes-Oxley was enacted in "anger" and "haste" in response to "public outrage" over the collapse of Enron and WorldCom and other massive accounting scandals. Tom Fowler, Following the Rules, Houston Chronicle, Jan. 29, 2006, at 1.

the law largely intact despite its constitutional infirmities is one more illustration that it does not have a pro-business tilt. Indeed, the Court in recent years has generally been more hostile to business than the lower federal courts.

In the *Free Enterprise Fund* case, the Supreme Court essentially ruled that Congress cannot create an *independent* agency overseen by another independent agency—but it can create a new subordinate agency whose members are subject to removal at will by an existing independent agency. The Court's ruling will promote accountability by strengthening the government's ability to fire hundreds if not thousands of high-ranking bureaucrats and lawyers. But it may also open the door to messy appointment processes at independent agencies.

The Court struck down tenure protections for leaders of an agency created by Sarbanes-Oxley, the Public Company Accounting Oversight Board.[5] The law prohibited removal without cause of members of the PCAOB—colloquially pronounced "peek-a-boo"—which regulates the auditing of public companies.[6] Under the statute, any decision to remove PCAOB members had to be made not by the president, but by another independent agency whose members can also only be removed for cause, the Securities and Exchange Commission.[7] Thus, two layers of removal restrictions insulated the PCAOB from any accountability to the president. The Court held that such dual for-cause limitations on removal of government officials violate the Constitution's separation of powers, which vests executive power in the president.[8]

The Court refused to strike down the Sarbanes-Oxley Act as a whole, however, instead merely severing the unconstitutional removal limitations.[9] It did so even though Sarbanes-Oxley lacks a severability clause and the removal provisions were central to it.

---

[5] See 15 U.S.C. §§ 7211(e)(6), 7217(d)(3) (2006).

[6] 15 U.S.C. § 7211(e)(6) (2006) (PCAOB members can be removed only "for good cause shown").

[7] 130 S. Ct. at 3148–49; see also SEC v. Blinder, Robinson & Co., 855 F.2d 677, 681 (10th Cir. 1988) (SEC commissioners removable only for good cause).

[8] 130 S. Ct. at 3151, 3153–54.

[9] *Id.* at 3161–62.

The Court then rejected a challenge to the PCAOB under the Constitution's Appointments Clause, which requires that the president, and no one else, pick the principal federal officers (with Senate approval), while permitting "Heads of Departments" to pick so-called inferior officers, who are supervised and directed by principal officers.[10] PCAOB members are picked not by the president, but by the SEC commissioners as a group.[11] By striking down the restrictions on removing PCAOB members, and thus making them subject to termination at will by the SEC, the Court was able to render PCAOB members inferior officers who could be validly picked by someone other than the president under the Appointments Clause. In effect, it used one constitutional violation to cure another, and limit the reach of its decision as narrowly as possible.

Even after the Court's decision, the PCAOB members, whose pay exceeds the president's,[12] retain considerable power. The PCAOB has the power to write regulations controlling the auditing of all public companies, which the SEC is supposed to approve as long as they are consistent with Sarbanes-Oxley or the public interest.[13] The PCAOB has the power to inspect, investigate, and punish accounting firms and accountants for violating its regulations, professional standards, or federal laws.[14] It can fine an accountant up to $100,000 or an accounting firm up to $2 million for a single, inadvertent violation of its rules, although the SEC has plenary power to review and reverse such sanctions.[15] And the PCAOB finances itself with a tax, the accounting support fee, which it levies on all public companies in the United States (although the SEC must first approve its budget).[16] The PCAOB is, in effect, "an enforcement body that is at once lawmaker, tax collector, inspector, sheriff, prosecutor, judge and jury."[17]

---

[10] U.S. Const. art. II, § 2, cl. 2. See Free Enter. Fund, 130 S. Ct. at 3162–64.

[11] *Id.* at 3147, 3163–64.

[12] *Id.* at 3147 n.1 (PCAOB members are paid $547,000 or more).

[13] Sarbanes-Oxley Act, 15 U.S.C. §§ 7213, 7217(b)(2),(5) (2006).

[14] See *id.* §§ 7214, 7215.

[15] See *id.* §§ 7215(c)(4)(D)(i), 7215(e), 7217(c)(3).

[16] See *id.* §§ 7219(c)–(d), 7219(b),(d)(1).

[17] Ilya Shapiro & Travis Cushman, Peekaboo, I See a Constitutional Violation, The American, Dec. 5, 2009, available at http://www.american.com/archive/2009/december-2009/peekaboo-i-see-a-constitutional-violation.

I. History of the Case

The case began after the PCAOB inspected the small Nevada accounting firm of Beckstead & Watts, and "released a report critical of its auditing procedures."[18] The firm's principal, Brad Beckstead, responded with a letter objecting to the report. He criticized the PCAOB bureaucrats for applying a gold-plated, one-size fits-all standard to auditing—a standard that would require small public companies to spend ruinously large amounts of their scarce resources on "additional audit steps" and "documentation requirements" as if money were no object, threatening "the entire existence of that segment of the marketplace."[19]

When I saw his letter on the internet in October 2005, I gave it to my colleague, Sam Kazman, who contacted Mr. Beckstead that week and convinced him to pursue a constitutional challenge to the PCAOB. Later that year, the three of us got together with the Jones Day law firm, which was already planning to challenge the PCAOB on behalf of a nonprofit organization called the Free Enterprise Fund.

In February 2006, Jones Day filed a lawsuit against the PCAOB on behalf of the Free Enterprise Fund and our client, Beckstead & Watts, with Sam and me serving as "of counsel." The lawsuit challenged the PCAOB structure as a violation of both the Appointments Clause and the separation-of-powers principles that vest executive power in the president—because the PCAOB members were not removable except for cause, and removable only by the SEC, not the president, who was thus left virtually powerless over the PCAOB.[20]

The trial judge found that the plaintiffs had standing to sue over these alleged violations because Beckstead was regulated by the PCAOB but rejected our lawsuit on the merits.[21] He found that the

---

[18] 130 S. Ct. at 3149.

[19] See Letter from Brad Beckstead to George H. Diacont of the PCAOB, at 2 (June 24, 2005) (on file with author), also available at PCAOB, Inspection of Beckstead and Watts, LLP, http://pcaobus.org/Inspections/Reports/Documents/2005_Beckstead _and_Watts.pdf, at 11 (last visited Aug. 15, 2010); see also Brad Beckstead, Commentary: Sarbanes-Oxley: The Impact on the Smaller Accounting Firm Industry, Accounting Today, Sept. 2006, at 6 (advocating reforms to help small public companies).

[20] See U.S. Const. art. II, § 1, cl. 1.

[21] Free Enter. Fund v. Pub. Co. Accounting Oversight Bd., No. 06-0217 2007 WL 891675 (D.D.C. Mar. 21, 2007).

PCAOB members were inferior officers who didn't have to be picked by the president, but rather could be picked by the head of a department under the Appointments Clause. He agreed with us that the relevant head of department who could pick officers for the SEC was not the SEC commissioners as a group (whom Sarbanes-Oxley vests with picking PCAOB members), but rather the SEC's chairman (who picks the SEC's own high-ranking officials, subject to the approval of the SEC commissioners as a whole).[22] But that made no difference in our case, he said, since "the SEC chairman has voted for each PCAOB member" who was selected by the SEC commissioners voting as a group.[23] In essence, he found that any Appointments Clause violation was harmless.

The trial judge also found no problem with Sarbanes-Oxley's removal restrictions. The president, he concluded, has not been "completely stripped of his ability to remove PCAOB members, because SEC commissioners can be removed by the president for cause, and PCAOB members can be removed by the SEC 'for good cause shown[.]'"[24] Moreover, he reasoned, PCAOB members were not "purely executive" officials that the president or his subordinates needed to have the power to remove at will, but rather independent agency employees who could reasonably be protected against removal without cause.[25]

The Supreme Court's precedents provided no clear answer as to whether these removal restrictions were permissible.[26] It had struck down restrictions on presidential removal of purely executive officers like postmasters in a 1926 decision, reasoning that the president has been stripped of his constitutional power to "faithfully execute" the law if he cannot choose the very people on whom he relies to carry it out.[27] But shortly thereafter it upheld restrictions on the

[22] *Id.* at *4 ("Multi-member bodies may, on occasion, properly constitute heads of departments for Appointments Clause purposes, but the SEC is not one of them.").

[23] *Id.* at *5.

[24] *Id.* at *5 (internal citations omitted).

[25] *Id.* at *5 (quoting Morrison v. Olson, 487 U.S. 684, 690 (1988)).

[26] Free Enter. Fund, 130 S. Ct. at 3167 (Breyer, J., dissenting) (arguing that the PCAOB was entirely constitutional, but admitting that "the question presented lies at the intersection of two sets of conflicting, broadly framed constitutional principles. And no text, no history, perhaps no precedent provides any clear answer.").

[27] Myers v. United States, 272 U.S. 52, 132–34 (1926); Compare U.S. Const. art. II, § 3 (President shall "take Care that the Laws be faithfully executed").

removal of independent agency heads in its 1935 *Humphrey's Executor* decision, citing their need to be "independent in character" to perform their "quasi-legislative," "quasi-judicial" role.[28] In 1988, it upheld the independent counsel statute, which protected prosecutors charged with investigating administration officials against removal without cause.[29] Despite the prosecutors' clearly executive function, the Court concluded that the removal restrictions did not hamper the president's ability to perform his constitutional duties.[30]

The Free Enterprise Fund and Beckstead appealed the dismissal of their lawsuit to the U.S. Court of Appeals for the D.C. Circuit. At oral argument in April 2008, it looked like the appeals court might strike down the PCAOB.[31] But in August 2008, it ruled in favor of the PCAOB in a 2–1 decision[32] that was aptly described by the *Harvard Law Review* as "contradicted by its own reasoning"[33] and by the *Wall Street Journal* "a ruling at odds with itself."[34]

First, the court held that PCAOB members are inferior officers, not principal officers, because, it claimed, the PCAOB is just "a heavily controlled component of an independent agency," not a truly independent agency.[35] The court conceded, however, that if

---

[28] Humphrey's Ex'r v. United States, 295 U.S. 602, 619, 629 (1935) (upholding requirement that Federal Trade Commission members cannot be removed without cause).

[29] Morrison v. Olson, 487 U.S. 654 (1988).

[30] *Id.* at 691–93.

[31] Jonathan Weil, SOX Appeal Judge Offers Peek Underneath His Robe, Bloomberg News, May 28, 2008, available at http://www.bloomberg.com/apps/news?pid= 21070001&sid= aYZZ9vduqaMU.

[32] Free Enter. Fund v. Pub. Co. Accounting Oversight Bd., 537 F.3d 667, 680 (D.C. Cir. 2008).

[33] D.C. Circuit Holds That the SEC Chairman Is Not the "Head" of the SEC—*Free Enterprise Fund v. Public Co. Accounting Oversight Board,* 122 Harv. L. Rev. 2267, 2271 (2009) (discussing in detail why the SEC's chairman is its "head" both in practical terms and for the purposes of, and the rationale behind, the Constitution's Appointments Clause).

[34] Editorial, Sarbox and the Constitution: Supreme Scrutiny for a Harmful Law, Wall St. J., May 19, 2009, at A16.

[35] Free Enter. Fund, 537 F.3d at 680; but see Free Enter. Fund, 130 S. Ct. at 3159 (approvingly citing Judge Kavanaugh's then-description of the PCAOB as an "independent agency . . . removable only for cause by another independent agency") (quoting Free Enter. Fund, 537 F.3d at 669 (Kavanaugh, J., dissenting)). Note that the General Accounting Office at the time Sarbanes-Oxley was enacted had conceded that "the PCAOB is an independent board with sweeping powers and authority." U.S. Gen. Accounting Office, Rep. No. GAO-03-339, Securities and Exchange Commission:

"the Board is itself an independent agency. . . . the dissent's conclusion that the Board's structure is unconstitutional conveniently follows."[36]

The appeals court then contradicted itself about who really runs the SEC: its chairman or the commissioners as a group. As the *Wall Street Journal* put it: "To reject the Appointments Clause challenge, the court held that the SEC Commissioners, rather than the Chairman alone, serve as the collective 'head' of the agency and can therefore pick PCAOB members without violating the Constitution. But to reject the separation of powers challenge, the same ruling suggests that the SEC chairman is in fact the head of the agency,"[37] because he "dominate[s] commission policymaking," "select[s] most staff, set[s] budgetary policy," and "command[s] staff loyalties."[38] Moreover, the Court reasoned that since the SEC's chairman, unlike its commissioners, serves at the president's pleasure, the PCAOB is indirectly accountable to the White House. Having begun by claiming that the chairman was "simply one commissioner" among several, and a mere "administrative" figurehead,[39] it ended by implying that he so dominated the SEC that he effectively controlled it, thereby in turn giving the president abundant influence over the PCAOB.[40]

By selectively touting the chairman's dominance when it was convenient, the court was able to play up the president's purported influence over the SEC's actions (like its oversight of the PCAOB), because the president has more influence over the SEC's chairman than he does over other commissioners. For example, the president can reassign at will which commissioner acts as chairman, but he cannot remove a commissioner from the commission without cause.[41] By virtue of the president's alleged influence over the SEC, which can remove wayward PCAOB members for cause, the Court felt that the president's authority to execute the laws and oversee the

---

Actions Needed to Improve Public Company Accounting Oversight Board Selection Process, at 6 (2002), available at http://www.gao.gov/products/GAO-03-339.

[36] See Free Enter. Fund, 537 F.3d at 680 n.9.

[37] Sarbox and the Constitution, *supra* note 34 at A16.

[38] Free Enter. Fund, 537 F.3d at 680.

[39] *Id.* 537 F.3d at 678.

[40] *Id.* at 680.

[41] SEC v. Blinder, Robinson & Co., 855 F.2d 677, 681–82 (10th Cir. 1988).

PCAOB had not been "unduly" encumbered by its removal restrictions.[42]

In dissent, Judge Brett Kavanaugh argued that PCAOB members were "principal officers" who had to be picked by the president, largely because they could be removed "only for cause," not "at will."[43] His conclusion that PCAOB members were principal officers was consistent with a number of legal scholars, who pointed to the fact that the SEC lacked the tool of removal at will to fully control the PCAOB.[44]

He also concluded that the removal restrictions, which "completely stripped" the president of any ability to remove rogue PCAOB members,[45] violated separation-of-powers principles[46] reflected in Article II of the Constitution, which vest the executive power in the presidency and give the president the sole authority and duty to "take Care that the Laws be faithfully executed."[47]

Judge Kavanaugh rejected the majority's argument that these removal restrictions were sanctioned by *Humphrey's Executor*, which permitted independent agency leaders to be protected against presidential removal without cause.[48] He noted that no one had "identified any independent agency other than the PCAOB that is appointed by and removable only for cause by another independent agency."[49] He observed that a ruling in favor of the PCAOB was not "*Humphrey's Executor* redux," but "*Humphrey's Executor* squared," because the PCAOB was insulated from presidential influence by not just one layer of removal protection (like most agencies), but two

---

[42] Free Enter. Fund, 537 F.3d at 682, 684 n.14.

[43] *Id.* at 687, 709 (Kavanaugh, J., dissenting).

[44] See, e.g., Donna M. Nagy, Is the PCAOB a "Heavily Controlled Component" of the SEC?: An Essential Question in the Constitutional Controversy, 71 U. Pitt. L. Rev. 361, 396, 400 (2010) (citing Edmond v. United States, 520 U.S. 651, 662 (1997)); Whitney Innes, The Unaccountability of the Accounting Regulators: Analyzing the Constitutionality of the Public Company Accounting Oversight Board, 42 J. Marshall L. Rev. 1019, 1036 (2010).

[45] Free Enter. Fund, 537 F.3d at 698 (Kavanaugh, J., dissenting) (quoting Morrison, 487 U.S. at 692).

[46] *Id.* at 689, 701–04.

[47] U.S. Const. art. II, § 3.

[48] Humphrey's Ex'r, 295 U.S. at 629–30.

[49] Free Enter. Fund, 537 F.3d at 699 (Kavanaugh, J., dissenting).

(one layer protecting the SEC from the president and another protecting the PCAOB from the SEC), meaning that the "'power to remove an executive official has been completely stripped from the President.'"[50]

The full D.C. Circuit then denied rehearing by a razor-thin margin of 5–4.[51]

II. The Supreme Court's Decision

In another 5–4 decision, the Supreme Court struck down the statutory restrictions on removing PCAOB members as a violation of the Constitution's separation of powers but upheld the process by which they are appointed against a challenge under the Appointments Clause.[52]

Echoing Judge Kavanaugh's dissent below, the Court noted that while it had previously upheld a law restricting removal of leaders of independent agencies in *Humphrey's Executor*, that ruling nevertheless left presidents with some influence over agencies by allowing removal of their leaders for cause. By contrast, PCAOB members cannot be removed by the president at all and could only be removed for cause by the SEC, a body which itself can only be removed by the president for cause.

Concluding that "two layers are not the same as one," the Court held that this structure deprived the president "of adequate control over the Board, which is . . . the primary law enforcement authority for a vital sector of our economy."[53] The president was, under the circumstances, unable "to execute the laws" by "holding his subordinates accountable for their conduct."[54]

The Court's ruling was based partly on the fear that presidents would acquiesce in removal restrictions precisely to avoid taking the blame for government failures—noting that the result was "a Board that is not accountable to the President, and a President who is not responsible for the Board."[55] Accountability is a major rationale

---

[50] *Id.* at 686, 697.

[51] *See* Innes, *supra* note 44, at 1020.

[52] Free Enter. Fund v. Pub. Co. Accounting Oversight Bd., 130 S. Ct. 3138 (2010).

[53] *Id.* at 3157, 3161.

[54] *Id.* at 3154.

[55] *Id.* at 3153.

behind separation of powers: the principle that "the buck stops with the President," and that "the President cannot escape responsibility for his own choices by pretending that they are not his own."[56]

The Court reasoned:

> The Constitution that makes the President accountable to the people for executing the laws also gives him the power to do so. That power includes, as a general matter, the authority to remove those who assist him in carrying out his duties. Without such power, the President could not be held fully accountable for discharging his own responsibilities; the buck would stop somewhere else. Such diffusion of authority "would greatly diminish the intended and necessary responsibility of the chief magistrate himself."[57]

Accordingly, it struck down the restrictions on removal, marking the first time in 84 years—and only the second time ever—that the Supreme Court had found a removal restriction invalid.

After declaring the removal provisions unconstitutional, the Court decided to sever them from the remainder of Sarbanes-Oxley, rather than striking down the law as a whole.[58] This was an unexpected development because courts commonly strike down an entire law if one of its central provisions is invalid, even if it contains a severability clause.[59] That practice would seem apt here given that Sarbanes-Oxley's "very purpose" was "to create an accounting board that would operate" independently "from the SEC, not one that would

---

[56] *Id.* at 3152, 3155. Both the Bush and Obama administrations had defended the removal restrictions in court. The justices may have been aware that politicians had taken credit for Sarbanes-Oxley and its purported successes, while conveniently blaming its failures and excessive costs on unaccountable PCAOB regulators. See Scott Leibs, Five Years and Accounting, CFO Magazine, July 1, 2007, at 11 (Bush defends Sarbanes-Oxley, even while criticizing the way it was implemented); Newt Gingrich & David W. Kralik, Repeal Sarbanes-Oxley, S.F. Chronicle, Nov. 5, 2008, at B17 (law's cosponsor Oxley blamed PCAOB for the expense of Sarbanes-Oxley's rules).

[57] Free Enterprise Fund, 130 S. Ct. at 3164 (quoting The Federalist No. 70, at 428 (Alexander Hamilton) (Clinton Rossiter ed., 1961)).

[58] *Id.* at 3161–62.

[59] See, e.g., Carter v. Carter Coal Co., 298 U.S. 238 (1936) (wholly invalidating a law some of whose provisions violated the "non-delegation doctrine"—fundamentally a separation-of-powers notion—despite the presence of a severability clause). See also EEOC v. CBS, 743 F.2d 969, 973 (2d Cir. 1984); Hotel Employees v. Davis, 981 P.2d 990, 1010 (Cal. 1999).

be 'directed and supervised' by the SEC," since Congress felt that "the successful operation of the Board depends upon its independence."[60] Indeed, commentators had frequently suggested that the act as a whole should be invalidated if it contained a separation-of-powers violation because Sarbanes-Oxley does not contain a severability clause[61] and the invalid removal provisions were central to the PCAOB's creation.[62] Yet the Court chose to preserve as much of the Sarbanes-Oxley statute as it possibly could, a decision that contrasts sharply with earlier cases in which it struck down laws in their entirety even when they had "a broad severability clause."[63]

The Court then used its finding of a removal violation to make the broader Appointments Clause violation retroactively disappear. Although Judge Kavanaugh, below, had found PCAOB members to be principal officers largely because of their protections against removal, the Court analyzed whether they were principal officers based on their status *after* the Court had excised those very protections against removal—leaving them firmly subordinate to the SEC.[64]

---

[60] Free Enter. Fund, 537 F.3d at 687 (Kavanaugh, J., dissenting) (quoting S. Rep. No. 107-205, at 6 (2002); 148 Cong. Rec. S6331 (daily ed. July 8, 2002) (statement of Sen. Paul Sarbanes) ("[W]e need to establish this oversight board . . . to provide an extra guarantee of its independence. . . .")).

[61] See, e.g., Editorial, Sarbanes-Oxley on Trial, Wall St. J., December 4, 2009, at A24 ("[A] ruling against the PCAOB could bring down the whole law because Sarbox does not have a 'severability clause.'"); Jane Bryant Quinn, Lawsuit Threatens Sarbanes-Oxley Act, Wash. Post, July 20, 2008, at F1 ("Linda Lord, head of legislative and regulatory affairs for the banking giant UBS, called it 'highly likely' that PCAOB would lose the case. . . . 'SOX in its entirety will fall.'").

[62] Free Enter. Fund, 537 F.3d at 687–88 (Kavanaugh, J., dissenting) ("Members of Congress designed the PCAOB to have 'massive power, unchecked power.'") (quoting 148 Cong. Rec. S6334 (daily ed. July 8, 2002) (statement of Sen. Phil Gramm)); *id.* at 709 ("[T]he whole point of this statute—as evidenced in the statutory text and history—was to create an Accounting Board that would not be part of the SEC and not be subject to direction and supervision by the SEC.")

[63] See, e.g., Thornburgh v. Am. Coll. of Obstetricians & Gynecologists, 476 U.S. 747, 764–65 (1986) (abortion case); see also Am. Booksellers v. Hudnut, 771 F.2d 323, 332 (7th Cir. 1985), aff'd, 475 U.S. 1001 (1986).

[64] Free Enter. Fund, 130 S. Ct. at 3162. See also Gordon Smith, Donna Nagy on Free Enterprise Fund v. Public Company Accounting Oversight Board, Conglomerate Blog, June 28, 2010, http://www.theconglomerate.org/2010/06/donna-nagy-on-free-enterprise-fund-v-public-company-accounting-oversight-board.html ("The Court's decision to excise from the SOX the restrictive removal provisions also allowed for a quick rejection of the Appointments Clause challenge. Here, instead of analyzing the statute as written, the Court analyzed its new post-surgery version. . . . Had the

Having thus retroactively rewritten the law to move the goalposts, the Court then found that the PCAOB members were inferior officers who could be picked by the head of a department rather than the president. It then concluded that the SEC, despite not being a cabinet department, qualified as a "department" for Appointments Clause purposes and that the SEC commissioners, collectively, were the "head" of that "department." Thus, the commissioners, rather than the SEC's nominal head, its chairman, could constitutionally pick PCAOB members.[65]

The Supreme Court thus rejected plaintiffs' Appointments Clause challenge even though the logic of its decision suggested that the board had operated in violation of that clause from its inception all the way until the Court's decision,[66] and even though the Constitution deems such violations to be intrinsically menacing to liberty.[67]

In a dissent for four justices, Justice Stephen Breyer argued that the PCAOB's removal and appointment mechanisms were entirely constitutional because they insulated "experts" from "political influence" and supposedly had little "practical" effect on the president's exercise of executive authority.[68] Indeed, he claimed that the removal restrictions would help the president "regulate through impartial regulation" by safeguarding the PCAOB's independence.[69] Breyer's claim ignored empirical evidence that the PCAOB's independence had instead "resulted in widespread policy failures" and a "lack of coordination with other agencies" like the SEC that "created duplicative and overly burdensome regulation" as a result.[70] For

---

Court not excised the restrictive removal provisions, it is unlikely that it could have [rejected the challenge]").

[65] Free Enter. Fund, 130 S. Ct. at 3162–64.

[66] See Keith Bishop, PCAOB Unconstitutional: So What?, S.F. Recorder, July 26, 2010, at 34, available at 2010 WLNR 14862387 (Under the Supreme Court's own logic, "[t]he PCAOB's constitutional infirmity was present at birth. Simply put, the PCAOB never was a constitutional entity" before the Court's decision.).

[67] Pub. Citizen v. U.S. Dep't of Justice, 491 U.S. 440, 468 (1989) (Kennedy, J., concurring) ("liberty is always in peril" when structural safeguards like separation of powers are violated); Bowsher v. Synar, 478 U.S. 714, 730 (1986).

[68] Free Enter. Fund, 130 S. Ct. at 3170, 3174 (Breyer, J., dissenting).

[69] Id. at 3169.

[70] Brief for the Cato Institute and Professors Larry Ribstein and Henry Butler as Amici Curiae in Support of Petitioners at 17, 24, Free Enter. Fund v. Pub. Co. Accounting Oversight Bd., 130 S. Ct. 3138 (2010) (No. 08-861), 2009 WL 2406376 (citing studies).

example, "[t]he SEC and PCAOB have issued two sets of guidance rules to perform the same assessment task . . . resulting in unnecessary confusion and complexity for management,"[71] and the PCAOB imposes duplicative rules governing banks' internal controls.[72]

Breyer lamented that many high-ranking bureaucrats in other independent agencies might be rendered removable in the future under the Court's decision. The PCAOB members were not unique, he noted, in being subject to for-cause removal only by officials who were themselves protected against removal except for cause: "Hundreds, perhaps thousands of high-level government officials [are] within the scope of the court's holding, putting their job security and their administrative actions and decisions constitutionally at risk."[73] At least 573 members of the Senior Executive Service working for independent agencies were now removable at will as a result of the Supreme Court's decision, he said, including the executive directors of the Nuclear Regulatory Commission, Federal Trade Commission, and Federal Energy Regulatory Commission, "virtually all of the leadership of the Social Security Administration," and "the general counsels of the Chemical Safety Board, the Federal Mine Safety and Health Review Commission, and the National Mediation Board."[74]

Chief Justice Roberts responded by arguing that rule by unaccountable bureaucrats was a much bigger danger than political influence over the bureaucracy, and that multiple layers of for-cause removal could ultimately shift the federal government's "vast power" to remote and arbitrary bureaucratic mandarins:

> One can have a government that functions without being ruled by functionaries, and a government that benefits from expertise without being ruled by experts. Our Constitution was adopted to enable the people to govern themselves, through their elected leaders. The growth of the Executive Branch, which now wields vast power and touches almost every aspect of daily life, heightens the concern that it may

---

[71] *Id.* at 25 (citing Press Release, IMA Responds to SEC and PCAOB Exposure Drafts on SOX: Much More Is Needed to Get It Right (Feb. 27, 2007)).

[72] *Id.* at 24 (quoting Rep. Oxley, cosponsor of the act).

[73] Free Enter. Fund, 130 S. Ct. at 3179 (Breyer, J., dissenting).

[74] *Id.* at 3180.

slip from the Executive's control, and thus from that of the people.[75]

The Court's decision broke down along ideological lines, with the four "liberal" justices in dissent and the more "conservative" justices in the majority. This voting breakdown is perhaps understandable in that, over the long run, a ruling that enables high-ranking bureaucrats to be removed more easily may benefit conservative presidents more than liberal ones because bureaucrats tend to be liberal.[76]

Moreover, bureaucrats tend to favor expanded regulation by their agency, reflecting their inherent incentive to maximize their agency's budget.[77] The PCAOB is perhaps an extreme example. Even Sarbanes-Oxley's cosponsor, Rep. Michael Oxley, has said that the PCAOB's rules "gave the accounting industry 'almost carte blanche to do almost everything they wanted to do, which turned out to be far more expensive than anticipated. . . . They just went crazy.'"[78] The Obama administration also tacitly recognized that the PCAOB had overregulated when it joined Republicans and moderate Democrats in backing an exemption to the PCAOB's internal-controls rules for small public companies.[79]

III. The *Free Enterprise Fund* Ruling Shows That the Court Is Not "Pro-Business"

The Court's ruling excised as little as it could of a law that is incredibly costly to business and retroactively rewrote it to rehabilitate an otherwise unconstitutional regulatory structure that existed

---

[75] *Id.* at 3156.

[76] See., e.g., James Q. Wilson, American Government: Brief Edition 276 (9th ed. 2009); Joel D. Aberbach & Bert A. Rockman, Clashing Beliefs within the Executive Branch: The Nixon Administration Bureaucracy, 70 Am. Pol. Sci. Rev. 456, 461–63 (1976).

[77] Mark Seidenfeld, Why Agencies Act: A Reassessment of the Ossification Critique of Judicial Review, 70 Ohio St. L.J. 251, 280 (2009). See also generally William A. Niskanen, Bureaucracy and Representative Government (1971).

[78] Liz Alderman, A Second Look at Sarbanes-Oxley, Int'l Herald-Tribune, Mar. 3, 2007, at 16.

[79] Investors Beware, N.Y. Times, Nov. 6, 2009, at A22. Ironically, that exemption later became law as part of a financial "reform" bill that otherwise expanded the reach of federal regulation. Dodd-Frank Wall Street Reform and Consumer Protection Act, Pub. L. 111-203, § 989G, 124 Stat. 1376 (July 21, 2010).

from Sarbanes-Oxley's very inception.[80] By doing so, the Court demonstrated that it is not "pro-business," as liberal politicians and journalists falsely claim.[81]

A classic example of the false meme that the Supreme Court is "pro-business" comes from *Slate*'s Dahlia Lithwick. She breathlessly reported that in the Supreme Court, "big business always prevails, environmentalists are always buried, female and elderly workers go unprotected, death row inmates get the needle, and criminal defendants are shown the door."[82] This claim was strikingly divorced from reality. On the criminal law side alone, over the last dozen years, the death penalty has been dramatically cut back, and Supreme Court rulings have invalidated literally thousands of criminal sentences.[83]

More importantly for this article, business has lost ground repeatedly. Environmentalists have won many cases at the business community's expense, including one of the most economically significant decisions ever, *Massachusetts v. EPA* (2007)[84]—which potentially opened the door to Environmental Protection Agency regulation of virtually every economic activity on the grounds that virtually all activity emits carbon dioxide. That decision even created a special rule to allow state attorneys general to bring lawsuits that would otherwise be dismissed for lack of standing.[85] Similarly, the Supreme Court recently allowed businesses to be sued even for products the

---

[80] Bishop, *supra* note 66.

[81] See, e.g., Jarrett Wampler, Liberal Fairy Tales about A Mythical "Pro-Business" Supreme Court; Senator Patrick Leahy's False Meme, Freedom Action, July 29, 2010, http://www.freedomaction.net/profiles/blogs/liberal-fairy-tales-about-a (Sen. Leahy bashed the Supreme Court as "pro-business" by distorting "the facts of many recent Supreme Court decisions," including *Free Enterprise Fund v. PCAOB*).

[82] Dahlia Lithwick, Spoonfuls of Sugar: Americans' Continued Love Affair with the John Roberts Court, Slate, Sept. 26, 2009, http://www.slate.com/id/2229517/.

[83] See, e.g., Roper v. Simmons, 543 U.S. 551 (2005) (barring executions of minors); Atkins v. Virginia, 536 U.S. 304 (2002) (barring execution of the retarded); Ring v. Arizona, 536 U.S. 584 (2002) (only juries, not judges, can impose death sentences); United States v. Booker, 543 U.S. 220 (2005) (gutting the U.S. Sentencing Guidelines); Blakely v. Washington, 542 U.S. 296 (2004) (striking down state sentencing guidelines similar to those in many states).

[84] 549 U.S. 497 (2007).

[85] *Id.* at 520.

Food and Drug Administration deems to be safe and effective.[86] And it has steadily expanded businesses' liability and damages for the most common forms of discrimination, such as gender and age discrimination, in rulings that reversed lower courts and overturned the weight of federal appellate precedent.[87]

The Supreme Court's refusal to invalidate Sarbanes-Oxley despite important constitutional defects (and despite its lack of a severability clause) contrasts sharply with other courts' willingness to strike down pro-business laws in their entirety based on the presence of a few putatively unconstitutional provisions, even when the challenged law contains many unobjectionable provisions as well as a severability clause.[88] If the Supreme Court had any sympathy for American business at all, it would have struck the law down in its entirety.

The Court bent over backward not to do that, however, by engaging in radical judicial surgery that fundamentally changed the future relationship between the SEC and the PCAOB. While that surgery

---

[86] Wyeth v. Levine, 129 S. Ct. 1887 (2009); Roger Pilon, Into the Pre-emption Thicket: *Wyeth v. Levine*, 2008-2009 Cato Sup. Ct. Rev. 85 (2009); see also Ted Frank, Wyeth v. Levine, Overlawyered, Mar. 4, 2009 (describing this ruling as the "worst anti-business decision" in 43 years) (http://overlawyered.com/2009/03/wyeth-v-levine/); Michael Kinsley, Drug Regulators in the Jury Box, Wash. Post, March 13, 2009, at A17 (even liberal commentator says Court went too far in allowing "regulation by lawsuits").

[87] For example, it rejected limits on punitive damages recognized by the vast majority of federal appeals courts. Kolstad v. Am. Dental Ass'n, 527 U.S. 526 (1999). It expanded the definition of sexual harassment, rejecting longstanding limits on lawsuits where there is no economic or psychological harm, Harris v. Forklift Systems, 510 U.S 17 (1993), and overturned earlier limits on vicarious liability, Faragher v. City of Boca Raton, 524 U.S. 775 (1998). It also allowed businesses to be sued for unintentional "discrimination" against elderly workers. Smith v. Jackson, 544 U.S. 228 (2005). It expanded the statute of limitations for racial discrimination claims, Jones v. R.R. Donnelley & Sons, 541 U.S. 369 (2004), and disparate-impact claims of all types. Lewis v. City of Chicago, 130 S. Ct. 2191 (2010). It broadened the definition of discriminatory "retaliation." Burlington Northern v. White, 548 U.S. 53 (2006) (rejecting limits on retaliation claims accepted in every circuit but the Ninth Circuit). Whether or not correct as a matter of law, all these rulings reversed lower-court "pro-business" decisions.

[88] See, e.g., Best v. Taylor Machine Works, 698 N.E.2d 1057 (Ill. 1997) (invalidating tort reform law in its entirety, based on certain provisions deemed to violate separation of powers and the state constitution, and holding that the provisions deemed invalid would not be severed from remainder of the law despite the law's severability clause).

may fix the Appointments Clause problems going forward, it does nothing about past constitutional violations. As one lawyer noted,

> The PCAOB's constitutional infirmity was present at birth. Simply put, the PCAOB never was a constitutional entity. Moreover, the PCAOB's lack of accountability infected all of its actions *ab initio*. To allow the PCAOB's actions to stand may be the least disruptive remedy, but it hardly promotes the constitutional rule of law.[89]

Yet the Court effectively treated that constitutional violation as trivial.

Doing that was particularly inappropriate in the context of the Appointments Clause, which the Framers regarded as one of the Constitution's most crucial provisions. They drafted it as an essential check on overweening bureaucracy. As English colonists, they had seen offices created by both the king and Parliament spawn what the Declaration of Independence called a "multitude of new offices" and "swarms of officers to harass our people and eat out their substance."[90] In its 1991 *Freytag* decision, the Supreme Court cited historian Gordon Wood, who wrote that "the power of appointment to offices" was considered by the American revolutionary generation to be "the most insidious and powerful weapon of eighteenth-century despotism."[91] Thus, the clause "reflects our Framers' conclusion that widely distributed appointment power subverts democratic government."[92]

IV. Effect of the Decision on Sarbanes-Oxley and the PCAOB: More Bureaucratic Accountability

Despite its narrowness, the Supreme Court's ruling does have certain concrete ramifications for how the PCAOB functions and manages itself. It will make the PCAOB more accountable to the SEC and introduces various constitutional safeguards.

---

[89] Bishop, *supra* note 66.

[90] The Declaration of Independence para. 12 (U.S. 1776).

[91] Freytag v. Comm'r of Internal Revenue, 501 U.S. 868, 883 (1991) (quoting Gordon Wood, The Creation of the American Republic, 1776–1787 at 79, 143 (1969)).

[92] Freytag, 501 U.S. at 883.

A. The Board's Rules

The Court's decision should give the SEC more ability, by relying on the unstated threat of removal, to prod the PCAOB into revising burdensome rules that SEC commissioners have come to view as flawed but not so flagrantly wrong as to warrant wholesale repeal. While the SEC can theoretically veto PCAOB rules if they are contrary to Sarbanes-Oxley and not in the public interest,[93] SEC commissioners are usually not accounting specialists and the enormous costs of the PCAOB's accounting rules became clear only after the SEC approved them.

A classic example is the PCAOB's "internal controls" rules, widely criticized as wasteful and unduly burdensome.[94] These vague rules have been interpreted as requiring micromanagement of company trivia, such as the number of letters in employee passwords.[95] Section 404 of Sarbanes-Oxley authorizes the board to regulate companies' "internal controls"—a provision that Sarbanes-Oxley's cosponsor notes was just "two paragraphs long" in the statute, but which the PCAOB used to issue "330 pages of regulations" that were "far" more "expensive than anyone anticipated."[96]

These rules' estimated cost of $35 billion a year is 20 to 30 times higher than what was originally projected.[97] The compliance cost has been "wildly in excess of the per-firm cost estimated by the SEC."[98] Yet the PCAOB's rules did nothing, on balance, to improve

---

[93] 15 U.S.C. §§ 7217(b)(2)&(5) (2006).

[94] See, e.g., Stephen Barlas, Jury Is Still Out on AS5 Impact, Investment Dealers' Digest, Oct. 29, 2007, available at 2007 WLNR 21290970 ("[C]ompanies and auditors" criticized PCAOB's "reviled Auditing Standard 2" for focusing on "insignificant controls" and "minutiae.").

[95] Paul Tharp, Sarbanes-Oxley Ruling Is Costly, N.Y. Post, June 29, 2010, at 24; Steve Forbes, Evil Agency—and It Ain't the CIA, Forbes Magazine, Jun. 22, 2009, at 15.

[96] Stephen Taub, Oxley: I'm Not Happy with Sarbox, CFO Magazine, Apr. 6, 2007, at 2 (quoting Rep. Oxley).

[97] Hon. Frank H. Easterbrook, The Race for the Bottom in Corporate Governance, 98 Va. L. Rev. 685, 696 (2009); Ken Small, Octavian Ionici & Hong Zhu, Size Does Matter: An Examination of the Economic Impact of Sarbanes-Oxley, Review of Business, Apr. 1, 2007, at 47.

[98] Roberta Romano, Does the Sarbanes-Oxley Act Have a Future?, 26 Yale J. on Reg. 226, 240 (2009); see also Joseph A. Grundfest & Steven E. Bochner, Fixing 404, 105 Mich. L. Rev. 1643, 1645–46 (2007).

corporate governance[99] or to detect the accounting failures that contributed to the 2008 financial crisis, such as the faulty valuation of subprime mortgage-backed securities.[100] Countrywide Financial, a shady subprime mortgage lender at the epicenter of the financial crisis, was a celebrated paragon of Sarbanes-Oxley compliance.[101]

If the SEC had had the power to remove PCAOB members at will, a chastened PCAOB would likely have made major revisions to those internal-controls rules, which SEC commissioners viewed as being too sweeping and onerous.[102] But secure against the possibility of removal, the PCAOB did the absolute minimum necessary to appease the SEC, making only minor revisions to its rules, and reportedly rebuffing the SEC's chairman when he suggested that they "exempt some small firms" from the most burdensome aspects of those rules.[103]

---

[99] Roberta Romano, The Sarbanes-Oxley Act and the Making of a Quack Corporate Governance, 114 Yale L. J. 1521, 1529–43 (2005) (reviewing 50 studies and finding Sarbanes-Oxley's provisions to be ineffective in improving corporate governance or investor protection).

[100] Forbes, *supra* note 95 ("[T]he PCAOB was out to lunch on the biggest economic/accounting issue of our time: the subprime mortgage disaster," preoccupied with "such minutiae as which workers in a company can have office keys."); Editorial, Sarbox Routed in House, Wall St. J., Dec. 12, 2009, at A18 ("the law wasn't of much use to investors in" mismanaged companies like "Bear Stearns, Lehman Brothers, AIG"); William M. Sinnett, Does Internal Control Improve Operations and Prevent Fraud?, Financial Executive, Dec. 1, 2009, at S32 (article answers its title's question with a resounding no).

[101] See Eric Krell, Inflection Point: How to Chart Your Path Beyond SOX, Business Finance, Sept. 1, 2007, at 22; John Berlau, Freedom and Its Digital Discontents, The Economist, Mar. 17, 2008, available at http://cei.org/op-eds-and-articles/freedom-and-its-digital-discontents ("In 2007, the Institute of Internal Auditors' Research Foundation profiled" Countrywide Financial in a laudatory "case study" that "described in breathless tones how the company's unique risk management software featured '530 risk matrices, 9,500 risks, and 27,000 controls.'").

[102] See Andrea James, SEC Unanimously Votes for New Rules to Lower Audit Costs, Seattle Post-Intelligencer, July 26, 2007, at E1 (Auditing Standard 2(AS2) was replaced with new Auditing Standard 5 (AS5) in July 2007; SEC chairman called the old rule "unduly expensive and inefficient," while "Commissioner Paul Atkins said he was 'happy to put [it] out of its misery'").

[103] Roberta Romano, Does the Sarbanes-Oxley Act Have a Future?, 26 Yale J. on Reg. 229, 243 & n.53 (2009); Stephen Barlas, Jury Is Still Out on AS5 Impact, Investment Dealers' Digest, Oct. 29, 2007 (critics called the change "weak gruel," not meaningful reform, and Sarbanes-Oxley's cosponsor said, "It does not go far enough").

As one commentator explained, "After the PCAOB produced their 'Audit Standard 2,' 'all five' SEC commissioners were in favor of 'radical' changes to it, and yet it took the SEC years to even make 'some' changes to the auditing standards due in part to PCAOB recalcitrance."[104] The SEC's "power" at the time was "not plenary" over the PCAOB, but rather akin to "pushing on a string."[105]

But even in the aftermath of the Supreme Court's decision, major reform of these PCAOB rules is unlikely. The SEC's composition has since changed, as the terms of the biggest advocates of such reforms, such as Paul Atkins, have expired. Sitting on the SEC in their place are commissioners who blame the current financial crisis entirely on (mythical) deregulation under the George W. Bush administration, despite the fact that regulation vastly expanded under Bush due to Sarbanes-Oxley.[106] Such commissioners are unlikely to use their added sway over the PCAOB to push for further major revisions to its internal-controls rules.[107] In short, the SEC's expanded authority over the PCAOB may come too late for advocates of Sarbanes-Oxley reform.

The SEC's stance may change, however, if a more market-friendly administration comes to power in Washington. In 2008, many Republican presidential contenders were critical of the cost of the

---

[104] Jonathan Moore, Peekaboo! PCAOB More Powerful and Less Accountable than Government Claims, OpenMarket.Org, Dec. 4, 2009, available at http://www.openmarket.org/2009/12/04/peekaboo-pcaob-more-powerful-and-less-accountable-than-government-claims (quoting SEC Commissioner Paul S. Atkins's remarks at a December 3, 2009, panel discussion at the American Enterprise Institute entitled "Public Company Accounting Oversight Board: A Preview"). Video of this event can be found at the following link, which subdivides the panel discussion by speaker: http://www.aei.org/video/101187. I also spoke at the event, which is described at http://www.aei.org/event/100177.

[105] Id.

[106] Aguilar Calls for Strong Financial Reform and Enforcement Measures, Banking & Financial Services Policy Report, July 2010, at 27 ("Commissioner Luis Aguilar, in remarks at a recent Compliance Week conference, blamed years of deregulation for the financial crisis."); Robert Hardaway, The Great American Housing Bubble: Re-Examining Cause and Effect, 35 U. Dayton L. Rev. 33 (2009) (discussing federal policies, regulations, and subsidies that spawned the financial crisis; debunking "deregulation" as a "simplistic explanation").

[107] See, e.g., Floyd Norris, U.S. Justices Vote to Keep Regulatory Committee, Int'l Herald-Tribune, June 29, 2010, at 18 ("There is no indication that the S.E.C. has any desire to fire any board members.").

PCAOB's rules, which have been widely criticized for undermining American competitiveness and driving business, initial public offerings, and financial jobs overseas to countries with less burdensome regulations.[108] Indeed, so much financial activity moved from New York to London that City bankers wanted "to erect a solid gold statue in honor of the legislators who sponsored [Sarbanes-Oxley], for their efforts . . . certainly resulted in shifting a massive proportion of the mergers and acquisitions boom to Britain."[109]

The logic of the Court's decision also suggests that rules influenced by the SEC's limited influence over the PCAOB can be challenged by private parties as constitutionally tainted.[110] But except with regard to the PCAOB's controversial internal-controls rules, such influence would probably be hard to show as to any particular rule. Indeed, the challengers in *Free Enterprise Fund* did not raise objections to "any of its auditing standards," which were putatively subject to exhaustion.[111] Beckstead did complain, however, of the PCAOB's "uncomplimentary inspection report."[112]

In theory, the board's rules adopted before *Free Enterprise Fund* should be considered null and void. If the PCAOB members were principal officers before the Court's decision expanding SEC authority over them—as legal commentators and Judge Kavanaugh in fact argued—then, purely as a matter of logic, the PCAOB's rules from that period were adopted by invalidly appointed officers.[113] But the

---

[108] See, e.g., Rick Merritt, Tech Off Radar in '08 Race, Electronic Engineering Times, Jan. 28, 2008, at 1 ("Both [former New York Mayor Rudolph] Giuliani and [former Massachusetts Governor Mitt] Romney call for reining in the excesses of Sarbanes-Oxley, particularly for small businesses.").

[109] Claire Berlinski, There Is No Alternative: Why Margaret Thatcher Matters 148–49 (2008).

[110] See, e.g., Allen v. Carmen, 578 F. Supp. 951, 969 (D.D.C. 1983) (holding that unconstitutional legislative veto used by one House of Congress to disapprove agency's regulation required invalidation of agency's subsequently adopted regulations, which were influenced and thus "tainted" by the veto).

[111] Free Enter. Fund, 130 S. Ct. at 3150 (narrowing reach of exhaustion doctrine).

[112] Free Enter. Fund, 130 S. Ct. at 3150; see also *id.* at 3164 (challengers entitled to order against enforcement by agency not constitutionally "accountable to the Executive"). See also Columbus Educ. Ass'n v. Columbus City Sch. Dist., 623 F.2d 1155 & n.1 (6th Cir. 1980) (expunging government reprimand, which was sufficient injury for suit).

[113] See Williams v. Phelps, 482 F.2d 669, 671 n.3 (D.C. Cir. 1973) (labor union could sue to challenge policies harming employees carried out by improperly appointed agency head); Freytag v. Comm'r of Internal Revenue, 501 U.S. 868, 879 (1991).

question is largely academic because the PCAOB would likely simply readopt any such rules if they were called into question. The Supreme Court held that the petitioners were "not entitled to broad injunctive relief against the Board's continued operations,"[114] and that "the Sarbanes-Oxley Act remains 'fully operative as a law'" going forward.[115]

Moreover, the regulated entities with the resources to bring far-reaching challenges to PCAOB rules adopted when it was not operating as a constitutional agency—that is, the big accounting firms—have no incentive to do so. They are the beneficiaries of the PCAOB's burdensome rules, not its victims. They "have reaped huge profits" due to all the PCAOB's red tape, and have vigorously defended the PCAOB's most burdensome auditing rules for that very reason.[116] Even if they were not enriched by its rules, however, as parties regulated by the PCAOB, there would be little point in their offending the board by challenging rules it could simply readopt going forward.

Finally, a law enacted just after the Supreme Court's decision, the massive Dodd-Frank financial overhaul, moots some potential challenges by exempting from the PCAOB's "internal controls" rules the small public companies most heavily burdened by them.[117] Added in response to prodding from financial regulation scholars like my colleague John Berlau,[118] Section 989G of that law exempts publicly traded companies with market capitalizations of less than $75 million from internal-controls audits under Sarbanes-Oxley.[119]

---

[114] Free Enter. Fund, 130 S. Ct. at 3164.

[115] *Id.* at 3161 (quoting New York v. United States, 505 U.S. 144, 186 (1992)).

[116] See, e.g., Eric Dash, S.E.C. Revises Its Standards for Corporate Audits, N.Y. Times, May 24, 2007, at C3; Stephen Labaton, U.S. Commission Set to Ease Audit Rules for Small Companies, Int'l Herald-Tribune, Dec. 12, 2006, at 14.

[117] Romano, 114 Yale L.J. at 1588 ("SOX imposed a far more significant burden on small than on large firms"); William J. Carney, The Costs of Being Public After Sarbanes-Oxley: The Irony of "Going Private," 55 Emory L.J. 141, 151 (2006) (same).

[118] John Berlau, Obama's Latest Monstrosity, American Spectator, July 21, 2010, available at http://spectator.org/archives/2010/07/21/obamas-latest-monstrosity; John Berlau, Obama Can Aid Small Businesses by Providing Regulatory Relief, Daily Caller, Feb. 2, 2010, available at http://dailycaller.com/2010/02/02/obama-can-aid-small-businesses-by-providing-regulatory-relief/.

[119] Dodd-Frank Wall Street Reform and Consumer Protection Act, Pub. L. 111-203, § 989G, 124 Stat. 1376 (July 21, 2010), adding Sarbanes-Oxley Act, Section 404(c), 15 U.S.C. § 7262(c).

B. Investigations and Inspections of Accounting Firms

The PCAOB publicly styles itself as a private entity immune from constitutional constraints, a claim parroted by gullible journalists.[120] It does this even though, in the Supreme Court, its lawyers admitted the obvious, "that the Board is 'part of the Government' for constitutional purposes," and "that its members are 'Officers of the United States' who 'exercise significant authority'" under federal law.[121] Sarbanes-Oxley itself declares the PCAOB to be "private," but the Supreme Court held years ago that such statutory labels are meaningless.[122]

The fact that the PCAOB is, in reality, a government agency means that it must respect constitutional rights in its investigations and rulemaking. As Donna Nagy, the leading PCAOB scholar, has explained, one such right is the Fifth Amendment right against self-incrimination.[123] Thus, the PCAOB could not force an accountant with a reasonable fear of criminal prosecution to testify in an investigation or subject him to discipline solely for his failure to cooperate— although it could draw a negative inference from that failure to testify.[124] That right may also affect the enforceability of the "consents" to cooperation that accountants are required to sign as a condition of their employment with a registered accounting firm.[125] Such consents will be limited by the well-established "doctrine of 'unconstitutional conditions,'" which prohibits requiring waivers of constitutional rights as a condition of government benefits.[126] Similarly, PCAOB inspections should be subject to Fourth Amendment

[120] PCAOB website, http://pcaobus.org/Pages/default.aspx (last visited, July 28, 2010) (claiming the "PCAOB is a private sector, non-profit corporation"); AP Washington Daybook, July 13, 2010 (repeating PCAOB claim that "the PCAOB is a private-sector, non-profit corporation").

[121] Free Enter. Fund, 130 S. Ct. at 3148 (quoting Lebron v. National Railroad Passenger Corporation, 513 U.S. 374, 397 (1995)).

[122] Lebron, 513 U.S. at 397 (Amtrak is a government-controlled corporation bound by the Constitution, even though federal law declares it to be private.).

[123] Donna M. Nagy, Playing Peekaboo with Constitutional Law: The PCAOB and Its Public/Private Status, 80 Notre Dame L. Rev. 975, 1044–48 (2005).

[124] Id. at 1045–46 (citing cases).

[125] Id. at 1046.

[126] Dollan v. City of Tigard, 512 U.S. 374, 385 (1994); see, e.g., Garrity v. New Jersey, 385 U.S. 493 (1967) (state may not condition continued public employment on relinquishment of right to invoke Fifth Amendment privilege against self-incrimination). Constitutional safeguards apply with greater force to "regulated entities" like

limits,[127] and the PCAOB's investigations would have to respect accountants' right to counsel and right to due process.[128] When the PCAOB imposes large monetary sanctions, subsequent sanctions by the SEC or Justice Department could be barred in extreme cases as a violation of the Fifth Amendment's Double Jeopardy Clause.[129] Finally, PCAOB auditing standards can be challenged if they restrict an accountant or accounting firm's right to free speech or association.[130]

C. Employment and Contracting by the PCAOB

Since it is now recognized as a government agency for constitutional purposes, the PCAOB must now afford its employees and contractors various rights that do not apply against private employers, but do apply against government agencies. For example, it will have to put up with controversial speech on matters of public concern by its employees, since that is protected by the First Amendment.[131] It will also be liable for a wider range of discrimination against employees and contractors, since the Constitution is not limited to protected classes covered by civil rights statutes,[132] and

accounting firms than they do to the government's own employees. Carepartners LLC v. Lashway, 545 F.3d 867, 880 (9th Cir. 2008); see also Waters v. Churchill, 511 U.S. 661, 671 (1994).

[127] Nagy, Playing Peekaboo, *supra* note 123 at 1046 (citing cases). Consents executed by accountants would not change this. A.F.G.E. v. Weinberger, 651 F. Supp. 726, 736 (S.D. Ga. 1986) ("Advance consent to future unreasonable searches is not a reasonable condition of employment.").

[128] Nagy, Playing Peekaboo, *supra* note 123, at 1046–48.

[129] *Id.* at 1047–48.

[130] *Id.* at 1048. See Edenfield v. Fane, 507 U.S. 761 (1993) (invalidating accounting board's rule restricting unsolicited phone calls); Pfizer v. Giles, 46 F.3d 1284 (3d Cir. 1995) (holding that a state may not use means of imposing liability that hamper free association if less restrictive means are available).

[131] Nagy, Playing Peekaboo, *supra* note 123, at 1048 (citing cases). Congress has preempted constitutional lawsuits with administrative remedies for many federal employees, but such preemption doesn't apply to the PCAOB, because it is nominally private, even though it is in fact a federal agency. Sculthies v. Nat'l Passenger R.R. Corp., 650 F. Supp.2d 994, 999 (N.D. Cal. 2009) (Amtrak employee could bring free speech claim because Amtrak is a de facto government agency; judicial remedy not preempted because Amtrak, like PCAOB, is nominally private).

[132] See, e.g., Peightal v. Metro. Dade County., 26 F.3d 1545 (11th Cir. 1991) (affirmative action plan upheld under Title VII but not under the Constitution); Brunet v. City of Columbus, 1 F.3d 390, 405 (6th Cir. 1993) (plan held unconstitutional despite its possible validity under Title VII).

since the Constitution—unlike Title VII of the Civil Rights Act—allows employees to sue not just the agency that employs them but also the individual government officials who engage in discrimination.[133] The PCAOB is now clearly subject to Fourth Amendment limits on things like random employee drug testing.[134] And it must respect due process by not firing those employees who have a reasonable expectation of continued employment without first giving them notice and an opportunity to be heard, and by not disciplining them in ways that contravene its written policies and procedures.[135]

V.   The Decision Strengthens the Government's Ability to Fire Mediocre and Recalcitrant Officials

The Supreme Court's holding directly governs only independent agencies, which can now remove high-ranking civil servants at will. But its logic is not limited to independent agencies. Over the long run, it will probably also affect other executive branch employees, such as those who work for the 15 cabinet departments.

Free Enterprise Fund breathed new life into the Supreme Court's previously eroded 1926 decision in *Myers v. United States*, which gave the president the ability to remove executive-branch officers like postmasters without Senate approval.[136] Indeed, the *Free Enterprise Fund* Court explicitly relied on *Myers* even though dicta in subsequent cases suggested that *Myers* had been largely overruled and limited to the context "where Congress granted itself removal authority over Executive Branch officials."[137] By applying *Myers*'s

---

[133] Compare Fantini v. Salem State Coll., 557 F.3d 22, 30 (1st Cir. 2009) (Title VII does not hold individual supervisors liable) with Alexander v. Estepp, 95 F.3d 312, 317 (4th Cir. 1996) (individual supervisors liable for "reverse discrimination" against white employees under Constitution).

[134] Nagy, Playing Peekaboo, *supra* note 123, at 1045.

[135] *Id.* at 1047 (citing cases); see Wilkinson v. Legal Servs. Corp., 27 F. Supp. 2d 32, 62 (D.D.C. 1998) (despite statutory language calling it a "private" corporation, the LSC is a government actor that must provide due process).

[136] 272 U.S. 52, 162 (1926).

[137] Compare Free Enter. Fund, 130 S. Ct. at 3152 (relying on "the landmark case of *Myers*" and its removal principles) with *id.* at 3167, 3176 (Breyer, J., dissenting) (stating that *Humphrey's Executor* "explicitly disapproved of most of the reasoning in *Myers*") (citing Wiener v. United States, 357 U.S. 349, 357 (1950)); Morrison v. Olson, 487 U.S. 654, 686 (1988) (*Myers* held "the Constitution prevents Congress from draw[ing] to itself . . . the power to remove") (quoting *Myers*, 272 U.S. at 161).

holding to a statute where Congress did not seek to expand its power over the executive branch—but rather sought to limit its *own* authority[138]—*Free Enterprise Fund* shows that *Myers's* principles cannot be so easily cabined, and that the president and his cabinet secretaries likely have broad constitutional authority to fire executive officers at will.

If that is so, then the Court's decision may empower administrations to remove administrators, lawyers, and other civil servants who flout their policies. For example, liberal Justice Department lawyers have routinely resisted the policies of Republican administrations, pressing for race-based redistricting and nullification of state voter-identification laws even when doing so cuts against administration policy and Supreme Court rulings.[139] As civil-service employees, these officials "are almost impossible to fire," despite the theoretical possibility of dismissal for cause.[140] But if high-ranking civil servants are officers of the United States—as Justice Breyer's dissent laments[141]—then they may logically be removable at will under *Myers*, which upheld the removal without cause of an "inferior officer" whose authority was no greater than theirs (a postmaster).[142]

Low-level bureaucrats do not qualify as federal "officers" removable at will under *Myers*, since they are mere "employees," not "officers" for constitutional purposes.[143] But many Justice Department lawyers clearly do qualify as federal officers, since they either

---

[138] Free Enter. Fund, 130 S. Ct. at 3176 (Breyer, J., dissenting) (Congress sought to limit its own influence over the PCAOB by not selecting its leaders and by "providing the Accounting Board with a revenue stream independent of the Congressional appropriations process.").

[139] See, e.g., LULAC v. Perry, 548 U.S. 399 (2006) (upholding all but one district in the 2003 Texas redistricting plan); Crawford v. Marion County. Election Bd., 553 U.S. 181 (2008) (upholding state's voter ID requirement); Voter-Fraud Activist on Election Panel Faces Hearings, NPR All Things Considered, June 12, 2007 (Bush appointee approved Texas redistricting plan and voter ID over resistance from career Justice Department lawyers), available at http://www.npr.org/templates/story/story.php-?storyId= 10991498.

[140] Carl Nolte, Bush Aides Scramble for Federal Jobs, S.F. Chronicle, Nov. 30, 1992, at A1 (also noting that civil service includes bureaucrats who "head up nationwide or department wide program"); Jim Balow, Raises Not Big, But Jobs Secure, Houston Chronicle, Aug. 8, 2000, at 1 (few employees with "poor" ratings ever get fired).

[141] Free Enter. Fund, 130 S. Ct. at 3179 (Breyer, J., dissenting).

[142] Buckley v. Valeo, 424 U.S. 1, 126 (1976) (postmaster in *Myers* was an inferior officer).

[143] Free Enter. Fund, 130 S. Ct. at 3160.

possess "significant authority"[144] or meet alternative tests for officer status. Under Supreme Court precedent, "officers" include *each* of the following categories of federal employees: "'(1) those charged with 'the administration and enforcement of the public law,' . . . (2) those granted 'significant authority,' . . . and (3) those with 'responsibility for conducting civil litigation in the courts of the United States.'"[145] Government lawyers commonly meet one or more of those tests.

Indeed, federal lawyers typically have far more authority than many minor officials whom the Supreme Court long ago held to be officers within the meaning of the Appointments Clause, such as "thousands of clerks" and an "assistant surgeon."[146] The fact that civil-service regulations may purport to bar their removal without cause does not change this; indeed, the Supreme Court in *Myers* noted that "a vast majority of all civil officers" as defined in the Constitution were covered by the Civil Service Law.[147]

VI. The Decision Opens the Door to Messy Selection Processes at Independent Agencies

To reject petitioners' Appointments Clause challenge, the Supreme Court embraced contradictory reasoning that is not sustainable in the long run and could undermine agencies' efficiency. The Court held that the members of the PCAOB can validly be picked by the SEC commissioners as a group, rather than by the SEC's chairman, based on the dubious theory that the commissioners are collectively the SEC's true "head" and thus constitutionally authorized to make appointments within their department.

But with the exception of the PCAOB members, all key appointments made by the SEC (like its general counsel) are made by its chairman, not by the SEC commissioners as a group.[148] If the Supreme Court is right that the SEC's chairman is not its "head," then he has no authority to make these other appointments under the Appointments Clause. That situation is troubling for independent agencies

---

[144] *Id.* at 3148 (quoting Buckley v. Valeo, 474 U.S. 1, 125–26 (1976)).

[145] *Id.* at 3179–80 (Breyer, J., dissenting) (quoting Buckley, 474 U.S. at 126, 139–40).

[146] *Id.* at 3179 (Breyer, J., dissenting) (citing examples from Supreme Court precedent).

[147] Myers, 272 U.S. at 173.

[148] SEC Chairman Is Not the "Head" of the SEC, *supra* note 33, at 2273 (quoting SEC v. Blinder, 855 F.2d 677, 681 (10th Cir. 1988)).

because virtually all of them—not just the SEC—vest appointments in their chairman. Taken to its logical conclusion, *Free Enterprise Fund* would call into question virtually all important appointments made by independent agencies.

The Supreme Court sought to finesse this problem by noting that appointments by the SEC's chairman are subject to approval by a majority of SEC commissioners. The Court then declared in dicta that such after-the-fact approvals rendered the chairman's pick the group-appointment of the commissioners.[149] But that's like saying that the Senate's approval of the president's judicial nominations makes judges senatorial appointees!

Not only is this dictum unpersuasive, it contradicts what the Court said earlier in its opinion, when it noted that it was improper to "assume . . . that the Chairman would have made the same appointments acting alone" as the full commission, merely because "no member of the Board has been appointed over the Chairman's objection."[150] In short, the Supreme Court itself admitted that there is a big difference between appointing someone and merely consenting to his or her appointment. For example, many Democratic senators voted to confirm Chief Justice Roberts but no one seriously believes that they would have appointed him if it were their choice.

The Supreme Court claimed that petitioners had effectively conceded that approval was the same as appointment by not asking the Supreme Court to overturn its past decisions in cases like *United States v. Hartwell*, which deemed an officer's appointment valid even though he was selected by a department head's subordinate, and then approved by that department head.[151] But there is a big difference between a busy department head's delegating a selection to one of his subordinates—who is eager for his approval and likely to carry out his every wish—and stripping officials of their appointment power and transferring it to a colleague who may have very different wishes (like shifting appointments from the SEC commissioners to the SEC's chairman). For example, federal appellate judges

---

[149] Free Enter. Fund, 130 S. Ct. at 3163 n.13.

[150] *Id.* at 3163 n.12.

[151] *Id.* at 3163 n.13 (citing, e.g., United States v. Hartwell, 73 U.S. (6 Wall.) 385, 393–94 (1868)).

are informally selected by "judge-pickers" subordinate to the president, who make sure that such selections reflect the president's judicial philosophy.[152] That is very different from having judges formally picked by the president's political competitors, like the Senate, and then approved by the president.

In a future case, the Court should remedy its contradictory Appointments Clause holding by ruling that an independent agency is headed by its chairman, not its commissioners as a group. Such a ruling would both affirm the validity of the vast majority of independent agency appointments and vindicate one of the purposes of the Appointments Clause, which was aimed precisely at "the lack of accountability in a multimember body."[153] As the *Harvard Law Review* notes, treating the commissioners of independent agencies as their collective heads is both factually wrong and contrary to the purpose of the Appointments Clause, which seeks to prevent "widely distributed appointment power" and maximize officials' accountability to democratically elected leaders.[154] It is factually wrong because the SEC's chairman, like other independent agency chairs, "'exerts far more control than [her] one vote would seem to indicate' because she 'controls key personnel, internal organization, and the expenditure of funds'"; because "every important position in the SEC is appointed by the chairman," including the general counsel, the chief accountant, and the chief economist; and because the SEC chairman is listed as the SEC's "head" and "chief executive" on the SEC's own website and in the *Federal Register*.[155]

Moreover, "vesting the appointment power in the multimember Commission violates the Appointments Clause's intent by not reserving the appointment power in the SEC's most politically accountable actor, the Chairman."[156] Unlike other SEC commissioners—but like cabinet secretaries, the paradigmatic department

---

[152] See, e.g., Jonathan Groner, Judiciary Battles Start Anew, Legal Times, Jan. 13, 2003, at 10.

[153] Freytag, 501 U.S. at 904–05 (Scalia, J., concurring).

[154] SEC Chairman Is Not the "Head," *supra* note 33, at 2273 (quoting Freytag, 501 U.S. at 885).

[155] *Id*. at 2272 (quoting S.E.C. v. Blinder, 855 F.2d at 681 and citing lists of agency "heads" published in the *Federal Register* by the Office of Management and Budget, which show independent agencies' chairmen are their "heads").

[156] *Id*. at 2270.

heads—the SEC's "chairman serves at the pleasure of the president," making him the most democratically accountable member of the SEC.[157] "This removal power is critical for political accountability, for 'it is only the authority that can remove him . . . that [an officer] must fear and, in the performance of his functions, obey.'"[158]

It is that accountability that makes the SEC's chairman, but not other SEC commissioners, qualify as a potential department head for Appointments Clause purposes: "According to the Supreme Court, appointment power can be vested in department heads because they are 'subject to the exercise of political oversight and share the President's accountability to the people.'"[159] The SEC's chairman is subject to such oversight, but that is manifestly not true of other SEC commissioners, who can be removed from their positions only for cause. Treating them as a department head for purposes of the Appointments Clause defeats its purpose of accountability.

The PCAOB's own history illustrates the foolishness of letting groups act as if they were an independent agency's "head." Sarbanes-Oxley's requirement that SEC commissioners as a group agree on the appointment of PCAOB members triggered a messy and divisive process for selecting the initial board members. As the General Accounting Office later found, "The selection process broke down in early October [2002] when the Commission was unable to agree on a consensus candidate for chairman."[160] Different commissioners backed different candidates, and this "inability to choose a final slate of candidates until the eve of the Commission's vote resulted in the appointment of PCAOB members who had not been fully vetted."[161] Retired Judge William Webster, the first PCAOB chairman, resigned shortly after he was appointed when his service on the audit board of U.S. Technologies, a company under SEC investigation for accounting problems, became public.[162] The SEC's own chairman, Harvey Pitt, was blamed for withholding this information from his fellow commissioners, and he ended up resigning

---

[157] *Id.* at 2274 n. 81 (citing Free Enter. Fund, 537 F.3d at 680).

[158] *Id.* at 2274 (quoting Bowsher v. Synar, 478 U.S. 714, 726 (1986)).

[159] *Id.* at 2273 (quoting Freytag, 501 U.S. at 886).

[160] U.S. Gen. Accounting Office Rep. No. GAO-03-339, *supra* note 35 at 4.

[161] *Id.* at i.

[162] *Id.* at 13–16.

as well. Yet the GAO found that no one, not even Pitt, knew of this information before the vote, because no commissioner was really in charge of the selection. Moreover, the SEC's chief accountant did not view this information as relevant and "did not inform the SEC chairman or other commissioners about certain matters concerning Judge Webster."[163] This is precisely the lack of accountability that the Framers sought to guard against through the Appointments Clause, and the Supreme Court was wrong to countenance such a messy appointment process.[164]

Conclusion

The Supreme Court's willingness to bend over backward to preserve as much of the Sarbanes-Oxley Act as it could—despite its serious constitutional flaws and massive cost to the economy and American business—is one more illustration that the Court is not "pro-business." Nonetheless, the Court's ruling striking down the act's removal restrictions will promote government accountability in two ways: First, it will place the wasteful, red-tape-obsessed PCAOB more firmly under SEC control by enabling the SEC to fire PCAOB members at will. Second, it will strengthen the government's ability to get rid of high-ranking bureaucrats and lawyers who are intractable, headstrong, or mediocre. This strengthened accountability may improve financial regulation—and the U.S. economy—in the long run.

---

[163] *Id*. at 3.

[164] See Freytag, 501 U.S. 868, 904–05 (Scalia, J., concurring).

Federal Misgovernance of Mutual Funds

Larry E. Ribstein*

Introduction

As Congress enacts another round of financial regulation in response to the most recent financial crisis, it is worth evaluating where we have been. An appropriate occasion for this evaluation is the Supreme Court's recent decision in *Jones v. Harris Associates*,[1] where the Court had to contend with the structure of the Investment Company Act—crafted in 1940 and revised in 1970 to deal with the financial circumstances of the 1920s and 1960s, respectively—in light of the vastly different financial marketplace of 2010. *Jones* should serve as a warning against the dangers of federal regulation of firms' structure and governance.

Jones interpreted section 36(b) of the Investment Company Act of 1940, which provides that "the investment adviser of a registered investment company shall be deemed to have a fiduciary duty with respect to the receipt of compensation for services, or of payments of a material nature" from the investment company or its investors.[2] The section also authorizes an action by the Securities and Exchange Commission or an investor in the fund against the investment adviser, among others, for breach of fiduciary duty as to this compensation.[3]

Since 1982, most federal courts applying section 36(b) have purported to apply the standard set forth in *Gartenberg v. Merrill Lynch Asset Management, Inc.*:

---

* Associate Dean for Research and Mildred Van Voorhis Jones Chair, University of Illinois College of Law. Thanks to Jill Fisch, Bruce Johnsen, and John Morley for very helpful comments.

[1] 559 U.S. ___, 130 S. Ct. 1418 (2010).

[2] 15 U.S.C. § 80a-35(b) (2006).

[3] *Id.*

> To be guilty of a violation of § 36(b). . . . the adviser-manager must charge a fee that is so disproportionately large that it bears no reasonable relationship to the services rendered and could not have been the product of arm's-length bargaining.[4]

When *Jones* reached the U.S. Court of Appeals for the Seventh Circuit, Judge Frank Easterbrook's panel opinion affirmed summary judgment for the defendant investment adviser.[5] Noting that "judicial price-setting does not accompany fiduciary duties" and the existence of vigorous competition among mutual funds, the court disapproved *Gartenberg* and articulated a new test:

> A fiduciary must make full disclosure and play no tricks but is not subject to a cap on compensation. The trustees (and in the end investors, who vote with their feet and dollars), rather than a judge or jury, determine how much advisory services are worth.[6]

The Seventh Circuit's denial of rehearing *en banc* prompted a sharp dissent from Judge Richard Posner, writing for four colleagues:

> The panel bases its rejection of *Gartenberg* mainly on an economic analysis that is ripe for reexamination on the basis of growing indications that executive compensation in large publicly traded firms often is excessive because of the feeble incentives of boards of directors to police compensation. . . . Competition in product and capital markets can't be counted on to solve the problem because the same structure of incentives operates on all large corporations and similar entities, including mutual funds.[7]

The Supreme Court, faced with a circuit split and two prominent market-oriented jurists' disagreement about the nature of the mutual fund market, took the bait and granted certiorari. The unanimous opinion by Justice Samuel Alito endorsed *Gartenberg* and vacated

---

[4] 694 F.2d 923, 928 (2d Cir. 1982). For citations and analysis of decisions applying *Gartenberg* see Lyman Johnson, A Fresh Look at Director "Independence": Mutual Fund Fee Litigation and *Gartenberg* at Twenty-Five, 61 Vand. L. Rev. 497, 538-42 (2008).

[5] Jones v. Harris Assocs., 527 F.3d 627, 635 (7th Cir. 2008).

[6] *Id.* at 632–33.

[7] Jones v. Harris Assocs., 537 F.3d 728, 730 (7th Cir. 2008).

and remanded the Seventh Circuit decision, concluding that the Easterbrook-Posner debate "regarding today's mutual fund market is a matter for Congress, not the courts."[8]

Justice Alito was correct that the issue in *Jones* is properly for Congress to decide. However, the issue reaches beyond the viability of the market for mutual funds to the federal role in regulating the structure of business. The problems highlighted in section 36(b) litigation do not stem from inadequate enforcement of investment advisers' fiduciary duty in setting fees, but rather from the very existence of this duty and the corporate structure from which it springs. Moreover, the perpetuation of this dysfunctional structure points to its even more basic problem of being embedded in a federal law that lacks state corporate law's safety valve of interstate competition and experimentation.

Part I of this article discusses the background of *Jones v. Harris Associates*, placing the case in the context of the statutory scheme and the pre-*Jones* litigation. This part shows that the section 36(b) fiduciary duty has served the interests of investment advisers and trial lawyers more than those of investors.

Part II links the problems with the fiduciary duty applied in *Jones* to mutual funds' corporate structure established in the original ICA. This structure conflicts with investors' right to cash out of open-end mutual funds at will. The redemption right renders the whole panoply of corporate shareholder-protection devices, particularly fiduciary duties, not only unnecessary but even counterproductive. Mutual fund investors buy a product rather than investing in a firm, and the law should treat investors accordingly.

Part III asks where to go from here, and takes a deeper look at the problems that led to *Jones*. The ICA's dysfunctional mutual fund governance regime could have been sustained only by a federal law, which lacks the competitive discipline that applies to state regulation of firms' internal governance. Federal regulation of financial markets should stick to the model established in the early 1930s for the original federal securities laws in which states establish governance structures and federal law requires firms to disclose these structures and other facts to investors. Whether or not disclosure is adequate to support a fully efficient market for mutual funds, the history of

---

[8] Jones, 130 S. Ct. at 1431.

mutual fund regulation shows that federal constraints on firms' governance are no solution.

I. The "Fiduciary Duty" Problem in Mutual Funds

The basic problems involved in *Jones* begin with the section 36(b) "fiduciary duty" the case was applying. Unlike traditional fiduciary duties, which have evolved through centuries of case law to meet firms' needs, section 36(b) used fiduciary duties as a makeshift political compromise. This part begins by placing fiduciary duties in a theoretical perspective. It then discusses the legislative history of the section 36(b) fiduciary duty and the duty's evolution through *Gartenberg* and *Jones*.

A. The Theory of Fiduciary Duties

Courts have interpreted the term "fiduciary duty" in many different professions (from doctors to corporate directors) to refer to a broad constellation of duties, including loyalty, care, the amorphous category of "good faith," and maintaining confidences. One leading commentator despaired of "confusion and uncertainty in applying the fiduciary principle to disparate fact situations."[9]

Perhaps the most famous judicial expression of fiduciary duties is by Justice Benjamin Cardozo in *Meinhard v. Salmon*:

> Joint adventurers, like copartners, owe to one another, while the enterprise continues, the duty of the finest loyalty. Many forms of conduct permissible in a workaday world for those acting at arm's length, are forbidden to those bound by fiduciary ties. A trustee is held to something stricter than the morals of the market place. Not honesty alone, but the punctilio of an honor the most sensitive, is then the standard of behavior. As to this there has developed a tradition that is unbending and inveterate. Uncompromising rigidity has been the attitude of courts of equity when petitioned to undermine the rule of undivided loyalty by the "disintegrating erosion" of particular exceptions [citation omitted]. Only thus has the level of conduct for fiduciaries been kept at a level higher than that trodden by the crowd. It will not consciously be lowered by any judgment of this court.[10]

---

[9] J.C. Shepherd, The Law of Fiduciaries 7 (1981).
[10] 164 N.E. 545, 546 (N.Y. 1928).

Justice Cardozo accurately describes the fiduciary duty as one of unselfishness. This insight helps define the situations in which the duty should rise. Given the extraordinary nature of a fiduciary duty in a commercial economy that generally assumes self-seeking behavior, we would expect this duty to arise only in extraordinary circumstances—specifically, where the beneficiary delegates to the fiduciary broad power that is not amenable to alternative disciplinary mechanisms.[11] The duty is not justified simply because one party to a transaction relies on another's expertise as long as the empowered party is subject to enough constraints that an intense duty of unselfishness is unnecessary. For example, fiduciary duties usually are unnecessary in general partnerships—the form of business involved in *Meinhard*—unless, as in that case, one partner functions as the manager.

Strong policy concerns justify excluding from the fiduciary category many situations where duties might seem necessary to protect a vulnerable party. Fiduciary duties are best seen as only one of several devices intended to control "agency costs"—that is, the costs of an owner's delegating discretion to manage her property. These duties may be costly because judges are poor business managers and judicial scrutiny can interfere with other aspects of parties' contracts. The parties need not incur these costs where market and reputational constraints and other governance devices are effective to constrain cheating. Fiduciary duties entail judicial intervention only as a last resort, and only to the limited extent of keeping the fiduciary from extracting selfish gain from the beneficiary.

The publicly held corporation illustrates when fiduciary duties are justified. Here, dispersed and rationally apathetic investors lack practicable ways to fully control managerial conduct. Although investors can sell their shares, the sale price reflects any mismanagement. Shareholders can vote, but small holders cannot easily coordinate and lack incentives to become well-informed. Accordingly, directors of publicly held firms are accountable for unauthorized self-interested transactions. Managers' disinterested conduct is left to discipline by capital markets, shareholder voting, and board supervision.

---

[11] See Larry E. Ribstein, Are Partners Fiduciaries?, 2005 U. Ill. L. Rev. 209.

Bringing the discussion closer to the issue in *Jones*, managerial compensation, including investment adviser fees, generally is not governed by the *default* fiduciary duties discussed above because fiduciaries commonly opt out of default duties and bargain over compensation. Corporate-type firms bargain through a board of directors or other managers who are subject to fiduciary rules requiring disinterested conduct. (Part II considers whether these constraints are appropriate for mutual funds.)

Finally, it is worth emphasizing that fiduciary duties traditionally emerge from state common law. Accordingly, fiduciary duties arising in federal statutes like section 36(b) raise special problems of meshing state fiduciary law with the specific aims of the federal statute.

B. Mutual Fund Governance under the Investment Company Act

The "fiduciary duty" in section 36(b) results from the corporate structure of mutual funds Congress imposed in the ICA, which in turn borrowed heavily from the industry as it existed in 1940. Analysis of the duty therefore must begin with the history of the mutual fund industry.

The investment companies formed in the 1920s were mostly "closed-end" funds, meaning their size and shares were fixed at birth. Investors could exit such funds only by finding somebody to buy their shares. Few pre-1940 mutual funds were "open-end" like the one in *Jones*, which continually sold new shares and let investors cash out by redeeming their shares from the fund.[12]

The most important feature of the mutual funds of the 1920s and early 1930s for present purposes is the typical, though not universal, corporate structure of the closed-end funds that dominated the early mutual fund industry. Because promoters established these funds mainly to earn fees from selling securities, they were unconcerned with devising the most efficient structure for managing money.[13] Mutual funds' corporate structure was never inevitable. Investment companies established in the United Kingdom since the 1800s have

---

[12] For a discussion of the pre-1930 mutual fund industry outlining the nature and roles of closed- and open-end funds, see Peter J. Wallison & Robert E. Litan, Competitive Equity: A Better Way to Organize Mutual Funds, 24–27 (2007).

[13] See *id.* at 25.

not used a corporate form,[14] and some U.S. funds as of the time of the ICA were organized as common-law trusts. When it came time to establish a regulatory structure for the investment company industry, Congress might have followed the disclosure approach that it had used in the Securities Act of 1933 and the Securities Exchange Act of 1934 and left firms' structure for the market to decide. Instead, Congress imposed the corporate-type structure that many funds used at the time.

There was little basis in 1940 for believing that the corporate structure was appropriate for mutual funds given the industry's limited history from the end of the 1920s stock market boom. In particular, Congress had had little opportunity to analyze the corporation's suitability for open-end funds which were only a small part of the industry in 1940. As we will see, the ICA's mandatory corporate structure was particularly inappropriate for open-end funds because of investors' power to cash out at will. The 1940 Act exempted the trusts that existed as of 1940,[15] and prevented further structural development of the industry thereafter.[16]

C. The Section 36(b) Fiduciary Duty

Since the ICA initially lacked an express fiduciary remedy, investors sued fund directors in state court. The courts applied a "waste" standard that made it virtually impossible for plaintiffs to win a challenge.[17] Opposition to the ICA regulatory structure began developing in the early 1960s. A report by the Wharton School in 1962 suggested that investment advisers were pocketing the fruits of increasing scale economies, abetted by inadequate competition among investment advisers.[18] There ensued eight years of legislative

---

[14] *Id.* at 24. This difference between the United States and the United Kingdom partly reflects the generally different roles played by the corporate form in the two countries. Larry E. Ribstein, The Rise of the Uncorporation 65–94 (2010).

[15] Investment Company Act of 1940 §16(c), 15 U.S.C. § 80a-16(c) (2006).

[16] See Wallison & Litan, *supra* note 12, at 24–25.

[17] See, e.g., Saxe v. Brady, 184 A.2d 602 (Del. Ch. 1962).

[18] Wharton Sch. of Fin. & Commerce, A Study of Mutual Funds, H.R. Rep. No. 87-2274, at 1 (1962).

proposals and bargaining between the SEC and the Investment Company Institute, the industry group that represented, and still represents, a vast majority of the industry.[19]

The Wharton report initially recommended subjecting fees to judicial review for reasonableness. The ICI opposed such rate regulation. A 1967 Wharton conference produced the compromise of imposing a fiduciary obligation on the adviser.[20] A 1968 Senate bill added a rebuttable presumption of reasonableness of fee agreements approved by shareholder and independent director vote.[21] The following year the ICI and the SEC agreed to key elements of the final version of section 36(b)—a fiduciary duty, with the burden on the plaintiff to prove a breach.[22]

Several elements of the final version of section 36(b) suggest that the so-called fiduciary duty, on which Congress placed so much weight, was not really a fiduciary duty at all in the sense discussed in Part I.A. First, the subsection imposes the duty not on the fund's board, which technically exercised the control that is fundamental to fiduciary duties, but rather on the adviser with whom the board is contracting.[23] The subsection states that "the investment adviser of a registered investment company shall be deemed to have a fiduciary duty with respect to the receipt of compensation for services,"[24] and "no damages or other relief shall be granted against any person other than the recipient of such compensation or payments."[25] Second, the section avoids imputing misconduct to the investment adviser for receiving excessive fees by providing that no judicial finding of a breach of fiduciary duty under the subsection is a basis for violation of or remedies under other specified sections of the

---

[19] For general reviews of the legislative history summarized below, see William P. Rogers & James N. Benedict, Market Fund Management Fees: How Much Is Too Much?, 57 N.Y.U. L. Rev. 1059 (1982); Amy Yeung & Kristen J. Freeman, *Gartenberg, Jones*, and the Meaning of Fiduciary: A Legislative Investigation of Section 36(b), 35 Del. J. Corp. L. (forthcoming 2010), available at http://ssrn.com/abstract=1557349.

[20] See The Mutual Fund Management Fee, 115 U. Pa. L. Rev. 726 (1967) (conference transcript).

[21] S. 3724, 90th Cong. § 8(d) (1968).

[22] See Yeung & Freeman, *supra* note 19, at 26-27. 23 15 U.S.C. § 80a-35(b) (2006).

[23] 15 U.S.C. § 80a-25(b) (2006).

[24] *Id.*

[25] *Id.* § 35(b)(3).

securities laws.[26] Third, section 36(b) provides that "the plaintiff shall have the burden of proving a breach of fiduciary duty" although the strict prohibition against self-dealing and the presumed information asymmetry between the fiduciary and the beneficiary support imposing the burden of proof on the fiduciary.[27]

Section 36(b) was born to fail. Given fund directors' practical difficulty of firing the investment adviser that established the fund, as well as the close relationship between advisers and boards,[28] a court cannot realistically assume that the fee was negotiated by a fully disinterested board.[29] Yet the fiduciary duty added in 1970 was too weak to provide the discipline such boards needed. This set the stage for the 40 years of litigation to follow.

D. *Post-36(b) Litigation and the* Gartenberg *Standard*

The previous section shows that section 36(b)'s fiduciary duty was conceived as a political compromise, in contrast to the carefully constrained functional role of fiduciary duties that developed under the common law. Congress did not fully consider how much judicial supervision was justified given the overall structure of mutual funds, or even what the structure of mutual funds should be. Moreover, it is unlikely that Congress or anyone else had a clear idea of what the fiduciary duty might entail. The courts were left to work out the details.

The Second Circuit's articulation of the *Gartenberg* standard established an equilibrium that survived for 30 years until Judge Easterbrook provoked a reevaluation.[30] The equilibrium was tenuous because the standard was never clear. The rule seems to stress the size of the fee—that is, whether it is disproportionate to the services rendered. This is at odds with section 36(b)'s legislative history discussed above, which shows that Congress adopted the fiduciary duty approach as a way to avoid rate regulation. The *Gartenberg* test arguably can be squared with this history by interpreting the

---

[26] *Id.* § 35(b)(6).

[27] *Id.* § 35(b)(1).

[28] See Camelia M. Kuhnen, Business Networks, Corporate Governance, and Contracting in the Mutual Fund Industry, 64 J. Fin. 2185 (2009) (finding connections between fund directors and advisers that cause them to hire one another).

[29] See Johnson, *supra* note 4.

[30] Jones v. Harris Assocs., 527 F.3d 627 (7th Cir. 2008).

standard as using the size of the fee only as circumstantial evidence of the board's independence and the existence of "arm's-length bargaining."[31] However, the court's use of "and" separates the "disproportionate" and "arm's-length bargaining" aspects of the test.[32] Moreover, *Gartenberg* admits consideration of other factors, including the amount and role of funds' competition for investors and the process of approving the fees.[33] Courts accordingly have significant leeway under *Gartenberg* as to what factors to emphasize.[34]

Gartenberg's "so disproportionately large" standard coupled with its placement of the burden of proof on the plaintiff has proved an insuperable hurdle for plaintiffs. Not one has won at trial in hundreds of post-*Gartenberg* cases.[35] Nevertheless, the cases are still costly. Todd Henderson's study of 36(b) litigation estimates that cases applying the *Gartenberg* standard "likely involved over 1600 lawyers filing nearly 1000 motions and about 1500 legal briefs, and generating over 1400 judicial orders," that defendants' total costs in cases tried post-*Gartenberg* are about $1.3 billion, and that cases filed and settled before a written judicial opinion cost defendants an additional $21.6 billion for a total post-*Gartenberg* cost of $23 billion.[36] Despite these costs, section 36(b) litigation probably has little effect on investment adviser behavior. The amounts work out to a litigation "tax" of about $125,000 per year for each of 8,000 mutual funds, which may not be a large enough portion of the investment advisers' revenue to motivate them to significantly change their practices.[37]

---

[31] Gartenberg v. Merrill Lynch Asset Mgmt., Inc., 694 F.2d 923, 928 (2d Cir. 1982).

[32] *Id.;* See Yeung & Freeman, *supra* note 19, at 34 n.203.

[33] 694 F.2d 923, 929–30. See John C. Coates IV & R. Glenn Hubbard, Competition in the Mutual Fund Industry: Evidence and Implications for Policy, 33 J. Corp. L. 151, 209-10 (2007). However, courts have given evidence of the extent of market competition little or no weight. *Id.* at 209 n.207.

[34] For a critical analysis of *Gartenberg* and its flawed economic understanding, see Br. for Cato Institute as Amicus Curiae Supporting Resp't 27-31, Jones v. Harris Assocs., 559 U.S. _____, 130 S. Ct. 1418 (2010) (No. 08-586), available at http://www.cato.org/pub_display.php?pub_id=10508.

[35] Johnson, *supra* note 4, at 500, 519; James D. Cox & John W. Payne, Mutual Fund Expense Disclosures; A Behavior Perspective, 83 Wash. U. L. Q. 907, 923 (2005).

[36] M. Todd Henderson, Justifying Jones, U. Chi. L. Rev. (forthcoming) (Univ. of Chi. Law Sch. John M. Olin L. & Econ., Working Paper No. 491 at 12, 2009), available at http://ssrn.com/abstract=1499410.

[37] *Id.* at 13 & n.42.

Moreover, Henderson reports conversations with fund board members indicating that they ignore litigation risk in management decisions because they view the incidence and cost of litigation as unrelated to the merits of individual cases.[38]

This system's biggest beneficiaries are plaintiffs' lawyers, who collect from settlements even without any wins at trial. Indeed, then-leading plaintiffs' lawyer Abe Pomerantz had a seat at the table when section 36(b) was being drafted.[39] Plaintiffs' lawyers can extract at least some of defendants' avoided discovery costs in settlement, particularly if the case survives a motion to dismiss or summary judgment.

Investment advisers might seem to have a significant incentive to fight this "tax" by banding together to fight the suits, thereby raising plaintiffs' costs. They can easily coordinate over litigation or a political fix because almost all of them are members of the ICI. Why do they not press for more judicial supervision of settlements, or for a statutory amendment that eliminates or sharply restricts litigation? One potential reason is that mutual fund advisers might rather pay a litigation tax and agree to "prophylactic" settlements prescribing breakpoints in fees than risk the rate regulation the fiduciary duty was intended to avoid.[40]

Other interest groups also have reason to support, or at least not oppose, the current regulatory structure and the fiduciary litigation that flows from it. The SEC gets to use fund boards to maintain at least the appearance of regulation, without actually having to devote more of its limited budget to actively policing fees at thousands of mutual funds.[41] Lawyers and others get to serve on these boards,

---

[38] *Id.* at 13-14.

[39] Yeung & Freeman, *supra* note 19, at 19 n.100.

[40] See Henderson, supra note 36, at 20-21 (noting that mutual funds would prefer a small litigation tax to focusing political attention on the problem of adviser pay); John Morley & Quinn Curtis, Taking Exit Rights Seriously: Why Governance and Fee Litigation Don't Work in Mutual Funds, Yale L.J. (forthcoming) (Yale L. & Econ. Res. Paper No. 403 at 66, 2010), available at http://ssrn.com/abstract=1547162 (noting that investment companies might prefer to "cultivate regulators' faith in boards as a way of convincing them that more invasive regulation is unnecessary").

[41] See John C. Coates IV, Reforming the Taxation and Regulation of Mutual Funds: A Comparative Legal and Economic Analysis, 1 J. Legal Analysis 591, 629 (2009) (noting that the SEC would rather spend its limited budget on enforcement of existing law than on reform).

legal academics get to work as litigation experts and consultants, and Congress avoids revisiting a regulatory tangle on which it spent eight years in the 1960s. Sophisticated investors have little reason to protest because they can easily choose and exit funds, including hedge funds and other vehicles. The only relevant group that does not seem to be accounted for in this regulatory process is the unsophisticated investors for whose benefit the ICA supposedly was enacted.

E. Jones v. Harris Associates: *Seventh Circuit*

It was left to Judge Easterbrook and his Seventh Circuit panel to cast doubt on the *Gartenberg* equilibrium. *Jones* involved fees paid by Oakmark Fund to its adviser, Harris Associates. Plaintiff investors argued for rejection of *Gartenberg* because this test would wrongly emphasize the fees paid by similar funds (a test Harris probably would pass) over one that compared Oakmark's fees with those Harris charged its unaffiliated institutional clients (which Harris might flunk).[42]

Faced squarely with the issue of *Gartenberg*'s validity, Judge Easterbrook threw out the test and replaced it with one that was even less friendly to plaintiffs. Easterbrook reasoned that "just as plaintiffs are skeptical of *Gartenberg* because it relies too heavily on markets, we are skeptical about *Gartenberg* because it relies too little on markets."[43] Rather than worrying about the fund board's control over the adviser's fees or the difference between fund and institutional fees, Easterbrook emphasized the apparently vigorous competition among fund companies for investors.[44] Since returns depend on fees, he said, "mutual funds have a powerful reason to keep [fees] low unless higher fees are associated with higher return on investment."[45] Firms must cater at least to "sophisticated investors who . . . create a competitive pressure that protects the rest."[46]

Consistent with his emphasis on markets, Judge Easterbrook rejected the idea that section 36(b)'s fiduciary duty required fees to

[42] Jones, 527 F.3d at 631.

[43] *Id.* at 632.

[44] *Id.* at 633.

[45] *Id.* at 632.

[46] *Id.* at 634 (citing Alan Schwartz & Louis Wilde, Imperfect Information in Markets for Contract Terms, 69 Va. L. Rev. 1387 (1983)).

"be 'reasonable' in relation to a judicially created standard."[47] Rather, he said:

> A fiduciary duty differs from rate regulation. A fiduciary must make full disclosure and play no tricks but is not subject to a cap on compensation. The trustees (and in the end investors, who vote with their feet and dollars), rather than a judge or jury, determine how much advisory services are worth.[48]

The federal securities laws help ensure full disclosure, and no one complained about disclosure. Judge Easterbrook also found support in the rules for corporations and attorneys' fees, where there is also no reasonableness review because markets constrain executive and attorney compensation just as they do the compensation of fund advisers.[49]

Although Judge Easterbrook emphasized competition in the market for mutual funds, there is reason to believe that he was actually more concerned with the problem of excessive litigation under *Gartenberg* discussed above.[50] Easterbrook noted that "regulating advisory fees through litigation is unlikely to do more good than harm,"[51] and that even imperfect markets "remain superior to a 'just price' system administered by the judiciary. However weak competition may be at weeding out errors, the judicial process is worse—for judges can't be turned out of office or have their salaries cut if they display poor business judgment."[52]

Todd Henderson explains *Jones* primarily in light of this concern with the judicial process.[53] Skepticism with judicial review could explain why Easterbrook swept away the *Gartenberg* multi-factor standard, rather than merely tinkering with it.

Judge Easterbrook's description of mutual fund markets may be more a response to plaintiffs' emphasis on Congress's supposed

---

[47] Jones, 527 F.3d at 632.

[48] *Id.*

[49] *Id.* at 633.

[50] See Henderson, *supra* note 36, at 6.

[51] 527 F.3d at 634 (citing Coates & Hubbard, *supra* note 33).

[52] *Id.* at 633.

[53] Henderson, *supra* note 36.

concern with the market of the late 1960s than positive support for a limited fiduciary duty. Easterbrook noted plaintiffs' position

> that because many members of Congress deemed competition inadequate (and regulation essential) in 1970, we must act as if competition remains weak today. Why? Congress did not enact its members' *beliefs;* it enacted a text. A text authorizing the SEC or the judiciary to set rates would be binding no matter how market conditions change. Section 36(b) does not create a rate-regulation mechanism, and plaintiffs' proposal to create such a mechanism in 2008 cannot be justified by suppositions about the market conditions of 1970.[54]

Easterbrook thus stressed that Congress did not, in fact, enact rate regulation—whatever market conditions may have been in 1970. He only secondarily observed that, even if those conditions might once have informed congressional intent, they have changed.

While Judge Easterbrook had ample justification for rejecting *Gartenberg,* problems with his analysis undermined his ability to establish a post-*Gartenberg* equilibrium. First, limiting the rule to disclosure essentially assumes that the fund or its investors are directly negotiating the fee in their own interests. Corporate law requires approval by disinterested directors. This leaves an opening for critics to argue that a stricter rule is necessary for mutual funds given the effective lack of arm's length bargaining between funds and advisers.[55]

Second, Easterbrook's tight constraint on liability has a loophole:

> It is possible to imagine compensation so unusual that a court will infer that deceit must have occurred, or that the persons responsible for decision have abdicated—for example, if a university's board of trustees decides to pay the president $50 million a year, when no other president of a comparable institution receives more than $2 million—but no court would inquire whether a salary normal among similar institutions is excessive."[56]

---

[54] 527 F.3d at 633 (emphasis in original).

[55] See Johnson, *supra* note 4.

[56] 527 F.3d at 632.

Thus, in *Jones* as in *Gartenberg*, the amount of the fee can circumstantially indicate breach of the board's duty. The difference between the cases lies mainly in Easterbrook's emphasis on evidence of clear wrongdoing and his willingness to accept a "salary normal among similar institutions" to show the absence of wrongdoing. Because charging a "normal" fee helps insulate the adviser from liability, this test facilitates a kind of rate regulation by the industry. Although this addresses Easterbrook's concern with excessive litigation by enabling the development of a clear and predictable rule, it hamstrings free-wheeling competition by advisers. Indeed, we will see below that this problem inheres in having boards set fees subject to judicial review.

Third, Judge Easterbrook's discussion of the market for mutual funds created an unfortunate sideshow to his argument based on legislative intent. The market was a hard sell in 2009 given the financial crisis and mounting skepticism concerning executive compensation. This enabled critics of the market for mutual funds to turn the sideshow into the main event.

Judge Posner, dissenting from the court's denial of rehearing en banc, argued that "[t]he panel bases its rejection of *Gartenberg* mainly on an economic analysis that is ripe for reexamination on the basis of growing indications that executive compensation in large publicly traded firms often is excessive because of the feeble incentives of boards of directors to police compensation."[57] Posner then cites a host of articles critical of corporate executive compensation by everybody from Lucian Bebchuk to Ben Stein,[58] concluding that "[c]ompetition in product and capital markets can't be counted on to solve the problem because the same structure of incentives operates on all large corporations and similar entities, including mutual funds."[59]

Posner also emphasized the deficiencies in mutual funds' hiring of advisers, citing evidence of favoritism and networks and the absence of arm's-length bargaining.[60] Because advisers face a real market for pension funds and other institutional clients, Posner suggested that this market provides a better standard than the suspect

---

[57] Jones, 537 F.3d at 730.

[58] *Id.*

[59] *Id.*

[60] *Id.* at 730-31.

market for mutual fund fees.[61] Posner concluded that "the one-sided character of the panel's analysis," together with the issue's importance and the circuit split, warranted hearing the case *en banc*.[62]

The circuit split resulting from Judge Easterbrook's rejection of *Gartenberg*, plus the sharp disagreement between two leading market-oriented jurists, made it almost inevitable that the Supreme Court would take the case. If Easterbrook hoped this would lead to the adoption of a less litigation-friendly standard, he was disappointed.

F. Jones v. Harris Associates: *Supreme Court*

The Court's unanimous opinion authored by Justice Alito rejected the Easterbrook rule and accepted *Gartenberg's* "basic formulation of what 36(b) requires."[63] This is not surprising given the fact that both parties and virtually all of the amici rejected Easterbrook's approach and endorsed *Gartenberg*. The Court's opinion found support in a famous Supreme Court corporate case involving the fiduciary duties of controlling shareholders, which looked for the "earmarks of an arm's-length bargain," holding that "this formulation expresses the meaning of the phrase 'fiduciary duty' in §36(b)."[64]

Although the Supreme Court seems to adopt the *Gartenberg* rule and reject the Easterbrook test, it actually endorses a new rule that, like Easterbrook's rule, reflects concern with the open-ended way the courts had applied *Gartenberg* and the litigation costs resulting from that approach. The Court warns that the *Gartenberg* standard "does not call for judicial second-guessing of informed board decisions," at least in the sense of "precise calculation of fees representative of arm's-length bargaining."[65] Justice Clarence Thomas's concurring opinion reinforces this point, calling attention to the above language and the Court's emphasis on the "degree of deference that is due a board's decision to approve an adviser's fees."[66] Thus,

---

[61] *Id.* at 731-32.

[62] *Id.* at 732-33.

[63] Jones v. Harris Assocs., 130 S. Ct. 1418, 1426 (2010).

[64] *Id.* at 1427 (citing Pepper v. Litton, 308 U.S. 295, 306-07 (1939)).

[65] *Id.* at 1430. This is consistent with Alito's concern with litigation costs as a federal appeals judge. See Larry E. Ribstein, Justice Alito on Business, Forbes.com, Jan. 13, 2006, http://www.forbes.com/2006/01/13/alito-ribstein-comentary-cx_lr_0116alito.html.

[66] Jones, 130 S. Ct. at 1431 (Thomas, J., concurring).

according to Justice Thomas, the Court did *not* "endorse the '*Gartenberg* standard'" and "does not countenance the free-ranging judicial 'fairness' review of fees that *Gartenberg* could be read to authorize."[67]

Despite the Court's recognition of the need for deference to board decisions, the continued existence of an open-ended, multi-factor standard left lower courts with significant freedom to question those decisions, thereby generating litigation, settlements, and attorneys' fee awards. While plaintiffs probably still cannot win at trial, which should please investment advisers, they can at least still sue and thereby purchase a lottery ticket that can get them a share of defendants' discovery costs. Faced with a motion to dismiss or for summary judgment, a judge can employ either the board-discretion-burden-on-plaintiff approach and grant the motion or the possibly-disproportionate-non-arm's-length approach and deny it. The Supreme Court's rejection of the Easterbrook rule, if not its reasoning, could make courts reluctant to accept compliance with industry standards as a safe harbor. *Jones*'s only effect may be to reduce defendants' chances of actually losing at trial compared with prior law, and thereby increase their freedom to charge what the market will bear subject to section 36(b)'s litigation tax.

Although the Supreme Court's resolution in *Jones* is not ideal, the Court cannot do much more. The basic problem with section 36(b) is the corporate governance structure Congress has imposed on open-end mutual funds. Given the corporate framework's unsuitability in this context, it should not be surprising that the courts have not been able to turn the statute into something that works in the real world.

II. The Mismatch of Corporate Governance and Investor Exit

A basic problem with regulation of mutual funds under the Investment Company Act is Congress's assumption that mutual funds should be governed like corporations. This assumption is faulty because mutual funds lack the critical corporate feature of "capital lock-in," or rules that protect managers' control of the cash from investors' reach.[68] The corporate structure was designed to deal with

---

[67] *Id.* at 1431 (majority opinion).

[68] See Margaret M. Blair, Locking in Capital: What Corporate Law Achieved for Business Organizers in the Nineteenth Century, 51 UCLA L. Rev. 387 (2003).

the far-flung business enterprises created during the Industrial Revolution to coordinate the production and sale of products.[69] This task
required giving control of the firm's resources and investors' money
to the firm's managers. Unlike typical partnership-based firms, corporate shareholders could not unilaterally dissolve the firm or otherwise take their money out.[70] Managers' power over corporate
resources necessitates mechanisms ensuring the managers' accountability to investors in exercising this power, including investors'
power to vote, sell their shares, and sue for breach of fiduciary duty.

Given corporations' importance to industrial development, it may
be easy to forget that the corporate form is not the only feasible
structure for organizing even large-scale businesses. What I have
called "uncorporate" business forms—including general or limited
partnership and limited liability companies—provide for a lower
level of "capital lock-in" by promising to repurchase investors'
shares, dissolve under certain circumstances or at a particular time,
or regularly distribute cash to investors.[71] These devices apply the
discipline of the capital markets by effectively forcing managers to
induce current owners to keep their cash in the firm, or to continually
raise cash from outside investors. Unlike corporate shareholders,
who are generally limited to selling their shares for a value that
reflects the buyer's continued exposure to the firm's current management, uncorporate owners have some ability to free their cash from
managers' control. A corporate shareholder, by contrast, can accomplish this only by taking control of the company in which he owns
shares and replacing its managers. The choice between corporate
and uncorporate forms involves an overall meshing of provisions.
It may make little sense for a firm to both forgo the benefits of
corporate-type capital lock-in by adopting the uncorporate form
and incurring the costs of corporate-type accountability, particularly
including voting and fiduciary duties.

This background enables a full appreciation of the difference
between a mutual fund and a corporation. An open-end mutual

---

[69] See generally Alfred D. Chandler Jr., The Visible Hand: The Managerial Revolution
in American Business (1977).

[70] For an analysis of this corporate feature and comparison with partnerships, see
Ribstein, *supra* note 14, at 65–94.

[71] See *id.* at 15-38.

fund is the extreme form of an uncorporation, or what might be called an un-uncorporation. Unlike partners or limited liability company (LLC) members, who can sell only at particular times or on certain conditions, mutual fund investors' redemption rights usually are subject to few restrictions.[72] Thus, while some uncorporations, such as hedge funds organized as limited partnerships, need some corporate-type protections, mutual fund investors do not because they have the ultimate power to discipline managers by simply removing capital from managers they do not like whenever they want. Accordingly, it has been said that, "[f]rom an economic perspective, the protection of redeemable shares is arguably more important in supporting competition than any other aspect of the current legal framework."[73] The protection provided by the right of exit accordingly eliminates the need not only for fiduciary duties but also for the board itself.[74] The price investors pay for this accountability is managers' inability to engage in long-term enterprise building because the firm's cash can fly away at any minute. But this is a small price in an open-end mutual fund whose main objective is achieving portfolio diversification rather than long-term asset management.

A possible response to the argument that mutual funds can dispense with corporate accountability mechanisms is that this may leave unsophisticated mutual fund investors who do not take advantage of their exit right even worse off than unsophisticated corporate shareholders. Unlike in corporations, sophisticated mutual fund investors have little interest in changing the management of their mutual funds on behalf of all the investors because the sophisticates

---

[72] This observation is subject to potential exit costs from taxes or back-end "load" fees. However, for many investors these costs are low or minimal. The contrast between open-end mutual funds and other unincorporated business entities suggests that the regulatory distinction between mutual funds and hedge funds is backwards. While mutual funds are subject to detailed requirements regarding the board of directors, see 15 U.S.C. § 80a-10 (2006)), and shareholder voting, *id.* § 80a-13, there are no such requirements for domestic hedge funds. However, since hedge fund limited partners normally are subject to restrictions on withdrawal, they arguably should have more governance rights than mutual fund investors, rather than fewer.

[73] Coates & Hubbard, *supra* note 33, at 162 (noting that it is corporate-type capital lock-in that creates a need for a "mediating hierarch" who can watch out for locked-in investors).

[74] See Morley & Curtis, *supra* note 40.

can cash out whenever they want.[75] However, even if the "left behind" investors need some protection from high fees, fiduciary duties are not the answer. For the same reason that sophisticated investors have no incentive to help the unsophisticated investors by changing the fund's management, they have no incentive to use their fiduciary rights to fix the fund's fees.[76] Plaintiffs' lawyers step into the role of the unsophisticated shareholders' "protectors" in bringing derivative suits, but without the potential for discipline that large shareholders bring to corporate securities class actions.[77]

The problems with the mutual fund derivative suit under section 36(b) were analyzed in a Delaware state court action involving a hedge fund organized as a Delaware limited partnership that was not subject to section 36(b).[78] The partnership invested in publicly traded securities and revalued the limited partners' capital accounts daily. The limited partners sued the general partner for over-withdrawing its capital account. Although actions devaluing the partnership's assets normally would give rise to a derivative claim on behalf of the partnership, the court characterized the suit as a direct action on behalf of the individual partners. The court reasoned "that the operation and function of the Fund as specified in the Agreement diverge so radically from the traditional corporate model that the claims made in the complaint must be brought as direct claims."[79] Specifically, that because the partners redeem their shares rather than sell them, the court noted devaluation of partnership assets

---

[75] See Donald C. Langevoort, Private Litigation to Enforce Fiduciary Duties in Mutual Funds: Derivative Suits, Disinterested Directors and the Ideology of Investor Sovereignty, 83 Wash. U.L.Q. 1017, 1031 (2005).

[76] See Morley & Curtis, *supra* note 40. This is not necessarily to say that unsophisticated mutual fund investors are not injured or that they should not be able to sue for deception or outright theft. Rather, the point here is that fiduciary litigation is ineffective to deal with excessive fund fees, the specific problem addressed by section 36(b).

[77] Supervision of litigation by large shareholders has been regarded as a possible solution to the problem of improvident securities class actions. See Elliott Weiss & John S. Beckerman, Let the Money Do the Monitoring: How Institutional Investors Can Reduce Agency Costs in Securities Class Actions, 104 Yale L.J. 2053 (1995). This article spurred the "lead plaintiff" provision of the Private Securities Litigation Reform Act of 1995. See 15 U.S.C. § 78u- 4(a)(3) (2006).

[78] Anglo Am. Sec. Fund, L.P. v. S.R. Global Int'l Fund, L.P, 829 A.2d 143 (Del. Ch. 2003).

[79] *Id.* at 152.

affects only current partners and not later partners.[80] Moreover, later partners would get a windfall if the partnership were to recover damages after the partners' admission on account of a pre-admission injury. Therefore, said the court, "[c]haracterizing the plaintiffs' claims as derivative would thus have the perverse effect of denying standing (and therefore recovery) to parties who were actually injured by the challenged transactions while granting ultimate recovery (and therefore a windfall) to parties who were not."[81] In other words, because the limited partnership functioned like an open-end mutual fund, a remedy on behalf of the fund was inappropriate.

In short, given open-end funds' redemption right, Georgetown University law professor Donald Langevoort is correct in describing mutual funds as "products—no different, really, from health care, insurance, bank deposits, residential real estate, and other important settings where consumers are often less than diligent."[82] University of Pennsylvania law professor Jill Fisch also argues for the product analogy.[83] It arguably follows that consumers of mutual fund products no more need the protection of directors than do consumers of other products.

The mutual fund governance structure that the ICA imposes on mutual funds is not only the wrong way to protect mutual fund investors, but it levies an additional cost in deterring competition among investment advisers. The corporate governance model, including empowering the board to protect mutual fund investors, necessarily entails judicial supervision of directors via fiduciary duties. Since the adviser establishes and finances the fund, it is unrealistic to expect the adviser–fund director relationship to be purely arm's-length,[84] and therefore the fund board to be disinterested.[85] Accordingly, the board's existence necessarily creates a conflict, which in turn requires judicial oversight. However, courts,

---

[80] *Id.*

[81] *Id.* at 153.

[82] Langevoort, *supra* note 75, at 1037.

[83] Jill E. Fisch, Rethinking the Regulation of Securities Intermediaries, 158 U. Pa. L. Rev. (forthcoming 2010) (Univ. of Pa. Law Sch. Inst. for L. & Econ., Research Paper No. 10-04), available at http://papers.ssrn.com/sol3/papers.cfm?abstract_id=1573768##.

[84] See Wallison & Litan, *supra* note 12, at 14 (noting that the adviser expects control because it sets up the fund).

[85] See Johnson, *supra* note 4 (questioning the disinterest of independent fund directors who are considered "independent" under current law).

wary of their ability to second-guess board decisions, necessarily look for some benchmark to apply, such as the funds' costs,[86] or the industry norms. Fund managers then might rather hew to the benchmark than look for profits in new efficiencies that the courts might force them to disgorge.

Langevoort laments that mutual fund advisers and directors have adopted the "ideology of consumer sovereignty" and so feel less obligated to act as real fiduciaries.[87] He accordingly suggests making the duty more fiduciary-like, including by tightening the standards for dismissing derivative claims, thereby encouraging the development of more fiduciary-like norms of investment adviser and mutual fund director conduct. But, like it or not, mutual funds are fundamentally like products given investors' exit rights, as Langevoort himself recognizes.[88] Applying the fiduciary duty to what seem to be ordinary market transactions therefore might have little effect on behavior and might even weaken fiduciary norms by confusing them with consumer norms.[89]

The lesson of the above discussion is that the courts cannot fix the section 36(b) duty simply by changing the standard because the problems with the duty are inherent in Congress's misbegotten imposition of a corporate governance structure on open-end mutual funds. Congress added the fiduciary duty when it became obvious that directors and other corporate trappings could not adequately protect investors. Loosening the standard would ignore the conflict built into the board's role in mutual fund governance. Tightening the standard would impose still more costly judicial supervision and constraints on competition that are unnecessary in light of investors' ability to exit mutual funds. The only viable solution is to dismantle the corporate governance structure in the Investment Company Act.

III. The Deeper Problem with Federal Regulation of Mutual Funds

We have seen that the basic problem in *Jones* lies not with the courts' approach to applying section 36(b) but with the statute the

---

[86] See Wallison & Litan, *supra* note 12, at 76–80.

[87] Langevoort, *supra* note 75, at 1019.

[88] See *supra* text accompanying note 75.

[89] See generally Larry E. Ribstein, Law v. Trust, 81 B.U. L. Rev. 553 (2001) (analyzing the law's effect on social norms).

courts had to apply. The problem lies deeper than section 36(b)'s fiduciary duty, which itself responded to the Investment Company Act's dysfunctional corporate governance structure. This part suggests that the problem goes even deeper than the particular governance structure Congress imposed on mutual funds, encompassing the entire concept of federal regulation of mutual funds' internal governance. Congress should stick with what the federal government does best in financial regulation—giving investors the facts and letting them decide where to invest. Even if disclosure does not fully protect investors, the alternative of federally mandating governance structure is doomed to costly failure, as the sad history of *Jones* has shown.

A. State vs. Federal Regulation of Governance

Critics of captive boards and empty duties in mutual funds[90] should ask how such dysfunction could arise in what "may be the most heavily regulated sector of the financial services industry."[91] The federal government did not just happen to get mutual fund regulation wrong in 1940 and 1970, but it continues to err as long as it attempts to regulate the internal governance structure of mutual funds or, for that matter, any business associations.

The problem is not that Congress is particularly error-prone, but that it lacks the error-correction mechanism inherent in the state market for internal governance of firms. In the absence of federal regulation of governance structure, states could provide various structures from which investment companies could choose. States' ability to provide choice and experimentation derives from the "internal affairs" choice of law rule, which ensures that each firm's choice of state law is enforced wherever its place of business and investors are located.[92] This rule enables firms to choose the law that best fits their needs. States can develop a broad menu of firms that evolves over time to meet changing business needs. Investment funds can experiment with different structures that, for example, trade off investor exit rights with investor voice and fiduciary litigation, and provide for different types of compensation. States can

---

[90] See Wallison & Litan, *supra* note 12; Morley & Curtis, *supra* note 40.

[91] Coates & Hubbard, *supra* note 33, at 162.

[92] See generally, Larry E. Ribstein & Erin Ann O'Hara, Corporations and the Market for Law, 2008 U. Ill. L. Rev. 661.

compete regarding not only the substance of their laws but also their legal infrastructures of courts, legal rules, and lawyers. Moreover, investment companies themselves can experiment with variations within general state statutory frameworks.

The flexibility, variation, and experimentation facilitated by the state system are necessary for the efficient governance of firms. A business association statute entails choosing provisions from a broad range of potential alternatives and assembling them into a coherent whole.[93] We have seen that the basic problem with federally dictated mutual fund governance is that investor redemption rights do not mesh well with the corporate trappings of boards, voting, and fiduciary duties. Legislatures must also decide, among other things, which terms are default rules and which are mandatory, the choices they will offer investors, and which types of firms to design terms for. No single legislature has enough information to get this right even at the time the statute is passed. Also, legislation necessarily is produced by contending interest groups rather than by disinterested lawgivers determined to maximize social welfare. And even if a legislature did come up with the right law as of the time of enactment, the business world changes rapidly. Accordingly, it is critical for competing jurisdictions to be able to fix mistakes and adapt to changing times.

The federal system's dynamic quality has been particularly evident with respect to the evolution of business associations.[94] U.S. law initially offered firms the choice between the corporate form designed for large, often publicly traded firms, and the partnership form for small firms. Tax and other laws and the evolving nature of firms have complicated these choices. The states provided new organizational forms, and firms' choices changed over time. During the mid-20th century the dominant business form for smaller firms was the closely held corporation. The LLC rapidly emerged from obscurity over 20 years and by the 2000s began to replace the corporate form for closely held firms.

To be sure, there is no guarantee that optimal business forms and state laws ultimately will dominate under a state system. States might cater to fund sponsors by designing structures that attract

---

[93] See generally, Ribstein, *supra* note 14, at 15–38.
[94] See *id.* at 39–136 (tracing this evolution).

funds, fees, and business for local lawyers.[95] Also, investment advisers might favor structures such as corporate boards and fiduciary duties that provide the appearance but not, as we have seen, the reality of discipline. Unsophisticated mutual fund investors may pay little attention to organizational form or applicable law. Accordingly, a state system may end up as a "race to the bottom," toward laxity rather than reasonable regulation.

However, before concluding from these undesirable possibilities that a mandatory federal regime is better than a state system, it is important to consider the former's defects. Imperfect competition may be better than no competition at all. The ICA locked mutual fund governance into the model that had developed in the nascent mutual fund industry during the 1920s despite numerous major changes in the investment industry since 1940, including the rise of open-end funds and significantly increased competition. Instead of 51 jurisdictions enacting new or revised laws from which investment companies could choose, the evolutionary process was left to a single modestly funded agency, the Securities and Exchange Commission, which has viewed its own power narrowly.[96] Although funds are technically formed under and governed by state law (mainly Delaware, Maryland, and Massachusetts),[97] the corporate structure built into the ICA constricts the range within which state laws can compete. Federal regulation is interpreted exclusively by federal courts throughout the country with only rare intervention by the Supreme Court. This system subjects mutual funds to different standards across the circuits, applied haphazardly based on where plaintiffs' lawyers choose to litigate. Changing financial regulation requires moving proposals through the cumbersome federal legislative process, and generally occurs in the panicked atmosphere of a financial bust.[98]

---

[95] See Langevoort, *supra* note 75, at 1036.

[96] Coates, *supra* note 40, at 627.

[97] For discussions of competing state structures for mutual funds, see John H. Langbein, The Secret Life of the Trust: The Trust as an Instrument of Commerce, 107 Yale L.J. 165, 187-88 (1997); Robert H. Sitkoff, Trust as "Uncorporation": A Research Agenda, 2005 U. Ill. L. Rev. 31. See also Wallace Wen Yeu Wang, Corporate versus Contractual Mutual Funds: An Evolution of Structure and Governance, 69 Wash. L. Rev. 927 (1994) (providing an international comparison between the U.S. "corporate" approach to mutual fund governance and the "contractual" approach in other countries).

[98] See Larry E. Ribstein, Bubble Laws, 40 Hous. L. Rev. 77 (2003).

Congress, the courts, and the SEC—no matter how wise, informed, and well meaning they are—cannot create a dynamic system comparable to the market for state law. Accordingly, efforts to fix federal law will inevitably fall short. For example, Peter Wallison and Robert Litan propose a new structure they call a "managed investment trust," an actively managed version of the unit investment trusts that antedated the Investment Company Act.[99] This is a move in the right direction under this article's approach because it would eliminate the board, which is an unnecessary corporate trapping. However, the dysfunction in the existing mutual fund structures created by Congress would remain. Moreover, adding one more choice would not alone create a dynamic system that can keep any structure updated to current business developments.

B. The Appropriate Scope of Federal Regulation: Beyond Disclosure

Beyond regulation of the governance of investment companies such as mutual funds, there is still arguably a role for the federal regulation of disclosure. This is essentially the approach taken by the federal securities laws. As William O. Douglas, chair of the SEC before serving on the Supreme Court, said of the Securities Act of 1933: "All the Act pretends to do is to require the 'truth about securities' at the time of issue, and to impose a penalty for failure to tell the truth. Once it is told, the matter is left to the investor."[100]

The main argument against relying on disclosure for mutual funds is that it may not fix what some believe to be a fundamentally defective market for investment adviser fees.[101] To some extent, the problem is that many investors are inexperienced or unsophisticated and therefore are suckers for advertising or the manipulation of disclosures. There is evidence, for example, that high fees actually

---

[99] Wallison & Litan, *supra* note 12, at 99-120.

[100] William O. Douglas & George E. Bates, The Federal Securities Act of 1933, 43 Yale L.J. 171, 171 (1933).

[101] For arguments critical of the market for investment adviser fees, see William A. Birdthistle, Investment Indiscipline: A Behavioral Approach to Mutual Fund Jurisprudence, 2010 U. Ill. L. Rev. 61; Alan R. Palmiter & Ahmed E. Taha, Mutual Fund Investors: Divergent Profiles, 2008 Colum. Bus. L. Rev. 934; Br. of Robert Litan, Joseph Mason & Ian Ayers as Amici Curiae Supporting Pet'rs, Jones v. Harris Assocs., 559 U.S. ____, 130 S. Ct. 1418 (2010) (No. 08-586), 2009 WL 1759017.

correlate with bad performance,[102] and that investors with below-average financial literacy feel overwhelmed by the information required to choose funds and are attracted to high-cost advertised and broker-sold funds.[103] One leading study shows that investors avoid front-end load fees or commissions but are not less likely to buy funds with higher expenses and are actually *more* likely to buy funds with higher marketing expenses, suggesting that they are sensitive to advertising and to more salient fees but are not otherwise very sophisticated about fees.[104] More experienced mutual fund investors are less likely to pay front-end loads than first-time buyers, but even these investors do not avoid high operating expenses. Mutual fund advisers apparently have figured all this out, since over the last 40 years operating expenses generally have increased while funds have tended to drop or lower front-end load fees.

Problems in the mutual fund market may not be limited to unsophisticated investors. Professors James Choi, David Laibson, and Brigitte Madrian conducted an experiment of mutual fund purchases by Harvard staff members, Wharton MBA students, and college students recruited on the Harvard campus.[105] The staff members were overwhelmingly college educated, and 60 percent also had graduate school education. The MBA and undergraduate subjects reported average SAT scores in the 98th and 99th percentiles, respectively, and all three groups had above-average financial literacy. The subjects were told to invest in S&P 500 Index funds; were given the funds' prospectuses, which disclosed fees; and were rewarded for maximizing the returns on their portfolios, which meant reducing expenses since the returns were based on the same index. The subjects generally failed to minimize fees.[106] Only the MBAs thought

---

[102] See Mark M. Carhart, On the Persistence in Mutual Fund Performance, 52 J. Fin. 57 (1997); Javier Gil-Bazo & Pablo Ruiz-Verdú, The Relation between Price and Performance in the Mutual Fund Industry, 64 J. Fin. 2153 (2009) (modeling how this result can occur even with competition).

[103] John A. Haslem, Why Does Mutual Fund Advertising Work? Some Complementary Evidence (July 1, 2009) (unpublished, available at http://papers.ssrn.com/sol3/papers.cfm?abstract_id = 1428620) (summarizing studies).

[104] Brad M. Barber, Terrance Odean & Lu Zheng, Out of Sight, Out of Mind: The Effects of Expenses on Mutual Fund Flows, 78 J. Bus. 2095 (2005).

[105] James J. Choi, David Laibson & Brigitte C. Madrian, Why Does the Law of One Price Fail? An Experiment on Index Mutual Funds, 23 Rev. Fin. Stud. 1405 (2010).

[106] *Id.* at 1407.

fees mattered most to their decisions, and even they did not choose significantly lower-fee funds than the college students. The subjects emphasized annualized returns of the fund—although prospectus returns were not comparable across funds—and relying on returns caused subjects to pay higher expenses.

A different picture of mutual fund fees arguably emerges from examining the overall structure of competition in the mutual fund market. Professors John Coates and R. Glenn Hubbard note the vast increase in the size of the mutual fund industry since the 1960s and summarize evidence consistent with competition in the industry.[107] They explain contrary evidence by such factors as differences in investor search costs and changes in how funds are distributed, including through mutual fund supermarkets, which are more convenient but costly to maintain.[108]

Part of the difficulty of reconciling this evidence is trying to determine what mutual fund investors want. As Coates and Hubbard discuss, some funds cost more than others because investors value their services, such as one-stop-shopping and easy exchange. Also, even if higher costs do not buy better service, they may serve as a bond to protect investors.[109] This reasonably assumes that investors are looking mainly for safety and reasonable returns rather than the highest possible returns. Since investors cannot easily determine safety and the likelihood of mismanagement from publicly available information, they would want advisers to have a lot of profits to lose if they do cheat. The bonding theory complicates any determination of when fund fees are too high.

There is a further question of whether any problems with the mutual fund market are distinct from those affecting consumer markets generally. For example, Florencia Marotta-Wurgler examines the extent to which consumers read online software contracts.[110]

---

[107] Coates & Hubbard, *supra* note 33, at 173-84.

[108] *Id.* at 184-201.

[109] See Benjamin Klein & Keith B. Leffler, The Role of Market Forces in Assuring Contractual Performance, 89 J. Pol. Econ. 615 (1981); D. Bruce Johnsen, Myths about Mutual Fund Fees: Economic Insights on Jones v. Harris (George Mason Univ. L. & Econ. Research Paper Series No. 09–49, 2009), available at http://ssrn.com/abstract=1483862.

[110] Florencia Marotta-Wurgler, Does Disclosure Matter? (March 16, 2010) (working paper, on file with author).

Strikingly, consumers tend not to read these contracts even when the internet makes them readily available; they are no more likely to read more accessible contracts or ones with more one-sided terms. If mutual funds should be regulated despite thousands of competitors and very low industry concentration,[111] this implies a need to increase regulation of all consumer markets.

Even if there really is something wrong with the mutual fund industry, the problem may lie in the regulation of the industry rather than in the market. This has at least superficial plausibility given the already quite detailed regulation of mutual funds.[112] Thus, Wallison and Litan observe the "paradox" of dispersion in pricing in a seemingly competitive industry that should exhibit more convergence as consumers find the best values.[113] As discussed above, the culprit may be the benchmarking inherent in fiduciary litigation. This hypothesis is supported by the fact that fee dispersion shows up much more in the United States than in the United Kingdom, where the consumers are likely similar to those in the United States but the regulation does not require mutual funds to adopt a corporate structure.

Better-designed disclosure regulation conceivably could address at least some of the problems in the market for mutual funds. For example, Fisch recommends an approach in which funds must explain their departure from a federally prescribed menu.[114] Perhaps there is some justification for specific substantive regulations such as debt limits and redemption rules. However, federally prescribed regulation of the *governance* of mutual funds is likely to lead to even worse mistakes than consumers would make under a disclosure-only regime. Indeed, future-Justice Douglas made this point in his defense of the securities laws.[115] The costs of mandating a particular governance structure for mutual funds, and of specifically adjudicating a "fiduciary duty" within that structure, have been high. Even if Congress initially took the right approach, the market evolved

---

[111] See Wallison & Litan, *supra* note 12, at 48 (noting that while a concentrated industry has an Herfindahl-Hirschman Index of over 1000, the mutual fund industry's HHI is only 400).

[112] See *id.* at 75.

[113] *Id.* at 48.

[114] Fisch, *supra* note 83, at 105-117.

[115] Douglas & Bates, *supra* note 100, at 171-73.

enough over time to render that approach obsolete. Yet Congress lacks the will to deregulate financial structures, the SEC lacks the resources and power to make adequate modifications, and the courts can do no more than tinker around the margins. Moreover, it is important to keep in mind that Congress, the SEC, and the federal courts are subject to the same sorts of heuristic errors as investors.[116]

Conversely, even if the laboratory of state law is defective and subject to interest-group capture, it can hardly be much worse than what Congress has done with investment companies. At least there is always an opportunity for some state to create a structure that would better suit modern needs than that crafted in the 1930s and 1960s. A vibrant market populated by self-interested investors at least stands some chance of fixing errors, while Congress and federal agencies are not subject to the same corrective pressures.

Conclusion

The central problem in *Jones v. Harris Associates* is not the issue that confronted the Court—that is, whether to adopt the *Gartenberg* standard for applying the fiduciary duty in section 36(b)—but instead the whole regulatory structure that gave rise to this duty. Judge Easterbrook addressed the problem but could not fix it without actually rewriting the Act. The Supreme Court's decision, while recognizing the problem with litigation under existing regulation, basically leaves things just as they were before *Jones*. The only effective fix is for Congress to scrap the existing approach of imposing a corporate governance model on decidedly non corporate mutual funds. More generally, *Jones* should stand as a lesson of the dangers of federal regulation of the governance of firms. *Jones*'s most important words, therefore, may be Justice Alito's closing comment that the relevant debate "is a matter for Congress, not the courts."[117]

It might seem quixotic to advocate scaling back federal financial regulation given the recent expansionary trend. Indeed, as part of its massive financial reform law, Congress authorized the SEC to establish a new fiduciary duty for brokers and dealers in selling

---

[116] See Stephen J. Choi & A.C. Pritchard, Behavioral Economics and the SEC, 56 Stan. L. Rev. 1 (2003).

[117] Jones, 130 S. Ct. at 1431.

securities.[118] This new duty could generate at least as much uncertainty and litigation as the fiduciary duty at issue in *Jones v. Harris.*

However, in the long run Congress will have to confront the fact that U.S. financial regulation must compete with regulations around the world, such as those in Luxembourg, with respect to mutual funds.[119] Also, no regulator can hope to keep pace with the market's endless inventiveness. Numerous investment vehicles already compete with mutual funds, including common trusts, separately managed accounts, and exchange-traded funds.[120] Continuing with misguided legislation in an unresponsive system ultimately will drive investment dollars to these competitors. The result may be a flow of investments out of the United States or to investment forms that leave investors even worse off than they are in mutual funds.

The United States has an inherent advantage over other countries: a robust federal system that provides an internal laboratory for refining regulation. The most promising regulatory path for the United States is to build on that system rather than slowly dismantling it.

---

[118] See Dodd-Frank Wall Street Reform and Consumer Protection Act, (H.R. 4173) §913(g). See also, Statement of Larry E. Ribstein, United States Senate Committee on the Judiciary, Subcommittee on Crime and Drugs, Hearing on "Wall Street and Fiduciary Duties: Can Jail Time Serve as an Adequate Deterrent for Willful Violations," May 4, 2010, http://judiciary.senate.gov/pdf/10-05-04RibsteinsTestimony.pdf (criticizing proposal to impose fiduciary duties on investment bankers with criminal sanctions for breach).

[119] See Coates, *supra* note 40, at 654-55.

[120] See Wallison & Litan, *supra* note 12, at 51-60.

Forward to the Past

*Michael Risch**

Introduction

The Supreme Court's decision in *Bilski v. Kappos*[1]—banning all patents claiming "abstract ideas," but refusing to categorically bar any particular type of patent—represents a return to the Court's past patentable subject matter jurisprudence. In so returning, the Court determined that business methods could potentially be patentable. The decision reverses an attempt by the Federal Circuit Court of Appeals to draw bright-line subject matter rules that had the effect of limiting patentable subject matter.

The Court's preference for a flexible but uncertain standard is not surprising given recent patent decisions. In the last few years, the Court has struck down several of the Federal Circuit's bright-line rules; instead, it required case-by-case consideration to determine obviousness, application of the doctrine of equivalents, and injunctive relief.[2]

In *Bilski*, however, the Federal Circuit's chosen line was not terribly bright, and it potentially limited a wide range of patentable subject

* ©2010 Michael Risch, associate professor of law, Villanova University School of Law. The author thanks Colleen Chien, Anne Lofaso, Adam Mossoff, Josh Sarnoff, David Schwartz, and Shashank Upadhye for their helpful comments. Valuable research assistance was provided by Jonathan Lombardo and Jenny Maxey.

[1] 561 U.S. ____, 130 S. Ct. 3218 (2010) [hereinafter Bilski II].

[2] See generally KSR Int'l Co. v. Teleflex Inc., 550 U.S. 398 (2007) (holding patent invalid for being obvious); MedImmune, Inc. v. Genentech, Inc., 549 U.S. 118 (2007) (holding that a licensee was not required to breach license agreement before seeking declaratory judgment of patent invalidity); eBay Inc. v. MercExchange, L.L.C., 547 U.S. 388 (2006) (typical four-factor test for injunctive relief applies to disputes under the Patent Act); Festo Corp. v. Shoketsu Kinzoko Kogyo Kabushiki Co., 535 U.S. 722 (2002) (claim amendment is not an absolute bar to infringement under the doctrine of equivalents).

matter in both historic and modern technologies.[3] This was the great fear of modern technology companies: that the Court would use this case to strike down all software patents.

In the end, then, the Court's vagueness may be preferable to the Federal Circuit's vagueness cloaked in bright-line clothing. The Court clearly struggled to apply an unambiguous statute in a way that would not create overbroad and underinventive patents that thwart innovation—while at the same time leaving open the possibility that new intangible technologies might be patentable.

This review considers these issues in four parts.

Part I discusses Mr. Bilski's patent application and the Court's ruling that it is an unpatentable abstract idea.

Part II takes a step back and considers how the law led to the growth of business methods patents. In particular, this part discusses how the Federal Circuit applied Supreme Court precedent to Bilski's application in an effort to reign in business methods.

Part III critically analyzes the Federal Circuit's opinion, the Supreme Court's granting of certiorari, and oral argument. It shows how lower courts have struggled to apply unclear Supreme Court precedent—precedent that is really concerned with patentability standards unrelated to eligible subject matter.

Part IV describes in further detail the Court's various opinions in *Bilski* and their reasoning. The discussion shows that the majority— as in previous cases—reached the right result through unprincipled, contradictory, and ultimately unrepeatable reasoning. Indeed, the Court based its ruling on the very same cases that led to the Federal Circuit's rule rejected here.

Part V discusses *Bilski*'s implications for the future of patent jurisprudence and innovation.

I. *Bilski* and Abstract Ideas

Bernard Bilski and Rand Warsaw (referred to collectively as Bilski) claim to have invented a method of hedging risk in commodities trading. The primary claim at issue includes the following steps:

> (a) initiating a series of transactions between said commodity provider and consumers of said commodity wherein said

---

[3] In re Bilski, 545 F.3d 943 (Fed. Cir. 2008) [hereinafter Bilski I].

consumers purchase said commodity at a fixed rate based upon historical averages, said fixed rate corresponding to a risk position of said consumers;

 (b) identifying market participants for said commodity having a counter-risk position to said consumers; and

 (c) initiating a series of transactions between said commodity provider and said market participants at a second fixed rate such that said series of market participant transactions balances the risk position of said series of consumer transactions.[4]

The method involved selling commodities at a fixed price to consumers and "transacting" with other market participants at a fixed price. The second set of transactions is not specified, and thus might be buying, selling, or trading options and futures. Hedging, in general, is well known, though the inventors here claim to have come up with a better way to calculate prices. Because hedging is not new, the claim as written appears non-inventive; it is not limited to the "better" way to calculate prices.

Furthermore, while the patent application's description of the hedging process clearly requires a computer,[5] the claim is not so limited and could quite easily encompass ordinary hedging transactions.

A. Bilski as a Test Case

Despite its apparent weakness on a variety of fronts, the U.S. Patent and Trademark Office chose to use Bilski's patent application as a vehicle to obtain judicial guidance about what *types* of inventions can be patentable. Thus, the patent application was rejected by the PTO as not embodying patentable subject matter, *and for no other reason*.

In the past, applications were rejected on multiple grounds, and the Federal Circuit—the only court that hears appeals from PTO proceedings—rarely rejected patents solely on subject matter grounds. By rejecting this patent based on its subject matter alone, rather than on its merits, the court was required to consider the "patentable subject matter" question.

---

[4] Bilski II, 130 S. Ct. at 3223–24.

[5] See Mark A. Lemley et al., Brief Amici Curiae of 20 Law and Business Professors in Support of Neither Party, Bilski II, 1305 S. Ct. 3218 (2010) (No. 08-964).

The PTO thus rejected Bilski's application because the claims were not the type of claims allowed by the Patent Act. Understanding why requires some discussion about patentable subject matter.

B. Patentable Subject Matter

Section 101 of the Patent Act sets forth the type of inventions that can be patented: "Whoever invents or discovers any new and useful process, machine, manufacture, or composition of matter, or any new and useful improvement thereof, may obtain a patent therefore, subject to the conditions and requirements of this title."[6] The statutory phrase "conditions and requirements" encompasses traditional criteria: novelty, non-obviousness, utility, description, and enablement.

Because of its procedural posture, the sole issue before the Court was the type of invention and not any of these other requirements. The question, at bottom, is whether Section 101 bars Bilski's (or anyone else's) patent application because of its subject matter, no matter how novel, non-obvious, or useful it may otherwise be. As discussed further below, however, the traditional requirements invariably become entwined with the subject matter question.

The words of the statute do not end the inquiry. While it appears that Congress has authorized patenting all processes, machines, manufactures, and compositions of matter, the Court has limited the statute. Several Supreme Court decisions state that abstract ideas, natural phenomena, and products of nature are not patentable subject matter.[7]

Unfortunately, it seems that no one can figure out what constitutes abstract ideas, natural phenomena, or products of nature. Prior Supreme Court and Federal Circuit cases provide little and sometimes contradictory guidance: Abstract ideas are only patentable if they are part of a physical process—but perhaps not if the physical process involves human business transactions. Combining two products of nature can be patentable, except in some cases where the two products continue to do what they always did. Extracting part

---

[6] 35 U.S.C. §101 (2006).

[7] See Bilski II, 130 S. Ct. at 3253 (Stevens, J., concurring) ("For example we have held that no one can patent 'laws of nature, natural phenomena, and abstract ideas.'") (quoting Diamond v. Diehr, 450 U.S. 175 (1981)). See also Parker v. Flook, 437 U.S. 584 (1978); Funk Bros. Seed Co. v. Kalo Inoculant Co., 333 U.S. 127 (1948).

of a product of nature can be patentable, unless the extraction does not sufficiently purify and isolate the new composition from existing material, a difficult and contentious inquiry. Applying a natural phenomenon can be patentable, except that "simple" application might be excluded, even though no one had discovered it before.

Bilski is thus the latest in a long line of cases trying to draw the line between patent-eligible processes and unpatentable abstractions that are undeserving of protection no matter by how much the invention clears the patent-issuance bar. It is an important case, however, because it is the first Supreme Court opinion to consider the question in nearly 30 years. *Bilski* caught the attention of many legal observers in part due to the amount of time that has passed without any new subject matter opinions despite the exponential growth of software patenting.

The stakes are quite high for affected industries, in this case software companies. Researchers estimate that between 1987 and 1996 the number of successful software patent applications increased by 16 percent per year,[8] and from 11,143 granted in 1998 to 21,224 in 2008.[9] It is no surprise that 68 amicus briefs were filed in this case, including from IBM, Eli Lilly and Company, and American Express.[10] Indeed, the definition of process might also affect manufacturing, biotechnology, medical diagnostics, and pharmaceutical companies.[11]

C. *The Court's Ruling in a Nutshell*

The Supreme Court unanimously voted to deny Bilski's patent application as outside the scope of Section 101. A majority of five

---

[8] James Bessen & Robert M. Hunt, An Empirical Look at Software Patents 16, (Research on Innovation, Working Paper No. 03-17/R, 2004), available at http://www.researchoninnovation.org/swpat.pdf.

[9] United States Patent & Trademark Office, Patent Counts by Class by Year, (May 5, 2009) available at http://www.uspto.gov/web/offices/ac/ido/oeip/taf/cbcby.htm (calculating the total software patents granted in 1998 and 2008 under classes 700 through 717).

[10] Sara Mason, Amicus Briefs for the In re Bilski Case, http://works.bepress.com/cgi/viewcontent.cgi?article= 1003&context= faye_jones (last visited March 24, 2010).

[11] See, e.g., Classen Immunotherapies v. Biogen Idec., 561 U.S. ___, 130 S. Ct. 3541 (2010) and Mayo Collaborative Servs. v. Prometheus Labs., 561 U.S. ___, 130 S. Ct. 3543 (2010) (both granting certiorari and vacating underlying judgment, with remand to reconsider in view of *Bilski* for patents relating to medical treatment and pharmaceutical processes respectively).

justices explained that the concept of hedging is no more than an abstract idea, and that application of the concept to particular commodities or using particular pricing formulas does not render the claims patentable. The majority also refused to bar all business methods, instead holding that non-abstract methods might be patentable. The remaining four justices would have gone further, banning all business methods patents. Even so, the minority also agreed that Bilski's claims were unpatentable as abstract ideas.

This ruling is consistent with long-standing Supreme Court pronouncements barring patents claiming abstract ideas. Indeed, it marks a return to those general rules from the more complex and rigid rules developed by the Federal Circuit.

Despite—or perhaps because of—the decision's simplicity, its implementation will be problematic. First, it provides no guidance about what an abstract idea might be. Second, it might arguably lead to over- or under-patenting, depending on how lower courts apply it.

The remaining sections provide the background and detailed analysis to understand these problems, beginning with the growth of business methods patents and ending with the future's likely course in light of *Bilski*.

II. The Rise of Business Methods

While the Court's decision is deceptively simple, understanding its importance and implications requires a closer look at the growth of business methods and the Federal Circuit's response in this case.

A. Software at the Supreme Court

Though *Bilski* is not technically a software case, understanding business methods and the Federal Circuit's decision in the case begins with the history of software at the Supreme Court. The Court first addressed software patentability in a series of three cases between 1972 and 1981. Analysis of these cases reveals just how difficult it is for courts to apply judicially developed limitations on patentable subject matter, a pattern that continues in *Bilski*.

In *Gottschalk v. Benson*, the Court considered a patent relating to the mathematical conversion of "binary coded decimals" into binary number representations, a conversion that was known and could be done by pencil and paper, though one of the claims at issue used "shift registers" and was therefore tied to a machine.[12] The Court ruled that both the machine-implemented claim and the intangible claim were too abstract to be patentable, as they would preempt all uses of the mathematical algorithm.[13]

Despite the subject matter discussion, the opinion's text implies that the Court was more concerned with the inventor's failure to describe the process in such a way that made clear that the applicant actually invented the claimed invention. The real concern appeared to be that the claim fell short of the specification and novelty requirements.[14] Furthermore, a mathematical algorithm with no practical application was not practically useful as required by 35 U.S.C. §101 and Supreme Court precedent.[15] Though the numeric conversion was used in all computers, on its own it did nothing in particular. Its generality made it potentially useful when applied by others but not presently useful as claimed by the applicant.

In *Parker v. Flook*, the Supreme Court considered a claim related to catalytic converters.[16] The claimed method determined the level of temperature, pressure, or flow rate necessary to trigger an alarm; it included a mathematical algorithm to determine the proper "alarm limit." The claim was indisputably tied to a machine: the catalytic converter and its computer controller. The Court ruled that the only allegedly "new" part of the three-step method was the mathematical algorithm. All the other parts of the claim were "insignificant post-solution activity" that could not change the nature of the mathematical step in the process.

The Court then held that discovery of a mathematical algorithm cannot be novel even if the algorithm was previously unknown: "Whether the algorithm was in fact known or unknown at the time of the claimed invention, as one of the 'basic tools of scientific and technological work' . . . it is treated as though it were a familiar part of the prior art."[17] In other words, the Court ruled that a scientific

---

[12] 409 U.S. 63, 73–74 (1972).

[13] *Id.* at 68.

[14] *Id.* at 70–72.

[15] For further discussion of the practical utility of mathematical algorithms, see Michael Risch, Everything Is Patentable, 75 Tenn. L. Rev. 591 (2008) and Michael Risch, New Uses for Patent Utility (working paper, 2010).

[16] 437 U.S. 584 (1978).

[17] *Id.* at 591–92 (quoting Gottschalk, 409 U.S. at 67).

principle cannot be novel, because it must have existed in nature. The *Flook* Court admits that its rule is not bright: "The line between a patentable 'process' and an unpatentable 'principle' is not always clear."[18]

Only three years later, in *Diamond v. Diehr*, the Court again considered whether a patent should issue where a claim used a mathematical algorithm, this time as part of a method for manufacturing rubber.[19] Part of the process implemented a well-known formula relating to the time required to cure rubber. The patent applicant argued, and the Court agreed, that the process could be novel and useful because the claimed invention was more than just the algorithm.[20] Thus, the Court ruled that the patent could not be rejected on subject matter grounds. The Court was unconcerned that the mathematical algorithm was well known; the process could have just as easily (and might have) contained a non-mathematical step that was well known. Instead, what was important was that the known step became novel and non-obvious *when combined with the other elements of the claim*. Thus, *Diehr*'s requirement that the claim as a whole be considered was at least an implicit rejection of *Parker v. Flook*'s "point of novelty" rule.[21]

These three cases show the difficulty (even folly) of trying to apply judicially created restrictions to computer software. It is easy to say that a mathematical algorithm is unpatentable, but every software program boils down to an algorithm of one type or another. How do we know whether the algorithm is part of a *Diehr* process or whether it is a *Flook* principle of nature or a *Gottschalk* abstract idea? Do we follow *Flook*'s point-of-novelty analysis to isolate the algorithm, or do we follow *Diehr*'s holistic analysis to see how the algorithm is part of a more complex process? And how should any of this apply to non-software processes that might incorporate intangible steps?

The directly contradictory outcomes of *Flook* and *Diehr* show that courts have great difficulty applying an uncertain standard. Many would say that *Flook* is simply wrongly decided, but that case has

---

[18] *Id.* at 589.
[19] 450 U.S. 175 (1981).
[20] *Id.* at 188–89.
[21] See *Id.* at 189 n.12.

never been overruled and is still cited today—including in the *Bilski* decision.

B. *Software and Business Methods*

Diehr is commonly interpreted as allowing software patents. After all, every computer with software installed is a machine, and a machine as a whole is patentable. The Federal Circuit cemented this interpretation in cases such as *In re Alappat*, which held that mathematical calculation circuitry combined to form a machine.[22]

Additionally, the Patent Act explicitly defines a process to include a new use for an existing machine.[23] Software that allows a new use for computers satisfies this requirement; most software is technically a patentable process so long as it can be implemented by a computer.

The Federal Circuit expanded on *Alappat* in later cases. In the 1998 case *State Street Bank* and its progeny, the court generally held that a "useful, concrete and tangible result" was sufficient for a process to be eligible subject matter.[24] Thus, methods of managing money by computer or measuring heart rhythms, and so forth, were useful, concrete and tangible.

State Street's rationale led to a trend over the last decade[25] toward patents claiming processes that are disembodied from a computer. These claims might be implemented by a computer, but need not be. Such claims are often called business methods. This circumstance reveals a definitional imprecision about what a business method is, and what role computers play in such methods. While a computer is not required to infringe business methods, such claims usually require a computer to be implemented with any reasonable speed.

Another definition of a business method is a process used to perform non-manufacturing tasks, such as money management, sales transactions, or other steps that do not transform a physical object.[26] This type of business method may or may not require a

---

[22] 33 F.3d 1526, 1544 (Fed. Cir. 1994) (en banc).

[23] 35 U.S.C. §100(b) (2006).

[24] See State St. Bank & Trust Co. v. Signature Fin. Group, Inc., 149 F.3d 1368, 1375 (1998) (quoting Allapat, 33 F.3d at 1544).

[25] Bilski, for example, filed his application in 1997.

[26] Michael Risch, Dealing with Controversial Patent Subjects, PrawfsBlawg (Oct. 29, 2008, 07:52 EST), http://prawfsblawg.blogs.com/prawfsblawg/2008/10/dealing-with-co.html.

computer. For example, one often-criticized business-method type is the tax-planning method—claims to tax savings by taking certain steps that minimize taxes under the Internal Revenue Code. These patents could be implemented by hand, but likely require a computer to be efficiently implemented.

Indeed, there are plenty of other intangible methods that are not really business related. Medical diagnostic and treatment patents are ostensibly not business methods. Even sports moves such as the Fosbury flop are a method for achieving a goal using only the human body. While not really "business" methods, patenting of such intangible methods might be affected by the same subject matter restrictions applied to business methods.

Regardless of how business methods are defined, their existence has been widely criticized by many businesses, scholars, and even some judges as not only contrary to law but harmful to innovation. Others, however, believe that business-methods patents are critical to investment. The policy debate is discussed further below.

C. Machine or Transformation Test

Against this backdrop of Supreme Court precedent and the growth of intangible methods, the Federal Circuit in *Bilski* sought to define just which claims should be patent eligible and which ones should be excluded.

The *en banc* Federal Circuit held, 11–1, that Bilski's claim was not patentable subject matter.[27] In so ruling, the Federal Circuit overruled *State Street* and all its other precedent that relied explicitly on a useful, concrete, and tangible test.[28]

Instead, the court announced an exclusive rule called the "machine-or-transformation" test: to be patent eligible, a process must either be tied to a machine or be a transformation of something physical.[29]

However, the court ruled that insignificant "post-solution" machines or transformations are ineligible, so that one cannot pass

---

[27] While there were three dissents, only Judge Pauline Newman would have found the claims to be patentable subject matter.

[28] Bilski I, 545 F.3d at 959–60.

[29] *Id.* at 961–62. The transformation can also be a transformation of data representing something physical, such that processing heart rhythm data is a transformation, while processing money data is not a transformation.

the test simply by adding a machine or transformation that is unrelated to the inventiveness of the claim.[30]

The Federal Circuit reached this test by attempting to assimilate the Supreme Court precedent discussed above, as follows. First, the Court has held that fundamental principles such as historical abstract ideas, products of nature, and principles of nature are not patentable.[31] To make them so would preempt use of such principles.

Second, it is difficult to determine whether a claim is a fundamental principle that might be preempted. The Court has held, however, that there are two ways to tell if something is *not* a fundamental principle. If a claim is tied to a machine or if a claim transforms some subject matter, then it is *not* a fundamental principle.[32]

Third, therefore, the *only* way for a process to be patent eligible is to be tied to a machine or to transform subject matter.[33]

Fourth, in order to make sure all fundamental principles are excluded, insignificant post-solution machines or transformations cannot save a non-machine and non-transformative process.

The Federal Circuit meant this test to apply to *any* process; it has since applied this rule to pharmaceutical process claims relating to the metabolization of drugs in the body.[34] If a process met the test, then it was eligible. If it did not meet the test, then it was not eligible.

Using this test, the Federal Circuit then ruled that Bilski's claims were not a patent-eligible process: a) they were not tied to a machine (though no human could efficiently do the calculations in many of the patent claims); b) the transformations involved are of legal obligations and not anything physical; and c) any physical activity contemplated by the claim was "post-solution."[35]

III. Certiorari and Oral Argument

The Federal Circuit's ruling had potentially wide-ranging consequences—consequences that led the Supreme Court to reconsider this area after a 30-year hiatus.

---

[30] *Id.* at 957.

[31] *Id.* at 960.

[32] *Id.* at 961.

[33] *Id.*

[34] Prometheus Labs., Inc. v. Mayo Collaborative Servs., 581 F.3d 1336 (Fed. Cir. 2009), rev'd 561 U.S. ___ 130 S. Ct. 3543 (2010) (summary certiorari grant and reversal in light of *Bilski*).

[35] Bilski I, 545 F.3d at 965–66.

A. Aftermath of the Federal Circuit Ruling

Many commentators immediately reacted to the new rule—that eligible processes must either be tied to a machine or transform something physical—and considered it problematic in many respects.

First, the rule is contrary to the statute, which states that "[t]he term 'process' means process, art, or method, and includes a new use of a known process, machine, manufacture, composition of matter, or material."[36] The Federal Circuit explicitly read this definition out of the statute. The opinion states that because the statutory definition of process includes the word "process," it is circular, and thus the entire definition—including the inclusion of new uses of processes, machines, and compositions of matter—may be ignored.[37]

Even if limiting subject matter is a preferred normative policy, interpretation of a statute to exclude an explicit definition defies the most flexible statutory interpretation principles. Many statutes are written to expand the definition of a word to include other words, just as "process" was written to include not only a process, but also an "art" or a "method."[38]

Thus, even if one were to argue, as the Supreme Court ultimately found, that historical limitations should apply to the term "process," simply ignoring the definition altogether was problematic.

Second, it is a rigid rule, which the Supreme Court has disfavored. Recent cases have overturned rigid Federal Circuit rules relating to obviousness,[39] declaratory relief,[40] injunctions,[41] and the doctrine of equivalents.[42]

Third, the logic used to justify a rigid rule is deeply flawed. The Federal Circuit held that Supreme Court precedent allowed patenting of machines or transformations, and thus *only* machines or transformations are patentable. The logical fallacy is apparent—just

---

[36] 35 U.S.C. § 100(b).

[37] Bilski I, 545 F.3d at 951 n.3, 957.

[38] For example, 35 U.S.C. § 100(d) states: "The word 'patentee' includes not only the patentee to whom the patent was issued but also the successors in title to the patentee."

[39] KSR Int'l Co. v. Teleflex Inc., 550 U.S. 398, 421–22 (2007).

[40] MedImmune, Inc. v. Genentech, Inc., 549 U.S. 118, 132 n.11 (2007).

[41] eBay Inc. v. MercExchange, L.L.C., 547 U.S. 388, 393–94 (2006).

[42] Festo Corp. v. Shoketsu Kinzoko Kogyo Kabushiki Co., 535 U.S. 722, 739 (2002).

because a machine or transformation is eligible subject matter, this does not mean that *nothing else* is eligible.

Fourth, the decision unsettled expectations about software patenting that were at least 10 years old, if not older. The court gave little indication of whether patents that were previously upheld, such as *State Street Bank*, would continue to be patentable.

Fifth, in its effort to deal with high technology, the court abandoned low technology. There are many patented processes that have nothing to do with machines or transformations—methods for measuring fabric, methods for harvesting fruit, and methods for manufacturing products by hand (for example, forming wrought iron). At worst, these types of historically patentable inventions would now be unpatentable. At best, determining what is patentable and what is excluded became much more difficult.

Sixth, rather than achieve the Federal Circuit's stated goal of identifying unpatentable fundamental principles,[43] the test transforms ordinary processes into fundamental principles. The opinion makes clear that the machine-or-transformation test should determine whether a claimed process is more than a "fundamental principle."[44] By finding that *Bilski* fails the test, the court effectively ruled that the claimed process must, therefore, be preempting a fundamental principle. But is the process of hedging through fixed-price contracts, even if obvious and overbroad, really a fundamental principle? Is it really part of the scientific landscape for all to use in whatever "applied" way they choose? Does this particular process really preempt a field of math, science, or technology?[45] Despite its failings, Bilski's claim does not rise to the level of gravity, relativity, or even the numeric conversion in *Gottschalk*. The machine-or-transformation test attempts to shoehorn an otherwise square claim into round subject matter rejection.

Seventh, and perhaps most important practically, although the test is supposedly bright-line, renewed emphasis on "insignificant

[43] Bilski I, 545 F.3d at 954 ("The question before us then is whether Applicants' claim recites a fundamental principle and, if so, whether it would pre-empt substantially all uses of that fundamental principle if allowed.").

[44] *Id.*

[45] See, e.g., Bilski II, 130 S. Ct. at 3235 (Stevens, J., concurring) ("The patent now before us is not for '[a] principle, in the abstract,' or a 'fundamental truth.'") (quoting Flook, 437 U.S. at 589).

post-solution activity" makes the patentability determination indefinite—any computer software could be invalidated if the computer were considered "insignificant." For example, data gathering may be physical, but courts could ignore such activity as unrelated to the solution. This hearkens back to the suspect "point of novelty" analysis of *Parker v. Flook* that was rejected only a few years later in *Diehr*.

Similarly, it is unclear which transformations involve physical data rather than intangible data. For example, financial processes involve money—which surely can be converted to physical dollar bills. It is unclear why programs that count heart rhythms should be sufficiently physical, but programs that count money should not.

Thus, the Federal Circuit's guidance about determining whether a process is tied to a machine is unhelpful. The appellate opinion cites *Mackay Radio* as a prime example of a machine-implemented mathematical formula.[46] But *Mackay* illustrates the imprecision of the Federal Circuit's test. There, a well-known equation predicted the optimal wire lengths for receiving radio signals. The patentee (who did not discover the equation) claimed an antenna using these lengths. The Supreme Court held that the antenna was patent eligible because it was an application of the well-known principle. Under the Federal Circuit's test, however, there is no principled way to separate the antenna from the formula under the insignificant post-solution activity rule. One could easily argue that the antenna was simply an insignificant "post-solution" part of the claim because the "real" solution was the mathematical formula, which is a process. In short, the Federal Circuit test might well consider the antenna ineligible when the Supreme Court long ago ruled to the contrary. Indeed, calling the antenna a manufacture rather than a process does not solve the problem, because computers are certainly manufactures/machines and they can be disregarded under the machine-or-transformation test.

It is this approach—point-of-novelty analysis and insignificant post-solution activity—that most threatened software and software patenting. Those considering an investment in a software-based business would not know *ex ante* whether their inventions would be entitled to possible patent protection. Any new software claim

---

[46] Mackay Radio & Tel. Co. v. Radio Corp. of Am., 306 U.S. 86 (1939).

might be considered simply a transformation of non-physical data, and its execution in a computer considered insignificant.

B. Certiorari

Given the difficulties of the Federal Circuit's test, the best test case for subject-matter limitations is a business method that a) need not be implemented on a computer (ever) but is still valuable, and b) is otherwise novel, nonobvious, useful, described, and enabled. Courts have yet to consider such a patent on subject matter grounds, and *Bilski* is no exception; though Bilski's broadest claim might have been practiced without a computer, that claim surely fell short of several patentability requirements. Until courts see such a patent, "insignificant post-solution activity" and the computer/non-computer divide will continue to invite uncertainty.

It may be unfair to criticize the Federal Circuit for the failings of its *Bilski* ruling. After all, it had vague Supreme Court precedent to deal with. Even so, there is no precedential basis for such a rigid test; even the Supreme Court cases relied on by the Federal Circuit explicitly state that a machine-or-transformation test is not exclusive.[47] Indeed, one interpretation of the opinion is that the Federal Circuit deliberately implemented a rigid rule in order to achieve Supreme Court review. The opinion implicitly invites such review.[48]

Even so, a desire for Supreme Court review was not unanimous, in part because *Bilski* is not the ideal vehicle for considering these difficult questions.

Furthermore, the news was not all bad for software patenting. The Federal Circuit reaffirmed that business methods and any other method—including software—that meet the test are patentable.[49] Of course, those favoring the elimination of software patents would

---

[47] Bilski I, 545 F.3d at 955–56; but see Gottschalk, 409 U.S. at 70; Diehr, 450 U.S. at 192; Flook, 437 U.S. at 589. See also, Bilski II, 130 S. Ct. at 3221 ("The Court of Appeals incorrectly concluded that this Court has endorsed the machine-or-transformation test as the exclusive test.").

[48] Bilski I, 545 F.3d at 956 ("Thus, we recognize that the Supreme Court may ultimately decide to alter or perhaps even set aside this test to accommodate emerging technologies.").

[49] The opinion made clear that "transformation" is not limited to physical items, but could also include data about physical items, such as heart rhythms or earth movement.

say that the opinion did not go far enough by banning all business methods or even all software.[50]

Because *Bilski* was not the best test case, and because it did not eliminate software patents, some people were surprised that the Court even agreed to review the case. Many believe that weak, non-computerized claims such as Bilski's could easily be sacrificed in the future given the Federal Circuit's affirmation of software patentability.[51] The fear, therefore, was that the Supreme Court would issue an opinion that would ban software patents.[52]

In fact, the solicitor general urged the Court to deny certiorari.[53] During oral argument, counsel mentioned this opposition, to which Justice Anthony Kennedy replied, "You thought we—you thought we'd mess it up."[54]

These fears were not unjustified. The *Bilski* claims were incredibly weak on the merits, and the Court could have made bad policy invalidating a bad patent for the wrong reasons.[55]

Nor were these fears lost on the Court. Oral argument demonstrated that many of the justices were grappling with what ruling would disallow "bad" patents but keep "good" patents. Even those justices who eventually voted to bar all business methods patents asked pointed questions to ensure that such a ruling might not go too far.

---

[50] *Id.* at 1007 (Mayer, J. dissenting) ("Allowing patents to issue on business methods shifts critical resources away from promoting and protecting truly useful technological advances.").

[51] *Id.* at 1000 (Mayer, J., dissenting).

[52] A humorous "Hitler Reacts to the Granting of Certiorari in *Bilski*" video posted on YouTube makes this point. *Bilski* Movie Spoof, http://271patent.blogspot.com/2009/11/bilski-movie-spoof.html (November 11, 2009, 16:26 EST); see also Studio Plots Downfall of Hitler Meme on YouTube, http://www.popeater.com/2010/04/20/hitler-meme-downfall-removed-youtube/ (Apr. 20, 2010, 11:45 EST).

[53] See generally Brief for the Respondent in Opposition, Bilski v. Doll, No. 08-964 (May 1, 2009).

[54] Transcript of Oral Argument at 47, Bilski v. Kappos, 130 S. Ct. 3218 (2010) (No. 08-964), available at http://www.supremecourt.gov/oral_arguments/argument_transcripts/08-964.pdf [hereinafter Transcript].

[55] See Michael Risch, The Idea's the Thing, Legal Times (May 12, 2008), available at http://law.wvu.edu/r/download/9874; John Duffy, Bilski, Kenny Rogers, and Supreme Court Rule 46, Patently-O Blog (June 25, 2010, 07:43 EST), http://www.patentlyo.com/patent/2010/06/bilski-kenny-rogers-and-supreme-court-rule-46.html.

For example, Justice Stephen Breyer noted:

> In the 19th century, they made it one way in respect to machines. Now you're telling us: Make it today in respect to information. And if you ask me as a person how to make that balance in respect to information, if I am honest, I have to tell you: I don't know. And I don't know whether across the board or in this area or that area patent protection will do no harm or more harm than good.[56]

Similarly, Justice Samuel Alito telegraphed the rationale for the majority opinion: "If you—if you are right [that this claim is an abstract idea], is this a good case for us to get into these—into the very broad issue that Petitioner has raised?"[57] Justice Sonia Sotomayor posed the question differently—that perhaps outlawing business methods would leave software patenting intact.[58]

This question led to the most surprising discussion of the argument: the solicitor—charged with seeking affirmance of the machine-or-transformation test—made clear that the United States did not support the banning of business methods patents. Deputy Solicitor General Malcolm Stewart responded to Justice Sotomayor's question:

> I think that would be incorrect, and it would create problems of its own. That is, the—the innovation that was held to be patent eligible in *State Street Bank* was not a process.
>
> [intervening questions omitted]
>
> [Though claimed as a machine, *State Street* is still considered a business method.] So, to say that business methods are categorically ineligible for patent protection would eliminate new machines, including programmed computers, that are useful because of their contributions to the operation of businesses.[59]

---

[56] Transcript, *supra* note 54, at 20; see also *Id.* at 31–32 (expressing concern about machine-or-transformation test).

[57] *Id.* at 28.

[58] *Id.* at 29.

[59] *Id.* at 29–30.

This statement interested the Court. Chief Justice John Roberts later asked about a similar statement in the government's brief:

> [Y]ou say this is not simply the method isn't patentable because it doesn't involve a machine. But then you say that it might be if you use a computer. . . . That's like saying if you use a typewriter to type out the—the process, then it is patentable. I—I—that takes away everything that you spent 53 pages establishing.[60]

When pressed by the Chief Justice, Stewart made clear that software should be patentable.[61] In fact, the government eventually argued explicitly that the *State Street Bank* decision—considered by most to have opened the business methods patent floodgates—would have come out exactly the same under a machine-or-transformation test because the method was implemented in a machine.[62]

Several justices appeared perplexed by this argument. After all, how could *Bilski* be the Court's chance to limit business methods patents if the quintessential business method case would be decided the same way? And how could the machine-or-transformation test have any relevance if it did not ban patenting on machines implementing business methods? How can a court tell the difference between hardware and software, especially when a software claim can easily be re-written as a computer claim? Why is a DVD player with software a new patentable machine while a general-purpose computer with software is not a new machine?

The government's nuanced argument about *State Street*—that the claimed software was both a business method and patent-eligible when implemented in a machine—was the right one as a matter of statutory interpretation, computer engineering, and patent policy. Nonetheless, the fine—and potentially irrelevant—distinction between processes and computers likely had two critical effects on the Court's thinking:

---

[60] *Id.* at 33–34.

[61] *Id.* at 36–37 ("[W]e don't want the court, for instance, in the area of software innovations or medical diagnostic techniques to be trying to use this case as the vehicle for identifying the circumstances in which innovations of that sort would and would not be patent eligible, because the case really doesn't present any—any question regarding those technologies.").

[62] *Id.* at 44–45.

1. A machine-based test alone is inadequate to eliminate "bad" patents, so some form of the insignificant post-solution activity rule must be reiterated; and

2. It would make little sense to ban patentability of all computer software when neither party was asking for it.

The combination of these two points leads to one conclusion: the Court was likely to allow software patents but leave a vague standard that would eliminate those deemed unworthy. The Court's struggle with this question took some time, however. Though argued on November 9, 2009, the opinion did not issue until the last decision day of the term, June 28, 2010, leading many to speculate that the majority shifted at some point.

IV. Analysis of the Supreme Court Opinions

A. The Court's Rulings

The Court's judgment was not a surprise: many had predicted a 9–0 defeat for Bilski. The rationale was debated, however, though as the date approached observer consensus seemed to be that Justice John Paul Stevens, who had authored *Flook*, would write the majority opinion.[63] This meant that the opinion was likely to significantly limit patentable subject matter.

The opinions that finally issued were therefore a surprise, causing some to speculate that Justice Stevens lost a vote somewhere along the way.[64] Of course, there may be many other explanations for the vote distribution.

Instead, Justice Anthony Kennedy wrote the majority opinion, which became a plurality opinion in two sections where Justice Antonin Scalia did not join. Justice Stevens authored a long concurrence on behalf of four justices. Justice Breyer issued a separate, shorter concurrence (joined in part by Justice Scalia) that sought to identify agreement among all justices. The following is a summary of the opinions and concurrences in the case:

---

[63] See Duffy, *supra* note 55.

[64] See, e.g., Tom Goldstein, Business Method Patents Nearly Bite the Dust, SCOTUS-blog (July 6, 2010, 12:54 EST), http://www.scotusblog.com/2010/07/business-method-patents-nearly-bite-the-dust/ ("[I]t seems quite likely to me that Justice Stevens was originally going to author the Court's opinion in *Bilski* but subsequently lost his majority to Justice Kennedy.").

1. As discussed above, all justices agreed that the Bilski claims are abstract ideas, and thus not patentable.

2. The Bilski claims are abstract even if they are limited by field of use or if "token" activities are undertaken outside the abstract idea. The majority held without much discussion that Bilski's additional claims limiting application to energy markets and performing "well-known random analysis techniques to help establish some of the inputs to the equation" did not add enough to the abstract idea to merit patent eligibility. This was the majority opinion of five justices: Kennedy, Roberts, Scalia, Thomas, and Alito. The other justices may have agreed, though it is difficult to tell as the concurrence criticizes the majority's methodology, as discussed below.

3. Limiting patentable processes to only those that use a machine or transform matter is a useful test but is not the *only* test. All nine justices appeared to agree on this point. None of the opinions state whether a process that meets the test is definitively or even presumptively eligible.

4. Section 100(b) defines process, and nothing in that definition excludes business methods per se or makes "machine or transformation" the only test. Section 273 (which provides a defense for potential infringers of business methods) is evidence that the statute contemplates at least some business methods patents. That section would be meaningless if business methods were excluded. The five-justice majority applied this rationale to reject the machine-or-transformation (or any other) rigid test.

5. The absence of business methods patents issuing early in America's history does not mean that they should not issue now with changing times and technology. Only four justices joined this portion of the Court's opinion: Kennedy, Roberts, Thomas, and Alito.

6. A high bar should be set for business methods, or else they may harm innovation. Lower courts might define broader categories of business methods that are abstract ideas, and therefore be consistent with the Court's opinion. The same four justices also joined this portion of the Court's opinion: Kennedy, Roberts, Thomas, and Alito.

7. The concurrence argues that in addition to being unpatentable as an abstract idea, the term "process" should not be read in the ordinary sense, but instead should be interpreted in light of history, context, and patent policy goals to exclude business methods. It also asserts that Section 273 is a red herring—Congress was merely

reacting to a court decision rather than defining patentable subject matter. Four justices joined this concurrence with the judgment: Stevens, Breyer, Ginsburg, and Sotomayor.

8. The majority gives no further guidance about identifying an unpatentable abstract process. Justice Breyer's concurrence with the judgment, joined only by Justice Scalia, argues that the Court unanimously agreed on the following principles. First, that Section 101 is not without limit. Second, that "machine-or-transformation" is a *clue* to patentability. Third, the machine or transformation test has never been the *sole* test of patentability. Fourth, that *State Street*'s "useful, concrete, and tangible result" test does not necessarily yield patentable subject matter.

B. Analysis

This section takes a closer look at the doctrinal rationale for the opinion and its likely application by lower courts through a series of questions.

1. What is an abstract invention?

This is the most important and least answerable question arising from the opinion. The answer is anyone's guess. One patent examiner memorably comments on the difficulty: "I'll tell you what, I wish I could write 101 rejections with as little supporting analysis as the Supreme Court did in the *Bilski* decision. A little discussion of precedential caselaw[], some hand-waving, and the conclusion that the claims at issue are drawn to an abstract idea."[65] The Court gives no guidance other than to say this "concept" of hedging is abstract.[66] Apparently, the Court knows abstractness when it sees it, and this is it.[67]

Indeed, the Court does not address (in detail) several other of Bilski's proposed patent claims which are much more specific than

---

[65] *Bilski* Fallout, http://just-n-examiner.livejournal.com/44111.html (June 30, 2010). (The quote continues: "Actually, it didn't even seem like a conclusion, it very much seemed as if the decision that the claims were drawn to an abstract idea was the starting point of the Court's deliberations. What that means, unfortunately, is that there was no analysis of how they reached that conclusion, and I really would like to have seen that type of analysis.").

[66] Bilski II, 130 S. Ct. at 3231.

[67] With apologies to Justice Potter Stewart, Jacobellis v. Ohio, 378 U.S. 184, 197 (1964) (Stewart, J., concurring).

the claim quoted above, implying that such claims are also abstract. This may create the greatest uncertainty of all: the reemergence of "insignificant post-solution activity" restrictions without describing what they are.[68] As a result, lower courts are left to guess which aspects of any given claim—even Bilski's claims—make them abstract.

In fact, Justice Stevens points out the indeterminacy of "token" activities in his concurrence.[69] Even if Justice Stevens's concurrence were the majority, however, the answer would still be uncertain. Defining a business method is extremely difficult. It cannot simply be data manipulation; otherwise, certain medical, physical, and electronic diagnostic tools might be barred when most seem to agree that such patents fall within Section 101. Further, as discussed above, many methods are implemented in a computer, so distinguishing between machines that qualify and those that are merely "insignificant" would be incredibly difficult.

2. What becomes of the machine-or-transformation test?

While the Court was unanimous that implementing a method using a machine or transforming matter is a "clue" to patent eligibility rather than the sole test, the fate of the test and how it should apply is hazy.

It is tempting to assume that the test can approve a method but cannot be used to reject a method. This assumption, however, is incomplete because the test includes the unpredictable "insignificant post-solution activity" component. Thus, methods like that implemented in *State Street* may turn out to be unpatentable despite the government's assertion that the method passes the machine-or-transformation test.

Indeed, Supreme Court precedent does not necessarily require a machine to identify a non-abstract idea. The applicants in both *Benson* and *Flook* indisputably tied their processes to machines but still were denied patents. It makes no sense to say that a process tied to a machine is necessarily eligible when all the Supreme Court's precedent involved machines regardless of outcome. Lack of machinery

---

[68] Bilski II, 130 S. Ct. at 3230.

[69] *Id.* at 3235 (Stevens, J., concurring).

could not have driven the Court's rationale in those cases, and thus cannot be the binding precedent that the Federal Circuit implied.

Consider, for example, the method at issue in *In re Comiskey*, a case involving a patent application for a method of dispute resolution, including the steps of submitting a matter to arbitration, arbitrating the matter, and reaching a final and binding resolution.[70] The Federal Circuit barred all claims that were not limited to implementation by a computer, but allowed the same process implemented through a computer system to be considered under other patentability criteria such as novelty.[71]

A rejection based on failure to include a computer in the claim limitations superficially makes sense. After all, a computer is a machine, so that a programmed computer falls within Section 101. Scratching the surface, however, shows that rejection solely on this basis is problematic. First, the definition of process is not limited to computers. The *Comiskey* claims included the use of paper if not a computer, and there is no basis under the statute to allow new uses of a computer but not new uses of paper, which is an "article of manufacture" under the statute. The court provides no principled basis for distinguishing the use of a machine from the use of an article of manufacture.

Furthermore, the *Comiskey* claims were not intangible human activity; they clearly contemplate physical movement of some sort as part of the transaction and arbitration, even if it is the act of signing and delivering a piece of paper (which was surely typed on a computer). The arbitration could not happen if nobody did anything physical. Here, too, the statute does not distinguish between physical activity to make things and physical activity to accomplish other ends. Readers of *Comiskey* are left trying to understand just what is patentable and what is not.

Cases like *Comiskey* reveal a general problem with any machine test—even if a claim is intangible on its face, the true invention, if there is one, is most likely computer-based. For example, considering Comiskey's claims without considering a computer makes little sense for three reasons. First, the process described in the patent

---

[70] In re Comiskey, 554 F.3d 967, 970 (Fed. Cir. 2009).

[71] *Id.*; Bilski I, 545 F.3d at 960–61 (discussing its holding in *Comiskey* and reaffirming that *Comiskey* was decided under the machine-or-transformation test).

disclosure was implemented by a computer, and no other way. Second, implementing the process without a computer would be so cumbersome as to be useless. Third, without the use of a computer, the claimed process so clearly fails a novelty test as to be absurd; it would be remarkable if this is what the applicant intended. A focus on the existence of a computer cannot drive analysis in a principled way.

A further reason to not use computerization as the dividing line is that computerized business methods will still run into patentability problems unrelated to subject matter. First, computerizing something that is known to be done without a computer, like *Comiskey's* online arbitration, is obvious—the Supreme Court addressed this nearly 35 years ago in *Dann v. Johnston*.[72] Even if the task was never done manually, it might still be obvious if it is something anyone skilled in the area might think of if only they had a computer.

In sum, it is unclear what it means for a test to be a "clue." Typically, clues are used to solve mysteries. The Court here created rather than solved a mystery and might leave Federal Circuit judges guessing whether Colonel Mustard used a lead pipe or a computer to invent a new process.

3. What becomes of the useful, concrete, and tangible result test?

Justice Breyer's final assertion—that all justices agreed that *State Street's* useful, concrete, and tangible result test cannot qualify patentable subject matter—may be the most controversial of his four points.[73] The majority opinion merely communicates "non-endorsement" of the test, rather than rejection of it. Theoretically, if the Federal Circuit were to explain why *every* claim meeting that test were non-abstract, then perhaps the majority would reconsider.

Then again, given that four justices explicitly rejected the test in Justice Stevens's concurrence, and that Justice Scalia joined Justice Breyer and did not join the part of the majority opinion suggesting that the Federal Circuit might come up with bright-line rules that implement an abstract idea test, a majority of the Court did, in fact, explicitly reject the "useful, concrete, and tangible result" test.

---

[72] Dann v. Johnston, 425 U.S. 219 (1976).
[73] Bilski II, 130 S. Ct. at 3259 (Breyer, J., concurring).

It is quite likely that that test will be abandoned, especially given that the Federal Circuit had already done so.

4. Was the majority's rationale sound?

The majority's rationale, while better than the alternatives, is internally inconsistent. The broad statutory reading is certainly reasonable. Even if one agrees with the policy of Justice Stevens's concurrence, it is difficult to simply ignore both the breadth of the definition of process and Section 273's explicit acknowledgment that some business methods might be patented. Thus, it is no surprise that the textualists on the Court relied on Section 100(b).[74]

In fact, ignoring Section 100(b) was the largest problem with the machine-or-transformation test, which required that *all* processes be tied to a machine or transform matter. Many patented processes from 1790 onward are new uses of manufactures or matter but are not tied to machines and did not "transform" matter in the way the Federal Circuit seemed to envision. Iron working, glass blowing, medical diagnostics, and some new uses for old drugs or tools are all historically patentable processes despite not satisfying the machine-or-transformation test.

And, in fact, that's how the majority saw things. The Court said:

> Section 101 similarly precludes the broad contention that the term "process" categorically excludes business methods. The term "method," which is within §100(b)'s definition of "process," at least as a textual matter and before consulting other limitations in the Patent Act and this Court's precedents, may include at least some methods of doing business. *See, e.g.*, Webster's New International Dictionary 1548 (2d ed. 1954) (defining "method" as"[a]n orderly procedure or process . . . regular way or manner of doing anything; hence, a set form of procedure adopted in investigation or instruction"). The Court is unaware of any argument that the "'ordinary, contemporary, common meaning,'" Diehr, *supra*, at 182, of "method" excludes business methods.[75]

---

[74] See Michael Risch, Bilski Argument: Procedure and Substance, PrawfsBlawg (Nov. 10, 2010, 09:58 EST), http://prawfsblawg.blogs.com/prawfsblawg/2009/11/bilski-argument-substance-and-procedure.html ("I was extremely disappointed that . . . there was not *one single mention* of 35 USC 100(b), *which states the statutory definition of process*. I would think that a court filled with textualists would want to know what the text of the statute says.") (emphasis in original).

[75] Bilski II, 130 S. Ct. at 3222.

Justice Stevens complained that the statutory term "process" should not have been interpreted in an ordinary and common sense, and much of his concurrence was directed at showing why process must have a narrower meaning. Some have argued that the reasoning used by Justice Stevens is suspect as a matter of history[76] and of statutory interpretation.[77] Indeed, the famous 19th-century case *O'Reilly v. Morse*—remarkably left almost entirely out of all *Bilski* opinions—upheld a patent for the business method of "the system of signs . . . in combination with machinery for recording them, as signals for telegraphic purposes."[78]

Even if one agrees with Justice Stevens, though, it is not outside the bounds of reason to disregard history when interpreting the plain language of a statute written and amended well after the historical opinions. After all, Congress frequently clarifies statutes in response to historical court opinions.

Beyond the plain reading, however, the majority's rationale becomes inconsistent. After all, the Court ruled that the claims were not, in fact, patent-eligible processes. In order to reach this result, remain true to the statute, yet reject this patent, the majority had to embrace a broad reading while finding some way to except these particular claims. To get there, Justice Kennedy writes:

> The Court's precedents provide three specific exceptions to §101's broad patent-eligibility principles: "laws of nature, physical phenomena, and abstract ideas." While these exceptions are not required by the statutory text, they are consistent with the notion that a patentable process must be "new and useful." And, in any case, these exceptions have defined the reach of the statute as a matter of statutory *stare decisis* going back 150 years. The concepts covered by these exceptions are "part of the storehouse of knowledge of all men . . . free to all men and reserved exclusively to none."[79]

---

[76] See, e.g., Adam Mossoff, Who Cares What Jefferson Thought about Patents? Reevaluating the Patent "Privilege" in Historical Context, 92 Cornell L. Rev. 953 (2007) (showing that historical account of patent rights is incorrect).

[77] See, e.g., Eric Guttag, Section 273 is NOT a Red Herring: Stevens' Disingenuous Concurrence in *Bilski*. IPWatchDog (June 30, 2010, 22:55 EST), http://www.ipwatchdog.com/2010/06/30/stevens-disingenuous-concurrence-in-bilski/id = 11457/ (arguing that Section 101 must be read in conjunction with Section 273).

[78] O'Reilly v. Morse, 56 U.S. 62, 86 (1853).

[79] Bilski II, 130 S. Ct. at 3225.

Thus, the Court remains true to the statute, except for these three exceptions, which are so old that they define the statute. The inconsistency is that there is no reason these, and only these, exceptions should define the statute, nor that these, and only these, exceptions are proper simply because they are consistent with Section 101's new and useful requirement. Indeed, Justice Breyer adds mental process in his concurrence, despite disagreement about the issue in lower courts.[80] In fact, there is no principled reason why business methods should be excluded from this *stare decisis* category where, as Justice Stevens notes, they were historically rare and where many thought they had been barred since the early 20th century.

Furthermore, the exclusion of laws of nature, physical phenomena, and abstract ideas is not so clear as a matter of *stare decisis*. The Court has repeatedly announced this rule but never barred a patent solely because it fell into one of those categories.[81] In legal terms, the exclusion has mostly been dicta. As discussed below, though the abstraction exclusion is applied in *Bilski*, it too is a proxy for other concerns about the patent application.

Thus, while the majority preached fidelity to the statute, it departed from that fidelity in a critical way. However, it appears that the Court has limited divergence from the statute to *only* abstract ideas, laws of nature, and physical phenomena.

5. Is subject matter a constitutional question?

One interesting and potentially important question was whether the Court would limit subject matter as a constitutional matter. The "Intellectual Property Clause" in the Constitution authorizes Congress to promulgate patent laws to promote the progress of the useful arts.[82] The Court could have ruled that business methods fail to promote the progress of the useful arts, and are thus barred.

Such a ruling would have had two important effects. First, it would have barred Congress from amending the statute—and courts from interpreting it—to expand patentable subject matter beyond the Court's limitations. In other words, Congress can arguably

---

[80] *Id.* at 3233 (Stevens, J., concurring).

[81] See generally, Risch, Everything Is Patentable, *supra* note 15.

[82] U.S. Const. art. I, § 8, cl. 8 (Congress has the power "To promote the Progress of Science and useful Arts, by securing for limited Times to Authors and Inventors the exclusive Right to their respective Writings and Discoveries. . . ").

amend the statute to allow patenting of abstract ideas without offending the Constitution. Second, it would have opened the door for Courts to look more specifically at patent subjects, and perhaps even individual patents, to see if they "promote the progress."

The Court did not elevate patentable subject matter to the level of constitutionality. The majority treated the historical exclusions as a matter of historical statutory interpretation. Despite the historical analysis, Justice Stevens also implied that its constitutional purpose was a tool to determine how to interpret "process" in the statute rather than a constitutional question:

> [A]lthough it is for Congress to "implement the stated pur-
> pose of the Framers by selecting the policy which in its
> judgment best effectuates the constitutional aim" . . . absent
> a discernible signal from Congress, we proceed cautiously
> when dealing with patents that press on the limits of the
> "'standard written into the constitution,'" [] for at the
> "fringes of congressional power," "more is required of legis-
> latures than a vague delegation to be filled in later . . . ."[83]

The concurrence thus implies that Congress can (and perhaps should) clearly delineate subject matter that it believes is in line with the constitutional mandate, and that such determinations would be given wide latitude so long as they are not vague. Of course, where the statute is not vague—as the majority found—then patentable subject matter is statutorily determined. The majority did not even respond to the concurrence's constitutional discussion.

Thus, it does not appear that the Court mandated testing each patent against the constitutional goal of promoting the progress of the useful arts.

6. Did the justices vote as predicted?

After oral argument, predictions were nearly unanimous that Bilski would lose 9–0, even if the scope and rationale of the eventual opinion might have been a surprise.[84] For the most part, the votes

---

[83] Bilski II, 130 S. Ct. at 3252–53 (Stevens, J., concurring).

[84] Josh Sarnoff predicted a narrow decision with a Stevens concurrence. *Bilski*—The Oral Argument, Inherently Sarnoff (Nov. 9, 2009, 19:16 EST), http://inherentlysarnoff.blogspot.com/2009/11/bilski-oral-argument.html.

matched expectations. For example, one would have expected Justices Stevens and Breyer to limit subject matter based on their opinions in prior cases, with Justices Ginsburg and Sotomayor probably following.[85] One might have also expected Chief Justice Roberts and Justices Scalia, Thomas, and Alito to adopt a textualist reading of the statute. This left Justice Kennedy as the swing vote on different issues. Justice Kennedy asked questions at oral argument that implied he could have accepted a bar on business methods.

More surprisingly, the opinions seem to indicate that Justice Scalia was a partial swing vote, and that his vote was unpredictable. First, as a self-avowed originalist, he might have been expected to limit subject matter based on the lack of business methods patents at the nation's founding. Indeed, he asked that very question at oral argument. Further, he did not join the majority regarding the need to change standards as part of changing times. More surprising, however, was his adoption of Justice Breyer's summary of the opinions, which means that he was at least partially persuaded by Justice Breyer's policy viewpoint.

Thus, it could be considered a surprise that Scalia the originalist voted in favor of broad subject matter. Perhaps Scalia the textualist won the internal argument, with the scale tipping toward the historic "abstract ideas" exception that resolved the case. Ironically, "living constitutionalists" on the Court relied on history and tradition to propose limited subject matter.

Looking to the future, with Justice Elena Kagan replacing Justice Stevens, it is unlikely that the Court will swing toward a more restrictive view of patentable subject matter.

7. Is the opinion consistent with the Court's recent patent jurisprudence?

The Court's rejection of the strict machine-or-transformation test is consistent with other recent opinions. The Federal Circuit has, over recent years, promulgated many bright-line tests in various areas. The Court has consistently reversed such tests, opting instead for standards that should apply on a case-by-case basis. For example,

---

[85] Conventional wisdom holds that liberal justices generally disfavor strong IP rights. This is not necessarily so, however. See Matthew Sag, et al., Ideology and Exceptionalism in Intellectual Property: An Empirical Study, 97 Cal. L. Rev. 801, 849–850 (2009) (finding that conservatives generally favor strong IP, but liberals are split in IP cases).

the Court recently overturned rigid Federal Circuit rules relating to obviousness,[86] declaratory relief,[87] injunctions,[88] and the doctrine of equivalents.[89] This decision is consistent with each of the others, embracing uncertain flexibility over certain rigidity.

V. Future Implications

Though *Bilski* did not fundamentally change patentable subject matter jurisprudence, the decision leads to important implications for the future of patent law.

A. Forward to the Past

Bilski simultaneously stops a recent trend of narrowing patentable subject matter and returns to the Court's past. The PTO had sought to limit patentable subject matter to the "technological arts." The Federal Circuit rejected this narrow test, but instead opted for a machine-or-transformation limit. Ironically, both tests would have excluded inventions considered patentable in the distant past, such as methods for manufacturing tools. The Supreme Court's test would not so limit subject matter.

The ruling marks a return not only to past technology but also to past precedent. The majority opinion simply reaffirms decades-old case law—both the substance and the resulting uncertainty. The time after *Benson* and *Diehr* led to much discussion about how to treat intangible methods, and *Bilski* restarts that discussion.

The future of patentable subject matter is thus in the past. The Federal Circuit must restart its jurisprudence in this area without the benefit of the useful, concrete, and tangible result test. The Federal Circuit's ruling effectively wiped out the last 10 years of patentable subject matter jurisprudence and the Supreme Court extended that erasure to 30 years! Lower courts and the PTO must forge a new reality based on the very same precedent they used (and perhaps misused) before.

B. An Undefinable Standard

Courts will struggle now as they did then as they forge this new reality. This is unsurprising because patentable subject matter jurisprudence—not just abstract ideas, but also natural products and

---

[86] KSR Int'l Co. v. Teleflex Inc., 550 U.S. 398 (2007).

[87] MedImmune, Inc. v. Genentech, Inc., 549 U.S. 118 (2007).

[88] eBay Inc. v. MercExchange, L.L.C., 547 U.S. 388 (2006).

[89] Festo Corp. v. Shoketsu Kinzoko Kogyo Kabushiki Co., 535 U.S. 722 (2002).

phenomena of nature—is a mess that can never be cleaned up.[90] While *Bilski's* return to the past does not make the mess any worse, it hardly tidies things.

As noted above, the Court could barely muster a majority for a specific line to draw, and that majority may have shifted at some point. A decision unanimous in outcome but yielding a 5-4 (and arguably 4–4–1) split in rationale is good evidence that defining a stable, consistently applicable, and clear standard is impossible.

Indeed, though he adds little clarity, Justice Stevens rightly points out that the majority opinion fails to provide a way to identify abstract ideas. As he says, the *Bilski* claims are far more complex and concrete than the simple and "abstract" mathematical formulas the Court previously rejected. Nonetheless, the concurrence provides no clear solution by suggesting a business methods patents ban without defining what a business method might be. Finally, neither the majority nor concurring opinions identify what post-solution activity is sufficient to make a claim non-abstract.

There are strong arguments that favor abandoning this sort of line drawing. The better approach is to plainly read "process" as the statute defines it but to do away with the supposed historical limitation on abstractness.[91] Instead, a direct application of the statutory categories "process, machine, manufacture, or composition of matter" should define patentable subject matter.[92] If rigorously applied, other patentability requirements such as novelty, obviousness, utility, description, and enablement are more than sufficient to weed out undesirable patents.

In fact, these other patentability requirements were implicitly considered by the *Bilski* Court. The Court justified its use of an abstract-idea exception in part on Section 101's requirement that inventions be new and useful. Perhaps the claims were not new and useful in the eyes of the Court.

---

[90] See generally, Risch, Everything Is Patentable, *supra* note 15.

[91] *Id.*

[92] See *Id.* (arguing that the broad statutory categories should be the exclusive test for patentable subject matter). See also, Mobil Oil Corp. v. Higginbotham, 436 U.S. 618, 625 (1978) ("There is a basic difference between filling a gap left by Congress' silence and rewriting rules that Congress has affirmatively and specifically enacted.").

The most basic claims here lacked any new practical utility: they did not do anything that provided a direct benefit to the public.[93] Instead they claimed a series of transactions that could have been any series of transactions conducted by anyone. It is not even clear who was to benefit from the claims—presumably the commodities seller benefits, but other participants in the transactions might have only benefited in some circumstances. The Court calls this the "concept" of hedging, and in fact the first claim is for no more than that.

Relatedly, the claimed methods were not definite. They cannot be practiced repeatedly in the same way to achieve the similar results. While a claim can certainly have leeway for circumstance, it should not depend on the ability to find people willing to contract at particular prices.

Also, the claims to the specific types of hedging (in addition to general hedging) were likely obvious. The Court discusses the patent's "use of well-known random analysis techniques."

Furthermore, the broader claims were not enabled or described. The patent specification describes a particular application with a particular formula tied to a very particularized set of data, but it did not describe how that formula might apply to *every* type of commodity and *every* set of consumers, and *every* group of third parties, which was required in order to support the broadest claim.

Some disagree with applying these patentability criteria. They argue that we should apply subject matter limitations even though such patents are surely invalid on other grounds. The rationale is that even if subject matter limits are proxies for other patentability criteria, categorical exclusions can be a more efficient way to reject low-quality patents.

Arguments in favor of subject-matter-as-proxy assume, however, that exclusionary rules can accurately identify which patents should be disallowed. To date no proffered test has shown the ability to do so in a principled way. Thus, the introduction of subject matter

---

[93] See, e.g., Brief for the State of Oregon as Amicus Curiae in Support of Neither Party, at 12, Bilski v. Doll, No. 08-964 (Aug. 6, 2009) ("There is no manifestly useful outcome, no palpable product, no given result. It is not clear how the process is performed, what the tangible outcome is, or even who benefits."). For further discussion about practical utility and patentable subject matter, see also Risch, Everything Is Patentable, *supra* note 15, and Michael Risch, New Uses for Patent Utility (working paper, 2010).

limitations injects unnecessary uncertainty into the process despite claims to the contrary.

Until the judges see the wisdom of abandoning line drawing, cases like *Bilski* will continue to vex courts, the PTO, scholars, attorneys, and inventors. Given the Court's reiteration of the abstract idea exception, however, it is unlikely that lower courts will eschew unwritten exceptions in favor of strict application of other patentability criteria any time soon.

In light of the continued uncertainty in patentable subject matter, perhaps the PTO and Federal Circuit will define abstractness by looking to other patentability criteria as a guide rather than as a replacement. The Court sanctioned this by importing the new and useful requirement to support its abstract idea exception. Importing other criteria means that obvious patent applications that lack practical utility and that are overbroad and underdescribed are more likely to be abstract than non-obvious claims that reach practical ends that are no broader than what the inventor teaches in the patent specification.[94]

C. Patent Standards at the Federal Circuit

Both the majority and the concurrence tell the Federal Circuit to avoid a rigid approach. Indeed, Justice Kennedy's statements that the Federal Circuit might develop special rules to identify abstract inventions failed to garner a majority. Even Justice Stevens recognized that barring business methods would leave some room in each case to determine what claims are business methods.

Of course, the Court arguably sent a clear message after each of the prior cases that rejected a rigid rule. But the other cases involved doctrine that developed over time, and represented different judges writing panel opinions that developed into a rigid rule. The Court intervened to reverse these rules where their application started to yield undesirable results. In *Bilski*, on the other hand, the Federal Circuit announced the rigidity of its rule with no precedential support in a single *en banc* opinion—one practically begging for Supreme Court review.[95] It is quite possible, therefore, that the lower court

---

[94] See Lemley et al., *supra* note 5, at 31 (arguing that *Bilski* claim is abstract because it is not enabled).

[95] See Bilski I, 545 F.3d at 956 ("Thus, we recognize that the Supreme Court may ultimately decide to alter or perhaps even set aside this test to accommodate emerging technologies.").

received prior messages loud and clear, and expected—even wanted—the Court to hear the case to give some guidance.

Three observations result from this insight: First, that the Court granted certiorari is perhaps not the surprise commentators thought. Second, the Federal Circuit sought guidance and received little more than a return to prior non-guiding precedent. Third, as a result, the Federal Circuit may be less likely to promulgate rigid rules in the future.

D. Implications for Business

This review has thus far focused on legal analysis, but even more important is the effect of *Bilski* on business research and development. Alas, it is difficult to predict and too soon to tell what effect *Bilski* will have in practice. First, resetting the debate back to earlier precedent leaves much uncertainty and potentially more litigation in the process, both of which hamper investment.

Second, even so, uncertainty may be better for investment in particular types of technology than banning business methods patents altogether. After all, some chance is better than no chance. Risk-averse companies can always rely on secrecy as they would have under a ban.

Third, there is deep division among interested parties about the effect of business methods patents on investment. A simple examination of the amicus briefs filed in the case illustrates this division. The briefs were numerous: 17 supporting Bilski, 24 supporting the PTO, and 25 favoring neither party. Parties supporting Bilski included Novartis (medical diagnostics); Borland Software (software); Double Rock Corporation (financial services); and Accenture and Pitney Bowes (business operations). Parties supporting the government included Adams Pharmaceutical and the American Medical Association (medical diagnostics); Microsoft and the Business Software Alliance (software); Bloomberg and Bank of America (financial services); and Internet Retailers (business operations). Briefs supporting neither party were filed by a variety of interest groups and took very different positions regarding the scope of patentable subject matter. Some argued for very broad subject matter, while others argued for limits even greater than those sought by the government.

Although it is early, I offer a conservative prediction: investment incentives will change little over the next decade or so. There will, however, be an increased cost and uncertainty associated with prosecuting patents relating to intangible subject matter. On the whole, the news is probably good for two reasons.

First, software patents seem to be clearly patentable unless they are too simple. Software patents were certainly not rejected.

Second, business methods (methods involving less software and more human activity) *might* be patentable, but they also might not be. This could appease all sides. Aggressive inventors can seek patents, and opponents can continue to argue that such patents are too abstract. This may be more costly to inventors than a clear rule that allowed all patents and more costly to potential defendants than a clear rule that disallowed all patents. However, the result is certainly less costly for either side than the worst alternative.

How one ultimately views *Bilski*'s effect on research and development depends on how one values the role of intangible method patents and how one predicts lower courts will implement the "abstract idea" standard. University of San Diego law professor Ted Sichelman sums up the issues nicely:

> Assuming the Federal Circuit and the PTO do not go astray in implementing *Bilski*—which admittedly leaves many doors open to do so—the opinion will allow startups to continue to use patents to garner financing and will, hopefully, set an appropriate balance on the patentability of non-technological inventions.
>
> . . .
>
> And while *Bilski* ultimately holds that business methods are not per se unpatentable, the practical effect of the outcome will be to place unapplied business methods into the precluded "abstract idea" category. If implemented properly, such an approach will ensure that startups—and, indeed, larger and more established companies—are not unnecessarily subject to overly broad patents while maintaining robust incentives to innovate.[96]

Sichelman's predictions are optimistic. A pessimistic story can also be told for each side. If you think that patents are critical to

---

[96] See, e.g., Ted M. Sichelman, Why *Bilski* Benefits Startup Companies, Patently-O (June 29, 2010, 08:19 EST), http://www.patentlyo.com/patent/2010/06/guest-post-why-bilski-benefits-startup-companies.html.

innovation—as I tend to—then this ruling is a bad thing to the extent that it increases patenting costs now and might overly limit patenting later. If you think patents are unnecessary or even harmful for innovation, then you are probably not thrilled with this decision, but it could have been worse: the *Bilski* claims might have been allowed. Further, courts might allow too much patenting of intangible claims in the future.

In the end, this decision is a draw: It does not expand eligibility, but it also puts a halt to the trend of limiting eligibility—which result appears to be exactly the Court's intent. The Court did not want to foreclose the debate nor invalidate a large number of existing patents, and did the best it could short of rejecting all non-statutory exceptions. Justice Kennedy wrote: "Rather than adopting categorical rules that might have wide-ranging and unforeseen impacts, the Court resolves this case narrowly . . . ."[97]

The Court's discussion seems to imply that it simply does not know what effect a broad limitation might have, and thus leaves the determination up to a case-by-case review. The result is not surprising given its recent rulings in other patent cases that also advocate a case-by-case analysis. Though not the best, it is also the better course.[98]

Conclusion

Given that many consider the opinion a non-event, *Bilski v. Kappos* is remarkably important. First, it is another in a recent line of cases emphasizing flexible interpretation of a broad statute. Second, it represents a return to old precedent and reopens the debate about how to interpret that precedent. Third, with Justice Stevens's retirement, it may represent that last, best hope that opponents of software patents had to ban software or even business methods at the judiciary. Fourth, it strikes a balance—albeit an uncertain one—between two important types of innovation: that innovation driven by the exclusivity that patents bring, and that driven by implementing combinations of valuable but non-pioneering intangible methods.

---

[97] Bilski II, 130 S. Ct. at 3229.

[98] See Risch, Everything Is Patentable, *supra* note 15, at 595 ("[T]he judiciary should not limit the subject matter of *all* patents based on *any single case* at bar, and it certainly should not do so without concrete evidence of the supposed harm that an entire class of patents might allegedly cause.") (emphasis in original).

Antitrust Formalism Is Dead! Long Live Antitrust Formalism! Some Implications of *American Needle v. NFL*

Judd E. Stone* and Joshua D. Wright**

Introduction

Few cases before the Supreme Court have been preceded by so many rival interpretations and grand predictions—from the death of modern antitrust policy to the end of professional football[1]—as *American Needle v. National Football League*.[2] The Court's decision reversed the U.S. Court of Appeals for the Seventh Circuit, which had held that with regard to licensing NFL intellectual property, the NFL and its constituent teams constituted a single-entity outside the reach of Section 1 of the Sherman Act. Thus, the Court held, American Needle's claims would survive another day, remanded to the district court for evaluation under the Rule of Reason. While unanimous, the Court raised nearly as many questions as it resolved; observers have depicted the opinion as everything from an antitrust sea change[3] to an idiosyncratic application of a niche doctrine with

* Research Fellow, International Center for Law and Economics.

** Associate Professor, George Mason University School of Law and Department of Economics. We thank Isaac Gruber for valuable research assistance and Bruce Kobayashi, Steve Salop, and Ilya Shapiro for helpful comments and discussions.

[1] Drew Brees, Saints' Quarterback Drew Brees Weighs In on NFL's Supreme Court Case, Wash. Post, January 10, 2010, available at http://www.washingtonpost.com/wp-dyn/content/article/2010/01/07/AR2010010702947.html?sid=ST2010052401943 ("The gains we fought for and won as players over the years could be lost, while the competition that runs through all aspects of the sport could be undermined.").

[2] Am. Needle, Inc. v. NFL, 560 U.S. ____, 130 S. Ct. 2201 (2010).

[3] See Press Release, American Antitrust Institute, AAI Applauds Supreme Court's Decision in *American Needle* (May 24, 2010), available at http://www.antitrustinstitute.org/Archives/Needle_Decision.ashx ("This decision shows that the Supreme Court is still capable of rejecting extreme pro-defendant positions, and should be a cautionary tale for defendants that seek to short-cut sound antitrust analysis . . . .").

little practical relevance.[4] Advocates of a more interventionist competition policy accurately note that *American Needle* represented the
first plaintiff's victory in an antitrust suit before the Supreme Court
in several years. Accordingly, one line of reasoning goes, the Court's
unanimous narrowing of the "intra-enterprise conspiracy immunity," or *Copperweld* immunity,[5] portends a break from several
decades of antitrust excessively concerned with over-deterrence and
a newfound confidence in judicial application of the Rule of Reason
without potentially competition-chilling error. In contrast, those perplexed over the sound and fury surrounding *American Needle* contend that the doctrine contains virtually no practical importance at
all. Under this construction, *American Needle* narrowed a doctrine
with roots preceding the modern architecture of mergers and acquisitions. By this line of logic, the few firms that might have availed
themselves of *Copperweld* immunity can obviate Sherman Act Section
1 liability (anti-competitive agreements by rival firms) by consolidat-
ing diffuse operations into a formal single-entity.

Both polar interpretations of *American Needle*, however, are premature. Depicting the case as a seismic shift in competition policy
ignores two major components of the Court's antitrust jurisprudence: first, a respect for the relative costs of over-deterring versus
under-deterring potentially anti-competitive conduct, referred to as
"error costs"; and second, a history of preferring readily administrable antitrust rules. That it was of little practical consequence, however, understates the increasing complexity of businesses and entrepreneurial arrangements and the critical importance of screening
mechanisms to the error-cost framework. The *American Needle* decision will, at minimum, affect credit card companies, franchising
firms, sports leagues, and interdependent combinations of all kinds;
to the extent it represents a greater reliance on alternate screening
methods, it could affect all antitrust litigation.

We offer an explanation of *American Needle* simultaneously more
modest yet less dismissive. Rather than a wholesale rejection of

---

[4] See Posting of Ted Frank to Point of Law, http://www.pointoflaw.com/archives/
2010/05/american-needle.php (May 24, 2010, 12:21 EST) (*"American Needle* . . . isn't
a tenth as important as everyone is going to be telling you over the next few days.").

[5] In this paper, we use the terms "intra-enterprise conspiracy immunity," "*Copperweld*
immunity," and "single-entity defense" interchangeably. All three terms refer to
prohibiting antitrust suits under Section 1 based on intra-firm arrangements.

error-cost concerns, *American Needle* represents the Supreme Court's understandable decision to abandon an antitrust "filter" that proved perennially problematic in its practical application. The role of this filter is to allow judges a doctrinal basis for dismissing at early stages, including prior to substantial discovery, claims alleging agreements that simply do not raise antitrust concerns. For example, consider the hypothetical price-fixing claim alleging that separate but not wholly owned subsidiaries of Coca-Cola Enterprises, Coca-Cola, and Coke Zero, are engaged in an illegal price-fixing scheme.[6] In light of the Court's recent decision in *Bell Atlantic v. Twombly*,[7] much of the work of the *Copperweld* doctrine has been subsumed by the "plausibility" pleading requirement, consistently applied at the earliest stages of an antitrust case.[8] Read in a vacuum, the Court's misguided emphasis on the unmanageable "unity of interests" test harkens to earlier days of antitrust formalism despite its protestations otherwise. The choice to narrow the intra-enterprise immunity doctrine in light of *Twombly*, however, is completely consistent with the error-cost principle of employing relatively low-cost screens to dismiss meritless antitrust claims in order to maximize consumer welfare. *American Needle* unraveled *Copperweld* immunity from two pressures: first, the unmanageable vagaries of the "unity of interests" language raised the costs of maintaining *Copperweld*, and second, *Twombly* dismissals for lack of economic plausibility at the pleading stage reduced *Copperweld*'s necessity.

This article proceeds in five parts. Part I discusses the legal history of *Copperweld* immunity from claims under Section 1 of the Sherman Act. Part II explains the error-cost framework and the economic justification for *Copperweld* immunity as a screen to reduce the error costs of Section 1 liability. Part III demonstrates how *American Needle* was the product of error-cost analysis of the relative merits of *Copperweld* immunity as a tool to remove comparatively marginal antitrust claims. Nonetheless, the stated logic of the Court's opinion reflects a perverse formalism with regard to the theory of the firm and to

[6] See Coke Sues Coke Zero for Infringement, July 26, 2006, available at http://www.youtube.com/watch?v= pv8YgrqUCVU.

[7] Bell Atl. Corp. v. Twombly, 550 U.S. 544 (2007).

[8] See Herbert Hovenkamp, The Pleading Problem in Antitrust Cases and Beyond, 95 Iowa L. Rev. Bull. 55 (2010), available at http://www.uiowa.edu/~ilr/bulletin/ILRB_95_Hovenkamp.pdf.

corporate organization more broadly. Part IV explains *American Needle* in light of the error-cost framework and how, in light of the "plausibility" pleading requirements presented in *Twombly* and *Iqbal*,[9] the Court's opinion reflects an imperfect attempt to substitute away from *Copperweld* immunity in favor of increased reliance on *Twombly* pleading and the Rule of Reason as screening mechanisms. We conclude with a review of *American Needle's* broader implications.

I. The Law and History of *Copperweld* Immunity

A. The Historical Origin of Copperweld

The Supreme Court has long held that Section 1 of the Sherman Act is impossible to construe literally; Justice Sandra Day O'Connor noted that "[a]lthough the Sherman Act, by its terms, prohibits every agreement 'in restraint of trade,' this Court has long recognized that Congress intended to outlaw only unreasonable restraints."[10] Indeed, the text of the act criminalizes every "contract, combination . . . , or conspiracy, in restraint of trade".[11] By necessity, of course, every contract restrains trade—that is precisely the purpose of a contract. The Supreme Court first narrowed the scope of the act by declaring that only contracts, combinations, or conspiracies in "unreasonable" restraint of trade violated it.[12] Subsequent statutes and cases extracted other conspiracies on various grounds. Unions and collective-bargaining agreements were exempted for expressly political reasons,[13] while Major League Baseball retained immunity from Section 1 scrutiny for reasons expressly historical.[14] Some of the most vexing of these agreements involved entities that commonly would not be expected to compete against one another: sister corporations,

---

[9] Ashcroft v. Iqbal, 556 U.S. ____, 129 S. Ct. 1937 (2009).

[10] State Oil Co. v. Khan, 522 U.S. 3, 10 (1997).

[11] Sherman Antitrust Act, 15 U.S.C § 1 (2004).

[12] Am. Needle, 130 S. Ct. at 2210. See also Standard Oil Co. v. United States, 221 U.S. 1, 87–88 (1911).

[13] Clayton Act § 6, 15 U.S.C. § 17 (1914) ("Nothing contained in the antitrust laws shall be construed to forbid the existence and operation of labor . . . organizations . . . ").

[14] Fed. Baseball Club of Baltimore, Inc. v. Nat'l League of Prof'l Baseball Clubs, 259 U.S. 200 (1922).

franchisor/franchisee relationships, and multiple divisions of an overarching business.

Before antitrust law became moored to economic analysis in the mid-1970s, intra-enterprise agreements were adjudicated under Section 1 formally by the statute's terms: individuals could conspire in violation of Section 1 despite being "affiliated or integrated under common ownership."[15] That multiple "instrumentalities of a single manufacturing merchandising unit" existed under "common ownership and control"[16] did not immunize the single unit from Section 1 scrutiny. Taken at face value, Section 1 called on courts to adjudicate not only the contracts between businesses but interactions entirely within firms. Under this antiquated, formalistic conception of Section 1, a single firm could as easily constitute a cartel as multiple firms, and the minimal requirement for an anti-competitive agreement was two entities of any sort—regardless of common ownership, control, or interests.

As economic analysis increasingly informed antitrust law and policy, however, both courts and enforcement agencies began to recognize, on economic grounds, that some set of agreements should nonetheless remain beyond Section 1 scrutiny. The doctrine was severely criticized because its focus on whether a parent and subsidiary had functioned in an integrated fashion was "unconnected to antitrust policy, [and] hopelessly vague."[17] While the purely formalistic model of Section 1 embraced by *United States v. Yellow Cab* required courts to make such examinations, enforcement agencies and academics increasingly recognized the condemnation of intra-enterprise conspiracies as fundamentally orthogonal to the central antitrust mission.[18] With Section 2 available to target unilateral decisions with anti-competitive effects, intra-enterprise conspiracy claims represented the triumph of formalism over economic substance. The availability of such claims enabled competitors to wield antitrust scrutiny against rivals and deter behavior with competitively neutral or pro-competitive implications.

[15] United States v. Yellow Cab Co., 332 U.S. 218, 227 (1947).

[16] Kiefer-Stewart Co. v. Joseph E. Seagram & Sons, 340 U.S. 211, 215 (1951).

[17] Phillip Areeda, Intraenterprise Conspiracy in Decline, 97 Harv. L. Rev. 451, 469 (1983).

[18] *Id*. at 462–63 ("The main effects of the intraenterprise conspiracy doctrine have been to confuse litigants and courts and to lengthen and complicate antitrust litigation.").

With the advancement of economic analysis displacing previously long-standing, formalistic models in antitrust, ranging from merger analysis to the use of vertical restraints and vertical integration,[19] the intra-enterprise conspiracy doctrine thus appeared to be a vestige discredit of formalism. Less than a year after Professor Phillip Areeda predicted the doctrine's collapse, the Supreme Court granted certiorari in *Copperweld v. Independence Tube*.[20]

B. Copperweld Corp. v. Independence Tube Corp.

In *Copperweld*, a defendant pipe corporation, Copperweld, purchased a freestanding division from a separate conglomerate, Lear Siegler.[21] Lear Siegler agreed not to compete with Copperweld in pipe manufacturing for five years after the purchase.[22] After an employee of the acquired division left to form the plaintiff corporation, Independence Tube, Copperweld and its subsidiary contacted pipe customers and suppliers to discourage their dealing with Independence.[23] Independence Tube claimed that Copperweld and its subsidiary "conspired . . . in restraint of trade" within the meaning of Section 1, and a jury agreed at trial, awarding treble damages against both the parent and subsidiary.[24] The Seventh Circuit affirmed as to both the parent and subsidiary corporations.[25]

The Supreme Court reversed, rejecting the awkward formalism exemplified by *Yellow Cab*.[26] The Sherman Act made a fundamental distinction between "unilateral" and "concerted" conduct and refused to condemn "coordinated conduct among officers or employees of the same company."[27] The Court noted that because

---

[19] See generally Ronald H. Coase, The Nature of the Firm, 4 Economica 386 (1937); Benjamin Klein, Robert G. Crawford, & Armen A. Alchian, Vertical Integration, Appropriable Rents, and the Competitive Contracting Process, 21 J.L. & Econ. 297 (1978); Oliver E. Williamson, Markets and Hierarchies: Analysis and Antitrust Implications (The Free Press, 1975).

[20] Copperweld Corp. v. Independence Tube Corp., 467 U.S. 752 (1984).

[21] *Id*. at 756.

[22] *Id*.

[23] *Id*. at 756–57.

[24] *Id*. at 757–58.

[25] *Id*. at 758–59.

[26] *Id*. at 760–61.

[27] *Id*. at 769.

parent and subsidiary corporations constituted a "single economic unit"[28] that enjoyed "ultimate interests . . . [that] are identical,"[29] the officers of each firm were not "separate economic actors,"[30] rendering Section 1 inapplicable.[31] Independence Tube's implausible claim motivated the Supreme Court to reexamine the formalism of *Yellow Cab* in a manner that would enable future judges to summarily dismiss similar claims without requiring extensive discovery or the strictures of the Rule of Reason. *Copperweld* immunity provided an easily articulated rationale that mapped onto straightforward economic intuition: a parent and wholly owned subsidiary neither could nor should be expected to behave as potential competitors might. Rival firms predicating Section 1 claims on wholly internal behavior are therefore unlikely to increase net consumer welfare by doing so, and courts should be unwilling to entertain these claims.

The contours of *Copperweld*'s exemption from Section 1 scrutiny, however, remained uncertain—as did the exact grounds for the Supreme Court's justification. Forcing parent-subsidiary corporate groups into a single firm in order to avoid antitrust scrutiny merely subsidized inefficient mergers. Nevertheless, *Copperweld* presented only the narrowest circumstance, where a parent corporation entirely owned a subsidiary division, permitting the Court to alternatively declare the origin of the exemption to be the firms' "unity of interests" and their status as commonly controlled actors. While these two factors were interchangeably cited in *Copperweld*, they need not appear simultaneously. Indeed, in nearly any other business arrangement, a "unity of interests" and common control would not necessarily follow each other. Members of an oligopolistic cartel certainly enjoy a "unity of interests" at least in the short run; various directors of divisions within a single corporation hold at least partially divergent interests with regard to future business strategies for their divisions and the company as a whole.[32] Similarly, franchisees, companies owned partially in common, and members of a league

---

[28] *Id*. at 772 n.18.

[29] *Id*.

[30] *Id*. at 769.

[31] See *Id*. at 768.

[32] See Part II, *infra*; Chicago Prof'l Sports Ltd. v. NBA, 95 F.3d 593, 598 (7th Cir. 1996) ("Even a single firm contains many competing interests.").

or overarching business organization may be subject to great or even total common control while enjoying divergent economic interests. The irreconcilable tension between unified interests and common control as bases for *Copperweld* immunity sprang into existence no sooner than the publication of the opinion validating it.[33]

C. *Post*-Copperweld *and* Major League Soccer

The Supreme Court had the luxury of dismissing Independence Tube's meritless claim on the cryptic grounds that *Copperweld* and its subsidiary acted as a "single economic unit" under a "unity of interests."[34] Subsequent lower courts, however, wrestled with consistently implementing this excessively vague language. Wholly owned subsidiaries and their parent companies routinely mapped their firm structures directly onto the facts of *Copperweld* so as to avail themselves of *Copperweld* immunity.[35] Similarly, several circuit courts of appeals granted wholly owned sister corporations—subsidiaries subject to a common parent's control—*Copperweld* immunity.[36] A handful of courts slightly broadened or narrowed this structure: at least one case extended *Copperweld* immunity to a chain of

[33] As Benjamin Klein and Andres Lerner point out, *Copperweld*'s "unity of interest" language is best interpreted as measuring indicia of control rather than incentive alignment. That interpretation also has the benefit of being consistent with at least one strand of the modern economic theory of the firm. Benjamin Klein & Andres Lerner, "The Firm in Economics and Antitrust Law," Issues in Competition Law and Policy 1, 249 (W. Collins, ed., American Bar Association Antitrust Section, 2008) ("[T]he economic definition of the firm that corresponds most closely with the legal definition and common usage focuses on control rights. . . . Whether one places the label of a firm on these various contractual arrangements is less important to an economist than an understanding of the economic motivation and effects of the particular contractual arrangement. However, classifications of alternative contractual arrangements are important for antitrust law.").

[34] Copperweld, 467 U.S. at 772 n. 18.

[35] See Eichorn v. AT&T Corp., 248 F.3d 131, 138 (3d Cir. 2001) (Lucent held to be a subsidiary of AT&T, and thus incapable of Section 1 conspiracy); Russ' Kwik Car Wash, Inc. v. Marathon Petroleum Co., 772 F.2d 214, 216 (6th Cir. 1985) (transfer of products between a parent and subsidiary granted Section 1 immunity under *Copperweld*); Rosen v. Hyundai Group, 829 F. Supp. 41, 45 n. 6 (E.D.N.Y. 1993) (an American subsidiary of a foreign corporation immune under Section 1).

[36] See Davidson Schaaf, Inc. v. Liberty Nat. Fire Ins., 69 F.3d 868, 871 (8th Cir. 1995) (two wholly-owned subsidiaries of the same parent cannot conspire under Section 1); Century Oil Tool, Inc. v. Prod. Specialties, Inc., 737 F.2d 1316, 1317 (5th Cir. 1993) (a group of individuals with joint ownership over a parent company and its two subsidiaries have Section 1 immunity).

separately owned theaters on the grounds that the "economic reality" of their common franchise rendered Section 1 inapplicable.[37] Conversely, one federal court strictly limited *Copperweld* to the parent-subsidiary structure, even excluding sister corporations.[38] Regardless, the implementation of *Copperweld* to wholly owned companies proved relatively straightforward.

Smaller equity stakes in a subsidiary, however, began to separate *Copperweld*'s "unity of interests" rationale from its "common control" rationale. Some district courts implemented a "complete common ownership" interpretation of *Copperweld*, allowing immunity only for total common ownership, subject only to a *de minimis* exception. This exception generally allowed firms with extremely high equity stakes in another entity, ranging from 90 percent to 95 percent, to avail themselves of *Copperweld*.[39] Most district courts, however, recognized substantially lower ownership stakes to provide the requisite common control necessary for *Copperweld* immunity, ranging from 70 percent down to a bare minimum of majority common ownership. These decisions generally cited the parent company or common owner's ability to exercise great control over its subsidiary as the economic purpose grounding *Copperweld*. The District Court for the Northern District of Georgia, for example, held that "[t]he 51% ownership retained by [a parent company] assured it of full control over [a partially owned subsidiary] and assured it could intervene at any time that [the subsidiary] ceased to act in its best interests."[40] If applicable corporate law permitted multiple firms to formally arrange themselves separately, yet to subject one (or more) to a single parent's control, antitrust sanctions for "coordinated action" of these firms merely served to encourage consolidation under a formal single-entity.

Courts handled more esoteric business arrangements somewhat less predictably, fashioning different rationales to ascertain common control absent a sufficient ownership stake to render common control obvious. *Williams v. I.B. Fischer Nevada* was one of the first attempts

---

[37] See Orson, Inc. v. Miramax Film Corp., 862 F. Supp. 1378, 1386 (E.D. Pa. 1994).

[38] See Aspen Title & Escrow, Inc. v. Jeld-Wen, Inc., 677 F. Supp. 1477, 1486 (D. Or. 1987).

[39] See Leaco Enters., Inc. v. Gen. Elec. Co., 737 F. Supp. 605, 608–09 (D. Or. 1990)

[40] Novatel Commc'ns Inc. v. Cellular Tel. Supply, Inc., 1986 U.S. Dist. LEXIS 16017, *25–26 (N.D. Ga.).

to address franchises under the *Copperweld* rubric.[41] In *Fischer*, a terminated Jack-in-the-Box manager brought suit against his former employers, both the franchisee, and the franchisor, premised on a clause in the franchise agreement restricting co-franchisees from hiring terminated employees for six months.[42] The defendant franchisor justified the clause as "prevent[ing] franchises from 'raiding' one another's management employees after time and expense have been incurred in training them."[43] The district court agreed, holding a franchisee and franchisor incapable of a Section 1 conspiracy for several separate reasons. First, though franchisees may exercise independent action on business decisions, such as price, this ability arises from territorial division rather than a competitive relationship.[44] Additionally, separate incorporation could not constitute evidence of a "conspiracy," particularly where the common franchise policies are dictated by an overarching corporate policy.[45] Ultimately, the court held that, despite the declared "independent contractor" relationship between franchisor and franchisee, the degree of control exerted by the franchisor corporation—including opening hours, insurance requirements, and processes by which retail goods would be made—rendered the franchisor and franchisee a "single enterprise" within the meaning of *Copperweld*.[46]

Courts ultimately relied on proxies for control, such as ownership and restrictive covenants, because the "unity of interests" test as frequently applied proved not only unwieldy but economically irrelevant. As Seventh Circuit Judge Frank Easterbrook noted in *Chicago Professional Sports v. National Basketball Association*, even a fully integrated single firm contains "many competing interests."[47] Rival divisions within a single firm pursue broadly different agendas, especially when one or more of these divisions are regulated or mandated by another dictate of federal law. For example, environmental regulations compel U.S. car manufacturers to offer lines of hybrid and

---

[41] Williams v. I.B. Fischer Nevada, 794 F. Supp. 1026 (D. Nev. 1992), aff'd, 999 F.2d 445 (9th Cir. 1993).

[42] *Id.* at 1029.

[43] *Id.*

[44] *Id.* at 1031.

[45] *Id.* at 1031–32.

[46] *Id.* at 1032.

[47] Chicago Prof'l Sports Ltd. v. NBA, 95 F.3d 593, 598 (7th Cir. 1996).

low-emissions cars in order to raise the average fuel efficiency of their fleets—even though these vehicles are not profitable due to expensive manufacturing processes and modest demand.[48] By contrast, sport-utility vehicles and light trucks remained popular throughout the 1990s and 2000s, allowing carmakers to reap a profit sufficient to support their otherwise flagging hybrid divisions.[49] This cross-subsidy alone indicates that General Motors' SUV and hybrid car divisions hardly enjoy a perfect "unity of interests" under *Copperweld*—yet a plaintiff that sought to bring suit under Section 1 claiming a conspiracy to inflate the price of sport-utility vehicles would rightly be summarily dismissed even prior to discovery. This is the main economic advantage of *Copperweld* immunity: to provide a low-cost screen by which judges may dismiss claims of collusive behavior that are, in fact, the product of wholly firm-internal decisionmaking.

Economists Benjamin Klein and Andres Lerner demonstrated that *Copperweld*'s reliance on a "unity of interests," and lower court applications of the "unity of interest" test that have focused on complete alignment of incentives rather than control, reflected a basic ignorance as to the modern economic theory of the firm. A firm was not simply the formal boundaries dictated by articles of incorporation or various partnership agreements; rather, a firm existed in order to serve two economic purposes.[50] First, firms allocate control in order to prevent holdup problems inherent in making asset-specific investments.[51] Second, firms allocate residual profits as incentives for performance. The precise legal relationships within a firm follow, rather than lead, the economic relationships; firms will tend to gravitate toward organizational structures that minimize transaction costs in order to maximize these residual profits.[52] It is insufficient for

---

[48] Holman Jenkins Jr., Yes, Detroit Can Be Fixed: A CAFE Tweak Can Bust the UAW Labor Monopoly, Wall St. J., Nov. 5, 2008, at A21.

[49] *Id.* ("For 30 years, to make and sell the large vehicles that earn their profits, the Detroit Three have been effectively required to build small cars in high-wage, UAW factories, though it means losing money on every car.").

[50] See Klein & Lerner, *supra* note 33, at *15.

[51] *Id.* at *5.

[52] See *id.*; Benjamin Klein, Robert G. Crawford, & Armen A. Alchian, Vertical Integration, Appropriable Rents, and the Competitive Contracting Process, 21 J. L. & Econ. 297 (1978); Oliver E. Williamson, Transaction Cost Economics: The Governance of Contractual Relations, 22 J. L. & Econ. 233 (1979).

antitrust purposes, then, to describe a firm by its legal boundaries; instead, contracts can be viewed as firms themselves. Where multiple businesses or parties organized themselves with centralized control in order to reduce transaction costs, those actors operated as a single economic unit deserving of, and generally receiving, immunity from Section 1 sanctions. Yet multiple firms could enter into such an arrangement despite thoroughly heterogeneous interests, similar to how multiple divisions within a single corporation might have wildly divergent incentives, despite clearly existing as part of the same firm. That many lower courts interpreted the "unity of interests" test crafted in *Copperweld* to require an examination of the internal motives of each participant proved more psychologically than economically useful.

Perhaps no case exposed how ultimately unworkable *Copperweld*'s "unity of interests" language had become as First Circuit Court of Appeals Judge Michael Boudin's opinion in *Fraser v. Major League Soccer*.[53] In *Major League Soccer*, the plaintiff players sued the defendant franchisee/investors claiming that Major League Soccer entered into an unlawful conspiracy not to compete for players' services in violation of Section 1.[54] While MLS availed itself successfully of *Copperweld* immunity at the trial level, the First Circuit found *Copperweld* unavailing.[55] The court struggled with the unusual structure of MLS in applying *Copperweld*, as the league consisted of owner/investors, while MLS proper retained formal "ownership" over all the teams.[56] MLS represented something of "a hybrid arrangement, somewhere between a single company . . . and a cooperative arrangement between existing competitors."[57] In declining to apply *Copperweld*, Judge Boudin noted the extreme complexity of interpreting *Copperweld* in light of hybrid business arrangements.[58]

Judge Boudin also presaged the very substitution that would come to pass through *American Needle*.[59] "The law," he wrote, "could

---

[53] Fraser v. Major League Soccer, LLC, 284 F.3d 47 (1st Cir. 2002).

[54] *Id.* at 54–55.

[55] *Id.* at 59.

[56] *Id.* at 57–58.

[57] *Id.* at 58.

[58] *Id.* at 56–57.

[59] *Id.* at 58.

develop along either or both of two different lines. One could expand upon *Copperweld* to develop functional tests or criteria for shielding . . . such hybrids . . . it would also prevent claims, clearly inappropriate in our view . . . .The other course is to reshape Section 1's Rule of Reason toward a body of more flexible rules for interdependent multi-party enterprises."[60] Judge Boudin noted the heretofore unresolved dilemma in developing intra-enterprise conspiracy immunity: either the substantial expansion of a new layer of analysis was needed in order to determine the propriety of *Copperweld*, or an alternative screen based on Rule of Reason analysis. Frustrated with the vagaries of a "complete unity of interests," the First Circuit nonetheless ruled in favor of MLS but on alternate grounds.[61] Judge Boudin, who periodically teaches antitrust at Harvard Law School, could make little use of *Copperweld*'s "unity of interest" requirements in the context of an interdependent sports league—and it turns out the Supreme Court would fare no better.

II. Error Costs and the Economic Rationale for the Single-Entity Defense

While much is said about the evolution of the single-entity defense in antitrust law, both before and after *Copperweld*, less often discussed is the function of such a defense in antitrust, a system of rules aimed at protecting consumers from the creation and exercise of market power. A proper evaluation of the implications of *American Needle* requires an understanding of how the single-entity defense "fits" in the antitrust framework. The primary role of such a rule is to supply a much-needed method for courts to provide for early resolution of antitrust claims concerning business arrangements that are not likely to trigger the core antitrust concern: consumer harm caused by the creation or exercise of market power. The single-entity defense provides courts an instrument to efficiently dismiss these cases while avoiding the host of social costs associated with engaging in discovery, motions, and trial for such claims. And of course, allowing such cases to proceed to discovery (and beyond) creates the possibility of judicial error, which in turn creates its own social costs.

---

[60] *Id.*

[61] Specifically, the court held that Fraser's appeal was barred as a matter of law by the jury's special verdict on Fraser's alternate, Section 2 claim. *Id.* at 71.

The optimal system of antitrust rules would balance the benefits of their application with the error and administrative costs of their implementation. This approach to evaluating antitrust rules is often described as "the error cost" approach and, as discussed below, is frequently associated with Frank Easterbrook's seminal article, "The Limits of Antitrust."[62] In this part, we discuss the role of the single-entity doctrine in modern antitrust as an efficient filter for claims involving business activity sufficiently unlikely to cause antitrust harms that the investment in judicial and societal resources, and the risk of judicial error, render further discovery or trial unproductive.

A. A Brief Primer on the Error-Cost Approach to Antitrust[63]

The error-cost framework is one of the most influential contributions to antitrust law and economics in large part because it paved the way for the incorporation of the powerful tools of decision theory (or "error-cost analysis"), into the optimal design of antitrust rules. The error-cost framework in antitrust originates with Easterbrook's seminal analysis, itself built on twin premises: first, that false positives are more costly than false negatives, because self-correction mechanisms mitigate the latter but not the former; and second, that errors of both types are inevitable, because distinguishing pro-competitive conduct from anti-competitive conduct is an inherently difficult task in the single-firm context.[64] At its core, the error-cost framework is a simple but powerful analytical tool that requires inputs from state-of-the-art economic theory and empirical evidence about the competitive consequences of various types of business conduct and produces outputs in the form of legal rules.

The error-cost approach is one borne out of a true melding of law and economics. Legal scholars typically avoid rigorous attempts to work through the available economic theory and evidence when discussing the optimal design of legal rules. Economists, meanwhile, frequently fail to assess their analyses in realistic institutional settings and therefore neglect to incorporate the social costs of erroneous enforcement decisions into their analyses and recommendations

---

[62] Frank H. Easterbrook, The Limits of Antitrust, 63 Tex. L. Rev. 1 (1984).

[63] For a more complete discussion of the error-cost approach to modern antitrust, on which Part II relies, see Geoffrey A. Manne & Joshua D. Wright, Innovation and the Limits of Antitrust, 6 J. Comp. L. & Econ. 153 (2010). See also Fred S. McChesney, Easterbrook on Errors, 6 J. Comp. L. & Econ. 11 (2010).

[64] Easterbrook, *supra* note 62, at 3, 7.

for legal rules. Thus, it is unsurprising that the error-cost framework lies at the heart of modern economic and legal debates surrounding antitrust analysis of business arrangements. The key policy tradeoff, Easterbrook explained, was that between Type I ("false positive") and Type II ("false negative") errors. Table 1 presents a matrix laying out the types of errors that occur in antitrust litigation.[65]

Table 1. Possible Errors in Antitrust Assessment of Business Practices

Competitive Impact	Illegal	Legal
Harmful to Competition	Percentage of cases correctly condemning anti-competitive practices	Percentage of cases falsely absolving anti-competitive practices ("false negatives")
Not Harmful to Competition	Percentage of cases falsely condemning legitimate practices ("false positives")	Percentage of cases correctly absolving legitimate practices

From simple legal and economic assumptions, Easterbrook provided a powerful framework for thinking about the optimal design of antitrust rules in the face of expected errors. The assumptions were as follows: (1) both types of errors were inevitable in antitrust cases because of the difficulty in distinguishing efficient, pro-competitive business conduct from anti-competitive behavior;[66] (2) the social costs associated with Type I errors would generally be greater than the social costs of Type II errors because market forces offer at least some corrective with respect to Type II errors and none with regard to Type I errors, or, as Easterbrook articulated it, "the economist's system corrects monopoly more readily than it corrects judicial [Type

---

[65] Table 1 originally appeared in David S. Evans & Jorge Padilla, Neo-Chicago Approach to Unilateral Practices, 72 U. Chi. L. Rev. 73, 84 (2005).

[66] These are two separate components of the error-cost approach. The first is the inevitability of errors with decision by legal rule generally. See Easterbrook, *supra* note 62, at 14–15 (reiterating that "one cannot have the savings of decision by rule without accepting the costs of mistakes."). The second point is that the likelihood of antitrust error depends crucially on the development of economic science to produce techniques and methods by which we can successfully identify conduct that harms consumers. See generally Frank H. Easterbrook, Workable Antitrust Policy, 84 Mich. L. Rev. 1696 (1986).

II] errors;"[67] and (3) optimal antitrust rules will minimize the expected sum of error costs subject to the constraint that the rules be relatively simple and reasonably administrable.[68]

From those simple assumptions, Easterbrook argued that a number of simple-to-apply rules, or "filters," could be used to minimize the sum of errors and administration costs. Among those error-cost filters that Easterbrook discussed were requirements that a plaintiff demonstrate that the firm at issue had market power, that the practices could harm consumers, whether firms in the industry used different methods of production and distribution, whether the evidence was consistent with a reduction in output, and whether the complaining firm was a rival in the relevant market.[69]

The notion that antitrust rules must be sensitive to both error costs and the costs of administering them was not exclusive to Easterbrook, or even Chicago. Then-Judge Stephen Breyer's well-known admonition in *Town of Concord v. Boston Edison Co.* that antitrust rules "must be administratively workable and therefore cannot always take account of every complex economic circumstance or qualification,"[70] shared the view that the real power of economics in antitrust was not found in its ability to improve decisionmaking on a case-by-case basis by making judges more like economists, but in generating simple rules that contained economic content.[71]

---

[67] Easterbrook, *supra* note 62, at 15.

[68] *Id.*

[69] Easterbrook, *supra* note 62, at 18. For a discussion of these filters as applied to the Microsoft litigation, see William H. Page, Microsoft and the Limits of Antitrust, 6 J. Comp. L. & Econ. 33 (2010).

[70] 915 F.2d 17, 22 (1st Cir. 1990). The Chicago School of antitrust has traditionally shared with Breyer's Harvard School a preference for using economics to generate simple and administrable rules rather than overly sophisticated economic tests. See Joshua D. Wright, The Roberts Court and the Chicago School of Antitrust: The 2006 Term and Beyond, 3 Competition Pol'y Int'l 25, 27 (2007), available at http://papers.ssrn.com/sol3/papers.cfm?abstract_id= 1028028; William E. Kovacic, The Intellectual DNA of Modern U.S. Competition Law for Dominant Firm Conduct: The Chicago/Harvard Double Helix, 2007 Colum. Bus. L. Rev. 1, 32-35 (2007). For further discussion of the Chicago and Harvard Schools in the context of modern antitrust jurisprudence, see Daniel A. Crane, *linkLine's* Institutional Suspicions, 2008–2009 Cato Sup. Ct. Rev. 111 (2009).

[71] The error-cost framework has been applied to identify optimal rules for a host of business arrangements ranging from vertical restraints to horizontal mergers. See generally Joshua D. Wright, Overshot the Mark? A Simple Explanation of the Chicago School's Influence on Antitrust, 5 Competition Pol'y Int'l 179 (2009); Keith N. Hylton

The key point is that the task of distinguishing anti-competitive behavior from pro-competitive behavior is a Herculean one imposed on enforcers and judges, and that even when economists get it right before the practice is litigated, some error is inevitable. The strength of the error-cost framework is that it allows regulators, judges, and policymakers to harness the power of economics to form simple and sensible filters and safe harbors rather than converting themselves into amateur econometricians, game theorists, or behaviorists.[72]

Within the error-cost framework, the promise of any bright-line rule depends on its qualities as a filter that can reliably distinguish claims involving business activities that are not likely to generate antitrust harms from those that might upon further inspection and analysis. The market power requirement in Section 2 of the Sherman Act, for example, is the signature error-cost filter because, while there are close and complex cases on the margins, it can be applied to reliably rule out allegations of competitive harm arising out of business activities by firms with small market shares. The filter is linked closely to economic theory and empirical evidence, which tells us that non-standard contractual arrangements such as exclusive dealing, "tying," and vertical restraints involving firms without market power are highly unlikely to result in consumer losses and likely promote competition.

Yet another error-cost filter that is less obvious, but more interesting for the purposes of discussing *Copperweld* immunity, is the two-product requirement in tying cases under Section 2 of the Sherman Act. Of course, much like the one-half economic and one-half metaphysical inquiry concerning the boundaries of the firm undergirding

---

& Michael Salinger, Tying Law and Policy: A Decision Theoretic Approach, 69 Antitrust L.J. 469 (2001); C. Frederick Beckner III & Steven C. Salop, Decision Theory and Antitrust Rules, 67 Antitrust L.J. 41 (1999); James C. Cooper, Luke M. Froeb, Dan O'Brien & Michael G. Vita, Vertical Antitrust Policy as a Problem of Inference, 23 Int'l J. Indus. Org. 639 (2005). See also Keith N. Hylton, The Law and Economics of Monopolization Standards, in Antitrust Law and Econ. 82 (Edward Elgar Publishing, Hylton ed., 2010).

[72] For empirical evidence that basic economic training improves judicial decision-making in relatively simple antitrust cases, lowering appeal and reversal rates for district court judges, see Michael R. Baye & Joshua D. Wright, Is Antitrust Too Complicated for Generalist Judges? The Impact of Economic Complexity & Judicial Training on Appeals, 54 J. L. & Econ. (forthcoming 2010), available at http://papers.ssrn.com/sol3/papers.cfm?abstract_id= 1319888##.

the single-entity defense, the judicial determination of whether shoes and shoelaces or operating systems and browsers amount to "single" products or are truly separate products creates some concern.[73] But note that the substantive economic content of the "single-product" defense to a tying claim turns on whether consumers have a separate and distinct demand for the tied good, apart from the tying good. As commentators have pointed out, and the D.C. Circuit Court of Appeals recognized in *United States v. Microsoft*, the "single product" test is a proxy for the net efficiencies: when consumers demand the two products bundled together, there are likely efficiencies to the bundling.[74] Looking to consumer demand for evidence of efficiencies can be a low-cost alternative to the fact-specific inquiry involved in understanding how a particular bundle reduces distribution costs, or the effects of integrating browser code into an operating system. Thus, while the simple rule has its imperfections, as rules must, it provides a reliable mechanism to identify agreements that are not likely to cause competitive harm at relatively low cost and in a manner that is linked to economic theory and empirical learning.

The single-entity defense as an error-cost filter has the potential to operate much the same way. Indeed, as we explain below, before turning to the implications of *American Needle* for the single-entity defense and antitrust more generally, the error-cost approach discussed above illuminates the potentially productive and efficient role the single-entity defense plays in antitrust.

B. The Single-Entity Defense as an Error-Cost Consistent Filter for Meritless Claims

The role of the single-entity defense embodied in *Copperweld* is to provide a relatively efficient mechanism for terminating Section 1 claims involving business arrangements that are highly unlikely to enable the creation or exercise of market power. The test has a functional origin based on the critical distinction in antitrust law

---

[73] See Jefferson Parish Hospital Dist. No. 2 v. Hyde, 466 U.S. 2, 11–12 (1984).

[74] United States v. Microsoft Corp., 253 F.3d 34, 135 (D.C. Cir. 2001) ("On the supply side, firms without market power will bundle two goods only when cost savings from joint sale outweigh the value consumers place on separate choice. So bundling by all firms implies strong net efficiencies."); see David S. Evans, A. Jorge Padilla, & Christian Alborn, The Antitrust Economics of Tying: A Farewell to Per Se Illegality, 49 Antitrust Bull. 287 (2004).

between unilateral and concerted conduct, with the latter class of conduct treated with greater suspicion because it "deprives the marketplace of independent centers of decisionmaking," reduces the diversity of entrepreneurial interests and, therefore, actual or potential competition.[75] This economic distinction lies at the very core of antitrust law and economics. The challenge for the law has been whether it is capable of developing a rule that leverages the economic theory of the firm in a way that allows courts to move beyond corporate "form" and consistently identify those business arrangements that "functionally" are associated with negative welfare consequences of cartels rather than the generally welfare-neutral or positive actions of the single firm.

Alone, *Copperweld's* instruction that the substance and not the form of an economic arrangement determined whether the arrangement fell within the scope of Section 1 does not imply this "filtering" role for the single-entity defense. But, when the Supreme Court elaborates on the type of functional inquiry it has in mind, the promise of the single-entity defense as a bright-line rule that fits within the "error-cost" framework of modern antitrust, in other words, a rule that minimizes the sum of the social cost of judicial errors and administrative costs, becomes apparent.

As discussed above, *Copperweld's* focus on control provides an analytical basis consistent with the economic theory of the firm upon which to base such a rule. Before *American Needle*, however, the single-entity jurisprudence was in disarray, with lower courts applying different versions of *Copperweld's* unity of interest test—some in a manner consistent with the "control" notion of the firm and others with a less economically sound rule that focused on incentive conflicts between entities. The unity of interest standard applied in a fashion untethered from "control" leads to absurd results. As Judge Easterbrook has pointed out:

> Although the [unity of interest] phrase appears in *Copperweld*
> . . . [a]s a proposition of law, it would be silly. Even a single
> firm contains many competing interests. One division may
> make inputs for another's finished goods. The first division
> might want to sell its products directly to the market, to
> maximize income (and thus the salary and bonus of the

---

[75] Copperweld Corp. v. Independence Tube Corp., 467 U.S. 752, 769 (1984).

division's managers); the second division might want to get its inputs from the first at a low transfer price, which would maximize the second division's paper profits. Conflicts are endemic in any multi-stage firm, such as General Motors or IBM . . . but they do not imply that these large firms must justify all of their acts under the Rule of Reason. . . . *Copperweld* does not hold that only conflict-free enterprises may be treated as single entities.[76]

Given the disarray in the lower courts applying *Copperweld* concepts, hopes that the single-entity doctrine could evolve to provide a useful method for courts to apply a filter to resolve claims unlikely to generate antitrust harms had already been greatly diminished, but not eliminated.[77]

The single-entity defense, of course, is not the only error-cost filter available to judges in cases involving horizontal restraints otherwise reviewable under the Rule of Reason. The Rule of Reason itself requires plaintiffs to define a relevant market, demonstrate competitive harm, and offer proof that efficiencies do not dominate anticompetitive effects. In addition to these filters within the Rule of Reason, pleading standards provide yet another filter for claims of antitrust conspiracies unlikely to generate competitive harms. The relative attractiveness of applying the *Copperweld* single-entity filter declines as the complexity of the analysis increases.

Consider, for example, Judge Boudin's discussion of the tradeoff between the single-entity analysis and the Rule of Reason in *Major League Soccer*:

> Once one goes beyond the classic single enterprise, including *Copperweld* situations, it is difficult to find an easy stopping point or even decide on the proper functional criteria for hybrid cases. To the extent the criteria reflect judgments that a particular practice in context is defensible, assessment under section 1 is more straightforward and draws on developed law. Indeed, the best arguments for upholding MLS's

---

[76] Chicago Prof'l Sports Ltd. v. NBA, 95 F.3d 593, 598 (7th Cir. 1996).

[77] See Transcript of Oral Argument at 60, Am. Needle, Inc. v. NFL, 130 S. Ct. 2201 (2010) (No. 08-661) (respondent NFL's counsel argued that the single-entity defense was important because under the modern Rule of Reason, "defending a claim like [American Needle's] on the merits involves an investment of tens of millions of dollars, thousands of hours of executive time, hours and hours of court time.").

restrictions—that it is a new and risky venture, constrained in some (perhaps great) measure by foreign and domestic competition for players, that unquestionably creates a new enterprise without combining existing competitors—have little to do with its structure.[78]

Judge Boudin eloquently characterizes the somewhat frustrating state of the single-entity doctrine prior to *American Needle*. The purpose of the doctrine as a tool to prevent claims for which further discovery is unlikely to unearth evidence of antitrust harms, coupled with the imprecise unity of interest standard, allowed the single-entity defense to be exported into cases involving hybrid organizational forms such as leagues and franchises. However, as Judge Boudin pointed out, reliable and functional criteria for those cases remained elusive and, thus, *Copperweld* remained a less comfortable ground for decision than Section 1 Rule of Reason precedent.

The tradeoff between these two courses for antitrust jurisprudence concerning hybrid organizations with apparent efficiencies invokes the choice between rules and standards in antitrust.[79] The single-entity defense offers the hope of a bright-line, low-administrative-cost safe haven for these arrangements contrasted with the fact-intensive Rule of Reason, which offers the hope of reduced error at the cost of higher cost of application. But whatever the uncertainty of the Rule of Reason approach in resolving complex economic issues,[80] there is no advantage in a single-entity defense that is equally fact-intensive, though focused on functional criteria with a less certain relationship to whether the business activity at issue is likely to generate competitive harms.

As we discussed above, in *Major League Soccer*, Judge Boudin presented two alternative approaches to the error-cost framework. On the one hand, the Court could develop a more thorough set of simply administrable tests that could serve as a prefatory examination to Section 1 liability under *Copperweld*. Alternatively, the Court could instead expand Rule of Reason treatment to take account of the economic realities surrounding complicated, interdependent

---

[78] Fraser v. Major League Soccer, 284 F.3d 47, 59 (1st Cir. 2002).

[79] See Daniel A. Crane, Rules versus Standards in Antitrust Adjudication, 64 Wash. & Lee L. Rev. 49 (2007).

[80] See Baye & Wright, *supra* note 72.

enterprises. These broadly mapped onto the advantages and disadvantages of employing bright-line rules versus flexible standards in antitrust suits. As *Major League Soccer* showed, however, *Copperweld* provided the untailored and occasionally arbitrary results one expects from a bright-line rule while imposing nearly all the costs of an exploratory standard. Aptly describable as neither rule nor standard, *Copperweld* immunity begged for stark revision. As we discuss below, in *American Needle* the Supreme Court indeed revised *Copperweld*—but along narrow lines that echo antitrust formalism harkening back to the days of *Yellow Cab*.

III. Antitrust Formalism Is Dead! Long Live Antitrust Formalism: *American Needle* and *Copperweld* Immunity

A. American Needle v. NFL

If the dominant interpretation of the holding in *American Needle* is amiss, the conventional wisdom that the case ultimately punished the NFL's hubris is surprisingly reasonable.[81] In 1963, all the NFL's teams came together to establish National Football League Properties to develop, license, and market the NFL's intellectual property. For nearly 40 years, NFLP granted vendors and manufacturers licenses to create and sell team-branded apparel of all sorts. In 2000, pursuant to NFLP's bylaws, the NFL's constituent teams voted to grant Reebok an exclusive license to manufacture team-branded headwear.[82]

Seven years into Reebok's 10-year agreement, American Needle brought suit in the Northern District of Illinois, claiming violations of both Sections 1 and 2 of the Sherman Act. While American Needle did not argue the formation of NFLP itself was illegal, the company contended that the agreement by which NFLP conveyed to Reebok an exclusive license was an illegal conspiracy to restrain trade in violation of Section 1. The NFL, as expected, immediately claimed single-entity status in response to these claims. The district court permitted limited discovery on the *Copperweld* question but eventually accepted the NFL's characterization of its business architecture

---

[81] Posting of Randy Picker to the University of Chicago Law School Faculty Blog, Supreme Court Blitzes NFL in *American Needle*, http://uchicagolaw.typepad.com/faculty/2010/05/supreme-court-blitzes-nfl-in-american-needle.html (May 24, 2010, 17:13 CST).

[82] Am. Needle, 130 S. Ct. at 2207.

and dismissed American Needle's Section 1 claim pursuant to *Copperweld* and a closely related Seventh Circuit case.[83] The NFL, NFLP, and respective NFL teams qualified as a "single-entity," and were therefore incapable of conspiring in violation of Section 1.

American Needle appealed to the Seventh Circuit, which affirmed the district court, albeit somewhat more modestly. The appellate court held that with regard to licensing of NFL intellectual property, the NFL and its constituent teams constituted a single-entity worthy of *Copperweld* immunity.[84] Accordingly, the NFL prevailed on all of American Needle's claims. In the vast majority of such cases—and in several similar cases against other professional sports leagues—the story of American Needle would have ended before the Seventh Circuit panel. Predictably, American Needle petitioned the Supreme Court for certiorari. Despite winning on all claims against them, however, the NFL surprisingly supported American Needle's petition for review, also seeking reversal of the Seventh Circuit—seeking a holding that the NFL (and other professional sports leagues) could not be implicated under Section 1 under any circumstances whatsoever via *Copperweld*.[85] The solicitor general, whose advice on such matters the Court conventionally follows, recommended denial. The Court obliged the NFL so far as the petition for certiorari, but no further.

At oral argument, the Court repeatedly stressed its concerns with the relative efficiency and utility of Rule of Reason analysis, including various filters that might apply to screen out low-quality claims, versus the theoretically simpler—but heretofore unpredictable—*Copperweld* screen. The Court began by exploring American Needle's proposed Rule of Reason inquiry. Justice Ruth Bader Ginsburg's first question pressed American Needle's counsel as to whether everything the NFL did was necessarily subject to the Rule of Reason, or whether some internal decisions would, by operation of some screening mechanism, "escape, entirely, antitrust analysis."[86] Justice

---

[83] See Chicago Prof'l Sports Ltd. v. NBA, 95 F.3d 593 (7th Cir. 1996).

[84] See Am. Needle, 130 S. Ct. at 2207–08 (citing Am. Needle, Inc. v. NFL, 538 F.3d 736 (7th Cir. 2008)).

[85] Brief for the NFL Respondents at 4, Am. Needle, 130 S. Ct. 2201, No. 08-661 (Jan. 21, 2009) ("NFL Respondents are taking the unusual step of supporting certiorari in an effort to secure a uniform rule.").

[86] Transcript of Oral Argument at 6, Am. Needle, 130 S. Ct. 2201 (No. 08-661).

Anthony Kennedy immediately followed up by probing the potential costs of subjecting all NFL actions to antitrust scrutiny by posing a hypothetical about the competitive implications of the NFL's changing game rules.[87] He emphasized error-cost concerns in so doing: "the owners sit around the room [for a rule change], they are liable for a conspiracy. I mean, this is serious stuff. Triple damages."[88] Justice Kennedy accordingly asked American Needle to identify "a zone where we are sure Rule of Reason inquiry . . . would be inappropriate."[89] The Chief Justice expressed yet further concern over the expensive nature of an expansive Rule of Reason treatment, and struck at the heart of the matter from an error-cost perspective, questioning where the Court should "rest the inefficiency and confusion" of an antitrust case between a prefatory *Copperweld* analysis and a Rule of Reason examination under Section 1.[90]

Copperweld immunity fared no better with the Court at oral argument. Justice Breyer questioned its usefulness as applied to the NFL, construing the doctrine as applying to a relatively narrow set of circumstances.[91] Justice Sonia Sotomayor framed granting the NFL *Copperweld* immunity as "an absolute bar to an antitrust claim."[92] Justice Antonin Scalia attempted to pose a question to the NFL's counsel he viewed as "reduc[ing *Copperweld*] to the absurd," only to find the NFL's position demanded that the *Copperweld* screen would permit price fixing on even the sales of NFL teams themselves.[93] Whatever dissatisfaction it found with the Rule of Reason, the Court to its credit was very much focused on the "compared to what?" question. In the end, it surmised that *Copperweld* analysis was nearly as expensive as the Rule of Reason and, finding no meaningful limit to the *Copperweld* screen offered by the NFL, appeared prepared to reject the single-entity defense altogether.

And the Court did reject the NFL's construction of *Copperweld*. Writing for the unanimous Court, Justice John Paul Stevens began

---

[87] *Id*. at 7.
[88] *Id*.
[89] *Id*.
[90] *Id*. at 23.
[91] *Id*. at 44–45.
[92] *Id*. at 49.
[93] *Id*. at 64.

his last antitrust opinion by reiterating two cornerstones of modern antitrust: the non-literality of the Sherman Act and the "distinction between concerted and independent action."[94] Though "concerted activity is [to be] judged more sternly than unilateral activity"[95] under the Sherman Act, Justice Stevens maintained that the Court "eschewed such formalistic distinctions"[96] as to whether the parties are "legally distinct entities" in determining whether behavior constitutes "concerted action."[97] In reiterating the Court's functional test, Justice Stevens traced the long and somewhat ignominious history of the intra-enterprise theory of liability under Section 1, beginning with *Yellow Cab* and ending with *Copperweld*.[98] Up until this point in the opinion, one might have reasonably foreseen the Court adopting something similar to the NFL's position or the first option of Judge Boudin's dichotomy: expounding a rule for regarding an integrated multi-component firm as a single actor for purposes of Section 1 and perhaps shifting the unity of interest inquiry away from incentive alignment and toward control rights, consistent with the economic theory of the firm. The latter strategy in particular would have been consistent with the Roberts Court's antitrust jurisprudence thus far, much of which has been in the spirit of "updating" the law to reflect modern economics and empirical learning.[99]

The Court proceeded, however, in nearly the opposite way. Reiterating the functionality of the test, Justice Stevens wrote that while it was not determinative to the concerted conduct inquiry that two or more entities had maintained legal separation, it was similarly not dispositive that they had "organized themselves under a single umbrella or into a structured joint venture."[100] He then summarily declared the 32 teams of the NFL to be "separate corporate consciousnesses" whose interests were "not common."[101] That the NFL had

---

[94] Am. Needle, 130 S. Ct. at 2208–09.

[95] *Id.* at 2209.

[96] *Id.*

[97] *Id.* at 2212.

[98] *Id.* at 2210–11.

[99] See Wright, *supra* note 70.

[100] Am. Needle, 130 S. Ct. at 2212.

[101] *Id.*

amalgamated its intellectual property into NFLP was "not dispositive," despite being "similar in some sense to a single enterprise
that owns several pieces of intellectual property and licenses them
jointly."[102] As the teams' "interests [were] not necessarily aligned"—
that they did not completely unite the teams' economic interests, in
the parlance of *Copperweld*—the NFL's teams remained independent
centers of decisionmaking, subject to Section 1.[103] Even NFLP itself
remained subject to Section 1—though this was, admittedly, a closer
decision for the Court.[104] While typically the Court heavily presumes
that intrafirm decisions are independent and motivated by the maximization of profits, "in rare cases, that presumption does not
hold"—as it did not for NFLP.[105] As the teams retained distinct
economic interests despite their equal participation in NFLP, and
because NFLP's decisions required more than typical shareholder
participation, NFLP merely served as an instrument for the separate
team decisionmaking, rather than acting as a single source of economic power itself.[106] The opinion noted in epilogue that there may
well have been justifications for the NFL's and NFLP's conduct;
indeed, that would be measured by the Rule of Reason, and potentially quite briefly, but only upon remand.[107]

B. American Needle: *Some Practical Implications*

As an initial observation, *American Needle*—and the justices' questioning during oral argument—leave open the extent to which *Copperweld* immunity itself remains at all. The opinion extensively cited
Copperweld's reliance on a "complete unity of interests" in order to
combine multiple entities into a single economic unit and noted
approvingly that wholly owned sub-entities could not conspire
under the meaning of Section 1.[108] The opinion even undermines
these faint implications, however, by carefully hedging that formal
single-entity status did not guarantee an exemption from Section

---

[102] *Id.* at 2213.
[103] *Id.*
[104] *Id.* at 2214–15.
[105] *Id.* at 2215.
[106] *Id.*
[107] *Id.* at 2216–17.
[108] *Id.* at 2212.

1.[109] During oral argument, Justice Kennedy went so far as to remark that the case appeared to call for abandoning the entire strain of *Copperweld* and the "single-entity theory" in the first place vis-à-vis Section 1.[110] Before *American Needle*, lower courts agreed that complete common ownership was a sufficient condition for single-entity status but not, perhaps, a necessary one.[111] Following *American Needle*, complete common ownership now appears to be a necessary condition for single-entity status, but not a sufficient one.

A key question is what types of cases will be more likely to occur due to the Court's decision. In other words, does *American Needle* change anything? Consider that *Copperweld* had foreclosed, in different circuits, suits between parents and wholly owned subsidiaries,[112] co-owned sister corporations,[113] "unofficially merged" companies or effective mergers between corporations and unincorporated associations,[114] suits against a franchisor and franchisee,[115] between a hospital and medical staff,[116] and between trade associations and their members.[117] *American Needle* presents the first decision in some time that effectively broadens, rather than reduces, the scope of the Sherman Act. These types of cases involving organizational structures that are short of full common ownership now fall outside the protection of *Copperweld* immunity and will be resolved under the Rule of Reason. One obvious and high-profile subset of such cases involves the credit card networks, and in particular MasterCard and Visa, because those firms altered ownership structure through initial

---

[109] *Id.* at 2216–17.

[110] Transcript of Oral Argument at 7, Am. Needle, Inc. v. NFL, 130 S. Ct. 2201 (No. 08-661).

[111] See, e.g., Leaco Enterprises, Inc. v. Gen. Elec. Co., 737 F. Supp. 605, 608–09 (D. Or. 1990) (creating a *de minimis* exception to the single-entity defense).

[112] See Eichorn v. AT&T Corp., 248 F.3d 131, 138 (3d Cir. 2001) (concluding that a subsidiary is incapable of Section 1 conspiracy); Russ' Kwik Car Wash, Inc. v. Marathon Petroleum Co., 772 F.2d 214, 216 (6th Cir. 1985) (holding that transfers between a parent company and its subsidiary were not a Section 1 conspiracy).

[113] Orson, Inc. v. Miramax Film Corp., 862 F. Supp. 1378, 1385 (E.D. Pa. 1994).

[114] Int'l Travel Arrangers v. NWA, Inc., 991 F.2d 1389, 1398 (8th Cir. 1993).

[115] Williams v. I.B. Fischer Nevada, 794 F. Supp. 1026 (D. Nev. 1992), aff'd 999 F.2d 445 (9th Cir. 1993).

[116] Levi Case Co. v. ATS Products, Inc., 788 F. Supp. 428, 432 (N.D. Cal. 1992).

[117] Am. Council of Certified Podiatric Physicians & Surgeons v. Am. Bd. of Podiatric Surgery, Inc., 185 F.3d 606, 622 (6th Cir. 1999).

public offerings in order to increase their likelihood of obtaining immunity.[118]

Will shifting these cases from resolution under *Copperweld* to evaluation by the Rule of Reason change litigation outcomes or affect consumer welfare? Even where the single-entity defense is rejected, plaintiffs appear to generally lose cases in which a single-entity defense is credibly raised.[119] This outcome is unsurprising because plaintiffs rarely win Rule of Reason cases.[120] *Copperweld* immunity served to dismiss relatively implausible cases—such as that a firm and its 91.9 percent owned subsidiary conspired to violate Section 1[121]—before getting into extensive discovery. In short, it is unclear that *American Needle*'s severe cabining of *Copperweld* will encourage successful cases, but it is likely that it will encourage substantially more discovery by plaintiffs. That outcome is probably not a positive development.

Perhaps the great contradiction of *American Needle* is the decision's repeated protestations—predicated on adherence to *Copperweld*—that its analysis was functional when the heart of *American Needle*'s construction of *Copperweld* is relentlessly formal.[122] *American Needle* simultaneously embraces *Copperweld*'s "unity of interest" rhetoric while pinioning the NFL in a seemingly impossible situation. On the one hand, the Court notes that its functional analysis as to whether the various teams consisted of one or more economic decisionmaking centers would largely depend on the extent to which those centers had "shared interests" sufficient to make them effectively constitute a single enterprise, shying away from *Copperweld*'s

---

[118] See generally, Joshua D. Wright, Mastercard's Single Entity Strategy, 12 Harv. Negot. L. Rev. 225 (2007); Herbert Hovenkamp, American Needle and the Boundaries of the Firm in Antitrust Law (Working Paper, June 2010), available at http://papers.ssrn.com/sol3/papers.cfm?abstract_id= 1616625.

[119] See *supra*, notes 112–17 (all cases in which the defendant's single-entity defense led to summary judgment on plaintiff's antitrust claims).

[120] Michael A. Carrier, The Rule of Reason: An Empirical Update for the 21st Century, 16 Geo. Mason L. Rev. 827, 829–30 (2009).

[121] See Leaco Enterprises, Inc. v. Gen. Elec. Co., 737 F. Supp. 605 (D. Or. 1990).

[122] See, e.g., Am. Needle, 130 S. Ct. at 2209 (" . . . we have eschewed such formalistic distinctions in favor of a functional consideration of how the parties involved in the alleged anti-competitive conduct actually operate . . . "); *id*. at 2210 (" . . . we now embark on a more functional analysis."); and *id*. at 2213 ("they are not similar in the relevant functional sense . . . ").

focus on control.[123] On the other hand, that the various teams had assembled themselves into something approaching a single enterprise through NFLP was also not determinative, as they based their decisions for NFLP on their individual, outside agendas.

The Court's decision went so far as to distinguish NFLP from a typical corporation with typical shareholders based on, in part, the fact that NFLP required a supermajority vote in order to grant exclusive licenses like the one in question to Reebok.[124] The opinion fails to make clear, either through an articulated theory of the firm or any economic analysis whatsoever, why such a detail reflects anything but a basic formalistic suspicion of a specific term of NFLP's bylaws. This line of reasoning regrettably ignores in its functional analysis that, as noticed by the trial court, American Needle at no point attempted to deal with any of the NFL teams as individual, independent organizations. The irony of this inversion must not be lost on the NFL: in pursuit of being declared a single-entity as a matter of law in the face of a plaintiff that had dealt with its constituent teams effectively as a single-entity, the Supreme Court not only reversed the Seventh Circuit's declaration for a determination as to whether the NFL enjoyed single-entity status as a matter of fact, but declared the NFL not a single-entity as a matter of law.

It is ultimately difficult to avoid the conclusion that the Court redefined the single-entity defense to Judge Easterbrook's dystopian scenario, immunizing conflict-free organizations and inadvertently subsidizing full mergers and internal unanimity out of reverence for the single-entity form. *American Needle* thus serves as a perverted end of *Copperweld*, given that *Copperweld* held that "separate incorporation does not necessarily imply a capacity to conspire" and that "a business enterprise should be free to structure itself in ways that serve efficiency of control."[125] An acute observer might respond that *Copperweld* also said that separate incorporation does not necessarily imply a capacity to conspire, but that integrated incorporation did not deny it as well. This notation, while true, is of small consolation

---

[123] The seemingly most important functional "fact" is that NFLP had been doing business within this arrangement for 47 years. See Am. Needle, 130 S. Ct. at 2207.

[124] *Id.* at 2215 ("Unlike typical decisions by corporate shareholders, NFLP licensing decisions effectively require the assent of more than a mere majority of shareholders . . . ").

[125] Copperweld, 467 U.S. at 773.

to the NFL teams which, by virtue of their separate incorporation and upon purely appellate review based on an exceptionally limited record, were declared multiple entities ipso facto.

Antitrust's central goal, though, is not the preservation of the single-entity defense or *Copperweld*; instead, it is the maximization of consumer welfare through rules that account for error costs and administrative costs. The elimination or limitation of the single-entity defense is neither necessarily positive nor negative for antitrust law. While it is true that it is the first decision in some time that expands the scope of the Sherman Act, the critical question is also a broader one: what will judges do with antitrust claims once barred by *Copperweld*? Judge Boudin's dilemma posed two possibilities: the expansion of *Copperweld* to form rules for hybrid entities or an increased lenience of the Rule of Reason to recognize the interdependent and complicated nature of many modern firms. To the extent that *Copperweld* and its progeny proved maladapted for implementation in the vast spectrum of cases involving anything short of complete common ownership or a complete subsidiary structure, the implications of *American Needle* for consumer welfare are generally more complex than has been assumed by much of the antitrust community.

IV. Explaining *American Needle* within the Error-Cost Framework

If the Court's dismantling of the single-entity defense was somewhat equivocal, then reactions from the interventionist sphere of antitrust commentators were anything but. The American Antitrust Institute described the Court's decision as a "solid touchdown not only for sports fans, but all consumers" as Justice Stevens "sought to ensure the antitrust laws remain[ed] vibrant."[126] Dissatisfied with the Court's consistent support for the error-cost framework, the AAI heralded *American Needle* as a "reject[ion of] extreme pro-defendant positions, and [the case] should be a cautionary tale for defendants that seek to short-cut sound antitrust analysis, as the NFL did."[127] Tulane law professor Gabriel Feldman wrote that "for all conceivable purposes, and after decades of litigating the issue, the single-entity

---

[126] American Antitrust Institute, *supra* note 3.
[127] *Id.*

argument for professional sports leagues is dead."[128] The *New York Times, Sports Illustrated,* and the *Washington Post* similarly ran editorials before and after the decision noting that *American Needle* exposed professional sports leagues to Sherman Act liability and asserting that this would be beneficial for consumers.[129] The common thrust of these responses is twofold: that *American Needle* represents a rejection of the "extreme pro-defendant" positions of the last decade—largely associated with error-cost protections enjoying supermajority Supreme Court support—and that a wider reach of the Sherman Act will increase consumer welfare. While the latter is ultimately an empirical question, the former is certainly premature.

The interventionist hypothesis only holds at a superficial level. *American Needle* was the first case since 1992 that the Supreme Court resolved in favor of a private antitrust plaintiff.[130] Furthermore, the Court decided the case unanimously, and in so doing exposed more, rather than fewer, business arrangements to Sherman Act scrutiny. This does in fact contrast with a long line of recent cases—such as *Brooke Group,*[131] *Credit Suisse,*[132] *linkLine Communications,*[133] and *Trinko*[134]—applying error-cost and other filters to exculpate defendants. The interventionist interpretation is flawed due to both the inherent failings of *Copperweld* and as the justices' articulated administrative cost concerns in oral argument and the final opinion. In this part, we explain the error-cost function of *Copperweld,* how its administrative costs ultimately led to its displacement, and how *American Needle* reflects a substitution away from *Copperweld* and toward *Twombly*'s requirement of "plausibility" in pleading an antitrust complaint.

---

[128] Gabriel A. Feldman, The Supreme Court Puts to Rest the NFL's Single Entity Defense in American Needle, Huffington Post (May 24, 2010), available at http://www.huffingtonpost.com/gabriel-a-feldman/the-supreme-court-puts-to_b_588086.html.

[129] See, e.g., Editorial, Throwing the Rule Book at the N.F.L., N.Y. Times, May 27, 2010 at A34; Steven Pearlstein, Trust-Busting the NFL, Wash. Post, Oct. 21, 2009 ("Americans would be better off if professional sports leagues and their teams were forced to compete—on the field and off . . . ").

[130] Eastman Kodak Co. v. Image Technical Servs., Inc., 504 U.S. 451 (1992).

[131] Brooke Group Ltd. v. Brown & Williamson Tobacco Corp., 509 U.S. 209 (1993).

[132] Credit Suisse Sec. (USA) LLC v. Billing, 127 S. Ct. 2383 (2007).

[133] Pac. Bell Tel. Co. v. linkLine Commc'ns, Inc., 129 S. Ct. 1109 (2009).

[134] Verizon Comm's, Inc. v. Law Offices of Curtis V. Trinko, LLP, 540 U.S. 398 (2004).

A. American Needle *and the Substitution of* Copperweld

Interpreting *American Needle*'s limitation of *Copperweld* to only wholly owned entities as a fundamental philosophical change ignores the Supreme Court's recognition of the fundamental problems lower courts encountered in applying *Copperweld*. *Copperweld*'s conceptual comparative advantage was as a low-cost, pre-discovery screening device. As increasingly complicated businesses attempted to avail themselves of *Copperweld*, however, no uniform rule arose that proved capable of consistent judicial application in addressing even partial-equity stakes, much less patent licensees, franchisees, and so on.[135] As courts wildly diverged from one another in the application of *Copperweld*, the single-entity defense's value as a quick, inexpensive proxy for filtering meritless claims necessarily declined. Rather than permitting parties to dismiss cases of dubious merit before expensive discovery disputes, parties unpredictably litigated a precursor stage to Section 1 litigation, embodied by *Major League Soccer*.[136]

It bears mention now that the Court's apparent limitation of *Copperweld* to effectively conflict-free enterprises affected a strikingly formalistic mistake. Lower courts understandably struggled with the correct equity stake percentage to deem multiple formal entities a "single economic unit." As Judge Boudin noted, this exercise did not necessarily require *Copperweld*'s marginalization: instead, the Court could have laid out a clear if imperfect test for single-entity status in interconnected franchises or leagues. Alternatively, the Court could have established a multifaceted set of factors that informed Rule of Reason treatment specifically with regards to interdependent enterprises. Instead, the Court retained *Copperweld* immunity, but only at the strictest of margins, seemingly refusing an even *de minimis* exception as many courts had allowed.

This approach is questionable. Before *American Needle*, complete common ownership was a sufficient condition for *Copperweld* immunity, but not a necessary one; after *American Needle*, it is at least necessary, and possibly not sufficient. It is not at all obvious that two enterprises under 99 percent common ownership would be able to engage in conduct in violation of Section 1 the prosecution of

---

[135] See *supra* notes 111–21 and accompanying text.

[136] Fraser v. Major League Soccer, LLC, 284 F.3d 47 (1st Cir. 2002).

which would increase total consumer welfare. The same could likely be said for 98 percent common ownership. There is certainly some percentage of common ownership at which point another marginal amount might seriously call into question anti-competitive effects; this would be the point at which *Copperweld* immunity ought no longer apply as a matter of law (though it potentially could as a question of fact). The "all-or-nothing" retention of *Copperweld* echoes *Yellow Cab*-like formalism, in which the structure of the firm—and nothing else—can be completely dispositive as to the propriety of Section 1 liability. Yet such an error hardly suggests a willing ignorance as to comparative administrative costs, much less error costs.

In order to appreciate the intended substitution we believe *American Needle* represents, one must first examine the Court's stated attitude toward both *Copperweld* immunity and the progression of an antitrust case more broadly. Several times the justices expressly referred to the potential utility of *Copperweld* as a screen for obviously low-quality antitrust claims. During oral argument, Justice Breyer admitted that though he found both sides' arguments "very confusing" on the points raised, his understanding was that "we have Copperweld to deal with the case that we don't make booths in department stores compete in price against each other."[137] Similarly, when counsel for American Needle proposed that a number of Section 1 inquiries could be disposed of summarily under the Rule of Reason, Chief Justice Roberts said that if a given arrangement "would be an easy case under the Rule of Reason," it would instead "make sense to carve those out at the outset, rather than at the end of the case."[138] This is, in other words, a Court that certainly understands the economics of judicial decisionmaking in the context of complex commercial litigation.

The Court also correctly and insightfully viewed its decision as involving a trade-off between submitting marginal single-entity defense claims to scrutiny under the Rule of Reason versus dismissing them out of hand. The Chief Justice remarked that the difficulty of the Rule of Reason versus *Copperweld* vis-à-vis Section 1 was

---

[137] Transcript of Oral Argument at 44, Am. Needle, Inc. v. NFL, 130 S. Ct. 2201 (2010) (No. 08-661).

[138] *Id.* at 23–24.

where to allocate the "inefficiency and confusion" in the trial court.[139] Accordingly, an analysis of the interdependence of businesses engaging in challenged conduct could occur as a part of the "concerted conduct inquiry" or within a conventional Rule of Reason application.[140] The two acted as direct substitutes for each other. Indeed, American Needle's counsel specifically suggested that the latter was a more appropriate venue for scrutinizing (and screening out) comparatively weak Section 1 claims.[141] The Court asked counsel about the costly nature of antitrust discovery,[142] the economic consequences of potentially condemning certain combinations among firms, and whether the plaintiff's claims as to the NFL's business structure were based on actual empirical data concerning economic harms versus benefits of the NFL's challenged contracts.[143] From the Court's inquiry, then, we would expect a close substitute for *Copperweld* immunity to both (1) be designed to allow judges to summarily dismiss claims that do not meaningfully articulate a substantial threat to consumer welfare and (2) be grounded in economic

[139] *Id.*

[140] *Id.* at 24.

[141] *Id.* at 23–24.

[142] *Id.* at 22.

[143] *Id.* at *51. Some have cited anecdotal evidence in support of the proposition that the price of NFL logo hats increased after the Reebok exclusive dealing arrangement. See, e.g., Brees, *supra* note 1 ("If you want to show support for your team by buying an official hat, it now costs $10 more than before the exclusive arrangement."). Even assuming prices have increased, such evidence must be read in conjunction with a simultaneous increase in price and output. A price increase after an exclusive dealing contract is consistent with the role of exclusives in facilitating the supply of promotional investments and preventing free-riding. See Benjamin Klein & Andres V. Lerner, The Expanded Economics of Free-Riding: How Exclusive Dealing Prevents Free-Riding and Creates Undivided Loyalty, 74 Antitrust L. J. 473 (2007). The Supreme Court has recently affirmed its recognition of the fundamental antitrust principle that consumer welfare can be enhanced by business arrangements that facilitate promotion, leading to both higher prices and increased output. See Leegin Creative Leather Prods., Inc. v. PSKS, Inc., 551 U.S. 877, 896–97 (2007) ("[m]any decisions a manufacturer makes . . . can lead to higher prices. A manufacturer might . . . hire an advertising agency to promote awareness of its goods. Yet no one would think these actions violate the Sherman Act."). Indeed, there is some evidence that Reebok's exclusive deal with the NFL increased sales by 21 percent by the end of 2002. See John Gibeaut, A League of Their Own: The NFL Wants to Run Up the Score on Its Antitrust Exemption, ABA Journal (January 1, 2010), available at http://www.aba-journal.com/magazine/article/a_league_of_their_own.

theory backed by empirical data when possible. As it turns out, counsel—for the plaintiffs, no less—suggested such a substitute.

B. *Implications for* Twombly *as an Antitrust Filter*

As American Needle pointed out in its briefs, "antitrust plaintiffs seeking to challenge 'ordinary business decisions' . . . have to surmount . . . the need, under *Bell Atlantic Corp. v. Twombly*, to allege a 'plausible' Rule of Reason claim, including anti-competitive effects in a cognizable market . . . ."[144] *Twombly* dismissals indeed satisfy both components of a workable substitute for *Copperweld* immunity—they both allow for an early dismissal of marginal antitrust cases and force antitrust plaintiffs to articulate theories of anti-competitive harm solidly grounded in economics. *Twombly* partially subsumes both of Judge Boudin's alternatives presented in *Major League Soccer* by forcing a plaintiff to articulate a theory of competitive harm that nonetheless accounts for hybrid enterprise arrangements with more sophistication than an unsubstantiated presumption of consumer harm. Moreover, *Twombly* analysis takes place at the pleading stage, prior to potentially years of costly discovery, thereby addressing several of the justices' concerns. During the *Twombly* oral arguments, for example, Justice Breyer expressed concern about lower pleading standards' granting an antitrust plaintiff "a ticket to conduct discovery,"[145] and *Twombly* itself stated that " . . . proceeding to antitrust discovery can be expensive."[146]

Copperweld held the potential to act as a uniform Section 1 screen possessing the virtue of at least some level of economic sophistication with regard to the theory of the firm. By the time *American Needle* came before the Court, however, judicial application of *Copperweld* had largely devolved into a psychological and metaphysical inquiry. The *Twombly* pleading filter, by contrast, is much broader and enables the early dismissal of cases by putting the court and defendants on notice not just to the challenged conduct at hand but to a coherent theory of anti-competitive harm so as to justify the heavy

---

[144] Reply Brief of Petitioner at 19, Am. Needle, Inc. v. NFL, 130 S. Ct. 2201 (2010) (No. 08-661) (internal citations omitted).

[145] Transcript of Oral Argument at 33, Bell Atl. Corp. v. Twombly, 550 U.S. 554 (2007) (No. 05-1126).

[146] Twombly, 550 U.S. at 558.

costs associated with antitrust sanctions.[147] *Twombly* thus can play a similar role to what Justice Breyer envisioned for *Copperweld* immunity, but also more broadly, facilitating dismissals and reducing the chilling effect of false positives by assuring firms that they have at least some latitude to engage in transaction cost-reducing restructuring without necessarily implicating antitrust concerns.[148]

Without defending *Twombly* pleading standards in all contexts, and acknowledging the criticism that *Twombly* and *Iqbal* have received—that they pose problems for notice pleading generally and require information of plaintiffs that would be most easily obtained during discovery[149]—in the antitrust context, the plausibility requirement creates value by preventing unwarranted judicial intrusion into business enterprises without at least a cursory presentation of economically coherent harm.[150] The economic literature on the theory

[147] William H. Page, *Twombly* and Communication: The Emerging Definition of Concerted Action under the New Pleading Standards, 5 J. Comp. L. & Econ. 439 (2009) (arguing that *Twombly* should be interpreted in Section 1 context to require actual communication between the parties).

[148] As discussed above, *Copperweld* could nonetheless have acted as a complement to *Twombly*. Indeed, according to one source, 111 of 170 (nearly two-thirds) post-*Twombly* motions to dismiss antitrust claims have been successful. See Heather Lamberg Kafaele & Mario M. Meeks, Antitrust Digest: Developing Trends and Patterns in Federal Antitrust Cases after *Bell Atlantic Corp. v. Twombly* and *Ashcroft v. Iqbal* (April 2010), available at http://www.shearman.com/files/upload/AT-041910-Antitrust-Digest.pdf. Consistent with our analysis, district court judges have made liberal usage of *Twombly* to dismiss antitrust claims at the pleading stage, including several on the grounds that the complaint did not adequately plead facts that rendered plausible an agreement between two separate entities. See, e.g., Williams v. Citigroup, No. 08-CV-9208, 2009 U.S. Dist. LEXIS 105864 (S.D.N.Y. 2009); Nichols v. Mahoney, 608 F. Supp. 2d 526 (S.D.N.Y. 2009); Westmoreland D.O. v. Pleasant Valley Hosp., Inc., No. 3:08-1444, 2009 U.S. Dist. LEXIS 52947 (S.D.W. Va. 2009); Perinatal Med. Group, Inc. v. Children's Hosp. Cent. Cal., No. 09-1273, 2009 U.S. Dist. LEXIS 36694 (E.D. Cal. 2009).

[149] See Adam M. Steinman, The Pleading Problem, 62 Stan. L. Rev. 1293 (2010); A. Benjamin Spencer, Plausibility Pleading, 49 B.C. L. Rev. 431, 433, 446–47 (2008); Scott Dodson, Pleading Standards after *Bell Atlantic Corp. v. Twombly*, 93 Va. L. Rev. In Brief 135, 137–41 (2007).

[150] See Richard A. Epstein, *Bell Atlantic v. Twombly*: How Motions to Dismiss Become (Disguised) Summary Judgments, 25 Wash. U. J. L. & Pol'y 61, 81–92 (2007); Keith N. Hylton, When Should a Case Be Dismissed? The Economics of Pleading and Summary Judgment Standards, 16 Sup. Ct. Econ. Rev. 39, 41 (2008) ("[E]arly dismissals, by eliminating low-merit claims before they become costly, offer benefits to society in comparison to late dismissals."); Robert G. Bone, *Twombly*, Pleading Rules, and the Regulation of Court Access, 94 Iowa L. Rev. 873 (2009).

of the firm teaches us that former *Copperweld*-availing firms typically structure their business architecture in order to minimize transaction costs.[151] By discouraging antitrust suits targeting nominal agreements between such firms that, in reality, represent unilateral action, *Twombly* allows these firms to pass on welfare gains through lower prices and increased innovation. We suggest that the strengthening of the pleading-stage antitrust filter in *Twombly* enabled the Court to provide a reasonable answer to Chief Justice Roberts's inquiry about where the Court should allocate antitrust's "inefficiency." In other words, *Twombly* allowed the Court to expand the scope of the Sherman Act for the first time in nearly two decades without fear of a large increase in the marginal cost of operating the "antitrust system" in the form of the error and administrative costs associated with the Rule of Reason.

But what of *Twombly* itself? One potential response to *Twombly* already proposed in multiple circles is simple legislation codifying the previous pleading requirements. This action would presumably lead to a large increase in cases at the margin between, as *Twombly* put it, merely "conceivable" versus "plausible."[152] These cases would be by necessity among the weakest antitrust suits present, requiring the most extensive discovery in order to vindicate the least obvious consumer harms. Antitrust has seen this pattern play out before, however; it was due to the massive proliferation of private actions that inspired much of the error-cost protections not only ensconced in the consumer harm requirements of Section 2 but narrowing Section 2's scope altogether. To borrow a phrase, the cautionary tale for repealing *Twombly* is that opening the floodgates to all conceivable antitrust claims is a strategic maneuver that will favor plaintiffs in only the very shortest of temporal horizons—before the antitrust "system" of rules reacts accordingly.

The expectation that *American Needle* represents a permanent shift toward more expansive antitrust enforcement is thus misguided. The narrowing of *Copperweld* was made possible by the successful implementation of the *Twombly* filter, and necessitated by *Copperweld*'s failure in application. The Court's decision to broadly scuttle

---

[151] See Williamson, *supra* note 19; Klein, Crawford & Alchian, *supra* note 19.

[152] Twombly, 550 U.S. at 569.

the single-entity defense was heavily informed by error-cost principles, if unfortunately implemented in a particularly formalistic way, and does not insinuate sweeping pro-plaintiff changes to Section 1 for the foreseeable future. Indeed, even as *American Needle* was argued, Chief Justice Roberts maintained substantial hesitancy over even the use of the Rule of Reason, which remained "a continuing project of [the] Court."[153] This work will almost certainly continue as it has for the last 30 years: motivated by a sincere concern for error costs and consistency with economic learning and empirical data.[154]

---

[153] Transcript of Oral Argument at 24, Am. Needle, Inc. v. NFL, 130 S. Ct. 2201 (2010) (No. 08-661).

[154] See Douglas H. Ginsburg & Leah Brannon, Antitrust Decisions of the U.S. Supreme Court, 1967 to 2007, 3 Comp. Pol'y Int'l 3 (Autumn 2007).

Looking Ahead: October Term 2010

Erik S. Jaffe*

It will hardly come as news that the most interesting aspect of the coming October Term 2010 will be the presence of a new justice on the bench: former Solicitor General Elena Kagan, replacing Justice John Paul Stevens. Confirmed on August 5, 2010, by a vote of 63–37, she will be the only sitting justice to arrive at the Court without any prior judicial experience. While opinions are divided on whether her different career path to the Court is a plus or a minus, nobody seriously questions her general abilities or that she will quickly gain ample on-the-job judicial experience.

Given Justice Kagan's clerkships for Judge Abner Mikva and Justice Thurgood Marshall, her appointment by President Obama, and what can be gleaned from her career to this point, most people reasonably assume that she will lean toward the left of the Court. But her addition to the Court is unlikely to cause a meaningful short-term change in outcome on the issues that tend to divide the Court along "political" lines given that she replaces a reliable vote on the left. She could, however, add an interesting perspective on a variety of less political issues. Indeed, her lack of judicial experience might allow her to take a fresh look at any number of questions while she evolves her own jurisprudence. Court watchers thus may find more of interest in Justice Kagan's overall approach to deciding cases than in the particular substantive decisions she makes. Of course, the early terms of any new justice involve a steep learning curve, so we should not be too quick to leap to conclusions based on her conduct during this one. It nonetheless will be difficult to resist the temptations and pleasures of trying to read the tea leaves of Justice Kagan's first year on the Court, and the cases granted thus far should provide us sufficient opportunity to engage in such sport.

* Solo appellate attorney, Erik S. Jaffe, P.C., Washington, D.C.

Turning to the substance of the upcoming term, while it is hardly shaping up as a blockbuster, it nonetheless has a number interesting cases—six of the ten discussed below coming from the Ninth Circuit Court of Appeals—in areas ranging from preemption, to the First Amendment, to copyright law.[1]

Preemption

The amount of leeway remaining to the states to regulate in areas partially occupied by federal law is at issue in several cases this term. While none is likely to break significant jurisprudential ground for preemption in general, each case is important within its own specific substantive area.

In *Williamson v. Mazda Motor of America*, the Court will consider whether federal safety standards regarding the type and placement of seatbelts in automobiles preempts a common-law claim of negligence for failing to exceed those federal safety standards.[2] The case involves the use of a lap-only seatbelt rather than a combination lap/shoulder belt in a rear aisle seat of a minivan. The use of a lap-only belt at that position is permissible under federal safety standards, though it is less safe for the passenger than a combination lap/shoulder belt. A passenger sitting in the aisle seat with a lap-only belt died following an accident when her body "jackknifed" around the lap-belt, causing internal injuries.

The California Court of Appeal, Fourth Appellate District, held that the state-law claim was preempted.[3] The California Supreme Court denied review. In finding the negligence claim preempted, the court of appeal relied on the U.S. Supreme Court's decision in *Geier v. American Honda Company, Inc.*, which held that federal safety standards giving car manufacturers a choice regarding front-seat passive restraints preempted state tort suits for the failure to choose airbags rather than passive seat belts.[4] Petitioners argue that the more relevant precedent is *Sprietsma v. Mercury Marine*, which held

---

[1] The discussions of the cases below are based on the petitions and other filings in those cases. Those materials are expertly collected and available on SCOTUSblog, organized by term and case.

[2] Williamson v. Mazda Motor of Am., Inc., 130 S. Ct. 3348 (2010) (No. 08-1314).

[3] Williamson v. Mazda Motor of Am., Inc., 167 Cal. App. 4th 905, 905–07 (Cal. Ct. App. 4th Dist. 2008).

[4] See *id.* at 907 (citing Geier v. Am. Honda Co., 529 U.S. 861, 870–72 (2000)).

that a federal agency's decision not to mandate a particular safety device does not preempt suits based on the failure to use such a device unless it reflects a federal policy *against* using such a device.[5]

In this case, petitioners seem to have the better of the argument. The applicable federal statute expressly provides that compliance with a motor vehicle safety standard does not exempt a person from liability at common law.[6] The mere existence of several options for satisfying a federal safety standard hardly conflicts with state-law duties that might require the safer of the available options. That is the very nature of a minimum standard: the fact that it is possible to *exceed* the minimum. While the same savings provision also applied in *Geier*, the historical circumstances and agency concerns favoring a slower phase-in of airbags were quite different from the circumstances and concerns that led the agency to allow the option of lap-only belts at inboard seating positions. Indeed, as noted by the solicitor general in response to an invitation by the Court, the agency that promulgated both safety standards—the National Highway Traffic Safety Administration—agrees with the petitioners that its lap-belt standard does not preempt state-law negligence suits. The solicitor general's brief further agreed with petitioners that the lower courts were reading *Geier* in an overly broad fashion.

Given that then-Solicitor General Kagan was counsel of record on the government's amicus brief at the certiorari stage, Justice Kagan will recuse herself from this case.

The Court will also consider preemption in the context of federal immigration law in *Chamber of Commerce v. Candelaria*, which involves an Arizona statute regulating how employers verify a prospective employee's work-authorization status and imposing penalties on employers who hire unauthorized aliens.[7] While not quite as controversial or high-profile as the direct clash between Arizona and the federal government over state police questioning and potential arrest of suspected illegal aliens in *United States v. Arizona*,[8] the

---

[5] See Petitioners' Brief at 43–44, Williamson v. Mazda Motor of Am., Inc., No. 08-1314 (U.S. July 30, 2010) (citing Sprietsma v. Mercury Marine, 537 U.S. 51, 61–68 (2002)).

[6] 49 U.S.C. § 30103(e) (2006).

[7] Chamber of Commerce of the United States v. Candelaria, 78 U.S.L.W. 3762 (U.S. June 28, 2010) (No. 09-115).

[8] United States v. Arizona, No. CV 10-1413-PHX-SRB, 2010 WL 2926157 (D. Ariz. July 28, 2010) (order granting preliminary injunction).

issues in this case could certainly influence the trailing case should it reach the Court later this or next term.

The Arizona statute at issue in *Chamber of Commerce* requires employers to use a computerized federal system (the so-called E-Verify system) to check the work-authorization status of prospective employees and imposes penalties—including the potential revocation of a company's articles of incorporation—on employers that hire unauthorized aliens.[9] Federal law, however, makes the use of the E-Verify system optional and expressly preempts state or local laws imposing civil or criminal sanctions "other than through licensing and similar laws" on those who hire unauthorized aliens.[10]

The Ninth Circuit held that the Arizona law was not preempted.[11] The court relied on an earlier Supreme Court case finding no preemption of state law prior to the enactment of the current federal statute governing employment of unauthorized aliens.[12] It also held that the penalties imposed on employers who hire illegal aliens fell within the current statute's savings clause for penalties imposed through "licensing" laws.[13]

The case has drawn considerable interest from groups spanning the political spectrum. At the invitation of the Court, the solicitor general filed a brief supporting certiorari only for the employer-penalties issue. The brief agreed with petitioners that both aspects of the law were preempted but argued that the E-Verify system was subject to change and hence that issue was not yet appropriate for review.[14] The Court, however, granted certiorari on both aspects of the Arizona law. Although the amicus brief was filed under Acting Solicitor General Neal Katyal's name, it is possible that then-Solicitor General Kagan had some involvement in the case before her nomination to the Supreme Court. It is thus unclear at this point whether Justice Kagan will recuse herself.

---

[9] Arizona Workers Act, Ariz. Rev. Stat. § 23.211–216 (2009).

[10] 8 U.S.C. §§ 1324a notes, 1324a(h)(2) (2006).

[11] Chicanos Por La Causa, Inc. v. Napolitano, 544 F.3d 976 (9th Cir. 2008), reh'g denied, 558 F.3d 856 (9th Cir. 2009) (amending and superseding initial opinion).

[12] Chicanos Por La Causa, 558 F.3d at 864–67 (citing De Canas v. Bica, 424 U.S. 351, 355–65 (1976)).

[13] *Id.* at 868–69.

[14] See Brief for the United States as Amicus Curiae at 9–21, Chamber of Commerce of the United States v. Candelaria, No. 09-115 (U.S. May 28, 2010).

The petitioners seem to have the better argument in this case as well, though it is a close call on both the E-Verify and employer-sanctions issues. Congress set up E-Verify as a pilot program and seems intentionally to have made participation voluntary while the federal government works through any potential issues with that system. The option given to employers here thus seems much closer to the intentionally phased transition to passive restraints in *Geier* than does the minimum seatbelt standard at issue in *Williamson*, discussed above. On the other hand, the solicitor general's tepid approach to this issue—and the government's prior inconsistent position regarding Arizona's E-Verify requirement in a suit involving a similar requirement imposed by a federal agency[15]—tend to undermine any claim that Arizona's requirement conflicts with a federal interest in *not* making the use of E-Verify mandatory.

The penalties imposed on employers who hire unauthorized aliens also are a close question given that an express exception to the statute's preemption clause allows states to penalize such conduct through licensing and other similar laws.[16] While it seems a stretch to call the Arizona statute here a licensing law—and an overly broad reading of the preemption exception could swallow the general rule—the very existence of the exception for at least some type of penalty tends to undercut the argument for sweeping preemption. The difficulty will be in drawing a coherent line between permissible and impermissible penalties, and it is hard to predict how the Court will draw that line.

Veteran Supreme Court litigator Carter Phillips is counsel of record for the Chamber of Commerce, along with a host of co-counsel, including Steven Shapiro of the ACLU, on behalf of the other petitioners.

Arbitration

In yet another preemption case, though in a category worthy of its own heading, the Federal Arbitration Act makes another of its frequent appearances at the Court in *AT&T Mobility v. Concepcion*.[17]

---

[15] See Stewart Baker, The Solicitor General Lays an Egg, http://volokh.com/2010/05/29/the-solicitor-general-lays-an-egg (last visited Aug. 13, 2010).

[16] 8 U.S.C. § 1324a(h)(2) (2006).

[17] AT&T Mobility LLC v. Concepcion, 130 S. Ct. 3322 (2010) (No. 09-893).

The Court will consider whether the FAA precludes states from forbidding class-arbitration waivers as unconscionable components of arbitration agreements.

Notwithstanding the FAA's mandate that arbitration agreements are valid and enforceable, arbitration agreements may be invalidated or rendered unenforceable on such grounds as are applicable to the revocation of "any contract."[18] California case law makes agreements to arbitrate (or to litigate) certain types of consumer claims unenforceable unless they permit class-wide arbitration.[19] The Ninth Circuit held that an agreement requiring individual arbitration in the consumer context was unconscionable under such precedent favoring class actions.[20] The court further held that there was no preemption because the rule also applied to agreements to litigate and would not decrease the efficiency or speed of arbitration in general.[21]

The narrow though important legal issue presented by this case is whether the fact that state law also forbids class-litigation waivers, in addition to class-arbitration waivers, renders the ground for unenforceability one that applies to "any contract." If the Ninth Circuit is correct, states would seemingly be free to impose all manner of litigation procedures on arbitration on the theory that such procedures were equally non-waivable in litigation agreements.

But as the petitioner correctly notes, class-wide arbitration is very risky given the broad consequences and limited judicial review of a class-wide arbitration ruling.[22] Many arbitration agreements, therefore, require that arbitration be conducted on an individual basis. As a matter of both the text and policy of the FAA, the petitioner seems to have the better argument that a policy-based restriction specific to dispute resolution agreements does not constitute grounds for unenforceability of "any" contract and that requiring arbitration to use the same procedures as litigation contravenes core FAA policies. Far from involving a mere application of general

---

[18] 9 U.S.C. § 2 (2006).

[19] See, e.g., Discover Bank v. Superior Ct., 113 P.3d 1100, 1110 (Cal. 2005); Shroyer v. New Cingular Wireless Services, 498 F.3d 976, 981–84 (9th Cir. 2007) (applying Discover Bank).

[20] See Laster v. AT&T Mobility LLC, 584 F.3d 849, 852 (9th Cir. 2009).

[21] Id. at 857–58 (quoting Shroyer, 498 F.3d at 989–91).

[22] See Brief for Petitioner at 21–23, AT&T Mobility LLC v. Concepcion, No. 09-893 (U.S. Aug. 2, 2010).

unconscionability rules, the particulars of the case suggest that the arbitration agreement was anything but unconscionable, and in fact may have been more favorable to individual consumers even if it provided less of a potential deterrent to the company.[23] Coupled with the Supreme Court's recent decision in *Stolt-Nielsen v. Animal Feeds Int'l*, which forbade arbitrators from imposing class arbitration where the agreement is silent on the subject, it should not require any heavy lifting to find preemption.[24] However, the empathetic lure of class-action remedies for consumers—combined with the 5–3 decision in *Stolt-Nielsen*[25]—might well result in a 5–4 split along the usual lines.

Veteran Supreme Court litigator Ken Geller is counsel of record for the petitioner. Public Citizen Litigation Group takes the laboring oar for the respondents.

ERISA

In *CIGNA Corporation v. Amara*, the Court will consider whether the terms of an Employee Retirement Income Security Act—required summary plan description ("SPD") or summary of material modifications ("SMM") can trump the terms of the actual ERISA plan.[26] The Second Circuit summarily affirmed the district court, which held that an inconsistent SPD or SMM will be deemed to modify the actual ERISA plan if a participant can demonstrate some "likely harm" to the class of plan beneficiaries even absent any individual showing of reliance, prejudice, or actual harm.[27] The district court went on to hold that a deficient SMM and SPD—regarding a conversion from a traditional defined benefit plan to a "cash balance" plan—required modification of the new plan to provide substantially greater benefits and preserved at least a part of the prior benefits.[28]

---

[23] See Laster v. AT&T, 584 F.3d at 853 ("Under this clause, AT&T will pay a customer $7,500 if the arbitrator issues an award in favor of a California customer that is greater than AT&T's last written settlement offer made before the arbitrator was selected.").

[24] Stolt-Nielsen S.A. v. Animal Feeds Int'l Corp., 559 U.S. ___, 130 S. Ct. 1758, 1775 (2010).

[25] Justice Sotomayor did not participate in the case.

[26] CIGNA Corp. v. Amara, 78 U.S.L.W. 3762 (U.S. June 28, 2010) (No. 09-804).

[27] Amara v. CIGNA Corp., 348 F. App'x 627 (2d Cir. 2009) (unpub.) (affirming 559 F. Supp.2d 192 (D. Conn. 2008) and 534 F. Supp.2d 288 (D. Conn. 2008)).

[28] Amara, 559 F. Supp.2d at 210–14.

The Second Circuit's holding takes a middle ground between six circuits that require a showing of reliance or prejudice before a deficient SMM or SPD can lead to modification of an ERISA plan and three circuits that require no showing of harm at all.[29]

While the legal issue itself is rather technical and lacks much jurisprudential interest, the consequences of the case are of considerable importance to employers and employees both. As the petitioner notes, the issue of when allegedly deficient SPDs can alter ERISA plans arises often and, for national companies with employees in multiple circuits, the inconsistent standards can be administratively burdensome.[30] As a practical matter, multi-circuit companies would likely be forced to accommodate the standard most favorable to plaintiffs—no requirement of prejudice or harm at all—given that such standard could apply to at least a portion of their employees or even all of them via a class action filed in a favorable circuit. The potentially high cost of unintended plan modifications based on allegedly flawed SPDs could have significant effects on the decisions of companies to adopt or retain ERISA plans, as well as on the potential solvency of existing plans.

Before granting certiorari, the Court called for the views of the solicitor general. Per Acting Solicitor General Katyal, the government recommended denying review, agreed with the standard applied below, and noted that the specific issue in the case regarding conversion to cash balance plans has been addressed by statute such that the remedy ordered by the district court is now the required method of calculating benefits for such conversions.[31] It is not currently clear whether then-Solicitor General Kagan had any involvement in this case or the government's amicus brief sufficient to trigger her recusal.

Apart from the specifics of cash balance plans, the broader issue of when SPDs or SMMs can modify an ERISA plan remains significant. Given the absurdity of awarding plan participants windfall benefits

[29] Petition for a Writ of Certiorari at 12–17, CIGNA Corp. v. Amara, No. 09-804 (U.S. Jan. 4, 2010) (discussing cases from the First, Fourth, Seventh, Eighth, Tenth, and Eleventh Circuits, which require a showing of reliance or prejudice, and cases from the Third, Fifth, and Sixth Circuits, which do not require a showing of harm).

[30] *Id.* at 11.

[31] Brief for the United States as Amicus Curiae at 10, Amara v. CIGNA Corp. and CIGNA Corp. v. Amara, Nos. 09-784 & 09-804 (U.S. May 27, 2010).

where they neither relied upon nor were prejudiced by the supposedly deficient summaries, and given that then-Judge Stephen Breyer was the author of an early First Circuit decision staking out the majority position requiring reliance or prejudice,[32] it seems more likely that the Supreme Court will endorse the majority view and require some showing of reliance or prejudice.

Veteran Supreme Court litigator and former Solicitor General Ted Olson is counsel of record for the petitioners.

Copyright

In *Costco v. Omega*, the Court will consider whether copyright law's "first-sale" doctrine applies to imported goods manufactured abroad.[33] Under that doctrine, embodied in 17 U.S.C. § 109(a), the owner of a copy "lawfully made under this title" may resell that copy without the permission of the copyright holder. The Copyright Act, however, also contains a provision, 17 U.S.C. § 602(a)(1), relating directly to importation of goods into the United States, which provides that absent authority of the copyright owner, importation of copies acquired outside the United States infringes the exclusive right to distribute copies under § 106. The Supreme Court in *Quality King Distributors v. L'Anza Research*, held the first-sale doctrine applicable to copies manufactured in the United States, sold abroad, and then re-imported, notwithstanding § 602(a)(1).[34]

The Ninth Circuit in this case, however, held that the first-sale doctrine did not apply to goods originally manufactured abroad, first sold abroad, and then imported into the United States for resale.[35] The court distinguished *Quality King* based on a brief solo concurrence by Justice Ruth Bader Ginsburg in that case suggesting that the treatment of foreign-manufactured goods under the first-sale doctrine remained an open question.[36] The court then applied its own earlier precedent to hold that the first-sale doctrine did not apply to goods manufactured abroad, that a contrary ruling would render

---

[32] Govoni v. Bricklayers, Masons & Plasterers Int'l Union of Am., 732 F.2d 250, 252 (1st Cir. 1984) (Breyer, J.).

[33] Costco Wholesale Corp. v. Omega S.A., 130 S. Ct. 2089 (2010) (No. 08-1423).

[34] Quality King Distributors, Inc. v. L'Anza Research Int'l, Inc., 523 U.S. 135 , 145 (1998).

[35] Omega S.A. v. Costco Wholesale Corp., 541 F.3d. 982, 988–90 (9th Cir. 2008).

[36] *Id.* at 989 (quoting Quality King, 523 U.S. at 154 (Ginsburg, J., concurring)).

the importation limits in § 602(a)(1) meaningless, and that extending the doctrine to foreign-made copies would constitute extraterritorial application of U.S. copyright laws.[37]

The issue has significant consequences for manufacturers and distributors of high-end goods that sell for a premium in the United States and for discount resellers who seek to import such goods less expensively from abroad. Such importation is often referred to as the "gray market," and imports of copyrighted materials constitute tens of billions of dollars of goods per year.[38]

The case has attracted considerable attention from amici curiae. Then-Solicitor General Kagan signed the amicus brief for the United States recommending that certiorari be denied and arguing that the decision below was consistent with *Quality King*.[39] Justice Kagan thus will recuse herself from hearing this case.

At first blush, the stronger argument seems to be that *Quality King* resolves the matter, notwithstanding Justice Ginsburg's individual reservation of the issue. That the Court granted certiorari notwithstanding the position of the solicitor general also tends to suggest some doubt regarding the decision below. But the question whether the production of copies abroad is a function of the U.S. copyright (making such copies lawfully made under "this title" for purposes of the first-sale doctrine) or instead is a function of foreign copyrights, hence rendering the first-sale doctrine inapplicable, is a more interesting question than might first appear. Dicta in *Quality King* distinguished the category of copies made pursuant to foreign law as not constituting copies lawfully made under this title, and hence not subject to the first-sale doctrine.[40] That interpretation, however, threatens to eviscerate the first-sale doctrine absent an extra-textual extension of the doctrine to copies lawfully "sold" in the United States under the Copyright Act, in addition to those lawfully "made" under the act. The issue is thus closer than it first seems, with both sides having difficulties in their construction of the Copyright Act.

---

[37] *Id.* at 987–90 (citing Miller v. Gamme, 335 F.3d 889, 900 (9th Cir. 2003); Suba-films, Ltd., v. MGM-Pathe Communications Co., 24 F.3d 1088, 1096 (9th Cir. 1994)).

[38] Petition for Writ of Certiorari at 20–21, Costco Wholesale Corp. v. Omega S.A., No. 08-1423 (U.S. May 18, 2009).

[39] Brief for the United States as Amicus Curiae at 5–8, 17–22, Costco Wholesale Corp. v. Omega, S.A., No. 08-1423 (U.S. Mar. 17, 2010).

[40] See Quality King, 523 U.S. at 145 n.14.

Supreme Court veteran Roy Englert is counsel of record for the petitioner, while Michael Kellogg is counsel of record for the respondent.

First Amendment

The Free Speech Clause makes two appearances this term in cases involving violent or offensive speech.

In *Schwarzenegger v. Entertainment Merchants Association*, the Court will consider whether the First Amendment protects the sale of violent videogames to minors.[41] California law prohibits the sale of certain videogames to minors where the violent content of such games appeals to a deviant or morbid interest of the minors, offends community standards as to what is suitable for minors, and lacks serious literary, artistic, scientific, or political value as a whole.[42] California's effort to equate violence with sex for First Amendment purposes was rejected by the Ninth Circuit, which struck down the law as a violation of the First Amendment.[43] The court rejected the state's analogy to sexually explicit materials and rejected application of the more lenient standards for restricting the sale of such materials to minors.[44] Applying strict scrutiny, the Ninth Circuit held that the state had failed to prove a causal connection between the violent videogames and the harms it sought to avoid and, in any event, the statute was not the least restrictive means of accomplishing the state's goals.[45]

Before the Supreme Court, California seeks the more lenient standards applicable to restrictions on sales of sexually explicit materials to minors and, in the alternative, seeks more lenient treatment even under strict scrutiny of its inferences that violent videogames are harmful to minors.[46]

The expansion of a conceptually questionable line of precedent regarding sexual materials to encompass violent materials merely

---

[41] Schwarzenegger v. Entm't Merchs. Ass'n, 130 S. Ct. 2398 (2010) (No. 08-1448).

[42] Cal. Civ. Code §§ 1746–1746.5 (2009).

[43] Video Software Dealers Ass'n. v. Schwarzenegger, 556 F.3d 950, 953 (9th Cir. 2009).

[44] *Id.* at 958–60.

[45] *Id.* at 964–65.

[46] See Petitioners' Brief at 7–10, Schwarzenegger v. Entm't Merchs. Ass'n, No. 08-1448 (U.S. July 12, 2010).

because the state believes that such speech is harmful is an important question. The notion that speech can be restricted because it leads to disfavored thoughts among minors seems to contradict a core premise of the First Amendment—that it is not the state's place to dictate or seek to control how people think. Insofar as the law is limited to direct sales to minors, but does not restrict a parent's ability to purchase the same materials and allow their minor children access, however, it might be viewed as simply facilitating parental control rather than forbidding minor's access to such speech per se. However, to the extent it is a first step in declaring violent speech unprotected at all, and hence allowing the state to substitute its judgment for that of the parents, it constitutes a more meaningful assault on First Amendment principles and is a different matter altogether. That the state claims the right to say when an interest in violence is "deviant" or "morbid" should be troubling to civil libertarians. Similarly, that the state gets to decide the artistic or social value of speech, or to allow local community tastes to dictate the content of speech, is just as troubling here as it is in the context of sexually themed speech.

Furthermore, the state's desire to minimize its burden of proof under strict scrutiny threatens to weaken the scrutiny of restrictions across a variety of substantive speech areas. Although in some cases the Supreme Court has suggested a degree of deference to the government's predictive judgments of future events, the Ninth Circuit in this case rejected the state's claims that violent videogames caused psychological and neurological harm because the evidence presented by the state was entirely based on correlation rather than causation.[47] The quality of proof required as justification for regulating speech seems to be the more important question contained herein.

It is hard to predict which way the Supreme Court will go on this issue given that the California law is aimed at "protecting" children, who generally get less consideration under the First Amendment. It will be interesting to see how Justice Kagan approaches this case given that the First Amendment is an area in which she has considerable academic background—though her writings do not suggest

---

[47] Video Software Dealers Ass'n., 556 F.3d at 964.

how she might view this case other than that she seems to take a generally strong view of the First Amendment.[48]

Supreme Court veteran Paul Smith is counsel of record for the respondents.

The Court will also take up the First Amendment in *Snyder v. Phelps*,[49] in which the Fourth Circuit held that an offensive anti-gay, anti-Catholic, anti-military protest staged near the funeral of a fallen marine was protected by the First Amendment.[50] The court of appeals reversed a verdict against the protestors for intentional infliction of emotional distress and invasion of privacy by intrusion upon seclusion.[51] It found that the protests related to matters of public concern and contained only rhetorical hyperbole—rather than assertions of actual facts—that was absolutely protected by the First Amendment under cases such as *Hustler Magazine v. Falwell* and *Milkovich v. Lorain Journal.*[52]

The petitioner argues that the First Amendment is inapplicable or less protective where the speech is directed at a private, rather than a public, figure; where there is a captive audience attending a funeral; and where the relevant tort is intentional infliction of emotional distress, which, unlike defamation, does not necessarily turn on the presence of false factual assertions.[53]

Given the sensitive context in which the speech in this case took place, and the broad implications of the rule proposed by the petitioner, it is not surprising that it has attracted the interest of numerous amici. A group of 42 senators filed an amicus brief in support of the petitioner, though, ironically, their brief tends to demonstrate the public and expressive nature of military funerals rather than the purely private nature of such events.[54] It also spends considerable

---

[48] See, e.g., Elena Kagan, Private Speech, Public Purpose: The Role of Government Motive in First Amendment Doctrine, 63 U. Chi. L. Rev. 413 (1996).

[49] Snyder v. Phelps, 130 S. Ct. 1737 (2010) (No. 09-751).

[50] Snyder v. Phelps, 580 F.3d 206, 226 (4th Cir. 2009).

[51] *Id.* at 211, 221.

[52] *Id.* at 218–22 (citing Hustler Magazine, Inc. v. Falwell, 485 U.S. 46, 53 (1988) and Milkovich v. Lorain Journal Co., 497 U.S. 1 (1990)).

[53] Brief for Petitioner at 18–21, Snyder v. Phelps, No. 09-751 (U.S. May 24, 2010).

[54] See Brief of Senators Harry Reid, Mitch McConnell, and 40 Other Members of the U.S. Senate as Amici Curiae in Support of Petitioner, Snyder v. Phelps, No. 09-751 (U.S. May 28, 2010).

time defending the less restrictive and content-neutral statutory alternatives that limit *any* demonstrations—pro or con—within a defined time and place around a funeral. A brief by the Foundation for Individual Rights in Education and several law professors in support of respondents notes that petitioner's positions would have severe consequences for free speech on university campuses and that the public/private figure dichotomy makes little sense where the speech is on matters of public concern.[55]

The most interesting legal issue in this case is the delineation of the public/private dichotomy as it relates to private figures entangled—whether willingly or not—in matters of public concern. Unlike wholly private funerals, military funerals tend to be more publicly expressive events. The soldiers' families, the government, and the press often use such funerals to convey a variety of public messages relating to patriotic service, sacrifice, the painful costs of war, or simply remembrance of a person lost. Regardless whether any individual soldier thereby becomes a public figure under prevailing legal standards, fallen soldiers certainly become public symbols in connection with any number of issues of public concern. Thus, while a soldier's funeral is an indisputably solemn occasion, and can be protected from *direct* interference no less than any other public or semi-public gathering, it is often a publicly expressive event. As such, the funeral's favored symbolic meanings for the surviving family, the government, and the public cannot be immunized from any and all counter-speech seeking to give it different symbolic content or purpose. That the family and the government find such counter-speech offensive and even hurtful does not justify ceding control to the family and the government of the public meaning and symbolism of military funerals. While there undoubtedly are content- and viewpoint-neutral time, place, and manner limitations that can maintain the solemnity of the occasion, the intentional infliction of emotional distress tort at issue here is far too content- and viewpoint-discriminatory to pass First Amendment muster. Moreover, the invasion of privacy tort reaches too broadly given that the protestors were in public space a considerable distance from the

---

[55] Brief of Amici Curiae the Foundation for Individual Rights in Education and Law Professors Ash Bhagwat, David Post, Martin Redish, Nadine Strossen, and Eugene Volokh, Snyder v. Phelps, No. 09-751 (U.S. July 14, 2010).

funeral itself and apparently not in violation of Maryland's statutory time, place, and manner limitations relating to funerals.[56]

Despite how this case ought to come out, it is a bit more difficult to be confident that the Supreme Court will in fact agree. Cases with patriotic overtones can often be difficult notwithstanding fairly clear principles, as the flag-burning case demonstrated.[57] The case could also put Justice Kagan in a potentially uncomfortable position given the sharp questioning she received about her positions regarding military recruiting while she was dean at Harvard Law School. A vote in favor of the offensive speech and against the deceased soldier's family would no doubt be used by many to bolster their claims that she is anti-military. While I cannot imagine that any such potential criticism would directly influence her decision in this case, it will provide for ample political theater and commentary when the case is argued and decided.

Establishment Clause and Taxpayer Standing

A different clause of the First Amendment is at issue in two consolidated petitions regarding Arizona's tax credit for contributions to various private tuition scholarship funds used to pay for private schooling of Arizona students. In *Arizona Christian School Tuition Organization v. Winn* and *Garriott v. Winn* the Court will consider whether such tax credits violate the Establishment Clause and whether taxpayers have standing to challenge such an alternative to school vouchers.[58]

Unlike voucher programs funded directly by the government, Arizona's program simply provides a tax credit to individuals who contribute to qualified non-profit scholarship funds.[59] The private scholarship funds are generally free to decide which schools and students are eligible for their scholarships and a fund may limit its scholarships to religious schools if it so chooses. Parents and students

---

[56] See Snyder, 580 F.3d at 230.

[57] Texas v. Johnson, 491 U.S. 397 (1989).

[58] Arizona Christian School Tuition Organization v. Winn, 130 S. Ct. 3350 (2010) (No. 09-987); Garriott v. Winn, 130 S. Ct. 3324 (2010) (No. 09-991). This is the second time this case has been to the Supreme Court. The previous time, in *Hibbs v. Winn*, 542 U.S. 88 (2004), the Supreme Court affirmed a Ninth Circuit holding that the suit was not barred by the Tax Injunction Act, 28 U.S.C. § 1341.

[59] Ariz. Rev. Stat. § 43-1089 (2010).

select which private schools to attend and whether to apply for a scholarship. A majority of scholarships from such contributions go to students attending religious schools.[60]

The Ninth Circuit held that taxpayers had standing to challenge the tax credit for contributions to such scholarship funds and reversed the district court's dismissal of the Establishment Clause claim, holding that respondents could bring an as-applied challenge to the tax credit program.[61] Despite the facial neutrality of the statute, the court found that the Arizona program would be a sham and would have the impermissible purpose and effect of advancing religion if the majority of contributions eligible for the tax credit went to funds that selectively awarded scholarships for religious schooling.[62] The court denied a petition for rehearing en banc over the dissent of eight judges.[63]

The consolidated petitions granted by the Court ask whether the various layers of private choice by contributors, scholarships funds, students, and parents are sufficient to render Arizona's tax credits religiously neutral for purposes of the Establishment Clause even when those choices tend, perhaps predictably, to favor religious schools. The Supreme Court will also face the question whether taxpayers have standing to challenge a tax credit for such private contributions rather than a direct expenditure of government funds. Unlike government programs that expend government funds already extracted from taxpayers, however, the Arizona program reduces the taxes of those who contribute to qualified funds but does not directly spend tax money already obtained from the citizenry.

The merits of the Establishment Clause claim seem fairly straightforward in that the tax-credit program is neutral on its face and leaves the making of contributions, the terms of the scholarships, and the enrollment in particular schools entirely to private choice. That some of those choices are made by private donors and private scholarship organizations—which choices then affect the available

---

[60] See Winn v. Arizona Christian Sch. Tuition Org., 562 F.3d 1002, 1017 (9th Cir. 2009) (at the time of plaintiffs' complaint, over 85 percent of students receiving scholarship money under the program attended religious schools).

[61] Id. at 1010–11, 1023.

[62] Id. at 1012–23.

[63] Winn v. Arizona Christian Sch. Tuition Org., 586 F.3d 649 (9th Cir. 2009) (opinions on denial of rehearing en banc).

scholarships from which parents and students may choose—would not seem to convert the program into government-directed support for religion for purposes of the Establishment Clause. While this case, like previous voucher cases, will no doubt be contentious, the merits seem to fall easily within the neutrality parameters of those earlier cases.

The standing question, however, is more interesting and more difficult at least at a theoretical level. The essential fungibility of tax credits and direct expenditures from a budget perspective lends a certain appeal to the Ninth Circuit's standing holding. The government's ability to impose conditions on the tax credits—and hence to control to some extent the use to which any contributions are put—strengthens the analogy even though the government cannot guarantee that the tax-credited contributions will be made at all or control the contributions to the same degree as direct expenditures. Petitioners' observation that the net revenue and budgetary effects of the tax credit may be uncertain—given offsetting reductions in public school costs, unknown political responses to potentially reduced tax revenues, and other factors—does little to distinguish the program here from direct expenditures on vouchers, which have similarly uncertain net effects on state budgets, revenues, and hence taxes.[64] On the other hand, the Court generally has been hostile to taxpayer standing and may be reluctant to extend such standing to situations where the government declines to collect a portion of its potential taxes as opposed to expends taxes already collected from objecting taxpayers.[65]

It will be interesting to see how Justice Kagan deals with both the substantive Establishment Clause question and the jurisprudentially broader standing question, at least the first of which has tended to divide the Court along political lines.

[64] Petitioner Gale Garriott's Brief on the Merits at 44–45, Arizona Christian Sch. Tuition Org. v. Winn, No. 09-991 (U.S. July 30, 2010).

[65] See Winn v. Ariz. Christian Sch., 562 F.3d at 1008 ("It is well established that individuals do not generally have standing to challenge governmental spending solely because they are taxpayers, because 'it is a complete fiction to argue that an unconstitutional federal expenditure causes an individual federal taxpayer any measurable economic harm.'") (quoting Hein v. Freedom From Religion Found., Inc., 551 U.S. 587, 593 (2007) (plurality opinion); see also Flast v. Cohen, 392 U.S. 82, 88 (1968) (recognizing a narrow exception to the general prohibition to taxpayer standing when the plaintiff contends that a use of funds violates the Establishment Clause).

Privacy

In *NASA v. Nelson*, the Court will consider the extent to which the federal government may inquire into the backgrounds of employees of federal contractors where the information will be used for employment purposes but otherwise held private.[66]

The Ninth Circuit held that portions of such background checks likely violated the contract employees' substantive due process right to informational privacy and issued an injunction pending appeal.[67] The court initially found that most of the background check questions, including a question concerning prior drug use, likely did not violate the employees' rights.[68] But it went on to hold that asking whether an employee was receiving *counseling* for prior drug use went too far and was likely unconstitutional. The court also held that asking an employee's references for "any adverse information" regarding the employee was too broad and open-ended, and thus not narrowly tailored to the government's interest in seeking information relevant to employment.[69]

In its petition, NASA does not take direct issue with the potential existence of a right to informational privacy. Instead, NASA argues that any such constitutional right is inapplicable in the context of the diminished expectation of privacy that accompanies employment at a federal facility pursuant to a federal contract and that an employee's interest in avoiding the dissemination of private information was adequately protected by the Privacy Act, which limits the information's use.[70]

This case is noteworthy not merely because it potentially limits the scope of background checks for numerous employees of government contractors but also because its reasoning seems to apply to the background checks used for direct government employees as well. It is also important in that it extends any putative privacy right beyond the right to prevent disclosure of certain information, to

[66] NASA v. Nelson, 130 S. Ct. 1755 (2010) (No. 09-530).

[67] Nelson v. NASA, 530 F.3d 865 (9th Cir. 2008), reh'g denied, 568 F.3d 1028 (9th Cir. 2009) (opinions concurring in and dissenting from denial of rehearing en banc).

[68] Nelson v. NASA, 530 F.3d at 878–79.

[69] *Id.* at 879–81.

[70] See Petition for a Writ of Certiorari at 3–4, 16–20, NASA v. Nelson, No. 09-530 (U.S. Nov. 2, 2009).

include the right to prevent the collection of information even from non-private sources.

On the other side of the coin, it seems that the inquiries being made by NASA, and the criteria used by NASA regarding suitability for employment, were broad enough to include information of a psychological and sexual nature, increasing the privacy interests at stake yet often having little obvious relevance to job suitability. The employees in question in this case likewise are conceded to be in low-risk positions dealing with non-classified materials and had been employed in their positions for years prior to the demand for new background checks.[71]

Given that then-Solicitor General Kagan was counsel of record for NASA, now-Justice Kagan will recuse herself from the case. Former Assistant Solicitor General Paul Wolfson is co-counsel for the respondents.

DNA Testing

Finally, in *Skinner v. Switzer*, the question presented is whether a convicted prisoner seeking access to evidence for the purposes of DNA testing in support of a claim of innocence may proceed via a civil action under 42 U.S.C. § 1983, or rather is limited to a petition for habeas corpus.[72] Applying the rule from *Heck v. Humphrey*— which bars § 1983 civil rights suits that, if successful, would necessarily imply the invalidity of the prisoner's conviction or sentence— the Fifth Circuit summarily affirmed the district court's decision that petitioner could only seek his relief in a habeas petition.[73]

The petitioner makes the persuasive argument that a suit merely seeking access to DNA evidence for testing—the results of which tests are obviously unknown at the time of the suit—does not necessarily imply that his conviction or sentence is invalid and hence is not barred by *Heck*.[74] It is possible, however, that such a § 1983 suit implies the withholding of potentially exculpatory evidence were such evidence available prior to trial, which conduct alone may

---

[71] See Brief for the Petitioners at 10, NASA v. Nelson, No. 09-530 (U.S. May 20, 2010).

[72] Skinner v. Switzer, 130 S. Ct. 3323 (2010) (No. 09-9000).

[73] Skinner v. Switzer, 363 F. App'x. 302, 303 (5th Cir. 2010) (citing Heck v. Humphrey, 512 U.S. 477, 487 (1994)).

[74] See Petition for Writ of Certiorari at 21–24, Skinner v. Switzer, No. 09-9000 (U.S. Feb. 12, 2009).

have a bearing on the conviction or sentence—but given the *ex ante* uncertainty of the test results, even that seems unlikely. The respondent's brief opposing certiorari did not even bother to cite or discuss *Heck* or to defend the reasoning of the decisions below, despite the existence of a 5–2 circuit split on the issue, with the Fourth and Fifth Circuits in the minority.[75]

The support of a majority of the circuits to have considered the issue, as well as the Supreme Court's narrow reading of the *Heck* rule in *Wilkinson v. Dotson*, seems to favor petitioner in this case.[76] The Fifth Circuit's inadequate reasoning regarding the *Heck* issue, its less-than-stellar history of obstruction in criminal cases, and the poor briefing in opposition to certiorari reinforce that conclusion. And while respondent has changed counsel for the merits stage— bringing on former Texas Solicitor General Gregory Coleman—new counsel will still be fighting an uphill battle.

Future Cases

In addition to the cases already before the Court, two recent district court decisions concerning gay marriage and immigration enforcement have the potential to be late entries on the docket if their appeals are expedited and promptly decided.

In *Perry v. Schwarzenegger*, the district court struck down as unconstitutional California's Proposition 8, which banned gay marriage.[77] The district court entered only a limited stay of its ruling, but the Ninth Circuit recently extended the stay and ordered expedited

---

[75] Respondent's Brief in Opposition to Petition for Writ of Certiorari at 8–12, Skinner v. Switzer, No. 09-9000 (2009). The Second, Third, Seventh, Ninth, and Eleventh Circuits all have allowed § 1983 suits seeking access to DNA evidence for testing. See McKithen v. Brown, 481 F.3d 89, 99 (2d Cir. 2007); Grier v. Klem, No. 06-3551, 2010 WL 92483, at *5 (3d Cir. Jan. 12, 2010); Savory v. Lyons, 469 F.3d 667, 672 (7th Cir. 2006); Osborne v. Dist. Att'y's Office, 423 F.3d 1050, 1054 (9th Cir. 2005), rev'd on other grounds, 129 S. Ct. 2308 (2009); Bradley v. Pryor, 305 F.3d 1287, 1290–91 (11th Cir. 2002). The Fourth and Fifth Circuits hold such suits barred under *Heck*. See Harvey v. Horan, 278 F.3d 370, 374–78 (4th Cir. 2002); Kutzner v. Montgomery County, 303 F.3d 339, 341 (5th Cir. 2002). The Supreme Court has previously granted certiorari on *Heck*'s application to post-conviction suits seeking DNA evidence, but resolved the case on other grounds, in Dist. Attorney's Office v. Osborne, 557 U.S., 129 S. Ct. 2308, 2318–19 (2009).

[76] Wilkinson v. Dotson, 544 U.S. 74, 79 (2005).

[77] Perry v. Schwarzenegger, No. C 09-2292 VRW, 2010 WL 3025614 (N.D. Cal., Aug. 4, 2010).

briefing with oral argument to be held on December 6, 2010.[78] A quick decision and an expedited petition to the Supreme Court might just squeeze the case onto its docket this term. However, questions concerning whether supporters of Proposition 8 have standing to appeal, and the refusal of California state officials to defend the suit or appeal the ruling, may derail the case entirely or push it into next term.

United States v. Arizona, in which the district court struck down portions of an Arizona statute adopting aggressive measures targeting illegal immigrants, also has the potential to make it onto the docket if things move sufficiently quickly.[79] Briefing on the case in the Ninth Circuit is already expedited, with argument to be held during the week of November 1, 2010. Given the political heat generated by the law and the lawsuit, it seems highly probable that whichever side loses will seek quick review in the Supreme Court. With *Chamber of Commerce v. Candelaria* already on its docket, the Court would have a convenient double-header in which to sort out uncertain issues involving immigration and preemption.

*   *   *

With roughly half the Court's expected docket for the term filled, there are already a number interesting cases to hold our attention. While perhaps not yet the most exciting term in recent memory, further grants over the next several months could change the term's character. In any event, the presence of new justice Elena Kagan is sure to make the term worth watching.

---

[78] Perry v. Schwarzenegger, No. 10-16696, 2010 WL 3212786 (9th Cir. Aug. 16, 2010).

[79] United States v. Arizona, No. CV 10-1413-PHX-SRB, 2010 WL 2926157 (D. Ariz. July 28, 2010) (order granting in part and denying in part motion for preliminary injunction).

Contributors

Hans Bader is a senior attorney at the Competitive Enterprise Institute, specializing in constitutional law. He is a 1994 graduate of Harvard Law School, where he served as an editor for the *Harvard Journal of Law and Public Policy*. Before joining CEI, Bader worked at the Center for Individual Rights, where he litigated federalism, First Amendment, and civil rights cases including *United States v. Morrison* (2000) and *Gratz v. Bollinger* (2003). He has also worked at the U.S. Department of Education and the law firms of Skadden, Arps, Slate, Meagher & Flom, LLP, and Nossaman, Buthner, Knox & Elliot, LLP. After graduating from law school, Bader served as law clerk to the late federal district judge Larry Lydick.

Josh Blackman is a law clerk for the Hon. Kim R. Gibson of the U.S. District Court for the Western District of Pennsylvania and a teaching fellow at the Pennsylvania State University Dickinson School of Law. Blackman has published articles in prominent law reviews on diverse topics, including constitutional law, information privacy law, property law, national security law, and civil rights. In 2009, he launched the internet's first Supreme Court fantasy league, FantasySCOTUS.net—which boasts over 5,000 members and which CNN's Supreme Court producer called the "hottest new fantasy-league game." He has also been interviewed by ABC News Radio and the Wall Street Journal Law Blog, has been featured on numerous websites, and blogs on legal topics at JoshBlackman.com. Blackman is the president and co-founder of the Harlan Institute, an organization that seeks to make legal learning interesting and accessible to high school students across the country. He graduated *magna cum laude* from the George Mason University School of Law, where he was an articles editor for the *George Mason Law Review*.

James Bopp Jr. is general counsel at the James Madison Center for Free Speech and has a national constitutional law practice with the law firm of Bopp, Coleson & Bostrom. His practice areas include First Amendment Law, Campaign Finance Law, Constitutional Law, Election Law, Civil Litigation, Appellate Practice and U.S. Supreme Court practice. Bopp has successfully argued several cases before the Supreme Court including *FEC v. Wisconsin Right to Life* ("*WRTL II*"), *Randall v. Sorrell*, and *Republican Party of Minnesota v. White*. He has numerous professional affiliations, including co-chairman of the election law subcommittee of the Federalist Society, commissioner for the National Conference of Commissioners of Uniform State Laws, and special advisor to the American Bar Association Working Group on the First Amendment and Judicial Elections. He holds a B.A. from Indiana University and a J.D. from the University of Florida. He is a member of the Indiana and U.S. Supreme Court Bars.

Richard E. Coleson is an attorney with Bopp, Coleson & Bostrom in Terre Haute, Indiana. His practice focuses on constitutional litigation and appeals. He has been counsel in numerous campaign-finance cases, including the Supreme Court cases of *Doe v. Reed*, *Citizens United v. FEC*, *WRTL II*, *Wisconsin Right to Life v. FEC*, *McConnell v. FEC*, *FEC v. Beaumont*, and *Republican Party of Minnesota v. White*. He has contributed a variety of articles, including several on campaign-finance law. One of these—James Bopp & Richard E. Coleson, *Distinguishing "Genuine" from "Sham" in Grassroots Lobbying: Protecting the Right to Petition During Elections* (Campbell Law Review 2007)—was published contemporaneously with Bopp and Coleson's Supreme Court briefing in *WRTL II* and referenced by the Court. Coleson has served on a county election board, as general counsel for a state advocacy group, and as pastor to several churches, and taught biblical literature at Oklahoma Wesleyan University. His education includes a year studying in Jerusalem and degrees from Indiana Wesleyan University, Asbury Theological Seminary, and Indiana University School of Law—Indianapolis.

Richard A. Epstein is the Laurence A. Tisch Professor of Law at New York University and James Parker Hall Distinguished Service Professor of Law at the University of Chicago, where he has taught since 1972. He has also been the Peter and Kirstin Bedford Senior Fellow at the Hoover Institution since 2000. Before joining the University of Chicago Law School faculty—where he also served as interim dean in 2001—he taught law at the University of Southern California. Epstein received an LLD, *hc*, from the University of Ghent, 2003, has been a member of the American Academy of Arts and Sciences since 1985 and a senior fellow of the Center for Clinical Medical Ethics at the University of Chicago Medical School since 1983. He served as editor of the *Journal of Legal Studies* from 1981 to 1991, and of the *Journal of Law and Economics* from 1991 to 2001. At present he is a director of Chicago's John M. Olin Program in Law and Economics. His books include *Antitrust Decrees in Theory and Practice: Why Less Is More* (AEI 2007); *Overdose: How Excessive Government Regulation Stifles Pharmaceutical Innovation* (Yale University Press 2006); *How Progressives Rewrote the Constitution* (Cato 2006); *Cases and Materials on Torts* (Aspen Law & Business; 8th ed. 2004); *Skepticism and Freedom: A Modern Case for Classical Liberalism* (University of Chicago 2003): *Cases and Materials on Torts* (Aspen Law & Business; 7th ed. 2000); *Torts* (Aspen Law & Business 1999); *Principles for a Free Society: Reconciling Individual Liberty with the Common Good* (Perseus Books 1998): *Mortal Peril: Our Inalienable Rights to Health Care* (Addison-Wesley 1997); *Simple Rules for a Complex World* (Harvard 1995); *Bargaining with the State* (Princeton, 1993); *Forbidden Grounds: The Case against Employment Discrimination Laws* (Harvard 1992); *Takings: Private Property and the Power of Eminent Domain* (Harvard 1985); and *Modern Products Liability Law* (Greenwood Press 1980). Epstein has also written numerous articles on a wide range of legal and interdisciplinary subjects.

Alan Gura is a constitutional attorney at the law firm of Gura & Possessky, PLLC. He began his career as a law clerk to the Hon. Terrence W. Boyle, United States District Judge for the Eastern District of North Carolina. Subsequently, as a deputy attorney general for the State of California, Gura defended the state and its employees from all manner of lawsuits, in state and federal courts, at trial and on appeal. He then entered the private practice of law at the Washington, D.C. office of Sidley & Austin LLP. In February 2000, he left the firm to serve for a year as counsel to the U.S. Senate Judiciary Committee, Subcommittee on Criminal Justice Oversight. Gura is admitted to the bars of the District of Columbia, Virginia, and California, and is admitted to practice before the U.S. Supreme Court and numerous other federal courts. In 2009, he was named one of Washington's "Top 40 Lawyers Under 40" and a "Champion of Justice" by the *Legal Times*. Gura is a graduate of the Georgetown University Law Center and Cornell University, where he earned a B.A. in Government, with distinction in all subjects.

Erik S. Jaffe is a solo appellate attorney in Washington, D.C., whose practice emphasizes the First Amendment and other constitutional issues. He is a graduate of Dartmouth College and Columbia Law School, where he was the articles editor of the *Columbia Law Review*. Following law school, he clerked for Judge Douglas H. Ginsburg on the U.S. Court of Appeals for the D.C. Circuit, practiced for five years at Williams & Connolly LLP in Washington, D.C., clerked for Justice Clarence Thomas on the U.S. Supreme Court, and then began his solo private practice. Since 1999, Jaffe has been involved in 24 cases at the merits stage before the Supreme Court. He represented one of the successful respondents in the First Amendment case of *Bartnicki v. Vopper* and authored Cato's amicus briefs in *Wisconsin Right to Life v. FEC*, *Randall v. Sorrell*, *McConnell v. FEC*, and *New York State Board of Elections v. Lopez Torres*. Jaffe has also authored amicus briefs in cases such as *Republican Party of Minnesota v. Kelly* (judicial speech), *Zelman v. Simmons Harris* (vouchers), *Watchtower Bible and Tract Society v. Village of Stratton* (anonymous speech), *Veneman v. Livestock Marketing Association* and *United States v. United Foods, Inc.* (compelled advertising), *Boy Scouts of America v. Dale* (freedom of expressive association), and *United States v. Morrison* (Commerce Clause). He is the chairman of the Federalist Society's free speech and election law practice group.

Michael W. McConnell is the Richard and Frances Mallery Professor of Law at Stanford Law School and a leading authority on freedom of speech and religion, the relation of individual rights to government structure, originalism, and various other aspects of constitutional history and constitutional law. He is author of numerous articles and co-author of two casebooks: *The Constitution of the United States* (Foundation Press) and *Religion and the Constitution* (Aspen). In addition to teaching, he is the director of the Stanford Constitutional Law Center, which was founded in 2006 to explore and improve public understanding of the most pressing constitutional issues. McConnell brings wide practical experience to bear on his teaching and scholarship. Before joining Stanford in 2009, he served as a federal judge on the U.S. Court of Appeals for the Tenth Circuit and was frequently mentioned as a possible nominee to the Supreme Court. He is the only full-time professor of law in the nation who has previously served as a federal judge. He also has been involved in extensive appellate litigation, including arguing 12 cases in the U.S. Supreme Court, including one during October Term 2009. Before his appointment to the bench, McConnell was Presidential Professor of Law at the S.J. Quinney College of Law at the University of Utah, and before that the William B. Graham Professor of Law at the University of Chicago Law School. He has taught five times as a visiting professor at Harvard Law School. McConnell served as law clerk to then-Chief Judge J. Skelly Wright of the U.S. Court of Appeals for the D.C. Circuit, and to Supreme Court Justice William J. Brennan Jr. McConnell was an assistant general counsel at the Office of Management and Budget and an assistant to the Solicitor General in the Department of Justice under President Ronald Reagan. He is also a senior fellow at the Hoover Institution.

Roger Pilon is the vice president for legal affairs at the Cato Institute. He holds Cato's B. Kenneth Simon Chair in Constitutional Studies and is the founder and director of Cato's Center for Constitutional Studies. Established in 1989 to encourage limited constitutional government at home and abroad, the Center has become an important force in the national debate over constitutional interpretation and judicial philosophy. Pilon's work has appeared in the *New York Times, Washington Post, Wall Street Journal, Los Angeles Times, Legal Times, National Law Journal, Harvard Journal of Law & Public Policy, Notre Dame Law Review, Stanford Law & Policy Review, Texas Review of Law and Politics* and elsewhere. He has appeared, among other places, on ABC's Nightline, CBS's 60 Minutes II, National Public Radio, Fox News Channel, CNN, MSNBC, CNBC. He lectures and debates at universities and law schools across the country and testifies often before Congress. Before joining Cato, Pilon held five senior posts in the Reagan administration, including at State and Justice. He has taught philosophy and law and was a national fellow at Stanford's Hoover Institution. Pilon holds a B.A. from Columbia University, an M.A. and a Ph.D. from the University of Chicago, and a J.D. from the George Washington University School of Law.

In the 1989, the Bicentennial Commission presented him with the Benjamin Franklin Award for excellence in writing on the U.S. Constitution. In 2001, Columbia University's School of General Studies awarded him its Alumni Medal of Distinction.

Larry E. Ribstein is the Mildred Van Voorhis Jones Chair in Law and the Associate Dean for Research, University of Illinois College of Law. He is the author of leading treatises on limited liability companies and partnership law, as well as two business associations casebooks. His books also include *The Sarbanes-Oxley Debacle* and *The Constitution and the Corporation* (both with Henry Butler), *The Law Market* (with Erin O'Hara), *The Rise of the Uncorporation* and *The Economics of Federalism*. From 1998-2001 he was co-editor of the *Supreme Court Economic Review*. Ribstein has written or co-authored approximately 150 articles on subjects including corporate, securities and partnership law, constitutional law, bankruptcy, film, the internet, family law, professional ethics and licensing, uniform laws, choice of law and jurisdictional competition. Ribstein holds a B.A. from Johns Hopkins University and earned his J.D. from the University of Chicago Law School.

Michael Risch is an associate professor of law at Villanova University School of Law. Before coming to Villanova, Risch taught at West Virginia University College of Law, where he directed the Entrepreneurship, Innovation and Law Program. Risch's teaching and scholarship focuses on intellectual property and cyberspace law, with an emphasis on patents, trade secrets and information access. His articles have been published in the *Indiana Law Journal, Tennessee Law Review, West Virginia Law Review, University of Pennsylvania Law Review* (forthcoming), *Harvard Journal of Law and Technology*, and *Yale Law Journal Online*, among others. Risch received his A.B. with honors and distinction in public policy and with distinction in quantitative economics from Stanford University, and his J.D. with high honors from the University of Chicago Law School. At Chicago, he was elected to the Order of the Coif and was an Olin Fellow in Law & Economics and a Bradley Fellow in Law & Economics. Before beginning his academic career, Risch was a partner at the intellectual property boutique Russo & Hale LLP in Palo Alto, California, and served as an Olin Fellow in Law at Stanford Law School. At Villanova, he will teach the intellectual property survey course, patent law, and cyberlaw.

Monica R. Shah practices in the areas of criminal defense and civil litigation at the law firm of Zalkind, Rodriguez, Lunt & Duncan LLP. During law school at Columbia University, Shah served as an articles editor on the *Columbia Law Review* and as a teaching assistant in constitutional law. She also interned with the Asian American Legal Defense & Education Fund, Neighborhood Defender Services of Harlem, the civil rights firm of Neufeld Scheck & Brustin, LLP, and the NAACP Legal Defense & Educational Fund, where she worked on an amicus curiae brief in *Roper v. Simmons*, the case in which the Supreme Court struck down the juvenile death penalty. Following her clerkship with Judge Allyne Ross in the U.S. District Court for the Eastern District of New York, Shah received the Johnnie L. Cochran Jr. Fellowship from Neufeld Scheck & Brustin and served as an associate for the firm, where she represented victims of wrongful convictions and police misconduct in civil rights actions in federal and state courts around the country.

Ilya Shapiro is a senior fellow in constitutional studies at the Cato Institute and editor-in-chief of the *Cato Supreme Court Review*. Before joining Cato, he was a special assistant/advisor to the Multi-National Force in Iraq on rule of law issues and practiced international, political, commercial, and antitrust litigation at Patton Boggs LLP and Cleary Gottlieb LLP. Shapiro has contributed to a variety of academic, popular, and professional publications, including the *Harvard Journal of Law & Public Policy*, *L.A. Times*, *Washington Times*, *Legal Times*, *Weekly Standard*, *Roll Call*, and *National Review Online*, and from 2004 to 2007 wrote the "Dispatches from Purple America" column for *TCS Daily.com*. He also regularly provides commentary on a host of legal and political issues for various TV and radio outlets, including CNN, Fox News, ABC, CBS, NBC, Univision, "The Colbert Report," and American Public Media's "Marketplace." He lectures regularly on behalf of the Federalist Society and other educational and professional groups, is a member of the board of visitors of the Legal Studies Institute at The Fund for American Studies, was an inaugural Washington Fellow at the National Review Institute, and has been an adjunct professor at the George Washington University Law School. Before entering private practice, Shapiro clerked for Judge E. Grady Jolly of the U.S. Court of Appeals for the Fifth Circuit, while living in Mississippi and traveling around the Deep South. He holds an A.B. from Princeton University, an M.Sc. from the London School of Economics, and a J.D. from the University of Chicago Law School (where he became a Tony Patiño Fellow). Shapiro is a member of the bars of New York, D.C., and the U.S. Supreme Court. He is a native speaker of English and Russian, is fluent in Spanish and French, and is proficient in Italian and Portuguese.

Harvey A. Silverglate is an adjunct scholar at the Cato Institute. He is a graduate of Princeton University, *cum laude*, and Harvard Law School. Silverglate, counsel to Boston's Zalkind, Rodriguez, Lunt & Duncan LLP, specializes in criminal defense, civil liberties, academic freedom and student rights. He has taught at Cambridge Rindge & Latin School in Massachusetts, University of Massachusetts College III, and Harvard Law School. He has served the Massachusetts state ACLU affiliate as a member of its board of directors for over three decades, serving two terms as its president. His law practice has ranged widely and has included drug prosecutions, draft and riot cases in the 1960s and 1970s, bank and securities fraud, bribery and extortion, espionage, tax evasion, police misconduct, murder and manslaughter, habeas corpus proceedings, money laundering, and desertion in a case tried at a court martial during the Vietnam War. Silverglate is a long-time criminal law and civil liberties columnist for *The Boston Phoenix*, an independent "alternative" weekly, and, more recently, was the regular bimonthly civil liberties columnist for the *National Law Journal*. He writes frequently on legal issues for *forbes.com*. Silverglate's articles, book reviews, and other writings have been published in the *Harvard Law Review, New York Times Book Review, Massachusetts Lawyers Weekly, Harvard Civil Rights–Civil Liberties Law Review, Wilson Quarterly, Chronicle of Higher Education, Wall Street Journal, Boston Globe, Philadelphia Inquirer*, and *Reason* magazine, among others. *The Shadow University* (Free Press, 1998), with Alan Charles Kors, was his first full-length book. Silverglate, with Kors, co-founded the Foundation for Individual Rights in Education, a nonprofit foundation dedicated to preserving academic freedom, due process, freedom of speech, and freedom of conscience on American college campuses. Silverglate has lectured at colleges and universities throughout the country and has appeared on local and national electronic media discussing legal issues. He is the author, most recently, of *Three Felonies a Day: How the Feds Target the Innocent* (Encounter Books, 2009).

Steve Simpson is a senior attorney at the Institute for Justice. He litigates primarily free speech cases in state and federal courts across the country. He is currently lead counsel in *SpeechNow.org v. FEC*, a challenge to the federal campaign finance laws that prevent individuals from banding together to spend money on speech for or against candidates. Simpson is also lead counsel in two challenges to Colorado's campaign finance laws, and has been involved in a wide variety of other cases, including IJ's challenge to New York's ban on direct shipping of wine, which resulted in a win before the U.S. Supreme *Court* in *Granholm v. Heald*. Simpson's views and writings have been published in a number of print and on-line newspapers and journals, including the *Legal Times*, *Washington Post*, *Chicago Tribune*, and *Washington Times*. Before joining IJ, he spent five years as a litigator with the international law firm Shearman & Sterling LLP. He has authored and co-authored articles and practice guides on federal securities laws, the non-delegation doctrine, and the First Amendment. Simpson is a graduate of New York Law School, where he was a managing editor and articles editor of the law review. After law school, he spent two years clerking for Judge Lenore C. Nesbitt on the U.S. District Court for the Southern District of Florida. Simpson is a member of the bars of New York, New Jersey, and D.C.

Ilya Somin is an associate professor at George Mason University School of Law. His research focuses on constitutional law, property law, and the study of popular political participation and its implications for constitutional democracy. Somin currently serves as co-editor of the *Supreme Court Economic Review* and his work has appeared in numerous scholarly journals, including the *Yale Law Journal*, *Stanford Law Review*, *Northwestern University Law Review*, *Georgetown Law Journal*, *Critical Review*, and others. He has also published articles in a variety of popular press outlets, including the

L.A. Times, Wall Street Journal OpinionJournal.com, South China Morning Post, Legal Times, National Law Journal, and *Reason.* He has been quoted or interviewed by the *New York Times, Washington Post,* BBC, and the Voice of America, among other media. In July 2009, he testified on property rights issues at the U.S. Senate Judiciary Committee confirmation hearings for Supreme Court Justice Sonia Sotomayor. Somin writes regularly for the popular Volokh Conspiracy law and politics blog. He has served as a visiting professor of law at the University of Pennsylvania Law School, the University of Hamburg, Germany, and the University of Torcuato Di Tella in Buenos Aires, Argentina. Before joining the faculty at George Mason, he was the John M. Olin Fellow in Law at Northwestern University Law School and clerked for the Hon. Judge Jerry E. Smith of the U.S. Court of Appeals for the Fifth Circuit. Somin earned his B.A., *summa cum laude*, at Amherst College, M.A. in political science from Harvard University, and J.D. from Yale Law School.

Judd E. Stone is a research fellow for the International Center for Law and Economics and is currently clerking for Justice Daniel E. Winfree of the Alaska Supreme Court. Stone is a recent graduate, *magna cum laude*, of the Northwestern University School of Law, where he was an associate editor of the law review and active in the Federalist Society. In fall 2011, Stone will begin a clerkship for Chief Judge Edith H. Jones of the U.S. Court of Appeals for the Fifth Circuit. Stone's research focuses on antitrust, industrial organization, and regulation in the banking, consumer protection, and financial services sectors.

Nadine Strossen is professor of law at New York Law School and has written, lectured, and practiced extensively in the areas of constitutional law, civil liberties, and international human rights. From 1991 through 2008 she served as president of the ACLU, the first woman to head the nation's largest and oldest civil liberties organization. Strossen is now a member of the ACLU's National Advisory Council. In 2005, Strossen was honored by the University of Tulsa College of Law and the *Tulsa Law Review,* which made her scholarly work the subject of their Fifth Annual Legal Scholarship Symposium titled "Nadine Strossen: Scholar as Activist." She comments frequently on legal issues in the national media, having appeared on virtually every national news program. In October 2001, Strossen made her professional theater debut as the guest star in Eve Ensler's award-winning play, *The Vagina Monologues*, during a week-long run at the National Theatre in Washington, D.C. Professor Strossen's writings have been published in many scholarly and general interest publications. Her book, *Defending Pornography: Free Speech, Sex, and the Fight for Women's Rights* (Scribner, 1995; NYU Press, 2000), was named by *The New York Times* as a "Notable Book" of 1995. Her coauthored book, *Speaking of Race, Speaking of Sex: Hate Speech, Civil Rights, and Civil Liberties* (NYU Press, 1995), was named an "outstanding book" by the Gustavus Myers Center for the Study of Human Rights in North America. Strossen graduated Phi Beta Kappa from Harvard College and *magna cum laude* from Harvard Law School, where she was an editor of the *Harvard Law Review*. Before becoming a law professor, she practiced law for nine years in Minneapolis and New York City. She is a member of the Council on Foreign Relations.

Joshua D. Wright is an associate professor at the George Mason University School of Law and Department of Economics. His research focuses on antitrust law and economics, the intersection of intellectual property and antitrust, consumer protection, and contracts. His publications have appeared in leading academic journals, including the *Journal of Law and Economics, Antitrust Law Journal, Competition Policy International, Supreme Court Economic Review, Yale Journal on Regulation, Journal of Competition Law and Economics, Review of Law and Economics, Harvard Journal of Law and Public Policy,* and the *UCLA Law Review*. Wright is also the co-editor of *Pioneers of Law and Economics* (Elgar Publishing) and *Regulating Innovation: Competition Policy and Patent Law under Uncertainty* (forthcoming, Cambridge Press). He was the inaugural Scholar in Residence at the Federal Trade Commission, where he served until fall 2008. Wright was a visiting professor at the University of Texas School of Law and a visiting fellow at the Searle Center at the Northwestern University School of Law during the 2008-09 academic year. Before coming to George Mason, Wright clerked for the Hon. James V. Selna of the U.S. District Court for the Central District of California and taught at the Pepperdine University Graduate School of Public Policy. He has also testified at the joint Department of Justice/FTC Hearings on Section 2 of the Sherman Act, the FTC's "FTC at 100" conference, the FTC Workshops on Resale Price Maintenance, and the Department of Justice/FTC Workshop on the Horizontal Merger Guidelines. Wright is the co-editor of the *Supreme Court Economic Review*, and serves on the editorial board of the *Antitrust Law Journal*, *Global Competition Policy*, and *Competition Policy International*. He is a co-founder of the Microsoft/George Mason Annual Conference on the Law and Economics of Innovation, a member of the National Science Foundation Advisory Panel for Law and Social Sciences, a Senior Fellow at the George Mason Information Economy Project, and a regular contributor to *Truth on the Market*, a blog dedicated to academic commentary on law, business, and economics. Wright received both a J.D. and a Ph.D. in economics from UCLA, where he was managing editor of the *UCLA Law Review*, and a B.A. in economics with highest departmental honors at the University of California, San Diego.

ABOUT THE CATO INSTITUTE

The Cato Institute is a public policy research foundation dedicated to the principles of limited government, individual liberty, free markets, and private property. It takes its name from *Cato's Letters,* popular libertarian pamphlets that helped to lay the philosophical foundation for the American Revolution.

Despite the Founders' libertarian values, today virtually no aspect of life is free from government encroachment. A pervasive intolerance for individual rights is shown by government's arbitrary intrusions into private economic transactions and its disregard for civil liberties.

To counter that trend, the Cato Institute undertakes an extensive publications program that addresses the complete spectrum of policy issues. It holds major conferences throughout the year, from which papers are published thrice yearly in the *Cato Journal,* and also publishes the quarterly magazine *Regulation* and the annual *Cato Supreme Court Review.*

The Cato Institute accepts no government funding. It relies instead on contributions from foundations, corporations, and individuals and revenue generated from the sale of publications. The Institute is a nonprofit, tax-exempt educational foundation under Section 501(c)(3) of the Internal Revenue Code.

ABOUT THE CENTER FOR CONSTITUTIONAL STUDIES

Cato's Center for Constitutional Studies and its scholars take their inspiration from the struggle of America's founding generation to secure liberty through limited government and the rule of law. Under the direction of Roger Pilon, the center was established in 1989 to help revive the idea that the Constitution authorizes a government of delegated, enumerated, and thus limited powers, the exercise of which must be further restrained by our rights, both enumerated and unenumerated. Through books, monographs, conferences, forums, op-eds, speeches, congressional testimony, and TV and radio appearances, the center's scholars address a wide range of constitutional and legal issues—from judicial review to federalism, economic liberty, property rights, civil rights, criminal law and procedure, asset forfeiture, tort law, and term limits, to name just a few. The center is especially concerned to encourage the judiciary to be "the bulwark of our liberties," as James Madison put it, neither making nor ignoring the law but interpreting and applying it through the natural rights tradition we inherited from the founding generation.

CATO INSTITUTE
1000 Massachusetts Ave., N.W.
Washington, D.C. 20001

陳從周先生百年誕辰紀念

2018 年，因中国著名古典园林与建筑艺术家陈从周先生的百年诞辰而非同寻常。

为了这份特别的纪念，我们将陈从周先生的四部经典学术著作《苏州园林》《苏州旧住宅》《扬州园林（与住宅）》《中国名园》汇集再版。文字的重新录入与勘校，照片、测绘图的重新查找与制作……我们倾注满腔心血，将崇敬之情融入每段文字、每张图片的编排与设计之中。

为了明晰文字内容与图片之间的逻辑关系，我们在忠于原书稿素材的基础上，重新调整了图文次序，并对四本书中的照片和测绘图较原版做了局部删减。另外，因新寻找到陈从周先生当年拍摄的扬州园林照片，《扬州园林与住宅》（原《扬州园林》）较原版做了约 50 张图片的增补。

由于汇集再版的四部著作的原版来自不同的年代、不同的英文译者、不同的出版社，因此译文风格与专有名词译法迥异。加之目前园林等专有名词尚未有统一的官方译法（政府部门、景点官网、国际组织、民间等各方的译法不一），作为"纪念版"，为了尽量保持原版的历史风貌与体系完整，对于专有名词的英译，我们只做了所属书内的统一。

四部久负盛名的经典著作，再现一位建筑前辈的魁奇风骨。

——编者按

2018 is a very special year because of the centenary of a great man in the field of Chinese architecture.

To memorize the extraordinary significance, we are going to republish Mr. Chen's four classic academic works: *Suzhou Gardens*, *Traditional Suzhou Residences*, *Yangzhou Gardens (and Traditional Residences)*, and *Famous Chinese Gardens*. We have put great effort into these books, typing and proofreading texts, collecting photos and drawings, editing images... We designed and arranged the layout and pictures with the highest respect for the author.

While trying our best to maintain the authenticity of the contents, we have adjusted the sequence of the contents and deleted some photos and drawings compared to the original, so as to better clarify the relationship between texts and pictures. In addition, due to the newly discovered photos of Yangzhou gardens taken by the author, about 50 pictures in *Yangzhou Gardens and Traditional Residences* (originally *Yangzhou Gardens*) were added.

Since the original editions of the four reprinted works are from different time, translated by different translators into English, and published by different publishers, the translation styles are not alike, and the proper nouns are translated in different ways. Currently, there is no unified official translation for the proper nouns. For example, for gardens, government departments, official websites of the scene spots, international organizations, and the general public have their own English translations. As the four books published this time are "Centenary Edition", the original historical features and complete system of which should be maintained as much as possible, we have only made the translations of proper nouns consistent within each book.

The four classic works on classical Chinese gardens and residences are revived, reflecting the distinguished character of a trailblazing Chinese architectural master.

— The Editors